Hereditary Order of
Descendants of Colonial Governors

1980

Founded January 1896
by
Miss Mary Cabell Richardson

CLEARFIELD

REGISTER

HEREDITARY ORDER OF

DESCENDANTS OF COLONIAL GOVERNORS

HEREDITARY ORDER OF

DESCENDANTS OF COLONIAL GOVERNORS

Edited by

Robert Glenn Thurtle

Publication Committee

John Frederick Dorman, Chairman

Charles Owen Johnson,
Governor General

Robert Glenn Thurtle,
Assistant Genealogist General

Reprinted for
Clearfield Company, Inc. by
Genealogical Publishing Co., Inc.
Baltimore, Maryland
2002

International Standard Book Number: 0-8063-5087-3

Made in the United States of America

iii

CONTENTS

This lineage book was prepared to immortalize the principal objective of the Hereditary Order of Descendants of Colonial Governors, to wit: "To commemorate the services of those men who, prior to July 4, 1776, singly exercised supreme executive power in the American colonies and who laid in them the foundations of stable government and of the respect for civil law and authority which made the maintenance of their future independence possible."

It is hoped that this book will be of value in preserving lineage records and in serving as a guide and source of information to people seeking a lineage back to a Colonial Governor. The book contains the lineage record of the current members who have presented to the Society a proven descent from one or more of the accepted Colonial Governors.

Membership numbers 1 to 1020 are the members of the original order to whom numbers were assigned for insignia permits; numbers M-1 to M-605 are members of the original order who were not assigned numbers for insignia permits; numbers 1-B and out are members accepted since 1954. A number preceded by an "S" indicates a successor whose membership has been inherited.

A brief biographical sketch is given for approved members in good standing. It is edited for uniformity and conciseness. For those who did not respond to the questionnaire sent to all members, the biographical sketch is limited to the data in the permanent records of the Registrar General of the Society. These sketches are followed by the name of the Colonial Governor Ancestor by right of descent from whom the member attained membership and the details of his line of descent as shown on the application approved by the Genealogist General. Supplemental lineages approved by the Genealogist General of the Society are given down to the generation in common with the member's original or other supplemental lineage. When the supplemental line appears in the second generation it is not shown separately but marked "Supplemental." Thus any member descended from Governor Nicholas Easton is also descended from Governor John Coggeshall through his daughter Anne Coggeshall who married Peter Easton; Governor Simon Bradstreet married Anne Dudley, daughter of Governor Thomas Dudley and his son Samuel Dudley married Mary Winthrop, daughter of Governor John Winthrop; William Stone's daughter Elizabeth Stone married William Calvert, son of Governor Leonard Calvert; John Haynes' daughter, Ruth Haynes married (1st) Samuel Willys, son of Governor Samuel Willys and Governor Thomas Smith's granddaughter Justina Smith married John Moore, son of Governor James Moore.

The left hand column in the lineage shows the ancestor in each generation through whom the Colonial Governor lineage was inherited whether a man or woman. The right hand column is for the spouse. The center column shows the place and date of marriage. For the ancestor and the spouse, the first line is for the place and date of birth and the second line is for the place and date of death. The lineage data were copied from the Original Application or Supplemental Application which was approved by the Genealogist General. To keep the lineage data within the limitations of type space as much as possible, titles such as Gen., Col, Rev., Dr., Judge, et cetera, have been

omitted. Abbreviations for the state of birth, death, and
marriage data have not been repeated. The various Societies to
which our members belong have been abbreviated.

Since vital data for the same ancestor shown in different
lineages may have been from a variety of published or unpublished
records, they may not have agreed precisely, for example, Bethia,
Bithia and Bethula Mansfield are all the same person. Such
errors may be due to clerical or typographical errors. Every
effort has been made to keep slight differences to a minimum.

There are several lines of descent shown by an asterisk
(*) which were accepted prior to 1980, such as George Reade of
Virginia Colony and William Bradford, Jr. of Plymouth Colony.
Later research has shown that they did not act as Governors of
their respective colonies. Also there were some lines of descent
from Governors William Stone and William Claiborne of Maryland
and Governors John West, Edward Digges and Samuel Matthews of
Virginia that may have broken lines of descent from their respective Governors. These questioned lines of descent which are
published herein,may be disallowed at a later date when
prospective members apply on the same lines. Further research
may help to establish these lines correctly and it is our hope
that future applicants will take the opportunity to research and
correct the questioned lines of descent. The asterisk is shown
at the point where the line appears to break.

We are indebted to our Honorary Governor General John
Frederick Dorman for his assistance on the lineage questions on
the Virginia and Maryland lines. A special thank you to our
Governor General Charles Owen Johnson for his expertise and to
our Assistant Genealogist General Robert Glenn Thurtle for his
work on this Register.

For those members elected after this book goes to press
but before being printed or bound an addendum section was added
following the main lineage section.

The necrology covers only members who have died in the
past ten years.

GOVERNORS GENERAL

FOUNDED
1896

Miss Mary Cabell Richardson	1896
Mrs. Henry Whipple Skinner	1897 – 1907
Miss Gail Treat	1907 – 1944

Reorganized in 1954

Mrs. Hermann August Knorr	1954 – 1961
Mr. William Young Pryor	1961 – 1963
Mr. Grahame Thomas Smallwood, Jr.	1963 – 1967
Mrs. Frederick Tracy Morse	1967 – 1970
Mr. Warren Smith Hall, Jr.	1970 – 1973
Mr. John Frederick Dorman	1973 – 1976
Mrs. Russell Francis Barker	1976 – 1979
Mr. Charles Owen Johnson	1979 –

OFFICERS

1958 - 1961

Governor General	Mrs. Hermann August Knorr
1st Deputy Governor General	Mrs. Samuel Green Biggs
2nd Deputy Governor General	Mrs. Harry Clark Boden, IV
Secretary General	Mrs. Joseph Barnett Paul
Treasurer General	Mrs. Margaret Scruggs Carruth
Registrar General	Mrs. George Castleman Estill

1961 - 1964

Governor General	Mr. William Young Pryor (1961-1963)
1st Deputy Governor General	Mr. Grahame T. Smallwood, Jr.
2nd Deputy Governor General	Hon. Charles S. Whitman, Jr.
Secretary General	Mrs. Joseph Barnett Paul
Treasurer General	Mr. John Daskam Leet
Registrar General	Mrs. Frederick Tracy Morse
Chaplain General	Mrs. George Castleman Estill

1964 - 1967

Governor General	Mr. Grahame T. Smallwood, Jr. (1963-1967)
1st Deputy Governor General	Hon. Charles S. Whitman, Jr.
2nd Deputy Governor General	Mrs. Helen Denny Howard
3rd Deputy Governor General	Mrs. Joseph Barnett Paul
Secretary General	Mrs. Russell Francis Barker
Treasurer General	Hon. Henry Whitcomb Sweeney
Registrar General	Mrs. Frederick Tracy Morse
Chaplain General	Mrs. George Castleman Estill
Chancellor General	Hon. Charles F. Stein, Jr.
Genealogist General	Rev. Dr. Harold Eugene Mayo

1967 - 1970

Governor General	Mrs. Frederick Tracy Morse
1st Deputy Governor General	Mr. Warren Smith Hall, Jr.
2nd Deputy Governor General	Mrs. George Castleman Estill
3rd Deputy Governor General	Hon. Charles F. Stein, Jr.
Secretary General	Mrs. Russell Francis Barker
Treasurer General	Mr. Samuel Hendrixson Newsome
Registrar General	Mrs. Eldon Loring Howe
Chaplain General	Rev. Dr. Harold Eugene Mayo
Chancellor General	Hon. Henry Whitcomb Sweeney
Genealogist General	Mr. Charles Owen Johnson

1970 - 1973

Governor General	Mr. Warren Smith Hall, Jr.
1st Deputy Governor General	Mr. John Frederick Dorman
2nd Deputy Governor General	Col. J. Huntington Hills
3rd Deputy Governor General	Mr. George Harrison King
Secretary General	Miss Agnes Virginia Dodson (1970-1972)
	Mrs. Russell Francis Barker (1972-1973)
Treasurer General	Mr. Samuel Hendrixson Newsome
Registrar General	Mr. Charles Owen Johnson
Chaplain General	Mrs. Joseph Barnett Paul
Chancellor General	Hon. Charles F. Stein, Jr.
Genealogist General	Mr. Abell Archibald Norris

1973 - 1976

Governor General	Mr. John Frederick Dorman
1st Deputy Governor General	Mrs. Russell Francis Barker
2nd Deputy Governor General	Mr. Charles Owen Johnson
3rd Deputy Governor General	Mrs. Lloyd Franklyn Wheeler
Recording Secretary General	Mrs. Edward Lynn Westbrooke
Corresponding Secretary General	Mrs. Lawrence O. Kupillas
Treasurer General	Mr. Samuel Hendrixson Newsome
Registrar General	Mr. J. Orton Buck
Chaplain General	Mrs. Joseph Barnett Paul
Chancellor General	Hon. Charles F. Stein, Jr.
Genealogist General	Mr. Robert Glenn Thurtle

1976 - 1979

Governor General	Mrs. Russell Francis Barker (Deceased)
1st Deputy Governor General	Mr. Charles Owen Johnson
2nd Deputy Governor General	Mrs. Lloyd Franklyn Wheeler
3rd Deputy Governor General	Mr. Nicholas Donnell Ward
Recording Secretary General	Mrs. Elden Loring Howe
Corresponding Secretary General	Mrs. Lawrence O. Kupillas
Treasurer General	Mr. Samuel Hendrixson Newsome
Registrar General	Mr. J. Orton Buck
Chaplain General	Mr. Abell Archibald Norris
Chancellor General	Mr. Brynn F. Aurelius
Genealogist General	Mr. Robert Glenn Thurtle

BRIEF HISTORY OF THE ORDER

1896 - 1980

1896   The Hereditary Order of Descendants of Colonial
                Governors was founded by Miss Mary Cabell
                Richardson of Covington, Kentucky.

1897   Mrs. Henry Whipple Skinner (Henrietta Dana) of
                Harbor Springs, Michigan, was named President.

1907   Miss Gail Treat of East Orange, New Jersey, became
                President. At her death in 1944 all of the records
                vanished, including the account of the first
                incorporation in New Jersey in 1907.

1944-1954   The Order was inactive, with the records missing.

1954-1961   In 1956 the Order was reactivated and was incor-
                porated in the District of Columbia under the
                leadership of Mrs. Hermann August Knorr of Pine
                Bluff, Arkansas, assisted by Mrs. Marguerite duPont
                Boden, Mrs. Helen Newberry Joy, Miss Stella Pickett
                Hardy and Mrs. Agnes L. Lepper.

                Following the incorporation, Mrs. Knorr was elected
                President in 1956. Through her tireless efforts
                bylaws were adopted, membership increased, member-
                ship certificates instituted and insignia revived.
                Mrs. Knorr was assisted by the first three members
                of the revived Order: #1-B Mrs. George Castleman
                Estill, #2-B Mrs. Joseph Barnett Paul, #3-B Mr.
                George Harrison Sanford King. A policy was adopted
                of restoring colonial records, using interest from
                the savings account.

                In 1959 "Henrico County, Virginia, Deeds and Wills
                1688-1697" was restored in honor of the President,
                Mrs. Knorr.

                In 1960 "Richmond County, Virginia, Deed Book #9,
                1734-1741" was restored in honor of the First Vice
                President, Mrs. Samuel Green Biggs. In 1961
                "Fredericksburg, Virginia, Will Book 1761-1820" was
                restored in honor of the Second Vice President,
                Mrs. Harry Clark Boden.

1961-1963   Mr. William Young Pryor of Essex Fells, New Jersey,
                was elected Governor General. After serving two
                years, a serious eye operation forced him to resign.
                During that time the voluminous papers of Miss
                Treat's regime were recovered from a barn in Con-
                necticut. With the help of Mrs. Pryor and other
                members living nearby these were sorted, indexed
                and filed for storage.

                In 1962 "King George County, Virginia, Marriage
                Register #1, 1786-1850" was restored in honor of
                the Governor General, Mr. Pryor.

1963-1967   Mr. Grahame Thomas Smallwood, Jr., served as
             Governor General for the final year of Mr. Pryor's
             term and in 1964 was elected Governor General.
             Plans were made for the publication of "Colonial
             Governors and Chief Executives of America Prior to
             July 4, 1776," to be edited by Mr. Smallwood. This
             will contain a brief history of each governor and
             where possible a photograph or a reproduction of
             his signature. In 1966 the first Membership Roster
             was published by Mr. Smallwood.

             In 1966 the following records were restored: "Orange
             County, Virginia, Marriage Bonds, 1837-1842," in
             honor of Mrs. Knorr: "North Farnham Parish Register
             1668-1800, Richmond County, Virginia," in honor of
             Mr. George H. S. King; and "Marriage Register kept
             by the Rev. William Forrester 1802-1842 in Richmond,
             Westmoreland and Northumberland Counties, Virginia,"
             in honor of Mr. King.

1967-1970   Mrs. Frederick Tracy Morse of Charlottesville,
             Virginia, was elected Governor General. In 1967
             "Richmond County, Virginia, Deed Book #10" was
             restored in honor of Mr. Smallwood. In 1968 and
             1969 "Box 1 and Box 2 of the Addison Papers" at the
             Maryland Historical Society were restored in honor
             of Mrs. Morse.

1970-1973   Mr. Warren Smith Hall, Jr., of Morristown, New
             Jersey, was elected Governor General. In 1972 a
             Roster of the Order was published by Mr. Hall.
             Necessary work toward a revision of the Bylaws was
             instituted.

1973-1976   Mr. John Frederick Dorman of Washington, D.C., was
             elected Governor General. In 1974 new Bylaws were
             adopted. In 1975 a Roster of the Order was
             published by Mr. Dorman.

1976-1979   Mrs. Russell Francis Barker of Atlantic City, New
             Jersey was elected Governor General for a two-year
             term under the 1974 Bylaws. Due to legal techni-
             calities no election was held in 1978 and Mrs.
             Barker was Governor General until 1979. During the
             latter part of 1978, however, Mrs. Barker became
             ill and Mr. Charles Owen Johnson, of Arlington,
             Virginia served, at Mrs. Barker's request, as
             Acting Governor General.

1979-   Mr. Charles Owen Johnson was elected Governor
             General. In 1979 a new Membership Roster of the
             Order was published. Culminating many years of
             effort, this 1980 Register was published showing
             the lineages and biographical sketches of all
             current members.

OUR MEMBERS AND THEIR COLONIAL GOVERNOR LINEAGES

ABAIRE, MADELINE PHELPS (MRS. ORLANDO)

Nat. #105-B. Elected 4 Dec 1964. b. Enfield, IL 2 Sep 1903. m. Chicago, IL 18 Sep 1943, Orlando Z. Abaire, b. Barre, VT 10 Jun 1904. Educ: MacCormac College, Chicago. Member: Hereditary Order of Desc. of Colonial Governors; Dau. of American Revolution (Past Regent, Santa Ana Chap.); Dau. of American Colonists (Past Regent, Hannah Hatch Chap.); Colonial Dames XVII Century; Soc. of Mayflower Desc. in California (Registrar, Los Angeles Colony); Dau. of Founders and Patriots of America; New England Women in Los Angeles; Huguenot Soc. of California (Councilor on State Board); Women Desc. of the Ancient and Honorable Artillery Co. (Past President, California Court of Assistants, National Chairman Junior Membership); Magna Charta Dames; Desc. of Colonial Clergy; Dames of Court of Honor in California; Order of Washington; Desc. of Founders of Hartford; American Heritage Soc. Address: 22400 Butterfield Road, #413, Richton Park, IL 60471. Descended from:

1 Thomas Dudley, Governor of Massachusetts 1634-35; 1640-41; 1645-46; 1650-51.

2 Mercy Dudley   John Woodbridge
  England 27 Sep 1621   Hartford,CT   Stanton, Eng. 1613
  Newbury,MA 1 Jul 1691   c.1639   Newbury 17 Mar 1695

3 Timothy Woodbridge   Mabel (Wyllys) Foster
  Wiltshire,Eng.   Hartford   Hartford c.1658
    13 Jan 1656
  Hartford 29 Apr 1732   bf.1686   Hartford c.1697

4 Mary Woodbridge   William Pitkin
  Hartford bf.1692   Hartford   Hartford 30 Apr 1694
  Hartford 17 Feb 1766   7 May 1724   E.Hartford 1 Oct 1769

5 Timothy Pitkin   Temperance Clapp
  Hartford 13 Jan 1727   New Haven,CT   Windham,CT 29 Apr 1732
  Farmington,CT 8 Jun   9 Aug 1753   New Haven 19 May 1772
    1812

6 Catherine Pitkin   Nathan Perkins
  Farmington 22 Feb 1757 Hartford   Lisbon,CT 12 May 1748
  W.Hartford 13 Sep 1838 1774   W.Hartford 18 Jan 1838

7 Timothy Pitkin Perkins   (3)   Nancy Lee
  W.Hartford Aug 1779   W.Hartford   Lyme,CT 18 Nov 1790
  Troy,NY 21 Dec 1858   1819   Troy 8 Jan 1881

8 Timothy Pitkin Perkins   Ann Marie Carpenter
  W.Hartford 1 Jul 1820   Quincy,IL   Waterbury,VT 25 Oct 1816
  St.Louis,MO 1 Apr 1879 -----   St.Louis 13 Feb 1859

9 Lillian Sherman Perkins   Lorenzo Augustus Phelps
  St.Louis 29 Sep 1855   Muscatine,IA   Natchez,MS 11 Jun 1840
  bf.1910   16 Oct 1874   Cairo,IL 29 Jan 1910

10 Frederick Lorenzo Phelps   Grace Celeste Brockett
   Muscatine 22 Feb 1877 Enfield,IL   Enfield 8 Aug 1882
   Chicago,IL 30 Mar 1943 3 Jan 1899   Chicago 11 Sep 1949

ABELL, ELIZABETH AUSTIN PORTER (MRS. WALTER WILLIAM, II)

Nat. #51-B. Elected 24 Jul 1962. b. Montclair,NJ 2 Feb 1899.
m. 16 Oct 1924, Walter William Abell II, b. Baltimore,MD 15 Aug
1898. Issue: Elizabeth Andree Abell Petticrew, b. 27 Nov 1925;
Helene Porter Abell Loring, b. 30 Jun 1951; Caroline S. Abell
Ellis, b. 2 Jan 1935. Member: Hereditary Order of Desc. of
Colonial Governors. Address: 151 Versailles Circle, Baltimore,
MD 21202. Descended from:

1 John Webster, Governor of Connecticut 1656

2 Robert Webster   Susannah Treat
   Cossington,Eng. c.1628 Middletown,CT   Pitminster,Eng. 1629
   Hartford,CT 1676   c.1652   Hartford 1705

3 Elizabeth Webster   John Seymour
   -----   -----   Hartford 12 Jun 1666
   15 May 1754   19 Dec 1693   Hartford 17 May 1748

4 Timothy Seymour   Rachel Allyn
   17 Jun 1696   -----   20 Aug 1694
   8 Sep 1749   27 Apr 1727   -----

5 Timothy Seymour   Lydia Kellogg
   1 Feb 1728   -----   22 Jul 1729
   Hartford 21 Dec 1782 1 Dec 1748   Litchfield,CT 6 Nov 1810

6 Amny Seymour   Moses Goodman
   15 Oct 1756   -----   W.Hartford 20 Jun 1750
   W.Hartford 7 Oct 1814 21 Oct 1780   W.Hartford 17 Aug 1831

7 Timothy S. Goodman   Amelia Faxon
   Hartford 5 Nov 1787 -----   Hartford 12 May 1791
   Cincinnati,OH 8 May 1 Dec 1814   Cincinnati 9 Sep 1872
   1869

8 Henry H. Goodman   Ester Ann Langdon
   Amherst,MA 25 Feb 1818 -----   Cincinnati 15 Aug 1822
   Cincinnati 16 May 1880 2 Dec 1840   Providence,RI 30 Mar
                                            1879

9 Florence Goodman   John B. Hawes
   New York,NY 10 Jun   -----   New York City 15 Jun
   1847   1844
   Montclair,NJ 26 Jun 29 Jun 1870   Montclair 28 Feb 1914
   1921

10 Helen Hawes   Hiland Porter
   New York City 9 Mar -----   Montclair 10 Dec 1871
   1872
   Baltimore,MD 10 May 16 Oct 1895   Stuart,FL 1 Feb 1942
   1950

   Inheritor: Mrs. Thacher Loring, 10858 E. Tanque Verde Rd.,
             Tucson, AZ 85715

ADDIS, VIRGINIA BOWERS DOWNES (MRS. ROLAND TAYLOR)

Nat. #325-B. Elected 26 Jun 1978. b. Dover,DE 23 Jul 1900.
m. Philadelphia,PA 26 Nov 1923, Roland Taylor Addis, b. Chelten-
ham,PA 20 Jul 1899, d. Bryn Mawr,PA 2 Jan 1972. Educ: Smith
College. Member: Hereditary Order of Desc. of Colonial Governors;
Colonial Dames of America in Pennsylvania; Soc. for Preservation
of Landmarks; Lower Merion Historical Soc. Address: 544 Avonwood
Rd., Haverford,PA 19041. Descended from:

1 Thomas Harvey, Deputy Governor of North Carolina 1694-1698.

2 Mary Harvey   Robert West
    Albemarle Co.,NC   -----   c.1681-89
      20 Nov 1694
    bf. 10 Apr 1729   bf.7 Jul 1716 af.1757

3 Robert West Jr.   -----
    bf.1721   -----   -----
    Bertie Co.,NC   -----   -----
      btw.Apr-Dec 1771

4 George West   Elizabeth Clark
    c.1758   -----   c.1766
    Montgomery Co.,TN   -----   Montgomery Co.,
      28 Jun 1810   30 Apr 1817

5 Mary West   Parry Wayne Humphreys
    Bertie Co. 1 Dec 1785   Montgomery Co. Staunton,VA c.1777-78
    af.1840   31 Jan 1805   Hernando,MS 16 Feb 1839

6 Elizabeth H. Humphreys   William H. Bayliss
    Sailor's Rest,TX   -----   Columbia Co.,GA
      22 Sep 1809   12 May 1806
    Marshall,TX 4 Sep 1872   1835   Amite City,LA 13 Jun
                                               1867

7 Elizabeth W. Bayliss   (2)   Thomas Martin Bowers
      Vander Hurst
    Hernando,MS 5 Jan 1844   Marshall   Fayette Co.,TN 18 Mar
                                               1837
    bur.Paris,TX 16 Dec   20 Mar 1866   Narberth,PA 31 Mar 1916
      1912

8 Robert (Bobb) Bowers   John Lee Carroll Downes
    Carthage,TX 23 Jun   Palestine,TX   Talbot Co.,MD 1878
      1878
    Nice,France 13 Feb   16 Sep 1897   Atlanta,GA 1 Jun 1948
      1928

ALLEN, MAUREEN K. THURTLE (MRS. ROBSON HUGH)

Nat. #233-B. Elected 1 May 1974. b. Plainfield,NJ 17 Feb 1939.
m. Belmont,CA 20 Aug 1960, Robson Hugh Allen, b. San Francisco,
CA 11 Nov 1937. Issue: Katherine Anne Allen, b. Santa Monica,CA
24 Jan 1962; Lisa Marie Allen, b. Santa Monica 12 May 1963; Mary
Virginia (Molly) Allen, b. San Rafael,CA 19 Feb 1965; Robert Hugh
Allen, b. San Rafael 9 Mar 1966; Matthew Brendan Allen, b. Reno,
NV 17 Jun 1970. Educ: Dominican College, San Rafael, B.A.
Member: Soc. of Mayflower Desc. in D.C.; Hereditary Order of
Desc. of Colonial Governors. Address: 2100 Andromeda Way, Reno,
NV 89502. Descended from:

1 Thomas Mayhew, Governor of Martha's Vineyard 1647-1681.

2 Martha Mayhew   Thomas Tupper
   Watertown,MA c.1638   Sandwich,MA   Sandwich 16 Jan 1638
   Sandwich 15 Nov 1717   27 Dec 1661   Sandwich 26 Apr 1706

3 Israel Tupper   Elizabeth Gifford
   Sandwich 22 Sep 1666   Sandwich   Falmouth,MA 25 Feb 1664
   Sandwich 1745   c.1690   Sandwich 19 Oct 1701

4 Thankful Tupper   Josiah Clark
   Sandwich 9 Oct 1696   Sandwich   Plymouth,MA 1690
   -----   30 Oct 1718   -----

5 Israel Clark   Deborah Pope
   · Plymouth 10 Sep 1720 Plymouth   Sandwich 23 Feb 1725
   Plymouth Oct 1788   13 May 1742   -----

6 Abigail Clark   Josiah Cornish
   Plymouth 13 May 1756   Plymouth   Plymouth 15 Oct 1760
   -----   15 Dec 1786   Lee Center,NY 10 Oct
                                                    1844

7 Allen Cornish   Clarissa Cornish
                                                    (cousin)
   Plymouth 1 Sep 1789   Plymouth   Plymouth 2 Nov 1792
   Lee Center 6 Apr 1853 18 Apr 1808   Lee Center 9 Jun 1864

8 George Cornish   Mary Tucker
   Lee Center 28 May 1825 New York,NY   New York City 2 May
                                                    1831
   Lee Center 3 Dec 1894 c.1848   Rome,NY 28 Apr 1898

9 Alice Cornish   Patrick Henry O'Donnell
   Lee Center 5 Nov 1853 Rome   Newport,NY 6 Nov 1850
   Albany,NY 24 May 1916 16 Apr 1862   Rome 18 Apr 1916

10 Mary Catherine   Charles Herbert Thurtle
      O'Donnell
   Elgin,IL 16 Mar 1875   Lincoln,NE   Knowlesville,NY 12 Oct
                                                    1877
   Euclid,OH 28 Mar 1948 2 Jun 1906   Lincoln 13 May 1947

11 Robert Glenn Thurtle   Mary Virginia Doyle
   Lincoln 2 Aug 1908   Omaha,NE   Greeley,NE 8 May 1908
   (living)   5 Jun 1934   (living)

4

ALMOND, ROXANNE M. ELMQUIST (MRS. RICHARD WESTON)

Nat. #237-B. Elected 30 May 1974. b. St. Paul,MN 30 Oct 1931.
m. New York,NY 25 May 1957, Richard Weston Almond, b. New York
City 14 May 1934. Issue: Weston Meredith Finch Almond, b. New
York City 10 Aug 1971. Educ: Bennett Junior College; Art Insti-
tute of Chicago; Yale Graduate School of Drama; Columbia
University, B.S.; New York University Institute of Fine Arts;
University of London. Member: Hereditary Order of Desc. of
Colonial Governors; Dau. of American Revolution; Dau. of American
Colonists; Dau. of Colonial Wars; New England Women; Washington
Headquarters Assn.; New York Genealogical and Biographical Soc.
Address: 401 East 65 St., New York,NY 10021. Descended from:

1 Benedict Arnold, Governor of Rhode Island 1657-60, 1662-66,
1677-78.

2 Caleb Arnold   Abigail Wilbur
  Providence,RI 19 Dec   Newport,RI   -----
  1644
  Newport 9 Feb 1719   10 Jun 1666   Newport 17 Nov 1730

3 William Arnold   Hannah Nichols
  Portsmouth 31 May 1677 Portsmouth,RI 7 Aug 1674
  Portsmouth 22 Sep 1723 22 Feb 1694   1723

4 William Arnold   Anne Coggeshall
  Portsmouth 18 Mar 1694 Portsmouth   Portsmouth 30 Jul 1699
  -----   27 Jan 1718   -----

5 Mary Arnold   Benjamin Lawton
  Portsmouth 19 Mar 1719 Portsmouth   Portsmouth 15 Apr 1715
  Portsmouth c.1752   16 Jan 1738   Portsmouth

6 Mary Lawton   Exekiel Tripp
  Portsmouth 15 Sep 1745 Exeter,RI   Exeter 9 Mar 1743
  Duanesburg,NY Feb 1827 29 Apr 1765   Duanesburg 23 Jul 1827

7 Sarah Tripp   Alpheus Finch
  Exeter 25 Nov 1775   Schoharie,NY Fredericksburg,NY
                                          29 Oct 1769
  Quaker Lake,PA 8 Apr   27 Nov 1794   Conklin,NY 19 Feb 1858
  1823

8 Alpheus Finch   Phoebe J. Waterman
  Quaker Lake 31 May   Binghamton,NY Chenango,NY 1821
  1815
  Binghamton 22 Jan 1880 24 Apr 1839   Binghamton 11 Mar 1889

9 Justin Finch   Caroline I. Pearson
  Binghamton 10 Aug 1857 -----   Binghamton 24 Oct 1856
  St.Paul,MN 19 Oct 1936 1876   Salmon,ID 15 Jul 1916

10 Ora Edna Finch   Theodore F. Thurston
   Towanda,PA 26 Feb 1877 St.Paul   St.Paul 29 Jun 1867
   St.Paul 12 Nov 1962   9 Jun 1903   St.Paul 14 Mar 1942

11 Dorothee M. Thurston   Roy E. Elmquist
   St.Paul 3 May 1904   St.Paul   St.Paul 13 Nov 1901
   (living)   6 Aug 1925   (living)

5

ALPER, ALICE GASKINS (MRS. THEODORE)

Nat. #M-261. b. Philadelphia,PA 11 Jul 1903. m. Scranton,PA
11 May 1937, Theodore Alper, b. Budapest, Hungary 13 Oct 1909.
Member: Hereditary Order of Desc. of Colonial Governors.
Address: 1626 33rd Street, N.W., Washington,DC 20007.
Descended from:

1 William Bradford, Governor of Plymouth Colony, 1621-33, 1635-
   36, 1637-38, 1639-44, 1645-57.

2 William Bradford   Alice Richards
   Plymouth,MA 17 Jun   Plymouth   c.1627
     1624
   Plymouth 20 Feb 1703   -----   Plymouth 12 Dec 1671

3 John Bradford   Mercy Warren
   Plymouth 20 Feb 1652   Plymouth   Plymouth 23 Sep 1653
   Kingston,MA 8 Sep 1736 6 Jan 1674   Kingston Mar 1747

4 Alice Bradford   Edward Mitchell
   Plymouth 28 Jan 1677   Plymouth   -----
   Hingham,MA 14 Jul 1746 26 Aug 1708   Bridgewater,MA
                                           15 Mar 1716

5 Edward Mitchell   Elizabeth Cushing
   Bridgewater 7 Feb 1715 Hingham   Hingham 21 May 1714
   Bridgewater 25 Dec 1801 14 Dec 1739   Bridgewater 9 May 1799

6 Cushing Mitchell   Jennet Orr
   Bridgewater 8 Dec 1740 Bridgewater   Bridgewater 14 Apr 1748
   Bridgewater 4 Jun 1820 26 Sep 1765   Bridgewater 25 Feb 1774

7 Nahum Mitchell   Nabby Lazell
   Bridgewater 12 Feb 1769 Bridgewater   Bridgewater 11 Jun 1778
   Plymouth 1 Aug 1853   11 Jun 1794   Boston,MA 23 Feb 1860

8 Jones H. Mitchell   Harriet L. Augier
   Bridgewater 15 Nov 1812 -----   26 Nov 1814
   Bridgewater 30 Jun 1872 1833   Bridgewater 16 Mar 1873

9 Henry H. Mitchell   Mary T. Wheletwest
   Belfast,ME 25 Jun 1839 Norfolk,VA   Prince Anne Co.,VA
                                           3 Jan 1845
   Philadelphia,PA   26 Dec 1864   Norfolk 28 Dec 1930
     16 Mar 1887

10 Maud A. Mitchell   Charles T. Gaskins
   Norfolk 14 Jun 1891   -----   VA 20 Sep 1859
   -----   -----   Philadelphia 5 Apr 1926

AMOS, EUGENE PAUL

Nat. #339-B. Elected 10 Oct 1978. b. Liberal,KS 20 Aug 1930.
m. Leavenworth Co.,KS 8 Mar 1953, Margaret Mae Zoll, b. Leaven-
worth Co. 18 Jul 1930. Educ: Kansas City,MO Junior College, A.A.;
Kansas City College of Mortuary Science. Member: Hereditary
Order of Desc. of Colonial Governors; Shawnee Historical Soc.
and a founder of Old Shawnee Town, a replica of an 1880 frontier
town (Past President); Lenexa Historical Soc.; Shawnee Mission
Historical Soc.; Sons of American Revolution (Delaware Crossing
Chap.). Address: 5925 Bluejacket, Shawnee,KS 66203.
Descended from:

1 John Webster, Governor of Connecticut 1656-57.

2 Robert Webster   Susannah Treat
   Middletown,CT 1627   Weathersfield, 1629
   31 May 1676   CT   1652   1705

3 Jonathan Webster   Dorcus Hopkins
   Middletown 9 Jan 1657   -----   -----
   1735   11 May 1681   1695

4 Jonathan Webster   Esther Judd
   Hartford,CT 18 Mar 1681 Bernardston,MA 8 Feb 1686
   Hartford 18 Sep 1758   14 Dec 1704   22 Dec 1782

5 Sarah Webster   John Keeney
   13 Jan 1718   -----   1712 or 15
   -----   -----   -----

6 Mark Keeney   Abigail Beeman
   CT 1 May 1740   Litchfield,CT   28 Apr 1739
   PA 7 Oct 1840   -----   7 Jul 1804

7 Richard Keeney   Mercy Keeney
   PA 17 Jun 1762   Braintrim,PA   15 Feb 1770
   PA 11 Jul 1831   18 Sep 1788   PA 14 Jun 1856

8 Ezra Keeney   (2)   Almira Dexter
   PA 15 Aug 1806   Laceyville,PA   PA 4 Sep 1824
   Laceyville 30 Nov 1873 15 Mar 1848   Pawnee Co.KS 2 Oct 1889

9 Harriet Elizabeth Keeney   Jude Goodale
   Wyoming Co.PA 14 Mar   Wyoming Co.   PA 26 Jul 1843
      1849
   Larned,KS 4 Apr 1927   7 Sep 1867   Larned 28 Jul 1916

10 Allie Maud Goodale   Joseph Crane
   Laceyville 17 Feb   Larned   Muscatine,IA 24 Dec
      1873   1870
   Larned 9 Feb 1954   17 Nov 1889   Larned 29 Apr 1942

11 Hazel Maude Crane   Edward Paul Amos
   Pawnee Co.KS 16 Aug   Baldwin,KS   Cimarron,KS 10 Aug
      1907   1907
   (living)   25 Feb 1928   Merriam,KS 7 Jan 1977

   Inheritor: Gregg Edward Amos, son

7

ANDERSEN, ELIZABETH FARR O'HANLON (MRS. THOR BJORN)

Nat. #244-B. Elected 19 Oct 1974. b. Danville,IL 26 Aug 1922.
m. Newark,NJ 1 Dec 1956, Thor Bjorn Andersen, b. New York,NY
12 Dec 1927. Issue: Julia Mundorff Andersen; Astrid Johanne
Andersen. Educ: Barnard College, New York City. Member:
Hereditary Order of Desc. of Colonial Governors (3rd Deputy
Governor General); Dau. of American Revolution (Past State
Chr.); Dau. of 1812; New England Women; Children of American
Revolution (Past State Librarian-Curator); Col. Daughters XVII
Century; Sons and Daughters of the Pilgrims; Dau. of American
Colonists; Dames of the Court of Honor (Vice Regent, NJ); Dau.
of Colonial Wars; Soc. of Desc. of Colonial Clergy; Huguenot
Society; Flagon and Trencher; Magna Charta Dames; Connecticut
Soc. of Genealogists. Address: 41 Park Road, Maplewood,NJ
07040. Descended from:

1 Roger Ludlow, Governor of Connecticut 1635, 1636

2 Sarah Ludlow   Nathaniel Brewster
   CT c.1643/4   -----   England c.1622/3
   Setauket,NY af.1699   1654   Setauket 18 Sep 1690

3 Daniel Brewster   Anna Jayne
   NY c.1668   Brookhaven   NY 1676
   Brookhaven,NY 15 Jun   c.1693   Brookhaven
      1748

4 John Brewster   Charity Biggs
   Brookhaven 1 Nov 1705   -----   NY 1711
   Blooming Grove,NY   -----   Blooming Grove
      23 Aug 1778   19 Nov 1786

5 Edward Brewster   Experience Reeve
   Blooming Grove   Blooming Gr.   NY 1744
      26 Aug 1740
   Blooming Grove Mar 1775 -----   New Windsor,NY 14 Feb
                                                1826

6 Sarah Brewster   John Sayre
   Blooming Grove   Blooming Gr.   Blooming Grove
      11 Sep 1771   24 Jul 1767
   Romulus,NY 30 Nov 1853 20 Dec 1789   Romulus 4 Mar 1848

7 Ann Sayre   Samuel Gulick
   Romulus 18 Dec 1793   Romulus   Alexandria,NJ 21 Nov
                                                1790
   Lodi,NY 9 Dec 1871   3 Jan 1813   Lodi 20 Jan 1877

8 Jane Gulick   Peter J. Van Vleet
   Lodi 22 Sep 1816   -----   Ovid,NY 2 Mar 1815
   12 Apr 1904   9 Feb 1837   Ovid 2 May 1910

9 Clarissa Van Vleet   George O'Hanlon
   Ovid 5 Jan 1840   Ovid   Elmira 4 Jan 1826
   Elmira,NY 27 Feb 1919   3 Nov 1859   Elmira 29 Jul 1897

10 George O'Hanlon   Elizabeth Farr
   Elmira 4 May 1870   Big Flats,NY   Big Flats 17 Nov 1868
   Elmira 26 Jun 1962   19 Jul 1899   Big Flats 16 Oct 1958

11 James Farr O'Hanlon   Althea Grau Mundorff
      King's Ark,NY 12 Apr   Chicago,IL   New York,NY 4 Nov 1902
      1900
      Zanesville,OH 24 May   19 Nov 1921   (living)
      1968

      Inheritor: James Geoffrey Scheffler, 41 Park Road, Maplewood,
      NJ 07040

ANDERSON, JOHN SHERBURNE, M.D.

Nat. #112-B. Elected 3 Apr 1965. b. Elgin,IL 19 Sep 1905.
m. New Orleans,LA 15 Sep 1929, Mary Mildred Stone Ware, b. Belle
Grove Plantation,LA 24 Dec 1904. Educ: Louisiana State Univ.,
M.D.; Univ. of North Carolina, CPH. Member: Hereditary Order of
Desc. of Colonial Governors; Louisiana Huguenot Soc. (Pres.);
Louisiana Gen. & Hist. Soc. (Pres.); Sons of American Revolution;
Soc. of War of 1812 (Asst. Surgeon Gen.); Soc. of Colonial Wars;
Jamestowne Soc.; Soc. of Desc. of King William, the Conqueror;
Plantagenet Soc.; Soc. of the Order of the Crown; Americans of
Royal Descent; Camelot and Pendennis Clubs of New Orleans. Occup:
Capt. Medical Corps, U.S. Army, Ophthalmologist. Address:
4654 Westdale Drive, Baton Rouge,LA 70808. Descended from:

1   Thomas Dudley, Governor of Massachusetts 1634-35, 1640-41,
    1645-46, 1650-51.

2   Anne Dudley   Simon Bradstreet
    Northamptonshire,Eng.   Hardingston,   Lincolnshire,Eng.
       c.1612   Eng.   bp. Mar 1603
    Andover,MA 16 Sep 1672   c.1628   Salem,MA 27 Mar 1697

3   Samuel Bradstreet   Mercy Tyng
    -----   -----   -----
    c.1682   -----   -----

4   Mercy Bradstreet   James Oliver
    -----   Cambridge,MA   10 Mar 1659
    -----   -----   -----

5   Sarah Oliver   Jacob Wendell
    Cambridge 4 Sep 1697   Boston,MA   Albany,NY bp.5 Aug 1691
    -----   12 Aug 1714   Boston c.1761

6   Sarah Wendell   John Hunt
    Boston 3 Mar 1721   Boston   Boston 13 Nov 1715
    -----   28 Feb 1739   Boston 29 May 1784

7   Elizabeth Hunt   Solomon Hewes
    Boston Feb 1752   Boston   Boston 4 Dec 1734
    Boston c.1785   1 Jul 1773   Boston 15 Oct 1806

8   Sarah Hunt Hewes   John Alexander Etheridge
    Boston 20 May 1774   Boston   Boston c.1772
    Louisville,KY 30 Nov   c.1797   At sea 1799
    1863

9 John Alexander   Alce Caroline North
    Etheridge
    Boston 25 Feb 1798   Boston   London,Eng. 8 Apr 1795
    Louisville 1 Jun 1854   1 Jul 1821   Louisville 17 Apr 1875

10 Caroline Susan   Palmer Ormsby Watts
    Etheridge
    Boston 9 Jul 1830   Louisville   1812
    Longton,KS May 1910   9 Oct 1845   c.1875

11 Isabella Jane Watts   John MacIntosh Anderson
    Louisville 12 Aug 1850 St.Louis,MO   Woodstock,Can. 20 Sep
                                                1841
    Independence,KS   12 Jul 1871   Independence 22 Apr
      22 Apr 1915   1915

12 John Albert Anderson   Ethel Eugenia Gaulden
    Independence 12 May   Gloster,MS   Wilkinson,MS 30 Jun
      1875   1883
    Baton Rouge,LA 17 May   30 Aug 1904   Baton Rouge 29 Mar 1957
      1941

                          SUPPLEMENT NO. 1

1 Simon Bradstreet, Governor of Massachusetts 1679-86, 1689-92.

2 Samuel Bradstreet   Mercy Tyng

    Continue with Generation 3 of his lineage from Governor Thomas
    Dudley.

                          SUPPLEMENT NO. 2

1 Colonel Giles Brent, Governor of Maryland 1643-1644.

2 Katherine Brent   Richard Marsham
    Stafford Co.VA c.1649   Calvert Co.MD   England c.1638
    Calvert Co. c.1690   c.1665   Prince George's Co.MD
                                                c.1713

3 Katherine Marsham   (2)   Samuel Queen
    Calvert Co. c.1672   Pr.George's Co.-----
    Pr.George's Co. c.1712 c.1700   Pr.George's Co. 1711

4 Margaret Queen   John Belt
    Pr.George's Co. 1709   Pr.George's Co.Pr.George's Co. 13 Mar
                                                1707
    Pr.George's Co. 1767   4 Mar 1727/8   Pr.George's Co. af.1778

5 Catherine Belt   Benjamin Brashear
    Pr.George's Co. 18 Mar Pr.George's Co.Pr.George's Co. 19 Sep
      1729/30   1727
    Pr.George's Co. 1773   c.1750   Jefferson Co.MS af.1808

6 Tobias Brashear   Martha Brocus
    Pr.George's Co. c.1754 Kaskaskias,IL   c.1760
    Claiborn Co.MS   Oct 1780   Claiborn Co. Jan 1813
      Dec 1807

7   Martha Brashear   William Lindsay
    St.Clair Co.IL c.1788   Port Gibson   Pittsylvania Co.VA
                                                 1769
    Port Gibson,MS 17 Jul   1805   Claiborne Co. Dec 1817
    1821

8   Margaret Newton Lindsay   Eugene Amedee Sherburne
    Claiborne Co. 1816   Baton Rouge   St.Malo,France 1802
    Baton Rouge,LA 25 Jul   1832   Baton Rouge 2 Nov 1860
    1852

9   William Lindsay   Sarah Eliza Caston
    Sherburne
    Plaquemine,LA 21 May   Baton Rouge   Amite Co.MS 24 Jul 1844
    1835
    Zachary,LA 12 Feb 1872   3 May 1861   Amite Co. 8 Sep 1898

10 Martha Newton   Thomas Calvin Gaulden
    Sherburne
    Amite Co. 23 Jul 1864   Wilkinson Co.   Wilkinson Co. 21 Jul
                             MS   1853
    Mangham,LA 13 Dec   1 Mar 1882   Wilkinson Co. 27 Sep
    1955   1895

11 Ethel Eugenia Gaulden   John Albert Anderson

Continue with Generation 12 of his lineage from Governor
Thomas Dudley.

SUPPLEMENT NO. 3

1   Captain Thomas Wiggin, Governor of New Hampshire 1631-37.

2   Thomas Wiggin   Sarah Barefoot
    Squanscot Patent,NH   Dover,NH   -----
    Dover af.1700   -----   -----

3   Sarah Wiggins   Henry Sherburne
    Dover 1669   Portsmouth   Portsmouth 1666
    Portsmouth,NH af.1738   13 Mar 1693   Portsmouth Aug 1738

4   Catherine Sherburne   Samuel Sherburne
    Portsmouth Mar 1705   Portsmouth   Portsmouth c.1688
    Conway,NH Jan 1808   25 Aug 1734   Portsmouth af.1740

5   Henry Sherburne   Phebe Dennett
    Portsmouth bp.31 Jul   Portsmouth   -----
    1737
    Conway 1823   28 Oct 1765   -----

6   Samuel Sherburne   Rose Ursula DuBois de
                                                   Corbein
    Portsmouth bp.29 Apr   Nantes,   France
    1770   France
    Baton Rouge,LA 6 Oct   c.1798   Baton Rouge 9 Jun 1824
    1819

7   Eugene Amedee Sherburne   Margaret Newton Lindsay

Continue with Generation 8 of his lineage from Governor Giles
Brent.

Inheritor: Eugene Joseph Sherburne, 806 West Grant Street,
Baton Rouge,LA 70802.

ARMIN, SADIE COLLINS (MRS. LOT W.)

Nat. #252-B. Elected 7 Feb 1975. b. Spokane,WA 18 Apr 1891.
m. Spokane 17 Apr 1915, Lot Wilbur Armin, b. Lake Park,IA 22 Jan
1888, d. Sioux Falls,SD 4 Jan 1949. Issue: Dayton Armin, b.
Yale,SD 19 Feb 1916. Educ: Whitman College, Walla Walla,WA, A.B.
Member: Hereditary Order of Desc. of Colonial Governors; Magna
Charta Dames; Dau. of American Revolution; Dau. of Founders and
Patriots of America; John Howland Soc.; Women Desc. of Ancient
and Honorable Artillery; Soc. of Desc. of Colonial Clergy; Soc.
of Mayflower Desc.; Washington Family Desc.; Dau. of Pioneers of
Washington. Address: 205 West 18th Street, Apt. 33, Sioux Falls,
SD 57105. Descended from:

1 Peleg Sanford, Governor of Rhode Island 1680-83.

2 Ann Sanford   James Noyes
   Newport,RI 1675/6   Rhode Island   Stonington,CT 2 Aug
                                            1677
   Rhode Island   1703   Rhode Island 1718

3 Dorothy Noyes   John Brown
   RI 1 Oct 1712   Stonington   Newport 1702
   Stonington 16 Oct 1772 4 Jul 1728   Stonington 25 Sep 1782

4 John Brown   Mary Holmes
   Stonington 25 Jul 1735 Stonington   Stonington 8 Aug 1745
   Stonington 25 Jul 1777 2 Jul 1767   Stonington 12 Sep 1809

5 Clark Brown   Tabitha Moffatt
   Stonington 25 Jan 1771 Brimfield,MA   Brimfield 1 May 1780
   Maryland 12 Jan 1817   1 Dec 1799   Salem,OR 4 May 1858

6 Pherne Tabitha Brown   Virgil Kellogg Pringle
   Montpelier,VT 22 Mar   St.Charles,MO Harwinton,CT 29 Jul
     1805   1804
   Salem 21 May 1891   4 May 1827   Salem 24 Mar 1887

7 Clark Spencer Pringle   Catherine Carney Sager
   Warren Co.,MO 17 Apr   Salem   Union Co.,OH 15 Apr
     1830   1835
   Spokane,WA 19 Oct 1914 29 Oct 1851   Spokane 10 Aug 1910

8 Lucia Naomi Pringle   Dayton C. Collins
   Linn Co.,OR 24 Nov   Colfax,WA   Middlesex,NY 13 Jan
     1871   1855
   Shelton,WA 25 Dec 1944 22 Jun 1890   Seattle,WA 7 Oct 1940

Inheritor: Dayton Collins Armin, 1400 East 49th Street, Sioux
Falls,SD 57103

ATWOOD, ROSWELL LEVI

Nat. #221-B. Elected 5 Nov 1973. b. Salem,MA 20 Oct 1910.
m. Boston,MA 24 Dec 1933, Thelma Bowlby, b. Lexington,MA 24 Aug
1908. Issue: Alden Atwood, b. Boston 14 Jun 1935. Educ: Boston
University, A.B. 1934. Member: Hereditary Order of Desc. of
Colonial Governors; Soc. of Mayflower Desc. in D.C.; Sons of
American Revolution in D.C.; Soc. of Desc. of Colonial Clergy;
Sons of Revolution; Order of Founders and Patriots of America;
Desc. of Magna Charta Barons; Knights of the Garter; Order of the
Crown of Charlemagne; Soc. of War of 1812 in D.C. Occup:
Education Consultant, Writer; Author of "Atwood's Rules for
Meetings." Address: 1701 Massachusetts Ave., N.W., Washington,DC
20036. Descended from:

1 Thomas Prence, Governor of Plymouth Colony 1634-1673.

2 Hannah Prence   Nathaniel Mayo
  bf.1635   Eastham,MA   England c.1627
  bf. 23 Nov 1698   13 Feb 1650   Eastham 1662

3 Thomas Mayo   Barbara Knowles
  Eastham 7 Dec 1650   Eastham   Eastham 28 Sep 1656
  Eastham 23 Apr 1729   13 Jun 1677   Eastham 23 Feb 1714/5

4 Judah Mayo   Mary Hamilton
  Eastham 25 Sep 1691   Chatham   -----
  Chatham,MA 1761   27 Jan 1722   -----

5 Barbara Mayo   George Smith
  Eastham c.1730   Chatham   Chatham Dec 1731
  -----   16 Oct 1755   18 Jul 1763

6 Stephen Smith   Marjorie Crowell
  Chatham 8 Nov 1763/4   Chatham   Chatham 23 Jan 1763
  Chatham 14 Sep 1832   25 Aug 1791   Chatham 13 Aug 1850

7 Lucy Smith   Solomon Atwood
  Chatham 6 Sep 1793   Chatham   Chatham 6 Aug 1785
  Chatham 29 Nov 1868   8 Dec 1814   Chatham 26 May 1848

8 Levi Atwood   Phebe Mason Hatch
  Chatham 25 Mar 1824   Chatham   Andover,MA 20 Jan 1827
  Chatham 3 Sep 1898   26 Mar 1850   Chatham 18 Jan 1890

9 Roswell Atwood   Idella M. Smith
  Chatham 20 Oct 1855   Chatham   Chatham 25 Sep 1857
  Chatham 26 Dec 1909   25 Dec 1877   Chatham 25 Sep 1903

10 Henry Romine Atwood   (1)   Mabel Bailey
   Chatham 20 Dec 1879   Providence,RI   Claxton-on-Sea, Eng.
                                              31 Jun 1883
   Boston,MA 27 Dec 1929   6 May 1906   Boston 8 Mar 1919

AURELIUS, BRYNN FREDERIC

Nat. #142-B. Elected 14 May 1968. b. Ridgewood,NJ 19 Feb 1940.
m. Greenwich,CT 27 Aug 1966, Suzan Wren Kennard, b. San Antonio,
TX 26 Mar 1943. Issue: Dunham Moore Aurelius, b. Ridgewood
28 Jun 1970; Campbell Kennard Aurelius, b. Atlanta,GA 25 Feb
1972. Educ: College of William and Mary,A.B.; New York University of Law, LLB. Member: Hereditary Order of Desc. of Colonial
Governors (Chancellor General); Soc. of the Cincinnati; St.
Nicholas Soc. of New York City; Soc. of Colonial Wars in Texas;
The English Speaking Union; American Bar Assn. Occup: Attorney
at Law. Address: 5706 Lodge Creek Drive, Houston,TX 77040.
Descended from:

1 Simon Bradstreet, Governor of Massachusetts 1679-1692

2 Mercy Bradstreet   Nathaniel Wade
   Andover,MA 1650   Andover   1648
   Medford,MA 5 Oct 1715 31 Oct 1672   27 Nov 1707

3 Johnathan Wade   Mary
   5 Mar 1681   -----   -----
   -----   -----   -----

4 Nathaniel Wade   Ruth (Hopkins) Hawkins
   22 Feb 1706   Scituate,RI   14 Mar 1711
   29 Jun 1754   26 Jun 1731   23 Nov 1789

5 Dudley Wade   Katherine Alverson
   Scituate 11 Dec 1734   Gloucester,RI   -----
   Paris,NY 10 Apr 1803   1757   Oneida Co.NY 27 Dec
                                           1805

6 Lydia Wade   John Nichols
   -----   -----   Brimfield,MA 24 Aug
                                           1760
   Attica,NY   -----   Attica 18 Feb 1817

7 Oliva W. Nichols   Roswell H. Brown
   Brimfield 3 Apr 1790   -----   Whiting,VT 7 Sep 1791
   Union City,PA 7 Mar   Apr 1818   Union City Oct 1865
   1865

8 Catherine A. Brown   George A. Moore
   Attica 12 Mar 1819   Buffalo,NY   Fabius,NY 27 Mar 1814
   Hamburg,NY 16 Mar 1884 1 Jan 1839   Buffalo 28 Dec 1890

9 Anna M. Moore   Daniel W. Allen
   Buffalo 27 Oct 1855   Buffalo   N.Collins,NY 9 Mar
                                           1856
   Hamburg 21 Sep 1952   10 Jul 1879   Hamburg 29 Jun 1909

10 Carrie L. Allen   Frederick Dunham
   Buffalo 5 Jun 1880   Buffalo   Buffalo 22 Mar 1878
   Ridgewood,NJ 7 Jan 1959 10 Apr 1909   Hackensack,NJ 24 Dec
                                           1943

11 Elizabeth Dunham   William M. Aurelius
   Albany,NY 31 Aug 1914 Ridgewood   St.Paul,MN 20 Oct 1899
                          22 Feb 1937

14

BACON, RALPH HOYT

Nat. #113-B. Elected 15 May 1965. b. Kenosha,WI 16 Jul 1907.
Educ: Fordham University, A.B.; Columbia University, M.A.; New
York University, Ph.D. Member: Hereditary Order of Desc. of
Colonial Governors; Sons of the Revolution; Sons of American
Revolution (Registrar, Empire State Soc.); Gen. Soc. of Colonial
Wars (Historian); Order of Founders and Patriots of America
(Registrar, N.Y. Soc.); Baronial Order of Magna Charta; Soc. of
Desc. of Founders of Hartford; Soc. of Desc. of Colonial Clergy;
Connecticut Hist. Soc.; New England Hist. and Gen. Soc. Address:
Box 190, Brewster,NY 10509. Descended from:

1 Thomas Welles, Governor of Connecticut 1658-59.

2 Samuel Welles   Elizabeth Hollister
   England c.1630   Wethersfield   Wethersfield,CT
   Wethersfield 15 Jul   1659   Glastonbury,CT 1673
   1675

3 Ann Welles   James Steel
   Wethersfield 1668   Wethersfield   1664
   Wethersfield 1739   19 Jul 1687   15 May 1713

4 Prudence Steel   Josiah Deming
   Wethersfield 17 Jan   Wethersfield   Wethersfield 1688
   1693
   Newington,CT 10 Jul   8 Dec 1714   Newington 12 Aug 1761
   1752

5 Gamaliel Deming   Rebecca Kellogg
   Newington 1727   Newington   Newington 11 Jul 1732
   Arlington,VT 18 Dec   18 Jul 1751   Arlington 27 Aug 1816
   1802

6 Rebecca Deming   Joseph Curtis
   Newington 10 Nov 1756 Arlington   Newington 12 Apr 1756
   Egremont,MA 12 Mar 1825 15 Dec 1778   Egremont 16 May 1810

7 Rhoda Curtis   Levi Hare
   Egremont 11 May 1788 Egremont   Egremont 7 Feb 1780
   Egremont 3 Apr 1859   -----   Egremont 16 Jun 1860

8 Rebecca D. Hare   Samuel Bacon
   Egremont 18 Jun 1805 Egremont   Egremont 19 May 1799
   Binghamton,NY 11 Apr 29 Jan 1823   Newark,NJ 1 Jun 1894
   1861

9 Levi A. Bacon   Ellen B. Kiely
   Egremont 12 May 1833 Milwaukee   Kingston, Canada
                                          15 May 1844
   Milwaukee,WI 14 Sep   22 Jan 1861   Milwaukee 3 Jun 1895
   1888

10 Ralph F. Bacon   Mabel R. Hoyt
   Milwaukee 25 Feb 1876 Brooklyn,NY   Brooklyn 21 Jun 1876
   New Rochelle,NY 30 Aug 16 Oct 1906
   1942

1 John Steel, Governor of Connecticut 1635-36

2 Mary Steel
   -----   Farmington,
                      CT
   Farmington 12 Oct 1718 c.1658

William Judd
Cambridge,MA c.1632

Farmington 1690

3 Thomas Judd
   Farmington 13 Nov 1662 -----
   Waterbury,CT   9 Feb 1687/8
     4 Jan 1746/7

Sarah Freeman
Milford,CT c.1670
Waterbury 8 Sep 1738

4 Rachel Judd
   Waterbury 19 Nov 1694 Waterbury
   Southington,CT   27 Jan 1718
    13 Jul 1756

Thomas Upson
Waterbury 1 Mar 1692
Southington 29 Sep
  1761

5 Amos Upson
   Southington 17 Mar   Southington
    1734
   Southington 8 Jul   27 Feb 1766
    1819

Sarah Woodruff
Southington 13 Jul
  1740
Southington 13 Feb
  1797

6 Lucy Upson
   Southington 19 Nov   Southington
    1766
   Egremont,MA 24 Oct   29 Dec 1788
    1862

Andrew Bacon
Canaan,CT 19 Sep 1765

Egremont 23 Aug 1840

7 Samuel Bacon   Rebecca D. Hare

Continue with Generation 8 of his lineage from Governor
Thomas Welles.

Inheritor: Mary Susan Bacon Pratt (Mrs. Mark R.), 734 Bison
Drive, Houston,TX 77024.

BAILEY, MARY ETHEL (MISS)

Nat. #166-B. Elected 4 Jan 1971. b. Athens,GA 26 Dec 1902.
Educ: Georgia State Teachers College, B.S. in Educ.; University
of Georgia, B.S. in Home Economics; University of Tennessee, M.S.
Member: Hereditary Order of Desc. of Colonial Governors; Dau. of
American Revolution (First Vice-Regent, Chr. of Veteran Service,
Edward Buncombe Chap.); Sons and Daughters of the Pilgrims (Past
State Gov. and Rec. Sec'y, North Carolina); First Families of
Virginia; Jamestowne Society; Historical Society of N.C.;
Colonial Dames of XVII Century (Past Pres., Gov. Philip Ludwell
Chap., Past State Historian, Chaplain, and Pres.); Dau. of
American Colonists (Past State Regent); Dames of Court of Honor;
Magna Charta Dames. Occup: High School Teacher. Address:
89 Edgemont Road, Asheville,NC 28801. Descended from:

1   Richard Bennett, Governor of Virginia 1652-55.

2   Anna Bennett   Theodorick Bland
    Weyanoke,VA c.1642   -----   London,Eng. 16 Jan 1629
    Wharton's Creek,MD   1660   Charles City Co.,VA
      Nov 1687   23 Apr 1671

3   Richard Bland   (2)   Elizabeth Randolph
    Charles City Co. 11 Aug -----   Henrico Co.,VA c.1680
      1665
    Prince George's Co.,MD 11 Feb 1701   Charles City Co.
      10 Apr 1720   20 Jan 1719

4   Richard Bland   Ann Poythress
    Prince George's Co.   -----   Prince George's Co.
      6 May 1710   13 Dec 1712
    Prince George's Co.   21 Mar 1729   Prince George's Co.
      26 Oct 1776   9 Apr 1758

5   Ann Bland   Alexander Morrison
    Prince George's Co.   -----   Prince George's Co.
      15 Aug 1735
    Virginia   c.1755   Prince George's Co.

6   Alexander Morrison   Mary Ann -----
    Prince George's Co.   Virginia   VA c.1784
      c.1760
    Jackson Co.GA 6 Jan   -----   Jackson Co. 1839
      1839

7   Elizabeth B. Morrison   Alexander E. Bacon
    Jackson Co. 1812   -----   Jackson Co. 1812
    Jackson Co. 1 Jan 1901 7 May 1833   Nashville,TN 5 May 1862

8   Mary A. Bacon   John Sailors
    Jackson Co. 19 Mar   Jackson Co.   Jackson Co. 5 Aug 1837
      1835
    Clarke Co.GA 15 Mar   30 Jan 1867   Jackson Co. 7 Apr 1887
      1924

9   Florrie C. Sailors   Cicero F. Bailey
    Jackson Co. 28 Apr   Clarke Co.GA   Jackson Co. 18 Sep
      1876   1861
    Fulton Co.GA 15 Jul   23 Jun 1897   Clarke Co. 21 Jun 1926
      1948

    Inheritor: Miss Ashley Bailey, 4176 North Carmel Drive, Mobile,
               AL 36608

17

BAIRD, STELLA (MISS)

Nat. #200-B. Elected 20 Mar 1973. b. Ola, ID 18 May 1881.
Educ: University of Idaho and University of Washington.
Member: Hereditary Order of Desc. of Colonial Governors; Magna
Charta Dames; Soc. of Knights of the Most Noble Order of the
Garter; Plantagenet Soc.; Americans of Royal Descent; First
Families of Virginia; Dau. of American Colonists; Huguenot Soc.;
Colonial Dames of XVII Century; Dau. of American Revolution
(Recording Secretary, Registrar, Historian). Occup: U.S.
Government Secretary. Address: 1720 MacArthur Blvd., Oakland,
CA 94602. Descended from:

1 Richard Bennett, Governor of Virginia 1652-55.

2 Anna Bennett   (2)   St.Leger Codd
   Weyanoke,VA c.1642   -----   England 1635
   Wharton's Creek,MD   1671   MD 1707
      Nov 1687

3 St.Leger Codd   Mary Hanson
   VA 1680   Maryland   Kimballton,VA 16 Dec
                                                 1680
   Maryland   c.1700   -----

4 Mary St.Leger Codd   James Stout
   Maryland   Maryland   Hopewell,NJ 1709
   NJ 1787   Feb 1731   NJ 1785

5 St.Leger Stout   Susannah -----
   Hunterdon Co.NJ 1736   -----   -----
   Amwell,NJ 10 Feb 1767   -----   NJ 1770

6 St.Leger Stout   Ann Barcalow
   Amwell,NJ 1 Feb 1755   New Jersey   New Jersey
   Beverly,WV 5 Apr 1806   1794   Beverly af.1806

7 John Stout   Barbara Casner
   Randolph Co.WV 21 Dec   Randolph Co.   Randolph Co. 1799
      1795
   Ottumwa,IA 6 May 1858   8 Jan 1816   Albia,IA 20 May 1876

8 Clarissa Stout   Eber Taylor
   Randolph Co. 29 Apr   Van Buren Co. PA 6 Sep 1811
      1817   IA
   Junction City,OR   4 Apr 1841   Junction City 11 Aug
      20 Jul 1861   1886

9 Sarepta A. Taylor   Carroll Baird
   Ottumwa 3 Apr 1843   Monroe,OR   West Fork,AR 15 Jun
                                                 1838
   Oakland,CA 6 Oct 1929   25 Dec 1859   Long Beach,CA 6 Aug
                                                 1914

BARBARA, ELIZABETH ONATA MUNSEY (MRS. ANTHONY ANDREW)

Nat. #310-B. Elected 5 Apr 1977. b. New Castle,ME 4 Mar 1904.
m. Derry,NH 16 Mar 1938, Anthony Andrew Barbara, b. Somerville,
MA 16 Aug 1895, d. Wayland,MA 6 Sep 1960. Educ: Registered Nurse
with Post Graduate in Surgery. Member: Hereditary Order of Desc.
of Colonial Governors; Dau. of American Revolution (Chap. Regent,
State Registrar, Chaplain); Children of American Revolution
(Senior Pres., State Chaplain, Registrar); Dau. of Colonial Wars
(State Custodian, Councillor); Soc. of Desc. of Colonial Clergy;
Founders and Patriots (Chaplain); Magna Charta Dames; Colonial
Dames of 17th Century; Dames of Court of Honor; Ancient and
Honorable Artillery Co. Address: Sandy Burr Country Club, Box
396, Wayland,MA 01778. Descended from:

1 Tristram Coffin, Governor of Nantucket 1671-73.

2 Tristram Coffin   Judith (Greenleaf)
                                            Somerby
   Brixton,Eng. 1632   Newbury,MA   England 2 Sep 1625
   Newbury 4 Feb 1703   2 Mar 1653   Newbury 15 Dec 1705

3 Stephen Coffin   Sarah Atkinson
   Newbury 18 Aug 1664   Newbury   Newbury 27 Nov 1665
   Newbury 31 Aug 1725   8 Oct 1685   Newbury 20 Jan 1724/5

4 Benjamin Coffin   Miriam Woodman
   Newbury 14 Jun 1710   Newbury   Newbury 13 Mar 1715
   Newbury 30 Apr 1784   28 Oct 1731   -----

5 Benjamin Coffin   (2)   Anna Kincaid
   Newbury 6 Sep 1735   Wiscasset,ME   Wiscasset
   Wiscasset 1 Nov 1818   10 Mar 1763   -----

6 Miriam Coffin   Samuel Jackson
   Wiscasset 1772   Wiscasset   Wiscasset 1769/70
   Wiscasset 9 Feb 1841   11 Oct 1790   Wiscasset 10 Jul 1837

7 Malinda Jackson   (int)   Rollins Munsey
   Wiscasset 1798   Wiscasset   Wiscasset Dec 1803
   Wiscasset Aug 1846   21 Oct 1827   Wiscasset 13 Feb 1863

8 Horace B. Munsey   (2)   Hannah (Somes) Hall
   Wiscasset 14 May 1837 Edgecomb,ME   Edgecomb Jun 1845
   Edgecomb 17 Mar 1902   16 Dec 1873   New Castle,ME 13 Aug
                                              1907

9 Virdell Thomas Munsey   Minnie Etta Dodge
   Edgecomb 6 Feb 1879   Wiscasset   Boston,MA 25 Nov 1878
   -----   22 Dec 1898   Concord,MA 11 Feb 1970

BARKER, C. AUSTIN

Nat. #130-B. Elected 21 Jan 1968. b. Centralia,WA 2 Dec 1911.
m. Ridgefield,CT 29 Mar 1941, Mary Ellen Brown, b. Filer,ID
19 May 1914. Issue: Beverly Jean Barker, b. Shaker Heights,OH
16 Jul 1945; Steven Warner Barker, b. Shaker Heights 17 May 1948.
Educ: Stanford University, A.B.; New York University Grad. Sch.
of Business Administration, M.B.A. 1939. Member: Hereditary

Order of Desc. of Colonial Governors; Order of Founders and
Patriots of America (Treasurer, Chaplain); Sons of American
Revolution, Empire State Soc.   Occup: Vice Pres., Consulting
Economist - Hornblower & Weeks - Hemphill, Noyes Inc. Chartered
Financial Analyst.   Address: 2 Hickory Drive, Rye,NY 10580.
Descended from:

1 John Webster, Governor of Connecticut 1656.

2 Mary Webster   John Hunt
   -----   England   England
   bf.1659   -----   -----

3 Jonathan Hunt   Clemence Hosmer
   England 1637   -----   -----
   Northampton,MA 29 Sep   2 Sep 1663   Northampton 8 Jul 1689
      1691

4 Mary Hunt   Ebenezer Sheldon
   Northampton 24 Mar   Northampton   Northampton 1 Mar 1677
      1679
   Northampton 10 Nov   6 Dec 1701   Northampton 18 Mar
      1767   1755

5 Stephen Sheldon   Thankful King
   Northampton 2 Feb 1709   Southampton   MA 9 Feb 1712
   Southampton,MA 1781   1736   -----

6 Thankful Sheldon   Elihu Strong
   Southampton 1748   Northampton   Northampton 12 Aug 1744
   -----   1768   -----

7 Thankful Strong   Elisha Barker
   Northampton 16 Apr 1773 Methuen,MA   Methuen 1770
   Italy,NY 4 Mar 1850   24 Sep 1801   Italy

8 Orlando Barker   Fidelia Barker
   Methuen 2 Aug 1803   Methuen   Methuen 11 Feb 1805
   Whitewater,MI 16 Jun   1827   Whitewater 8 May 1869
      1869

9 Moses B. Barker   Lucy A. Marsh
   Italy 18 Aug 1831   Battle Creek,   Waterford,CT 21 Jun
                               MI   1835
   Forest,WA 19 Oct 1911   3 Nov 1855   Hillsdale,MI 4 Jun
                                               1865

10 Marcus G. Barker   Aletha J. Sharp
   Hillsdale 12 Sep 1858   Traverse City, Michigan 1856
                               MI
   Sacramento,CA 11 May   6 Oct 1881   Centralia,WA 28 Mar
      1944   1890

11 Clarence G. Barker   Susan M. McElroy
   Traverse City 13 Dec   Seattle,WA   Cedar Rapids,IA 14 Sep
      1882   1888
   Sacramento 26 Jun   27 Jul 1908
      1947

   Inheritor: Steven Warner Barker, son.

BARRINGTON, LAURENCE WALKER LIVINGSTON

Nat. #296-B. Elected 25 Sep 1976. b. New York,NY 4 Mar 1905.
m. Meriden,CT 13 Apr 1935, Lois Barbara Hall, b. Meriden 13 Jun
1908. Educ: Wesleyan University, B.A.; University of Maine,
M.A. Member: Hereditary Order of Desc. of Colonial Governors;
Sons of American Revolution; Desc. of Old Plymouth Colony;
Worcester Historical Society. Address: 130 Flagg Street,
Worcester,MA 01609. Descended from:

1 William Bradford, Governor of Plymouth Colony 1621-33; 1635-
   36; 1637-38; 1639-44; 1645-57.

2 William Bradford   Alice Richards
   Plymouth,MA 17 Jun 1624 -----   -----
   Plymouth 20 Feb 1703   -----   -----

3 Mercy Bradford   Samuel Steele
   Plymouth   -----   15 Mar 1652
   Hartford,CT 1720   16 Sep 1680   Hartford 1710

4 Daniel Steele   Mary Hopkins
   Hartford 3 Apr 1697 -----   -----
   West Hartford,CT   1725   -----
     28 May 1770

5 Timothy Steele   Sarah Seymour
   Hartford 1736   -----   1740
   Albany,NY 27 Dec 1808 -----   -----

6 Daniel Steele   Elizabeth Van Benthuy-
                                             sen
   Hartford 20 March 1772 -----   10 Mar 1777
   Albany 7 Jul 1828   15 Apr 1797   17 Mar 1825

7 Oliver Steele   Mary Augusta Livingston
   Albany 16 Aug 1800   Albany   1800
   -----   7 Mar 1826   11 Mar 1839

8 Lavinia Livingston   Amos Markham Kellogg
     Steele
   Albany 15 Dec 1832   Farmington,CT   Clinton,NY 4 Jun 1831
   New Rochelle,NY 28 Jan 6 Jul 1857   New Rochelle 3 Oct
     1910   1914

9 Amy Livingston Kellogg   Robert Walker
                                             Barrington
   Bergen,NJ 24 Feb 1867 Orange,NJ   New York,NY 9 Mar 1866
   Worcester,MA 13 Sep   7 Apr 1894   New Rochelle 17 Jul
     1944   1948

BARRINGTON, LOIS BARBARA HALL (MRS. LAURENCE W. L.)

Nat. #295-B. Elected 25 Sep 1976. b. Meriden,CT 13 Jun 1908.
m. Meriden 13 Apr 1935, Laurence W. L. Barrington, b. New York,
NY 4 Mar 1905. Educ: Smith College, A.B. Member: Hereditary
Order of Desc. of Colonial Governors; Dau. of American Revolution; New England Women; Desc. of Old Plymouth Colony; Women

Desc. of the Ancient and Honorable Artillery Co.; Soc. of Desc.
of Colonial Clergy; Worcester Historical Soc.; Friends of Old
Sturbridge Village. Address: 130 Flagg Street, Worcester,MA
01609. Descended from:

1 William Brenton, Governor of Rhode Island, 1666-69.

2 Sarah Brenton   Joseph Eliot
   Newport,RI 12 Dec 1677 -----   20 Dec 1638
   14 Nov 1703   -----   -----

3 Anne Eliot   Jonathan Law
   12 Dec 1677   -----   Milford,CT 6 Aug 1674
   -----   20 Dec 1698   6 Nov 1750

4 Anna Law   Samuel Hall
   Milford 1 Aug 1702   -----   Wallingford,CT 4 Oct
                                          1695
   23 Aug 1775   12 Jan 1725   Cheshire,CT 26 Feb 1776

5 Brenton Hall   (2)   Abigail (Baldwin) Guy
   Cheshire 2 Apr 1738   -----   1749
   Meriden,CT 25 Nov 1820 -----   5 May 1837

6 Anna Guy Hall   Orrin Hall
   Meriden 5 Jun 1792   Meriden   Meriden 5 Jun 1785
   Meriden 30 Nov 1880   18 Nov 1813   Meriden 7 Aug 1853

7 Russell Hall   Mary E. Baldwin
   Meriden 26 Jul 1835   Meriden   Meriden 10 Jan 1839
   Meriden 27 Mar 1922   28 Jan 1866   Meriden 30 Apr 1924

8 Howard Baldwin Hall   Gertrude Bertha Wetmore
   Meriden 1 May 1881   Wallingford,   Colchester,CT 15 Jul
                           CT   1879
   Meriden 24 Jul 1945   27 Apr 1905   Meriden 1 Apr 1973

BARTLETT, LEAH CLAGETT FORD (MRS. BRADFORD)

Nat. #207-B. Elected 14 Jun 1973. b. Washington,DC 1 Jul 1911.
m. Annapolis,MD 21 Nov 1942, Bradford Bartlett, b. Annapolis
26 Dec 1900. Educ: Gunston Hall; George Washington University.
Member: Hereditary Order of Desc. of Colonial Governors; Nat.
Soc. of Colonial Dames in the State of Maryland (Wash. Committee);
Daughters of the Cincinnati; Soc. of Desc. of Lords of Maryland
Manors; Order of Colonial Lords of Manors in America; Magna
Charta Dames; Soc. of Loyalists and Patriots; Knights of the
Temple of Jerusalem; Pilgrims of St. Mary's; Maryland Historical
Soc.; Stamford Genealogical Soc.; Washington Club, D.C.; Chevy
Chase Club, Maryland. Address: 3236 Peace Valley Lane, Falls
Church,VA 22044. Descended from:

1 Robert Brooke, Governor of Maryland 1652.

2 Thomas Brooke   Eleanor Hatton
   Battle,Eng. 23 Jun 1632 Maryland   England 1642
   Calvert Co.MD 1676   1659   Calvert Co. 1725

#			
3	Thomas Brooke Calvert Co. 1659 Prince George's Co.MD 7 Jan 1730/1	(1) Maryland c.1680	Anne ----- Maryland Maryland
4	Thomas Brooke Nottingham,MD 1683 Prince George's Co. 28 Dec 1744	Maryland 9 May 1705	Lucy Smith Maryland 1688 MD 15 Apr 1776
5	Eleanor Brooke 7 Mar 1718 Prince George's Co. 1771	Maryland 23 May 1734	Samuel Beall Montgomery Co.MD 1713 Washington Co.MD 1778
6	Richard Beall Montgomery Co. 1738 Frederick Co.MD 1778	Maryland 1758/9	Sarah Brooke Maryland 1739 MD 23 Dec 1797
7	Samuel Brooke Beall Georgetown,DC 1762 Amherst Co.VA 28 Mar 1842	Pr.Geo's Co. 3 Nov 1785	Eleanor Berry ----- -----
8	Otho Berry Beall Prince George's Co. 1791 Prince George's Co. 8 Nov 1853	Pr.Geo's Co. 1813	Mary Berry Brashears Prince George's Co. 1785 Prince George's Co. 1853
9	Washington Jeremiah Beall Prince George's Co. 17 Apr 1818 Prince George's Co. 11 Dec 1895	Pr.Geo's Co. 8 Jul 1840	Mary Ann Magruder Prince George's Co. 19 May 1823 Prince George's Co. 13 Jun 1884
10	Otho Richard Beall Prince George's Co. 6 Jul 1846 Washington,DC 16 Feb 1901	----- 18 Oct 1871	Alice Maude Thompson Montgomery Co. 11 Jan 1853 Washington,DC 20 Oct 1931
11	Arietta Maude Beall Prince George's Co. 10 May 1881 Washington,DC 1 Jan 1949	----- 10 Aug 1910	Walter Baldwin Ford Seymour,IN 6 Dec 1873 Elgin,IL 5 Sep 1936

BATCHELDER, CLARKE GILMAN

Nat. #93-B. Elected 3 Mar 1964. b. Arlington,MA 30 Aug 1919.
m. Delray Beach,FL 9 Mar 1954, Mary Josephine Luster, b.
Florence,SC 6 Feb 1926. Educ: William and Mary College; Embry-
Riddle Aviation Inst. in Miami,FL. Member: Hereditary Order of
Desc. of Colonial Governors; Sons of American Revolution; Sons
of Revolution; Order of Founders and Patriots of America; Soc. of
Desc. of Colonial Clergy; Desc. of the Mayflower. Occup: Sales
Rep. with Pan American Airways. Descended from:

1 William Bradford, Governor of Plymouth Colony 1621-33, 1635-36, 1637-38, 1639-44, 1645-57.

2 William Bradford   (1)   Alice Richards
  Plymouth,MA 17 Jun   Plymouth   c.1627
  1624
  Plymouth 20 Feb 1703   28 Jan 1650   Plymouth 12 Dec 1671

3 Thomas Bradford   Ann Raymond
  c.1657   -----   New London,CT 12 May
                       1664
  Windham,CT 1 Oct 1731 1681   Norwich,CT 8 May 1705

4 James Bradford   Susannah Adams
  Canterbury,CT 8 May   -----   Charlestown,MA 12 Mar
  1705   1692
  Canterbury 26 Mar 1762 7 Dec 1724   Canterbury 17 Mar 1752

5 Anna Bradford   Eleazer Cleveland
  Canterbury bp.10 Jul Canterbury Canterbury 26 May 1722
  1726
  -----   25 Apr 1749 -----

6 Mehitable Cleveland   Jacob Batchelder
  Canterbury 14 Jul 1756 Belmont,NH   Exeter,NH 14 Mar 1748
  18 Dec 1797   8 Oct 1789   Pittsfield,NH 19 May
                       1819

7 Jacob Batchelder   Mehitable Blake
  Loudon,NH 19 Aug 1792 -----   Epsom,NH
  Stanstead,Canada   -----   Stanstead 25 Sep 1866
  18 Dec 1862

8 Clarke Gilman   Huldah Priscilla
  Batchelder   Yeaton
  Franklin,NH 5 Feb 1810 Franklin   Exeter 22 Oct 1820
  Plymouth,NH 2 Apr 1883 21 Feb 1850 Cambridge,MA 25 Sep
                       1891

9 William Fitts Batchelder   Annie Laura Lawrence
  Plymouth 6 Jul 1859   -----   Nova Scotia
  -----   17 Mar 1885 -----

10 Warren Albert Batchelder   Emma Louise Lovejoy
  Cambridge 12 Feb 1891 Arlington,MA Lynn,MA 21 May 1892
  Brookline,MA 21 Mar   20 Nov 1912
  1943

Inheritor: Dana Clarke Bottcher

BAUERMANN, HELEN GAYNELL BENEDICT (MRS. WERNER FRITZ)

Nat. #337-B. Elected 12 Feb 1977. b. Bridgeport,CT 19 Dec 1913. m. Bridgeport 3 Apr 1934, Werner Fritz Bauermann, b. Solingen, Germany 18 Nov 1912. Issue: Richard Werner Bauermann, Sr. Member: Hereditary Order of Desc. of Colonial Governors; Dau. of American Colonists (Regent, Gov. Welles Chap.); Soc. of Mayflower Desc. in Connecticut; Dau. of American Revolution; Soc. of New England Women (Historian, New Haven Colony); Dames of Court of

Honor (Historian, Connecticut); Alden Kindred of America;
Sons and Daughters of the Pilgrims; Dau. of Founders and Patriots
of America; Magna Charta Dames. Address: 618 Clark Street,
Bridgeport,CT 06606. Descended from:

1 William Bradford, Governor of Plymouth Colony 1621-33, 1635-
36, 1637-38, 1639-44, 1645-57.

2 William Bradford   Alice Richards
  Plymouth,MA 17 Jun   Plymouth   Weymouth,MA 16 Jun 1627
  1624
  Plymouth 20 Feb 1703/4 c.1650   Plymouth 12 Dec 1671

3 Hannah Bradford   Joshua Ripley
  Plymouth 9 May 1662   Plymouth   Hingham,MA 9 Nov 1658
  Windham,CT 28 May 1738   28 Nov 1682   Windham 8 May 1739

4 Faith Ripley   Samuel Bingham
  Hingham 20 Sep 1686   Windham   Norwich,CT 28 Mar 1685
  Windham 11 Feb 1720/1   5 Jan 1708/9   Windham 1 Mar 1760

5 Lemuel Bingham   Hannah Perkins
  Windham 20 Sep 1713   Windham   Norwich 15 Dec 1717
  Windham 3 Nov 1788   28 Apr 1737   Windham 21 Oct 1793

6 Faith Bingham   Jesse Tracy
  Windham 27 Jan 1745   Norwich   Norwich 21 Dec 1745
  Norwich 10 Jul 1818   27 Sep 1770   Norwich 6 Nov 1828

7 Freeman Tracy   (2)   Dolly Reade
  Lisbon,CT 5 Mar 1775   Lisbon   Lisbon 17 Apr 1782
  Lisbon 24 Oct 1855   Jan 1802   Lisbon 5 Aug 1863

8 Ebenezer Tracy   Phoebe D. Rogers
  Lisbon 29 Jun 1822   Montville,CT   -----
  Bridgeport,CT 26 Feb   29 Oct 1849   Bridgeport 20 Jun 1881
  1875

9 Frank Ernest Tracy   Sarah Elizabeth Boggs
  Lisbon 31 Oct 1855   Union,ME   -----
  Bridgeport 12 Aug 1930   13 Oct 1884   -----

10 Helen Mae Tracy   Harold Gilbert Benedict
   Bridgeport 5 Aug 1885   Bridgeport   Bridgeport 8 Aug 1883
   Bridgeport 14 Jun 1973   4 Dec 1907   Bridgeport 22 Jan 1955

   Inheritor: Richard Werner Bauermann, Sr.

BEARD, TIMOTHY FIELD

Nat. #202-B. Elected 26 Mar 1973. b. Great Barrington,MA 19 Dec
1930. m. New York,NY 12 Sep 1963, Annette Knowles Huddleston, b.
Montgomery,AL 20 Sep 1933. Educ: Berkshire School; Williams
College, B.A. in History; Columbia University, M.S. in Library
Science. Member: Hereditary Order of Desc. of Colonial Governors
(Genealogist General); Sons of the Revolution (Examiner, NY
State); Soc. of Colonial Wars (Genealogist, NY State); St.
Nicholas Soc. of City of New York (Genealogist); Order of Colonial
Lords of Manors in America (Registrar); St. Andrews Society;

Americans of Royal Descent (Genealogist); Order of the Three
Crusades (Genealogist); Order of the Crown of Charlemagne;
Colonial Order of the Acorn. Occup: Librarian and Genealogist,
New York Public Library. Address: 38 Barrow Street, New York,NY
10014. Descended from:

1 Theophilus Eaton, Governor of the New Haven Colony 1639-58.

2 Hannah Eaton   William Jones
   London, Eng. 6 Oct   London   England c.1624
   1632
   New Haven,CT 4 May 1707 4 Jul 1659   New Haven 17 Oct 1706

3 Sarah Jones   Andrew Morrison
   New Haven 17 Aug 1662   New Haven   Scotland
   -----   21 Oct 1687   New Haven bf. 30 Jan
                                                   1702/3

4 Ann Morrison   Ebenezer Tallman
   New Haven 4 Nov 1693   Guilford,CT   Guilford 1 Sep 1692
   Guilford 4 Oct 1773   1 Sep 1714   Guilford 2 Sep 1770

5 Mary Tallman   David Dudley
   Guilford c.1724   Guilford   Guilford 27 Nov 1718
   Guilford 26 Mar 1778   17 Feb 1741/2   Guilford 17 Feb 1807

6 Anna Dudley   Timothy Field
   Guilford 13 Apr 1752   Guilford   E.Guilford 12 Nov
                                                   1743/4
   Madison,CT 7 Oct 1819   25 Nov 1767   Madison 1 Jan 1818

7 Timothy Field   Wealthy Bishop
   Guilford 28 Sep 1775   Madison   E.Guilford 9 Jul 1773
   Brattleboro,VT 22 Feb   3 Jan 1801   Westminster West,VT
   1844   17 Apr 1814

8 Alfred Bishop Field   Ann Field Beals
   Avon,NY 6 Oct 1801   Canandaigua,   Canandaigua 4 Dec 1805
   Canandaigua,NY 23 Feb   7 Mar 1833   Detroit,MI 5 Jan 1896
   1858

9 Louise Howell Field   Horace Marshall Finley
   Canandaigua 23 Oct   Canandaigua   Bristol,NY 23 Jan 1838
   1845
   Canandaigua 3 Apr 1917   4 Oct 1866   Canandaigua 17 Jul
                                                   1901

10 Gertrude Field Finley   Maximillian Cornelius
                                                   Beard
   Canandaigua 18 Jun   Canandaigua   Biloxi,MS 27 Nov 1864
   1896
   Sheffield,MA 20 Apr   25 Sep 1888   New Haven,CT 19 Feb
   1941   1924

11 Stuart-Menteth Beard   Natalie Sudler Turner
   Canandaigua 28 Nov   Asbury Park,   Wilmington,DE 20 Dec
   1893   NJ   1888
   Sheffield 8 Sep 1955   30 Jun 1921   Great Barrington,MA
                                                   7 Jan 1957

   Inheritor: Walter Johnson Beard, Russell Stage Road,
              Blanford,MA 01008

BELDING, SICILY AMELIA SPARKMAN (MRS. PAUL BROOKS)

Nat. #328-B. Elected 10 Aug 1978. b. Longview,TX 11 Oct 1906.
m.(1) 28 Dec 1925, Knowles Robison Melton (dec.). Issue: Jane
Eley Melton Cunningham, b. Longview 26 Jan 1927. m.(2) 16 Jul
1933, Joseph Jack Castleberry (dec.). Issue: Amelia Northcutt
Castleberry Tierney, b. Longview 26 Aug 1944. m.(3) 27 Nov 1959,
Paul Brooks Belding. Educ: Texas Women's University; Kilgore
College. Member: Hereditary Order of Desc. of Colonial Governors;
Dau. of American Revolution; Dau. of American Colonists (Regi-
strar); Soc. of Desc. of Colonial Clergy; Colonial Dames of
America; Magna Charta Dames (State Registrar); Order of First
Families of Virginia; Dau. of Founders and Patriots of America;
Gregg Co. Historical Commission (Chm.); Gregg Co. Historical
Soc.; Historical Foundation Board. Address: 602 Sylvan Drive,
Longview,TX 75602. Descended from:

1 William Brathwaythe (Brathwaite), Governor of Maryland 1644.

2 Margaret Braithwaythe   Alexander Macgreuther
  pb.England   England   Perthshire, Scotland
                                              bf.1605
  England/Maryland   -----   Calvert Co.MD 1677
    bf.1644

3 Samuel Magruder   Sarah Beall
  Maryland 1654   Maryland   Maryland
  Maryland 1711   -----   1734

4 Elizabeth Magruder   (2)   William Beall
  Maryland   Maryland   Maryland
  Maryland af.1761   -----   Maryland 1756

5 Nathaniel Beall   Ann Murdoch
  Prince George's Co.MD   Pr.Geo's Co.   -----
  Frederick Co.MD   -----   Maryland af.1760
    will 20 Jun 1757

6 William Beall   (2)   Elizabeth Murphy
  Frederick Co.MD   Lunenburg Co.   Virginia
                            VA
  Wilkes Co.GA 1805   -----   Jasper Co.GA
                                              4 Aug 1812

7 Frances Beall   Randolph Payne
  Wilkes Co. c.1800   Jasper Co.   Bedford Co.VA/
                                              Wilkes Co.GA
                                              c.1796
  pb.AL af.18 Aug 1850   8 Sep 1816   Columbus,GA 1838

8 Martha Alabama Payne   Algernon Sidney Eley
  Alabama 1826   Columbus,GA   Greene Co.GA 1812
  Longview,TX 1898   13 Apr 1841   Mt.Enterprise,TX
                                              Apr 1868

9 Amelia Eley   William Thomas Brooks
  Autauga Co.AL 15 Apr   nr.Shreveport,   Oglethorpe Co.GA 1828
    1845   LA
  Longview 6 Dec 1907   -----   Shreveport 1873

10 Martha Eley Brooks

    Marshall,TX 30 Jun 1868 Longview
    Jacksonville,TX 14 Jul   13 Apr 1884
    1930

    Joseph Marcellus
      Sparkman
    Pine Hill,TX 8 Nov 1861
    Longview 25 Jul 1897

11 Joseph Roy Sparkman
    Longview 9 Apr 1885   Acworth,GA
    Longview 8 Feb 1945   20 Nov 1905

    Ruth Northcutt
    Marietta,GA 11 Aug 1883
    Longview 11 Oct 1967

BENSON, NEWELL BARTON, JR.

Nat. #315-B.　Elected 8 Aug 1977.　b. Baltimore,MD 22 Jul 1924.
m. Towson,MD 4 Sep 1965, Betty Church, b. Baltimore 20 Dec
1929.　Issue:　Anne Damaris Benson,　b. 2 Aug 1966.　Educ:
Loyola College of Baltimore, B.S. in Chemistry 1948; University
of Baltimore Law School, J.D. 1952.　Member: Hereditary Order of
Desc. of Colonial Governors; Sons of American Revolution;
Colonial Order of the Crown; Baltimore Co. and Maryland Bar
Assns.　Occup: Assistant Attorney General for State of Maryland.
Address: 5 Midcrest Court, Towson,MD 21204.　Descended from:

1 Benedict Arnold, Governor of Rhode Island 1657-60, 1662-66,
    1669-72, 1677-78.

2 Oliver Arnold
    RI 25 Jul 1656   Jamestown,RI
    RI 6 Nov 1699   -----
    Phoebe Cook
    1655
    1732

3 Damaris Arnold
    30 Dec 1680   Bridgewater,MA
    -----   3 Mar 1700
    John Carey, III
    9 Dec 1674
    14 Jul 1721

4 Damaris Carey
    1701   New Port,RI
    1765   3 Apr 1726
    John Hull
    4 Dec 1694
    3 Mar 1765

5 Teddeman Hull
    1 Feb 1734   Harrison,NY
    1795   14 May 1758
    Elizabeth Franklin
    8 May 1735
    -----

6 Damaris Hull
    1769   Stanfordville,
            NY
    1808   1790
    Caleb Barton, Jr.
    1769
    Amenia,NY 20 Apr 1812

7 Henry Barton
    Amenia Sep 1803   Stanfordville
    Oct 1869   24 Mar 1825
    Rhoda Chase
    16 May 1804
    Stanfordville 2 Nov
      1862

8 Damaris Barton
    Stanfordville   Centerville,VA
      Nov 1827
    Baltimore,MD 13 May   1855
      1907
    Thomas James Benson
    Baltimore Co.MD 10 Nov
      1820
    Baltimore Co. 1 Nov
      1887

```
9  Sallie Williams Benson                     Joshua Lemmon Benson
   Centerville 26 Nov 1862 Baltimore          Baltimore Co. 20 Jan
                                                 1831
   Baltimore City 23 Dec    28 Jul 1897       Baltimore Co. 4 Aug
     1954                                       1910

10 N. Barton Benson, Sr.                       Edna Virginia Macey
   Baltimore Co. 28 Sep     Baltimore          Baltimore 30 Mar 1901
     1900
   Baltimore 4 Nov 1970     4 Sep 1923         Baltimore 28 Feb 1951
```

Inheritor: Anne Damaris Benson, daughter

BEYERS, BERNICE WEST (MRS. ROBERT ARTHUR)

Nat. #30-B. Elected 23 Nov 1960. b. New York,NY 26 Apr 1906.
m. St. Petersburg,FL 2 Mar 1940, Robert Arthur Beyers, b. New
York,NY 17 Sep 1904, d. 23 Feb 1962. Issue: Robert West Beyers,
b. New York,NY 10 Oct 1931; Arthur Lovette Beyers, b. Bronxville,
NY 10 Feb 1943. Educ: Bennett College; Theatre Guild School;
Archipenko's Ecole d'Art. Member: Hereditary Order of Desc. of
Colonial Governors; Dau. of American Revolution; Soc. of May-
flower Desc.; Magna Charta Dames; Colonial Order of the Crown;
Soc. of Desc. of the Most Noble Order of Knights of the Garter;
Plantagenet Soc.; Americans of Royal Descent; Women Desc. of the
Ancient and Honorable Artillery Co.; Old Plymouth Colony Desc.;
Colonial Dames of America; Soc. of New England Women; Dau. of
American Colonists; Dau. of Colonial Wars; Order of Washington;
Dau. of the Founders and Patriots of America. Occup: Sculptor.
Address: 10008 Meadowbrook Drive, Dallas,TX 75229. Descended fr:

```
1  John Webster, Governor of Connecticut 1656

2  Robert Webster                           Susanna Treat
   Warwickshire,Eng.c.1627 Middletown,CT    England 1629
   Hartford,CT 31 May 1676 1652             Hartford 1705

3  Jonathan Webster                         Dorcas Hopkins
   Middletown,CT Jan 1656   Hartford        -----
   Hartford 1735            11 May 1681     -----

4  Stephen Webster                          Mary Burnham
   Hartford Jan 1691        Hartford        bp. 19 Dec 1690
   Hartford 1724            6 Jun 1717      -----

5  Isaac Webster                            Ame White
   Hartford 15 Jun 1718     Hartford        c.1716
   W.Hartford 19 Sep 1801   11 Nov 1739     W.Hartford 26 Jun 1807

6  Ame Webster                              Ebenezer Goodwin
   Hartford bp.26 Jan 1746  Hartford        Hartford bp.29 May 1743
   W.Hartford 8 Jan 1835    c.1762/3        New Hartford 18 May
                                              1810

7  William Goodwin                          Abigail Crosswell
   Hartford 15 Oct 1776     Hartford        W.Hartford 20 Jan 1774
   New Hartford 20 Apr      12 Aug 1796     New Hartford 16 Aug
     1849                                     1852
```

8 Harley Goodwin   Maria Lorenda Smith
   W.Hartford 10 Mar 1797   Vermont   West Rutland,VT 27 Oct
                                                       1807
   Falls Village,CT   24 Nov 1828   W.Rutland 8 Apr 1843
     11 Jan 1855

9 Abigail Crosswell Goodwin   Edward H. Canfield
   New Marlboro,MA   S.Canaan,CT   Salisbury,CT 1 Jun 1822
     21 Feb 1830
   Sparta,WI 27 Apr 1907   10 Apr 1848   Sparta 12 Oct 1899

10 Mary Delamar Canfield   George Hegeman Palmer
   Sparta 1 Nov 1850   Sparta   West Troy,NY 11 Jun
                                                       1850
   Sparta 5 Sep 1901   12 Jun 1876   Sparta 16 Sep 1933

11 Bess Abigail Palmer   Lovette West
   Sparta 20 Feb 1885   London,Eng.   Lakeville,NY 19 Sep
                                                       1875
                             11 Jul 1903   Bronxville,NY 6 Mar
                                                       1944

BIRD, JACKSON

Nat. #336-B. Elected 27 Feb 1979. b. Wilmington,DE 18 Jul 1915.
m. Ashland,ME, Audrey Louise Campbell, b. Masardis,ME 31 Jul
1919. Educ: Harvard College, A.B. 1938. Member: Hereditary
Order of Desc. of Colonial Governors; Soc. of Mayflower Desc.;
Sons of American Revolution; Order of Founders and Patriots of
America; Huguenot Soc. of America; Soc. of Desc. of Colonial
Clergy; Desc. of Colonial Wars; Piscataqua Pioneers; National
Huguenot Soc.; Desc. of Illegitimate Sons and Dau. of Kings of
Britain. Occup: Headmaster, retired. Address: 6 New City St.,
Essex, CT 06426. Descended from:

1 Edward Winslow, Governor of Plymouth Colony 1633, 1636, 1644

2 Josiah Winslow   Penelope Pelham
   Marshfield,MA 1629   New England   Bures,Eng. bp. 1633
   Marshfield 18 Dec 1680   1657   Marshfield 7 Dec 1703

3 Isaac Winslow   Sarah Wensley
   Marshfield 1671   Boston,MA   Boston 11 Aug 1673
   Marshfield 14 Dec 1738   11 Jul 1700   Marshfield 16 Dec 1753

4 Penelope Winslow   (int.)   James Warren
   Marshfield 21 Dec 1704   Plymouth,MA   Plymouth 14 Apr 1700
   -----   27 Dec 1723   Plymouth 2 Jul 1757

5 Sarah Warren   (int.)   William Sever
   Plymouth 23 May 1730   Kingston,MA   Kingston 12 Oct 1729
   Kingston 15 Mar 1797   16 Aug 1755   Kingston 15 Jun 1809

6 William Sever   Mary Chandler
   Kingston 23 Jun 1759   Shrewsbury/   Worcester,MA 21 Dec
                               Worcester   1759
   Worcester 26/27 Oct   29/30 Oct 1785 -----
     1798

7	Anne Warren Sever Worcester 24 Oct 1789 Salem,MA 30 Jan 1843	Worcester 19 Apr 1821	John Brazer Worcester 29 Sep 1789 Charleston,SC 25 Feb 1846
8	Anne Warren Brazer Salem 10 Jun 1829 Wilmington,DE 22 Mar 1907	Dorchester,MA 24 Sep 1854	Henry Payson Ellis Boston,MA 1 Mar 1827 -----
9	Katherine Ellis Dorchester 7 Apr 1857 Bala,PA 13 May 1927	Dorchester 9 Oct 1883	Oscar Roland Jackson Boston 10 May 1855 Wilmington 10 Apr 1916
10	Anne Warren Jackson Chester,PA 25 Feb 1886 Philadelphia,PA 8 Jun 1938	Wilmington 8 Oct 1914	Benjamin Newcomer Bird Chester 20 Jun 1883 Bala 12 Feb 1931

BOGARDUS, ETHEL KENRICK SAMSON (MRS. EMORY A.)

Nat. #212-B. Elected 23 Jul 1973. b. Brooklyn,NY. m. Cliff-
side Park,NJ 23 Nov 1925, Emory Arthur Bogardus, b. Athens,NY.
Educ: Maxwell Teachers College; Cornell University. Member:
Hereditary Order of Desc. of Colonial Governors; Dau. of American
Revolution (NY Officers Club, Ex-Regents Assn.); Dau. of American
Colonists (NY Chairman, Natl. Defense); New England Women (Vice
Pres. Poughkeepsie Colony); Dau. of Founders and Patriots of
America; Women Desc. of Ancient and Honorable Artillery Co. (NY
Court of Assistants); Soc. of Desc. of Colonial Clergy; Dau. of
Colonial Wars; Sons and Dau. of the Pilgrims; New England
Historical and Genealogical Soc.; Rockland County Historical
Soc. Occup: Dir. of Public Health Assn., Retired. Address:
15 Briarwood Drive, New City,NY 10956. Descended from:

1 Thomas Danforth, Governor of Maine 1680-86.

2	Elizabeth Danforth Cambridge,MA 17 Feb 1664 Cambridge 4 Jul 1721	Cambridge 3 Oct 1682	Francis Foxcroft England 1657 Cambridge 31 Dec 1727
3	Francis Foxcroft Boston,MA 26 Jan 1694 Cambridge 28 Mar 1768	Boston 5 Nov 1722	Mehitable Coney Boston 1703 Andover 4 May 1782
4	Mehitable Foxcroft Cambridge 19 Aug 1723 Newton,MA 22 Apr 1770	Cambridge 25 Jan 1759	Jonas Meriam Lincoln,MA 1730 Newton 13 Aug 1780
5	Mehitable Meriam Newton 5 Jun 1760 Newton 20 Jan 1817	Newton 1779	John Kenrick Newton 6 Nov 1755 Newton 28 Mar 1833

6	Mehitable Kenrick
	Newton 22 Nov 1780
	
	3 Apr 1845
		Newton
		
		16 Jan 1814
			Abisha Samson
			Woodstock,VT 28 Oct
			  1783
			Washington,DC 19 Jan
			  1861

7   John K. Samson   Elizabeth Campbell
    Harvard,MA 22 Jan 1818   Milton,MA   Milton 13 Mar 1818
    Brooklyn,NY 28 Mar   19 May 1842   Brooklyn 18 May 1886
      1876   •

8   James C. Samson   Leanna Norman
    Brooklyn 24 Nov 1852   Brooklyn   Brooklyn 23 Sep 1854
    Brooklyn 22 Jul 1904   23 Sep 1875   Brooklyn 21 Jun 1908

9   John K. Samson   Alicia Riches
    Brooklyn 21 Dec 1876   Brooklyn   London,Eng. 12 Feb 1874
    New City,NY 2 Aug 1954   4 Aug 1902   Haverstraw,NY 10 Oct
                                                 1958

BRADSTREET, WILLIAM CARNER

Nat. #53-B.   Elected 28 Jul 1962.   b. Wichita Falls,TX 25 Jul
1924.   Educ: Baylor University, Waco,TX, BS; NY University
Graduate School of Business, MBA; Grad. Sessions at University
of Oklahoma and Columbia University.   Member: Hereditary Order
of Desc. of Colonial Governors (Councillor General); Sons of
American Revolution.   Address: Box 1189, Easton,PA 18042.
Descended from:

1   Simon Bradstreet, Governor of Massachusetts 1679-86, 1689-92

2   John Bradstreet   Sarah Perkins
    Andover,MA 22 Jul 1652   -----   Topsfield 11 Aug 1658
    Topsfield,MA 11 Jan   11 Jun 1677   Topsfield 7 Apr 1745
      1718

3   Samuel Bradstreet   Sarah Clarke
    Topsfield 4 Aug 1699   -----   Topsfield 1 Jan 1705
    Topsfield 1 Dec 1762   3 Apr 1722   Topsfield 19 Jun 1736

4   Samuel Bradstreet   Ruth Lamson
    Topsfield 8 Mar 1729   -----   Ipswich,MA 7 Feb 1733
    Topsfield 7 Jul 1777   5 Apr 1763   Topsfield 25 Jul 1777

5   Samuel Bradstreet   Martha Foster
    Topsfield 2 Jan 1764   -----   Topsfield 22 Aug 1765
    Topsfield 26 Nov 1816   14 Apr 1785   Topsfield 13 Apr 1820

6   Samuel Bradstreet   Mehitabel Gould
    Topsfield 26 Aug 1789   Topsfield   Boxford,MA 19 Mar 1791
    Irondequoit,NY   7 Oct 1810   Irondequoit 5 May 1875

7   Austin Bradstreet   Marietta Perrin
    Topsfield 6 Apr 1818   Irondequoit   25 Jul 1825
    Irondequoit 18 Apr 1860 May 1841   Irondequoit 15 Nov 1872

8   Jacob Gould Bradstreet   Angeline Jackson
    Irondequoit 25 Mar   Fairview,PA   Butler Co.PA 14 Apr
      1859   1866
    Muskogee,OK 27 Oct 1938 Jan 1887   Muskogee 15 Feb 1915

9   William H. Bradstreet   Alberta Carner
    Butler,PA 22 Mar 1889   Bartlesville,   Marietta,OH 23 May 1897
                             OK
    Avoca,TX 7 Jun 1961   15 Jun 1922

BROOKS, VIRGINIA F. WALTON (MRS. BERRY B.)

Nat. #5-B. Elected 17 Mar 1959. b. Jonesboro,AR 6 Aug 1904.
m. Blytheville,AR 27 Apr 1929, Berry Boswell Brooks, Jr., b.
Senatobia,MS 2 Feb 1902. Issue: Virginia W. Brooks Martin,
b. 4 Jun 1933. Educ: Lindenwood College, St. Charles,MO.
Member: Hereditary Order of Desc. of Colonial Governors; Children
of American Colonists (Hon. Nat. Pres. Gen.); Huguenot Soc. of
the Founders of Mannakin in the Colony of VA (Past Nat. Hist.);
Dau. of American Colonies (Vice Regent); Dau. of American Revolu-
tion (Past Regent, Ft. Assumption Chap.); Dau. of 1812; Dames of
Court of Honor (Organizing Pres. TN); Desc. of Lords of Maryland
Manors (Past Councillor); Colonial Order of the Crown (Vice
Sovereign); Dau. of Founders and Patriots of America (Past TN
Pres.); Jamestowne Soc.; United Dau. of Confederacy; Louisiana
Colonials; Dau. of Barons of Runnemede; Magna Charta Dames;
Americans of Royal Descent; Americans of Armorial Ancestry;
Order of Washington; Order of First Crusade; Plantagenet Soc.;
Memphis Genealogical Soc. (Founder). Occup: Explorer and Writer.
Address: 3661 James Rd., Memphis,TN 38128. Descended from:

1 Samuel Mathews, Governor of Virginia 1656-60.

2 Francis Mathews   -----
   c.1648   -----   -----
   16 Feb 1674/5   -----   -----

3 Baldwin Mathews   -----
   1670   -----   -----
   1737   -----   -----

4 Mary Mathews   J. Philip Smith
   York Co.VA c.1695   -----   Purton,VA 1 Jun 1695
   Fleet's Bay,VA   9 Feb 1711   1743

5 Mildred Smith   (2)   James Ball
   c.1725   -----   Lancaster Co. 31 Dec
                                                     1718
   Lancaster Co.VA 1 Dec · c.1744   Lancaster Co. 24 Nov
   1751   1789

6 Jesse Ball   Aggatha Conway
   c.1740   -----   Lancaster Co. c.1746
   Lancaster Co. 1778   9 Mar 1765   Lancaster Co. af.1773

7 John Smith Ball   Nancy Opie
   Lancaster Co. 1773   -----   VA c.1782
   MO 12 Apr 1849   8 Apr 1799   Lancaster Co. bf.21 Dec
                                                     1804

8 Nancy Opie Ball   Frederick Bates
   Lancaster Co. 19 Apr   -----   Henrico Co.VA 23 Jun
   1802   1777
   St.Louis,MO 16 Mar 1877 4 Mar 1819   MO 4 Aug 1825

9 Emily Caroline Bates   Robert Alfred Walton
   St.Louis 5 Jan 1820   -----   VA 27 Aug 1804
   St.Louis 23 Nov 1891   9 Aug 1838   St.Louis 20 Nov 1867

```
10  Frederick Bates Walton                      Louisa Conway
    St.Louis 4 Jun 1839      -----             St.Louis 24 Apr 1840
    Winterhaven,FL 24 Dec    3 Sep 1861        St.Louis 30 Jun 1895
    1907

11  Allan Walton                                Virginia Warren Feild
    St.Louis 4 Mar 1864      -----             Memphis,TN 21 Oct 1882
    Blytheville,AR 6 May     21 Oct 1903
    1919
```

Inheritor: Virginia Walton Brooks Martin (Mrs. Allen M.),
3661 James Rd., Memphis,TN 38128.

BRUMBAUGH, LT. COL. STILES DANIEL

Nat. #220-B. Elected 23 Oct 1973. b. Cleveland,OH 1 Jan 1912.
m. Rome,OH 19 Nov 1932, Garnett Evelyn Plantz, b. Cleveland
20 Jul 1912. Issue: Peter Paul Brumbaugh, b. 1 Dec 1935; Daniel
David Brumbaugh, b. 8 Feb 1940; William Billie Brumbaugh, b. and
d. 27 Dec 1943; Barbara A. Brumbaugh Zurat, b. 10 Nov 1945; all
b. Cleveland. Educ: Spencerian College, Cleveland; Command and
Staff School, Columbus,OH. Member: Hereditary Order of Desc. of
Colonial Governors; Desc. of Founders of Hartford,CT; Sons of
American Revolution; Huguenot Soc.; Founders and Patriots of
America; Military Order of Loyal Legion; Sons of Revolution;
Colonial Wars; Soc. of War of 1812; Western Reserve Historical
Soc., OH; Lancaster Co.PA Historical Soc. Military: Active Unit
5th Brigade,OH, 12 Apr 1946 to date; Lt.Col. 26 Mar 1973. Present
Assignment - Executive Officer, 5th Brigade,OH. Address:
4237 East 110th St., Cleveland,OH 44105. Descended from:

```
1  John Webster, Governor of Connecticut 1656.

2  Robert Webster                          Susannah Treat
   Cossington,Eng. c.1628  Middletown,CT   Pitminster,Eng. 1629
   Hartford,CT Jun 1676    1652            Hartford Nov 1705

3  Sarah Webster                           Joseph Mygatt
   Middletown 30 Jun 1655  Hartford        Hartford c.1656
   Hartford Feb 1744       15 Nov 1677     Mar 1697/8

4  Zebulon Mygatt                          Dorothy Waters
   Hartford 1 Nov 1693     Hartford        Hartford 28 Aug 1704
   CT c.1745               c.1722          CT c.1745

5  Sabra Mygatt                            Joseph Hosmer
   Hartford 1727           Hartford        Hartford 28 Nov 1705
   Southwick,MA 6 Jun 1789 17 Jan 1745     Southwick 27 Jun 1777

6  William Hosmer                          Elizabeth Barker
   Hartford 15 Dec 1745    Suffield,CT     Suffield,MA 18 Apr 1762
   Seville,OH 18 Jul 1839  15 Jul 1779     Seville 19 Aug 1838

7  Chester Hosmer                          Emeline S. Forbes
   Longyard,MA 20 Sep 1795 Seville         Truxton,NY 20 Jul 1807
   Seville 8 Oct 1882      21 Dec 1826     Seville 13 Dec 1889
```

8	Stiles A. Hosmer		Jane Nelson
	Seville 10 Mar 1829	Seville	Seville 13 Feb 1846
	Seville 12 Apr 1915	5 Nov 1863	Seville 17 Jul 1911
9	Mary Adell Hosmer		Hugh Harland Brumbaugh
	Seville 8 Nov 1877	Seville	Antrim,OH 12 Apr 1873
	Cleveland,OH 3 Oct 1956	14 Nov 1894	Cleveland 9 Nov 1929

BRYAN, LESLIE AULLS

Nat. #156-B. Elected 17 Feb 1970. b. Bath,NY 23 Feb 1900.
m. 22 Aug 1931, Gertrude C. Gelder, b. Forest City,PA 22 Feb
1907. Issue: Leslie A. Bryan, Jr., b. Syracuse,NY 1 Mar 1933;
George G. Bryan, b. Syracuse 28 Jun 1939. Educ: Syracuse
University, B.S., M.S., J.D.; American University, Ph.D.; Southwestern College, Sc.D. (Hon). Member: Hereditary Order of Desc.
of Colonial Governors; Sons of American Revolution (Genealogist
Gen.); Huguenot Society (President, Illinois); Soc. of War of
1812 (Director, Illinois); Soc. of Colonial Wars; Soc. of Desc.
of Colonial Clergy. Occup: Director of Institute of Aviation
and Professor of Management, Emeritus, University of Illinois.
Honors: Arents Medal, Syracuse Univ.; Letterman of Distinction,
Syracuse Univ.; Distinguished Alumni Award, American Univ.;
Silver Beaver and Silver Antelope, Boy Scouts of America.
Address: 34 Fields East, Champaign,IL 61820. Descended from:

1 John Webster, Governor of Connecticut 1656.

2	Thomas Webster		Abigail Alexander
	-----	-----	-----
	Northampton,MA 1686	16 Jun 1663	bf.1690
3	John Webster		Elizabeth Dewey
	Northampton 11 Sep 1672	-----	10 Jul 1677
	Lebanon,CT 2 Mar 1736	1698	af.1705
4	Josiah Webster		Hannah Hutchinson
	Lebanon 26 Jan 1705/6	-----	14 Sep 1709
	Lebanon 10 Apr 1751	21 Jul 1726	18 Jun 1773
5	Josiah Webster		Sarah Loomis
	Lebanon 5 Jan 1742/3	-----	Lebanon 15 Nov 1736
	6 Feb 1816	-----	c.1794
6	Josiah Webster		Abigail Babcock
	Lebanon 24 Nov 1774	-----	Lebanon 2 May 1775
	1 Sep 1852	8 Aug 1794	31 Dec 1861
7	Lydia Marinda Webster		Ephraim Aulls
	26 Jun 1812	-----	Wayne,NY 5 Nov 1810
	3 Jun 1884	19 Dec 1833	Nov 1849
8	Frank M. Aulls		Mary E. Rowlett
	26 Feb 1840	-----	8 Nov 1840
	25 Oct 1893	17 Dec 1863	25 Oct 1929
9	Anna Aulls		Daniel Beach Bryan
	18 Jan 1874	-----	7 Mar 1868
	21 Jul 1916	4 Nov 1897	13 Feb 1937

BUCK, JAMES ORTON

Nat. #133-B. Elected Aug 1968. b. Bridgeport,CT 1 Jul 1913.
m. NYC 19 Apr 1947, Nancy Gulley Foster, b. Hardy,AR 21 Feb 1910.
Issue: Clare B. Buck Dalva, b. NYC 7 Sep 1950. Educ: New York
School of Fine and Applied Arts. Member: Hereditary Order of
Desc. of Colonial Governors (Registrar General); Order of the
Crown of Charlemagne (Pres. Gen.); St. Nicholas Soc. of NYC
(Secretary); Baronial Order of Magna Charta (Surety); Soc. of
Colonial Wars (NY, Member of Council); Colonial Order of the
Acorn; Desc. of Illegitimate Sons and Dau. of Kings of Britain;
Americans of Armorial Ancestry; Sons of the Revolution (NY);
National Gavel Club; Co-compiler of Vol. II of "Pedigrees of Some
of Emperor Charlemagne's Descendants." Occup: Interior Design.
Address: Apt. 2, General Jackson Apts., 1907 Capers Ave.,
Nashville,TN 37212. Descended from:

1 Robert Treat, Governor of Connecticut 1683-98

2 Robert Treat   Abigail Camp
   Milford,CT 14 Aug 1654 Milford   Milford 28 Mar 1667
   Milford 20 Mar 1720   c.1687   Milford 20 Mar 1742

3 Abigail Treat   Jedediah Mills
   Milford c.1704   -----   Wintonbury,CT 23 Mar
                                         1697
   Huntington,CT 2 Nov   16 Jun 1726   Huntington 19 Jan 1776
   1775

4 Philo Mills   Elizabeth Riggs
   Huntington c.1735   Derby,CT   Derby 21 Nov 1733
   Derby 8 Mar 1765   19 Mar 1755   31 Oct 1824

5 Abigail E. Ann Mills   Ephraim Wooster
   Derby 24 Feb 1756   Huntington   Huntington 8 Apr 1755
   Huntington 29 Apr 1831 15 Dec 1776   Huntington 17 Aug 1838

6 Philo M. Wooster   Sarah Cogswell
   Huntington 6 Jan 1786   New Preston,CT New Preston 6 Jan 1792
   Huntington 14 Jul 1849 18 Sep 1817   Huntington 30 Mar 1819

7 William C. Wooster   Mary L. Gilbert
   Huntington 30 Mar 1819 Huntington   New Preston 18 May 1827
   New Preston 7 Aug 1864 22 Sep 1847   New Preston 13 Jun 1903

8 Albert M. Wooster   Fannie Brounley Bowen
   Chatham,NY 15 Apr 1850 Washington,DC Clark Co.VA 7 Jul 1850
   Bridgeport,CT 25 Nov   15 Apr 1875   Scarsdale,NY 11 Nov
   1945   1912

9 Myra Estelle Wooster   James Orton Buck
   Washington,DC 23 Jun   Bridgeport   Brantford,Canada
   1879   10 Sep 1880
                           5 Jun 1912   Lake Wales,FL 6 Mar
                                         1965

SUPPLEMENT NO. 1

1 Thomas Welles, Governor of Connecticut, 1655 and 1658

2   Sarah Welles   John Chester
    England c.1631   Wethersfield   3 Aug 1634
    Wethersfield,CT   Feb 1653/4   Wethersfield 23 Feb
       12 Dec 1698   1698

3   Stephen Chester   Jemima Treat
    Wethersfield 26 May   Wethersfield   Wethersfield 15 Mar
       1660   1667/8
    Wethersfield 9 Feb   17 Dec 1691   Wethersfield 25 May
       1697/8   1727

4   Dorothy Chester   Martin Kellogg
    Wethersfield 5 Sep   Wethersfield   Deerfield,MA 1685
       1692
    Wethersfield 26 Sep   13 Jan 1716   Newington,CT 13 Nov
       1754   1753

5   Dorothy Kellogg   Eliphalet Whittlesey
    Wethersfield 24 Dec   -----   Newington 10 May 1714
       1716
    Washington,CT 14 Apr 16 Dec 1736   Washington 12 Jul 1786
       1772

6   Anna Whittlesey   William Cogswell
    Newington 27 Jan 1744 -----   Ipswich,MA 22 Dec 1734
    New Preston,CT 10 Jan 4 Nov 1762   New Preston 19 Feb
       1810   1786

7   Stephen Cogswell   Anna Camp
    New Preston 1 Sep 1771 New Preston   Connecticut
    New Preston 29 Oct   May 1791   New Preston 22 Oct
       1837   1810

8   Sarah Cogswell   Philo Mills Wooster

    Continue with Generation 6 of his lineage from Governor
    Robert Treat.

    Inheritor: Clare Bowen Buck Dalva (Mrs. D. M. Morrison)

BUONASSISI, LOUISA CARTER FROST (MRS. CHARLES B.)

Nat. #128-B. Elected 27 Mar 1967. b. Plattsburg,MO 1 Sep 1916.
m. (1) Kansas City,MO 22 Feb 1942, Marshall Earl Turley, b.
Lindale,GA 29 Sep 1909. Issue: Anne Fitzhugh Turley, b. Rio de
Janeiro, Brazil 30 Mar 1953; Marshall Frost Turley, b. Kansas
City 14 Dec 1945. m. (2) 29 Dec 1971, Charles B. Buonassisi,
b. 3 Oct 1918. Educ: University of Missouri, B.J. 1939; University of Delaware, Art History. Member: Hereditary Order of Desc.
of Colonial Governors; Americans of Royal Descent; Order of
Charlemagne; Order of the Three Crusades. Occup: Art Commenta-
tor. Address: Plaza Apts. 805, 1303 Delaware Ave., Wilmington,
DE 19806. Descended from:

1 Robert Carter, Governor of Virginia 1726-27.

2　Landon Carter　　　　　　　　　　　　　Elizabeth Wormeley
　　Lancaster Co.VA 1709　　Middlesex Co.　　Middlesex Co.VA 1713
　　Virginia 1778　　　　　　24 Nov 1732　　Virginia 31 Jan 1740

3　John Carter　　　　　　　　　　　　　　Janet Hamilton
　　Richmond Co.VA 1739　　Richmond Co.　　-----
　　Loudoun Co.VA 1789　　　1760　　　　　　-----

4　William F. Carter　　　　　　　　　　　Elizabeth L. Ball
　　15 Aug 1783　　　　　　-----　　　　　16 Aug 1791
　　Fairfax Co.VA 15 Aug　　5 Mar 1807　　Fairfax Co. Mar 1855
　　　1836

5　Elizabeth L. Carter　　　　　　　　　　John Frost
　　Fairfax Co. Apr 1811　　Fairfax Co.　　Washington,DC 17 Apr
　　　　　　　　　　　　　　　　　　　　　　1811
　　Plattsburg,MO 8 Apr　　9 Jun 1829　　Mississippi 15 Jan
　　　1897　　　　　　　　　　　　　　　　　1855

6　Fitzhugh C. Frost　　　　　　　　　　　Sarah C. Birch
　　Fairfax Co. 19 Nov　　Clinton Co.MO　Fayette,MO 17 Jun 1836
　　　1834
　　Plattsburg 11 Apr 1900　26 Aug 1856　　16 Apr 1883

7　Daniel H. Frost　　　　　　　　　　　　Sallie Hoskins
　　Plattsburg 11 May 1868　Knoxville,TN　25 May 1888
　　Plattsburg 3 Jun 1934　12 Feb 1912　　-----

Inheritor: Anne Fitzhugh Turley, Marshall Frost Turley

BURDEN, ORDWAY PARTRIDGE

Nat. #263-B.　Elected 22 Sep 1975.　b. New York,NY 20 Nov 1944.
Educ: Harvard College, A.B., Magna Cum Laude, 1966; Harvard
University Graduate School of Business Administration, M.B.A.,
1968.　Member: Hereditary Order of Desc. of Colonial Governors;
Order of Colonial Lords of Manors; Soc. of Colonial Wars (NY);
St. Nicholas Soc. of New York City; Order of the Crown of Charle-
magne; Americans of Royal Descent; Order of Three Crusades; Sons
of American Revolution (Ch., Law Enforcement Comm.); Desc. of
Colonial Physicians and Surgeons; International Assn. of Chiefs
of Police; The Florence V. Burden Foundation.　Honors: Law
Enforcement Commendation Medal.　Occup: Investment Banking.
Address: 250 East 87th St., New York,NY 10028.　Descended from:

1　Rip Van Dam, Governor of New York 1731-32.

2　Sarah Van Dam　　　　　　　　　　　　Walter Thong
　　NYC bp.31 Oct 1686　　-----　　　　-----
　　NYC bf.17 Feb 1720　　lic.16 Oct　　New York bf.2 Nov 1724
　　　　　　　　　　　　　　1704

3　Mary Thong　　　　　　　　　　　　　　Robert Livingston
　　Albany,NY 3 Jun 1711　　NYC　　　　Albany 18 Dec 1708
　　Livingston Manor,NY　　20 May 1731　Clermont,NY 27 Nov
　　　30 May 1765　　　　　　　　　　　　　1790

4	Walter Livingston 27 Nov 1740 NYC 14 May 1797	----- 1769	Cornelia Schuyler bp. 26 Jul 1746 -----
5	Robert L. Livingston bpt. 6 May 1775 Clermont 7 Jan 1843	 Clermont 10 Jul 1799	Margaret Marie Livingston 11 Apr 1783 8 Mar 1818

6	Cornelia Louisiana
	  Livingston
	24 Dec 1802
	Washington,DC 22 Dec
	  1830
		
		Clermont
		1 Dec 1822
			Charles Goodwin
			  Ridgely
			Baltimore,MD 2 Jul 1784
			Baltimore 4 Feb 1848

7	Margaret Marie Ridgely 11 Apr 1824 NYC 25 Nov 1863	----- 2 Jul 1846	James Schott, Jr. ----- NYC 26 May 1860

8	Rebecca Cornelia Schott
	NYC 24 Nov 1850
	
	NYC 11 May 1935
		
		Philadelphia
		
		1 Sep 1870
			William Engels Schott
			Philadelphia,PA 1 Sep
			  1847
			Philadelphia 22 Feb
			  1882

9	Margaret Ridgely Schott
	
	Philadelphia 5 Oct
	  1872
	NYC 26 Dec 1963
		
		Venice,Italy
		
		14 Jun 1905
			William Ordway
			  Partridge
			Paris,France 11 Apr
			  1861
			NYC 22 May 1930

10	Margaret Livingston
	  Partridge
	NYC 6 Mar 1909
		
		NYC
		16 Feb 1931
			William Armistead Moale
			  Burden
			NYC 8 Apr 1906

Inheritor: William A. M. Burden, IV, (nephew) Seachange,
Northeast Harbor, ME

C

CAREY, ALMA RETHA RISDON (MRS. ORA FOREST)

Nat. #283-B. Elected 1 Mar 1976. b. Iowa Co.,IA 27 Mar 1897.
m. Adel,IA 5 Jul 1919, Ora Forest Carey,b. Iowa Co. 27 Jun 1898,
d. Encinitas,CA 29 Jan 1956. Educ: Iowa State Teachers College,
Cedar Falls,IA; Highland Park College, Des Moines,IA. Member:
Hereditary Order of Desc. of Colonial Governors; Dau. of American
Revolution, Past and Present Chapter Regents' Assn.; Colonial
Dames XVII Century; Magna Charta Dames; Women Desc. of Ancient
and Honorable Artillery Company; Huguenot Society of California;
Southern California Genealogical Soc.; North San Diego County
Genealogical Soc. Address: 540 Balour Drive, Encinitas,CA
92024. Descended from:

1 Samuel Gorton, Governor of Rhode Island 1651-52.

2 Ann Gorton   John Warner
   -----   -----   1 Aug 1645
   -----   7 Aug 1670   22 Apr 1712

3 Ann Warner   (Jacob) Jabez Browne
   -----   -----   Providence,RI 1675
   Providence 25 Feb 1727   -----   Providence 9 Sep 1724

4 William Browne   Patience Arnold
   Providence 1708   -----   -----
   Smithfield,RI 27 Jan   c.1728   -----
     1756

5 Eleazer Browne   Sarah Scott
   Smithfield 31 Dec 1736   Smithfield   Smithfield 18 Oct 1738
   Fayette Co.PA 23 Mar   14 Dec 1758   -----
     1822

6 Joseph Browne (Brown)   Sarah Hewitt
   Smithfield 10 Jun 1764   Fayette Co.   Pennsylvania
   Stark Co.OH   8 Apr 1802   Stark Co.

7 Eliza Brown   Jesse Hawley
   1806   -----   Chester Co.PA 10 Feb
                                                     1796
   Stark Co. 1852   c.1827   Cedar Co.IA 31 Jul 1880

8 Elvira Hawley   Thomas Maudlin
   Stark Co. 14 Mar 1838   -----   Wayne Co.IN 28 Aug 1818
   Ladora,IA 14 Oct 1928   16 Feb 1860   Iowa Co.IA 10 Feb 1896

9 Euretha Maudlin   William J. Risdon
   Iowa Co. 13 May 1873   Iowa Co.   Iowa Co. 28 Apr 1873
   Iowa Co. 15 Feb 1919   1 Jan 1894   Riverside,CA 15 Sep
                                                     1937

CARPENTER, MILDRED E. CARVER (MRS. CLOVIS LEON)

Nat. #117-B. Elected 22 Jan 1966. b. Putnam,CT 8 Oct 1890.
m. Putnam 18 Oct 1916, Clovis Leon Carpenter, b. 18 Jun 1890.
Member: Hereditary Order of Desc. of Colonial Governors; Dau. of
War of 1812; Soc. of Mayflower Desc.; Magna Charta Dames; Dau.
of Colonial Wars; Dau. of American Revolution (Past Regent,
Worcester,MA); Soc. of Desc. of Colonial Clergy; New England
Women; Huguenot Soc. of CT and RI (Organizing Pres. of both);
Huguenot Memorial Soc. of Oxford; New England Historic and
Genealogical Soc.; National Genealogical Soc. of Washington,DC;
Dau. of Founders and Patriots of America. Address: 12 Rexhame
Rd., Worcester,MA 01606. Descended from:

1 William Coddington, Governor of Rhode Island 1640-47

2 Mary Coddington   Peleg Sanford
   Newport,RI 16 May 1654   Newport   Newport 10 May 1639
   Newport Mar 1693   1 Dec 1674   Newport 1701

<table>
<tr><td>3</td><td>Ann Sanford
Newport

-----</td><td>

1702</td><td>James Noyes
Stonington,CT 2 Aug 1677
Stonington 1718</td></tr>
<tr><td>4</td><td>Bridget Noyes
Stonington 25 Mar 1710
Stonington 24 Oct 1774</td><td>
Stonington
23 Nov 1727</td><td>Nathan Chesebrough
Stonington 2 Aug 1707
Stonington 10 Aug 1769</td></tr>
<tr><td>5</td><td>Bridget Chesebrough
23 Sep 1722
1 Jan 1831</td><td>
-----
2 Feb 1766</td><td>Charles Chesebrough
Stonington 6 Jun 1736
In Prison 1780</td></tr>
<tr><td>6</td><td>Phebe Chesebrough
Stonington 9 Mar 1772
-----</td><td>
-----
29 Nov 1792</td><td>Rainsford Hempstead
Stonington 1771
-----</td></tr>
<tr><td>7</td><td>Fanny Hempstead
Stonington
Mystic,CT 26 Mar 1872</td><td>

-----</td><td>Oliver Bennett
Mystic 29 Mar 1793
Mystic 8 Feb 1841</td></tr>
<tr><td>8</td><td>Miranda Bennett
Mystic 13 Oct 1824
Mystic 1898</td><td>(2)
Mystic
21 Jun 1840</td><td>Rhodes Burrows
Mystic 1 Jul 1819
Mystic 1 Feb 1876</td></tr>
<tr><td>9</td><td>Fanny M. Burrows
Mystic 7 May 1842
Worcester,MA 30 Dec 1906</td><td>
Warwick,RI
21 Jun 1859</td><td>Francis M. Brayton
Albion,RI 27 Jul 1837
Providence,RI 10 Jun 1932</td></tr>
<tr><td>10</td><td>Evangeline Brayton
Warwick 5 Nov 1865
Putnam 23 May 1916</td><td>
Putnam,CT
4 Jun 1884</td><td>Hermon G. Carver
Putnam 16 Nov 1862
Putnam 6 Feb 1937</td></tr>
</table>

CARRUTH, MARGARET SCRUGGS (MRS.)

Nat. #865. Elected 17 Jul 1923. b. Dallas,TX 18 Feb 1892.
m. Dallas 6 Jun 1912, R. F. Carruth. Issue: Walter Scruggs
Carruth, b. Dallas 15 Jul 1914. Educ: Bryn Mawr College;
Southern Methodist University, B.A. and M.A. Member: Hereditary
Order of Desc. of Colonial Governors; Dau. of American Colonists;
Dau. of American Revolution; Colonial Dames of America (Past Nat.
Secretary); Colonial Dames of XVII Century; Order of the Crown;
Lords of Maryland Manors; New England Women; Dau. of Founders and
Patriots; Dames of the Court of Honor. Occup: Illustrator,
Lecturer and Professor at So. Methodist Univ. (Ret.). Address:
4524 Edmondson Ave., Dallas,TX 75205. Descended from:

1 Robert Brooke, Governor of Maryland 1652

<table>
<tr><td>2</td><td>Roger Brooke
20 Sep 1637
8 Apr 1700</td><td>(2)

-----</td><td>Mary Woolsey

-----</td></tr>
<tr><td>3</td><td>Anne Brooke

-----</td><td>
Calvert Co.MD
1702</td><td>James Mackal
Calvert Co. 1667
-----</td></tr>
</table>

4 John Mackal   Martha Duke
   Calvert Co. c.1710   -----   1715
   -----   -----   -----

5 Ann Mackal   Ralph Briscoe
   Calvert Co. c.1748   -----   Charles Co.MD 24 Nov
                                              1747
   Maryland c.1790   c.1765   Missouri

6 James M. Briscoe   Mary Bruner
   Frederick Co.MD   -----   Maryland 19 Jan 1783
     15 Nov 1779
   -----   7 May 1801   -----

7 Ann M. Briscoe   Gross F. Scruggs
   Scott Co.KY 18 Jul 1814 -----   Scott Co. 22 Nov 1808
   -----   21 Sep 1832   Dallas,TX 8 Jan 1897

8 James B. Scruggs   Mary I. Hastings
   Scott Co. 10 Oct 1835   Robertson Co. -----
                               TX
   Dallas,TX 10 May 1910   14 Sep 1865   -----

9 Gross R. Scruggs   Marian S. Price
   Robertson Co. 5 Jan   Dallas   -----
     1868
   -----   18 Nov 1890   -----

CHADWICK, MARGARETTA LYTLE WOODBRIDGE (MRS.)

Nat. #287-B. Elected 4 May 1976. b. Wilmington,DE 27 Feb 1919.
m. Wilmington 23 Oct 1943, George William Chadwick (marriage
dissolved). Educ: Sarah Lawrence College, Bronxville,NY, B.A.
1941. Member: Hereditary Order of Desc. of Colonial Governors;
Colonial Dames of America; Americans of Royal Descent; Soc. of
Dau. of Colonial Wars; Dau. of American Revolution; Dau. of
Barons of Runnemede; Dutch Colonial Soc. of Delaware; Order of
Desc., Colonial Physicians and Chirurgiens. Address: 2407 West
17th Street, Wilmington,DE 19806. Descended from:

1 Walter Clarke, Governor of Rhode Island 1686, 1696-98

2 Mary Clarke   (2)   Ralph Chapman
   Newport,RI 11 Jan 1661   Newport   Marshfield,MA 165-
   Newport 10 Aug 1711   af.1694   -----

3 Catherine Chapman   James Sheffield
   -----   -----   Newport 1694
   12 Mar 1769   1 Mar 1714   Newport 20 Apr 1762

4 Mary Sheffield   Nathaniel Coffin
   Newport 21 Sep 1716   Newport   Nantucket,MA 9/19 Jul
                                               1711
   Nantucket 25 Aug 1778   6 Feb 1735   Nantucket 7/10 Jun 1800

5 Walter Coffin   (2)   Sarah Bristow
   Nantucket 20 Nov 1748   Newport   -----
   at sea 1 Nov 1785   26 Sep 1774   -----

6	Mary Coffin Nantucket 1783 Chester 26 Feb 1826	New York 8 Sep 1798	Samuel Lytle, II Chester,PA 1773 Chester 1 Dec 1859
7	Samuel Lytle, III Chester 1816 Camden 26 Oct 1871	Camden,NJ 2 May 1841	Mary Cole(s) Hammell 1820 Elwood,NJ 9 Mar 1891
8	Mary Coffin Lytle Camden 27 Nov 1855 Wilmington,DE 23 Jan 1921	Camden 20 Dec 1877	George Elliot Whall Boston,MA 2 May 1853 Auburndale,MA 23 Sep 1883
9	Ethel Lytle Whall Dorchester,MA 31 May 1879 Wilmington 6 Jul 1967	Waltham,MA 5 Jul 1911	Richard George Woodbridge, Jr. Iowa City,IA 18 Mar 1885 Wilmington 7 Nov 1946

CHATFIELD, BENJAMIN VANTINE

Nat. #290-B. Elected 14 Jun 1976. b. Bridgeport,CT 2 Nov 1929. m. Juneau,AK 26 Jul 1958, Rilda Mae Swiger, b. Auburn,MO 23 Sep 1930. Issue: Margaret Swiger Chatfield, b. Juneau 11 Aug 1960; Benjamin Vantine Chatfield, Jr., b. Palo Alto,CA 19 May 1967. Educ: Stanford University, Palo Alto, B.S. 1951, M.S. 1959, Ph.D. 1969. Member: Hereditary Order of Desc. of Colonial Governors; Soc. of Desc. of Colonial Clergy. Occup: Professional Engineer. Address: 5509 Thirty-second Street North, Arlington,VA 22207. Descended from:

1 Robert Treat, Governor of Connecticut 1683-98

2	Abigail Treat Milford,CT 1660 Milford 25 Dec 1727	Milford -----	Samuel Andrew Cambridge,MA 29 Jan 1655/6 Milford 24 Jan 1737/8
3	Jonathan Andrew bp.Milford 24 Aug 1701 Milford Sep 1739	Milford 5 Jan 1727	Elizabeth Smith ----- -----
4	Abigail Andrew bp.Milford Mar 1732 -----	Milford 10 Apr 1753	Ebenezer Buckingham Milford 10 Dec 1727 Oxford,CT 6 Oct 1798
5	Ebenezer Buckingham Milford 28 Nov 1764 Oxford Sep 1839	Milford 28 Oct 1792	Olive Woodruff Milford 7 May 1768 Oxford 1 Nov 1849
6	Clarissa Buckingham Milford 29 Aug 1794 Oxford 20 Dec 1840	Milford 1 Jan 1815	Chester Chatfield Oxford 7 Jul 1794 Oxford 18 Jul 1881
7	Henry Chatfield Oxford 6 May 1819 New Haven,CT 23 Jan 1908	Milford 6 May 1844	Jennet Beach Milford 2 Oct 1819 New Haven 17 Apr 1890

8 Frederick Chatfield   Edith Belle Smith
   New Haven 8 May 1860   New Haven   New Haven 13 Aug 1865
   New Haven 7 Apr 1927   7 Apr 1885   Bound Brook,NJ 13 Feb
                                                 1937

9 Chester Hart Chatfield   Florence Marie Van Tine
   New Haven 22 Sep 1896   Long Branch,NJ Long Branch 8 Sep 1897
   Stamford,CT 6 Jul 1963 20 Sep 1924   (living on 9 May 1976)

   Inheritor: Benjamin Vantine Chatfield, Jr.

CHATFIELD, FLORENCE VAN TINE (MRS. CHESTER HART)

Nat. #92-B.   Elected 3 Mar 1964.   b. Long Branch,NJ 8 Sep 1897.
m. Long Branch 20 Sep 1924, Chester Hart Chatfield, b. New Haven,
CT 22 Sep 1896, d. 6 Jul 1963.   Issue: Chester Hart Chatfield,Jr.
b. 23 Oct 1925; Benjamin Vantine Chatfield, b. 2 Nov 1929; Edwin
Bruce Chatfield, b. 4 Feb 1935; all b. Bridgeport,CT.   Educ:
State Normal School, Trenton,NJ.   Member: Hereditary Order of
Desc. of Colonial Governors; National Huguenot Soc. (Past
Registrar Gen.); Huguenot Soc. of Connecticut; Fellow Huguenot
Soc. of London; Magna Charta Dames; Americans of Royal Descent;
Dau. of American Revolution (Nat. Vice Chairman, Genealogical
Records); Connecticut State Officers and Regents Club; Children
of American Revolution; Founders and Patriots of America (Past
State Registrar,CT); Dames of Court of Honor (Librarian Gen.);
Dau. of American Colonists (Regent, Gov. Thomas Welles Ch.,
Bridgeport); Sons and Dau. of the Pilgrims; New England Women;
Vermont Soc. of Colonial Dames; Nat. Genealogical Soc.; New York
Genealogical and Biographical Soc.; N.E. Historic and Genealogi-
cal Soc.   Occup: Former Teacher.   Address: 80 Cartright St.,
Apt. 3-M, Bridgeport,CT 06604.   Descended from:

1 Gerardus Beekman, Governor of New York 1710

2 Christopher Beekman   Marie DeLancy
   Flatbush,NY 4 Jan 1681 New Amsterdam, Albany,NY c.1684
                           NY
   New York,NY 6 May 1724 28 Jan 1704   New Jersey af.1724

3 Gerardus C. Beekman   Catherine Van Dyke
   Somerset Co.NJ 6 Aug   Somerset Co.   New Brunswick,NJ
     1707   12 Apr 1708
   Somerset Co. 4 Aug 1777 -----   Somerset Co. c.1777

4 Mary Beekman   Thomas Skillman
   Harlingen,NJ   -----   Newtown,NY 1727
   New Jersey Jun 1819   1751   -----

5 Jacob Skillman   (2)   Mary Hageman
   Harlingen 28 Aug 1764   New Jersey   NJ 18 Apr 1767
   Three Mile Run,NJ   af.1796   Six Mile Run,NJ
     13 Apr 1854   25 Oct 1840

6 Ellen Skillman   Peter Van Tine
   Six Mile Run 5 Sep   Six Mile Run   Six Mile Run 23 Aug
     1801   1789
   Six Mile Run 13 Mar   30 Jun 1819   Six Mile Run 23 Nov
     1882   1852

7   Isaac Van Tine   Mary Butler
    Three Mile Run 29 Nov   Trenton,NJ   Sheffol,Eng. 1838
      1821
    Harbourton,NJ 18 May   31 Dec 1856   Trenton 7 Aug 1922
      1913

8   Isaac Van Tine   Sallie Millaway
    Hunterdon Co.NJ 10 Jan Philipsburg,NJ Smyrna,DE 24 Mar 1871
      1862
    Long Branch,NJ 14 Nov   13 Jul 1891   29 Nov 1963
      1934

    Inheritor: Edwin Bruce Chatfield, 31 Medbury Rd., Wallingford,
    PA 19086

CHERRY, CHARLOTTE E. SPENCER (MRS. LEE WILLIAM)

Nat. #167-B. Elected 4 Jan 1971. b. Massilon,OH 7 Aug 1906.
m. Massilon 7 Aug 1930, Lee William Cherry, b. Canton,OH 28 Sep
1903. Issue: Eugene Spencer Cherry, b. Canton; Muriel Lee Cherry
McConoughey, b. Canton. Educ: College of Wooster,OH; Kent State,
OH; Ohio State. Member: Hereditary Order of Desc. of Colonial
Governors; Dau. of American Revolution (Vice-Regent, Martha
Pitkin Ch.). Occup: High School teacher. Address: 324 Maple
Ave., Lakeside,OH 43440. Descended from:

1   John Webster, Governor of Connecticut 1656

2   Robert Webster   Susanna Treat
    Warwickshire,Eng.   Middletown,CT   England 1629
      c.1627
    Hartford,CT 31 May   1652   Hartford 1705
      1676

3   Jonathan Webster   Dorcas Hopkins
    Middletown 2 Jan 1656   Hartford   -----
    Hartford 1735   11 May 1681   -----

4   Jonathan Webster   Esther Judd
    Hartford 18 Mar 1681/2 Connecticut   CT 6 Feb 1686
    Glastonbury,CT 18 Sep   14 Dec 1704   Bernardstown,MA 22 Dec
      1758   1782

5   David Webster   Lydia Andrus
    Glastonbury 29 Jan   Newington,CT   -----
      1720/1
    Newington 12 May 1806   20 Jun 1750   -----

6   Amos Andrews Webster   Mabel Andrews
    Newington 30 Aug 1750   Newington   -----
    Newington 10 Jan 1827   18 Dec 1777   -----

7   Chloe Webster   Henry Fuller
    Newington 30 Dec 1795   Berlin,CT   -----
    Saugerties,NY 15 Mar   23 Mar 1815   -----
      1880

8 Susan Fuller   Martin Spencer
  CT 6 May 1817   Chatham,MA   -----
  Saugerties 26 Nov 1911   24 Jun 1838   -----

9 Selden Spencer   Aurelia Platt
  Quarreyville,NY 29 Nov   Myersburg,PA   North Towanda,PA 5 May
  1849   1855
  Waverly,NY 19 Nov 1904   4 Jul 1871   N.Towanda 29 Jan 1897

10 Ralph Kenneth Spencer   Lilian K. Schott
   Towanda,PA 22 Aug 1880   Massilon,OH   25 May 1880
                                  15 Jun 1905   9 Feb 1956

   Inheritor: Dr. Eugene Spencer Cherry, 321 Princewood, Dayton,
   OH 45421.

CLARK, JANET COLLIER (MRS. RICHARD GILMAN)

Nat. #294-B. Elected 25 Sep 1976. b. Billerica,MA 28 May 1908.
m. Billerica 28 Oct 1939, Richard Gilman Clark, b. Strong,ME
14 May 1903. Educ: Lake Erie College, A.B.; Boston University;
University of Vermont. Member: Hereditary Order of Desc. of
Colonial Governors; Dau. of American Revolution; Dau. of Founders
and Patriots of America; Dau. of Colonial Wars; Women Desc. of
Ancient and Honorable Artillery Co.; Dau. of 1812; Colonial
Dames of XVII Century; Dau. of American Colonists; New England
Women; Old Plymouth Colony Desc.; Soc. of Desc. of Colonial
Clergy; Dames of the Court of Honor; National Huguenot Soc.
Address: (summer) 216 North Church St., Rutland,VT 05701;
(winter) 67 Crystal Dr., DeBary,FL 32713. Descended from:

1 Tristram Coffin, Sr., Governor of Nantucket 1671-72

2 Tristram Coffin, Jr.   Judith (Greenleaf)
                                                        Somerby
  Brixton,Eng. 1632   Newbury   England 2 Sep 1625
  Newbury,MA 4 Feb 1704   2 Mar 1652/3   Newbury 15 Dec 1705

3 Lydia Coffin   (2)   John Pike
  Newbury 22 Apr 1662   Newbury   Newbury 28 Dec 1671
  Newbury 25 Mar 1719   18 Mar 1695   Newbury 13 Aug 1714

4 Joanna Pike   Thomas Thurlow
  Newbury 17 Dec 1700   Newbury   Newbury 11 Dec 1701
  -----   12 Mar 1722/3   Newbury 28 Aug 1789

5 Abraham Thurlow   (int)   Lydia Boynton
  Newbury 14 Jul 1743   Newburyport,MA   Coventry,CT 10 Feb 1743
  Newbury 31 Aug 1786   20 May 1763   Newbury 1820

6 David Thurlow   Mercy Trundy
  Newbury 18 Oct 1774   Deer Isle,ME   Deer Isle 1779
  Deer Isle 5 Apr 1857   1798   Deer Isle 17 May 1859

7 Elvira Thurlow Raynes   Charles Collier
  Deer Isle 2 Jan 1812   Charlestown,   Bristol,Eng. 23 Apr
                                  MA   1817
  Charlestown 3 Mar 1864   1 Nov 1838   Charlestown 27 Jun 1891

8 Abram Thurlow Collier   Addie Isabelle Foster
   Charlestown 17 May 1848 Chelsea,MA   Boston,MA 17 Sep 1847
   Watertown,MA 2 Feb   8 Oct 1874   Winchester,MA 30 Dec
     1921   1915

9 Forrest Foster Collier   Lucy Janette Bryant
   Chelsea 14 Jul 1875   Billerica,MA   Concord,MA 20 Oct 1877
   Miami,FL 7 Dec 1970   29 Oct 1903   Boston 20 Aug 1947

CLELAND, RUTH HILTON (MRS.)

Nat. #342-B. Elected 17 Jul 1979. b. Starks,ME 20 Apr 1902.
m. Athens,Greece 10 Apr 1928, Paul Swift Cleland, b. Bridgeport,
CT 19 Nov 1903; d. Camarillo,CA 7 Oct 1956. Member: Hereditary
Order of Desc. of Colonial Governors; Soc. of Mayflower Desc.;
Dau. of Colonial Wars; Soc. of Desc. of Colonial Clergy; Flagon
and Trencher; Dau. of American Revolution; Dau. of American
Colonists; Colonial Dames XVII Century; New England Women;
Pilgrim John Howland Soc.; Ancient and Honorable Artillery Co.;
Magna Charta Dames; Aux. to Sons of Union Veterans of Civil War.
Address: 521 West Meadow Ave., Rahway,NJ 07065. Descended from:

1 Thomas Mayhew, Sr., Governor of Martha's Vineyard 1647-81

2 Thomas Mayhew, Jr.   Jane Paine
   England c.1620   -----   c.1625
   at sea 1651   c.1645   af.1658

3 Matthew Mayhew   Mary Skiffe
   Martha's Vineyard,MA   -----   Martha's Vnyd. 24 Mar
     1648   1650
   Martha's Vnyd. 19 May   1 Mar 1674   Martha's Vnyd. 1 May
     1710   1690

4 Paine Mayhew   Mary Rankin
   Martha's Vnyd. 31 Oct   Boston   Boston,MA 1676
     1677
   Martha's Vnyd. 8 May   8 Dec 1699   Martha's Vnyd. 17 Feb
     1761   1753

5 Mary Mayhew   Jethro Athearn
   Martha's Vnyd. 26 Sep   Martha's Vnyd.   Martha's Vnyd. 10 Jun
     1700   1692
   Martha's Vnyd. 7 Apr   8 Sep 1720   Martha's Vnyd. 3 Feb
     1778   1784

6 Zerviah Athearn   Benjamin Manter
   Martha's Vnyd. 17 Aug   Martha's Vnyd.   Martha's Vnyd. 17 Jan
     1723   1711
   Martha's Vnyd. 11 Jan   9 Dec 1742   Martha's Vnyd. 18 Mar
     1810   1796

7 James Manter   Mary Butler
   Martha's Vnyd. 29 Jun   Martha's Vnyd.   Martha's Vnyd. 1751
     1746
   pb.Industry,MA 26 Dec   28 Nov 1771   Martha's Vnyd. 22 May
     1796   1845

8 Elizabeth Manter   Benjamin Hilton
   Martha's Vnyd. 17 Mar   -----   Wiscasset,ME 21 Mar
     1775   1772
   Anson,ME 8 Aug 1869   26 Jul 1798   Anson 28 Jul 1845

9 Benjamin Hilton   Margaret Athearn
   Anson 3 Feb 1803   Anson   Castine,ME 21 May 1805
   Starks,ME 2 Oct 1891   2 Jul 1829   Starks 23 Jul 1862

10 Benjamin Franklin Hilton   Mary E. Furber
   Starks 9 Feb 1832   -----   Athens,ME 13 Jun 1840
   Starks 21 Mar 1909   20 Nov 1860   Starks 11 Apr 1900

11 Ernest Hilton   Viola Izetta Piper
   Anson 3 Dec 1861   Portsmouth,NH   Starks 26 Oct 1865
   Starks 8 Aug 1923   8 Mar 1898   Morristown,NJ Apr 1944

   Inheritor: Debra Davidge Cleland, 444 East Glaucus, Leucadia,
   CA 92024.

CONKEY, CDR CLEMENT SNOWDEN

Nat. #240-B. Elected 17 Oct 1974. b. Kansas City,MO 22 Apr 1915.
m. Washington,DC 25 Nov 1942, Pauline Adair Howell, b. Brunswick
Co.,VA 11 Aug 1910. Issue: Clement Snowden Conkey, Jr. Educ:
Columbia University, New York,NY; George Washington University,
Washington,DC; Benjamin Franklin University, Washington,DC
(B.C.S.); Columbus University, Washington,DC (M.F.A.). Member:
Hereditary Order of Desc. of Colonial Governors; Desc. of Lords
of Maryland Manors (Member of Council); Sons of American Revolu-
tion; Jamestowne Society; Soc. of the Pilgrims of St. Mary's
(President); Huguenot Soc. of Washington,DC (President); seven
Masonic orders. Address: 1507 Baylor Ave., Rockville,MD 20850.
Descended from:

1 Edward Digges, Governor of Virginia 1655-56

2 William Digges   Elizabeth (Warton)
                                             Sewall
   Belleville,VA   -----   -----
   Prince George's Co.,MD   1676   1716
     1697

3 Charles Digges   Susanna M. (Darnall)
                                             Lowe
   Prince George's Co.   -----   -----
     1676
   Prince George's Co.   -----   -----
     1742

4 Mary Digges   Clement Hill, III
   Prince George's Co.   -----   Prince George's Co.
     17 Jan 1715   4 Jan 1707
   Prince George's Co.   11 Jan 1737   Prince George's Co.
     16 Jan 1756   12 Feb 1782

```
5  Clement Hill                                    Eleanor Brent
   Prince George's Co.      Pr.Geo.Co.            Charles Co.MD
      6 Nov 1743
   Prince George's Co.      13 Dec 1774           Prince George's Co.
      6 Feb 1807                                     28 May 1827

6  Charles Hill                  (3)              Anne E. (Hall) Snowden
   Prince George's Co.      Pr.Geo.Co.            Roxbury Mills,MD
      22 Dec 1786                                    31 Jul 1808
   Prince George's Co.      4 Oct 1836            Prince George's Co.
      18 Sep 1868                                    15 Jul 1847

7  Francis E. Hill                                Minnie Waldo
   Prince George's Co.      Washington,DC         Independence,MO
      27 Jan 1845                                    23 Sep 1856
   Kansas City,MO           23 Nov 1881           Washington,DC
      8 Apr 1926                                     25 Dec 1940

8  Lula E. Hill                                   George L. Conkey
   Prince George's Co.      Kansas City           Maysville,KY 28 Oct
      4 Feb 1884                                     1882
   Kansas City 15 Apr 1923 4 Oct 1906            Kansas City 24 Nov
                                                    1924
```

COOKE, ROBERT GEORGE

Nat. #226-B. Elected 4 Apr 1974. b. Sturgis,MI 1906. m. North
St. Paul,MN 1935, Helen Marie Mullery. Issue: Mary Alice Cooke
Leaper, b. 1936. Educ: University of Minnesota; Minneapolis
College of Art; College of St. Thomas, B.A. Member: Hereditary
Order of Desc. of Colonial Governors; Order of Crown of Charle-
magne in the U.S.A.; Americans of Royal Descent; Soc. of
Colonial Wars (Alabama); Sons of American Revolution; Baronial
Order of Magna Charta; Order of Three Crusades; Americans of
Armorial Ancestry. Occup: Publisher and former teacher of
English, Art, Journalism and History. Knighted by King Peter
II, of Yugoslavia and by the Republic of San Marino. Address:
515 S. Lexington Pkwy., #105, St. Paul, MN 55116. Descended fr:

```
1  Charles Calvert, Governor of Maryland 1675-1715

2  Benedict Leonard Calvert                       Charlotte Lee
      21 Mar 1679              -----              1678
      16 Apr 1715             2 Jan 1698/9        1720/1

3  Jane Calvert                                   John Hyde
      13 Nov 1703            London,Eng.          1695
      Jul 1778               9 Jun 1720           1746

4  Mary Calvert Hyde                              George Mitchell
      -----                   -----              -----
      -----                  c.1766               -----

5  George Calvert Mitchell                        -----
      Ireland c.1772          -----              -----
      France c.1825           -----              -----
```

6 George Baltimore Mitchell   Rhoda Pamelia Fenn
   New York 15 Jun 1810   -----   Rutland,VT 27 Jul 1816
   Royalton,NY 26 Mar 1838 -----   Colon,MI 27 Mar 1865

7 George Marvin Mitchell   Mary A. Walrath
   Royalton 6 Aug 1836   Barry Co.NY   Herkimer Co.NY 23 Dec
                                                    1834
   7 Mar 1883   5 Jul 1858   Sturgis,MI 3 Sep 1901

8 Cora May Mitchell   Joseph R. Cooke
   Middleville,MI 4 Oct   Middleville   Barry Co. 7 Jul 1858
     1864
   Goshen,IN 14 Aug 1949   29 Dec 1886   Sturgis 3 Apr 1910

Inheritor: Mary Alice W. Cooke Leaper (Mrs. Percy F.), 1 Alta
Vista Drive, Princeton,NJ 08540.

CORNETT, ROBERT FIELDING JR.

Nat. #38-B. Elected 30 Aug 1961. b. Bluefield,WV 13 Mar 1929.
Educ: Exmoor School and University of Miami, both at Coral
Gables,FL. Member: Hereditary Order of Desc. of Colonial
Governors; Soc. of Mayflower Desc., MA; Sons of American Revolu-
tion, FL; Sons of Revolution, FL; Huguenot Soc.; Founders of
Manakin in the Colony of Virginia; Sons of Confederate Veterans.
(From Society's Records). Address: Box 1495, Bluefield,WV
24701. Descended from:

1 John Alden, Governor of Plymouth Colony 1663-64; 1667

2 Elizabeth Alden   William Peabody
   Plymouth,MA 1624   Duxbury,MA   c.1619
   Little Compton,RI   6 Dec 1644   Little Compton 13 Dec
     31 May 1717   1707

3 Ruth Peabody   Benjamin Bartlett
   Duxbury 27 Jun 1658   -----   27 Jun 1658
   Duxbury btw.25 Apr   c. Nov 1678   Duxbury 27 Aug 1720
     1724 and 1725

4 Ruth Bartlett   John Murdock
   Duxbury c.1690   -----   Plymouth 8 Jun 1691
   Plymouth 27 Mar 1725   c.1710   Plymouth 17 Sep 1756

5 Janet Murdock   Stephen Tilson
   Plymouth 10 Dec 1711   Plymouth   Plymouth 6 Apr 1717
   Plymouth bf.1759   13 Nov 1740   Plymouth af.1763

6 William Tilson   Mary Ransom
   Plymouth 15 Mar 1741   -----   -----
   Virginia c.1825   1 Apr 1763   Erwin,TN c.1820

7 Thomas Tilson   Eunice Hubbell
   St.Clair,VA 15 Jun 1767 Smyth Co.VA   Smyth Co. 1 Jun 1773
   St.Clair 24 Nov 1829   3 May 1792   St.Clair 11 Jan 1846

8	Rachel Tilson St.Clair 4 Feb 1812 Marion,VA 19 Oct 1884	St.Clair 20 Jun 1832	Thomas Copenhaver Marion 22 Dec 1811 Marion 3 Jan 1882
9	Eunice M. Copenhaver Marion 17 Apr 1841 Wythe Co.VA 12 Dec 1934	Marion 19 Jan 1869	Fielding R. Cornett Elk Creek,VA 16 Oct 1835 Spring Valley,VA 20 Mar 1920
10	Walter M. Cornett Elk Creek 19 Jul 1874 Wythe Co. 7 Sep 1941	Princeton,WV 26 Oct 1898	Edna McClaugherty Giles Co.VA 16 Sep 1876 Wythe Co. 17 Apr 1958

COUDEKERQUE-LAMBRECHT, BEATRICE COWLES (MME. ANDRÉ de)

Nat. #201-B. Elected 16 Feb 1941. b. Cleveland,OH 29 Jul 1905.
m. New York,NY 2 Jan 1930, André de Coudekerque-Lambrecht, b.
27 Aug 1898, Rambouillet, France. Educ: The Bishop's School,
La Jolla,CA; Colorado College. Member: Hereditary Order of Desc.
of Colonial Governors; Union Interalliée, Paris; American
Women's Group of Paris (Pres.); Dau. of American Revolution
(State Regent for France); Comité France-Amerique, Paris.
Honors: Medaille de la Reconnaissance Francaise; Medaille de la
France Libre. Address: 11 Rue Cernuschi, 75012 Paris, France.
Descended from:

1 Thomas Dudley, Governor of Massachusetts 1634-35, 1640-41,
1645-46, 1650-51

This line has been lost by the Society.

COULTER, PHEBE DOUGLAS FROST (MRS. JOHN LEE)

Nat. #89-B. Elected 12 Oct 1963. b. Richmond,TX 9 Nov 1888.
m. Washington,DC 23 Sep 1911, John Lee Coulter, b. Mallory,MN
16 Apr 1881; d. Washington,DC 16 Apr 1959. Issue: John Lee
Coulter, Jr., b. Washington,DC 1 Aug 1912; Kirkley Schley Coulter
b. Nashville,TN 26 Jul 1914; David D. Creswell Coulter, b.
Fargo,ND 4 Apr 1928. Member: Hereditary Order of Desc. of
Colonial Governors; Dau. of American Revolution (Past Regent);
Colonial Dames of America, VA; U.S. Dau. of 1812; United Dau.
of the Confederacy (Past Pres. of Chapter); Americans of Royal
Descent; Order of First Families of Virginia; Dau. of the Barons
of Runnemede (Past Natl. Chaplain); Jamestowne Soc.; Desc. of
Lords of Maryland Manors (Past Treas.); Washington Family Desc.;
Assoc. for the Preservation of Virginia Antiquities; Washington
Club, D.C. Address: 2100 S Street, N.W., Washington,DC 20008.
Descended from:

1 John West, Governor of Virginia 1635-37

2 John West
    Bluefield,VA 1632   -----   Unity Croshaw
    King William Co.VA   c.1667   York Co. VA
    1689   -----

3 Anne West
    King William Co.   -----   Henry Fox
    -----   bf.1684   Virginia c.1650
                               King William Co. 1714

4 Anne Fox
    Virginia 20 May 1684 -----   Thomas Claiborne
    Virginia 4 May 1733   bf.1701   16 Dec 1680
                              16 Aug 1732

5 Leonard Claiborne
    1701   -----   Martha Burnell
    8 May 1785   -----   Virginia 1 Jan 1701
                              Virginia 3 Apr 1720

*6 Leonard Claiborne   -----
    c.1720   -----   -----
    Georgia bf.1772   -----   -----

7 Elizabeth Claiborne   (2)   David Douglas
    c.1750   -----   Augusta,GA
    -----   10 Jul 1777 -----

8 Samuel C. Douglas   Phoebe T. Creswell
    Washington,GA 1780   Richmond Co.GA Wilkes Co.GA c.1794
    Texas af.1853   11 Apr 1812 c.1820

9 Zemula W. Douglas   George H. Schley
    Georgia 1818   Georgia   Georgia by 1809
    Richmond,TX 1882   4 Apr 1836   Galveston,TX 1893

10 Mary W. Schley   Henry Frost
    Georgia 1851   -----   Houston,TX 1846
    Richmond 13 Feb 1904 May 1870   Richmond Aug 1889

COX, PAUL VERNON

Nat. #307-B. Elected 5 Apr 1977. b. Pickens,SC 17 Feb 1908.
m. Washington,DC 22 Aug 1936, Mary Elizabeth Bartholomew,
b. 13 Apr 1909. Educ: Benjamin Franklin University, Washington,
DC, B.C.S. Member: Hereditary Order of Desc. of Colonial Gover-
nors; Sons of Confederate Veterans; Order of the Stars and Bars;
Soc. of Desc. of Colonial Clergy; Sons of Revolution; Sovereign
Military Order of Temple of Jerusalem; all masonic bodies.
Occup: Vice President, Southland Life Insurance Co., retired.
Address: 11305 Riverview Rd., Oxon Hill,MD 20022. Descended fr:

1 Henry Vane, Governor of Massachusetts 1636-37

2 Frances Vane   John Grubb
    Kent,Eng. 1641   -----   Cornwall 1692
    -----   -----   New Castle,DE Mar 1708

* See Preface

3	Charity Grubb		Richard Beeson
	Grubb's Landing,DE	-----	7 Oct 1684
	29 Sep 1687		
	New Garden,NC 27 Nov 1761	26 Oct 1706	1 Jan 1777
4	Benjamin Beeson		Elizabeth Hunter
	Pennsylvania	-----	-----
	NC 14 Jun 1794	1738	-----
5	Ann Beeson		David Lewis
	30 May 1749	-----	21 Mar 1749
	7 Dec 1812	30 Jan 1768	Pendleton District,SC 23 Jun 1822
6	Jacob Lewis		Ailsie Leonard
	14 Jan 1772	-----	11 Oct 1771
	4 Aug 1857	22 Feb 1792	24 Oct 1857
7	James Lewis		Mary Stewart
	26 Jul 1807	-----	11 Oct 1811
	26 Mar 1883	28 Dec 1828	25 Mar 1883
8	Mary Malinda Lewis		James Madison Stewart
	14 Jun 1843	-----	16 May 1839
	14 Apr 1896	14 Nov 1865	26 Feb 1928
9	Lena Stewart		Francis Edward Cox
	11 Nov 1873	-----	2 Sep 1866
	8 Nov 1957	30 Dec 1896	8 Apr 1912

Inheritor: Dr. Henry Bartholomew Cox (son)

CRAM, HENRY SERGEANT

Nat. #314-B. Elected 8 Aug 1977. b. New York,NY 21 Jan 1907.
m. Ridgeland,SC 20 Apr 1950, Lucy Catherine Ladd, b. Dawkins,SC
12 Aug 1916. Educ: Browning School, NY; Hun School of Princeton,
NJ. Member: Hereditary Order of Desc. of Colonial Governors;
Order of Colonial Lords of Manors in America; Desc. of Lords of
Maryland Manors; Soc. of Colonial Wars,FL; Sons of American
Revolution,FL; Order of Founders and Patriots of America (FL,
Past Governor); Soc. of Desc. of Colonial Clergy; Baronial Order
of Magna Charta; Military Order of Loyal Legion of U.S.; Navy
League (Director). Military: World War II, U.S. Coast Guard.
Address: Devil's Elbow Island, Bluffton,SC 29910. Descended fr:

1	Robert Brooke, Governor of Maryland 1652		
2	Thomas Brooke		Eleanor Hatton
	Battle,Eng. 23 Jun 1632	Maryland	England 1642
	Calvert Co.MD 1676	1659	Calvert Co. 1725
3	Thomas Brooke		Barbara Dent
	Calvert Co. 1659	-----	1676
	Prince George's Co., MD 7 Jan 1730/1	-----	-----
4	Mary Brooke		Patrick Sim
	-----	-----	-----
	1758	-----	24 Oct 1740

```
5   Barbara Sim                                Clement Smith
    -----                    -----             1718
    -----                    -----             1792

6   Walter Smith                               Esther Belt
    1744                     -----             1744
    29 Aug 1796             -----              2 Mar 1814

7   Clement Smith                              Margaret Clare Brice
    1776                    Baltimore,MD       1783
    Georgetown,DC 7 Mar    12 Nov 1807         Georgetown 9 Oct 1862
      1838

8   Joseph Smith Bryce                         Elizabeth Stephens
    Georgetown 21 Sep 1808  -----              -----
    New York,NY 16 Apr 1901 -----              1880

9   Lloyd Stephens Bryce                       Edith Cooper
    Flushing,NY 20 Sep      NYC                NYC 1854
      1851
    Roslyn,NY 2 Apr 1917   31 May 1879         Roslyn 29 Apr 1916

10  Edith Clare Bryce                          John Sergeant Cram
    NYC 6 May 1880          NYC                NYC 18 May 1851
    NYC 29 Feb 1960        17 Jan 1906         NYC 18 Jan 1936
```

CRAYNE, LYNN MYERS

Nat. #277-B. Elected 10 Feb 1976. b. Jefferson,PA 6 Nov 1914.
m. Wellsburg,WV 10 Jun 1938, Kathryn Edith Guiher, b. Waynesburg,
PA 17 May 1915. Educ: Graduate of Waynesburg College, 1937.
Member: Hereditary Order of Desc. of Colonial Governors; Sons
of American Revolution. Address: Box 54, Jefferson,PA 15344.
Descended from:

```
1   Robert Treat, Governor of Connecticut   1683-98

2   Mary Treat                               Azariah Crane
    Milford,CT 1 May 1652    -----           East Haven,CT 1649
    East Jersey 12 Nov 1704 -----            East Jersey 5 Nov 1730

3   Azariah Crane                            Rebecca
    East Jersey 1682         East Jersey     1681
    East Jersey             c.1706           Montclair,NJ 15 Jun
                                               1739

4   Azariah Crane                            Phebe
    East Jersey             East Jersey      -----
    East Jersey 21 Nov 1752 -----            -----

5   Silas Crane (Crayne)                     Jane
    Essex Co.NJ 1737         -----           1748
    Morgan,PA 30 Jul 1835   -----            Morgan 25 Jan 1845

6   Samuel Crayne                            Mary Huss
    Washington,PA 30 Sep    Greene Co.PA     VA 15 May 1792
      1784
    Morgan 27 Oct 1853      -----            Morgan 14 Jun 1865
```

```
7  Stephen Crayne                              Mary Bell
   Washington 4 Jan 1813    Greene Co.         Morgan 26 May 1816
   Morgan 12 Mar 1909       18 Mar 1834        Morgan 16 Sep 1899

8  David Bell Crayne                           Mary Jane (Jennie) Bane
   Morgan 14 Nov 1851       Washington Co.     Amwell,PA 8 Jul 1855
                             PA
   Jefferson,PA 6 Jan       11 Nov 1877        Morgan 8 Jul 1944
     1929

9  Hallie Crayne                               Elizabeth Myers
   Morgan 15 Mar 1879       Jefferson          Garard's Fort,PA
                                                 23 Apr 1877
   Waynesburg,PA 26 Feb     24 Apr 1900        Jefferson 16 Jan 1938
     1960
```

Inheritor: Lynn Myers Crayne, II, R.D. #1, Jefferson,PA 15344

CROSS, J. ALAN

Nat. #274-B. Elected 1975. b. Chicago,IL 7 Dec 1906. m.
Stuart,FL 13 Oct 1928, Delta Deitz, b. Richwood,WV 11 Nov 1901.
Educ: United States Naval Academy; University of Miami, B.A. and
M.Ed. Member: Hereditary Order of Desc. of Colonial Governors;
Soc. of Mayflower Desc., FL; Sons of American Revolution, FL;
Sons of Revolution; Huguenot Soc. of Florida; Alden Kindred.
Address: 5401 S.W. 101 Street, Miami,FL 33156. Descended from:

1 John Alden, Governor of Plymouth Colony 1663-64, 1667

```
2  Elizabeth Alden                             William Pabodie
                                                 (Peabody)
   Plymouth,MA c.1624       -----              England c.1619
   Little Compton,RI        26 Dec 1644        13 Nov 1707
     31 May 1717

3  Lydia Peabody                               Daniel Grinnell
   Duxbury,MA 3 Apr 1667    Duxbury            Little Compton 1665
   Saybrook,CT 13 Jul 1748  1683               Saybrook 7 Jan 1740/1

4  George Grinnell                             Mary Post Bull
   Saybrook 12 Apr 1702     Saybrook           Saybrook 22 Apr 1708/9
   Saybrook 11 Nov 1759     31 Jan 1725/6      Saybrook 30 Sep 1775

5  Daniel Grinnell                             Ann Chapman
   Westbrook,CT 29 Apr      Westbrook          Westbrook 21 Mar 1731
     1729
   Greenfield,NY 21 Dec     1758               Greenfield 20 May 1814
     1801

6  Asenath Grinnell                            Ebenezer Couch
   22 Sep 1774              Greenfield         26 Feb 1768
   -----                    29 Mar 1792        Pompey,NY 20 Aug 1853

7  Asenath Couch                               Harrington Russ
   5 Mar 1805              Johnstown,NY        Galway,NY 1 Oct 1805
   Milton,NY 20 Sep 1846   -----              Pontiac,IL 28 Mar 1873
```

8	Alanson Bernard Russ		Anna Augusta Rathbone
	Milton 19 Jun 1835	Pontiac	Jersey City,NJ 9 Oct
			1849
	Canandaiqua,NY 26 Feb	13 Aug 1867	Ballston Spa,NY 17 Mar
	1920		1892
9	Nellie Holbrook Russ		James Franklin Cross
	Ballston Spa 13 Jul	Chicago,IL	Mission,KS 20 Sep 1869
	1881		
	Mission 6 Jul 1969	5 Oct 1904	Mission 26 Feb 1940

CROWELL, DELLA DODSON (MRS. CLYDE OREN)

Nat. #81-B. Elected 15 Jul 1963. b. Pilot Mountain,NC 26 Jul
1897. m. 9 Oct 1926, Clyde Oren Crowell, b. Monroe,NC 21 Jul
1897. Issue: Clyde Oren Crowell, Jr. Educ: Salem College,
Winston-Salem,NC, A.B. Member: Hereditary Order of Desc. of
Colonial Governors; Dau. of American Colonists; Colonial
Daughters of XVII Century. Occup: Former mathematics teacher.
Address: 2751 Pilgrim Court, Winston-Salem,NC 27106. (From
Society's Records). Descended from:

1 William Stone, Governor of Maryland 1649-54

2	John Stone		Elizabeth Warren
	Accomac Co.VA 1640	-----	-----
	Maryland 1698	-----	-----
3	Thomas Stone		Martha Hoskins
	Maryland 1677	-----	Charles Co.MD c.1680
	Virginia 1727	-----	-----
*4	Thomas Stone		Mary Butler
	Charles Co. c.1700	-----	-----
	Prince William Co.VA	c.1720	-----
	24 Nov 1748		
5	John Stone		Miss Corder
	Virginia c.1727	-----	-----
	Surry Co.NC	-----	-----
6	Enoch Stone		Nancy Anthony
	Surry Co.	Surry Co.	-----
	Surry Co. Sep 1823	c.1784	-----
7	Enoch Stone		Elizabeth Gordon
	Surry Co. 8 Nov 1791	Surry Co.	Surry Co. 28 Mar 1797
	Surry Co. 11 Oct 1874	21 Oct 1819	Surry Co. 26 Mar 1877
8	Rhoda E. Stone		John C. Dodson
	Surry Co. 1 Jun 1833	Surry Co.	Surry Co. 4 Apr 1831
	Surry Co. 20 Jul 1891	2 May 1861	Surry Co. 8 Aug 1891
9	James C. Dodson		Elizabeth L. Pepper
	Surry Co. 22 Jul 1869	Danbury,NC	Winston-Salem 29 Nov
			1867
	Winston-Salem,NC	-----	Winston-Salem 12 Dec
	30 Nov 1942		1951

Inheritor: Clyde Oren Crowell,Jr.,1101 Winona Rd.,Raleigh,NC
27609

CUMMINS, DR. JAMES WILLIAM

Nat. #353-B. Elected 25 Jul 1979. b. Arcadia,FL 18 Mar 1916.
m. Bellflower,CA 23 Jan 1943, Reland Marie Findlay, b. Anaheim,
CA 31 Dec 1920. Educ: University of Southern California, School
of Dentistry, D.D.S. 1942. Member: Hereditary Order of Desc. of
Colonial Governors; Soc. of Colonial Clergy; Soc. of Boones-
borough; Sons of American Revolution; Soc. of War of 1812; Sons
and Dau. of Pilgrims; Soc. of Valley Forge; Order of Crown of
Charlemagne in the USA; Most Noble Order of the Garter; St.
Nicholas Soc. of City of New York; New England Historic and
Genealogical Soc. Military: U.S. Navy, 11 years; USNR, retired
in 1972 as a Captain. Occup: Dentist. Address: 1200 West Rowan
St., Anaheim,CA 92801. Descended from:

1 George Wyllys, Governor of Connecticut 1642

2 Amy Wyllys   John Pynchon
   Fenny Compton,Eng.   Springfield,MA Springfield,Eng. 1621
     1621/25
   Springfield,MA 9 Jan   30 Oct 1645   Springfield,MA 17 Jan
     1699   1703

3 John Pynchon   Margaret Hubbard
   Springfield,MA 15 Oct Massachusetts Ipswich,MA 5 Oct 1647
     1647
   Springfield,MA 25 Apr -----   Springfield,MA 11 Nov
     1721   1716

4 John Pynchon   Bathsheba Taylor
   Ipswich 1674   Springfield   Westfield,MA 17 Jan
                                            1683
   Springfield 12 Jul 1742 18 Feb 1702   Springfield 20 Jun 1710

5 Elizabeth Pynchon   Benjamin Colton
   Springfield 27 Dec 1702 Massachusetts Longmeadow,MA 18 Jun
                                            1695
   Springfield 26 Sep 1776 16 Feb 1721   Springfield 6 May 1770

6 Benjamin Colton   Abiah Cooley
   Springfield 1 Feb 1722 Springfield   MA 11 Mar 1721
   Springfield 20 Jan 1808 24 Mar 1742   MA 30 Apr 1778

7 Eli Colton   Mary Crane
   Springfield 20 Jul 1750 Massachusetts MA Nov/Dec 1752
   Scipio,NY btw.1815-20   1774   Mount Pleasant,WI
                                            9 Jul 1848

8 Pliney Colton   Rizpha Minch (Murch or
                                            Marsh)
   MA 8 Jan 1787   Washington Co. CT 6 Aug 1791
                            NY
   Green Co.WI   Oct 1817   Exeter,WI 14 Oct 1876

9 Eliza A. Colton   Charles Ernest Rise
   North East,PA 24 May   Mount Pleasant Lima,NY 21 Jan 1817
     1828
   Santa Ana,CA 7 Jul   12 Aug 1847   Exeter,WI 10 Jan 1868
     1915

10 Mary Phyllesta Rice   James Winn Hockaday
   Green Co. 31 Dec 1861   Caldwell,KS   Plattsburg,MO
   Ontario,CA 7 Sep 1932   21 Aug 1881   Ontario 23 Mar 1923

11 Nina May Hockaday   Marcus Guy Cummins
   El Reno,OK 16 Apr 1895   Enid,OK   New Douglas 6 Jun 1890
   Anaheim,CA 10 Aug 1957   9 Apr 1915   Anaheim 3 Jun 1966

   Inheritor: Dr. James W. Cummins,Jr., 3021 James St.,
   San Diego,CA 92106.

CURTIUS, CATHERINE REBEKAH PELOT (MRS. BENJAMIN L., JR.)

Nat. #322-B. Elected 17 Feb 1978. b. Blackburn,MO 30 Jun 1920.
m. Marshall,MO 28 Oct 1943, Benjamin Luman Curtius, Jr., b.
Blackburn 28 Apr 1917. Member: Hereditary Order of Desc. of
Colonial Governors; Dau. of American Revolution; United States
Dau. of 1812; United Dau. of Confederacy; Sons and Dau. of the
Pilgrims; Plantagenet Soc.; Magna Charta Dames; Huguenot Soc.
of South Carolina; Soc. of Desc. of Colonial Clergy; Soc. of
Desc. of Knights of Most Noble Order of the Garter; Dau. of
Colonial Wars; Dau. of American Colonists; Colonial Order of
the Crown; Order of Crown of Charlemagne in U.S.A.; Colonial
Dames XVII Century; Order of Washington. Address: 5874 East
21st Place, Tulsa,OK 74114. Descended from:

1 Samuel Mathews, Governor of Virginia 1656-59/60

2 Francis Mathews   Miss Baldwin
   Virginia 1635   Virginia   -----
   Virginia 16 Feb 1675   -----   England

3 Baldwin Mathews   Mary Bushrod
   Virginia 1670   Virginia   -----
   Virginia Apr 1737   -----   -----

4 Mary Mathews   Philip Smith
   Virginia 1695   Virginia   Fleet's Bay,VA 1 Jun
                                                1695
   Virginia 1745   9 Feb 1711   4 Jun 1743

5 Sarah Smith   George Hale
   Virginia 2 Feb 1730   Virginia   Lancaster/Fauquier Co.
                                                VA
   Virginia 1806   30 Jan 1746   -----

6 Smith Hale   Nancy Douglass
   Fauquier Co. 31 Aug   -----   -----
     1765
   Woodford Co.KY 1817   -----   -----

7 Susannah Smith Hale   William Holman Martin
   Virginia 1802   -----   30 Dec 1801
   -----   10 Jun 1820   Scott Co.KY 21 Jun 1860

8 Solon Douglas Martin   Catherine Harriet
                                                  Pinkerton
   Woodford Co. 1825   Woodford Co.   Bethany,VA 27 Jul 1827
   Kansas City,MO   30 Jun 1847   Marshall,MO 14 Apr
     10 Aug 1907   1902

9 Rebekah Martin   Henry Spencer Hopkins
   Midway,KY 1 Jun 1848   Sedalia,MO   Oxford,MD 22 Jan 1839
   Blackburn,MO 3 Mar 1948 3 Oct 1870   Blackburn 1 May 1917

10 Lulu LaMar Hopkins   Henry J. Pelot
   Blackburn 18 Sep 1879   Blackburn   Blackburn 17 Apr 1861
   Waverly,MO 10 Apr 1976   28 Jun 1905   Blackburn

CUSTER, CAROLINE HALLETT (MRS. JACQUES RICHARD)

Nat. #225-B. Elected 24 Jan 1974. b. Lima,Peru 1 Apr 1927.
m. Lima 6 Aug 1946, Jacques Richard Custer, b. Huancayo, Peru
30 Nov 1919. Issue: Richard Custer, b. 10 Jul 1949; Andres
Custer, b. 20 Oct 1952; Philip Custer, b. 27 May 1954; all b.
Lima. Educ: Wellesley College, MA, 1948. Member: Hereditary
Order of Desc. of Colonial Governors; Soc. of Mayflower Desc. in
DC; Lima Wellesley Club (Founder and Pres.); Accion Comunitaria
del Peru (Vice Pres.); International Council Museum of Modern
Art, NY; Instituto Cultural Peru and Norte Americano (Director).
Occup: Portrait Sculptor. Address: Apartado 681, Lima,
Peru S. A. Descended from:

1 Thomas Prence, Governor of Plymouth Colony 1634-73

2 Mercy Prence   John Freeman
   Plymouth,MA c.1631   Eastham,MA   Billinghurst,Eng.
                                                     28 Jan 1626
   Eastham 28 Sep 1711   13 Feb 1649   Eastham 28 Oct 1719

3 Thomas Freeman   Rebecca Sparrow
   Eastham Sep 1653   Eastham   Eastham 30 Oct 1655
   Harwich,MA 9 Feb 1715   31 Dec 1673   Harwich Feb 1740

4 Mercy Freeman   Paul Sears
   Eastham 30 Oct 1674   Harwich   Yarmouth,MA 15 Jun 1669
   Harwich 30 Aug 1747   c.1693   Harwich 14 Feb 1739

5 Edmund Sears   Hannah Crowell
   Yarmouth 6 Aug 1712   Yarmouth   Yarmouth 19 Sep 1725
   Harwich 12 Aug 1796   7 Apr 1743   Harwich 22 Jun 1802

6 Edmund Sears   Hannah Taylor
   Yarmouth 3 Jan 1743   Yarmouth   1753
   Brewster,MA 16 Mar 1832 24 Jan 1771   Brewster 7 Jul 1828

7 Sally Sears   Paul Crowell
   Yarmouth 26 Jan 1780   Dennis,MA   Dennis 27 Mar 1778
   W.Sandwich,MA 14 Aug   4 May 1797   Sandwich 26 Aug 1866
      1861

8 Sally Crowell   William Swift
   Dennis 26 Dec 1804   W.Sandwich   Sandwich 22 Sep 1795
   W.Sandwich 15 Jan 1885   9 Jan 1822   W.Sandwich 9 Dec 1868

9 Caroline Beale Swift   Josiah Blossom Hallett
   Sandwich 9 Apr 1835   Sandwich   Chatham,MA 7 Nov 1832
   Bridgeport,CT 18 Sep   5 May 1853   Bridgeport 12 Oct 1917
      1909

10 Herbert Francis Hallett   Annie Yutzler
   Sandwich 5 Mar 1854   W.Cornwall,CT   W.Cornwall 1 Oct 1859
   Bridgeport 25 Mar 1898   24 Nov 1883   W.Cornwall 22 May 1901

11 George Herbert Hallett   Julia Fredricks Albes
   Bridgeport 22 Nov 1892   Lima   Decatur,AL 28 Jul 1892
   Lima Peru 19 Dec 1967   29 May 1922

                              D

DARLINGTON, THOMAS

Nat. #84-B. Elected 15 Jul 1963. b. New York,NY 10 Mar 1926.
m. Bronxville,NY 26 Apr 1952, Marcia Willetts McMichael. Issue:
Thomas Darlington, b. 9 Mar 1955. Educ: Columbia University,
1951. Member: Hereditary Order of Desc. of Colonial Governors;
St. Nicholas Society of New York; Soc. of Colonial Wars, NJ and
NY; Sons of Revolution, NY; St. Anthony Club; St. Andrews Soc.
of NY; Newcomin Soc.. Address: 55 Lake View Dr., Short Hills,NJ
07078. (From Society's Records). Descended from:

1 James Bishop, Governor of Connecticut 1683-84

2 John Bishop   Abigail Willet
   New Haven,CT 1662   -----   Hartford
   Hartford,CT   -----   Hartford

3 John Bishop   Susannah
   Hartford 1693   -----   -----
   Bolton,CT   -----   New York

4 Anna Bishop   Griffin Wilde
   Hartford 1738   -----   New York 1737
   Jackson,NY 1822   -----   -----

5 James Wilde   Phoebe Rainous
   Kinderhook,NY 1770   New York   Dutchess Co.NY 1772
   Manchester 1816   1792   Cornwall,NY 1828

6 Maria Wilde   Peter Darlington
   Poughkeepsie,NY 1800   -----   Scotland 1793
   NYC 1900   -----   NYC 1851

7 Thomas Darlington   Hannah A. Goodliffe
   Salisbury,NY 1826   -----   England 1830
   1903   -----   NYC 1900

8 Thomas Darlington   Josephine A. Sargent
   Brooklyn,NY 24 Sep 1858 -----   1864
   1945   -----   1890

9 Clinton P. Darlington   Florence A. Brush
   10 Mar 1887   -----   1901
   2 Feb 1952   -----

   Inheritor: Thomas Darlington

DAVIS, ELLSWORTH MARCUS

Nat. #341-B. Elected 12 Jul 1979. b. New Haven,CT 25 Dec 1907.
m. New Haven 10 Oct 1936, Virginia Eleanor Trench, b. New Haven
31 Mar 1916; d. 17 Sep 1966. Member: Hereditary Order of Desc.
of Colonial Governors; Society of the Cincinnati; Soc. of
Colonial Wars; Sons of American Revolution; Sons of the Revolu-
tion; Order of Founders and Patriots of America; Soc. of Desc.
of Colonial Clergy; Soc. of Desc. of Founders of Hartford,CT;
Order of Americans of Armorial Ancestry; National Huguenot Soc.;
Desc. of Illegitimate Sons and Dau. of Kings of Britain; Baronial
Order of Magna Charta; Flagon and Trencher; Soc. of Desc. of John
Davis of Wales (President); Botsford, Frisbie, Welles, Hawley
Family Assns.; Guilford Keeping Soc. Address: 40 Juniper Knoll,
Leete's Island, Guilford,CT 06437. Descended from:

1 Thomas Welles, Governor of Connecticut 1655-56, 1658

2 Mary Welles   Timothy Baldwin
  1618   -----   -----
  31 Jul 1647   1642   -----

3 Hannah Baldwin   Elnathan Botsford
  16 Aug 1644   Milford,CT   -----
  -----   12 Dec 1667   -----

4 Hannah Botsford   John Prindle
  30 Apr 1674   -----   -----
  -----   21 Dec 1699   -----

5 Hannah Prindle   Nathan Smith
  Derby,CT 4 Dec 1700   -----   Derby 4 Feb 1696
  Derby 1784   27 Jun 1720   Derby

6 Nathan Smith   Sarah Northrup
  Derby 19 Sep 1724   -----   Milford,CT 28 Nov 1728
  Derby 24 Feb 1798   4 Nov 1747   Derby 25 Jun 1757

7 Sarah Smith   Jeremiah Gillette
  Derby 18 Apr 1750   -----   Milford 18 Dec 1734
  1777   -----   -----

8 Anson Gillette   Betsey Mansfield
  Derby 3 Feb 1773   -----   Seymour,CT 30 Nov 1777
  Seymour 12 Jun 1846   10 Mar 1801   Derby 31 Jan 1863

9 Eli Gillette   Eliza Bassett
  Seymour 1 Jun 1810   Seymour   Oxford,CT
  Seymour 22 Aug 1899   18 Sep 1834   Seymour 18 Sep 1894

10 Mary Gillette   Edward James Davis
   Seymour 12 Oct 1859   Seymour   Seymour 7 Sep 1859
   New Haven,CT 22 Nov   9 Oct 1879   Seymour 5 Sep 1893
     1932

11 Clarence Marcus Davis   Charlotte Clarissa
                                         Bartholomew
   Seymour 24 Feb 1885   New Haven   New Haven 2 Feb 1883
   Derby 31 Jan 1973   26 Apr 1905   New Haven 23 Sep 1956

DAVIS, THE REVEREND RALPH MILTON

Nat. #313-B. Elected 1977. b. Rutland,VT 1897. Educ: Nashotah College, WI, Bachelor and Master of Divinity. Member: Hereditary Order of Desc. of Colonial Governors; Sons of American Revolution; Soc. of Desc. of Knights of Most Noble Order of Garter; Magna Charta Barons; Sovereign Colonial Soc. of Americans of Royal Descent; Historical Soc. of Pennsylvania. Address: Bridgeboro Road, The Evergreens, Moorestown,NJ 08057. Descended from:

1 Thomas Welles, Governor of Connecticut 1655-56, 1658-59

2	Anna Welles		Thomas Thompson
	1619	-----	England 1617
	1680	14 Apr 1646	1655
3	Thomas Thompson		Elizabeth Smith
	1651	-----	1653
	1705	-----	1695
4	Anna Thompson		John Norton
	1689	-----	1684
	-----	6 May 1708	1752
5	Ruth Norton		Josiah Burnham
	26 Feb 1724	-----	Halifax,Nova Scotia
			1716
	1762	1740	1800
6	Lucy Burnham		James Porter
	1750	Berlin,CT	1743
	1784	1771	Long Island,NY 1781
7	James Burnham Porter		Hephzibah Wheelock
	Long Island 1780	Whitehall,NY	Rutland,VT 1787
	1854	1806	1866
8	James Burnham Porter		Harriet Griggs
	1806	Brookline,MA	1808
	1879	1834	1876
9	James Edward Porter		Jennie Stanhope Lovell
	1842	-----	1850
	1918	1872	1933
10	Caroline Griggs Porter		Walter Milton Davis
	1873	Rutland,VT	Rutland 1867
	Rutland 1910	1890	Orange,NJ 1921

DENNY, JOSEPHINE (MISS)

Nat. #10-B. Elected 4 Aug 1959. b. Waynesburg,PA 31 Aug 1893. Educ: Waynesburg College, B.A.; University of Besancon, Paris, France. Member: Hereditary Order of Desc. of Colonial Governors; Dau. of 1812; Dau. of American Revolution; Desc. of Lords of Maryland Manors; Order of First Families of Virginia; Jamestowne Soc.; Dau. of American Colonists; Dau. of Colonial Wars; Colonial

Dau. of XVII Century; New England Women; Royal Order of the Crown; Magna Charta Dames; Americans of Royal Descent; Colonial Dames of America; Dau. of Barons of Runnemede; Greene County, PA Historical Soc. Address: 145 West High St., Waynesburg,PA 15370. Descended from:

1 William Stone, Governor of Maryland 1649-54

2 Mary Stone   Robert Doyne
   Accomac Co.VA 1642   Charles Co.   England 1640
   Charles Co.MD 1685   1674   Charles Co. 1689

3 Mary Doyne   Nicholas Dawson
   Charles Co. 1683   Charles Co.   St.Mary's Co.MD 1682
   Prince George's Co.MD   1706   Prince George's Co.
     1734   1727

4 Thomas Dawson   Elizabeth Lowe
   Prince George's Co.   Oxon Hill,MD   Prince George's Co.
     1708   27 Dec 1712
   Montgomery Co.MD 1800   1740   Montgomery Co. 1802

5 Sarah Dawson   William Blackmore
   Prince George's Co.   Dawsonville   Prince George's Co.
     1748   1746
   Dawsonville,MD 1800   1771   Pennsylvania 1790

6 Rebecca Blackmore   Robert Adams
   Prince George's Co.   Washington,PA   Pennsylvania 1769
     1778
   Waynesburg,PA 1853   1796   Waynesburg 1864

7 Sarah Adams   William Inghram, Jr.
   Waynesburg 1799   Waynesburg   Waynesburg 1794
   Waynesburg 1830   1816   Waynesburg 1843

8 Eliza Inghram   John T. Hook
   Waynesburg 13 Jul 1817 Waynesburg   Waynesburg 20 Jan 1814
   Waynesburg 1 May 1901   14 Jan 1836   Waynesburg 13 Nov 1883

9 Sarah Hook   Josiah Inghram
   Waynesburg 26 Oct 1836 Waynesburg   Waynesburg 5 Oct 1819
   Waynesburg 22 Nov 1913 31 Oct 1861   Waynesburg 8 Aug 1879

10 Louise Inghram   Eleazer Luse Denny
   Waynesburg 27 May 1867 Waynesburg   Waynesburg 18 Sep 1865
   Waynesburg 14 Apr 1956 16 Oct 1890   Waynesburg 1 Apr 1910

DIES, EDWARD JEROME

Nat. #43-B. Elected 8 Feb 1962. b. Springfield,OR 23 May 1891. m. St. Paul,MN 29 May 1912, Mareeta Cole. Issue: Douglas Dies. Member: Hereditary Order of Desc. of Colonial Governors; Huguenot Soc. of Washington,DC; Sons of the Revolution; Union League Club, Chicago; Capitol Hill Club; City Tavern Club, Georgetown. Occup: Journalist and Author. Address: 2111 Jefferson Davis Highway, Arlington,VA 22202. Descended from:

1 John Winthrop, Governor of Massachusetts 1629-34, 1637-40, 1642-44, 1646-49

```
2  Mary Winthrop                              Samuel Dudley
   c.1610/11              -----               England 30 Nov 1608
   12 Apr 1643            -----               10 Feb 1682

3  Ann Dudley                                 Edward Hilton
   1641                  -----                Exeter 1623
   Exeter,NH c.1699      -----                Exeter 28 Apr 1699

4  Richard Hilton                             Ann Hilton
   Portsmouth,NH 1662    -----                Portsmouth
   af.1739               c.1687               af.1719

5  Benjamin Hilton                            -----
   -----                 -----                -----
   af.1731               -----                -----

6  Jeremiah Hilton       (2)                  Abigail Hunkin
   Exeter c.1736         -----                Haverhill,MA 6 Apr 1744
   Sandwich,NH c.1800    c.1766               Sandwich af.1800

7  Benjamin Hilton                            Ruth Brown
   Sandwich 20 Mar 1780  -----                c.1790
   Maine c.1842          -----                Corinna,ME 3 Sep 1835

8  Benjamin F. Hilton    (3)                  Martha E. Lumpkin
   Corinna 23 Oct 1817   Grant Co.WI          Giles Co.VA 1833
   Luce,NE 12 Dec 1889   31 Dec 1851          Nebraska 1883

9  Martha Hilton                              Allen Lewis Dies
   Grant Co. 7 Apr 1862  Nebraska             Olmstead Co.MN 17 Feb
                                                1860
   Glendale,CA 2 Oct 1942  17 Nov 1883        Los Angeles,CA 12 Dec
                                                1935
```

SUPPLEMENT NO. 1

1 Thomas Dudley, Governor of Massachusetts 1634-51

2 Mary Winthrop   Samuel Dudley

   Continue with Generation 2 of his lineage from Governor
   John Winthrop.

   Inheritor: Douglas Hilton Dies

DODSON, LOIS ELIZABETH (MISS)

Nat. #144-B. Elected 20 Jun 1968. b. Walnut Cove,NC 24 Jun
1918. Educ: Draughan Business College. Member: Hereditary
Order of Desc. of Colonial Governors; Dau. of American Revolu-
tion; Colonial Dau. of XVII Century. Occup: Administrative
Assistant of Bank. Address: 2731 Pilgrim Court, Winston-Salem,
NC 27106. (From Society's Records). Descended from:

1 William Stone, Governor of Maryland 1649-54

64

```
 2  John Stone                                    Elizabeth Warren
    Accomac Co.VA 1640        -----              -----
    Maryland 1698             -----              -----

 3  Thomas Stone                                  Martha Hoskins
    1677                      -----              Charles Co.MD c.1680
    1727                      -----              -----

*4  Thomas Stone                                  Mary Butler
    Charles Co. c.1700        -----              -----
    Prince William Co.VA      c.1720             -----
      24 Nov 1748

 5  John Stone                                    Miss Corder
    Virginia c.1727           -----              -----
    Surry Co.NC c.1780        -----              -----

 6  Enoch Stone                                   Nancy Anthony
    Surry Co.                 Surry Co.          -----
    Surry Co. Sep 1823        c. 1784            -----

 7  Enoch Stone                                   Elizabeth Gordon
    Surry Co. 8 Nov 1791      Surry Co.          Surry Co. 28 Mar 1797
    Surry Co. 11 Oct 1874     21 Oct 1819        Surry Co. 26 Mar 1877

 8  Rhoda E. Stone                                John C. Dodson
    Surry Co. 1 Jun 1833      Surry Co.          Surry Co. 4 Apr 1831
    Surry Co. 20 Jul 1891     2 May 1861         Surry Co. 8 Aug 1891

 9  Wesley G. Dodson                              Salome Dair
    Surry Co. 27 Nov 1867     Walnut Cove,NC     Madison,NC 9 Sep 1881
    Walnut Cove 23 Sep 1924   17 May 1916        Walnut Cove 24 Oct 1956
```

Inheritor: Mrs.W. Deane Taylor (Elizabeth Louise Hamner),
3246 Paddington Lane, Winston-Salem,NC 27106.

DORMAN, JOHN FREDERICK

Nat. #28-B. Elected 1 Oct 1960. b. Louisville,KY 25 Jul 1928.
Educ: University of Louisville, A.B., 1950; Emory University,
M.A., 1955. Member: Hereditary Order of Desc. of Colonial
Governors (Hon. Governor General); Soc. of the Cincinnati in the
State of Virginia; Soc. of War of 1812; Sons of the Revolution
(Registrar, D.C.); Sons of American Revolution (Past Natl.
Trustee); Soc. of Colonial Wars (Deputy Registrar General);
Children of American Revolution (Hon. Senior Natl. Vice Presi-
dent); Jamestowne Soc.; Soc. of Desc. of Lords of Maryland Manors
(Registrar); Order of the Stars and Bars; Hereditary Order of the
Desc. of Loyalists and Patriots of America; Kentucky Historical
Soc.; Virginia Historical Soc.; National Trust for Historic
Preservation; American Soc. of Genealogists (Fellow). Occup:
Professional Genealogist and Publisher of "The Virginia Geneal-
ogist," 1957-date. Address: 2022 Columbia Road, N.W.,
Washington,DC 20009. Descended from:

1 Robert Brooke, Governor of Maryland 1652

2 Thomas Brooke
   Battle, Eng. 23 Jun   Maryland   Eleanor Hatton
   1632   England 1642
   Calvert Co.MD 1676   1659   Calvert Co. 1725

3 Thomas Brooke   (1)   Anne
   Calvert Co. 1659   Maryland   Maryland
   Prince George's Co.,   1680   Maryland
   MD 7 Jan 1730/1

4 Thomas Brooke   Lucy Smith
   Nottingham,MD 1683   Maryland   1688
   Prince George's Co.   9 May 1705   MD 15 Apr 1776
   28 Dec 1744

5 Eleanor Brooke   Samuel Beall
   7 Mar 1718   Maryland   Montgomery Co.,MD 1713
   Prince George's Co.   23 May 1734   Washington,MD 1778
   1771

6 Walter Beall   (1)   Susannah
   1740   Maryland   -----
   Nelson Co.KY 1810   11 Feb 1768   -----

7 Susannah Beall   Edward Slaughter
                                             Pendleton Thomas
   c.1770   -----   Orange Co.VA bf.1765
   Nelson Co. af.1818   -----   Nelson Co. 1820/22

8 Lucinda Beall Thomas   William Elliott
   Nelson Co. 11 Mar 1805 Nelson Co.   Garrard Co.KY 27 Apr
                                             1798
   Nelson Co. 27 Aug 1882 11 May 1824   New Haven,KY 11 Dec
                                             1896

9 John Darwin Elliott   Susan Duncan Carpenter
   New Haven 28 Aug 1826 Bardstown,KY   Bardstown 25 Apr 1834
   New Haven 21 Sep 1897 26 Jun 1855   Louisville,KY 15 Jan
                                             1917

10 Lucinda Page Elliott   Leonard Samson Miller
   Bardstown 22 Apr 1860 Bardstown   Oldham Co.KY 11 May
                                             1842
   Louisville 29 Sep 1950 17 Sep 1889   Louisville 19 Jul 1910

11 Sue Carpenter Miller   John Frederick Dorman
   Bardstown 10 Sep 1893 Louisville   Louisville 4 Oct 1875
   Louisville 4 May 1969 27 Jan 1927   Louisville 11 Jun 1952

DuBOIS, FREDERIC MARSHALL

Nat. #256-B. Elected 15 May 1975. b. Englewood,NJ 8 Jun 1906.
m. Philadelphia,PA 17 Jun 1935, Katherine Wiener, b. Philadelphia
3 May 1911. Educ: Hotchkiss School, Lakeville,CT; Harvard
College. Member: Hereditary Order of Desc. of Colonial Governors;
Huguenot Soc. (IA, Pres.); Soc. of Desc. of Colonial Clergy; The
Huguenot Soc. of New Paltz (Duzene). Address: 5700 Waterbury Rd.,
Des Moines,IA 50312. Descended from:

1 John Reading, Governor of New Jersey 1747, 1757-58

2	Richard Reading		Catharine Reid
	Amwell,NJ 8 Dec 1732	New Jersey	New Jersey
	Canada bf.11 Nov 1801	20 Dec 1757	New York

3	Thomas Reading		Catharine Stout
	Spotswood,NJ 11 Aug 1773	New Jersey	NJ 17 Apr 1778
	NY 21 Aug 1802	c.1797	Harlem,NY 20 Sep 1842

4	Richard Augustine Reading		Elizabeth Sarah Floy
	NYC 6 Nov 1801	New York,NY	NYC 13 Mar 1810
	Harlem 7 Jun 1871	8 Dec 1831	Harlem 4 Jan 1871

5	Katherine Barclay Reading		Cornelius DuBois
	NYC 9 Jun 1851	NYC	NYC 27 Mar 1851
	NYC 3 Jan 1913	22 Apr 1874	NYC 22 May 1921

6	Floy(d) Reading DuBois		Rosilla Marshall
	NYC 15 Nov 1878	NYC	NYC 29 Aug 1882
	NYC 23 Oct 1952	14 Nov 1902	Old Lyme,CT 7 Aug 1960

Inheritor: Peter Cornelius DuBois, 340 East 72nd Street, New York,NY 10021.

DYER, ELEANOR E. FOLSOM (MRS. WILLIAM W., JR.)

Nat. #111-B. Elected 3 Apr 1965. b. Schenectady,NY 19 Apr 1905. m. Pittsburgh,PA 28 Dec 1928, William Washington Dyer, Jr., b. Washington,DC 14 Jul 1908. Issue: Penhallow Folsom Dyer, b. Washington,DC 24 Apr 1935. Educ: William and Mary; George Washington University; American University, A.B. Member: Hereditary Order of Desc. of Colonial Governors; Dau. of American Revolution (Registrar, Secretary, Historian); Dau. of Confederacy; Dau. of Founders and Patriots of America; Magna Charta Dames; Piscataqua Pioneers; Desc. of Colonial Clergy; New England Women; Dau. of Colonial Wars. Occup: Art teacher and Genealogist. Descended from:

1 Simon Bradstreet, Governor of Massachusetts 1679-86, 1689-92

2	Anne Bradstreet		Andrew Wiggin
	Andover,MA	-----	c.1633
	c.1707	3 Jun 1659	Exeter,NH 1710

3	Andrew Wiggin		Abigail Follett
	6 Jan 1672	-----	c.1678
	23 Jan 1756	-----	-----

4	Bradstreet Wiggin		Phebe Sherburne
	21 Feb 1713/4	-----	Portsmouth,NH
	Stratham,NH af.1744	c.1736	-----

5	Andrew Wiggin		Mary (Jewett) Weeks
	Stratham 5 May 1737	Exeter,NH	Rowley,MA 6 Oct 1733
	Stratham 16 Sep 1778	15 Oct 1760	Stratham 24 Jan 1834

6 Anna Wiggin   Theophilus Smith
   Stratham 23 Jul 1761   Exeter   Exeter 12 Dec 1761
   Stratham 8 Feb 1845   c.1783   Stratham 7 Jun 1824

7 Mary Smith   Nathaniel Folsom
   Stratham 24 Dec 1786   -----   Dover,NH 13 Feb 1782
   Portsmouth 3 Oct 1853   10 Apr 1805 Portsmouth 12 Mar 1866

8 Nathaniel S. Folsom   Ann W. Penhallow
   Portsmouth 12 Mar 1806 -----   Portsmouth 22 Oct 1808
   Asheville,NC 10 Nov   30 Oct 1832 9 Apr 1885
     1890

9 Paris H. Folsom   Eleanor E. Lowry
   Providence,RI 12 Jan   Washington,DC Virginia 11 Feb 1840
     1840
   Asheville,NC 29 Apr   -----   Asheville 18 Aug 1913
     1904

10 Paris P. Folsom   Ida K. Snelson
   Washington,DC 6 Dec   Niagara Falls, Asheville 10 Oct 1872
     1871   NY
   Washington,DC 28 Jun   5 Sep 1903   Arlington,VA 25 May
     1921   1954

SUPPLEMENT NO. 1

1 Thomas Wiggin, Governor of New Hampshire 1631-37

2 Andrew Wiggin   Anne Bradstreet

   Continue with Generation 2 of her lineage from Governor
   Simon Bradstreet.

                              E

EDWARDS, ELSIE MAY DUNN (MRS. CHESTER E.)

Nat. #141-B. Elected 27 Apr 1968. b. Jameson,MO 27 Sep 1891.
m. Jameson 15 Jun 1920, Chester E. Edwards, b. Shawnee,OH 20 May
1887. Issue: Elsie Patricia Edwards, b. Grand Rapids,MI 18 Feb
1928; Chester Charles Edwards, b. Grand Rapids 19 May 1930.
Educ: Fort Hayes State College, Kansas, B.A.; University of
Michigan, M.A. 1948. Member: Hereditary Order of Desc. of
Colonial Governors; Soc. of New England Women; U.S. Dau. of 1812;
Soc. of Mayflower Desc.; Americans of Armorial Ancestry; Dau. of
American Revolution; Colonial Dames of America; Children of
American Revolution (Natl. Vice Pres.). Occup: Former Teacher
Training Director. (From Society's records). Descended from:

1 Thomas Hinckley, Governor of Plymouth Colony 1685-92

2 Melathiah Hinckley   Josiah Crocker
   Barnstable,MA 24 Nov   Barnstable   Barnstable 19 Sep 1647
     1648
   Barnstable Feb 1714   22 Oct 1668 Barnstable 2 Feb 1698

                              68

```
3   Thomas Crocker                                      Hannah Green
    28 May 1671          -----                          -----
    Apr 1728            25 Mar 1696                      23 Jun 1728

4   Seth Crocker                                        Temperance Thacher
    Barnstable 13 Jun 1708   Yarmouth,MA                Yarmouth 16 Sep 1711
    West Barnstable,MA       24 Jul 1734                W.Barnstable 11 Jul
       25 Mar 1770                                         1736

5   Thomas Crocker                                      Marcy Hamblen
    W.Barnstable 8 Jun 1735  Barnstable                 Barnstable 15 Nov 1737
    -----                    1756                        -----

6   Hannah Crocker               (2)                    John Winegar
    Barnstable 12 Oct 1778   Lee,MA                     Lee 10 Jun 1777
    Meredosia,IL 12 Oct      4 Dec 1805                 Meredosia 2 Sep 1842
       1838

7   Angeline Winegar                                    Harvey Dunn
    Lee 31 Jul 1809          Geauga Co.OH               Fabius,NY 12 Feb 1806
    Meredosia 8 May 1838     9 Feb 1831                 Chambersburg,IL 28 Dec
                                                           1868

8   John A. Dunn                                        Jane Loer
    Geauga Co. 7 Jun 1832    Chambersburg               Hamilton,OH 19 Oct 1835
    Pattonsburg,MO 19 Oct    28 Dec 1854                Jameson,MO 16 Jun 1907
       1908

9   Charles W. Dunn                                     Ruth J. Scott
    Chambersburg 8 Feb 1866  Jameson                    Davies Co.MO 9 Jun 1869
                             9 Oct 1890                 Davies Co. 31 Jul 1909
```

Inheritor: Cdr. Chester Charles Edwards, USN

ELKINS, WILLARD EUGENE

Nat. #210-B. Elected 21 Jun 1973.   b. Monessen,PA 28 Feb 1905.
m. Marion,IN 16 Jun 1929, Whilma Julia Redman, b. 13 Feb 1902,
d. 30 Mar 1970.   Educ: Purdue University, B.S.; DePaul University,
M.A.; Northwestern University, M.A. Member: Hereditary Order of
Desc. of Colonial Governors; Soc. of Desc. of Colonial Clergy;
National Huguenot Soc.; Huguenot Soc. of South Carolina; Magna
Charta Barons; Plantagenet Soc.; Colonial Order of the Crown;
Soc. of Desc. of Knights of The Most Noble Order of the Garter;
Soc. of Mayflower Desc. (Past Historian,IL); Sons of American
Revolution (Past President,FL); Pilgrim John Howland Soc.;
Pilgrim Richard Warren Soc.; Sons of American Colonists. Occup:
Personnel Director. Address: 1726 North Dormont Lane, Orlando,
FL 32804. Descended from:

1   Samuel Jennings, Governor of New Jersey 1681-84

```
2   Sarah Jennings                                      Edward Pennington
    Aylesburg,Eng. 10 Feb    Burlington                 England c.1645
       1679
    Burlington,NJ 6 Dec      16 Nov 1699                Philadelphia,PA 11 Nov
       1733                                                1701
```

3 Isaac Pennington   Rachel
   Philadelphia 22 Sep   -----   -----
      1700
   -----   -----   -----

4 Rachel Pennington   Edward Beeson
   England   -----   England 1652
   Mar 1714   -----   Chester Co.PA Mar 1714

5 Richard Beeson   Charity Grubb
   England Oct 1684   Nottingham,PA   Wilmington,DE 29 Sep
                                                           1687
   NC 1 Jan 1777   26 Oct 1706   NC 27 Nov 1761

6 Charity Beeson   Mordecai Mendenhall
   Chester Co. c.1715   -----   Chester Co. c.1713
   Guilford Co.NC 21 Sep   21 Mar 1735   Guilford Co. 13 Nov
      1809   1803

7 Isaac Mendenhall   Rachel Hoggatt
   Rowan Co.NC 10 Aug   Guilford Co.   Orange Co.NC 11 Dec
      1756   1761
   Guilford Co. 1 Aug   13 May 1778   Guilford Co. 19 Oct
      1833   1825

8 Mordecai Mendenhall   Mary M. Chipman
   Guilford Co. 24 Aug   Guilford Co.   Deep River,NC 9 Mar
      1791   1795
   Guilford Co. 15 Jun   6 Aug 1816   Guilford Co. 17 Dec
      1879   1840

9 Clementina Mendenhall   Cuthbert Hiatt
   Guilford Co. 15 Aug   Guilford Co.   Guilford Co. 17 Jan
      1822   1820
   Fairmont,IN 21 Apr   22 Feb 1851   Grant Co.IN 4 Mar 1902
      1880

10 Mary A. Hiatt   John S. Baker
   Guilford Co. 29 Jul   Grant Co.   Miami Co.OH 21 Jun 1852
      1857
   Grant Co. 5 May 1905   10 Oct 1875   Jefferson Co.AL 13 Jan
                                                           1933

11 Marguerite M. Baker   Willard L. Elkins
   Grant Co. 18 Apr 1878   Grant Co.   Marshall Co.IN 16 Nov
                                                           1874
   Syracuse,IN 19 Aug   17 Dec 1902   Goshen,IN 6 Nov 1953
      1966

Inheritor: Craig Elkins Thompson, 2841 N.E. 21st Ave.,
Lighthouse Point, Pompano Beach,FL 33064

EMERSON, MAXWELL

Nat. #164-B.   Elected 30 Mar 1971.   b. Newton Centre,MA 25 Mar
1903.   m.(1) NYC 18 Aug 1927, Mary Bryam Millet, b. Brockton,MA
23 Oct 1904.   Issue: David Millet Emerson, b. Boston,MA 10 Jul
1928.   m.(2) Memphis,TN 1 Aug 1945, Dorothy Jane Kerr, b.
Memphis,TN 16 Oct 1911.   Issue: June Alice Emerson, b. Ft. Mead,
MD 10 Oct 1947.   Educ: Dartmouth and Memphis State University,
M.A.   Member: Hereditary Order of Desc. of Colonial Governors;
Soc. of Mayflower Desc.; Soc. of Americans of Royal Descent;
Baronial Order of Magna Charta; Order of Crown of Charlemagne in
U.S.; Colonial Lords of Manors in U.S.A.; Soc. of Desc. of
Colonial Clergy; Colonial Wars (Past Secretary, TN); National
Huguenot Soc.; Military Order of Foreign Wars (State Cmdr.);
Sons of American Revolution (Past State Pres.).   Occup: Formerly
Assist Professor, Management.   Address: 223 Lorece Lane, Memphis,
TN 38117.   Descended from:

1   Thomas Mayhew, Governor of Martha's Vineyard 1647-81

2   Thomas Mayhew   Jane Paine
    Wilts,Eng. 1620   -----   England 1625
    At sea 1651   1645   af.1658

3. Thomas Mayhew   Sarah Skiffe
    Martha's Vnyd.MA 1650   Martha's Vnyd.   Martha's Vnyd. 12 Oct
                                              1646
    Martha's Vnyd. 21 Jul   c.1675   Martha's Vnyd. 30 Dec
    1715   1740

4   Zaccheus Mayhew   Susanna Wade
    Martha's Vnyd. 1684   Ipswich,MA   Ipswich 20 Feb 1692
    Martha's Vnyd. 3 Jan   12 Sep 1713   Martha's Vnyd. 23 May
    1760   1758

5   Sarah Mayhew   (2)   Samuel Palmer
    Martha's Vnyd. 13 Jan   Chilmark,MA   Middleboro,MA 8 Aug
    1719   1707
    Falmouth,MA 23 Jul 1812 3 Nov 1751   Falmouth 13 Apr 1775

6   Sarah Palmer   Andrew Croswell
    Falmouth 7 Nov 1752   Plymouth,MA   Plymouth 1737
    Falmouth 21 Feb 1819   1775   Plymouth 1 Nov 1796

7   Andrew Croswell   Susanna Church
    Plymouth 9 Apr 1778   Farmington,ME   Farmington 22 Jul 1789
    Mercer,ME 4 Jun 1858   22 Feb 1807   Mercer 3 Jul 1861

8   Emily Cox Croswell   John Perley Emerson
    Mercer 1 Dec 1817   Mercer   Bridgton,ME 16 Nov 1812
    Mercer 4 Aug 1852   29 Mar 1841   Baltimore,MD 5 Oct 1874

9   George Denny Emerson   Fannie Howard Macomber
    Mercer 1849   Boston,MA   Boston 12 Sep 1848
    Newton,MA 23 Jul 1878   19 Nov 1874   East Orange,NJ 7 Apr
                                              1911

10 Howard Emerson   Ada Maxwell
    Newton Centre,MA   Pittsburgh,PA   Pittsburgh 30 Jul 1878
      31 Aug 1875
    Newton Centre 4 May   24 Jan 1898   Brookline,MA 13 Jun
    1961   1963

1 John Endicott, Governor of Massachusetts 1629-1644/45,
  1649-65

2 Zerubbabel Endicott   Mary Smith
    Salem,MA 1635   Salem   Salem c.1636/38
    Salem Jan 1683/4   1654   Salem 20 Jun 1677

3 Mary Endicott   Isaac Williams
    Salem 1667   Salem   Salem 20 Dec 1662
    Salem   2 Aug 1685   Salem

4 Mary Williams   Thomas Massey
    Salem 19 Dec 1699   Salem   Salem 22 Mar 1677
    Salem   c.1716   Salem af.1730

5 Mary Massey   Samuel West
    Salem 1 May 1720   Salem   Salem 20 Jun 1722
    Salem af.1791   8 Oct 1747   Salem May 1774

6 Samuel M. West   Mary Young
    Salem 16 Dec 1750   Salem   Salem 7 Feb 1752
    Salem 1801   8 Sep 1773   Salem 23 Jan 1816

7 Abigail West   Ichabod Macomber
    Salem 2 Apr 1789   Salem   Bridgewater,MA 5 Nov
                                                 1777
    Boston,MA 20 May 1863 12 Jun 1820   Jamaica Plain,MA
                                                 1 Oct 1845

8 William Macomber   Mary Stedman T. Leeds
    Boston 3 Jul 1821   Boston   Boston 4 Aug 1827
    Newton Centre,MA   13 Mar 1845   Newton Centre 17 Dec
      5 Dec 1904   1872

9 Fannie Howard Macomber   George Denny Emerson

Continue with Generation 9 of his lineage from Governor Thomas
Mayhew.

ESTILL, ALICE D. GARTH (MRS. GEORGE C.)

Nat. #1-B. Elected 14 Aug 1958. b. Huntsville,AL. m. 25 Oct
1911, George Castleman Estill, b. Lexington,KY 27 May 1881.
Educ: Hollins College, VA. Member: Hereditary Order of Desc. of
Colonial Governors; Dau. of American Revolution; First Families
of Virginia; Colonial Dames of America; Magna Charta Dames;
Order of the Crown; Dau. of the Barons of Runnemede; Dau. of
American Colonists; Huguenots of Manakin Town; U.S. Dau. of 1812;
Dau. of the Confederacy. Address: 2127 Brickell Ave., Miami,FL
33129. (From Society's records). Descended from:

1 John West, Governor of Virginia 1635-37

2 John West   Unity Croshaw
    Bellfield,VA 1632   -----   -----
    King William Co.VA   1667   -----
      15 Nov 1689

3 Nathaniel West   Martha Woodward
  -----   -----   c.1683
  af. Oct 1723   -----   -----

4 Unity West   William Dandridge
  -----   -----   England
  9 Jul 1753   c.1719   Hanover Co.VA 1743

5 Nathaniel West Dandridge   Dorothea Spotswood
  7 Sep 1729   -----   1733
  16 Jan 1786   12 Sep 1764 25 Sep 1773

6 Nathaniel West Dandridge   Sarah Watson
  26 Oct 1765   -----   -----
  1810   -----   -----

7 Unity Spotswood   Jesse Winston Garth
    Dandridge
  May 1800   -----   17 Oct 1788
  7 Oct 1833   23 Aug 1821 7 Sep 1867

8 William Willis Garth   Marie Eliza Fearn
  28 Oct 1826   -----   9 Jan 1832
  25 Feb 1912   21 Jun 1855 6 Mar 1917

9 Winston Fearn Garth   Lena Garth
  26 Sep 1856   -----   19 Oct 1860
  31 Dec 1933   18 Apr 1883 30 Jan 1938

Inheritor: St. Julien Palmer Rosemond, Jr.

F

FARICY, NORMA ANITA HAUSER (MRS. WILLIAM THOMAS)

Nat. #357-B. Elected 2 Aug 1979. b. Elgin,IL 28 Jun 1894.
m. 6 Apr 1918, William Thomas Faricy, b. St. Paul,MN 7 Mar 1893.
Member: Hereditary Order of Desc. of Colonial Governors; Soc.
of Desc. of Colonial Clergy; Dau. of American Revolution.
Address: 4914 Glenbrook Rd., N.W., Washington,DC 20016. Descended
from:

1 Theophilus Eaton, Governor of New Haven Colony 1639-58

2 Hannah Eaton   William Jones
  London,England   London   London c.1624
    6 Oct 1632
  New Haven,CT 4 May 1707 4 Jul 1659 New Haven 17 Oct 1706

3 Isaac Jones   (1)   Deborah Clark
  Old Saybrook,CT   Old Saybrook New Haven 1672
    21 Jun 1671
  Old Saybrook 1741   c.1692   28 May 1735

4 Isaac Jones   Deborah Parker
  New Haven 23 Dec 1702 ----- Saybrook,CT 12 May 1704
  Old Saybrook 3 Aug bf.9 Nov 1726 -----
    1759

5 Mabel (Temperance) Jones   Ezekiel Butler
   Saybrook c.1732   -----   -----
   -----   c.1750   1781

6 Mabel Butler   Thomas Van Alstyne
   Saybrook 3 Jan 1768   Columbia Co.   -----
   Saybrook 10 Jan 1832   7 Apr 1791   Columbia Co.NY 10 Sep
                                                  1838

7 Maria Van Alstyne   Martin Barton
   Columbia Co. 2 Jun 1793 -----   Columbia Co. 1789
   Columbia Co.   14 Feb 1815   Hudson City,NY

8 Eveline Barton   Nathaniel Timotheus
                                                  Hauser
   Hudson City 17 Mar   Columbus,IN   Salem,NC 8 Mar 1822
     1828
   Minneapolis,MN 11 Nov   5 Sep 1848   St. Paul,MN 12 Aug 1905
     1886

9 Eric Van Alstyne Hauser   Nellie Anita Mason
   Minneapolis 10 Dec   Crookston,MN   Prescott,WI 22 May 1867
     1864
   Portland,OR 17 Jan   15 Nov 1883   St. Paul 24 Dec 1942
     1929

FENN, RUTH ANNA JONES (MRS. CLYDE BOSTWICK)

Nat. #85-B. Elected 19 Mar 1968. b. Syracuse,NY 16 Mar 1894.
m.(1) Syracuse 28 Jun 1917, Earle R. Powers, b. Sherburne,NY
20 Apr 1890. Issue: David Russell Powers, b. 9 Jun 1918; Barbara
Powers Longwell, b. 1 Jul 1923; Burr Stoddard Powers, b. 6 Feb
1929; all b. Syracuse. m.(2) Camillus,NY 8 May 1971, Clyde
Bostwick Fenn, b. Syracuse 20 Mar 1892. Educ: Syracuse University
College of Library Science. Member: Hereditary Order of Desc. of
Colonial Governors; Soc. of Mayflower Desc. (CT, Historian);
Women Desc. of the Ancient and Honorable Artillery Company (Natl.
Chaplain); Colonial Dames, CT; Dau. of Colonial Wars (CT, Chap-
lain); Soc. of Desc. of Colonial Clergy; Soc. of the Desc. of
Founders of Hartford (Genealogist); Dau. of American Revolution
(Chapter Librarian). Occup: Genealogist. Address: 105½ North
Hoopes Ave., Auburn,NY 13021. Descended from:

1 William Bradford, Governor of Plymouth Colony 1621-57

2 William Bradford   (2)   Mary Fitch Wiswall
   Plymouth 17 Jun 1624   Plymouth,MA   1643
   Plymouth 20 Feb 1703/4   c.1673   c.1681/2

3 Joseph Bradford   Anne Fitch
   Plymouth 18 Apr 1675   Lebanon,CT   Norwich,CT 1 Apr 1675
   New London,CT 16 Jan   5 Oct 1698   Lebanon 17 Oct 1715
     1747

4 Irene Bradford   Jonathan Janes
   Lebanon 19 Sep 1715   Lebanon   Lebanon 12 Mar 1713
   -----   18 Mar 1736   -----

5 Eliphalet Janes   Woodstock,CT   Elfleda Lyon
   Lebanon 23 Feb 1743   Woodstock 27 May 1749
   Sturbridge,MA 5 Jun   1768   Sturbridge 1 Mar 1792
     1835

6 Almarin Janes   Polly Fay
   11 Jul 1781   -----   Stratford,CT 23 Jul
                                              1784
   Little York,NY 5 May   1 Dec 1803   Seneca Falls,NY 28 Dec
     1813   1843

7 Diantha Janes   William Jackson
   Manlius,NY 30 Jul 1810   Manlius   Pompey,NY 15 Feb 1806
   Syracuse,NY 31 Dec   7 Sep 1827   Syracuse 23 Jul 1860
     1881

8 Charles R. Jackson   Ruth A. Stoddard
   Syracuse 1 Jan 1849   Syracuse   Syracuse 4 Mar 1849
   Syracuse 7 May 1925   31 Dec 1869   Syracuse 28 Oct 1926

9 Matie Jackson   Robert R. Jones
   Syracuse 30 Sep 1871   Syracuse   Waterbury,CT 26 Aug
                                              1857
   Bloomfield,CT 19 Sep   23 Jun 1892   Syracuse 20 Apr 1922
     1952

   Inheritor: David Russell Powers, 114 Kimry Moor, Fayetteville, NY 13088

FENTON, MARGARET STEELE HAINES (MRS. JOHN GIBBONS)

Nat. #280-B. Elected 1 Mar 1976. b. Fort Fairfield,ME 26 Apr
1902. m. 11 Jun 1927, John Gibbons Fenton, b. Spruce,WV 2 Jun
1900. Educ: Registered Nurse, Lakewood Hospital, Lakewood,OH
1923. Member: Hereditary Order of Desc. of Colonial Governors;
Dau. of American Revolution; Colonial Dau. of 17th Century;
New England Women. Occup: Supervisor of Nurses. Address:
8652 Thackeray St., Dallas,TX 75225. Descended from:

1 Thomas Dudley, Governor of Massachusetts 1634-35, 1640-41,
   1645-46, and 1650-51

2 Samuel Dudley   (3)   Elizabeth Hilton
   England 1610   -----   -----
   1683   -----   -----

3 Stephen Dudley   Sarah Gilman
   Exeter,NH   -----   -----
   -----   -----   -----

4 James Dudley   Mercy Folsom
   11 Jun 1690   -----   -----
   1749   -----   -----

5 Samuel Dudley   Mary Ladd
   Exeter 1720   -----   1722
   -----   -----   -----

6 Mary Dudley Exeter 30 Aug 1797	----- -----	John Haines Exeter 1738 1810
7 Daniel Haines 6 Nov 1779 2 Jul 1838	----- 10 Oct 1804	Betsy Wingate Sep 1784 - 21 Feb 1826
8 Joseph Wingate Haines 21 Jul 1805 30 Jan 1876	----- Mar 1828	Mary B. Briggs Jun 1805 May 1874
9 John W. Haines Aug 1837 Fort Fairfield,ME 1913	(2) ----- 1868	Mary Findland ----- -----
10 Charles Henry Haines 17 Aug 1879 6 Dec 1958	----- 13 Mar 1901	Prudence May Steele 6 Dec 1878 6 Jun 1958

FINLAY, LYDIA ROPES DOW (MRS. CHRISTOPHER A.)

Nat. #182-B. Elected 15 Nov 1971. b. Beverly,MA 18 Apr 1912.
m. Pelham,NH 27 Feb 1937, Christopher Alonzo Finlay, b. 24 Feb
1905. Issue: Susan Caroline Finlay, b. Melrose,MA 12 Mar 1942;
Carol Johann Finlay, b. Peabody,MA. Member: Hereditary Order of
Desc. of Colonial Governors; Soc. of Mayflower Desc.; Soc. of
Desc. of Colonial Clergy; Dau. of Colonial Wars; U.S. Dau. of
1812 (MA, State Pres.); Dames of Court of Honor; Dau. of American
Colonists; Dau. of Founders and Patriots of America; Dau. of
American Revolution (Past Ch. Regent); Women Desc. of Ancient and
Honorable Artillery; Flagon and Trencher; Desc. of Illegitimate
Sons and Dau. of Kings of Britain; Soc. of Old Plymouth Colony
Desc.; Magna Charta Dames; Soc. of Desc. of Knights of Most Noble
Order of the Garter; Colonial Order of the Crown; New England
Historic and Genealogical Soc.; Essex Institute; Peabody Museum;
Peabody Historic Soc. (Recording Secretary); Balch House Associ-
ates (Nat. Gen.); MA Ex-Regents DAR Club. Occup: Certified
American Lineage Specialist. Address: 48 Summit St., Peabody,
MA 01960. Descended from:

1 John Endicott, Governor of Massachusetts 1629-65

2 Zerubbabel Endicott Salem,MA c.1635 Salem Jan 1683/4	Salem 1654	Mary Smith Salem 1636 Salem 20 Jun 1677
3 Samuel Endicott 1659 1694	----- 1684	Hannah Felton bpt. 20 Jun 1663 -----
4 Ruth Endicott 1689 -----	----- 17 Jul 1710	Martyn Herrick Salem 26 Jan 1679 Salem 1739
5 Samuel Herrick 1713 Reading,MA 1792	----- 1742	Elizabeth Jones Woburn,MA 31 Aug 1720 1759

```
 6  Susanna Herrick                        Stephen Putman
    Reading 30 Jun 1750      Reading       Salem Village,MA 22 Feb
                                             1742
    Danvers,MA 25 Feb 1825   15 Dec 1774   Danvers 8 Jun 1809

 7  Eben Putman                            Betsey Webb
    Danvers 5 Feb 1785       Danvers       Danvers 11 Dec 1790
    Danvers 19 Oct 1876      8 Oct 1809    Danvers 19 Apr 1842

 8  Margaret D. Putman                     Joseph W. Ropes
    Danvers 24 Dec 1817      Danvers       Salem 14 Mar 1816
    Danvers 11 Jan 1895      8 Apr 1840    Danvers 24 Mar 1880

 9  Caroline E. Ropes                      John E. Dow
    Danvers 9 Dec 1847       Danvers       Quincy,MA 16 Sep 1846
    Danvers 19 Jan 1928      20 Mar 1873   Beverly,MA 28 Feb 1938

10  Waldo H. Dow                           Nettie C. Morgan
    Danvers 28 Jul 1882      Beverly       Beverly 19 Jul 1885
                             21 Aug 1907   Beverly 1 Oct 1964

    Inheritor: Carol Johann Finlay
```

FISHER, CLARA CARROLL KERBY (MRS. ADRIAN P.)

Nat. #50-B. Elected 18 Jul 1962. b. Oxon Hill,MD 16 Dec 1899.
m. 27 Jun 1929, Adrian Posey Fisher, b. Oxon Hill 26 Mar 1900.
Issue: Mary Eugenia Fisher. Educ: Private Boarding School.
Member: Hereditary Order of Desc. of Colonial Governors; Dau. of
American Revolution; Dau. of Founders and Patriots of America;
Magna Charta Dames; Lords of the Maryland Manors. Address:
6901 Livingston Road, Oxon Hill,MD 20021. (From Society's
Records). Descended from:

```
 1  Robert Brooke, Governor of Maryland 1652

 2  Thomas Brooke                          Eleanor Hatton
    Battle,Eng. 23 Jun 1632 Maryland       England 1642
    Calvert Co.MD 25 Oct    1659           Calvert Co. 1725
       1676

 3  Clement Brooke                         Jane Sewall
    Calvert Co. bf. Oct     -----          St.Mary's Co.MD
       1676
    Prince George's Co.,    bf.31 Aug 1704 Prince George's Co.
       MD 1737                                c.1761

 4  Henry Brooke                           Margaret
    Prince George's Co.     Maryland       -----
       1704
    Prince George's Co.     -----          Prince George's Co.
       1751                                   bf. 3 Jan 1792

 5  Nicholas Brooke                        Miss Hill
    Prince George's Co.     Maryland       Prince George's Co.
       1752
    Prince George's Co.     -----          -----
       1797
```

6 Clement Hill Brooke
    Prince George's Co.   Surratts-   Ann Carroll
      1778   ville,MD

6 Clement Hill Brooke		Ann Carroll
Prince George's Co. 1778	Surratts- ville,MD	Surrattsville c.1799
Silver Hill,MD 28 Aug 1854	-----	Silver Hill 23 Jul 1879
7 Clement Hill Brooke		Margaret E. Jenkins
Surrattsville 25 Feb 1832	Washington,DC	Surrattsville 15 Jan 1844
Silver Hill 4 Apr 1917	23 Dec 1869	Silver Hill 5 Dec 1915
8 Eugenia Brooke		John Henry Kerby
Silver Hill 10 Jul 1870	-----	Oxon Hill,MD 10 Aug 1864
Washington,DC 19 Nov 1954	7 Feb 1893	Oxon Hill 29 Jun 1936

Inheritor: Mary Eugenia Fisher

FISHER, ELVA J.B. PAUL (MRS. CRAIG BECKER)

Nat. #2-B-S.   Member: Hereditary Order of Desc. of Colonial
Governors. Address: 66 Ralph Avenue, White Plains,NY 10606.
Descended from:

1 Roger Conant, Governor of Massachusetts 1624-29

2 Lot Conant		Elizabeth Walton
Cape Ann,MA c.1624	Marblehead,MA	Eng. 27 Oct 1629
Beverly,MA 29 Sep 1674	c.1649	Marblehead 1668
3 John Conant		Bethula Mansfield
Beverly 15 Dec	Beverly	7 Apr 1658
Beverly 30 Sep 1724	7 May 1678	Lynn,MA 27 Jul 1720
4 Rebecca Conant		Benjamin Cleaves
5 May 1695	-----	Beverly 29 Oct 1695
-----	2 Jun 1718	Beverly 14 Dec 1775
5 Joshua Cleaves		Elizabeth Putnam
Beverly 27 Feb 1724	-----	Salem 19 Nov 1728
Salem,MA	26 Feb 1741/2	Salem 1786
6 Elizabeth Cleaves		Benjamin Jones
Ipswich,MA 20 Oct 1752	-----	Ipswich 13 Aug 1751
Lyndeboro 6 Jun 1819	18 Dec 1771/3	Lyndeboro,NH 12 Jan 1819
7 Elizabeth Cleaves Jones		Nehemiah Boutwell
Lyndeboro 11 Dec 1776	-----	Lyndeboro 20 Nov 1774
Lyndeboro 3 Jul 1856	28 Jul 1806	Lyndeboro 3 Oct 1855
8 Clark Crombie Boutwell		Aseneth Hills Bradford
Lyndeboro 22 Apr 1818	Hancock,NH	Hancock 30 Nov 1820
Manchester,NH 17 Jan 1892	30 Nov 1840	Nashua,NH 16 Feb 1880

9	Henry Thatcher Boutwell Hancock 20 Aug 1844 Santa Barbara,CA 21 Dec 1915	St.Louis,MO 25 Dec 1872	Helen Willis Walpole,NH 3 Apr 1846 Manchester 4 May 1894
10	John T. Boutwell St.Louis 1 May 1874 -----	Lawrence- ville,NJ 21 Jan 1910	Esther Miner Maysville,KY 13 Dec 1880 -----
11	Jean Miner Boutwell Santa Barbara 2 Feb 1911 -----	----- -----	Joseph Barnett Paul ----- -----

FLEMING, ELAINE BRIGGS (MRS. KENNETH SPRING)

Nat. #132-B. Elected 22 Jan 1968. b. Oak Grove,LA 23 Jul 1912.
m. Oak Grove 24 Jun 1937, Dr. Kenneth S. Fleming, b. Hubbard,OH
17 Nov 1908. Issue: Henry Briggs Fleming, b. Grove City,PA
14 Nov 1942. Educ: Whitworth College, Brookhaven,MS; Louisiana
State University. Member: Hereditary Order of Desc. of Colonial
Governors; Dau. of American Revolution (Past Nat. Chairman; OH,
Past Chaplain); Dau. of Colonial Wars (Nat. Chaplain); Dames of
the Court of Honor; Colonial Dau. of the XVII Century (OH,
Councillor); Soc. of Dau. of Founders and Patriots of America;
Order of First Families of Mississippi (Past Librarian Gen.);
United Dau. of the Confederacy; Soc. of Old Plymouth Colony
Desc.; Soc. of Desc. of Colonial Clergy; Order of Crown of
Charlemagne in the USA; Sovereign Colonial Soc. of Americans of
Royal Descent; Magna Charta Dames; Jamestowne Soc. Address:
255 Neff Drive, Canfield,OH 44406. Descended from:

1 John Coggeshall, Governor of Rhode Island 1647

2	Joshua Coggeshall Essex Co.Eng. c.1623 Portsmouth,RI	Newport,RI 22 Dec 1652	Joan West England 1631 24 Apr 1676
3	Humility Coggeshall Portsmouth 1670 af. 1719	Portsmouth c.1687	Benjamin Greene Rhode Island c.1665 East Greenwich,RI 1719
4	Henry Greene c.1696 E.Greenwich 21 Feb 1752	E.Greenwich 15 May 1724	Margaret Rathbone E.Greenwich 29 Nov 1700 28 Feb 1742
5	Job Greene E.Greenwich 2 Mar 1735 VT 25 Jan 1792	West Greenwich 3 Feb 1757	Meribah Carr W.Greenwich 3 Jul 1739 12 Jul 1785
6	Sarah Greene 1 Jan 1759 Augusta,NY 12 Feb 1849	Hancock,MA 28 Dec 1775	Michael Briggs E.Greenwich 16 Sep 1751 Burlington,NY 10 Feb 1828

```
7   Henry Briggs                                    Phoebe Parker
    c.1780                          -----           1 Oct 1787
    Otsego Co.NY 26 Jan             -----           af.1860
      1846

8   Michael P. Briggs                               Sophronia Matteson
    NY c.1808                       -----           NY c.1817
    Otsego Co. 21 Mar 1864   c.1832                 1857/60

9   Henry D. Briggs                                 Sarah E. Wright
    Otsego 6 Jan 1835        Floyd,LA               East Carroll,LA 11 May
                                                      1851
    Oak Grove,LA 20 Dec      19 Jan 1871            Oak Grove 10 Jan 1918
      1900

10  Ollie Briggs                                    Edna S. Harper
    Oak Grove 22 Feb 1887    Winn Parish,           Winn Parish 16 Dec
                               LA                      1890
    Oak Grove 8 Oct 1937     -----                  Oak Grove 9 Oct 1938
```

FOSS, PHILIP EMERY

Nat. #193-B. Elected 8 Aug 1972. b. Norway,ME 21 Mar 1896.
m. Auburn,ME 30 Dec 1922, Thelma Griswold Tracy, b. Auburn 14 Jun
1898. Issue: Richard Tracy Foss, b. Lewiston,ME 30 Oct 1923;
Mary M. Foss McDaniel, b. Hartford,CT 25 Dec 1929. Educ: Bowdoin
College, B.S.; Bates College, A.M. Member: Hereditary Order of
Desc. of Colonial Governors; Mayflower Soc., CT; Soc. of Desc.
of Colonial Clergy. Occup: H.S. Science Teacher, Co-author
"Social Biology" for Secondary Schools. Address: 29 Heritage
Drive, Apt. B, Windsor,CT 06095. Descended from:

```
1   William Bradford, Governor of Plymouth Colony 1621-33, 1635-
      36, 1637-38, 1639-44, 1645-57

2   William Bradford            (1)              Alice Richards
    Plymouth 17 Jun 1624    Plymouth,MA          c.1627
    Plymouth 20 Feb 1703/4  bf.28 Jan 1650  Plymouth 12 Dec 1671

3   Sarah Bradford                              Kenelm Baker
    Plymouth 1671           Plymouth             Marshfield 23 Mar 1657
    Marshfield,MA 18 Oct    1687                 Marshfield 1712/3
      1705

4   Kenelm Baker                                Patience Doty
    Marshfield 3 Nov 1695   Duxbury,MA           Plymouth 3 Jul 1697
    Marshfield 22 May 1771  22 Jan 1719          Marshfield 18 Feb 1784

5   John Baker                                  Ruth Barker
    Marshfield 18 Oct 1719  Marshfield           Scituate,MA 1720
    Marshfield 1 Jul 1804   24 Feb 1742/3   Pembroke,MA 15 Mar 1783

6   Ruth Baker                                  Charles Kent
    Marshfield 10 Oct 1755  Marshfield           Marshfield 7 Jan 1754
    Readfield,ME 10 Jun     27 Jan 1780          Readfield Mar 1825
      1838
```

7	Lucy Kent		John Morrison
	Marshfield 2 Jun 1785	Readfield	14 Sep 1779
	Wayne,ME 6 Mar 1865	15 Mar 1805	Wayne,ME 5 Jul 1852

8	Dorcas Morrison		Walter Foss
	Wayne 10 Aug 1806	Wayne	Leeds 18 May 1799
	Leeds 29 Apr 1882	21 Jul 1824	Leeds 12 Apr 1875

9	Sarah E. Foss		Emery Foss
	Leeds 19 Sep 1830	Leeds	Wayne 10 Apr 1823
	Wayne 4 Feb 1864	1 Feb 1852	Wayne 11 Sep 1872

10	Walter Emery Foss		Cora Estelle Chandler
	Wayne 29 Jul 1860	Wayne	Wayne 13 Aug 1862
	Norway,ME 29 Jul 1936	18 Dec 1882	Norway 17 Dec 1910

Inheritor: Tracy Foss McDaniel (Mrs. Albert W.)

FOSTER, GIRAUD VAN NEST

Nat. #86-B. Elected 16 Jul 1963. b. New York,NY 6 Jan 1904.
m.(1) NYC 22 Apr 1926. Issue: Giraud Vernam Foster, b. NYC
19 Jan 1928. m.(2) Warwick,NY 12 Aug 1946, Suzanne Holloway.
Issue: Jane DeMoret Foster, b. New Orleans,LA 8 Jun 1947. Educ:
Groton School; Harvard. Member: Hereditary Order of Desc. of
Colonial Governors; Sons of American Revolution; Soc. of Colonial
Wars; Huguenot Soc. of America; Order of Founders and Patriots of
America; Order of Americans of Armorial Ancestry. Occup: Cattle
and Timber Business (Ret.). Descended from:

1 Gerardus Beekman, Governor of New York 1710

2	Gerardus Beekman		Anna M. van Horne
	New York c.1693	New York	New York
	New York	12 Oct 1718	New York

3	Elizabeth Beekman		Lucas van Ranst
	New York 14 Dec 1720	New York	New York 25 Dec 1716
	New York	-----	New York 1788

4	Anna Maria van Ranst		George Codwise
	New York 8 Oct 1740	New York	New York
	New York	19 Jul 1760	New York

5	Marie Codwise		John Kane
	New York 14 Apr 1775	New York	New York
	New York	20 Nov 1793	New York

6	Marie A. Kane		John Hone
	New York 22 May 1798	New York	New York 30 Aug 1796
	New York 30 Oct 1869	12 Nov 1817	New York 1829

7	Emily Hone		Frederick G. Foster
	New York 3 Nov 1818	New York	New York 1810 *
	New York 5 Dec 1875	14 Nov 1844	New York 8 Jan 1879

8 Giraud Foster   Jean van Nest
   New York 8 Nov 1850   New York   New York 19 May 1860
   Lenox,MA 22 Sep 1945   19 Apr 1892   Aitken,SC 22 Apr 1932

   Inheritor: Jane Foster

FRASER, ALEXANDER HERBEMONT

Nat. #271-B.   Elected 11 Nov 1975.   b. San Antonio,TX 12 Jan 1910.
m. Orange,TX 5 Dec 1938, Clara Lee Kennedy, b. Williamson Co.,TX
26 Jul 1913. Issue: Charles Kennedy Fraser, b. 15 Jul 1930;
Dr. Clara Jane Fraser, b. 23 May 1941; Joan Fraser Gaedke, b.
22 Jun 1946; all b. San Antonio. Educ: Virginia Military Insti-
tute; University of Texas Law School, 1929-32. Member: Heredi-
tary Order of Desc. of Colonial Governors; Sons of American
Revolution (Pres., San Antonio Chap.); Soc. of Colonial Wars (Lt.
Governor,TX); Huguenot Soc. of South Carolina; Sons of Confederate
Veterans; Order of Stars and Bars; Sons of Republic of Texas;
Knights of Order of San Jacinto; Texas and San Antonio Bar Assns.;
Bexar County Historical Comm.; San Antonio Historical Soc. (Past
Pres.). Military: U.S. Army (WWII); Texas Nat'l. Guard; U.S.
Army Reserve; Major of Armor, USAR (ret.) Address: 1705 Alamo
National Bldg., San Antonio,TX 78205. Descended from:

1 James Moore, Governor of South Carolina 1700-02, 1719, 1721

2 James Moore   (2)   Carolina Elizabeth
                                                Bersford
   Barbados c.1678   -----   Barbados c.1680/6
   Charleston,SC 3 Mar   c.1700   Charleston af.1715
     1723

3 John Moore   Elizabeth Postell
   South Carolina c.1718   South Carolina   South Carolina c.1718
   South Carolina c.1761   c.1733   South Carolina c.1761

4 Elizabeth Moore   William Coachman
   South Carolina c.1735   South Carolina   South Carolina c.1725
   South Carolina c.1807   Mar 1755   South Carolina Mar 1770

5 Elizabeth Coachman   William Mathews
   South Carolina c.1757   South Carolina   South Carolina c.1756
   South Carolina Nov 1833 16 Jan 1777   Charleston Apr 1817

6 Ann Mathews   John Fraser
   South Carolina c.1780   Charleston   Inverness, Scotland
                                              c.1777
   South Carolina bf.1850 12 Jan 1808   Charleston 2 Jan 1854

7 John August Fraser   Mary A. Lenoir
   Charleston Nov 1808   Horatio,SC   Horatio 9 Feb 1830
   Camden,SC 1854   1848   San Antonio,TX 4 Sep
                                              1898

8 John Augustus Fraser   Zelime Susan Tobin
   Camden 29 Sep 1849   San Antonio   San Antonio 8 Jul 1855
   San Antonio 31 Jan 1932 8 Jan 1878   San Antonio 29 Jun 1911

9 Alexander Herbemont   Florence Agnes Clamp
     Fraser
   San Antonio 20 Sep   San Antonio   Bracketville,TX 10 Jun
     1886   1887
   San Antonio 28 Oct 1918 5 Jan 1909   (living in 1975)

FREEMAN, MYRON FREDERICK

Nat. #288-B. Elected 14 Jan 1976. b. Somerville,MA 22 Aug 1903.
m. Roslindale,MA 19 Sep 1928, Lillian Josephine Walker, b.
Jamaica Plain,MA 25 Feb 1904. Member: Hereditary Order of Desc.
of Colonial Governors; Soc. of Mayflower Descendants; Soc. of
Genealogists. Address: 1248 Farmington Ave., Apt. A6, West
Hartford, CT 06107. Descended from:

1 Thomas Prence, Governor of Plymouth 1634-35; 1638; 1657-73

2 Mercy Prence   John Freeman
     Plymouth c.1631   Eastham,MA   England 1627
     11 Sep 1711   13 Feb 1649   28 Oct 1719

3 Nathaniel Freeman   Mary Howland
     20 Mar 1669   -----   Dartmouth,MA 23 Feb
                                        1665/6
     4 Jan 1760   c.1690   29 Jan 1742/3

4 Lydia Freeman   Elisha Freeman
     14 Oct 1703   -----   9 Dec 1701
     1742   7 May 1725   -----

5 Simeon Freeman   Patience Wood
     Rochester,MA   -----   -----
     Liverpool, Nova Scotia 1776   -----

6 Nelson Freeman   Mary Whitman
     14 Jul 1764   Annapolis,NS 26 Mar 1763
     Nova Scotia 19 Mar Apr 1787   13 Feb 1828
       1819

7 Edward Perkins   Lucinda Hayes
     Freeman
     26 Jan 1811   Milton,NS   1812
     1895   12 Oct 1836   1901

8 William Edward Freeman   Tryphene Allison
     2 Sep 1837   Kempt,NS   1838
     Kempt 12 Oct 1912 25 Oct 1865   Kempt 3 Jul 1928

9 Janet Grace Freeman   Frederick Slocomb
                                  Freeman
     Kempt 5 Dec 1880   Kempt   South Brookfield,NS
                                        3 Dec 1880
     Boston,MA 19 Oct 1925 1 Oct 1902 Brookline,MA 17 Jul
                                          1943

FRISCHE, HARRIET CATHERINE ROSS (MRS. CARL A.)

Nat. #279-B. Elected 10 Feb 1976. b. Cherry Valley,IL 25 Jun
1907. m. Paola,KS 2 Jun 1930, Carl Alfred Frische, b. Freeport,
KS 13 Aug 1906. Educ: Baker University, Baldwin,KS. Member:
Hereditary Order of Desc. of Colonial Governors; Dau. of American
Revolution (NY State Historian); Soc. of Mayflower Desc.; Colonial
Dames XVII Century; Huguenot Soc. of New York; New England Women;
Order of Crown of Charlemagne in U.S.; Who's Who of American
Women. Address: 6642 Praying Monk Rd., Scottsdale,AZ 85253.
Descended from:

1 William Bradford, Governor of Plymouth Colony 1621-57

2 William Bradford   Alice Richards
   Plymouth,MA 17 Jun 1624 -----   Weymouth 14 Aug 1623
   Plymouth 20 Feb 1703/4   -----   Plymouth 12 Dec 1671

3 Hannah Bradford   Joshua Ripley
   Plymouth 9 May 1662   Plymouth   Hingham,MA 9 Nov 1658
   Windham,CT 28 May 1738   28 Nov 1682   Windham 8 May 1739

4 Faith Ripley   Samuel Bingham
   Hingham 20 Sep 1686   Plymouth   Norwich,CT 28 Mar 1685
   Windham 11 Feb 1720/1   7 Jan 1708/9   Windham 1 Mar 1760

5 Jerusha Bingham   Benjamin Robinson
   Windham 2 Feb 1709   Tisbury,MA 23 Feb
                            -----   1703/4
   Windham   4 Mar 1728/9   Windham

6 Irene Robinson   John Blodgett
   Windham 1 Nov 1733   Stafford,CT   Stafford
   Claremont,NH 12 Apr   4 Dec 1755   Claremont 13 Apr 1813
      1813

7 Irene Blodgett   Thomas Buell
   Stafford 3 Feb 1762   Stafford   Somers,CT 15 May 1756
   Earlville,NY 6 Mar 1839 27 Jan 1780   Earlville 1 Oct 1820

8 Chauncey Buell   Levina Willis
   Earlville 6 Mar 1803   Madison Co.NY   Winchester,NH 7 Feb
                                            1804
   Earlville 7 Oct 1864   c.1828   Earlville 25 Dec 1887

9 Celestia Levina Buell   (1)   Lafayette Muzzy
   Lebanon,NY 25 Jul 1831 Lebanon   NY 6 Sep 1824
   Grant Park,IL 12 Nov   6 Sep 1849   Earlville 17 Mar 1852
      1903

10 Addison Muzzy   Harriet Maria Wheeler
   Earlville 15 Jul 1850   Grant Park   Bennington,VT 8 Mar
                                            1847
   Grant Park 26 Jun 1914 25 Apr 1876   Grant Park 25 Jul 1907

11 Edith Mae Muzzy   Smiley Allen Ross
   Grant Park 6 Feb 1877   Grant Park   Blue Rock,OH 11 Oct
                                            1871
   Paola,KS 26 Mar 1932   31 Aug 1905   Paola 28 Jul 1973

FRYER, APPLETON

Nat. #251-B.   Elected 7 Feb 1975.   b. Buffalo,NY 25 Feb 1927.
m. Buffalo 16 May 1953, Angeline Dudley Kenefick, b. Buffalo
2 Jul 1932.   Issue: Appleton Fryer, Jr., b. 10 May 1954; Daniel
Kenefick Fryer, b. 6 May 1956; Robert Livingston Fryer, b. 4 Sep
1959; Catherine Appleton Fryer, b. 13 Nov 1960; all b. Buffalo.
Educ: Princeton University, B.A.   Member: Hereditary Order of
Desc. of Colonial Governors; Holland Soc. of New York (Vice
Pres.); Soc. of Mayflower Descendants (Regent, Buffalo Colony);
Sons of Revolution, NY;   Sons of American Revolution; Soc. of
Colonial Wars; Order of Colonial Lords of Manors in America; The
Order of the Crown of Charlemagne in the U.S.A.; Baronial Order
of Magna Charta; Huguenot Historical Soc., New Paltz,NY; Freer-
Low Family Assn.   Address: 85 Windsor Ave., Buffalo,NY 14209.
Descended from:

1   Rip Van Dam, Governor of New York 1731/2

2   Sarah Van Dam   Walter Thong
    New York,NY 31 Oct 1686 -----   -----
    NY 17 Feb 1720   c.16 Oct 1704   NY bf.2 Nov 1724

3   Mary Thong   Robert Livingston
    NY 3 Jun 1711   NYC   Albany,NY 18 Dec 1708
    NY 30 May 1765   20 May 1731   NY 27 Nov 1790

4   Peter Robert Livingston   Margaret Livingston
    NYC 27 Apr 1737   -----   NYC 4 Jul 1738
    13 Nov 1794   20 Jun 1758   Hudson,NY 31 Jul 1809

5   Robert Thong Livingston   Margaretta Livingston
    Livingston Manor,NY   -----   NYC Feb 1759
       4 Apr 1759
    Livingston Manor   15 Nov 1787   Livingston Manor
       20 Dec 1813   17 Oct 1817

6   Mary Livingston   Alexander Crofts
    Livingston Manor   Livingston   Dublin, Ireland 6 Aug
       19 Dec 1788   Manor   1781
    Albany 26 Feb 1865   20 Feb 1809   Livingston Manor
                                                22 Oct 1833

7   Margaret Livingston   William John Fryer
       Crofts
    Livingston Manor   Livingston   Guilderland,NY 1 Aug
       24 Nov 1811   Manor   1808
    Albany 11 Apr 1882   10 Feb 1836   Albany 22 Apr 1891

8   Robert Livingston Fryer   Melissa Dodge Pratt
    Albany 12 Dec 1847   Buffalo,NY   Buffalo 5 Mar 1854
    Buffalo 20 Oct 1915   7 Dec 1882   Buffalo May 1932

9   Livingston Fryer   Catherine Appleton
    Buffalo 4 Jan 1888   Buffalo   Buffalo 17 Oct 1900
    Buffalo 25 Jun 1960   7 Jul 1924

    Inheritor: Appleton Fryer, Jr. or Daniel K. Fryer (home address)

FRYER, LIVINGSTON, JR.

Nat. #250-B. Elected 7 Feb 1975. b. Buffalo,NY 9 Jan 1926.
Educ: Yale University, B.A. 1947. Member: Hereditary Order of
Desc. of Colonial Governors; The Holland Society, Saint Nicholas
Society of City of New York; Sons of the Revolution,NY; Order of
Colonial Lords of the Manors in America; Order of the Crown of
Charlemagne in U.S.A.; Baronial Order of Magna Charta; Soc. of
Mayflower Descendants; Huguenot Society; Freer-Low Family Assn.;
Elder William Brewster Soc.; Huguenot Historical Soc. Address:
55 East End Avenue, New York,NY 10028. Descended from:

1 Rip Van Dam, Governor of New York 1731/2

Continue with the lineage of his brother Appleton Fryer, Nat.
#251-B.

   Inheritor: Robert Livingston Fryer or Catherine A. Fryer

FULLER, EUNICE BOURNE LEE (MRS. WILLIAM H.)

Nat. #72-B. Elected 25 Mar 1963. b. Grosse Pointe Farms,MI
21 Mar 1922. m. Kansas City,MO 1 Jan 1943, William Hanscom
Fuller, b. Boston,MA 21 Jun 1913. Issue: William H. Fuller, Jr.
b. Westerly,RI 21 Jun 1944; Michael Bourne Fuller, b. Sarasota,
FL 24 Feb 1947; Bradford Newberry Fuller, b. Winter Haven,FL
6 Jul 1949. Educ: Emma Willard School, Lenox School. Member:
Hereditary Order of Desc. of Colonial Governors; Soc. of
Mayflower Desc.; Dau. of 1812; Dau. of American Revolution;
Women Desc. of Ancient and Honorable Artillery Co.; Soc. of
Colonial Dames. Address: Box 1487, Winter Haven,FL 33880.
Descended from:

1 William Bradford, Governor of Plymouth Colony 1621-33, 1635-57

2	William Bradford	(1)	Alice Richards
	Plymouth 17 Jun 1624	Plymouth,MA	c.1627
	Plymouth 20 Feb 1703/4	28 Jan 1650/1	Plymouth 12 Dec 1671
3	Alice Bradford Adams	(2)	James Fitch
	Plymouth 1661	Norwich,CT	Saybrook,CT 2 Aug 1649
	Canterbury,CT 15 Mar	8 May 1687	Canterbury 10 Nov 1727
	1745		
4	Ebenezer Fitch		Bridget Brown
	Norwich,CT 10 Jan 1689	Canterbury	-----
	Windham,CT 24 Nov 1724	18 Sep 1712	Windham
5	Alice Fitch		John Fitch
	Windsor,CT 30 Jan 1713	Windsor	Windham 18 Mar 1705
	1796	25 Jan 1730/1	Windsor 12 Feb 1760
6	James Fitch		Ann Hulbert
	Windham 9 Apr 1739	Windsor	Windham 14 Apr 1730
	Windsor 7 Nov 1815	23 May 1763	Windsor 3 Feb 1821

7 Anna Theresa Fitch   George Phelps
   Windham 16 Oct 1765   Windsor   Windsor 7 Dec 1755
   Windsor 29 Oct 1854   23 May 1784   Windsor 16 Feb 1807

8 Rhoda Phelps   Elihu Newberry
   Windsor 16 Aug 1793   Windsor   Windsor 3 Feb 1788
   Romeo,MI 16 Oct 1877   19 Dec 1815   Romeo 13 Mar 1860

9 John Stoughton Newberry   Helen Handy
   Waterville,NY 18 Nov   Cleveland,OH   Cleveland 15 Nov 1835
      1826
   Detroit,MI 2 Jan 1887   6 Oct 1859   Detroit 17 Dec 1912

10 Helen Hall Newberry   Henry Bourne Joy
   Detroit 9 Jun 1869   Grosse Pointe   Detroit 23 Nov 1864
                            Farms,MI
   Grosse Pointe Farms   11 Oct 1892   Grosse Pointe Farms
      13 Mar 1958   6 Nov 1936

11 Helen Bourne Joy   Howard Barker Lee
   Detroit 20 Mar 1896   Grosse Pointe   Detroit 13 Aug 1891
   -----   16 Jun 1917   Detroit 28 Feb 1962

FULLER, ROBERT STEVENS

Nat. #275-B. Elected 10 Feb 1976. Member: Hereditary Order of
Desc. of Colonial Governors. Address: 1914 Bellevue Road,
Harrisburg,PA 17104. Descended from:

1 William Bradford, Governor of Plymouth Colony 1621-33, 1635-57

2 William Bradford   Alice Richards
   Plymouth 17 Jun 1624   Plymouth,MA   16 Jun 1627
   Plymouth 20 Feb 1703/4   28 Jan 1650   Plymouth 12 Dec 1671

3 Hannah Bradford   Joshua Ripley
   Plymouth 9 May 1662   Plymouth   Hingham,MA 9 Nov 1658
   Windham,CT 28 May 1738   26 Nov 1682   Windham 8 May 1739

4 David Ripley   Lydia Cary
   Windham 20 May 1697   Windham   Bristol,RI 12 Feb 1705
   Windham 16 Feb 1781   21 Mar 1720   Windham 9 Apr 1784

5 Irene Ripley   Timothy Warner
   Windham 11 Feb 1728/9   Windham   Lebanon,CT 1 Dec 1724
   Windham 24 Feb 1804   11 Jan 1749/50   Windham 8 Apr 1760

6 Hannah Warner   Darius Peck
   Windham 23 Nov 1751   Windham   Norwich,CT 14 Mar 1749
   Norwich 16 Sep 1789   5 Nov 1772   Norwich 13 Apr 1804

7 Joseph Peck   Polly Collins
   Norwich 21 Jan 1782   Connecticut   c.1781
   Harford,PA 26 Nov 1867   c.1816   Harford 14 Nov 1853

8 Philura Peck
   Columbia,CT 14 Jun   Harford   James C. Powers
     1817   South Gibson,PA 12 Jul
   South Gibson 7 Aug   22 Sep 1836   1817
     1912   Rush,PA 15 Feb 1893

9 Mary Powers
   South Gibson 25 Jul   Gibson,PA   James Bacon Fuller
     1840   Lenox,PA 27 Feb 1837
   South Gibson 25 Sep   22 Sep 1868
     1914   Philadelphia,PA 7 Jan
                                                1927

10 Byron James Fuller
   South Gibson 25 Jun   Garrett,IN   Margaret Cummings
     1873   Ligonier,IN 18 Dec 1869
   Philadelphia 20 Apr   9 Sep 1896
     1954   Philadelphia 7 Jan 1958

11 Stanley Cummings Fuller
   Buffalo,NY 14 Dec 1897   Philadelphia   Isabelle Stevens
                                              Binghampton,NY 9 Nov
                                                1897
   11 May 1973   4 Sep 1926

FULLERTON, TOMMIE FAIRFAX TRIPLETT (MRS. SAMUEL BAKER, JR.)

Nat. #34-B. Elected 10 Apr 1961. b. Little Rock,AR 28 Aug 1934.
m. Pine Bluff,AR 31 Jul 1953, Samuel Baker Fullerton, Jr., b.
St. Louis,MO 10 Jul 1931. Issue: Samuel Baker Fullerton III.
Educ: Smith College, Northampton,MA. Member: Hereditary Order of
Desc. of Colonial Governors; Colonial Dames of America in
Arkansas. Address: 416 South Myrtle St., Warren,AR 71671.
(From Society's Records). Descended from:

1 Leonard Calvert, Governor of Maryland 1633-47

2 William Calvert   Elizabeth Stone
   England 1603   -----   Maryland 1603
   MD 10 Jan 1682   1621/2   MD af.1682

3 George Calvert   Elizabeth Doyne
   St.Mary's Co.,MD 1668   -----   -----
   af.1739   1690   -----

4 John Calvert   (1)   Jane
   MD 1690   -----   -----
   Prince William Co.,VA   1711   -----
     1739

5 George Calvert   Anne Crupper
   MD 1712   -----   -----
   Culpeper Co.,VA   c.1750   -----
     19 May 1782

6 Ann Calvert   William Lindsay
   1751   -----   Fairfax Co.,VA 1743
   1822   c.1766   Fairfax Co. 15 Sep 1798

7 Sarah Lindsay 1785 29 Apr 1837	----- 4 Dec 1805	George Triplett Fairfax Co. 1777 6 Oct 1821

8 Charles H. Triplett
Fairfax Co. 13 Aug
   1809
Pine Bluff,AR 22 Sep
   1887
	----- 	
	7 Feb 1833
		Virginia E. Dunlap
		Alexandria,VA 7 Jan
		   1811
		Marven,AR 7 Feb 1858

9 Charles H. Triplett
Jefferson Co.,AR
   12 Mar 1850
Pine Bluff 2 Nov 1837
	Pine Bluff
	15 Dec 1880
		Estelle Holland
		Sangamon Co.,IL 17 Jan
		   1852
		Pine Bluff 14 Jun 1895

10 Arthur F. Triplett Pine Bluff 20 Aug 1891 Pine Bluff 24 Nov 1958	Pine Bluff 15 Jan 1918	Vashti E. King Shreveport,LA 12 Dec 1897

SUPPLEMENT NO. 1

1 William Stone, Governor of Maryland 1649-54

2 Elizabeth Stone   William Calvert

Continue with Generation 2 of her lineage from Governor
William Calvert.

Inheritor: Samuel Baker Fullerton III

FULWEILER, SPENCER BIDDLE

Nat. #191-B. Elected 11 Jul 1972. b. West Chester,PA 26 Aug
1913. m. New York,NY 5 Oct 1946, Patricia Louise Platt, b.
NYC 19 Mar 1923. Issue: Marie Louise Fulweiler, b. 15 Dec 1949;
Pamela Spencer Fulweiler, b. 20 Jan 1953; Hull Platt Fulweiler,
b. 25 Oct 1954; Spencer Biddle Fulweiler, Jr., b. 14 Mar 1958;
all b. NYC. Educ: Harvard University, B.S. Member: Hereditary
Order of Desc. of Colonial Governors; St. Nicholas Soc. (Board
of Managers). Occup: USNR, Ret., Photo Control Chemist.
Address: 158 East 83nd St., New York,NY 10028. Descended from:

1 Thomas Mayhew, Governor of Martha's Vineyard 1647-81

2 Thomas Mayhew Wilts, England 1620 At Sea 1651	----- 1645	Jane Paine England 1625 af.1658
3 Jerusha Mayhew Martha's Vineyard,MA c.1654 -----	(2) ----- 12 Dec 1684	Thomas Eaton Shrewsbury,NJ 1660 Shrewsbury 26 Sep 1688
4 John Eaton Shrewsbury 26 Mar 1689 Shrewsbury 5 Oct 1750	----- 1721	Joanna Wardell ----- Jan 1770

5 Joanna Eaton   Elihu Spencer
   1728   -----   East Haddam,CT 1721
   Trenton,NJ 1 Nov 1791   15 Oct 1750   Trenton 27 Dec 1784

6 Lydia Spencer   William MacFunn Biddle
   Trenton 1766   -----   England 1764
   1858   Sep 1796   Philadelphia,PA
                                                     28 Aug 1809

7 Lydia MacFunn Biddle   Samuel Baird
   Carlisle,PA 4 Jul 1797   -----   Morristown,PA 1786
   Carlisle 3 Jun 1871   1815   Pottstown,PA 27 Jul
                                                     1833

8 Thomas Baird   Mary Bill
   PA 28 Oct 1831   -----   Norwich,CT 22 Feb 1840
   West Chester,PA   24 Jan 1872   W.Chester 1917
   29 Mar 1897

9 Lydia Spencer Baird   Walter Herbert Fulweiler
   Carlisle 7 Mar 1877   W.Chester   Philadelphia 3 Jan 1880
   Bryn Mawr,PA 25 Oct   28 Oct 1908   Bryn Mawr 22 Dec 1959
   1961

                                      G

GALLAGHER, GENEVIEVE SHERMAN (MRS. EDWARD ELMER)

Nat. #257-B. Elected 22 May 1975. b. Fargo,ND 28 Jun 1909.
m. Decatur,IL 24 Oct 1931, Edward Elmer Gallagher, b. Decatur
16 Jan 1907. Issue: Edward Sherman Gallagher, b. Decatur 28 Aug
1933. Educ: Interstate College, Fargo,ND. Member: Hereditary
Order of Desc. of Colonial Governors; Magna Charta Dames; Soc.
of Mayflower Descendants; Women Desc. of Ancient and Honorable
Artillery Co.; Colonial Dames XVII Century; Dau. of American
Revolution; General Federation of Women's Clubs. Address:
7702 East Pinchot Ave., Scottsdale,AZ 85251. Descended from:

1 John Alden, Governor of Plymouth Colony 1663-64, 1667

2 Rebecca Alden   Thomas Delano
   Plymouth,MA c.1630   Plymouth   Duxbury,MA 21 Mar 1642
   -----   1667   Duxbury 13 Apr 1723

3 Jonathan Delano   Hannah Doten
   Duxbury 1676   Duxbury   Plymouth 1675
   Duxbury 6 Jan 1765   12 Jan 1699   Duxbury 12 Apr 1764

4 Ruth Delano   John Peterson
   Duxbury 25 May 1707   -----   Duxbury 22 Aug 1701
   af.1756   21 Aug 1726   af.1765

5 Lucy Peterson Hathaway   Edward Sherman
   Freetown   Middleboro,MA   Dartmouth,MA 1726
   Middleboro 12 Jul 1812   21 Sep 1759   Middleboro 26 Nov 1804

6 Nathan Sherman   Rebecca Williams
   Middleboro 8 Dec 1765   Adams,MA   -----
   -----   8 Mar 1787   -----

                                     90

```
7  Sarah Sherman                           John Sherman
   1787                  Middleboro        New Jersey 1775/99
   -----                 -----             -----

8  David Thompson Sherman      (2)         Mary Ann (McCoy)
                                             Wheelock
   Whitingham,VT 31 May   Pontiac,IL       Keene,NH 10 Feb 1835
     1824
   Butler,IL 5 May 1913   25 Mar 1867      Butler 25 Mar 1923

9  William Busher Sherman      (2)         Cora Paulson
   Decatur,IL 18 Nov      Frazee,MN        Grove City,MN 30 Dec
     1872                                    1887
   Phoenix,AZ 9 Aug 1950  8 Sep 1908       (living)
```

Inheritor: Shannon Gay Gallagher (granddaughter)

GARRETT, MARGARET LOUISE ZELLER (MRS. CLARENCE JASPER)

Nat. #305-B. Elected 9 Mar 1977. b. Chebanse,IL 26 Nov 1902.
m. Topeka,KS 3 Jun 1950, Clarence Jasper Garrett, b. Burlington,
KS 16 Nov 1887, d. Emporia,KS 18 Feb 1974. Member: Hereditary
Order of Desc. of Colonial Governors; Mayflower Soc. (Deputy
Governor General for Kansas); Dau. of Founders and Patriots of
America (State Historian); Dames of Court of Honor (State Regi-
strar); U.S. Daughters of 1812 (State Registrar); Colonial
Daughters of Seventeenth Century (State Pres.); Women Desc. of
Ancient and Honorable Artillery Co. (President, Kansas); Dau. of
American Revolution (Librarian, Topeka Chap.); National Huguenot
Soc. (Past Pres., Kansas); Dau. of American Colonists (Chapter
Regent); Sons and Daus. of the Pilgrims (Historian, Kansas);
Order of Three Crusades; Order of Crown of Charlemagne in U.S.A.
Address: R. 3, Box 66, Burlington,KS 66839. Descended from:

1 William Hooke, Governor of Maine 1638-40

```
2  William Hooke                           Mary (Follonsby) Pike
   Kittery,ME c.1665      -----            -----
   1743                   c.1691           -----

3  Mary Hooke                              Stephen Bennett
   1710                   -----            20 Jan 1707
   18 Jun 1788            -----            Gloucester,MA 1790

4  Judith Bennett                          Ebenezer Bray
   2 Sep 1739             -----            18/19 Apr 1732
   30 Jan 1799            -----            24 Feb 1817

5  Thomas Bray            int.             Cynthia Record
   Turner,ME 21 Sep 1778  -----            20 Aug 1778
   27 Mar 1842            30 Dec 1797      20 Sep 1819

6  Cynthia Bray                            James Spaulding
   Minot,ME 25 Mar 1802   -----            Buckfield 10 Jun 1802
   Buckfield,ME 11 Dec    5 Jun 1825       Earlville,IL 31 Oct
     1864                                    1886
```

7	Emma Frances Spaulding		John Emory Bryant
	Buckfield 16 Feb 1844	Buckfield	Wayne,ME 13 Oct 1836
	Manteno,IL 2 May 1901	26 Jun 1864	New York,NY 27 Feb 1900
8	Emma Alice Bryant		Julius Christian Zeller
	Atlanta,GA 16 Nov	Mount Vernon,	Spring Bay,IL 15 Dec
	1871	NY	1871
	East Orange,NJ 26 Apr	1 Jan 1895	Kansas City,MO 10 Mar
	1946		1938

GETZINGER, VIRGINIA A. TARDY (MRS. PHILIP L.)

Nat. #225-B. b. Birmingham,AL 11 Sep 1929. m. Fort Monroe,VA 27 Sep 1963, Philip Leland Getzinger, b. Chicago,IL 10 Jun 1914. Issue: Margaret Anne Getzinger, b. Newport News,VA 1 Jun 1967. Educ: Jacksonville State Teachers College, Alabama. Member: Hereditary Order of Desc. of Colonial Governors; First Families of Virginia; Hampton Historical Soc. (Past Corr. Secretary). Occup: Formerly Radio and TV Writer. Address: 3748 Chesapeake Avenue, Hampton,VA 23369. Descended from:

1	Joseph Morton, Governor of South Carolina 1682-84, 1686		
2	Elizabeth Morton	-----	Christopher Wilkinson
3	Francis Wilkinson	-----	----- Brailesford
4	Ann Wilkinson		Edmund Peters
	-----	-----	Virginia 1733
	-----	1763	1789
5	Mary Peters		Gibson Southerne
	1761	-----	-----
	-----	-----	-----
6	John W. Southerne		Elizabeth Callahan
	1802	-----	1804
	1874	-----	1865
7	John P. Southerne		Mary W. Hollowell
	Greenville,SC 1825	Petersburg,VA	Huntsville,AL 1839
	Columbia,SC 1883	1865	Birmingham,AL 1918
8	Annie L. Southerne		Clarence Minge Tardy
	Petersburg,VA 4 Nov	-----	Mobile,AL 27 Mar 1864
	1866		
	Newport News,VA	29 Dec 1885	Birmingham 10 Apr 1944
	31 May 1949		
9	Matthews H. Tardy		Margaret Frances McDuffie
	Huntsville 29 Oct 1888	-----	Hawkinsville,GA 23 Oct 1896
	Hampton,VA 14 Jan 1967	30 Apr 1927	

GIBBS, JAMES WENRICH

Nat. #326-B. Elected 30 Jun 1978. b. Canton,OH 12 Dec 1915.
m. Cleveland,OH 12 Apr 1941, Mary Jewel Hellwig, b. Cleveland
17 Feb 1916. Educ: Yale University, B.A., 1938; University of
Michigan Law School; University of Pennsylvania Wharton Graduate
School. Member: Hereditary Order of Desc. of Colonial Governors;
St. Nicholas Soc. of New York; Sons of Revolution, PA; Sons of
American Revolution; Society of Colonial Wars; Soc. of Mayflower
Descendants; Colonial Society of PA; Soc. of Sons of St. George
of Philadelphia; Order of Lafayette; Old Plymouth Colony Desc.;
Sons & Daus. of Pilgrims; John Howland Soc.; Royal Soc. of St.
George, London, Eng.; PA Historical Soc.; Germantown Historical
Soc.; Valley Forge Historical Soc.; Newcomen Soc.; Royal Soc. of
Arts, London; Sovereign Military Order of Temple of Jerusalem.
Address: 5450 Wissahickon Ave., Philadelphia,PA 19144. Desc. fr:

1 John Endicott, Governor of Massachusetts 1629, 1644-49, 1651-
   53, 1655-64

2 Zerubbabel Endicott   Mary Smith
   Salem,MA 1635   Salem   -----
   Salem 1684   1654   -----

3 Hannah Endicott   Edward Gaskill
                                              (Gascoyne)
   Salem 1676   Salem   Salem 23 Oct 1667
   Mount Holly,NJ   10 Apr 1693   Mount Holly 1748

4 Samuel Gaskill   Theophila Cripps
   Mount Holly   Mount Holly   Burlington Co.,NJ
   -----   2 Aug 1727   -----

5 Samuel Gaskill   Sybilla Collins
   Burlington Sep 1731   -----   29 Jul 1743
   Burlington   19 Dec 1759   Burlington Co. 23 Oct
     w.p. 8 Feb 1825   1814

6 Mary Gaskill   Joshua Gibbs
   Burlington Co. 1 Dec   Monmouth,NJ   Burlington Co. 15 Jan
     1769   1764
   6 Mar 1846   14 Apr 1791   -----

7 Joshua Gibbs   Barbara Shaefer
   Trenton,NJ 5 Feb 1803 Canton,OH   Germany 14 Aug 1806
   Canton 15 Dec 1875   4 Oct 1829   Canton 16 Feb 1887

8 Lewis L. Gibbs   Caroline Bauerise
   Canton 16 Oct 1833   Canton   Illesheim,Bayern,Ger.
                                              1 Jan 1833
   Canton 16 Apr 1914   1 Jan 1856   Canton 7 May 1900

9 Alvin J. Gibbs   Eva Ann Wenrich
   Canton 28 Jan 1868   Wernersville,   Wernersville
                            PA   4 Nov 1873
   Canton 12 Sep 1958   12 Oct 1893   Canton 25 Jan 1962

   Inheritor: Stephen V. Gibbs (son)

GIBBS, MARION BARR JONES (MRS. FREDERICK R.)

Nat. #356-B. Elected 24 Aug 1979. b. 1 Nov 1900. m. Fairfield, CT 20 Apr 1941, Frederick R. Gibbs, b. Washington,DC 11 Jan 1889. Member: Hereditary Order of Desc. of Colonial Governors; Colonial Dames in District of Columbia; Daus. of Colonial Wars in District of Columbia. Address: 4450 Volta Place,N.W., Washington,DC 20007. Descended from:

1 John Cranston, Governor of Rhode Island 1678-80

2 Samuel Cranston   (1)   Mary Hart
   Newport,RI 16 Aug 1659 Newport   Newport 1663
   Newport 26 Apr 1727   1680   Newport 17 Sep 1710

3 John Cranston   Penelope Godfrey
   Newport 4 Aug 1684   Newport   1685
   Newport 15 Oct 1745   c.1700   Newport 18 Mar 1761

4 James Cranston   Eunice Richmond
   Jamestown,RI c.1712   Newport   Little Compton,RI
                                            23 Sep 1722
   bf.6 Oct 1740   14 May 1739   -----

5 Richmond Cranston   Sarah Hookey
   Newport 24 Dec 1740   Newport   Newport 17 Sep 1742
   Newport 12 Mar 1775   15 Jul 1765   af.1782

6 James Cranston   Anne Hempstead
   Newport 5 May 1768   Stonington,CT Stonington 26 Jun 1773
   Ontario,Can. 6 Jun 1814 Jul 1792   Stonington 3 Jul 1810

7 Richmond Cranston   Chloe Hyde Collier
   Stonington 27 Feb 1804 Norwich,CT   Norwich 13 Apr 1807
   Brooklyn,NY 30 Oct 1883 28 Jan 1827   Brooklyn 15 Dec 1880

8 Mary Cranston   Henry Augustus Jones
   Woolaston,MA 2 May 1835 New London,CT Boston,MA 19 Nov 1827
   20 Nov 1886   17 May 1859   New York,NY 20 Mar 1900

9 William Jones   Isabel Barr
   Roxbury,MA 25 Dec 1860 Geneva,Switz. Pittsburgh,PA 21 Mar
                                            1868
   -----   23 Aug 1893   -----

SUPPLEMENT NO. 1

1 Samuel Cranston, Governor of Rhode Island

2 John Cranston   Penelope Godfrey

   Continue with Generation 3 of her lineage from Governor John
   Cranston.

GIBSON, AIMEE B. FROST (MRS. ZACHARY L.)

Nat. #102-B. Elected 26 Jun 1964. b. Concord,MA 17 Jul 1894.
m. Hoboken,NJ 11 Feb 1926, Zachary Lewis Gibson, b. Louisville,
KY 4 Jul 1880. Issue: Lee Gibson Collison, b. Concord,NH 5 Aug
1931. Member: Hereditary Order of Desc. of Colonial Governors;
Dau. of American Revolution; Colonial Dames XVII Century (Past
Regent,FL); U.S. Dau. of 1812 (Past Treasurer,FL); Soc. of New
England Women (Past Pres.FL); Children of American Revolution;
Dau. of Founders and Patriots; Dau. of American Colonists; Dames
of Court of Honor; Women Desc. of Ancient and Honorable Artillery
Co. (Treasurer,FL); National Huguenot Soc.; Magna Charta Dames;
Soc. of Desc. of King William the First, Conqueror and His
Companions at Arms; Soc. of Desc. of Knights of Most Noble Order
of the Garter; Sovereign Colonial Soc. of Americans of Royal
Descent. Descended from:

1 Thomas Dudley, Governor of Massachusetts 1634-35, 1640-41,
  1645-46, 1650-51

2 Patience Dudley   Daniel Denison
  England c.1615   Ipswich,MA   Stratford,Eng. c.1611
  Ipswich 8 Feb 1689/90 18 Oct 1632   Ipswich 17 Oct 1682

3 Elizabeth Denison   John Rogers
  Ipswich 10 Apr 1642   -----   Coggeswell,Eng. 12 Jan
                                            1630
  Ipswich 13 Jun 1732   1660   2 Jul 1684

4 John Rogers   Martha Whittingham
  Ipswich 7 Jul 1666   Ipswich   Ipswich c.1670
  Ipswich 28 Dec 1745   4 Mar 1691   9 Mar 1759

5 John Rogers   Susannah Whipple
  Ipswich c.1692   -----   -----
  Ipswich c.1773   16 Oct 1718   22 Oct 1779

6 John Rogers   (3)   Abigail Woodward
  Ipswich 7 Aug 1719   -----   -----
  Ipswich 4 Oct 1782   2 Apr 1770   -----

7 Sarah Rogers   Theadore Stanwood
  1 Apr 1774   Gloucester,MA   Gloucester 26 Sep 1775
  Boston,MA 25 Jun 1825 22 Nov 1798   At sea 1814

8 Amelia Sargent Stanwood   Andrew Bigelow
  Gloucester 12 Sep 1806 Groton,MA   Groton 7 Apr 1795
  Boston 1 Oct 1893   26 Jan 1824   Boston c.1885

9 Timothy Bigelow   Louisa Jane Bennett
  15 Mar 1825   -----   Maine 4 Mar 1836
  Boston c.1898   7 Jan 1854   Boston Mar 1881

10 Aimee Stanwood Bigelow   William Lawrence Frost
   23 Dec 1864   -----   Boston 5 Apr 1868
   North Conway,NH   26 Apr 1893   Boston 27 Jul 1938
     30 Sep 1894

   Inheritor: Harry Warren Collison, Jr., Box 43, Maitland,FL
              32751

GOODELL, COL. RALPH HARMER, JR.

Nat. #268-B. Elected 11 Nov 1975. b. Kansas City,KS 23 Oct
1920. m. Kansas City,MO 29 Sep 1946, Olive Susan Bramlette, b.
Fresno,CA 23 Mar 1923, d. Sacramento,CA 7 Jan 1967. Issue:
Ralph Harmer Goodell, III, b. Albuquerque,NM 10 Oct 1950. Educ:
Park College, Parkville,MO, B.A. cum laude; graduate of Air War
College, Air University. Member: Hereditary Order of Desc. of
Colonial Governors; Society of Mayflower Descendants; Sons of
American Revolution; Soc. of Descendants of Colonial Clergy;
Desc. of Founders of Hartford; Huguenot Society, Sons of the
Revolution; Military Order of the Loyal Legion of the U.S.; Sons
of Union Veterans of the Civil War; Native Sons of Kansas.
Military: Colonel, Air Force (32 years active and reserve
service). Address: 5436 West 99 Terrace, Overland Park, KS
66207. Descended from:

1 John Webster, Governor of Connecticut 1656

| 2 | Robert Webster England 1627/8 | ----- | Susannah Treat Pitminster,Eng. Oct 1629 |
| | Hartford,CT 31 May 1676 | 1652 | Hartford 1705 |

| 3 | Jonathan Webster Middletown,CT 9 Jan 1656 | ----- | Dorcas Hopkins ----- |
| | Hartford 1735 | 11 May 1681 | Hartford 1695 |

| 4 | Jonathan Webster Hartford 18 Mar 1681 | ----- | Esther Judd 8 Feb 1686 |
| | Glastonbury 18 Sep 1758 | 14 Dec 1704 | Bernardston,MA 22 Dec 1782 |

| 5 | Jonathan Webster III Hartford 5 Oct 1705 | Hartford | Mabel Risley Hartford |
| | Glastonbury 14 Nov 1781 | Feb 1730 | Glastonbury 2 Jan 1781 |

| 6 | Elizur Webster Glastonbury 30 Sep 1743 | ----- | Ruth Densmore 24 Aug 1747 |
| | 26 Mar 1791 | ----- | 27 Jun 1829 |

| 7 | Elizur Webster E.Hartford 24 Aug 1767 | Hampton,NY | Elizabeth Warren 15 May 1774 |
| | Ripley,NY 8 Mar 1854 | c.1791 | Ripley 17 Dec 1848 |

| 8 | Horace Webster Warsaw,NY 3 Jan 1808 | Gainesville,NY | Mahitable Johnson Suffield,MA 2 May 1810 |
| | Edinboro,PA 18 Mar 1887 | 2 Apr 1833 | Crossingville,PA 1 Oct 1847 |

| 9 | Clorinda Hough Webster Edinboro 12 Jun 1836 | Edinboro | James Adolphus Goodell Edinboro 3 Aug 1835 |
| | Mattoon,IL 24 Oct 1919 | 2 Oct 1856 | Mattoon 13 Apr 1896 |

| 10 | Elmer Ellsworth Goodell Greenup,IL 24 Aug 1862 | Mattoon | Katherine M. Igoe Mattoon 9 Apr 1872 |
| | Kansas City,KS 9 Mar 1931 | 1 Jan 1889 | Los Angeles,CA 22 Feb 1938 |

11 Ralph Harmer Goodell   Jeannette Ethel Duvall
   Kansas City 17 Jun 1895 Olathe,KS   Kansas City 20 Jan 1898
   Kansas City 30 Jul 1953 29 Nov 1919

SUPPLEMENT NO. 1

1 John Alden, Governor of Plymouth Colony 1631-39

2 Elizabeth Alden   William Pabodie (Peabody)
   Plymouth   -----   -----
   -----   -----   -----

3 Elizabeth Pabodie   John Rogers
   Duxbury,MA 24 Apr 1647 Duxbury   c.1640
   Duxbury bf.21 Oct 1679 16 Nov 1666   Barrington,RI 23 Jun
                                             1732

4 Sarah Rogers   Nathaniel Searle
   Duxbury 4 May 1677   -----   Little Compton,RI 9 Jun
                                             1662
   Little Compton 10 Jan   c.1694   Little Compton 5 Feb
     1770   1750

5 Sarah Searle   Thomas Dring
   Little Compton 2 Apr   -----   23 Apr 1704
     1700
   -----   28 Jun 1725   -----

6 Philip Dring   Ruth Stoddard
   7 Sep 1730   -----   1 Oct 1733
   18 Jan 1796   -----   24 Jul 1816

7 Delaney Dring   Robert W. Woodworth
   30 Jun 1752   Little Compton   -----
   -----   27 Feb 1776   -----

8 Delaney Woodworth   Samuel Goodell
   Cambridge,NY 6 Jul   -----   Salem,MA 2 Jun 1778
     1786
   Hopkinton,NY 25 Apr   6 Feb 1804   Hopkinton 10 May 1822
     1859

9 Layton Bentley Goodell   Mary Goodell
                                             (first cousin)
   Hopkinton 4 Aug 1808   -----   c.1807
   Edinboro,PA 7 Jun 1894 c.1828   Edinboro 17 Jun 1877

10 James Adolphus Goodell   Clorinda Hough Webster

   Continue with Generation 9 of his lineage from Governor John
   Webster.

   Inheritor: Ralph Harmer Goodell III (son)

GOODSELL, PERCY HAMILTON

Nat. #974. Elected 22 Feb 1931. b. Hartford,CT 24 Sep 1910.
Educ: Yale University, B.A. 1934. Member: Hereditary Order of
Desc. of Colonial Governors; Desc. of Signers of Declaration of
Independence (Hon. Pres. Gen.); Society of Cincinnati, (CT, Past
Pres.); Soc. of Colonial Wars (Registrar General; NY, Past
Genealogist; CT, Past Gov.); Soc. of Mayflower Descendants; St.
Nicholas Soc. of the City of New York; Sons of the Revolution;
Huguenot Soc. of America; Soc. of War of 1812; Military Order of
Loyal Legion of the U.S.; Colonial Lords of Manors in America;
Desc. of Illegitimate Sons and Dau. of Kings of Britain; Desc. of
the Founders of Hartford; CT Soc. of Genealogists; NY Genealogi-
cal and Biographical Soc.; N.E. Historic and Genealogical Soc.;
CT Historical Soc.; Cheshire Historical Soc.; Antiquarian and
Landmarks Soc. of CT; Nat. Trust for Hist. Preservation.. Occup:
Genealogist. Address: "Pandemonium," Tress Road, Cheshire,CT
06410. Descended from:

1 William Bradford, Governor of Plymouth Colony 1621-57

2 William Bradford   (1)   Alice Richards
  Plymouth,MA 17 Jun 1624 Plymouth   Weymouth,MA 16 Jun 1627
  Plymouth 30 Feb 1703/4 28 Jan 1650   Plymouth 12 Dec 1671

3 Alice Bradford   William Adams
  Kingston,MA 1662   Plymouth   Ipswich,MA 27 May 1650
  Canterbury,CT 10 Mar   27 Mar 1680   Dedham,MA 17 Aug 1685
  1745

4 Elizabeth Adams   Samuel Whiting
  Dedham 21 Feb 1681   Norwich,CT   Hartford,CT 22 Apr 1670
  New Haven,CT 21 Dec   14 Sep 1696   Enfield,CT 21 Sep 1725
  1766

5 Mary Whiting   Thomas Clap
  Windham 24 Nov 1712   Windham,CT   Scituate,MA 26 Jun 1703
  New Haven 9 Aug 1736   23 Nov 1727   New Haven 7 Jan 1767

6 Temperance Clap   Timothy Pitkin
  Windham 29 Apr 1732   Farmington,CT   E.Hartford 13 Jan 1727
  Farmington 19 May 1772 9 Aug 1753   Farmington 8 Jul 1812

7 Katharine Pitkin   Nathan Perkins
  Farmington 22 Feb 1757 Farmington   Norwich 11 May 1748
  W.Hartford 13 Sep 1837 17 Nov 1774   W.Hartford 18 Jan 1838

8 Catherine Perkins   Charles Seymour
  W.Hartford 20 Jan 1782 Hartford   W.Hartford 17 Jan 1777
  Hartford 19 Feb 1848   20 Dec 1803   Hartford 21 Jan 1852

9 Catherine Seymour   Calvin Day
  Hartford 25 May 1806   Hartford   Westfield,MA 26 Feb
                                            1803
  Charleston,SC 3 Mar   5 Dec 1827   Hartford 10 Jun 1884
  1884

10 Katharine P. Day   Joseph C. Jackson
   Hartford 24 Feb 1837   Hartford   Newark,NJ 5 Aug 1835
   Hartford 25 Nov 1914   12 Oct 1864   New York,NY 22 May 1913

11 Katharine S. Jackson   Percy H. Goodsell
   NYC 21 Oct 1871   Hartford   NYC 13 Sep 1876
   Purchase,NY 1 Jun 1959 4 Dec 1909   Purchase 28 May 1950

SUPPLEMENT NO. 1

1 George Willys, Governor of Connecticut 1642

2 Samuel Willys   Ruth Haynes
   Fenny Compton,   -----   c.1639
     Warwickshire
   bp. Feb 1631
   Hartford 30 May 1709   1654   c.1688

3 Mabel Willys   Timothy Woodbridge
   c.1658   -----   Barford-St.Martins,
                                                  Wilts 13 Jan 1656
   21 Dec 1698   1685   Hartford 30 Apr 1732

4 Mary Woodbridge   William Pitkin
   Hartford bp.19 Jun 1692 -----   E.Hartford 30 Apr 1694
   E.Hartford 17 Feb 1766 7 May 1724   E.Hartford 1 Oct 1769

5 Timothy Pitkin   Temperance Clap

   Continue with Generation 6 of his lineage from Governor
   William Bradford.

SUPPLEMENT NO. 2

1 John Haynes, Governor of Connecticut 1639-54

2 Ruth Haynes   Samuel Willys

   Continue with Generation 2 of his lineage from Governor
   George Willys.

SUPPLEMENT NO. 3

1 Thomas Dudley, Governor of Massachusetts 1634-51

2 Mercy Dudley   John Woodbridge
   England 27 Sep 1621   -----   Stanton,Eng. 1613
   Newbury,MA 1 Jul 1691   1639   Newbury 17 Mar 1695

3 Timothy Woodbridge   Mabel Willys

   Continue with Generation 3 of his lineage from Governor
   George Willys.

SUPPLEMENT NO. 4

1 Thomas Welles, Governor of Connecticut 1655-58

2 Sarah Welles   John Chester
   1631   -----   Watertown,MA 3 Aug 1635
   Wethersfield,CT   Feb 1653/4   Wethersfield 23 Feb
     12 Dec 1698   1698

3 John Chester   Hannah Talcott
   Wethersfield 10 Jun   -----   1665
     1656
   Wethersfield 14 Dec   25 Nov 1686   Wethersfield 23 Jul
     1711   1741

4 Penelope Chester   Ebenezer Williams
   Wethersfield 18 Nov   -----   2 Aug 1690
     1693
   27 Jun 1764   24 May 1716   28 Mar 1753

5 Hannah Williams   Jabez Huntington
   Pomfret,CT 23 Jul 1726   -----   Norwich,CT 7 Aug 1719
   Norwich 25 Mar 1807   10 Jul 1746   Norwich 5 Oct 1786

6 Hannah Huntington   Joshua Huntington
   Norwich 3 Nov 1750   Norwich   Norwich 16 Aug 1751
   Norwich 23 Apr 1815   11 Dec 1771   Norwich 1 Feb 1821

7 Elizabeth Huntington   Frederick Wolcott
   Norwich 6 Mar 1774   Norwich   Litchfield,CT 2 Nov
                                                  1767
   Litchfield 2 Apr 1812   12 Oct 1800   Litchfield 28 May 1837

8 Elizabeth Wolcott   John P. Jackson
   Litchfield 6 Mar 1806   Litchfield   Acquackanonk,NJ 8 Jun
                                                  1805
   Newark,NJ 15 Oct 1875   22 May 1827   Newark 10 Dec 1861

9 Joseph C. Jackson   Katharine P. Day

Continue with Generation 10 of his lineage from Governor
William Bradford.

                          SUPPLEMENT NO. 5

1 Roger Wolcott, Governor of Connecticut 1750-64

2 Oliver Wolcott   Laura Collins
   S.Windsor,CT 20 Nov   -----   Guilford,CT 1 Jan
     1726   1732/3
   Litchfield 1 Dec 1797   21 Jan 1755   Litchfield 19 Apr 1794

3 Frederick Wolcott   Elizabeth Huntington

Continue with Generation 7 of his lineage from Governor
Thomas Welles.

                          SUPPLEMENT NO. 6

1 William Leete, Governor of Connecticut 1676-83

2 John Leete   Mary Chittenden
   Guilford,CT 1639   Guilford   Guilford 1647
   Guilford 25 Nov 1692   4 Oct 1670   Guilford 9 Mar 1712

3 Anne Leete   John Collins
   Guilford 5 Aug 1671   Guilford   Branford,CT 1 Mar 1665
   Guilford 22 Nov 1724   23 Jul 1691   Guilford 24 Jan 1751

```
4   Daniel Collins                              Lois Cornwall
    Guilford 13 Jun 1701    -----               bp. 8 Feb 1702
    8 Oct 1751              15 Mar 1725         Litchfield,CT 4 Jan 1768

5   Laura Collins                               Oliver Wolcott
    Guilford 1 Jan 1732/3   -----               S.Windsor,CT 20 Nov 1726
    Litchfield 19 Apr 1794  21 Jan 1755         Litchfield 1 Dec 1797

6   Frederick Wolcott                           Elizabeth Huntington
```

Continue with Generation 7 of his lineage from Governor Thomas
Welles.

SUPPLEMENT NO. 7

1   John Webster, Governor of Connecticut 1656

```
2   Robert Webster                              Susannah Treat
    c.1627                  Wethersfield,       Pitminster, Somerset
                           CT                  bp. 8 Oct 1629
    1676                   c.1652               1705

3   Elizabeth Webster                           John Seymour
    Hartford bp.8 Feb 1673  Hartford,CT         Hartford 12 Jun 1666
    Hartford 15 May 1754    19 Dec 1693         Hartford 17 May 1748

4   Timothy Seymour                             Rachel Alleyn
    W.Hartford 27 Jun 1696  W.Hartford          20 Aug 1694
    W.Hartford 8 Sep 1749   27 Apr 1727         1756

5   Charles Seymour                             Lucy Whitman
    W.Hartford bp.29 Jan    W.Hartford          W.Hartford 10 Jan 1745
      1738
    W.Hartford 16 May 1802  3 Dec 1767          W.Hartford 4 May 1810

6   Charles Seymour                             Catherine Perkins
```

Continue with Generation 8 of his lineage from Governor William
Bradford.

GREGG, COL. CLIFFORD CILLEY

Nat. #58-B. Elected 14 Jan 1963. b. Cincinnati,OH 9 Jul 1895.
m. Fowler,IN 8 May 1918, Marian Van Natta, b. Fowler 30 Nov 1897.
Issue: Frank VanNatta Gregg, b. Toledo,OH 21 Apr 1919; John B.
Gregg, b. Boston,MA 15 Dec 1921; Clifford C. Gregg, Jr., b. Park
Ridge,IL 27 Mar 1930. Educ: University of Cincinnati, B.Sc. and
LLD.; Willamette University, ScD. Member: Hereditary Order of
Desc. of Colonial Governors; Sons of American Revolution (Past
Pres.,IL); Soc. of Mayflower Desc. (Past Gov.,IL); Soc. of
Colonial Wars (Past Gov.,IL); Order of First Families of Virginia;
The Pilgrim John Howland Soc.; National Huguenot Soc. (Past Pres.
Gen.); Soc. of Desc. of Colonial Clergy (Member of the Council);
Baronial Order of Magna Charta; Order of Crown of Charlemagne in
U.S.A.; Military Order of Crusades; Huguenot Memorial Soc.,Oxford,
MA; New England Hist. and Genealogical Soc.; Military Order of
World Wars. Occup: Col. U.S. Army, Ret.; Past Director, Field
Museum of Natural History, Chicago,IL. Address: 7450 Olivetas Ave.
Apt. D-12, La Jolla,CA 92037. Descended from:

1 Thomas Mayhew, Governor of Martha's Vineyard 1647-81

2 Hannah Mayhew   Thomas Doggett
   Watertown,MA 15 Apr   -----   Watertown c.1630
   1635
   Martha's Vineyard 1722 1657   Martha's Vineyard 1691

3 Thomas Doggett   Elizabeth Hawes
   Martha's Vnyd.1658   Martha's Vnyd. 5 Oct 1662
   Martha's Vnyd. 25 Aug 22 Jan 1684   Martha's Vnyd. 1733
   1726

4 Jemima Doggett   Malachi Butler
   Martha's Vnyd. 1694   Martha's Vnyd. Martha's Vnyd. 1689
   Martha's Vnyd.   -----   -----

5 Benjamin Butler   Dorcas Abbot
   Windham,CT 9 Apr 1729 Andover,MA   Andover 11 May 1729
   Nottingham,NH 26 Dec   17 Apr 1754   Nottingham 19 Apr 1789
   1804

6 Dorcas Butler   Jonathan Cilley
   Nottingham 9 Oct 1766 Nottingham   Nottingham 8 Mar 1762
   Colerain,OH 22 Oct   5 Jun 1786   Colerain 1807
   1857

7 Bradbury Cilley   Harriet Hedges
   Nottingham 16 May 1798 Colerain   Morristown,NJ
   Colerain 19 Jul 1874   15 Feb 1834   -----

8 Elizabeth Ann Cilley   David Bedinger
   Colerain 12 Jul 1842   Colerain   Richwood,KY 13 Jun 1839
   Jackson,TN 20 Mar 1915 5 Feb 1862   Richwood 13 Mar 1874

9 Ann Elizabeth Bedinger   Ellis Bailey Gregg
   Richwood 27 Sep 1868   Richwood   Macedonia,OH 16 Apr
                                          1856
   Miami,FL 11 Feb 1948   27 Dec 1887   Cincinnati,OH 21 Sep
                                          1936

GRINNELL, HENRY STEPHEN

Nat. #344-B. Elected 22 Jul 1979. b. Franklin,MI 4 Oct 1904.
m. Detroit,MI 6 Jul 1933, Ruth Elizabeth Grinnell Neff,
b. Detroit 11 Nov 1908. Educ: University of Michigan, B.A. 1928.
Member: Hereditary Order of Desc. of Colonial Governors; Soc. of
Mayflower Descendants; Order of Founders and Patriots of
America; Sons of American Revolution. Address: 519 Dickemery
Dr., Akron,OH 44303. Descended from:

1 John Alden, Governor of Plymouth Colony 1664-77.

2 Elizabeth Alden   William Pabodie
   Plymouth 1623   Duxbury,MA   England 1619
   Little·Compton,RI   4 Apr 1644   Little Compton 13 Dec
   31 May 1717   1707

3 Lydia Pabodie   Daniel Grinnell
   Duxbury,MA 3 Apr 1667   Duxbury   Little Compton 1665
   Saybrook,CT 13 Jul 1748 1683   Saybrook 7 Jan 1740/1

4 George Grinnell   Mary Post Bull
   Saybrook 12 Apr 1702   Saybrook   Saybrook 22 Apr 1708
   Saybrook 11 Nov 1759   31 Jan 1725/6   Saybrook 30 Sep 1775

5 Daniel Grinnell   (2)   Ann Chapman
   Westbrook,CT 29 Apr   Westbrook   Westbrook 21 Mar 1731
     1729
   Greenfield,NY 21 Dec   1758   Greenfield 20 May 1814
     1801

6 Daniel Grinnell   Anna Everest
   Westbrook 25 Mar 1752   Westbrook   Westbrook
   -----   22 Feb 1777   -----

7 Daniel Grinnell   Anna Chase
   Saybrook 16 Jan 1789   Saybrook   RI 16 Jun 1785
   Franklin,MI 6 Jul 1855   -----   Franklin 1 May 1855

8 Henry Grinnell   Mary Jane Miller
   Middlebury,NY 16 Sep   Franklin   Howell,MI 1844
     1822
   Franklin 1901   1869   Franklin 21 May 1871

9 Henry Miller Grinnell,Jr.   Alice Atwood Reynolds
   Franklin 5 May 1871   Grosse Ile,MI   Grosse Ile 9 Dec 1872
   Franklin 24 Feb 1904   1894   Detroit,MI 23 Nov 1959

GROSS, MARTHA MaWHINNEY (MRS.)

Nat. #292-B. Elected 28 Apr 1976. b. Flint,MI 27 Sep 1947.
m. Bethesda,MD 18 Oct 1968, Gareth Kelly Gross, b. Vidalia,GA
4 Aug 1946. Member: Hereditary Order of Desc. of Colonial
Governors. Address: Rt. 3, 601 Bell Lake Road, Douglas,GA
31533. Descended from:

1 Thomas Welles, Governor of Connecticut 1655-58

2 Ann Welles   (2)   Anthony Hawkins
   Essex,Eng. c.1619   Farmington   England
   Farmington,CT bf.Dec   af.16 Jul 1656   Farmington 28 Feb 1674
     1680

3 Elizabeth Hawkins   Paul Brinsmade
   Hartford,CT 1659   Connecticut   Stratford,CT
   CT bf.1696   10 Oct 1678   bf. 15 Mar 1696

4 John Brinsmade   Abigail Wheeler
   Darby,CT c.1681   -----   Fairfield,CT 8 Feb 1683
   Milford,CT 19 Jan 1753 -----   -----

5 Mary Brinsmade   Ebenezer Howes
   Stratford Jul 1714   Stratford   Stratford c.1711
   -----   c.1731   -----

6	Sarah Howes	Josiah Burton
	Stratford Jun 1735 — Connecticut	Stratford 6 Jun 1732
	Manchester,VT 17 Jan — 25 Jan 1756	Manchester 28 May 1793
	1832	

6 Sarah Howes   Josiah Burton
    Stratford Jun 1735   Connecticut   Stratford 6 Jun 1732
    Manchester,VT 17 Jan   25 Jan 1756   Manchester 28 May 1793
     1832

7 Samuel Burton   Anne Chamberlain
    Stratford 11 Jul   Rutland,VT   Sandisfield,MA 13 Sep
     1767   1769
    Malone,NY 27 Jul 1834   22 Aug 1793   Malone 22 Dec 1828

8 Curtis Burton   Mabel Spencer
    Manchester 21 Jan 1795   Middlebury,VT   Hartford bf.1790
    E.Cleveland,OH 12 Oct   c.1818   E.Cleveland 14 Aug
     1861   1834

9 James Burton   (2)   Harriet Johnson
    Malone 16 Apr 1821   Fenner,NY   Fenner 23 Aug 1825
    Milwaukee,WI 13 May   c.1850   Fenner 31 Jan 1860
     1885

10 James E. Burton   Louise Bailey
    Milwaukee 28 Jun 1857   Whitewater,WI   Koshkonong,WI 4 Apr
                                       1858
    Whitewater 21 May 1927   1 Oct 1878   Milwaukee 11 Mar 1934

11 Frances-Eva Burton   William Thomas MaWhinney
    Whitewater 12 Feb 1891   Hammond,IN   Lima,WI 24 Aug 1886
    -----   3 Sep 1910   -----

12 William Dana MaWhinney   Madolin May Kelly
    Milwaukee 7 Oct 1919   Fenton,MI   Flint,MI 15 Dec 1917
    -----   21 Feb 1942   -----

GROSS, MIRIAM I. ZELLER (MRS. RUSSELL CHARLES)

Nat. #108-B. Elected 20 Feb 1965. b. Hennepin,IL 28 Oct 1895.
m. (2) Zelleria Plantations,MS 26 Nov 1927, Russell Charles
Gross, b. Philadelphia,PA 27 May 1892. Issue: Ruth Adora Gross.
Educ: Huntingdon College, B.A.; Temple University. Member:
Hereditary Order of Desc. of Colonial Governors; Dau. of Founders
and Patriots of America; Soc. of Mayflower Desc.; Women Desc. of
Ancient and Honorable Artillery Co. (Past Pres.NY); Huguenot Soc.
of America; U.S. Dau. of 1812 (Life Hon. Pres.NJ); Dau. of
American Revolution; Dames of Court of Honor. Address: C/O Bove-
3 Briarcliff Rd., Morris Plains,NJ 07950. Descended from:

1 William Hooke, Governor of Maine 1638-40

2 William Hooke   Mary (Follonsby) Pike
    Kittery,ME c.1665   -----   -----
    1743   c.1691   -----

3 Mary Hooke   Stephen Bennett
    1710   -----   20 Jan 1707
    18 Jun 1788   -----   Gloucester,MA 1790

4 Judith Bennett   Ebenezer Bray
    2 Sep 1739   -----   18/19 Apr 1732
    30 Jan 1799   -----   24 Feb 1817

5	Thomas Bray	int.	Cynthia Record
	Turner,ME 21 Sep 1778	-----	20 Aug 1778
	27 Mar 1842	30 Dec 1797	20 Sep 1819
6	Cynthia Bray		James Spaulding
	Minot,ME 25 Mar 1802	-----	Buckfield 10 Jun 1802
	Buckfield,ME 11 Dec	5 Jun 1825	Earlville,IL 31 Oct
	1864		1886
7	Emma Frances Spaulding		John Emory Bryant
	Buckfield 16 Feb 1844	Buckfield	Wayne,ME 13 Oct 1836
	Manteno,IL 2 May 1901	26 Jun 1864	New York,NY 27 Feb
			1900
8	Emma Alice Bryant		Julius Christian Zeller
	Atlanta,GA 16 Nov	Mount Vernon,	Spring Bay,IL 15 Dec
	1871	NY	1871
	East Orange,NJ 26 Apr	1 Jan 1895	Kansas City,MO 10 Mar
	1946		1938

Inheritor: Ruth Adora Gross

GUFFEY, VERITÉ L. GREENE (MRS.)

Nat. #114-B. Elected 15 May 1965. b. NYC 27 Oct 1921. m.
Seaford,NY 13 Jul 1946 (div.). Issue: Corinne Guffey Babcock,
b. Amityville,NY 21 Jun 1947. Member: Hereditary Order of Desc.
of Colonial Governors; Dau. of American Revolution; Dau. of
American Colonists; Sons and Dau. of the Pilgrims; Soc. of Desc.
of Colonial Clergy; New England Women; Colonial Dames of XVII
Century. Occup: Banking. Address: 5825 West Lazy "S" St.,
Tucson,AZ 85713. Descended from:

1 Thomas Welles, Governor of Connecticut 1655-1658

2	John Welles		Elizabeth Bourne
	England 1621	Stratford,CT	Stratford c.1627
	Stratford 1659	c.1647	-----
3	John Welles		Mary Hollister
	Stratford c.1648	-----	Wethersfield,CT
	Stratford 24 Mar 1713	c.1669	1732
4	Thomas Welles		Sarah Stiles
	-----	-----	3 Nov 1693
	1755	31 Aug 1710	-----
5	Gideon Welles		Eunice Walker
	CT 12 Nov 1719	-----	c.1720
	CT 19 Oct 1805	-----	Huntington,CT 18 Jan
			1805
6	Martha Welles		Blackleach Burritt
	Connecticut	-----	Stratford 1740/2
	1786	1765	Winhall,VT 27 Aug
			1792

7 Diantha Burritt   John Gray
  Poundridge,NY 9 Jan   Winhall   Canaan,NY 15 Dec 1769
  1776
  Sheridan,NY 14 Oct   26 May 1793   Forestville,NY 24 Apr
  1846   1859

8 Alfred W. Gray   Valeria E. Dodd
  Sherburne,NY 15 Apr   -----   Sacketts,NY
  1802
  Milwaukee,WI 8 Jan 1873 12 May 1823/5   -----

9 Mary E. Gray   Danford M. Crosby
  Watertown,NY 18 Jul   Jamestown,NY   Brattleboro,VT 19 Feb
  1830   1828
  Grand Rapids,MI 23 Apr   14 Jun 1849   Grand Rapids 19 Jan
  1898   1897

10 Hattie Valeria Crosby   Amos DeCourcey Greene
   Ionia,MI 12 Jan 1857   Grand Rapids   Huron Co.OH 29 Dec
                                                1853
   Grand Rapids 25 Mar   10 Oct 1877   Peoria,IL 1 May 1910
   1899

11 Alfred DeCourcey Greene   Lillian B. Peters
   Grand Rapids 31 Jul   Lansing,MI   Detroit,MI 26 Nov 1898
   1878
   Meadbrook,NY 12 Oct   23 Aug 1916   -----
   1949

   Inheritor: Corinne Yvonne Guffey Babcock

                                H

HADEN, EUNICE BARNARD (MISS)

Nat. #281-B. Elected 1 Mar 1976. Educ: Oberlin College,OH,
B.A. in Fine Arts. Member: Hereditary Order of Desc. of
Colonial Governors; Soc. of New England Women; Soc. of Desc. of
Colonial Clergy; Dau. of American Revolution; Women Desc. of
Ancient and Honorable Artillery Co.; American Clan Gregor Soc.;
Flagon and Trencher; Nantucket (MA) Historical Assn.; New
England Historic and Genealogical Soc.; National Trust for
Historic Preservation. Address: 5112 Connecticut Ave., N.W.,
Washington,DC 20008. Descended from:

1 Tristram Coffin (Coffyn), Governor of Nantucket 1671-73

2 James Coffin   Mary Severans
   England 12 Aug 1640   Salisbury,MA   Salisbury 5 Jun 1645
   Nantucket,MA 28 Jul   3 Dec 1663   Massachusetts
   1720

3 Dinah Coffin   Nathaniel Starbuck,Jr.
   pb.Nantucket May 1674   Nantucket   Nantucket 9 Aug 1668
   Nantucket 1 Aug 1750   20 Nov 1690   Nantucket 29 Nov 1752
                                                  or 9 Feb 1753

4   Elizabeth Starbuck   George Hussey, Sr.
    Nantucket 27 Nov 1698   Nantucket   Nantucket 21 Jun 1694
    Nantucket 9 Feb 1770   12 Sep 1717   Nantucket 7 Jun 1782

5   Deborah Hussey   Peter Coffin
    Nantucket 11 Aug 1721   Nantucket   Nantucket 26 Dec 1717
    Nantucket 9 Feb 1785   10 Feb 1738   Nantucket 4 Mar 1799

6   Elizabeth Coffin   int.   Andrew Myrick, Jr.
    Nantucket 25 Aug 1745   Nantucket   MA 15 Sep 1741
    Nantucket 27 Apr 1788   Dec 1763   Nantucket 10 Mar 1816

7   Elizabeth Myrick   Zophar Hayden (Haden)
    Nantucket 16 Dec 1781   Nantucket   England 1 Jul 1775
    Nantucket 16/7 Apr 1828   11 Jan 1799   New York,NY 31 Aug 1837

8   George Haden   Eunice S. Barnard
    Nantucket 11 Jun 1801   Nantucket   Nantucket 6 Jan 1803
    Union Co.IN 3 Jun 1878   7 Nov 1822   Union Co. 11 Jul 1853

9   Charles (William) Haden   (2)   Rhoda Virginia Mount
    Nantucket 27 Apr 1827   Guthrie Co.IA   Morgan Co.OH 28 Jun
                                                 1841
    Panora,IA 22 Jan 1907   25 Aug 1861   Panora 1 Nov 1933

10 Charles Franklin Haden   Susan Eudora Benton
    Guthrie Center,IA   Baltimore,MD   Washington,DC 18 Jun
      2 Jul 1862   1863
    Washington,DC 24 Sep   6 Nov 1889   Washington,DC 26 Jun
      1942   1951

HALBERSTADT, JAMES FRANKLIN, JR.

Nat. #343-B.   Elected 23 Jul 1979.   b. Pleasant Mills,IN 3 Oct
1912.   m. Jacksboro,TN 2 Oct 1939, Willodean Ellenberger, b.
Adams Co.IN 9 Feb 1916.   Member: Hereditary Order of Desc. of
Colonial Governors; Soc. of Colonial Wars,MS; Sons of Union
Veterans of Civil War,IN; Soc. of Desc. of Colonial Clergy; Soc.
of War of 1812,IL; Sons and Dau. of the Soddies Inc.   Address:
227 South First Street, Decatur,IN 46733.   Descended from:

1   Thomas Dudley, Governor of Massachusetts 1634-40, 1645-50

2   Anne Dudley   Simon Bradstreet
    England c.1612   England   Horbling,Eng. c.1603
    Andover,MA 16 Sep 1672   c.1628   Salem,MA 27 Mar 1697

3   John Bradstreet   Sarah Perkins
    Andover 22 Jul 1653   -----   MA 2 Mar 1657
    Topsfield,MA 17 Jan   11 Jun 1677   MA Apr 1745
      1717/18

4   Mercy Bradstreet   John Hazen
    2 Jun 1689   -----   Boxford,MA 23 Mar 1687
    Norwich,CT 22 Nov 1725   c.1710   24 Feb 1772

5 John Hazen   Deborah Peck
   Lyme,CT 21 Feb 1710/11 Lyme   -----
   -----   10 Mar 1736/7 -----

6 Nathaniel Hazen   Mary Bell
   Lyme 17 Mar 1745   -----   24 Oct 1748
   Beaver Co.PA 3 Nov 1835 27 Nov 1768   Beaver Co. 29 Dec 1834

7 John Hazen   Rebecca Townsend
   10 Nov 1773   -----   Washington Co.PA 1774
   Oreville,PA 12 Jun 1851 c.1798   Oreville 1 Apr 1868

8 John Hazen   Rebecca Caster
   North Sewickley,PA   -----   PA 5 Jul 1810
      7 Jun 1810
   Seymour,IL 19 Dec 1894   c.1830/1   Seymour 18 Mar 1893

9 James Louis Hazen   Adeline Davis
   Dearborn Co.IN 22 Feb   -----   Dearborn Co. Nov 1841
      1836
   Seymour 16 Apr 1907   20 Aug 1857   Sherwood,MI 3 Mar 1927

10 Anna Hazen   Franklin Pierce
                                                       Halberstadt
   Ripley Co.IN 19 Nov   -----   Franklin Co.IN 29 Sep
      1864   1853
   Pleasant Mills,IN   6 Jan 1881   Colon,MI 25 Feb 1940
      10 Dec 1945

11 James Franklin   Flava Ploughe
      Halberstadt, Sr.
   Champaign Co.IL 3 Jul   Clinton Co.IN   Tipton Co.IN 20 Jun
      1881   1886
   Van Wert Co.OH 1 Dec   15 Sep 1905   Ven Wert Co. 1 Jan 1971
      1969

   Inheritor: Byron Douglas Halberstadt, 125 Hickory Knoll,
   Buffton,IN 46714

HALL, CATHERINE E. (MISS)

Nat. #135-B. Elected 16 Feb 1968. b. Newark,NJ 27 Dec 1947.
Educ: Finch College,NYC. Member: Hereditary Order of Desc. of
Colonial Governors; Soc. of Desc. of Colonial Clergy; Dau. of
American Revolution; Colonial Lords of Manors in America. Occup:
Insurance Broker. Address: "Pinecroft," Harter Rd., Morristown,
NJ 07960. Descended from:

1 Thomas Mayhew, Governor of Martha's Vineyard 1647-81

Same lineage as her father, Warren S. Hall, Jr., 42-B.

HALL, MARGARET S. (MISS)

Nat. #137-B. Elected 16 Feb 1968. b. Morristown,NJ 24 Dec 1950.
Educ: Briarcliff College, NY, B.A. Member:Hereditary Order of
Desc. of Colonial Governors; Soc. of Desc. of Colonial Clergy;
Dau. of American Revolution; Colonial Lords of Manors in America.
Occup: Cartographer. Address: "Pinecroft," Harter Rd.,
Morristown,NJ 07960. Descended from:

1 Thomas Mayhew, Governor of Martha's Vineyard 1647-81

Same lineage as her father, Warren S. Hall,Jr., 42-B.

HALL, SARAH L. (MISS)

Nat. #136-B. Elected 16 Feb 1968. b. Montclair,NJ 21 Jul 1949.
Educ: University of Colorado, B.A., Spanish Major. Member:
Hereditary Order of Desc. of Colonial Governors; Soc. of Desc.
of Colonial Clergy; Dau. of American Revolution; Colonial Lords
of Manors in America. Occup: Assistant Buyer for Bloomingdale.
Address: "Pinecroft," Harter Rd., Morristown,NJ 07960. Descended from:

1 Thomas Mayhew, Governor of Martha's Vineyard 1647-81

Same lineage as her father, Warren S. Hall,Jr., 42-B.

HALL, WARREN SMITH, JR.

Nat. #42-B. Elected 26 Sep 1961. b. Allentown,PA 11 Feb 1906.
m. South Orange,NJ 11 Nov 1946, Rita Wismar Eichhorn, b. Newark,
NJ 22 May 1914. Issue: Catherine E. Hall, b. Newark 27 Dec
1947; Sarah L. Hall, b. Montclair,NJ 21 Jul 1949; Margaret S.
Hall, b. Morristown,NJ 24 Dec 1950. Educ: Stevens Institute of
Technology, Licensed Professional Engineer in NJ. Member:
Hereditary Order of Desc. of Colonial Governors (Hon. Governor
General); St. Nicholas Soc. of New York (Secretary-Member Board
of Managers); Colonial Lords of Manors in America; Soc. of
Colonial Wars in NY and NJ; Sons of American Revolution (NJ State
Registrar); Sons of the Revolution in NY and NJ; Soc. of Desc.
of Colonial Clergy; New England Soc. Occup: Engineering, Heavy
Construction. Honors: On staff of Port of New York Authority
Engineers that built the first tube of the Lincoln Tunnel.
Address: "Pinecroft," Harter Road, Morristown,NJ 07960.
Descended from:

1 Thomas Mayhew, Governor of Martha's Vineyard 1647-81

2	Hannah Mayhew		Thomas Doggett
	Watertown,MA 15 Apr	-----	Martha's Vnyd. c.1630
	1635		
	Martha's Vineyard,MA	c.1657	Martha's Vnyd. 1691
	1722		

```
3   John Doggett                            Sarah
    Martha's Vnyd. 1662      -----          -----
    Attleboro,MA 7 Sep 1724  c.1685         -----

4   Jane Doggett                            Caleb Hall
    c.1700                   Attleboro       c.1700
    -----                   9 Nov 1721      1 Oct 1791

5   Reuben Hall                             Sarah
    Attleboro 14 Mar        -----           -----
    1729/30
    Warwick,NY af.1800      -----           -----

6   John Hall                               Sarah Moore
    Peekskill,NY 9 May      -----           -----
    1758
    Orange Co.NY bf.1847    -----           -----

7   Nathan Hall                             Prudence McDonel
    New York c.1804         Warwick         -----
    New York                6 Dec 1827      bf.1850

8   Joel M. Hall                            Harriet Smith
    Warwick 19 Feb 1831     New York,NY     Orange Co. 10 Sep 1844
    Monroe,NY 19 Apr 1901   1869            Monroe 28 May 1878

9   Warren Smith Hall                       Jessie Magdalen Scanlon
    Monroe 12 Aug 1871      -----           Moscow,PA 8 Nov 1880
    Morristown,NJ 10 Mar    26 Apr 1905     Montclair,NJ 25 Dec
    1960                                    1955
```

HALLOWELL, THOMAS JEWETT, JR.

Nat. #110-B. Elected 3 Apr 1965. b. New York,NY 9 May 1908.
m. Ballston Spa,NY 8 Sep 1937, Marian Lavinia Hewitt, b. Plainfield,NJ 14 Mar 1910. Issue: Peter Sand Hallowell, b. 18 May
1938; Robert Hewitt S. Hallowell, b. 4 Jun 1941; Frederick
Hayward Hallowell, b. 17 May 1945; all b. NYC. Educ: St. Paul's,
Concord,NH; Westminster, Simsbury,CT. Member: Hereditary Order
of Desc. of Colonial Governors; Soc. of Colonial Wars,NY; Soc.
of Mayflower Desc.; Order of Founders and Patriots of America;
Sons of Revolution; Order of the Crown of Charlemagne; The
Plantagenet Soc.; Desc. of Armorial Ancestry; Desc. of Knights
of the Garter; Desc. of Americans of Royal Descent. Address:
R.D. #1, Box 845, Northport, L.I., NY 11768. (From Society's
Records). Descended from:

1   William Bradford, Governor of Plymouth Colony, 1621-33,
    1635-57

```
2   William Bradford            (1)         Alice Richards
    Plymouth,MA 17 Jun      Plymouth        Weymouth,MA 16 Jun
    1624                                    1627
    Plymouth 20 Feb 1703/4  28 Jan 1650     Plymouth 12 Dec 1671

3   Hannah Bradford                         Joshua Ripley
    Plymouth 9 May 1662     Plymouth        Hingham,MA 9 Nov 1658
    Windham,CT 28 May 1738  28 Nov 1628     Windham 8 May 1739
```

4	Leah Ripley	Samuel Cook
	Windham 17 Apr 1693	Windham	Cambridge,MA 3 Dec 1690
	-----	14 Mar 1716	-----
5	Rebecca Cook	Caleb Jewett
	Windham 20 Nov 1718	Scotland,CT	Norwich,CT 25 Jun 1710
	Sharon,CT 15 Jul 1764	3 Feb 1735	18 Jan 1778
6	Thaddeus Jewett	Ann Webster
	Sharon 17 Dec 1746	-----	Hartford Co.MD 6 Sep 1745
	At sea 1782	9 Apr 1772	Hartford Co.
7	John Jewett	Susanna Judge
	Deer Creek,MD 7 Mar 1777	-----	Uwchland,PA 21 Dec 1778
	Hartford Co. 28 Jan 1854	16 Jun 1808	Hartford Co. 13 Dec 1853
8	Thomas Lightfoot Jewett (2)	Ann Haines
	Hartford Co. 9 Apr 1809 Cadiz,OH	Cannonsburgh,PA 11 Dec 1812
	Darlington,MD 3 Nov 1876	18 May 1843	Zanesville,OH 13 Apr 1898
9	Nora Belle Jewett	Charles Hallowell
	Cadiz 7 Feb 1846	Steubens,OH	Philadelphia,PA 13 Aug 1842
	Irvington,NY 24 Apr 1923	21 Jan 1868	Philadelphia 3 Apr 1875
10	Thomas Jewett Hallowell	Marian Ricketson Slocum
	Steubensville 29 Dec 1869	N.Bedford,MA	N.Bedford 1 Aug 1886
	Bedford,MA 12 Feb 1958	15 Jun 1907	

Inheritor: Peter Sand Hallowell

HAMM, RUTH T. BITTING (MRS. JAMES JUSTIN)

Nat.. #242-B. Elected 18 Oct 1974. b. Torrington,WY 3 Jul 1915. m. Ellsworth,IL 22 Jul 1936, James Justin Hamm, b. Hudson,IL 2 Aug 1907. Member: Hereditary Order of Desc. of Colonial Governors; Dau. of American Revolution (Vice Pres. Gen. and IL Regent); Children of American Revolution (Nat. Vice Chmn.); Dau. of Founders and Patriots,IL; Colonial Dau. of Seventeenth Century (Rec. Sec.); Illinois State Genealogical Soc. (Rec. Sec.). Life promoter of CAR; Life member friends of DAR Museum. Honors: listed in Illinois Lives, Two Thousand Women of Achievement 1969. Address: 101 South Broadway, Hudson,IL 61748. Descended from:

1 John Webster, Governor of Connecticut 1656

2	Thomas Webster	Abigail Alexander
	Northampton,MA	Massachusetts	Northampton 1643
	Northfield,MA 1686	16 Jun 1663	bf.1690

3 John Webster   Elizabeth
   Northampton 11 Sep   Lebanon,CT   -----
     1672
   Lebanon 3 Nov 1735   c.1698   -----

4 John Webster   Mary Dewey
   Lebanon 10 Jul 1702   Lebanon   Lebanon 24 Oct 1704
   -----   20 Aug 1724   -----

5 John Webster   Mary Bliss
   Lebanon 29 Nov 1727   Lebanon   Lebanon
   10 May 1750   c.1747   af.1749

6 John Webster   Amy W. Martin
   Lebanon c.1747   Goshen,CT   -----
   Austerlitz,NY 1828   5 Aug 1771   Lebanon 8 Feb 1775

7 John M. Webster   Polly Graves
   Lebanon 8 Feb 1775   -----   6 Oct 1776
   Addison,NY 19 Feb 1842   1796   Mills,PA 13 Apr 1862

8 John M. Webster   Rebecca M. Bacon
   Smithville,NY 18 Apr   -----   1811
     1804
   af.1851   1829/30   1887

9 Marcus P. Webster   Sally Ann Taft
   Addison 9 Jul 1832   Addison   Addison 4 Mar 1835
   Bayard,NE 10 Mar 1914   20 Sep 1854   Bayard 11 Aug 1906

10 Florence A. Webster   Samuel Bitting
   Mankato,MN 8 Jan 1862   Bayard   PA 5 May 1853
   Bayard 25 Mar 1918   16 Jan 1880   Miami,FL 27 Nov 1940

11 Frank L. Bitting   Harriet B. Merwin
   Ft.Kearney,NE 20 Apr   Ellsworth,IL   Ellsworth 29 Sep 1900
     1887
   Normal,IL 15 Feb 1949   24 Jun 1914   (living)

HARDY, ANN RIDGELY (MISS)

Nat. #318-B. Elected 1977. b. New York,NY 10 Sep 1929. Educ:
Wells and Bennington Colleges. Member: Hereditary Order of Desc.
of Colonial Governors; Colonial Dames in State of New York; Dau.
of Founders and Patriots in State of New York. Address: Amenia
Union Rd., Sharon,CT 06069. Descended from:

1 Nicholas Greenberry, Governor of Maryland 1694

2 Katherine Greenberry   Henry Ridgely
   England Jul 1674   -----   Wardridge 3 Oct 1669
   29 Aug 1703   1689   Wardridge 19 Mar 1699

3 Nicholas Ridgely   Mary Vining
   Maryland 12 Sep 1694   Salem,NJ   Salem 5 May 1705
   Dover,DE 16 Feb 1755   23 Dec 1736   Dover 11 Dec 1761

4	Charles Greenberry Ridgely		Ann Moore
	26 Jan 1738	Chester Co.PA	Pennsylvania
	bur.Dover 25 Nov 1785	Jun 1774	-----

5	Henry Moore Ridgely		Sarah Banning
	Dover 6 Aug 1779	Dover	Dover 18 Feb 1787
	Dover 6 Aug 1847	21 Nov 1803	Dover 14 Jan 1837

6	Edward Ridgely		Elizabeth Comegys
	Dover 30 Jan 1831	Dover	Dover 23 Feb 1841
	Dover 17 Nov 1900	22 Jun 1859	Whitestone,NY 11 Nov 1927

7	Harriet Moore Ridgely		Daniel Harrison
	Dover 3 Mar 1862	Dover	Stratford,Canada 31 Aug 1852
	Whitestone 10 Oct 1933	21 Sep 1887	Whitestone 6 Jan 1927

8	Barbara Wyndham Harrison		John Alexander Hardy
	Whitestone 17 Sep 1900	Whitestone	Mt.Vernon,NY 10 May 1899
	Sharon,CT 15 Dec 1976	5 Jun 1926	(living in 1977)

Inheritor: Christopher Ridgely Hardy, 31 Hamilton Ave., Harborne, Birmingham 17, England.

HARRIS, EDWARD PARK

Nat. #179-B. Elected 29 Sep 1971. b. Warsaw,NY 18 Jan 1909. m. Dayton,OH 8 Aug 1934, Mary Elizabeth Smith, b. Springfield, OH 26 Nov 1907. Issue: Edward Park Harris III, b. Rahway,NJ 16 Aug 1942; Mary P. Harris Martin, b. Plainfield,NJ 10 Mar 1945. Educ: Cornell University, M.E. Member: Hereditary Order of Desc. of Colonial Governors; National Assn. Watch and Clock Collectors. Occup: Antique Clock Bus.; Formerly with General Motors Corp. and received 49 patents. Address: 1230 Wabash Avenue, Dayton,OH 45405. Descended from:

1 John Webster, Governor of Connecticut 1656

2	Robert Webster		Susannah Treat
	Cossington,Eng. 1627	Middletown,CT	Pitminster,Eng. 1629
	Hartford,CT May 1676	1652	Hartford,CT 1705

3	Jonathon Webster		Dorcas Hopkins
	Middletown 9 Jan 1656	Hartford	-----
	Hartford 1735	11 May 1681	-----

4	Jonathon Webster		Esther Judd
	CT 18 Mar 1681/2	Connecticut	CT 6 Feb 1686
	CT 18 Sep 1758	Feb 1704	Bernardstown,MA 22 Dec 1782

5	Jonathon Webster		Mabel Risley
	Hartford 5 Oct 1705	Connecticut	Connecticut
	Glastonbury,CT 14 Nov 1781	Feb 1730	Glastonbury 2 Jan 1781

6	Elizur Webster Glastonbury 30 Sep 1743 CT 26 Mar 1791	----- -----	Ruth Densmore 24 Aug 1747 27 Jun 1829
7	William Webster 4 May 1787 Warsaw,NY 17 Aug 1876	----- 28 Apr 1812	Charlotte Phelps ----- Warsaw 7 Jun 1878
8	William Webster Warsaw 15 Dec 1818 Warsaw 19 Sep 1893	Warsaw 10 Apr 1842	Calista Keeney Warsaw 25 May 1821 Warsaw 30 Sep 1893
9	Jay R. Webster Gainesville,NY 23 Jun 1844 Westfield,MA 6 May 1901	----- 18 Aug 1869	Jennie May Fluker ----- 1911
10	Lottie Belle Webster Silver Springs,NY 5 Jan 1871 Warsaw 18 Mar 1951	S. Warsaw,NY ----- 31 Dec 1890	Harry Nehemiah Harris ----- Warsaw 6 Dec 1941

HARRIS, FLORENCE E. CLARKE (MRS. FRANK L.)

Nat. #36-B. Elected 14 Apr 1961. b. Milwaukee,WI 27 Apr 1900.
m. Maryland 21 Feb 1921, Frank L. Harris, b. Wilmington,DE
15 May 1902. Issue: William Clarke Harris, b. 22 Jul 1922;
Frank L. Harris, Jr., b. 11 Sep 1923; both b. Wilmington. Educ:
University of Delaware. Member: Hereditary Order of Desc. of
Colonial Governors; Dau. of American Revolution (Hon. Regent,WI;
Executive Club); Children of American Revolution (Past Vice Pres.
Gen.); American Colonists (Past Pres.); Women Desc. of Ancient
and Honorable Artillery Co. (Past Pres. and Organizer); Magna
Charta Dames; Soc. of Mayflower Desc.; Soc. of Colonial Wars;
Colonial Dames of XVII Century; Racine Co. Historical Soc.
(Past Vice Pres.). Address: 17527 Two Mile Rd., Frankville,WI
53126. Descended from:

1 William Bradford, Governor of Plymouth Colony 1621-33,
   1635-57

2	William Bradford Plymouth,MA 17 Jun 1624 Plymouth 20 Feb 1703/4	(1) ----- 28 Jan 1650	Alice Richards Weymouth,MA 16 Jun 1627 Plymouth 12 Dec 1671
3	Samuel Bradford Plymouth Jul 1668 Duxbury 11 Apr 1714	Plymouth 31 Jul 1689	Hannah Rogers Duxbury,MA 16 Nov 1668 Milton,MA af.16 Jul 1733

4 Elizabeth Bradford   Charles Whiting
   Duxbury 15 Dec 1696   Hartford,CT   Hartford 5 Jul 1692
   Stonington,CT 10 May   10 Jan 1716/7   Montville,CT 7 Mar 1738
   1777

5 Gamaliel Whiting   Annie Gillette
   17 Sep 1727   Great   18 Feb 1738
                           Barrington
   Great Barrington,MA   18 Jun 1752   Great Barrington
   27 Nov 1790   27 Feb 1808

6 William Whiting   Lois Andrews
   Canaan,CT 11 Feb   -----   c.1760
   1757
   11 Mar 1838   4 May 1779   17 Jan 1829

7 Polly Whiting   William S. Smith
   12 Mar 1787   Lenox,MA   11 Jul 1787
   3 Oct 1853   10 Mar 1810   Lenox 14 Mar 1853

8 Mary Ann W. Smith   Ezra S. Clarke
   Lenox 10 Jan 1811   -----   Fairfield,NY 21 Mar
                                                   1811
   Brooklyn,NY 1882   1833   Brooklyn Dec 1892

9 William E. Clarke   Susan Weidau
   Oswego,NY 2 Dec 1848   Boyertown,PA   Boyertown 1852
   Brooklyn 4 Dec 1875   1871   Wilkes-Barre,PA 1900

10 Edward W. Clarke   Elizabeth Shaull
   Wilkes-Barre 9 Feb   Chicago,IL   Tiffin,OH 22 Oct 1863
   1872
   Wilmington,DE 13 Jun   30 Oct 1893   -----
   1946

Inheritor: Susan Elizabeth Harris (Mrs. Robert Ruland)

HATHAWAY, RUTH J. (MRS. CHESTER E.)

Nat. #24-B. Elected 2 Apr 1960. b. Yarmouth,ME 27 May 1896.
m. New York,NY 10 Sep 1921, Chester Erwin Hathaway, b. Somer-
ville,MA 5 Mar 1896. Issue: Susan Elizabeth Hathaway, b.
Portland,ME 24 Sep 1923, d. 27 Sep 1923; Marjorie J. Hathaway
Wall, b. NYC 2 Jan 1930. Educ: North Yarmouth Academy; New
England Conservatory of Music. Member: Hereditary Order of Desc.
of Colonial Governors; Dau. of Founders and Patriots of America
(Past Chaplain,CT); Dau. of American Revolution (Regent, MA and
RI; Chrm. of Gen. Records,CT); National Huguenot Soc.; Dau. of
Colonial Wars; Soc. of Desc. of Colonial Clergy; Soc. of
Mayflower Desc.; Women Desc. of Ancient and Honorable Artillery
Co. Address: 47 Keeney Ave., West Hartford,CT 06107. Descended
from:

1 Thomas Prence, Governor of Plymouth Colony 1634-35, 1638-39,
   1657-73

2 Mercy Prence   John Freeman
   Plymouth,MA 1631   Eastham   Eng. bp.28 Jan 1626/7
   Eastham,MA 28 Sep 1711   13/14 Feb   Eastham 28 Oct 1719
                             1649/50

3 Edmond Freeman   (2)   Sarah Mayo
   Eastham Jun 1657   Eastham   Boston,MA 19 Dec 1660
   Eastham 10 Dec 1717   c.1681   Eastham bf. 15 Mar 1745

4 Mary Freeman   Samuel Hinckley
   -----   Georgetown,ME   Barnstable,MA 24 Sep
                                                1684
   af.26 Mar 1736/7   c.1703   -----

5 Samuel Hinckley   Sarah Miller
   Harwich,MA 7 Feb 1711   -----   -----
   Georgetown 18 Jun 1767   -----   -----

6 Mary Hinckley   Timothy Batchelder
   Brunswick,ME 6 Nov   Georgetown   Kensington,NH 25 Jul
     1740   1744
   Phippsburg,ME 17 Dec   8 Jun 1766   Phippsburg 16 Jul 1816
     1817

7 Sarah Batchelder   Moses Titcomb
   Phippsburg 14 Jun 1772   -----   Falmouth 15 Jun 1767
   N.Yarmouth,ME 20 Dec   12 Apr 1796   N.Yarmouth 20 Oct 1843
     1830

8 Marie Batchelder   Nathaniel Jordan
     Titcomb
   N.Yarmouth 17 Jun 1804   -----   Lisbon,ME 23 Jan 1812
   Yarmouth 28 May 1888   17 Jan 1837   Yarmouth 20 Dec 1879

9 Charles Wilson Jordan   Elsie Medora Johnson
   N.Yarmouth 14 Sep 1850   N.Yarmouth   N.Yarmouth 6 Apr 1858
   Portland,ME 4 Jul 1922   1 Jan 1878   Athol,MA 20 Jul 1937

   Inheritor: Marjorie Hathaway Wall (Mrs. Gordon Baldwin),
   15 Garland Road, West Hartford,CT 06107

HEANEY, MARJORIE A. (MRS. RICHARD C.)

Nat. #327-B. Elected 28 Jun 1978. b. Haverhill,MA 31 Jan 1915.
m. Folkstone,GA 30 Apr 1952, Richard Collier Heaney, b. East
Rochester,NH, 23 Sep 1927, d. Roxbury,MA 10 Oct 1960. Educ:
New Eng. Conservatory of Music, Boston; Stetson University.
Member: Hereditary Order of Desc. of Colonial Governors;
Dau. of American Revolution (Past Regent); Soc. of Mayflower
Desc.; New England Women (Past Pres., Daytona Beach Colony);
Soc. of Desc. of Colonial Clergy; Huguenot Society of FL;
Colonial Dames XVII Century; Dau. of American Colonists; Magna
Charta Dames; Sovereign Colonial Soc. Americans of Royal Desc.;
Desc. of Knights of the Garter; Desc. of Illegitimate Sons and
Dau. of Kings of Britain; Sons and Daus. of First Settlers of
Newbury,MA. Address: Rte. 2, Box 660B, DeLand,FL 32720.
Descended from:

1   Thomas Dudley, Governor of Massachusetts 1634, 1640, 1645-50

2   Anne Dudley   Simon Bradstreet
    Northants,Eng. 1612   Northants   1603
    Andover,MA 16 Sep 1672 1628   Andover 27 Mar 1697

3   Hannah Bradstreet   Andrew Wiggin
    Andover c.1641   Andover   Hampton,NH 1635
    Exeter,NH bf. Apr 1707 3 Jun 1659   Exeter 9 Jan 1708/9

4   Dorothy Wiggin   John Gilman
    Exeter 13 Sep 1678   Hampton,NH   Exeter 7 Jun 1668
    Exeter bf. 2 May 1751   19 Nov 1695   Exeter w.2 May 1751

5   John Gilman   Abigail Thing
    Exeter c.1700   Exeter   Exeter 1 Dec 1700
    af. 1751   bf. 1720   af. 1748

6   Joanna Gilman   Antipas Gilman
    Exeter bp. 1733   Exeter   Brentwood 15 Jul 1730
    Gilmanton,NH Sep 1773   1755   Gilmanton 28 Feb 1801

7   Alice Gilman   Samuel Gilman
    Exeter 10 Sep 1758   Gilmanton   Newmarket 28 Oct 1748
    Gilmanton 1832   28 Dec 1775   Gilmanton

8   Joanna Gilman   Jonathan Dow
    Gilmanton 17 Dec 1777   Gilmanton   Epping,NH 1776
    15 Nov 1822   7 Jan 1796   af. 1822

9   William Harrison Dow   Fannie F. Ransom
    Gilmanton 8 Dec 1819   Walden,VT   Walden 1822
    Tuftonborough,NH   14 Mar 1844   Tuftonborough 19 Sep
       22 Dec 1901   1897

10 Emma K. Dow   Nathan Charles
                                                 Hazelton
    Coventry,VT 4 Jan 1845 Manchester,NH   Manchester 7 Mar 1843
    Manchester 1868   4 Jan 1864   Somerville,MA 1885

11 Lillian Emma Hazelton   Charles Edward Stubbs
    Pennacook,NH 6 Jun   Somerville   Winterport,ME 24 Aug
       1865   1858
    Brooks,ME 7 Aug 1937   20 Jan 1883   E.Providence,RI
                                                 4 Mar 1946

12 Walter Osgood Stubbs   Iva Lyle Randall
    Boston,MA 24 Sep 1886   Haverhill,MA   N.Nottingham,NH
                                                 16 Jul 1886
    Haverhill 26 Apr 1948   25 Apr 1906   Haverhill 19 Feb 1955

HEDRICK, GALE HOLBROOK II

Nat. #203-B. Elected 3 Apr 1973. b. Allison Park,PA 3 Jan 1919. m. La Grange,IL 28 Jun 1941, Shirley Elizabeth Ebert, b. La Grange 16 Mar 1918. Issue: Penelope Pate Hedrick, b. 10 Apr 1944; Twin sons: Gale Holbrook Hedrick III and Bradford Hunt Hedrick, b. 21 Dec 1945. Educ: Maryville College, Maryville,TN; University of Chicago Graduate School of Business. Member: Hereditary Order of Desc. of Colonial Governors; Sons of Revolution, (Treasurer,IL); Sons of American Revolution (Vice Pres.); Order of Crown of Charlemagne in the U.S.A.; Baronial Order of Magna Charta; Soc. of Desc. of King William I, the Conqueror and his Companions at Arms (Life Founder Member); Heraldry Soc. of London. Occup: Stock Broker. Address: 204 South Spring Ave., LaGrange,IL 60525. Descended from:

1 Thomas Dudley, Governor of Massachusetts 1634-1640/1

2	Samuel Dudley Northampton,Eng. 30 Nov 1606 Exeter,NH 10 Feb 1683	(2) ----- -----	Mary Winthrop 1612 1643
3	Dorothy Dudley ----- -----	Exeter 26 Oct 1681	Moses Leavitt Exeter 12 Aug 1650 Exeter 1731
4	Joseph Leavitt Exeter 23 Mar 1699 c.1792	----- -----	Mary Wadleigh Deerfield,NH 1702 1776
5	Jonathan Leavitt Exeter 1730 13 May 1824	----- -----	Ruth Cram Deerfield c.1735 Apr 1820
6	Dorothy Leavitt Exeter 1773 -----	----- -----	John Hunt ----- -----
7	John W. Hunt Sanbornton,NH 23 Nov 1791 20 Dec 1849	(2) ----- 7 Nov 1813	Nancy Lord Sanbornton 7 Jul 1796 Aug 1879
8	Charles J. Hunt Coeymans,NY 17 Apr 1832 Templeton,SD 9 Aug 1889	Coeymans 26 Oct 1855	Betsy A. Holbrook Coeymans 6 Oct 1838 Crafton,PA 4 Sep 1918
9	Mary A. Hunt Weston,OH 29 Nov 1866 Youngstown,OH 17 Feb 1952	Templeton,SD 2 Oct 1888	Peter H. Hedrick Grafton,WV 28 Jul 1864 Lakeland,FL 16 Dec 1933
10	Gale Holbrook Hedrick Ottumwa,IA 18 Dec 1895 -----	Allison Park, PA 10 Apr 1917	Margaret J. Sutter Allison Park 10 Mar 1896 -----

Inheritor: Bradford Hunt Hedrick, 1044 South Ashland Ave., LaGrange,IL 60525.

HIGGINS, MARY A. TYNG (MRS. CHARLES ASHLEY)

Nat. #154-B. Elected 1 Dec 1969. b. Hankow, China 20 Apr 1913.
m. Hong Kong, China 29 Aug 1939, Charles Ashley Higgins, b.
McAlpine,WV 8 Sep 1912. Issue: Charles Tyng Higgins, b. Hong
Kong 29 Jun 1940; Alexander Griswold Higgins, b. Cape Girardeau,
MO 25 Oct 1943; Lovell Ashley Higgins, b. Waco,TX 15 Apr 1946;
Dudley Atkins Higgins, b. Waco 25 Nov 1949; Stephen Tyng Higgins,
b. Waco 19 Nov 1953. Educ: Radcliffe College, B.A. Member:
Hereditary Order of Desc. of Colonial Governors; National League
of American Pen Women. Occup: Writer and Illustrator. Address:
Rt. #1, Sewanee, TN 37375. Descended from:

1 Thomas Dudley, Governor of Massachusetts, 1634-35, 1640-41,
1645-46

2 Joseph Dudley   Rebecca Tyng
  Roxbury,MA 23 Sep 1647   -----   13 Jul 1651
  Roxbury 2 Apr 1720   1668/9   21 Sep 1722

3 Mary Dudley   (2)   Joseph Atkins
  2 Nov 1692   -----   Sandwich,Eng. bp. 4 Nov
                                               1680
  19 Nov 1774   1730   Newbury,MA 25 Jan 1773

4 Dudley Atkins   Sarah Kent
  Newbury Jan 1731   -----   -----
  Newburyport,MA 24 Sep   4 May 1752   1810
    1767

5 Dudley Atkins Tyng   Sarah Higginson
  Newburyport 3 Sep 1760   -----   Salem,MA 11 Jun 1766
  Newburyport 1 Aug 1829   18 Oct 1792   Boston,MA 2 Nov 1808

6 Stephen Higginson Tyng   Anne Griswold
  Newburyport 1 Mar 1880   -----   5 Oct 1805
  Irvington,NY 3 Sep   5 Aug 1821   16 May 1832
    1885

7 Dudley Atkins Tyng   Catherine M. Stevens
  Prince George's Co.,MD   Castle Point,   Castle Point
    12 Jan 1825   NJ
  Philadelphia,PA   1847   21 Apr 1888
    20 Apr 1858

8 Stephen Higginson   Elizabeth Walworth
    Tyng
  Castle Point 2 Aug   Newton,MA   Boston 5 Aug 1852
    1851
  Cataumet, MA Sep 1911   8 Sep 1880   New York,NY 1937

9 Walworth Tyng   Ethel Atkinson Arens
  Dorchester,MA 3 Jan   Newburyport   Boston 25 Oct 1887
    1885
  Cambridge,MD 27 May   19 Jun 1912   -----
    1960

Inheritor: Charles Tyng Higgins

HILL, MARY MARGARET AYRES (MS.)

Nat. #163-B. Elected 4 Aug 1970. Member: Hereditary Order of
Desc. of Colonial Governors. Address: c/o Ayres Construction
Co., 243 Tillman, Memphis,TN 38112. Descended from:

1 John West, Governor of Virginia 1635-1636/7

2 John West   Unity Croshaw
   Chiskack,VA 1632   -----   -----
   Virginia c.1691   c.1667   -----

3 Henry Fox   Ann West
   Huntington,VA c.1650   -----   -----
   -----   -----   1714

4 Thomas Fox   Mary Tunstall
   King William Co.VA   -----   -----
   -----   c.1708   -----

5 Joseph Fox, Sr.   Mildred Fenton
   -----   -----   -----
   King William Co.   bf. 1746   -----
      1788

6 Nathaniel Fox   (1)   Mary Carver King
   1763   -----   -----
   1821   -----   -----

7 Mary Bailey Fox   (1)   Bowler F. Cocke
   Virginia 1799   Virginia   Virginia
   Memphis,TN 18 Oct 1847 c.1820   1825

8 Rebecca Cocke   William Park
   Virginia 20 Jan 1822   Memphis,TN   County Tyrone, Ireland
                                             8 Feb 1808
   Memphis 1 May 1894   18 Oct 1838   Memphis 3 Apr 1877

9 Mary Elizabeth Park   Charles Wesley Metcalf
   Memphis 18 Sep 1842   Memphis   Nicholasville,KY
                                             10 Apr 1840
   Memphis 15 Feb 1925   4 Dec 1866   Memphis 2 Apr 1923

10 Rebecca Park Metcalf   William Arthur McNeill
   Memphis 7 Oct 1867   Memphis   Rosedale,MS 17 Aug 1862
   Memphis 2 Apr 1945   19 Nov 1887   Memphis 18 Nov 1935

11 Margaret Metcalf   Willis Edward Ayres
      McNeill
   Memphis 21 Jul 1893   Chicago,IL   Osceola,AR 28 Nov 1881
   8 Apr 1970   8 Nov 1917   Memphis 8 Nov 1936

HILLS, COL. J. HUNTINGTON

Nat. #47-B. Elected 18 Mar 1962. b. Brooklyn,NY 23 Jul 1892. m. West Point,NY 20 Dec 1916, Vera Mae Kreger, b. Cherokee,IA 24 Dec 1893. Issue: Elizabeth M. Hills Culhane, b. 27 Apr 1921; Vera H. Hills Inskeep, b. 21 Jan 1931; both b. Washington,DC. Educ: Hamilton Institute,NYC; King School, Stamford,CT; Command and Gen Staff College and Army War College. Member: Hereditary Order of Desc. of Colonial Governors (Past 2nd Deputy Governor General); Soc. of the Cincinnati in CT; Sons of American Revolution (Nat. Trustee for Texas); Soc. of Mayflower Desc. (Dep. Governor General for Texas); Children of American Revolution (Sr. Nat. 2nd Vice Pres.); Soc. of Founders of Norwich,CT; Order of First Families of Virginia; National Huguenot Soc.; Magna Charta Barons; Soc. of Desc. of Knights of Most Noble Order of the Garter; New England Historic Genealogical Soc. Honors: Legion of Merit, Citation Medal with Oak Leaf Cluster, Purple Heart, New York State Conspicuous Service Cross. Served in all commissioned grades of U.S. Army to Colonel. Address: 405 Geneseo Rd., San Antonio,TX 78209. Descended from:

1 Benedict Arnold, Governor of Rhode Island 1657-59, 1662-65, 1669-71, 1677-78

2 Caleb Arnold   Abigail Wilbur
  Providence,RI   -----   -----
    18 Dec 1644
  Newport,RI 9 Feb 1719   10 Jun 1666   Newport 17 Nov 1730

3 Penelope Arnold   George Hazard
  Newport 3 Aug 1669   Rhode Island   Kingston,RI
  South Kingston,RI   -----   S.Kingston af.1743
    af.1742

4 George Hazard   Sarah Carder
  North Kingston 9 Oct   Rhode Island   RI 14 May 1705
    1700
  S.Kingston 24 Jun 1738   -----   RI 1738

5 Carder Hazard   (2)   Alice Hazard
  S.Kingston 11 Aug 1734   Rhode Island   S.Kingston 30 Aug 1737
  S.Kingston 24 Nov 1792   5 Mar 1761   S.Kingston 13 Jan 1793

6 George C. Hazard   (3)   Jane Hull
  S.Kingston 13 Apr 1763   S.Kingston   S.Kingston 24 Sep 1781
  S.Kingston 29 Sep 1829   16 May 1807   S.Kingston 13 Apr 1862

7 Carder Hazard   Elizabeth Watson
  20 Aug 1809   -----   3 Mar 1813
  3 Jul 1863   3 Mar 1834   -----

8 Ann Eliza Hazard   Jedediah Huntington
  Kingston 6 Jun 1837   Kingston   -----
  Fort McKinley,P.I.   6 Jun 1860   -----
    10 Dec 1928

9	Lillian Huntington		Henry Mayhew Hills
	Norwich,CT 28 Sep 1867	New York City	-----
	Puyallup,WA 12 Jul 1942	27 Apr 1891	-----

SUPPLEMENT NO. 1

1 William Hutchinson, Governor of Rhode Island 1639-40

2	Susanna Hutchinson		John Cole
	15 Nov 1633	Boston,MA	-----
	RI c.1713	30 Dec 1651	Wickford,RI c.1707

3	William Cole		Ann Pinder
	Kingston,RI 13 Jul 1671	-----	-----
	1734	1701	-----

4	John Cole		Ann
	1702	Narragansett, RI	-----
	c.1792	-----	-----

5	William Cole		Mary Hazard
	13 Mar 1737	-----	24 Aug 1758
	7 Aug 1823	-----	18 Sep 1841

6	Ann Cole		Elisha Watson
	1758	-----	1 Oct 1776
	27 Aug 1874	5 Jan 1806	7 Jul 1847

| 7 | Elizabeth Watson | | Carder Hazard |

Continue with Generation 7 of his lineage from Governor Benedict Arnold.

Inheritor: Inskeep, Vera Huntington Hills (Mrs. William Free), 913 Summit St., Sherman,TX
or
Culhane, Elizabeth Mae Hills (Mrs. Roger J.), 405 Geneseo Rd., San Antonio,TX

HOFMEISTER, VIRGINIA LEE HAGEMAN (MRS. GEORGE C., SR.)

Nat. #264-B. Elected 22 Sep 1975. b. Bennington,NE 30 Aug 1928. m. Pittsburgh,PA 19 Apr 1952, George Carl Hofmeister, b. Pittsburgh 26 May 1926. Issue: George Carl Hofmeister, Jr., b. 29 Aug 1954; Lisa Louise Hofmeister, b. 12 Jan 1957; Eric Lee Hofmeister, b. 2 Mar 1961; all b. Mt. Lebanon,PA. Educ: Duquesne University. Member: Hereditary Order of Desc. of Colonial Governors; Daus. of American Revolution (Baton Rouge,LA Chap.); Colonial Dames of XVII Century (Organizing Pres.,MI); Daughters of American Colonists (New Orleans and Organizing Regent in Baton Rouge). Address: 1718 Sherwood Forest Blvd., Baton Rouge, LA 70815. Descended from:

1 Andrew Ward, Governor of Connecticut 1635-36

2 Andrew Ward   Tryal Meigs
   Killingworth,CT 1645   -----   1646
   1690   1667/8   1690

3 Peter Ward   Mary Joy
   Killingworth 14 Oct   -----   17 Sep 1680
     1676
   18 Dec 1763   30 Mar 1699   -----

4 Pelethiah Ward   Jerusha Kelsey
   Killingworth 27 Dec   -----   Killingworth 1 Nov
     1699   1705
   -----   30 Dec 1727   -----

5 Mary Ward   John Griswold
   Killingworth 12 Mar   -----   Killingworth 6 Mar
     1730   1725
   -----   13 Jan 1748   Long Island,NY c.1776

6 Matthew Griswold   Lucy Morse
   Springfield,VT 28 Sep   Johnson,VT   Holden,MA 21 Nov 1774
     1771
   Morristown,VT 19 May   8 Oct 1792   Morristown 11 Mar 1837
     1846

7 Lucinda Griswold   Hiram Patch
   Johnson,25 Mar 1812   Johnson   Francestown,NH 15 Jan
                                                  1805
   -----   10 Nov 1832   Eden,VT 15 Apr 1880

8 Mary Ann Patch   Jairus Davis Clark
   Johnson 1 Apr 1835   Johnson   Corinth,VT 9 Sep 1839
   Randolph,VT 14 Aug   c.22 May 1868   Westfield,MA 1 Jan 1917
     1912

9 Perley Clark   Mary McLellan
   Eden 4 May 1869   Eden   Irasburgh,VT 16 Jan
                                                  1868
   Northfield 4 Aug 1956   16 Jan 1893   -----

10 Ruth Pearl Clark   (2)   Fred Hageman
   Brookfield,VT 10 Apr   Brooklyn,NY   Elkhorn,NE 11 Apr 1898
     1895
   -----   1 Feb 1925   Omaha,NE 28 Jul 1969

HOPE, CRAIG LEONARD

Nat. #245-B. Elected 19 Oct 1974. b. Philadelphia,PA 26 Sep
1943. Educ: West Chester College, A.B. Member: Sons of St.
George of Philadelphia; Sons of American Revolution; Soc. of Mayflower Descendants; Baronial Order of Magna Charta; Americans of
Royal Descent; Royal Society of St. George; Scottish Historical
Soc. of Delaware; Military Order of the Crusades; Soc. of Desc.
of Colonial Clergy; Hereditary Order of Desc. of Colonial Governors; Old Plymouth Colony Desc.; St. David's Soc. of New York;
Sons and Dau. of Pilgrims. Occup: Optician. Address: 2306 Kenil-
worth Rd., Ardmore,PA 19003 (Box #665, Ardmore,PA 19003).
Descended from:

1   Thomas Hinckley, Governor of New Plymouth 1681-92

2   Meletiah Hinckley   Josiah Crocker
      Barnstable,MA 25 Nov   Barnstable   Barnstable 19 Sep 1647
      1648
      Barnstable 2 Feb 1714   22 Oct 1668   2 Feb 1698/9

3   Thomas Crocker   Hannah Green
      Barnstable 28 May 1671   -----   MA 1676
      Barnstable Apr 1728   25 Mar 1696   23 Jan 1728/9

4   Joseph Crocker   Reliance Allen
      Barnstable 1714   -----   1718
      Orleans,MA 2 Mar 1772   13 Sep 1739   Orleans 30 Jun 1762

5   Anna Crocker   Simeon Williams
      Eastham,MA 1748   Weymouth,MA   Easton,MA 19 Jun 1743
      Easton 10 Aug 1823   1 Sep 1770   S.Weymouth 31 May 1819

6   Thomas Williams   Sarah P. Cushman
      S.Weymouth 11 Mar 1787   Taunton,MA   Taunton 28 Feb 1788
      Poland,ME 23 Nov 1846   16 Nov 1812   Washington,DC 30 Jul
                                                1867

7   George C. Williams   Anna Shields
      Brewer,ME 4 Apr 1819   Harrisburg,PA   Chester Co.PA 11 Oct
                                                1829
      Coatsville,PA 10 Mar   12 Oct 1848   East Brandywine,PA
      1870   18 Sep 1908

8   Howard Williams   Elizabeth Coffin
      Coatsville 28 Sep 1863   Philadelphia,   Philadelphia 3 Oct
                                PA   1867
      Atlantic City,NJ 5 May   15 Jan 1885   Philadelphia 6 Feb
      1932   1959

9   Wesley Williams   Elizabeth C. McDonald
      West Chester,PA 27 Aug   Baltimore,MD   Philadelphia 29 Jan
      1888   1895
      Miami,FL 5 May 1970   10 Dec 1917   Atlantic City 27 Aug
                                                1929

10 Margaret Williams   Leonard G. Hope
      Philadelphia 13 Sep   Philadelphia   Dalhousie,India
      1920   5 Aug 1904
                                18 Nov 1939

HOWARD, HELEN DENNY (MRS.)

Nat. #9-B. Elected 4 Aug 1959. b. Waynesburg,PA 26 Mar 1896.
m. Waynesburg 12 Nov 1924, Willis George Howard. Educ: Waynesburg College, B.A.; Bachelor of Music and Doctor of Music (Hon.).
Member: Hereditary Order of Desc. of Colonial Governors; U.S.
Daughters of 1812; Dau. of American Revolution; Desc. of Lords
of Maryland Manors; Order of First Families of Virginia; Jamestowne Soc.; Dau. of American Colonists (Hon. Nat. Pres.); Dau.
of Colonial Wars; Colonial Daughters of XVII Century; Women Desc.
of Ancient and Honorable Artillery Co.; New England Women; Order

of Crown in America; Magna Charta Dames; Americans of Royal
Descent; Colonial Dames of America; Dau. of Barons of Runnemede;
Order of Three Crusades. Address: 145 West High St., Waynesburg,
PA 15370. Descended from:

1 William Stone, Governor of Maryland 1649-54

2 Mary Stone   Robert Doyne
  Accomac Co.VA 1642   Charles Co.   England 1640
  Charles Co.MD 1685   1674   Charles Co. 1689

3 Mary Doyne   Nicholas Dawson
  Charles Co. 1683   Charles Co.   St.Mary's Co.MD 1682
  Prince George's Co.MD 1706   Prince George's Co.
   1734   1727

4 Thomas Dawson   Elizabeth Lowe
  Prince George's Co.   Oxon Hill,MD   Prince George's Co.
   1708   27 Dec 1712
  Montgomery Co.MD 1800 1740   Montgomery Co. 1802

5 Sarah Dawson   William Blackmore
  Prince George's Co.   Dawsonville   Prince George's Co.
   1748   1746
  Dawsonville,MD 1800   1771   PA 1790

6 Rebecca Blackmore   Robert Adams
  Prince George's Co.   Washington,PA   PA 1769
   1778
  Waynesburg,PA 1853   1796   Waynesburg 1864

7 Sarah Adams   (1)   William Inghram, Jr.
  Waynesburg 1799   Waynesburg   Waynesburg 1794
  Waynesburg 1830   1816   Waynesburg 1843

8 Eliza Inghram   John T. Hook
  Waynesburg 13 Jul   Waynesburg   Waynesburg 20 Jan 1814
   1817
  Waynesburg 1 May 1901 14 Jan 1836   Waynesburg 13 Nov 1883

9 Sarah Hook   Josiah Inghram
  Waynesburg 26 Oct   Waynesburg   Waynesburg 5 Oct 1819
   1836
  Waynesburg 22 Nov 1913 31 Oct 1861   Waynesburg 8 Aug 1879

10 Louise Inghram   Eleazer Luse Denny
  Waynesburg 27 May 1867 Waynesburg   Waynesburg 18 Sep 1865
  Waynesburg 14 Apr 1956 16 Oct 1890   Waynesburg 1 Apr 1910

Inheritor: Mrs. Timothy J. Wisecarver, Jr.

HOWE, HELEN DELANO BAILEY (MRS. ELDEN LORING)

Nat. #17-B. Elected 24 Nov 1959. b. Brookline,MA 3 Jul 1899.
m. Miami,FL 7 Jan 1966, Elden Loring Howe, b. 4 Oct 1894. Educ:
Fitchburg,MA Teachers College, B.S.Ed. Member: Hereditary Order
of Desc. of Colonial Governors; Women Desc. of Ancient and
Honorable Artillery Co. (Past Pres.); Dau. of Colonial Wars
(Past Nat. Treas.); Soc. of Mayflower Desc. in State of Florida
(Past Gov.); Alden Kindred of America (Past Pres.); Dau. of
American Colonists (Treas.); Soc. of U.S. Daughters of 1812;
Huguenot Soc. of Florida (Past Treas.). Address: 2514 Granada
Blvd., Coral Gables, FL 33134. Descended from:

1 John Alden, Governor of Plymouth Colony 1663-64, 1667

2 Mary Alden   Thomas Delano
  Duxbury,MA 1643   Duxbury   Duxbury 31 Mar 1642
  Duxbury bf. Sep 1688   bf. 1667   Duxbury 13 Mar 1723

3 Jonathan Delano   Hannah Doten
  Duxbury 6 Jan 1676   Duxbury   Plymouth,MA Dec 1675
  Duxbury 6 Jan 1765   12 Jan 1699   Duxbury 12 Jan 1699

4 David Delano   Abigail Chandler
  Duxbury 3 Jun 1720   Duxbury   Duxbury 1 Jul 1721
  In the Army 11 Jan   28 May 1740   -----
    1761

5 Oliver Delano   Mary Chandler
  Duxbury 17 May 1759   Duxbury   Duxbury 13 Oct 1760
  Duxbury 7 Jan 1846   6 Apr 1783   Duxbury 7 Oct 1846

6 Hosea Delano   Hannah Brewster
  Duxbury 18 Feb 1789   Duxbury   Duxbury 31 Mar 1798
  Venice,Italy   6 May 1817   Duxbury 25 Feb 1855

7 Deborah Brewster   Louis Martine
    Delano   Bailey, Jr.
  Duxbury 21 Dec 1825   Duxbury   Duxbury 12 May 1826
  Duxbury 30 Oct 1915   8 Apr 1849   Duxbury 16 Aug 1924

8 Arthur Hosea Bailey   Barbara Ella
                                                MacIntosh
  Duxbury 3 Aug 1859   Brookline,MA   Prince Edward Island
                                                2 Nov 1868
  Duxbury 25 Oct 1928   30 Jun 1898   -----

HOWLAND, McCLURE MEREDITH

Nat. #149-B. Elected 10 Feb 1969. b. New York,NY 4 Nov 1906.
m. (1) 6 Jun 1939, Jane Robb Murdoch, b. Pittsburgh,PA 18 Nov
1915. Issue: Grafton Dulany Howland, b. NYC 9 Mar 1943; Louisa
M. Howland Miller, b. NYC 25 Jan 1948; Katherine Murdoch Howland,
b. NYC 14 Sep 1951, d. NYC 28 Dec 1963. m.(2) NYC 14 Sep 1960,
Enid Gillett Irving. Educ: St. Paul's School; Harvard University; University of London. Member: Hereditary Order of Desc. of
Colonial Governors; Pilgrim John Howland Soc. (Pres.); Soc. of
Mayflower Desc. (Historian of NY Soc.); Soc. of Colonial Wars;

St. Nicholas Soc. of New York; Colonial Lords of Manors; Sons of
the Revolution; Soc. of Desc. of William I, the Conqueror;
Harvard Club, NY; Harvard Club, Spain (Pres.); Knickerbocker
Club; River Club. Occup: Free Lance Writer. Address:
224 Fisher Place, Princeton, NJ 08540. Descended from:

1 Thomas Southworth, Governor of Plymouth Colony 1655

2 Elizabeth Southworth   Joseph Howland
   Plymouth,MA   Plymouth   Plymouth
   Plymouth   7 Dec 1664   Plymouth Jan 1704

3 Nathaniel Howland   Martha Cole
   Plymouth 1671   Plymouth   -----
   Plymouth 29 Dec 1746   -----   -----

4 Nathaniel Howland   (2)   Abigail (Burt) Lane
   Plymouth 9 Jun 1705   Boston   Boston 28 Mar 1718
   Boston,MA 13 Jul 1766 1739   Boston 22 Jul 1766

5 Joseph Howland   Lydia Bill
   Boston 30 Sep 1749   Norwich,CT   Norwich 7 Jul 1753
   Greenburg,NY 11 Mar   26 May 1772   New York,NY May 1838
     1836

6 Gardiner G. Howland   (2)   Louise Meredith
   Norwich 4 Sep 1787   Baltimore   Baltimore 9 Nov 1810
   NY 11 Nov 1851   17 Jul 1829   NYC

7 Gardiner G. Howland   Mary Grafton Dulany
   NYC 22 Jul 1834   Baltimore   Baltimore 1835
   NY 9 May 1902   25 Nov 1856   NYC 1897

8 Dulany Howland   Marguerite McClure
   S.Island 27 Jun 1859 NYC   NYC 7 Mar 1876
   NYC 8 Apr 1915   Feb 1906   -----

   Inheritor: Grafton Dulany Howland

HULTANDER, ETHEL RUSSELL (MRS. MARTIN E.)

Nat. #78-B. Elected 3 Apr 1963. b. Hersey,MI 30 Apr 1904.
m. Bowling Green,OH 28 Feb 1930, Martin E. Hultander, b. Omaha,
NE 7 Mar 1905. Educ: Baker Bus. University. Member: Hereditary
Order of Desc. of Colonial Governors; Dau. of American Revolu-
tion; Soc. of Mayflower Descendants; Dau. of Founders and
Patriots of America (Past Councillor,MI); Order of Americans of
Armorial Ancestry; Women Desc. of Ancient and Honorable Artillery
Co. (Past First Vice Pres.,MI); Soc. of Desc. of Colonial Clergy;
Order of Three Crusades; Order of Crown of Charlemagne in the
U.S.A.; National Huguenot Soc. (Past Bd. of Dir.,MI); Magna
Charta Dames; Soc. of Desc. of King William I, the Conqueror;
Sons and Dau. of Pilgrims; Dau. of American Colonists; Dau. of
the Union. Address: 10232 North 109th Ave., Sun City,AZ 85351.
Descended from:

1 John Alden, Governor of Plymouth Colony 1663-67

2 Elizabeth Alden   William Pabodie
   Plymouth 1624   Duxbury,MA   c.1620
   Little Compton,RI   26 Dec 1644   Little Compton 13 Dec
     31 May 1717   1707

3 Elizabeth Pabodie   John Rogers
   Duxbury 24 Apr 1647   Duxbury   1640
   bf.1707   16 Nov 1666   Barrington, RI
                                               28 Jun 1732

4 Sarah Rogers   Nathaniel Searles
   Little Compton   Little Compton 9 Jun 1662
     4 May 1677
   Little Compton   1694   Little Compton
     19 Jan 1770   5 Feb 1750

5 Nathaniel Searle   Elizabeth Kinnicutt
   Little Compton   Little Compton 26 Apr 1701
     26 Apr 1703
   Little Compton   1725   11 Dec 1781
     8 Dec 1781

6 Constant Searle   Hannah Miner
   Little Compton   N.Stonington   North Stonington,CT
     17 Jun 1728   19 Dec 1731
   Wyoming Battlefield   16 Mar 1751   Pittston,PA
     3 Jul 1778   16 Aug 1813

7 Hannah Searle   Henry Harding
   Stonington 25 Jan 1753 Kingstown,   CT 22 Feb 1753
                          PA
   Williamson,NY   29 Feb 1776   Minisink,NY 2 Sep 1794
     2 Sep 1841

8 Lucretia Harding   Asa Williams Stoddard
   Williamson 3 Jun 1791 -----   CT 17 May 1790
   Williamson 5 Nov 1814 1809   Tuscola Co.MI 17 Aug
                                              1868

9 Eleanor L. Stoddard   Moses Benjamin Russell
   Williamson 22 Dec   -----   Williamson 13 Apr
     1810   1809
   Battle Creek,MI   13 Oct 1830   Colorado 3 Feb 1883
     10 Aug 1887

10 Allen S. Russell   Mary F. Norton
   Marion,NY 8 Jun 1834   Hersey,MI   Hersey 8 Feb 1869
   Hersey 23 Jan 1912   1 Jan 1899   Flint,MI 28 Jan 1950

JAKOBSSON, DONNA RAE JOHNSON (MRS.)

Nat. #349-B. Elected 10 Aug 1979. b. Jackson,IA 24 Nov 1928.
m. Jackson 16 Sep 1956, Lester Theodore Jakobsson, b. San Francisco,CA 15 Sep 1926. Educ: Sacramento Junior College, A.A.
Member: Hereditary Order of Desc. of Colonial Governors; Dau. of
American Revolution. Address: 2504 Rocky Branch Road, Vienna,VA
22130. Descended from:

1 Robert Treat, Governor of Connecticut 1683-98

2 Mary Treat   Azariah Crane
   Milford,CT 1 May 1652   -----   East Haven,CT 1649
   East Jersey 12 Nov 1704 -----   East Jersey 5 Nov 1730

3 Azariah Crane   Rebecca
   East Jersey 6-1682   East Jersey   1681
   East Jersey   c. 1706   Montclair,NJ 15 Jun
                                             1739

4 Azariah Crane   Phebe
   East Jersey   East Jersey   -----
   East Jersey 21 Nov   -----   -----
     1752

5 Silas Crane (Crayne)   Jane
   Essex Co.NJ 1737   -----   1748
   Morgan,PA 30 Jul 1835   -----   Morgan 25 Jan 1845

6 Jane Crayne   Stephen Ulrey
   Washington Co.PA 14 Oct -----   Washington Co. 17 Oct
     1789   1789
   Knox Co.OH 20 May   30 Nov 1809   Knox Co. 21 Nov 1850
     1878

7 Rachael Ulrey   Zephaniah Johnson
   Washington Co.   Morgan   Morgan 21 Dec 1812
     24 Feb 1819
   Morgan 21 Jul 1853   6 Mar 1837   Morgan 12 Jul 1895

8 George Johnson   Ellen Robertson
   Morgan 20 Oct 1842   Waterloo,IA   Dundee,IL 28 Jan 1850
   Jackson,IA 17 Jul 1914   12 Sep 1869   Jackson 22 Nov 1904

9 Lawrence Wayne Johnson   Claire Mary Baker
   Jackson 28 Sep 1892   Dodge,IA   Dodge 18 May 1896
   Jackson 19 Nov 1953   20 Nov 1920   -----

JOHNS, DOROTHY MAE (MISS)

Nat. #121-B. Elected 5 Jul 1966. b. Kansas City,KS 26 Aug 1897.
Educ: University of Chicago, Ph.B.; University of So. California,
M.S. Member: Hereditary Order of Desc. of Colonial Governors;
National Huguenot Soc.; Dau. of American Revolution; Soc. of
Mayflower Desc.; Soc. of New England Women; Sons and Dau. of the
Pilgrims; Colonial Dames of XVII Century; Women Desc. of Ancient
and Honorable Artillery Co.; Soc. of Desc. of Colonial Clergy;
Dau. of American Colonists; Magna Charta Dames; Dames of the
Court of Honor; Plantagenet Soc.; Soc. of Desc. of Knights of the
Most Noble Order of the Garter; Sovereign Colonial Soc. of
Americans of Royal Descent; Order of Washington; Phi Delta Phi;
Phi Kappa Phi. Occup: Teacher, UCLA (Ret.). Address: 750 - 47th
Ave., Space 48, Capitola,CA 95010. Descended from:

1 Thomas Prence, Governor of Plymouth Colony 1634-73

2 Jane Prence   Mark Snow
   Duxbury,MA 1 Nov 1637   Eastham,MA   Plymouth,MA 9 May 1628
   Harwich,MA c.1711   9 Jan 1660/1 Eastham 1695

3 Nicholas Snow   Lydia Shaw
   Eastham 6 Dec 1663   -----   -----
   Rochester,MA 1745   4 Apr 1689   -----

4 Prince Snow   Mary Sturtevant
   Rochester 26 Dec 1707   Rochester   Rochester 1705
   Rochester   31 Aug 1727   Rochester

5 Mary Snow   Samuel Sherman
   Rochester 30 Oct 1729   Rochester   Rochester 3 Jan 1724
   Ware,MA c.1752   20 Apr 1749   Ware 29 Jan 1811

6 Prence Sherman   Mary S. Rogers
   Ware 26 Feb 1753   -----   Ware 1755
   -----   1780   Kitley,Ont. c.1798

7 Ira Sherman   Phebe Edmunds
   Hinesburg,VT 1786   Leeds Co.Ont. Vermont 1796
   Geneva,WI c.1860   1817   Geneva c.1860

8 Sylvia Ann Sherman   Schuyler Mattoon
   Canada 18 Jan 1818   Hanover,NY   Warren Co.NY 1806
   -----   1838   -----

9 Amanda L. Mattoon   Noble Lovely Johns
   Silver Creek,NY   Walworth,WI   Williston,VT 14 Jul
     23 Sep 1840   1837
   Chicago,IL 4 Jun 1927   4 Jul 1859   Walworth 25 Oct 1920

10 Alvin L. Johns   Mary A. E. Cole
   Delavan,WI 13 Sep   Corliss,WI   London,Eng. 10 May
     1861   1860
   Delavan 27 Jan 1947   26 Nov 1891   Los Angeles,CA 16 Aug
                                           1940

Inheritor: Ralph W. Hinckley

130

JOHNSON, CHARLES OWEN

Nat. #125-B. Elected 24 Sep 1966. b. Monroe,LA 18 Aug 1926.
Educ: Tulane University, B.A.; Harvard University, LLB;
Columbia University, Master of Laws; Tulane University, J.D.
Member: St. Andrews Soc. of Washington,DC; Hereditary Order of
Desc. of Colonial Governors (Governor General); Soc. of Sons of
St. George, Philadelphia; Soc. of Cincinnati of South Carolina;
Soc. of War of 1812 (Pres., DC Soc.); St. David's Soc. of State
of New York; St. Nicholas Soc. of City of New York; Gen. Soc.
Sons of the Revolution (President, DC); Huguenot Soc. of South
Carolina; Nat. Soc. of Sons of American Revolution (National
Trustee, DC Soc.); Gen. Soc. of Colonial Wars (Deputy Secretary,
DC); Sons of Confederate Veterans; Sons of Union Veterans; Order
of Founders and Patriots of America (Past Genealogist General);
Order of Americans of Armorial Ancestry (Member of the Council);
Louisiana Colonials; Soc. of Desc. of Colonial Clergy; Hereditary
Order of Loyalists and Patriots (Past Governor General);
Jamestowne Society; Order of Stars and Bars (Cmdr, Jefferson
Davis Chap.); Desc. of New Jersey Settlers; National Huguenot
Soc.; Order of First Families of Mississippi (Past Governor
General); Colonial Order of the Crown; Soc. of Desc. of Knights
of the Most Noble Order of the Garter; Sovereign Colonial Soc.
of Americans of Royal Descent; Somerset Chapter, Magna Charta
Barons; Royal Soc. of St. George, England; Pilgrims of St. Mary's;
Mississippi Historical Soc.; Northern Neck of Virginia Historical
Soc.; Virginia Historical Soc.; Virginia Genealogical Soc.; Soc.
of King Charles the Martyr; National Gavel Club; National Lawyers
Club; Phi Beta Kappa; Sons and Dau. of the Pilgrims (Counselor);
Selden Soc.; American Judicature Soc.; Louisiana and Federal
Bar Assns.; Harvard Club of Washington; Pendennis Club of New
Orleans; Arts Club of Washington. Occup: Chief of the Court of
Appeals Branch, Tax Court Div., Chief Counsel's Office, Internal
Revenue Service. Address: 2111 Jefferson Davis Hwy., Apt. 109-S,
Arlington, VA 22202. Descended from:

1 John Coggeshall, Governor of Rhode Island 1647

2 Joshua Coggeshall   Joan West
   Essex Co.Eng. c.1623   Newport,RI   1631
   Portsmouth,RI 1 May   22 Dec 1652   24 Apr 1676
      1688

3 Humility Coggeshall   Benjamin Greene
   Portsmouth Jan 1670   Portsmouth   North Kingstown,RI
                                               c.1665
   af.1719   c.1695   bf. 5 Mar 1719

4 Henry Greene   Margaret Rathbone
   N.Kingstown c.1696   East Greenwich,E.Greenwich 29 Nov
                              RI   1700
   West Greenwich,RI   15 May 1724   28 Feb 1742
      21 Feb 1752

5 Job Greene   Meribah Carr
   E.Greenwich 2 Mar 1735 W.Greenwich   W.Greenwich 3 Jul 1739
   Vermont 25 Jan 1792   3 Feb 1757   12 Jul 1785

6 Sarah Greene   Michael Briggs
   1 Jan 1759   Hancock,MA   E.Greenwich 16 Sep
                                                      1751
   Augusta,NY 12 Feb 1849 28 Dec 1775   Burlington,NY 10 Feb
                                                      1828

7 Henry Briggs   Phoebe Parker
   1780   -----   1 Oct 1787
   Otsego Co.NY   -----   af. 1850
     bf. 26 Jan 1846

8 Michael Parker Briggs   Sophronia Matteson
   Otsego Co. c.1808/10   -----   Otsego Co. 1815
   Otsego Co. 21 Mar 1864 c.1832   af. 1857

9 Henry Delos Briggs   Sarah Elizabeth Wright
   Otsego Co. 6 Jan 1835   Floyd,LA   East Carroll Parish,LA
                                                      11 May 1851
   Oak Grove,LA 20 Dec   19 Jan 1871   Oak Grove 12 Jan 1917
     1900

10 Sue Sophronia Briggs   Jason Uriah Johnson
   Oak Grove 31 Mar 1878   Oak Grove   Chicot Co.AR 4 Jul 1866
   Monroe,LA 6 Dec 1926   15 Mar 1893   Clifford,AR 27 Dec 1906

11 Clifford Uriah Johnson   Laura Owen
   Oak Grove 10 Nov 1897   Owendale   Waco,TX 11 Jul 1898
                           Plantation,
                           LA
   Arlington,VA 24 Nov   21 Dec 1922   Monroe 14 Jan 1974
     1977

                           SUPPLEMENT NO. 1

1 John Greene, Governor of Rhode Island 1695-96

2 Phillis Greene   Caleb Carr
   Warwick,RI 7 Oct 1658   Warwick   Newport,RI c.1650
   af. 3 Mar 1690   c.1677   Jamestown,RI 1690

3 Caleb Carr   Joanna Slocum
   Jamestown 26 Mar 1679   Jamestown   Jamestown 2 Jan 1680/1
   W.Greenwich af. 1750   30 Apr 1701   Jamestown 30 Dec 1708/9

4 Caleb Carr   Sarah Richmond
   Jamestown 6 Nov 1702   -----   8 Nov 1711
   W.Greenwich 1769   -----   Nov 1798

5 Meribah Carr   Job Greene

   Continue with Generation 5 of his lineage from Governor
   John Coggeshall.

JOHNSON, ROSS BYRON

Nat. #197-B. Elected 1 Dec 1972. b. Ladd,IL 4 Jun 1919.
m. Princeton,IL 29 Jun 1942, Mary Louise Wallenhorst, b. Wagon
Mound,NM 2 Nov 1917. Educ: University of New Mexico, B.S. and
M.S. Member: Hereditary Order of Desc. of Colonial Governors;
Soc. of Desc. of Colonial Clergy; Huguenot Society; Soc. of
Mayflower Desc.; Sons of American Revolution; New Mexico Genea-
logical Soc.; Nat. Audubon Soc.; Soc. of Sigma Xi; Geological
Soc. of America. Occup: Research Geologist, U.S. Geological
Survey. Address: 240 Quay St., Lakewood,CO 80226. Descended fr:

1 John Coggeshall, Governor of Rhode Island 1647

2 Joshua Coggeshall   Joan West
   England c.1626   Portsmouth,RI   England c.1635
   Portsmouth 1 May 1688 22 Dec 1652   Portsmouth 24 Apr 1676

3 Humility Coggeshall   Benjamin Greene
   Portsmouth Jan 1670   Kingston,RI   North Kingston c.1655
   Portsmouth c.1719   c.1687   East Greenwich,RI
                                                c.1718

4 John Greene   Mary Ayleworth
   Quidnessett,RI c.1688 E.Greenwich   Quidnessett c.1688
   W.Greenwich 29 Mar   c.1708   W.Greenwich bf.1741
     1752

5 Joseph Greene   Margaret Greenman
   E.Greenwich c.1725   Westerly,RI   Charlestown,RI 17 Oct
                                                1725
   Berlin,NY af.1768   20 Sep 1747   Berlin 4 Dec 1808

6 Charles Greene   Waite Bailey
   Westerly 19 Jun 1749   W.Greenwich   E.Greenwich 9 Mar 1751
   Pinckney,NY 1 Jun 1810 24 Nov 1768   Pinckney 14 Mar 1791

7 Catherine (Greene)   (2)   Richard Dye
     Spencer
   W.Greenwich 3 Dec 1769 Brookfield,NY   Richmond,RI 18 Oct 1760
   New York 1849   1802   Rodman,NY 2 Apr 1856

8 Catharine Dye   Simon B. Taft
   Henderson,NY 19 Mar   Watertown,NY   Mendon,MA 18 Jul 1800
     1805
   Tunnel City,WI 20 Feb 20 Mar 1831   Tunnel City 11 Jun 1877
     1888

9 Delia L. Taft   Wilson Woodward
   Watertown 26 Sep 1836 Tilsonburg,   South Champion,NY
                            Can.   31 Dec 1831
   Tunnel City 7 Dec 1905 25 Feb 1855   Tunnel City 2 Feb 1903

10 Priscilla F. Woodward   Frank L. Johnson
   Watertown 23 Aug 1862 Eau Claire,WI   Sauk,WI 9 May 1853
   Tunnel City 15 Oct   9 May 1882   Tunnel City 26 Sep 1890
     1902

11 Ray B. Johnson   Katherine E. Wolfe
   Tunnel City 3 Aug   Ladd,IL   Kirkville,IA 1 Mar
      1885   1890
   Peoria,IL 11 May 1958   23 Dec 1912

SUPPLEMENT NO. 1

1 Caleb Carr, Governor of Rhode Island 1695

2 Elizabeth Carr   John Godfrey
   Newport,RI c.1684   Newport   Newport c.1680
   Newport af.1709   28 May 1701   Newport af.1709

3 John Godfrey   Katherine Davis
   Newport 31 Jan 1704   E.Greenwich   Newport c.1704
   St.Martins,W.I.   19 Jul 1722   E.Greenwich c.1740
      1 Apr 1756

4 Mary Godfrey   Caleb Bailey
   E.Greenwich c.1723   E.Greenwich   E.Greenwich 7 Sep 1720
   W.Greenwich Nov 1790   2 Apr 1744   W.Greenwich Aug 1803

5 Waite Bailey   Charles Greene

   Continue with Generation 6 of his lineage from Governor
   John Coggeshall.

SUPPLEMENT NO. 2

1 Jeremiah Clarke, Governor of Rhode Island 1648

2 Jeremiah Clarke   Ann Audley
   Newport,RI c.1643   Newport   Boston,MA c.1645
   Newport 16 Jan 1728   c.1665   Newport 15 Dec 1732

3 Jeremiah Clarke   Elizabeth Sisson
   Newport c.1667   Newport   Portsmouth,RI 18 Aug
                                                  1669
   South Kingstown,RI   c.1690   S.Kingstown
      10 Sep 1733

4 Sarah Clarke   Edward Greenman
   S.Kingstown c.1693   S.Kingstown   Newport c.1694
   Charlestown,RI af.1741   11 May 1721   Charlestown 21 Feb 1741

5 Margaret Greenman   Joseph Greene

   Continue with Generation 5 of his lineage from Governor
   John Coggeshall.

JONES, CERENO ST.CLAIR

Nat. #334-B.   Elected 1 Feb 1979.   b. Newton,MA 24 Apr 1897.
m. Oakland,CA 24 Jun 1924, Rosalin Carmela Christina Schultheis,
b. San Francisco,CA 15 Dec 1897.   Member: Hereditary Order of
Desc. of Colonial Governors; Royal Order of Scotland; Sons of
American Revolution; Sons and Daughters of Pilgrims; Desc. of
Loyalists and Patriots; Baronial Order of Magna Charta; Order of
Crown of Charlemagne; Soc. of Desc. of Colonial Clergy; Soc. of
Mayflower Desc.; Friends of St. George; Desc. of Knights of Most
Noble Order of the Garter; Military Order of Crusades; Knights
Templar; Order of Amaranth.   Address: 5500 Burling Court,
Bethesda,MD 20034.   Descended from:

1 William Bradford, Governor of Plymouth Colony 1621-57

2 William Bradford   Alice Richards
   Plymouth,MA 17 Jun   Weymouth   Weymouth,MA 16 Jun
     1624   1627
   Plymouth 20 Feb 1703/4 28 Jan 1650   Plymouth 12 Dec 1671

3 Samuel Bradford   Hannah Rogers
   Plymouth c.1668   Duxbury,MA   Duxbury 16 Nov 1668
   Duxbury 11 Apr 1714   31 Jul 1689   Milton,MA af.16 Jul
                                                1733

4 Hannah Bradford   Nathaniel Gilbert
   Plymouth 14 Feb 1689/90 Duxbury   Taunton,MA 19 Jul 1683
   Berkley,MA 28 Jan 1772 16 Jun 1709   Berkley 17 Aug 1763

5 Welthea Gilbert   Ebenezer Hathaway
   -----   -----   15 Jul 1718
   -----   -----   16 Jun 1791

6 Welthea Hathaway   Richard Ruggles
   -----   -----   Rochester,MA 4 Mar
                                               1743/4
   4 Dec 1825   1771   Annapolis,Nova Scotia
                                               21 Oct 1832

7 Sophia Ruggles   John Ryerson
   31 Jan 1785   New York,NY 25 Jan 1779
   -----   17 Feb 1803   Nova Scotia 10 Nov 1854

8 Abigail Hathaway   Frederick Davou Sterns
     Ryerson   Jones
   Annapolis 5 Sep 1814   St.John,   Weymouth,NS 8 May 1807
                            Brunswick
   Malden,MA 1892   10 Nov 1838   St.John,NB 1893

9 Gustavus Jones   Mary Elizabeth Bullock
                                               Robertson
   St.John 10 Nov 1838   St.John   St.John 26 Apr 1844
   Malden 9 May 1888   25 Apr 1864   Somerville,MA 29 Oct
                                               1916

10 Mary Emma Robertson   Cereno Percy Jones
     Jones
   Chelsea,MA 30 Aug 1869 Somerville,MA   Weymouth,NS 29 May 1870
   South Pasadena,CA   27 Jun 1896   South Pasadena 27 Apr
     2 Sep 1958   1946

JONES, MALCOLM MURRAY

Nat. #134-B. Elected 7 Feb 1968. b. Scarsdale,NY 24 Oct 1935.
m. Sudbury,MA 18 Jun 1966, Lesly Sheldon Weaver, b. Evanston,IL
7 Jul 1941. Issue: Oliver Neville Jones, b. 7 May 1968; Marbury
Joy Jones, b. 24 Mar 1973; both b. Lexington,MA. Educ:
Massachusetts Institute of Technology, B.S., M.S., and Ph.D.
1967. Member: Hereditary Order of Desc. of Colonial Governors;
Soc. of Colonial Wars; National Huguenot Soc.; Soc. of Old
Plymouth Colony Desc.; Flagon and Trencher; Soc. of Knights of
Most Noble Order of the Garter; Lexington Historical Soc.; listed
in Living Desc. of Blood Royal in America. Occup: Management
Consultant, Decision Technology; Consultant U.S. Dept of Defense.
Address: Double Tree at Heather Ridge, 2623 S. Vaughn Way,
Aurora,CO 80014. Descended from:

1 William Leete, Governor of Connecticut 1676-83

2 John Leete II   Mary Chittenden
   Guilford,CT 1639   Guilford   Guilford 1647
   Guilford 25 Nov 1692 4 Oct 1670   Guilford 9 Mar 1712

3 Anne Leete   John Collins III
   Guilford 5 Aug 1671   Guilford   Branford,CT 1 Mar 1665
   Guilford 2 Nov 1724   23 Jul 1691   Guilford 24 Jan 1751

4 Mercy Collins   Samuel Hopson, Jr.
   Guilford 19 Jan 1707 Guilford   Guilford 21 Oct 1710
   Wallingford,CT   bf.1734   Wallingford 3 May 1789
     22 Jan 1786

5 Simeon Hopson   Naomi Moss
   Wallingford 14 Oct   Wallingford   Wallingford 1 Oct 1754
     1747
   Oswego Co.NY   22 Feb 1776   Oswego Co. af.1830
     af. 4 Jul 1836

6 Simeon Hopson, Jr.   Ruth Cowing
   Northfield,CT   Lebanon,NY   Chesterfield,MA
     18 Dec 1786   10 Sep 1793
   Jefferson,WI 18 Mar   29 Dec 1813   Jefferson 30 Aug 1869
     1855

7 William Alonzo Hopson   (Hannah) Jane Scofield
   Mexico,NY 6 Aug 1817 New Haven,NY   Paris Hill,NY 30 Sep
                                              1818
   Fort Atkinson,WI   4 Mar 1841   Fort Atkinson 16 Feb
     10 May 1866   1888

8 Edgar DeLos Hopson   Mary Rebecca Colwell
   Fort Atkinson 16 Dec Milwaukee,WI   Farmington,WI 28 Nov
     1851   1856
   Madison,WI 11 Jun 1913 10 May 1881   Chestnut Hill,MA
                                              14 Nov 1930

9 Norma Joy Hopson   Samuel Murray Jones
   Fort Atkinson   Scarsdale,NY   Paterson,NJ 19 Mar 1901
     5 Apr 1900
                         2 May 1931   West Newton,MA 21 Jan
                                              1954

1 Stephen Goodyear, Deputy Governor of Connecticut 1643-58

2 Rebecca Goodyear
   London,Eng. c.1626   New Haven,CT   John Bishop
   Stamford,CT 1679   -----   England c.1612
                                  Stamford 12 Mar 1694

Rebecca Goodyear
London,Eng. c.1626 — New Haven,CT — ----- — Stamford,CT 1679

John Bishop
England c.1612 — Stamford 12 Mar 1694

3 Rebecca Bishop
   Stamford Feb 1663   -----   Joseph Whiting
   Southampton,NY   c.1682   Lynn,MA 6 Apr 1641
    26 Apr 1726   Southampton 7 Apr 1723

4 Joseph Whiting, Jr.
   Southampton bf.1694 Stamford   Abigail Holly
   Stamford c.1657   17 Apr 1720 Stamford 8 Jun 1700
                              Stamford 2 May 1733

5 Martha Whiting
   Stamford 2 Apr 1728 Stamford   Peter Selleck
   -----   18 Jan 1753 Stamford 2 May 1729
                              af.1790

6 Mary Selleck
   Stamford 5 Mar 1755 -----   Israel Scofield, Jr.
   Paris,NY 5 May 1836 22 Feb 1779 Stamford 19 May 1754
                              Paris 10 Jun 1833

7 Ira Scofield
   CT Nov 1787   Paris Hill,NY Anne Webber
   Fort Atkinson,WI   6 Jul 1814   Holland,MA 19 Jan 1794
    7 Nov 1853   New Haven,NY 30 Apr
                              1830

8 Hannah Jane Scofield   William Alonzo Hopson

Continue with Generation 7 of his lineage from Governor
William Leete.

Inheritor: Oliver Neville Jones (same address)

JONES, NORMA HOPSON (MRS. S. MURRAY)

Nat. #100-B. Elected 12 Sep 1964. b. Ft. Atkinson,WI 5 Apr 1900.
m. Scarsdale,NY 2 May 1931, Samuel Murray Jones, b. Paterson,NJ
19 Mar 1901, d. West Newton,MA 21 Jan 1954. Issue: Claire Jones
Royston, b. Scarsdale 31 Mar 1933; Malcolm Murray Jones, b. Scars-
dale 24 Oct 1935. Educ: Boston U., B.S.; Radcliffe College;
Harvard University. Member: Hereditary Order of Desc. of Colonial
Governors; Dau. of American Revolution (Past Chap. Regent); U.S.
Dau. of 1812; New England Women (Colony Historian); Dau. of
Founders and Patriots of America (Hon. State Pres.); Piscataqua
Pioneers; Old Plymouth Colony Desc. (Past Pres. Gen.); Dau. of
Barons of Runnemede; Dames of Court of Honor; Women Desc. of the
Ancient and Honorable Artillery Co. (State Color Bearer); Dau. of
Colonial Wars (State Historian); Soc. of Desc. of Colonial Clergy
(Councillor); National Huguenot Soc. (State Councillor); Flagon
and Trencher; Soc. of Desc. of Knights of the Most Noble Order of

the Garter; Magna Charta Dames; Order of Americans of Armorial
Ancestry; Doolittles of America; Bunker Hill Monument Assn.;
Huguenot Memorial Soc. of Oxford (Vice Pres.); Connecticut Soc.
of Genealogists; listed in Living Desc. of Blood Royal.
Address: 14 Concord Avenue, #307, Cambridge,MA 02138. Descended
from:

1 William Leete, Governor of Connecticut 1676-83

                              and

1 Stephen Goodyear, Deputy Governor of Connecticut 1643-58

   Continue with the lineages of her son Malcolm Murray Jones.

   Inheritor: Claire Joyce Jones Royston (Mrs. Richard H.),
   2230 West Orange Ave., Apt. 7, Anaheim,CA 92804.

                              K

KEMPER, JOHN WILLIAM

Nat. #299-B. Elected 2 Dec 1976. b. Ponca City,OK 20 Jan 1945.
Educ: Parsons College, B.A. Member: Hereditary Order of Desc.
of Colonial Governors; Baronial Order of Magna Charta; Soc. of
Mayflower Descendants; Soc. of Desc. of Colonial Clergy; Sons of
American Revolution; Pioneer Historical Society. Address:
20218 Tilstock Road, Katy, TX 77450. Descended from:

1 Thomas Prence, Governor of Plymouth Colony, 1633-34, 1636-37,
   1644-45

2 Mercy Prence   John Freeman
   Plymouth,MA 1631   Eastham,MA   Billinghurst,Eng.
                                            c.1621-27
   Eastham 28 Sep 1711 13 Feb 1649   Eastham 28 Oct 1719

3 Edmond Freeman   Ruth Merrick
   Eastham Jun 1655   Eastham   Eastham 15 May 1652
   Eastham 10 Dec 1717 Jan 1677   Eastham 1680

4 Ruth Freeman   Israel Doane
   Eastham 1680   Eastham   Eastham 1672
   Eastham 7 Jun 1728   1700   Eastham af.1732

5 Elnathan Doane   Martha Paddock
   Eastham 9 Apr 1709   Eastham   -----
   Doansburg,NY af.1778 -----   Doansburg

6 Daniel Doane   Elizabeth Merrick
   Eastham 4 Apr 1741   -----   Harwich,MA 23 Jul 1747
   Doansburg af.1787   -----   Plainfield,NY c.1798/9

7 Joseph Doane   Esther Markham
   Dutchess Co.NY 1773 Dutchess Co.   Enfield,CT 17 Feb 1778
   Lyon,MI 29 Mar 1847 1797   Lyon 18 Dec 1851

8	Erastus Doane		Hester Stringham
	Brookfield,NY 6 Jan 1798	Scipio,NY	Scipio 16 Feb 1802
	Green Oak,MI 13 Aug 1861	1827	Green Oak 27 Nov 1883

9	Jemima Zilla Doane		William Lloyd Webb
	Sempronius,NY 17 Aug 1828	South Lyon, MI	England 1823
	South Lyon 8 Apr 1908	10 Apr 1851	South Lyon 5 Mar 1867

10	Janet Webb		William Thomas Ramsey
	Northville,MI 16 Apr 1853	Butler Co.KS	Pittsylvania Co.,VA 16 Oct 1842
	Ripley,OK 2 Feb 1913	20 Sep 1875	Ripley 31 May 1913

11	John Newman Ramsey		Anna Stazia Jones
	Greenwood Co.KS 8 Apr 1880	Stillwater,OK	Marshfield,MO 28 Sep 1880
	Boise,ID 25 Jun 1964	20 Nov 1900	Ponca City,OK 26 Mar 1951

12	Mildred Marie Ramsey		William Kemper
	Orlando,OK 1 Dec 1914	Ponca City	Osage Co.OK 16 Oct 1909
	living in 1976	2 Oct 1938	living in 1976

KEMPER, MILDRED MARIE RAMSEY (MRS. WILLIAM)

Nat. #297-B. Elected 25 Sep 1976. b. Orlando,OK 1 Dec 1914. m. Ponca City,OK 2 Oct 1938, William Kemper, b. Osage Co.,OK 16 Oct 1909. Issue: John William Kemper, b. Ponca City 20 Jan 1945. Member: Hereditary Order of Desc. of Colonial Governors; Dau. of American Revolution; Dau. of American Colonists; Colonial Dames of XVII Century; Women Desc. of the Ancient and Honorable Artillery Co.; Soc. of Mayflower Descendants; Soc. of Desc. of Colonial Clergy. Address: 204 West State, Eagle Lake, TX 77434. Descended from:

1 Thomas Prence, Governor of Plymouth Colony, 1633-34, 1636-37, 1644-45

Continue with the lineage of her son John William Kemper.

KESSLER, ELIZABETH M. HILL (MRS. LEWIS HANFORD)

Nat. #215-B. Elected 15 Sep 1973. b. Antigo,WI 26 Apr 1903. m. Rockford,IL 3 Jan 1923, Lewis Hanford Kessler, b. South Haven, MI 12 Mar 1900. Issue: Gwendolyn L. Kessler John; Lewis Hanford Kessler, Jr.; Avery Bassett Kessler. Educ: University of Wisconsin, 1924. Member: Hereditary Order of Desc. of Colonial Governors; Dau. of American Revolution; Dau. of American Colonists; Dau. of Colonial Wars; New England Women; Dau. of

Founders and Patriots of America; Dames of the Court of Honor;
Women Desc. of the Ancient and Honorable Artillery Co.; Soc. of
Desc. of Colonial Clergy; Magna Charta Dames; Westport Histori-
cal Soc. Address: 6404 Sagamore Rd., Mission Hills,KS 66208.
Descended from:

1 John Mason, Governor of Connecticut 1659-60

2 Priscilla Mason   James Fitch
   Connecticut   Norwich,CT   England 24 Dec 1622
   Lebanon,CT   Oct 1664   Lebanon 18 Nov 1702

3 Daniel Fitch   Mary Sherwood
   Norwich 16 Aug 1665   Fairfield,CT   Fairfield
   Fairfield 3 Jun 1711 Mar 1698   -----

4 Daniel Fitch   Sarah Sherwood
   Montville,CT   Stratford,CT   -----
   -----   16 Nov 1732   -----

5 Ann Fitch   Elisha Fox
   Montville 1746   Montville   Montville 15 Oct 1743
   Montville 21 Aug 1836 1763   Montville 13 Apr 1800

6 Pamelia Fox   Jonathan Avery
   Montville 14 Nov 1763 Enfield,CT   Montville 10 Sep 1755
   E.Charlemont,MA   11 Dec 1782   E.Charlemont 14 Jun
    20 Jul 1853   1847

7 Annis Avery   Caleb Hill
   Enfield 14 Nov 1796   Charlemont,MA   Gardiner,MA 19 Dec
                                           1786
   Wauwatosa,WI 25 May   25 Dec 1815   Charlemont 18 Jun 1842
    1885

8 Homer Hill   Elizabeth Kiernan
   W.Springfield,MA   Chicago,IL   Ireland 11 Sep 1833
    16 Feb 1833
   Antigo,WI 23 Sep 1893 29 May 1856   Antigo 13 Aug 1883

9 Warren C. Hill   Ida R. Chadek
   Manitowoc,WI 2 Nov   New London,WI   Kewaunee,WI 14 Oct
    1866   1879
   Rhinelander,WI   27 Nov 1901   Antigo 3 Jun 1924
    9 Oct 1930

Inheritor: Miss Susan Victoria John, 6718 Oglesby, Chicago,IL
60649

KING, GEORGE HARRISON SANFORD

Nat. #3-B. Elected 15 Mar 1959. b. Fredericksburg,VA 2 Jan
1914. Educ: Virginia Polytechnic Inst., B.S. 1935. Member:
Hereditary Order of Desc. of Colonial Governors; Soc. of Desc.
of Henry Fox and wife, Ann West (Registrar); Order of First
Families of Virginia; American Soc. of Genealogists; Virginia,
Kentucky, and Maryland Historical Societies; N.E. Hist. and
Gene. Soc.; Assn. for Preservation of Virginia Antiquities; The
Mount Vernon Club; Country Club, Fredericksburg. Occup:
Genealogist. Address: 1303 Prince Edward St., Fredericksburg,
VA 22401. Descended from:

1 John West, Governor of Virginia 1635-37

2 John West   Unity Croshaw
   Bellfield,VA 1632   -----   -----
   King William Co.,VA   c.1667   -----
      15 Nov 1689

3 Ann West   Henry Fox
   -----   -----   King William Co. c.1650
   -----   -----   c.1714

4 Thomas Fox   Mary Tunstall
   King William Co.   -----   King William Co.
   -----   c.1708   -----

5 Thomas Fox   Philadelphia Claiborne
   c.1710   -----   King William Co.
   Oct 1792   -----   -----

6 Elizabeth Fox   John Frazer
   c.1762   -----   c.1756
   Apr 1795   16 Jan 1783   Nov 1793

7 Thomas Fox Frazer   Margaret Magee
   27 Nov 1783   -----   -----
   1841   3 Oct 1815   -----

8 Lucy Fox Frazer   Melzi Sanford
                                             Chancellor
   1817   Washington,DC   29 Jun 1815
   3 Sep 1884   23 Nov 1837   20 Feb 1895

9 Annastasia Chancellor   George Phillips King
   5 Sep 1840/1   Locust Grove,   29 Mar 1813
                             VA
   Nov 1912   25 Mar 1868   3 Dec 1876

10 George Phillips   Cora May Harrison
      King, Jr.
   Fredericksburg,VA   Prince George   7 Aug 1882
      20 Jan 1871   Co.,MD
   Fredericksburg   11 Aug 1908   25 Sep 1944
      21 Jun 1931

Inheritor: Anne Woodbury King Silver (Mrs. Ronald Craig),
Box 134, Rt. 2, Fredericksburg,VA 22401

KLEIN, CATHERINE CHILCOTE TAYLOR (MRS. GEORGE)

Nat. #161-B. Elected 28 Jul 1970. b. Baltimore,MD 15 Dec 1905.
m. Bel Air,MD 23 Jun 1925, George Klein, b. Baltimore 3 Jun
1903 (dec.). Issue: C. Dudley Klein Albright, b. Baltimore
3 Apr 1926. Member: Hereditary Order of Desc. of Colonial
Governors; The Jamestowne Soc.; Plantagenet Soc.; Colonial
Order of the Crown; Magna Charta Dames; U.S. Daughters of 1812;
Colonial Dames of America; Colonial Dames of XVII Century;
Soc. of Daughters of Colonial Wars; Dau. of American Revolution;
Woman's Eastern Shore Soc.; Maryland Historical Soc. Address:
8402 Charles Valley Court, Baltimore, MD 21204. Descended from:

1   Richard Bennett, Governor of Virginia 1652-55

2	Elizabeth Bennett Virginia c.1645 -----	----- -----	Charles Scarburgh c.1643 Accomack Co.,VA c.1701/2
. 3	Henry Scarburgh c.1678 4 Nov 1735	----- -----	Winefred Taylor ----- -----
4	Henry Scarburgh ----- -----	----- -----	Margaret Custis ----- -----
5	Tabitha Custis Scarburgh 6 Nov 1744 -----	----- 8 Jun 1769	Nathaniel Beavans 15 May 1748 17 Jan 1792
6	Tabitha C. Beavans 8 Oct 1781 Somerset Co.MD 21 Sep 1843	Accomack Co. 7 Feb 1815	William Hayward Waters 11 Feb 1778 10 Aug 1838
7	Mary W. Waters Somerset Co. 29 Oct 1816 6 Sep 1877	----- 21 Nov 1833	John W. Taylor 11 Oct 1811 Somerset Co. 26 Jun 1865
8	Jefferson Zachary Taylor Somerset Co. 29 Aug 1848 Baltimore,MD 8 Jan 1930	----- 4 Jan 1877	Hannah E. Evans 19 Jan 1858 Baltimore 17 Nov 1942
9	Paul D. Taylor Oxford,MD 17 Nov 1877 Nashville,TN 23 Oct 1954	Baltimore 19 Dec 1900	Mary T. Chilcote 7 May 1880 16 Jul 1966

Inheritor: C. Dudley Klein Albright (Mrs. John J., Jr.),
1008 Jamieson Rd., Lutherville,MD 21093

KNOWLES, GRACE FULLER (MRS. W. HERBERT)

Nat. #33-B. Elected 8 Apr 1961. b. La Salle,NY 6 Apr 1905.
m. Niagara Falls,NY 18 Sep 1926, William Herbert Knowles, b.
Americus,GA 27 Oct 1903, d. Richmond,VA 15 Jul 1956. Issue:
Lawrence Fuller Knowles, b. Buffalo,NY 17 Jan 1929. Educ:
American University and Richmond Professional Inst. Member:
Hereditary Order of Desc. of Colonial Governors; Dau. of Ameri-
can Revolution (Past Regent, Wm. Byrd Ch.); Dau. of American
Colonists (Past Regent, Pocahontas Ch.); Soc. of Mayflower
Descendants in VA (Historian); Jamestowne Society; Virginia
Genealogical Soc. (Member of Executive Board); Women Desc. of
Ancient and Honorable Artillery Co., DC; Dau. of Founders and
Patriots, VA; Colonial Dames of XVII Century. Occup: Genealo-
gist. Address: 1715 Bellevue Ave., B-901, Richmond,VA 23227.
Descended from:

1 John Alden, Governor of Plymouth Colony 1663-4, 1667

2 Rebecca Alden   Thomas Delano
   Plymouth,MA   Plymouth   Duxbury,MA 21 Nov 1642
   -----   1667   Duxbury 13 Apr 1723

3 Jonathan Delano   Hannah Doty
   Duxbury 1676   Duxbury   Plymouth Dec 1675
   Duxbury 6 Jan 1765   12 Jan 1698   Duxbury Apr 1764

4 Ruth Delano   John Peterson
   Duxbury 25 May 1707   Kingston,MA   Duxbury 22 Aug 1701
   -----   25 May 1726   -----

5 Nathan Peterson   Amy Tanner
   Middleboro,MA 1734   S.Kingstown   South Kingstown,RI
                                                      11 Oct 1729
   S.Kingstown bf.25 Sep   bf.1759   Richmond,RI 7 Jul 1817
      1796

6 John Peterson   Phebe Tanner
   S.Kingstown 15 May   S.Kingstown   S.Kingstown 11 May
      1769   1775
   Orleans Co.NY 9 Nov   Nov 1793   North Ridge,NY 4 May
      1831   1855

7 Phebe Peterson   Sylvester Himes
   Bristol,VT 17 Aug   -----   Clarendon,VT 6 May
      1797   1797
   Niagara Co.NY 4 Jan   -----   Niagara Co. 19 Jun
      1862   1868

8 Hanford Sylvester Himes   Julia Ann Abbott
   Ridgeway,NY 4 May 1823 Oswego Co.NY   Oswego Co. 25 Jul
                                                      1828
   Granby Center,NY   25 Aug 1847   Granby Center 20 Apr
      28 Dec 1880   1919

9 Adelaide Francelia   William Harrison Cole
      Himes
   Ridgeway 13 Feb 1849   Ransomville,NY Cambria,NY 24 Apr 1841
   Niagara Falls 25 Dec   3 Jan 1867   Granby Center 18 Jun
      1921   1915

10 Bessie Maude Cole   Merritt Goold Fuller
   Sanborn,NY 25 Oct 1882   Sanborn   Pekin,NY 1 May 1879
                        4 Sep 1901   Niagara Falls 19 Feb
                                         1933

   Inheritor: Lawrence Fuller Knowles (son)

KRANZ, YSABELITA H. J. (MRS. MARTIN E.)

Nat. #355-B. Elected 15 Jul 1979. b. New Orleans,LA 25 Dec
1905. m. New Orleans 15 Apr 1926, Martin Emile Kranz, b. New
Orleans 3 Mar 1900. Issue: Ysabelita Lillian Kranz Martin, b.
2 Sep 1927; Mary Appolonia Kranz Perilloux, b. 17 Oct 1928,
d. 23 Sep 1974. Educ: Grand Coteau College, Lafayette,LA.
Member: Hereditary Order of Desc. of Colonial Governors;
Dau. of American Revolution; Dau. of American Colonists;
U.S. Dau of 1812; Colonial Dames of XVII Century; Colonial
Order of the Crown; Magna Charta Dames; Ark and Dove Soc.;
Americans of Royal Descent; Knights of the Most Noble Order of
the Garter; Soc. of Desc. of Colonial Clergy; Physicians and
Chirurgeins; LA Historical Soc. Address: P.O. Box 1761,
Covington,LA 70433. Descended from:

1 Thomas Greene, Governor of Maryland 1647-48

2 Leonard Greene   -----
   England   Maryland   England
   Maryland 1651   -----   -----

3 Winifred Greene   Francis Wheeler
   St.Mary's Co.MD 1644 Maryland   c.1673
   St.Mary's Co. 1688   28 Aug 1690   -----

4 Mary Wheeler   Salome Noble
   Charles Co.MD   Charles Co.   England 17 Apr 1689
     14 Nov 1693
   -----   2 Feb 1708   Maryland 1749

5 Salome Noble   Joseph Edelen
   Prince George's Co., -----   Prince George's Co.
    MD 23 Apr 1724   14 Apr 1710
   Maryland   1740   Prince George's Co.
                                   1708

6 Theresa Celestia   Samuel McPherson
    Edelen
   Prince George's Co. Maryland   Charles Co. 1808
    1757
   Prince George's Co. 17 Jul 1828   St.Landry Parish,LA
    4 Jan 1833   13 Jun 1871

7 Augusta McPherson   John Ignatius Gardiner
   St.Landry Par.   St.Landry Par. Charles Co. 11 Sep 1811
    15 Jul 1834
   St.Landry Par.   14 Apr 1852   St.Landry Par.
    21 Dec 1890   18 Jul 1891

8 Josephine Marie   John Gardiner Hamilton
    Gardiner
  St.Landry Par.   New Orleans,LA Burlington,OH 22 Sep
    17 Jun 1861   1838
  St.Landry Par.   1 Nov 1883   New Orleans 4 Apr 1893
    3 Jul 1940

  Inheritor: Ysabelita L. K. Martin, Route 1, Box 27C,
  Covington, LA 70433

KUHN, VIRGINIA FLORENCE (MISS)

Nat. #73-B. Elected 30 Mar 1963. b. Malden,WV 22 Jul 1901.
Educ: Morris Harvey College, Kanawha College, Capital City Com-
mercial College. Member: Hereditary Order of Desc. of Colonial
Governors; Dau. of American Colonists; Magna Charta Dames; Dau.
of American Revolution; U.S. Daughters of 1812; Huguenot Society
of Founders of Manakin in the Colony of Virginia; Lords of
Maryland Manors; Colonial Dames of XVII Century; Dau. of the
Colonial Wars; Sovereign Colonial Soc. of Americans of Royal
Descent. Address: 1316 Virginia St., Charleston,WV 25301.
(From Society's Records). Descended from:

1 Leonard Calvert, Governor of Maryland 1633-47

2 William Calvert   Elizabeth Stone
   England c.1642   Maryland   Maryland 1603
   Maryland 10 Jan 1682   c.1661   Maryland af.1682

3 George Calvert   Elizabeth Doyne
   Maryland 1668   Maryland   -----
   Maryland af.1739   1690   -----

4 John Calvert   (2)   Elizabeth Harrison
   Maryland 1692   Pr.Wm.Co.   Prince William Co.
   Prince William Co.,VA 1711   -----
     1739

5 Jacob Calvert   Sarah Crupper
   Stafford Co.,VA 1720   Pr.Wm.Co.   -----
   Prince William Co. 1772 -----   -----

6 Francis Calvert   Elizabeth Witt
   Prince William Co. 1751 Bedford Co.VA Bedford Co. 1772
   Kanawha Co.WV   22 Dec 1791 Bedford Co. 1806
     11 Jul 1823

7 John L. Calvert   Elizabeth Anne Slack
   Bedford Co. 28 Apr 1803 Kanawha Co. Bedford Co. 7 Nov 1807
   Kanawha Co. 30 Apr 1863 30 Aug 1825 Kanawha Co. 12 Nov 1882

8 Sallie Anne Calvert   Joseph Jubal Kuhn
   Malden,WV 2 Jan 1837   Malden   Franklin Co.VA 1 Apr
                                         1830
   Marmet,WV 25 Oct 1909   14 Jun 1854 Marmet 11 Sep 1897

9 James Allen Kuhn   Icie Elizabeth Lee
   Malden 1 Jul 1868   Charleston   Mason Co.WV 9 Jan 1877
   Charleston,WV 7 Jul   17 May 1894
   1946

   Inheritor: Loughrey Roberts Kuhn, Llewellyn Fields Farm,
   950 Norwood Road, Silver Spring, MD 20904

KUPILLAS, MARY ANNA COATES MARTIN (MRS. LAWRENCE O.)

Nat. #160-B. Elected 27 Jul 1970. b. Gloucester Co.,NJ 4 Jan
1912. m.(1) Haddonfield,NJ 29 May 1931, Clyde Davis Martin,
b. Philadelphia,PA 6 May 1906, d. Jun 1945. Issue: William
Raymond Martin, b. Philadelphia 16 Oct 1939. m.(2) Washington,
DC 28 Oct 1950, Lawrence O. Kupillas, b. New York 1898. Educ:
Camden Community College, Pearce Business College, New York
University. Member: Hereditary Order of Desc. of Colonial
Governors (1st Deputy Governor General); Dau. of American
Revolution (State Chaplain); New England Women (Director
General); Dau. of Colonial Wars (State Corr. Secretary); Sorosis,
Inc. (President); Washington Headquarters Assn. (President).
Occup: Civic Worker, Restoring Historic houses in NYC. Address:
220 Madison Avenue, New York,NY 10016. Descended from:

1 Jeremiah Clarke, Governor of Rhode Island 1652

2 Jeremiah Clarke   Anne Dudley
   c.1643   -----   -----
   16 Jan 1729   -----   15 Dec 1732

3 Anne Clarke   William Greenman
   c.1676   -----   -----
   -----   c.1703   -----

4 Jeremiah Greenman   Sarah Blackman
   -----   -----   -----
   -----   -----   -----

5 Amey Greenman   Peter DuBois
   24 Oct 1727   -----   10 Apr 1734
   2 Jun 1807   1758   21 Aug 1795

6 Thomas DuBois   Sarah Foster
   Salem Co.NJ 16 Jul 1764 -----   26 Sep 1764
   19 Dec 1845   -----   1 Jul 1838

7 Phebe DuBois   Moses Richman
   Salem Co. 29 Dec 1796   Salem Co.   4 Jun 1797
   17 Sep 1882   18 Mar 1817   27 Aug 1862

8 Emily Richman   Harrison Johnson
   Salem Co. 19 Sep 1820   Salem Co.   2 Nov 1819
   5 May 1885   13 Mar 1845   -----

9 Alfred R. Johnson   Ruth Anna Dailey
   Salem Co. 28 Sep 1846   -----   28 Sep 1857
   Woodstown,NJ 20 Feb   26 Feb 1878   17 Jun 1947
      1923

10 Emily Johnson   Raymond Coates
   Salem Co. 28 Oct 1882   Harrisonville, Staytonsville,DE
                                   NJ   2 Dec 1877
   Salem Co. 22 Nov 1966   31 Jul 1900   Salem Co. 17 Jan 1965

   Inheritor: William Raymond Martin (son)

                                    L

LANE, ELIZABETH C. CHAPMAN (MRS. E. SAM)

Nat. #20-B. Elected 11 Mar 1960. m.(1) 23 Jun 1941, John Waltz
Salvage, d. 13 Nov 1942. Issue: John Waltz Salvage, Jr.,
b. 6 Oct 1942. m.(2) 8 Jul 1944, Ernest Sam Lane, Jr. Member:
Hereditary Order of Desc. of Colonial Governors; Dau. of Ameri-
can Revolution; United Daughters of the Confederacy; Dau. of
Barons of Runnemede. (From Society's Records). Address:
P.O. Box #253, Riverview Drive, Murfreesboro,TN 37130. Descended
from:

1 Alexander Spotswood, Governor of Virginia 1710-22

2 Dorothea Spotswood   Nathaniel West
                                                    Dandridge
   1733   7 Sep 1729
   25 Sep 1773   18 Jun 1747   16 Jan 1786

3 Elizabeth Dandridge   Philip Payne
   12 Sep 1764   29 Mar 1760
   26 Apr 1833   13 Nov 1783   7 Jul 1840

4 John Smith Payne   Susan Elwood Scott
   26 Jun 1786   -----   1794
   1872   -----   1826

5 Martha Harriet Payne   Marco Bozzaris Carter
   12 Apr 1835   -----   11 Apr 1826
   19 Jul 1875   25 Jan 1860   10 Dec 1874

6 Elizabeth Clark Carter   William Henry Adams
   19 Feb 1867   Jun 1865
   Aug 1944   27 Sep 1893   Jul 1932

7 Blanch Howard Adams   Lewis Linwood Chapman
   Newport News,VA   -----   6 Aug 1893
      12 Jul 1895
   22 Jul 1958   5 May 1917   Smithfield,VA 23 Mar
                                                    1956

   Inheritor: John Waltz Salvage II

                                   147

LEET, ERNEST DELOS

Nat. #366-B. Elected 30 Oct 1979. b. Jamestown,NY 9 Nov 1901.
m. Jamestown 18 Oct 1927, Mary Bailey, b. Bradford,PA 8 Oct
1901. Issue: Bethia Leet, b. Jamestown 8 Apr 1930; Frances
Bailey Leet, b. Jamestown 17 Apr 1932; Rosemary Leet, b. James-
town 30 Jan 1937. Educ: Cornell University, A.B.; Harvard Law
School, LLB and JD. Member: Hereditary Order of Desc. of
Colonial Governors; Sons of the American Revolution (Former Chrm.
Jamestown Chap.); Chautauqua Co. Historical Soc.; Jamestown Bar
Assn. (Past Pres.); Fenton Historical Soc.; American Legion.
Military: Lt. Cmdr.,U.S. Navy, World War II. Address: 58 Houston
Ave., Jamestown,NY 14701. Descended from:

1 William Leete, Governor of Connecticut 1676-83

2	John Leete		Mary Chittenden
	Guilford,CT 1639	Guilford	Guilford 1647
	Guilford 25 Nov 1692	4 Oct 1670	Guilford 9 Mar 1712

3	Pelatiah Leete		Abigail Fowler
	Leete's Island,CT	Guilford	Guilford 1679
	26 Mar 1681		
	Leete's Island	1 Jul 1705	Leete's Island
	13 Oct 1768		22 Oct 1769

4	Pelatiah Leete		Lydia Crittenden
	Leete's Island	Leete's Isl.	Guilford 4 Mar 1719
	7 Mar 1713		
	Leete's Island	26 Mar 1740	Leete's Island
	28 May 1786		13 Aug 1772

5	Simeon Leete		Zerviah Norton
	Leete's Island	Leete's Isl.	Guilford
	14 Apr 1753		
	Leete's Island	-----	-----
	19 Jun 1781		

6	Anson Leete		Abigail Dudley
	Leete's Island	Leete's Isl.	Guilford 27 Jan 1780
	21 May 1777		
	Point Chautauqua,NY	-----	Chautauqua Co.
	1843		2 Feb 1879

7	Franklin Leet		Sally Sumner
	Herkimer Co.NY	-----	14 Sep 1817
	20 Jul 1815		
	Jamestown,NY	31 Oct 1839	Sewittville,NY
	11 Dec 1907		4 Apr 1865

8	Fayette G. Leet		Helen E. Olds
	Stockton,NY	-----	Olds' Corners,NY
	15 May 1847		1 Sep 1847
	Jamestown 11 May 1934	30 Jun 1869	Jamestown 14 Oct 1918

9	Frank F. Leet		Emma A. Shannon
	Stockton 27 Feb 1873	Rutledge,NY	Conewango,NY 9 Jul 1870
	Jamestown 22 Apr 1931	31 Jul 1895	Jamestown 8 Mar 1954

LEET, IRENE HAINES (MRS. JOHN DASKAM)

Nat. #67-B. Elected 15 Mar 1963. b. Eldorado,KS 21 Apr 1906.
m. Daytona Beach,FL 25 Apr 1933, John Daskam Leet. Issue: Jaren
Forest Leet; Marilyn H. Leet Ray. Educ: Smith College; Parsons
(NY School of Fine and Applied Art). Member: Hereditary Order
of Desc. of Colonial Governors; Soc. of Colonial Dames of
America. Address: 1788 Oak Creek Drive #417, Palo Alto,CA
94304. (From Society's Records). Descended from:

1 Thomas Lloyd, Governor of Pennsylvania 1684-93

2 Rachel Lloyd   Samuel Preston
   North Wales 1667   -----   Maryland 1664
   -----   -----   Philadelphia,PA 1743

3 Hannah Preston   Samuel Carpenter
   1693   -----   Philadelphia 9 Feb
                                                   1688
   1772   1711   Philadelphia 7 Nov
                                                   1745

4 Preston Carpenter   Hannah Smith
   Philadelphia 1721   -----   Hedgefield,NJ 1723
   20 Oct 1785   1742   -----

5 Hannah Carpenter   Charles Ellet
   1743   -----   New Jersey
   1820   1768   -----

6 Charles Ellet   Mary Israel
   Salem Co.NJ 1777   -----   1779
   1847   1801   1870

7 John I. Ellet   (2)   Mary Skillman
   28 Aug 1811   St.Louis,MO   LA 19 Mar 1832
   Kansas City,MO   8 Aug 1849   -----
     30 Mar 1896

8 Thomas C. Ellet   Irene Tyler
   CA 12 Dec 1855   -----   Yazoo City,MS 26 May
                                                   1863
   Kansas City 5 Nov 1921   22 Apr 1882   Kansas City 8 Mar 1951

9 Mary S. Ellet   Forest H. Haines
   Yazoo City 9 Feb 1883   -----   Bigelow,MO 6 Mar 1877
                              1 Jun 1905   El Dorado,KS 20 Sep
                                                   1936

   Inheritor: Miss Laura Lee Ray, 18 Castle Drive, Potsdam,NY
   13676

LEET, JOHN DASKAM

Nat. #31-B. Elected 28 Feb 1961. b. Washington,DC 24 May 1906.
m. Daytona Beach,FL 25 Apr 1933, Irene Josephine Haines, b.
El Dorado,KS 21 Apr 1906. Issue: Jaren Forest Leet, b. 24 Dec
1937; Marilyn Haines Leet, b. 2 Oct 1960. Educ: Williams
College, 1928; University World Cruise 1926/27. Member: Heredi-
tary Order of Desc. of Colonial Governors; Sons of American
Revolution (Member of Color Guard); Soc. of Colonial Wars (NJ,
Member Junior Council); Sons of Revolution; Soc. of Order of
Founders and Patriots of America. Address: 1788 Oak Creek Drive,
#417, Palo Alto, CA 94304. (From Society's Records). Descended
from:

1 William Leete, Governor of Connecticut 1676-83

2 John Leete   Mary Chittenden
    Guilford,CT 1639   Guilford   Guilford 1647
    Guilford 25 Nov 1692 4 Oct 1670   Guilford 9 Mar 1712

3 John Leete   Sarah Allen
    Guilford 4 Jan 1674   Guilford   1676
    Guilford May 1730   c.1699   Guilford 8 Mar 1712

4 Gideon Leete   Abigail Rossiter
    Guilford 4 Feb 1703   Guilford   -----
    Chester,CT 1781   26 Sep 1727 -----

5 Allen Leete   Rachel Morgan
    Guilford 13 Oct 1728 Preston,CT   Preston 11 Feb 1732
    Chester 1783   22 Nov 1758 -----

6 Edward Allen Leete   Amy Morgan
    Chester 6 Oct 1762   Preston   Preston 20 Jun 1770
    Chester Mar 1841   22 Nov 1792 -----

7 Edward A. Leete   Mary W. Keller
    Chester 11 Aug 1805   Pittsburgh,PA -----
    Pittsburgh Aug 1874   23 Jul 1835 -----

8 George Keller Leet   Sarah Jane Bryan
    Pittsburgh 9 Jul 1836 Pittsburgh   -----
    Chevy Chase,MD   18 Feb 1864 9 May 1915
      26 Mar 1881

9 George Keller Leet   Edith Besse Daskam
    New York,NY   Washington,DC Washington,DC
      22 Jul 1872
    Montclair,NJ 7 Jan   25 Jan 1900
      1947

Inheritor: Jaren Forest Leet or Marilyn Haines Leet

LEWIS, A. SIDNEY

Nat. #96-B. Elected 8 Jun 1964. b. Newnan,GA 13 Mar 1898.
m. Atlanta,GA 17 Oct 1935, Marinet Beasley Carroll, b. Nashville,
TN 31 Dec 1892. Educ: Georgia Institute of Technology,B.S.M.E.
Member: Hereditary Order of Desc. of Colonial Governors; Sons of
American Revolution, GA; Colonial Order of the Crown; Soc. of
Desc. of Knights of the Garter; Somerset Chapter,Magna Charta
Barons; Sovereign Colonial Soc. Americans of Royal Descent; Soc.
of the Cincinnati, CT; Veteran World War I and II. Occup:
Co-owner Lewis and Co. Construction. Address: 310 Peachtree
Battle Ave., N.W., Atlanta,GA 30305. Descended from:

1 Thomas Welles, Governor of Connecticut 1655-58

2 John Welles   Elizabeth Bourne
  England 1621   Stratford   England c.1627
  Stratford,CT 1659   1647   -----

3 John Welles   Mary Hollister
  Stratford c.1648   -----   Wethersfield,CT
  Stratford 24 Mar   c.1669   1732
    1713/4

4 Elizabeth Welles   Joseph Curtis
  1682   -----   6 Nov 1687
  -----   5 Jul 1711   1738

5 Bethia Curtis   Abraham Beardsley
  Jan 1730   -----   28 Sep 1726
  4 Aug 1801   21 Oct 1753   13 Feb 1815

6 Curtis Beardsley   Mary Allen
  9 Aug 1754   -----   -----
  Stratford 13 Sep 1796 17 Apr 1777   Stratford 13 Oct 1822

7 Mary A. Beardsley   James Lewis
  Stratford 18 Feb 1780 -----   1779
  1857   1 Jun 1799   1822

8 Curtis Lewis   Jane G. Collier
  Stratford 11 Jul 1800 Greensboro,GA   Savannah,GA 3 Nov 1807
  Atlanta,GA 19 Jun 1882 12 May 1826   Griffin,GA 24 Oct 1861

9 James T. Lewis   Mary Rose
  Griffin 4 Apr 1827   Russel Co.AL   1833
  Newnan,GA 2 Sep 1908 -----   Newnan 8 May 1918

10 Homer T. Lewis   Aley C. Clarke
   Newnan 5 May 1854   Newnan   Newnan 4 Jun 1861
   Atlanta 8 Mar 1940   12 Jul 1882   Atlanta 11 May 1956

   Inheritor: Thomas Johnston Lewis, Jr.

LEWIS, MARY KATHARINE CURTIUS (MRS. LEROY R.)

Nat. #306-B. Elected 1977. b. Blackburn,MO 27 Jul 1915. m.
Adrian,MO 30 May 1935, Leroy Ramey Lewis, b. Alma,MO 4 Aug 1906.
Member: Hereditary Order of Desc. of Colonial Governors; Soc. of
Desc. of Colonial Clergy; Dau. of Founders and Patriots; Dau. of
1812; Soc. of Colonial Wars; Sons and Dau. of the Pilgrims; Dau.
of American Colonists; Dames of the Court of Honor (Past State
Pres.); Dau. of American Revolution; Children of American
Revolution (Life Promotor). Address: 115 East 14th Street,
Higginsville,MO 64037. Descended from:

1 Thomas Welles, Governor of Connecticut 1655-58

2 John Welles   Elizabeth Bourne
   England 1621   Stratford,CT   England c.1627
   Stratford 7 Aug 1659 1647   -----

3 Robert Welles   Elizabeth Goodrich
   1651   -----   -----
   22 Jun 1714   9 Jun 1675   Feb 1697/8

4 Prudence Welles   Anthony Stoddard
   1682   -----   9 Aug 1678
   May 1714   1 Mar 1701   6 Sep 1760

5 Eliakim Stoddard   Joanna Curtiss
   Woodbury,CT 3 Apr 1703 -----   Watertown,CT 5 Sep
                                            1708
   Woodbury 1750   4 Dec 1729   Woodbury 1749

6 John Stoddard   Mary Atwood
   Woodbury 26 Jan 1730 Woodbury   Watertown 20 Apr 1733
   Charlestown,NY   15 Apr 1751   Charlestown 16 Jan
     22 Jan 1795   1802

7 Mary Stoddard   (2)   Nathaniel Curtius
   11 Jan 1771   -----   Sharon,CT 9 Jun 1770
   Vienna,NY 27 Sep 1845 1806   Vienna 15 Nov 1840

8 Luman Curtius   Ellen Rosalie Beebe
   Duchess Co.NY 18 May Elkart,IN   Buffalo,NY 11 Aug 1818
     1808
   Carrollton,IL   -----   Carrollton 11 Nov 1870
     4 Nov 1895

9 Luman Beebe Curtius   Colville Mungall
   Carrollton 16 Sep   Cincinnati,OH   Palimont Sterlingshire,
     1852   Scotland 25 Feb 1858
   Blackburn,MO 13 Jul   26 Nov 1880   Blackburn 1 Apr 1947
     1938

10 Benjamin Luman Curtius   Sara Frances Maddox
   Carrollton 11 Dec 1888 Blackburn   Waverly,MO 26 Jun 1890
   Marshall,MO 11 Jun   28 Oct 1911   living in 1977
     1971

   Inheritor: Leroy Ramey Lewis, Jr. (son)

LEWIS, RUTH AHLERT (MRS. GEORGE SPENCER)

Nat. #308-B. Elected 5 Apr 1977. b. Dawson, Yukon Territory,
Canada 2 Mar 1906. m. Alhambra,CA 3 Feb 1951, George Spencer
Lewis, b. Detroit,MI 15 Jun 1907, d. Alhambra 9 Feb 1971. Educ:
Pasadena City College. Member: Hereditary Order of Desc. of
Colonial Governors; Dau. of American Revolution; Dau. of the
American Colonists; Dau. of Colonial Wars; Soc. of Desc. of
Colonial Clergy; Dames of the Court of Honor; U.S. Daus. of
1812; Colonial Dames XVII Century; Magna Charta Dames.
Address: 3204 Keats Street, Alhambra,CA 91801. Descended from:

1 William Leete, Governor of Connecticut 1676-83

2 John Leete   Mary Chittenden
   Guilford,CT 1639   Guilford   Guilford 1647
   Guilford 25 Nov 1692 4 Oct 1670   Guilford 9 Mar 1712

3 Anne Leete   John Collins
   Guilford 5 Aug 1671   Lebanon,CT   Saybrook,CT Jun 1665
   2 Nov 1724   23 Jul 1691   Lebanon 24 Jan 1751

4 Timothy Collins   Elizabeth Hyde
   Guilford 13 Apr 1699 Litchfield,CT   Lebanon 12 Dec 1703
   Litchfield 7 Feb 1777 16 Jan 1722/3   Litchfield af.1780

5 John Collins   Lydia Buell
   Litchfield 1 Jun 1739 Litchfield   Goshen,CT 11 Nov 1742
   Litchfield 25 Jun 1792 -----   Litchfield 26 Sep 1790

6 Norman Collins   Elizabeth Hulbert
   Litchfield 13 Dec 1769 -----   1769
   -----   1787   -----

7 Elizabeth Lewis   William Forsha
      Collins
   Hamilton Co.,OH   Cincinnati,OH   New York,NY 18 Apr
      28 May 1803   1796
   Unionville,MO   1 Jul 1824   Montecello,MO
      11 Dec 1882   10 Aug 1863

8 Stiles Ely Forsha   Adeline Campbell
   Oxford,OH 27 Jan 1831 Eddyville,IA   Windham,NH 26 Nov 1832
   Sawtelle,CA 3 Dec 1911 22 Apr 1852   Downey,CA 20 May 1899

9 Grace Louise Forsha   John Henry Frederick
                                               Ahlert
   Glenwood,MO 26 Jul   Los Angeles,CA   Osnabruck,Germany
      1871   15 Feb 1864
   San Gabriel,CA   1 Aug 1895   Alhambra,CA 23 Aug
      3 Feb 1856   1949

LINDSEY, JULIA EDMONIA HOBSON (MRS. CHARLES F.)

Nat. #90-B. Elected 12 Oct 1963. b. Abingdon,VA 29 Jun 1915.
m. Bluefield,VA 15 May 1946, Charles Francis Preston Lindsey,
b. 26 Oct 1901, d. Bluefield 31 Jul 1957. Educ: Randolph-Macon
Woman's College, Lynchburg,VA B.A. Member: Hereditary Order of
Desc. of Colonial Governors. Address: Box 42, Route 3, College
Drive, Bluefield,VA 24605. (From Society's Records). Descended
from:

1 Robert Carter, Governor of Virginia 1726-27

2 Elizabeth Carter   Nathaniel Burwell
  Lancaster Co.VA 1688   -----   Gloucester Co.VA 1680
  -----   -----   1721

3 Carter Burwell   Lucy Grymes
  Gloucester Co. 1712   -----   -----
  James City Co.VA 1756   5 Jan 1737/8   -----

4 Mary Burwell   (2)   Edmund Berkeley
  James City Co.   -----   VA 5 Dec 1730
  -----   23 Jan 1768   VA 21 Oct 1788

5 Lewis Berkeley   Frances Callender
                                              Noland
  Middlesex Co. 1777   -----   -----
  Loudoun Co.VA 1836   1821   -----

6 Edmund Berkeley   Mary L. Williams
  Loudoun Co. 1823   -----   -----
  Prince William Co.VA   c.1845   -----
    1915

7 Edmund Berkeley   Julia Ramsey
  Loudoun Co. 17 Apr   Jackson,TN   Jackson 6 Sep 1861
    1846
  Haymarket,VA 29 Nov   1878   Bluefield,WV May 1947
    1906

8 Mary L. Berkeley   Jennings W. Hobson
  Atlanta,GA 12 Aug 1887   Philadelphia,   Amherst,VA 15 Aug 1887
                             PA
  Bluefield 9 Jan 1947   5 Nov 1913   Bluefield 6 Dec 1955

  Inheritor: Miss Julia Hobson Lindsey, 1747 Link Road,
  Lynchburg,VA 24503

LIPSCOMB, MARGARET SMITH (MRS.)

Nat. #115-B. Elected 24 Jul 1965. b. Mullins,SC 18 Nov 1905.
m.(1) Mullins 10 Sep 1924, George Tweedie, b. Sandusky,MI 27 Apr
1898. Issue: Ann Tweedie Nye, b. Sandusky 24 Jul 1927. m.(2)
Chase City,VA 27 Dec 1937, Richard E. Lipscomb, b. 10 May 1912.
Educ: Emory University, A.B. Member: Hereditary Order of Desc.
of Colonial Governors; Colonial Dau. of XVII Century (Past Pres.
Gen.); Dames of the Court of Honor (Past First Vice Pres. Gen.);
Dau. of American Revolution (Past Vice Pres. Gen.); Soc. of
Colonial Wars (Past State Pres.); Dau. of American Colonists.

Occup: Real Estate. Outstanding Citizen of the year 1951,
Mullins,SC. Address: 152 South Main Street, Mullins,SC 29574.
Descended from:

*1 George Reade, Governor of Virginia 1638

2   Mildred Reade   Augustine Warner
    -----   -----   3 Jun 1642
    -----   -----   19 Jun 1681

3   Elizabeth Warner   John Lewis
    c.1672   -----   30 Nov 1669
    c.1719   c.1690   14 Nov 1725

4   John Lewis   Frances Fielding
    c.1702   -----   -----
    17 Jan 1754   c.1717   -----

5   Warner Lewis   Eleanor Bowles Gooch
    Tidewater,VA c.1720 -----   -----
    Gloucester Co.VA   -----   -----

6   John Lewis   Delilah Z. Powell
    VA 28 Nov 1754   -----   NC c.1755
    NC 1842   1770   Robeson Co.NC c.1842

7   James Lewis   Edith Walters
    NC 26 Nov 1772   North Carolina   NC 30 May 1780
    Robeson Co. 10 Jan 10 Jan 1796   Robeson Co. 5 Apr 1848
      1855

8   Delilah Lewis   Reddin Britt
    Robeson Co. 1 Jan 1812 -----   Robeson Co. 19 Sep 1801
    Robeson Co. 28 Apr 2 Jan 1828   Robeson Co. 14 Aug 1849
      1891

9   Mary A. Britt   Isaac Spivey
    Robeson Co. 10 Nov Robeson Co.   1819
      1829
    Marion Co.,SC 12 Oct 4 Nov 1844   Robeson Co. 4 Nov 1913
      1867

10 Sarah J. Spivey   Reddin Smith
    Robeson Co. 18 Mar Robeson Co.   Marion Co. 29 Jan 1845
      1846
    Marion Co. 11 Nov   1868   Marion Co. 12 Nov 1924
      1899

11 Thomas L. Smith   Isabel Perritt
    Marion Co. 28 Jan   Marion,SC   Marion Co. 25 Apr 1898
      1875
    Mullins,SC 4 May 1939 22 Dec 1932   Mullins 22 Dec 1932

*   See Preface

LOCKWOOD, RANDOLPH SCOTT DEWEY

Nat. #276-B. Elected 10 Feb 1971. b. Geneva, Switzerland 19 Mar 1913. Educ: U.S. Naval Academy; Harvard University Sc.B. cum laude 1940. Member: Hereditary Order of Desc. of Colonial Governors; Sons of American Revolution (TX, Past Pres.); Somerset Chapter, Magna Charta Barons; Sovereign Colonial Soc. of Americans of Royal Descent; Plantagenet Society; Retired Officer Assn.; American Legion; Pearl Harbor Survivors Assn.; Masonic Orders. Military: Retired from U.S. Marine Corps with rank of Lt. Col., 24 years service, 1960. Address: 214 Tuttle Road, Terrell Hills, San Antonio,TX 78209. Descended from:

1 John Webster, Governor of Connecticut 1656

2 Mary Webster   John Hunt
   England   -----   England
   CT/MA   -----   CT/MA

3 Jonathan Hunt   Clemence Hosmer
   Eng/Salem,MA 1637 -----   Hartford,CT
   Northampton,MA 30 Sep 3 Sep 1662   -----
     1691

4 Ebenezer Hunt   Hannah Clark
   Northampton 6/27 Feb -----   Northampton 5 May 1681
     1676
   Northampton/Lebanon 27 May 1698   -----

5 Abigail Hunt   Isaac II Bailey
   Northampton 16 Jul   Lebanon,CT   -----
     1708
   Northampton/Lebanon 1730   -----

6 Temperance Bailey   Daniel Dewey
   Lebanon 2 Feb 1731   -----   Lebanon 19 Jun 1731
   Lebanon 31 Mar 1795 22 Feb 1753   Lebanon 9 Mar 1816

7 Eliphalet Dewey   Rachel Ann Hyde
   Lebanon 13 Dec 1762 -----   Norwich,CT 3 Dec 1761
   Cadiz,OH 1838   25 Aug 1793   Cadiz 1847

8 Chauncey Dewey   Nancy Pritchard
   Norwich 27 Mar 1796 Cadiz   Cadiz 1804
   Cadiz 13 Feb 1880   11 Feb 1823   Cadiz 6 Sep 1897

9 Charles Paulson Dewey   Emma Scott
   Cadiz 24 Oct 1843   San Antonio,TX Louisville,KY 8 Jan
                                              1844
   Wheeling,WV 10 Jun   21 Jan 1875   Junction City,KS
     1904   25 Nov 1920

10 Emma Scott Dewey   Henry Brocton
                                              Lockwood
   Austin,TX 27 May 1880 Europe   England bf.1870
   Flora,IL 25 Nov 1952   by Jun 1912   1913

LOUCKS, BARBARA WILSON HAUPT (MRS. CHARLES ERNEST)

Nat. #266-B. Elected 22 Sep 1975. b. Bergen Co.,NJ 19 Dec 1926.
m. Annapolis,MD 8 Oct 1973, Maj. Gen. Charles Ernest Loucks, b.
Mayfield,CA 29 Jun 1895. Educ: Randolph-Macon Woman's College;
Rutgers Univ.; Georgetown Univ. Member: Hereditary Order of
Desc. of Colonial Governors; Dau. of American Revolution; U.S.
Daughters of 1812; Sons and Daughters of Pilgrims; Soc. of Desc.
of Colonial Clergy; Women Desc. of Ancient and Honorable Artil-
lery Company; Colonial Dames; Soc. of Founders of Norwich,CT.
Address: 1408 - 20th Street, South, Arlington,VA 22202. Descended
from:

1 Thomas Dudley, Governor of Massachusetts 1634-35, 1640-41,
   1645-46, 1650-51

2 Anne Dudley   Simon Bradstreet
   Northamptonshire,   Hardingston,   Lincolnshire, Eng.
     Eng. c.1612   Eng.   bp. March 1603
   Andover,MA 16 Sep 1672 c.1628   Salem,MA 27 Mar 1697

3 John Bradstreet   Sarah Perkins
   Andover 22 Jul 1653   -----   2 Mar 1657
   Topsfield,MA 17 Jan   11 Jun 1677   Apr 1745
     1717/8

4 Mercy Bradstreet   John Hazen
   Topsfield bp. 2 Jun   -----   Boxford,MA 23 Mar
     1689   1687/8
   Norwich,CT 22 Nov 1725 1710   24 Feb 1772

5 Samuel Hazen   -----
   Norwich 1 May 1713   -----   -----
   -----   -----   -----

6 Samuel Hazen   -----
   Litchfield,CT 5 Apr   -----   -----
     1749
   Sussex Co.NY   -----   -----

7 Hannah Hazen   Joseph Thorne Clement
   Woodbury,CT 12 Apr   Sussex Co.NJ   Flushing,NY 1774
     1785
   Sunbury,PA 25 Jun   11 Jun 1805   Fort Richmond,NY
     1868   6 Jun 1815

8 Ira Thorne Clement   Sarah Martz
   NJ 11 Jan 1813   Northumberland   Upper Augusta,PA
                            Co.PA   2 Feb 1813
   Sunbury,PA 28 Oct 1898 29 Mar 1834   -----

9 Hannah Louisa Clement   George Washington Haupt
   Sunbury 31 Aug 1845/7 Sunbury   Sunbury 21 Feb 1840
   Sunbury 12 Sep 1930   2 Apr 1867   Sunbury 18 Jan 1870

10 Wilson Haupt   Marie Louisa Schindel
   Sunbury 6 Aug 1869   Sunbury   Sunbury 18 Nov 1871
   Sunbury 16 Jul 1938   14 Jun 1899   La Plata,MD 6 Jan 1962

11 George Webster Haupt   Grace Eleanor Lee
                                                   Maines
   Sunbury 15 Jun 1900   Philadelphia   Richmond,VA 23 May 1900
   Philadelphia,PA   31 Jan 1925   (living in 1975)
   9 Jun 1955

SUPPLEMENT NO. 1

1 Simon Bradstreet, Governor of Massachusetts 1679-86, 1689-92

2 John Bradstreet   Sarah Perkins

   Continue with Generation 3 of her lineage from Governor Thomas
   Dudley.

SUPPLEMENT NO. 2

1 Brian Pendleton, Governor of Maine 1680-1681

2 James Pendleton   (2)   Hannah Goodenow
   Watertown,MA c.1628   Sudbury,MA   Sudbury 28 Nov 1639
   Stonington,CT 29 Nov   29 Apr 1656   Stonington af.1725
      1709

3 Ann Pendleton   Eleazer Brown
   Sudbury 12 Nov 1667   Stonington   Lynn,MA 5 Aug 1670
   Stonington 1723   18 Oct 1693   Stonington 30 Nov 1734

4 Ann Brown   Thomas Main
   Stonington Feb 1699/00   Stonington   Stonington 19 Jul 1700
   N.Stonington 11 Mar   20 Apr 1720   N.Stonington
      1766   w.p. 6 Sep 1771

5 Ezekiel Main   Deborah Meacham
   N.Stonington 8 Jul   Stonington   Norwich,CT 20 Apr 1746
      1742
   Bridgewater,PA   25 Nov 1763   -----
      btw. 1790-1800

6 Nehemiah Main(s)   Phebe Bunnell
   Bristol,CT bf.1774   Connecticut   af.1774
   Clearfield Co.PA   bf.1800   Clearfield Co.
      adm. 6 May 1841   af. May 1841

7 Seth Maines   Nancy Forcee/Forcey
   Centre Co.PA 1808   Clearfield Co.   Delaware 26 Oct 1799
   Clearfield Co.   bf.1829   Clearfield Co. 15 Sep
      w.p. 17 May 1859   1882

8 David B. Maines   Louisa C. Vought
   Clearfield Co. 1838   Clearfield Co.   Clearfield Co. 1844
   Amelia Co.VA   bf.1865   Amelia Co. Nov 1887
      22/23 Mar 1892

9 Edgar W. Maines   Tacey Elizabeth Glace
   Clearfield Co. btw.   Clearfield Co.   Lock Haven,PA 3 Feb
      15 Jun-6 Aug 1869   1872
   Clearfield Co. Dec/Jan   25 Oct 1892   Northumberland Co.PA
      1895/6   5 Aug 1936

10 Grace Eleanor Maines   George Webster Haupt

   Continue with Generation 11 of her lineage from Governor Thomas
   Dudley.

158

LOUCKS, MAJOR GENERAL CHARLES ERNEST

Nat. #367-B. Elected 31 Oct 1979. b. Mayfield,CA 29 Jun 1895.
m.(1) Manila,PI 13 Jan 1921, Pearl Reyburn, b. Clovis,CA 8 Jul
1894, d. Fort Belvoir,VA 8 Apr 1967. m.(2) Annapolis 8 Oct
1973, Barbara Wilson Haupt, b. Bergen Co.NJ 19 Dec 1926.
Member: Hereditary Order of Desc. of Colonial Governors; Order
of Founders and Patriots, DC; Desc. of Colonial Clergy; Sons of
American Revolution, VA; Sons of Revolution, DC; Soc. of
Mayflower Descendants, DC; Soc. of War of 1812, DC; Americans of
Armorial Ancestry; Military Order of Loyal Legion, DC; National
Huguenot Soc., VA; Ancient and Honorable Artillery Co.; Soc. of
Colonial Wars, DC; Desc. of Loyalists and Patriots; Military
Order of World Wars; Sons and Daus. of Pilgrims, VA; Old
Plymouth Colony Descs.; Clan Frazer. Address: 1408-20th Street,
Arlington,VA 22202. Descended from:

1 Samuel Gorton, Governor of Rhode Island 1651-52

2 Susanna Gorton   Benjamin Barton
  -----   Warwick,RI   Warwick 1645
  Warwick 28 May 1734   8 Jun 1669   Warwick w.p.9 Nov 1720

3 Phebe Barton   Henry Tucker
  -----   -----   Dartmouth,MA 30 Aug
                                                1680
  -----   bf. 1706   -----

4 Henry Tucker   Elizabeth Ricketson
  Dartmouth 8 Feb 1713   Dartmouth   Dartmouth 17 Mar 1715
  Dartmouth w.p. 15 Jun   18 Oct 1733   -----
    1763

5 Eliphal Tucker   Ebenezer Allen
  Dartmouth 28 Feb 1739   Dartmouth   Dartmouth 28 Jul 1739
  -----   29 Apr 1758/9   Dartmouth inv.1778

6 Meribah Allen   Thomas Sherman
  Westport,MA 1775   Westport   Portsmouth,RI 28 May
                                                1775
  Westport 17 Mar 1835   3 May 1800   Westport 29 Oct 1845

7 Peleg Sherman   Hannah Potter Case
  Westport 10 Oct 1804   Westport   Westport 1 Apr 1809
  S.Westport 14 Feb   12 Dec 1828   New Bedford,MA 28 Dec
    1862   1907

8 Charles Frederick   Martha White Snell
    Sherman
  S.Westport 10 Mar   Dartmouth   Westport 16 Jul 1842
    1835
  New Bedford 11 Nov   2 Feb 1862   Dartmouth 26 Dec 1896
    1915

9 Maria Letitia Sherman   Menzo Samuel Loucks
  Westport 17 Feb 1864   Stockton,CA   Walworth Co.WI 19 Aug
                                                1849
  Mountain View,CA   8 Sep 1893   Mountain View
    9 Jan 1941   5 Mar 1924

  Inheritor: Miss Karen Lynne Loucks

LOVEJOY, COL. CHARLES DOUGLAS, USA (Ret.)

Nat. #321-B.   Elected 17 Feb 1978.   b. Knoxville,TN 19 Jan 1918.
m. Claremont,MN 6 Jun 1942, Marion Florence Paukert, b. Bismark,
ND 13 Dec 1918.   Educ: University of Tennessee; University of
Nebraska BGE.   Member: Hereditary Order of Desc. of Colonial
Governors; Sons of the Revolution; Soc. of Desc. of Colonial
Clergy; Soc. of Colonial Wars; Sons of Confederate Veterans;
Roger Williams Family Assn.   Military: U.S. Army 1939-68.
Occup: Director, Fiscal and Property Division, Seattle Police
Dept.   Address: 2102 - 12 East, Seattle,WA 98102. Descended from:

1   Samuel Cranston, Governor of Rhode Island 1698-1727

2   John Cranston   Penelope Godfrey
    Newport,RI 4 Aug 1684   -----   1685
    Newport 15 Oct 1745   c.1700   Newport 18 Mar 1761

3   Caleb Cranston   Mary Gould
    Newport/Jamestown,RI   -----   -----
      c.1730
    North Kingston,RI   27 Aug (yr ?)   bf. 1790
      12 Oct 1800

4   Thomas Cranston   Sarah Northrup
    Jamestown 26 Apr 1757   -----   5 Apr 1767
    31 Aug 1825   -----   1831

5   Samuel Northrup   Hanna Kingsley
      Cranston
    N. Kingston 18 Mar (?)   -----   -----
    -----   -----   -----

6   Lucrectia Kingsley   Reynolds Hoxsie Jr.
      Cranston
    9 Sep 1808   -----   Richmond,RI 30 Jun 1803
    -----   -----   Allendale,RI 29 Mar
                                                 1865

7   James Baker Hoxsie   Zilpha Depue
    East Greenwich,RI   -----   Blanchville,NJ
      17 Dec 1832   25 Jun 1857
    Knoxville,TN 4 May   -----   Knoxville 24 Feb 1911
      1888

8   Buleah Bell Hoxsie   Isaac Winship Lovejoy
    Knoxville 10 Mar 1868   Knoxville   Atlanta,GA 8 Mar 1866
    Knoxville 4 Apr 1907   -----   Pennsylvania 1942

9   Hoxsie Winship   Mary Catherine Douglas
      Lovejoy
    Knoxville 17 Oct 1892   Cincinnati,OH   Albuquerque,NM
                                                 17 Jan 1885
    (living in 1978)   c.1910   Albuquerque 24 Sep
                                                 1959

160

MANN, VANDELIA DREW SMITH (MRS. WILLIAM M., JR.)

Nat. #185-B. Elected 3 Jan 1972. b. Raleigh,NC 3 Jan 1934.
m. Winston-Salem,NC 1 Aug 1960, William Marion Mann, Jr., M.D.,
b. Enfield,NC 7 Jan 1931. Issue: William Marion Mann, III, b.
Winston-Salem 2 Jun 1961; Benjamin Denton Mann, IV, b. Fort Sam
Houston,TX 12 Jul 1962; William Oliver Mann, b. Warren,PA 29 Apr
1967; Teressa Vandelia Mann, b. Warren 21 Jan 1969. Educ: St.
Mary's Junior College; Salem College; University of Innsbruck,
Austria. Member: Hereditary Order of Desc. of Colonial
Governors; Colonial Dames of America; Colonial Dames of XVII
Century; Dau. of the Revolution of 1776. Address: Box #249,
Warren,PA 16365. Descended from:

1 Thomas Roberts, Governor of New Hampshire 1640-41

2	Thomas Roberts		Mary Leighton
	Dover,NH c.1636	-----	-----
	-----	-----	-----
3	Mary Roberts		Thomas Young
	-----	-----	Dover c.1643
	1745	-----	-----
4	Lydia Young		John Cook
	29 Nov 1694	-----	5 May 1692
	-----	-----	c.1754/5
5	Hezekiah Cook		-----
	1 Jan 1717	-----	-----
	-----	-----	-----
6	Sarah Cook		Eleazer Davis
	-----	-----	Medbury,NH 23 Jan 1742
	-----	11 Apr 1771	-----
7	Charlotte Davis		John Drew
	21 Dec 1790	-----	Alton 27 Apr 1786
	Alton,NH 1870	4 Jan 1810	Alton 1867
8	George F. Drew		Amelia Dickens
	Alton	Columbus,GA	GA 24 Dec 1832
	Jacksonville,FL	28 Jan 1854	Jacksonville 26 Sep
	26 Sep 1900		1900
9	Franklin Drew		Lula R. Hooper
	Ellaville,FL 28 Mar	Swannee Co.FL	Tuckaseigee,NC 24 Apr
	1867		1872
	Luraville,FL 17 Jul	11 Aug 1890	Raleigh,NC 11 May 1956
	1932		
10	Vandelia E. Drew		William O. Smith
	Jacksonville	Live Oak,FL	Liberty,MO 28 Aug 1894
	24 Dec 1896		
		26 Oct 1921	near Lisbon, Portugal
			16 Jan 1960

Inheritor: Teressa Vandelia Mann (daughter)

MARMADUKE, VIRGINIA FRANCES CLAYTON (MRS. DONALD SHERMAN)

Nat. #330-B. Elected 15 Sep 1978. b. Lewistown,MT 14 Mar 1910.
m.(1) Douglas,WY 2 Jun 1930, Edward Arthur Reynolds, d. 1952.
Issue: Edward Arthur Reynolds, Jr., b. New Haven,CT 6 Jun 1931.
m.(2) Santa Fe,NM 28 Oct 1955, Donald Sherman Marmaduke, b.
Kansas City,MO 16 May 1920. Educ: University of Wyoming.
Member: Hereditary Order of Desc. of Colonial Governors; United
Dau. of Confederacy; Soc. of Desc. of Founders of Hartford;
Colonial Order of the Crown; Flagon and Trencher; Huguenot Soc.
of SC; National Huguenot Soc.; Dames of Court of Honor; Dau. of
American Revolution; Dau. of Colonial Wars; Dau. of Founders and
Patriots of America; Magna Charta Dames; Sons and Dau. of the
Pilgrims; U. S. Daughters of 1812; Order of Americans of Armorial
Ancestry; Plantagenet Soc.;Soc. of Desc. of Knights of Most
Noble Order of Garter; Soc. of Desc. of Colonial Clergy. Address:
500 Oneida Street, Denver,CO 80220. Descended from:

1 John Webster, Governor of Connecticut 1656-57

2	Robert Webster		Susannah Treat
	Cossington,Eng.	Wethersfield,	Pitminster,Eng.
	bp. 17 Nov 1619	CT	bp. 8 Oct 1629
	Hartford,CT c. May 1676	1652	Hartford 1705

3	Sarah Webster		Joseph Mygatt
	Middletown,CT	Hartford	Hartford c.1656
	30 Jun 1655		
	Hartford Feb 1744	15 Nov 1677	Hartford Mar 1698

4	Sarah Mygatt		Thomas King, Jr.
	Hartford 9 Mar 1691	Hartford	Northampton,MA
			3 Dec 1684
	Hartford 1744	6 Nov 1712	Hartford af.1729

5	Timothy King		Sarah Fitch
	Sharon,CT 20 Oct 1727	Windsor,CT	Windsor 1737
	Windsor 18 Jan 1812	19 Apr 1753	Windsor 20 May 1785

6	Roswell King		Catherine Barrington
	Windsor 3 May 1765	SanSavilla	SanSavilla Bluff, GA
		Bluff	22 Feb 1776
	Roswell,GA 15 Feb	14 Apr 1792	McIntosh Co.GA
	1844		23 Apr 1839

7	Barrington King		Catherine Margaret
			Nephew
	Darien,GA 9 Mar 1798	McIntosh Co.	McIntosh Co. 28 Feb
			1804
	Roswell 17 Jan 1866	30 Jan 1822	Roswell 7 Jul 1887

8	Clifford Alonzo King		Marie Eliza Hardee
	Roswell 16 Dec 1842	Savannah,GA	Savannah 1 Mar 1844
	Idaho Springs,CO	8 Mar 1864	Cripple Creek,CO
	31 Mar 1911		2 Mar 1897

9	Marie Hardee King		Ernest Mayer Clayton
	Dallas,TX 26 Oct 1885	Denver,CO	Beaver Falls,PA
			8 Jul 1883
	Douglas,WY 11 Jan 1972	2 Jun 1909	Douglas 7 May 1958

MARSH, ELIZABETH LOUISE DODSON (MRS.)

Nat. #174-B. Elected 11 Mar 1971. b. Winston-Salem,NC 9 Sep 1912. m. Danville,VA 23 Feb 1935, Alexander Wade Marsh, b. Randolph Co.,NC 28 Mar 1898. Issue: Robert Dodson Marsh, b. 24 Aug 1937. Educ: Applachian State University. Member: Heredi-tary Order of Desc. of Colonial Governors; Dau. of American Revolution; Daughters of American Colonists. Address: 406 Otteray Drive, High Point, NC 27262. Descended from:

1 William Stone, Governor of Maryland 1648-53

2 John Stone   Elizabeth Warren
  Accomac Co.VA 1640   -----   -----
  Charles Co.MD 1698   -----   -----

3 Thomas Stone   Martha Hoskins
  Charles Co. 1677   -----   Charles Co.
  Prince William Co.VA   -----   -----
    1727

4 Thomas Stone   Mary Butler
  -----   -----   Charles Co.
  Pr.Wm.Co. 24 Nov 1784   c.1720   -----

5 John Stone   Miss Corder
  Virginia c.1747   -----   Pr.Wm.Co.
  Surry Co.NC   -----   Surry Co.NC

6 Enoch Stone, Sr.   Nancy Anthony
  Surry Co.   -----   Surry Co.
  Aug/Sep 1823   c.1784   -----

7 Enoch Stone, Jr.   Elizabeth Gordon
  8 Nov 1791   Surry Co.   28 Mar 1797
  Surry Co. 11 Oct 1874 21 Oct 1819   Surry Co. 26 Mar 1877

8 Rhoda Elizabeth Stone   John Clayborn Dodson
  1 Jun 1833   -----   4 Apr 1831
  Surry Co. 20 Jul 1891 2 May 1861   Surry Co. 8 Aug 1891

9 Charles Robert Dodson   Carrie Lenora Angell
  Surry Co. 1 Sep 1874 Boonville,NC   Yadkin Co.NC 1 Aug 1884
  Wallburg,NC 27 Sep   30 Dec 1908   Winston-Salem,NC
    1940   7 Feb 1949

Inheritor: Chaun Alexanderea Gerard Marsh (granddaughter)

MARTELL, HELEN MARIE CONTEE (MISS)

Nat. #248-B. Elected 6 Feb 1975. b. Boston,MA 12 Mar 1906. Educ: B.A. and LLB, George Washington University, Washington,DC. Admitted to the Bar of the District Court of U.S. for the District of Columbia in 1938 and U.S. Court of Appeals in 1939. Member: Hereditary Order of Desc. of Colonial Governors; Colonial Dames of America, MD; Desc. of Lords of Maryland Manors (Recording Secretary); Order of the Coif. Occup: Former Treas-urer and Asst. Secretary of Potomac Electric Power Co. Address: 4201 Cathedral Ave., Washington,DC 20016. Descended from:

1 Robert Brooke, Governor of Maryland 1652

2 Thomas Brooke   Eleanor Hatton
   Battle,Eng. 23 Jun   Maryland   England 1642
   1632
   Calvert Co.MD 25 Oct   c.1658   Calvert Co. 1725
   1676

3 Thomas Brooke   Barbara Dent
   Prince George's Co.MD   -----   c.1676
   c.1659
   Calvert Co. 25 Jan   -----   c.1754
   1730

4 Jane Brooke   Alexander Contee
   -----   -----   Barnstable,Eng.
                                              Apr 1693
   Jun 1779   c.1720   Prince Geoge's Co.
                                              5 Jan 1740

5 John Contee   Margaret Snowden
   Prince George's Co.   -----   1726
   1722
   Prince George's Co.   1745   -----
   Jan 1796

6 Richard Alexander   Elizabeth Rawlings
   Contee
   Prince George's Co.   -----   -----
   1753
   Nov 1818   c.1790   1818

7 John Contee   Anne Louise Snowden
   Prince George's Co.   -----   MD Aug 1800
   7 Nov 1794
   Prince George's Co.   17 Feb 1824   Millersville,MD
   15 Nov 1839   10 Jun 1882

8 Charles Snowden Contee   Elizabeth Childs
                                               Bowling
   Prince George's Co.   Baltimore,MD   Aquasco 7 Apr 1841
   31 Oct 1830
   Aquasco,MD 18 Mar 1886 5 Jun 1860   Aquasco 26 Aug 1894

9 Helen Frances Contee   Charles Joseph Martell
   Contee Station,MD   Baltimore   Boston,MA 30 Apr 1874
   8 May 1877
   Washington,DC   5 Jun 1905   Boston 3 Feb 1920
   31 May 1952

MARTIN, CAROLYN A. ASHBURN (MRS. WARREN D.)

Nat. #192-B-s. Elected 18 Jul 1972. Member: Hereditary Order
of Desc. of Colonial Governors. Address: 301 Trail One,
Burlington,NC 27212. (From Society's Records). Descended from:

1 William Stone, Governor of Maryland 1648-53

2	John Stone		Elizabeth Warren	
	Accomac Co.VA 1640	-----	-----	
	Charles Co.MD 1698	-----	-----	
3	Thomas Stone		Martha Hoskins	
	Charles Co. 1677	-----	Charles Co. c.1680	
	Prince William Co.VA 1727	-----	-----	
*4	Thomas Stone		Mary Butler	
	-----	-----	Charles Co.	
	Pr.Wm.Co. 24 Nov 1784	c.1720	-----	
5	John Stone		Miss Corder	
	Virginia c.1747	-----	Pr.Wm.Co.	
	Surry Co.NC	c.1780	Surry Co.NC	
6	Enoch Stone, Sr.		Nancy Anthony	
	Surry Co.	-----	Surry Co.	
	Aug/Sep 1823	c.1784	-----	
7	Enoch Stone, Jr.		Elizabeth Gordon	
	8 Nov 1791	Surry Co.	28 Mar 1797	
	Surry Co. 11 Oct 1874	21 Oct 1819	Surry Co. 26 Mar 1877	
8	Francis R. Stone		Sarah C. Poindexter	
	Surry Co. 6 Mar 1828	-----	26 Dec 1833	
	Ararat,NC 30 Mar 1918	4 Mar 1851	Ararat 5 Jul 1911	
9	Caroline T. Stone		William J. Boyles	
	Surry Co. 29 Dec 1865	Surry Co.	Surry Co. 6 Oct 1863	
	Surry Co. 29 Jan 1887	Dec 1885	Pilot Mountain,NC 2 Mar 1944	
10	Nonnie May Boyles		Arthur L. Ashburn	
	Surry Co. 10 Jan 1887	Kernersville, NC 4 Aug 1907	Surry Co. 9 Apr 1885 Winston-Salem 26 Apr 1962	

MARTIN, WILLIAM RAYMOND

Nat. #224-B. Elected 24 Jan 1974. b. Philadelphia,PA 16 Oct
1939. m.(1) New Brunswick,NJ 8 Sep 1962, Roberta Smink, b.
23 Dec 1940, div. 20 Jan 1970. Issue: Jamie Davis Lawrence
Martin, b. 28 May 1969. m.(2) Philadelphia 16 Oct 1970, Margaret
Scouten, b. 17 Jul 1941. Issue: Mary Frances Martin, b. 2 Oct
1972. Educ: Lehigh University, B.S.M.E., 1960; Wharton School,
University of Pennsylvania, M.B.A. 1973. Member: Hereditary
Order of Desc. of Colonial Governors; Sons of Revolution, NYC;
Huguenot Historical Soc., New Platz,NY; Soc. of Automotive
Engineers; American Soc. of Mechanical Engineers; American Eco-
nomic Assn.; Transportation Research Forum; Sierra Club; Mensa.
Address: 10308 Great Arbor Drive, Potomac,MD 20854. Descended fr:

1 Jeremiah Clarke, Governor of Rhode Island 1652

2	Jeremiah Clarke		Anne Dudley
	c.1643	-----	-----
	16 Jan 1729	-----	15 Dec 1732
3	Anne Clarke		William Greenman
	c.1676	-----	-----
	-----	c.1703	-----
4	Jeremiah Greenman		Sarah Blackman
	-----	-----	-----
	-----	-----	-----
5	Amey Greenman		Peter DuBois
	24 Oct 1727	-----	10 Apr 1734
	2 Jun 1807	1758	21 Aug 1795
6	Thomas DuBois		Sarah Foster
	Salem Co.NJ 16 Jul 1764	-----	26 Sep 1764
	19 Dec 1845	-----	1 Jul 1838
7	Phebe DuBois		Moses Richman
	Salem Co. 29 Dec 1796	Salem Co.	4 Jun 1797
	17 Sep 1882	18 Mar 1817	27 Aug 1862
8	Emily Richman		Harrison Johnson
	Salem Co. 19 Sep 1820	Salem Co.	2 Nov 1819
	5 May 1885	13 Mar 1845	-----
9	Alfred R. Johnson		Ruth Anna Dailey
	Salem Co. 28 Sep 1846	-----	28 Sep 1857
	Woodstown,NJ 20 Feb	26 Feb 1878	17 Jun 1947
	1923		
10	Emily Johnson		Raymond Coates
	Salem Co. 28 Oct 1882	Harrisonville,	Staytonsville,DE
		NJ	2 Dec 1877
	Salem Co. 22 Nov 1966	31 Jul 1900	Salem Co. 17 Jan 1965
11	Mary Anna Coates	(1)	Clyde Davis Martin
	Gloucester Co.NJ	Haddonfield,	Iowa 6 May 1906
	4 Jan 1912	NJ	
		29 May 1931	Philadelphia,PA 12 Jun
			1945

MARTIN, YSABELITA L. KRANZ (MRS. JACK LOFTIN)

Nat. #354-B. Elected 20 Aug 1979. b. New Orleans,LA 2 Sep 1927. m. Jack Loftin Martin. Issue: Hamilton Loftin Martin, b. 1 Aug 1958; Ysabelita Mary Martin, b. 3 Feb 1961. Educ: Southwestern Louisiana University, B.A. Member: Hereditary Order of Desc. of Colonial Governors; Dau. of American Colonists; Ark and Dove; Louisiana Colonials; Soc. of Desc. of Colonial Clergy; Colonial Physicians and Chirurgiens; Colonial Dames XVII Century; U.S. Dau. of 1812; United Dau. of Confederacy; Dau. of American Revolution; Colonial Order of Crown; Magna Charta Dames; Americans of Royal Descent; Dau. of Colonial Wars; Order of Garter. Address: Route 1, Box 27C, Covington,LA 70433. Descended from:

1 Thomas Greene, Governor of Maryland 1647-48

Continue with the lineage of her mother, Ysabelita H. J. Kranz, #355-B.

Inheritor: Hamilton Loftin Martin, Route 1, Box 27C, Covington, LA 70433

MASON, JUDSON PHILIP

Nat. #194-B. Elected 8 Aug 1972. b. Elgin,IL 31 Oct 1914. m.
Clayton,MO 17 Mar 1945, Marian Frances Wilhite, b. St. Louis,MO
14 Feb 1918. Issue: Judith Ellen Mason, b. Washington,DC 6 Jan
1946; Judson Philip Mason, Jr., b. Joliet,IL 5 Jun 1947. Educ:
University of Illinois, B.S.; St. Louis University and U.S. Dept.
of Agriculture, graduate schools. Member: Hereditary Order of
Desc. of Colonial Governors (Corres. Secretary General); Soc. of
Mayflower Desc. (Past Governor, DC); Order of Founders and
Patriots of America (Treasurer, DC); Sons of American Revolution
(Membership Comm. and Auditing Comm., VA), (Vice Pres. and Chrm.
of Membership Comm., George Mason Chap.); Soc. of War of 1812;
Soc. of Desc. of Colonial Clergy; Flagon and Trencher; Magna
Charta Barons, Somerset Chap.; American Agricultural Economics
Assn.; International Assn. of Agricultural Economists; Washing-
ton Golf and Country Club. Occup: Director, Program Development
and Dept. of Economics, National Milk Producers Federation.
Address: "Heritage Point," P.O. Box 183, Lancaster,VA 22503.
Descended from:

1 John Coggeshall, Governor of Rhode Island 1647

2 John Coggeshall   Elizabeth Baulston
   Halstead,Eng. 1618   Newport,RI   Portsmouth,RI Aug 1639
   Newport 1 Oct 1708   17 Jun 1647   Portsmouth 1 Oct 1700

3 John Coggeshall   Elizabeth Timberlake
   Portsmouth 12 Feb 1649 Portsmouth   -----
   Portsmouth 9 Nov 1706   24 Dec 1669   -----

4 Mary Coggeshall   William Anthony
   Portsmouth 18 Sep 1675 Portsmouth   Portsmouth 31 Oct 1675
   Newport af.1739   14 Mar 1695   Newport 28 Dec 1744

5 John Anthony   Lydia Luther
   Swansea,MA 16 Nov 1708 Swansea   Swansea 19 Sep 1714
   8 Nov 1788   16 Dec 1733   12 Feb 1783

6 Avis Anthony   John Lee
   Swansea 11 Dec 1739   Swansea   Swansea 26 Nov 1726
   Swansea 19 Dec 1822   27 Aug 1758   Jamaica Island,Bahama

7 Sarah Lee   David Mason
   Swansea 12 Dec 1761   Rehoboth,MA   Rehoboth 14 Jun 1758
   17 May 1817   13 Feb 1780   -----

8 Edward Mason   Mary Pierce
   Swansea 5 May 1784   -----   Rehoboth 6 Jan 1788
   Savoy,MA 30 Oct 1824   c.1807   Savoy 20 Jul 1876

9 John Thomas Mason   Wealthy D. Kelsey
   Savoy 18 Feb 1816   Cuba,IL   Sheldon,NY 22 May 1826
   Elgin,IL 14 Jul 1876   15 Nov 1845   Elgin 6 Nov 1866

10 Judson P. Mason   Anna E. Fraser
   Elgin 31 Mar 1850   Rutland,IL   Rutland 1 Apr 1850
   Elgin 12 Mar 1927   -----   Chicago,IL 27 Apr 1923

11 Raymond Mason   Susie Gerber
   Elgin 5 Jun 1881   Chicago   Chicago 13 Sep 1884
   Elgin 24 Dec 1946   26 Jun 1907

   Inheritor: Judson P. Mason, Jr.

McCALL, BETH ADA (MISS)

Nat. #311-B. Elected 27 Jun 1977. b. Ogden,IA 27 Jan 1901.
Educ: University of Iowa, B.A.; University of Southern Califor-
nia, M.A. Member: Hereditary Order of Desc. of Colonial
Governors; Dau. of American Revolution; Dau. of Founders and
Patriots of America; Colonial Dames XVII Century; Women Desc. of
Ancient and Honorable Artillery Co.; Soc. of Desc. of Colonial
Clergy; Dames of Court of Honor; Dau. of American Colonists;
Dau. of Colonial Wars; Magna Charta Dames. Address: 103½ Elgin
Street, Alhambra, CA 91801. Descended from:

1 Thomas Welles, Governor of Connecticut 1655-58

2 Sarah Welles   John Chester
  England 1631   -----   5 Aug 1635
  12/16 Dec 1698   Feb 1653   23 Feb 1698

3 Stephen Chester   Jemima Treat
  Wethersfield,CT 26 May   -----   15 Mar 1677/8
    1660
  9 Feb 1698   17 Dec 1691   25 May 1727

4 Dorothy Chester   Martin Kellogg
  5 Sep 1692   Newington,MA   26 Oct 1686
  26 Sep 1754   26 Jan 1714   13 Nov 1758

5 Dorothy Kellogg   Eliphalet Whittlesey
  CT 24 Dec 1716   -----   Newington 10 May 1714
  Washington,CT 14 Apr   17 Dec 1736   12 Jul 1786
    1772

6 Eliphalet Whittlesey   Comfort Waller
  Newington 2 Jul 1748   -----   Kent,CT 15 Nov 1750
  Stockbridge,MA   25 Dec 1771   12 Jul 1786
    23 Jan 1823

7 David Whittlesey   Rebecca Smalley
  Stockbridge 4 Feb 1775   New Britain,CT 3 Dec 1778
  New Britain 21 Jul   15 Oct 1804   New Britain 8 Jan 1838
    1851

8 Mary Whittlesey   Dan Clark
  New Britain 2 Sep 1809   New Britain   New Britain 15 Jan
                                   1805
  Boonesboro,IA 18 Oct   4 Sep 1827   Boonesboro 29 Jan 1884
    1881

9 Elbert Cornelius Clark   Ada Theresa Hitchcock
   New Britain 30 Jul   Davenport,IA   Davenport 8 Sep 1845
     1838
   Des Moines,IA 2 Apr   8 Sep 1864   Franklin,OH 4 Apr 1905
     1918

10 Anna Cornelia Clark   Roselle Solomon McCall
   Durant,IA 25 Sep 1865   -----   Moingoina,IA 9 Jul 1866
   San Gabriel,CA 6 Feb   9 Jun 1892   San Gabriel 6 Jul 1941
     1940

Inheritor: Mrs. James Shepherd, 4843 N.E. 42nd St., Seattle,
WA 98105.

McCREA, BERNIE CHESLEY (MRS.)

Nat. #243-B. Elected 18 Oct 1974. b. Chesley Ranch, Stephens
Co., TX 14 Jan 1906. m. Fort Worth,TX 8 Jan 1927, Yancey J.
McCrea, b. 8 Aug 1907. Issue: Yancey J. McCrea, Jr.; Patsy L.
Isenhower; Bernie Ann Hale; Llewellyn Wentworth McCrea. Educ:
Texas Christian University. Member: Hereditary Order of Desc. of
Colonial Governors; Dau. of American Revolution (State Officers
Club, Past Treas.; State Regents Club, Past Pres.); New England
Women; Children of American Revolution (Natl. and State Promoter);
Colonial Dames XVII Century; Dau. of American Colonists; Taylor
County Historical Survey Comm.; Texas Federation of Women's
Clubs. Address: Box 5024, Abilene, TX 79605. Descended from:

1 Theophilus Eaton, Governor of New Haven 1639-58

2 Mary Eaton   Valentine Hill
   England c.1627   New Haven,CT   England c.1600
   Dover,NH 24 Apr 1708   bf. 1647   Oyster River,NH 1661

3 Nathaniel Hill   Sarah Nutter
   Oyster R. 1 Mar 1659   Dover   Dover c.1670
   Oyster R. c.1742   c.1690   Oyster River

4 Samuel Hill   Sarah Thompson
   Oyster R. c.1696   Oyster River,   Oyster River,NH c.1700
   Oyster R. bf.2 Apr 1767 12 Jun 1718   Durham,NH

5 Mary Hill   Thomas Chesley
   Oyster River bp.15 Feb -----   New Haven c.1718
     1719
   New Haven c.1810   -----   New Haven 1778

6 Benjamin Chesley   Deborah Randall
   Durham 24 Jan 1743   New Durham,NH   New Haven 24 Aug 1747
   Durham 5 Feb 1831   c.1763   New Haven 28 May 1830

7 Miles Chesley   Mary Furber
   New Durham 24 Jan 1770 New Durham   New Haven 15 Jul 1780
   New Durham 15 Apr 1861 28 May 1801   Durham 1 Aug 1860

8 Moses Horne Chesley   Abigail Ann Berry
   New Durham 6 Dec 1817   New Durham   New Durham 25 Jun 1816
   New Durham 4 May 1897   11 Jul 1843   New Durham 1 Apr 1854

9 John Elwood Chesley   Fannie Mary Sampson
   New Durham 7 Mar 1851   New Haven   New Haven 28 Jun 1863
   Cisco,TX 25 Jan 1932   13 Oct 1891   Cisco 2 Jan 1908

McDONNELL, GLADYS B. HOLCOMBE (MRS. JOSEPH F., JR.)

Nat. #234-B. Elected 1 May 1974. b. Brooklyn,NY 16 Nov 1904.
m. New York,NY 28 May 1938, Joseph Francis McDonnell, Jr., b.
Jenkintown,PA 23 Jul 1905. Member: Hereditary Order of Desc. of
Colonial Governors; Dau. of American Revolution; New England
Women; Colonial Dames XVII Century; Washington Headquarters Assn.
Address: 2851 So. Buchanan St., Arlington,VA 22206. Descended
from:

1 John Cranston, Governor of Rhode Island 1678-80

2 Samuel Cranston   Mary Hart
   Newport,RI 16 Aug 1659   Newport   Newport 1663
   Newport 26 Apr 1727   1680   Newport 17 Sep 1710

3 John Cranston   Penelope Godfrey
   Newport 4 Aug 1684   Newport   1685
   Newport 15 Oct 1745   c.1700   Newport 18 Mar 1761

4 James Cranston   Eunice Richmond
   Jamestown,RI c.1712   Newport   Little Compton,RI
                                                 23 Sep 1722
   bf.6 Oct 1740   14 May 1739   -----

5 Richard Cranston   Sarah Hookey
   Newport 24 Dec 1740   Newport   Newport 17 Sep 1742
   Newport 12 Mar 1775   15 Jul 1763/5   af.1782

6 James Cranston   Anne Hempstead
   Newport 5 May 1768   Stonington,CT   Stonington 26 Jun 1773
   Ontario,Canada   Jul 1792   Stonington 3 Jul 1810
     6 Jun 1814

7 Richmond Cranston   Chloe Hyde Collier
   Stonington 27 Feb 1804   Norwich,CT   Norwich 13 Apr 1807
   Brooklyn,NY 30 Oct   28 Jan 1827   Brooklyn 15 Dec 1880
     1883

8 Lucy Jane Cranston   Charles M. Holcombe
   29 Sep 1842   -----   Amwell,NJ 17 Aug 1812
   14 May 1884   21 Feb 1869   8 Apr 1879

9 Richmond C. Holcombe   Mary Wells Browning
   Brooklyn 26 Jul 1874   Brooklyn   6 Jun 1874
   Upper Darby,PA 1 Apr   3 May 1899   Rockville,NY 2 Oct
     1945   1950

   Inheritor: Joseph F. McDonnell,III, 6211 Collinsway Road,
   Baltimore, MD 21228.

170

McKAY, MARGARET IONE (MISS)

Nat. #153-B. Elected 14 Aug 1969. b. Frankfort,NY 17 May 1901.
Educ: Utica,NY School of Commerce. Member: Hereditary Order of
Desc. of Colonial Governors; Dau. of American Revolution; Women
Desc. of Ancient and Honorable Artillery Co. (Past 2nd Vice
Pres.); Dau. of American Colonists; Soc. of Desc. of Colonial
Clergy; New England Women; NY State DAR Officers Club; Flagon
and Trencher; Dau. of Founders and Patriots (Natl. Registrar);
Telephone Pioneers of America. Occup: NY Telephone Co. (ret.).
Address: 310 Second Ave., Frankfort,NY 13340. Descended from:

1 Thomas Mayhew, Governor of Martha's Vineyard 1647-81

2 Thomas Mayhew   Jane Paine
   Wilts, England 1620   -----   England 1625
   At sea 1651   1645   af.1658

3 Jedediah Mayhew   Benjamin Smith
   Martha's Vineyard 1656   Martha's Vnyd.   Martha's Vnyd. 7 Jan
                            MA   1658
   Martha's Vnyd. 6 Jan   c.1684   Martha's Vnyd. 4 Jul
      1736   1720

4 Abiah Smith   Thomas Claghorn
   Martha's Vnyd. Aug 1698 Martha's Vnyd.   Barnstable,MA 20 Mar
                                                1692
   Martha's Vnyd. 10 Feb   c.1721   Eastville,MA 10 Feb
      1730   1784

5 Benjamin Claghorn   Katherine Blackwell
   Eastville 1722   Sandwich,MA   Rochester,MA 16 Aug
                                                1725
   Vineyard Sound,MA   27 Feb 1746   Martha's Vnyd. 1 Jan
      9 Jun 1759   1804

6 Mary Claghorn   Abner Norton
   Martha's Vnyd. 7 Jan   Martha's Vnyd.   Martha's Vnyd. 19 Oct
      1751   1740
   -----   12 Apr 1770   c.1813

7 Isaac Norton   Katherine Caine
   c.1771   -----   c.1786
   Starks,ME c.1843   27 Nov 1806   af.1843

8 Sarah B. Norton   Peter McKay
   New Vineyard,ME 3 Nov   Starks   Hallowell,ME 17 Aug
      1816   1820
   Newport,ME 20 Apr 1891   10 Oct 1838   Newport 13 Jan 1894

9 Isaac Norton McKay   Lurana Barns Ballard
   Waterford,ME 10 Mar   Gloversville,   Carlisle,NY 6 Feb 1846
      1844   NY
   Sandown,NH 7 Sep 1927   22 Nov 1871   Derry,NH 7 Dec 1936

10 John Edwin McKay   Ida May Seamans
   Newport,ME 10 Jun 1874   Frankfort,NY   Dewitt,NY 4 Dec 1878
   Utica,NY 20 Sep 1953   10 Aug 1899   Utica 9 Nov 1963

McKNIGHT, ELISE McDANIEL (MRS. STEPHEN DOLLINSON)

Nat. #230-B. Elected 4 Apr 1974. b. 2 Sep 1910. m. 25 Jul 1935, Stephen Dollinson McKnight, b. 20 Mar 1909. Issue: Stephen Dollinson McKnight, Jr., b. 30 Jan 1937; Katherine Elise McKnight, b. 17 Jun 1946. Educ: Southwestern University, Memphis,TN B.S.; Middle Tennessee State University, Murfreesboro, TN M.A. Member: Hereditary Order of Desc. of Colonial Governors; Dau. of American Revolution; Dau. of American Colonists. Address: 2602 Loyd St., Murfreesboro,TN 37130. Descended from:

1 Leonard Calvert, Governor of Maryland 1633-47

2 William Calvert   Elizabeth Stone
 England c.1642/3 ----- -----
 Maryland 10 Jan 1682 c.1662 -----

3 George Calvert   Elizabeth Doyne
 St.Mary's Co.MD 1668 ----- -----
 af.1739   c.1690 -----

4 George Calvert   Sytha E. Harrison
 Stafford Co.VA 1707 ----- -----
 c.1771   1725   -----

5 William Calvert   Hannah
 Prince William Co.VA ----- -----
  22 Feb 1732
 KY 17 Aug 1812 c.1757 KY 17 Aug 1807

6 Landon Calvert   Anne Wood Howison
 Prince William Co. ----- 8 Jun 1766
  17 Mar 1763
 Lewis Co.KY 2 Jan 30 Jan 1787 28 Dec 1845
  1809

7 Nancy B. Calvert   John McDaniel
 5 Apr 1799   ----- 25 Jan 1799
 15 Sep 1873 16 Mar 1820 31 Oct 1869

8 Ambrose D. McDaniel   Marie E. Osborne
 6 Oct 1826   ----- -----
 6 Sep 1888   ----- 22 Jan 1889

9 Arthur J. McDaniel   Clyde Mae Conlan
 10 Jan 1875   ----- -----
 5 Jul 1957   15 Mar 1907 -----

Inheritor: Katherine Elise McKnight

McPECK, DOROTHY E. MOONEY (MRS. EDWIN KEYTE)

Nat. #213-B. Elected 23 Jul 1973. b. Trenton,NJ 23 Mar 1909.
m. Port Chester,NY 17 Sep 1929, Edwin Keyte McPeck, b. Kearny,NJ
27 Jan 1908. Educ: Antioch College, Yellow Springs,OH. Member:
Hereditary Order of Desc. of Colonial Governors; Dau. of American
Revolution; Colonial Dames of XVII Century; U.S. Dau. of War of
1812; Ancient and Honorable Artillery Co.; Magna Charta Dames;
Genealogical and Historical Soc. of Central Florida; Children of
American Revolution; Marquis Biographical Library Assn. Occup:
Antique dealer, appraiser and restorer of old homes. Address:
1259 Lakeview Drive, Winter Park, FL 32789. Descended from:

1 Roger Conant, Governor of Massachusetts 1624-28

2 Lot Conant   Elizabeth Walton
   Plymouth c.1624   Marblehead,MA   Eng. 27 Oct 1629
   Beverley,MA 29 Sep   1649   Lynn, MA c.1668
     1674

3 John Conant   Bethia Mansfield
   Salem,MA 15 Dec 1652   Beverley   Lynn 7 Apr 1658
   Beverley 30 Sep 1724   7 May 1678   Beverley 27 Jul 1720

4 Lot Conant   Martha Cleaves
   Beverley 1 Jun 1679   Beverley   Beverley 24 Jul 1681
   Concord,MA 20 Sep 1767 16 May 1698   Concord 15 Feb 1725

5 Robert Conant   Esther
   Beverley 26 Apr 1699   Chelmsford,MA   Chelmsford c.1703
   Stow,MA 27 Mar 1773   1721   Chelmsford c.1741

6 Peter Conant   Sarah Gibson
   Chelmsford c.1732   Stow   Stow 26 Aug 1732
   Stow 1785   18 Nov 1749   Stow 19 Aug 1825

7 Peter Conant   Elizabeth Fairbanks
   Stow 10 May 1760   Stow   Harvard,MA 13 Jan 1758
   Stow 22 Sep 1833   7 Dec 1780   Stow 2 Feb 1847

8 Betsy Conant   Paul Randall
   Stow 4 Oct 1787   Stow   Stow 11 Jan 1784
   Bolton,MA c.1850   9 Nov 1806   Stow 6 Jul 1842

9 Ann M. Randall   Henry T. French
   Stow 3 Jul 1826   Bolton,MA   Candia,NH 16 Nov 1826
   Hudson,MA 19 Mar 1916 c.1851   Hudson 16 Dec 1913

10 Hermon E. French   Lilla F. Stowe
   Hudson 19 Jun 1857   Hudson,MA   Hudson 15 Aug 1860
   Hudson 8 Jun 1940   30 Jan 1883   Marlborough,MA 23 Jan
                                                   1935

11 Ruby G. French   Harry M. Mooney
   Hudson 18 Sep 1887   Hudson   Brooklyn,NY 24 Feb 1886
   Hudson 14 Jun 1971   6 Apr 1908   Hudson 22 Oct 1952

McRAE, NANCY JANE (MISS)

Nat.#267-B. Elected 27 Oct 1975. b. Galena,IL 6 Oct 1905. Educ:
San Francisco State University, B.A. and M.A.; San Jose State
University, M.A. in Librarianship. Member: Hereditary Order of
Desc. of Colonial Governors; Magna Charta Dames; Sovereign
Colonial Soc. of Americans of Royal Descent; Descendants of
Knights of the Garter at Windsor Castle, England; Desc. of
Knights of the Garter; Plantagenet Society; Sovereign Order of
the Crown; Dau. of American Revolution; Colonial Dames of XVII
Century; Women Descendants of the Ancient and Honorable Artillery
Co. of Massachusetts; New England Women; Dau. of American
Colonists; National Society of Literature and the Arts; The Lotus
Club House. Occup: Teacher of Art and Librarianship; Enamel
Studio. Address: 1234 Bernal Avenue, Burlingame,CA 94010.
Descended from:

1 Thomas Dudley, Governor of Massachusetts 1634-35, 1640-41,
  1645-46, 1650-51

2 Samuel Dudley   Elizabeth Leget
  Northampton,Eng.c.1606   Exeter,NH   Exeter c.1628
  Exeter 10 Feb 1682/3   c.1652   af.1702

3 Dorothy Dudley   Moses Leavitt
  Exeter 1663   Exeter   Exeter 1650
  Exeter   26 Oct 1681   Exeter 1731

4 Joseph Leavitt   Mary Wadleigh
  Exeter 1699   Deerfield   -----
  Deerfield,NH 1793   -----   -----

5 Nathaniel Leavitt   Lydia Sanborn
  Deerfield 1727   Hampton,NH   Hampton 1737
  Exeter 1824   -----   Exeter 18 Nov 1827

6 Moses Leavitt   Ruth Leavitt
  Exeter 12 Jul 1759   -----   Exeter 22 Jan 1757
  Sanbornton,NH   1780   Sanbornton 26 Nov 1803
     3 Oct 1827

7 Miriam Leavitt   David Hunkins
  Sanbornton 22 Jul 1788 Sanbornton   Sanbornton 22 Jul 1785
  Sanbornton 31 Aug 1841 21 Dec 1809   Sanbornton 19 Jun 1865

8 Darius Hunkins   Ann McCarthy
  Sanbornton 29 Apr 1812 Galena,IL   Silver Lake,PA
                                                13 Feb 1821
  Galena 1 Mar 1881   28 Jun 1840   Galena 18 Jul 1862

9 Sydney Cassius Hunkins   Isaphene Mills
  Galena 2 Aug 1847   Prarie de   Matoon,IL 12 Jul 1852
                          Chien,WI
  Galena 11 Jul 1918   5 Jan 1872   Galena 16 Jun 1927

10 Miriam Hunkins   William Murdock McRae
   Galena 13 Jan 1874   Chicago,IL   Chicago 31 Jul 1866
   Burlingame,CA 4 Oct   2 Apr 1902   New York,NY 1912
      1947

MEYER, PAUL ROGERS

Nat. #247-B. Elected 3 Dec 1974. b. Chicago,IL 7 Nov 1938.
m. Grand Haven,MI 22 Jul 1967, Jean Arlene Schmidt, b. Grand
Haven 10 May 1940. Issue: Brent Rogers Meyer. Educ: Southern
Illinois University, B.A. Member: Hereditary Order of Desc. of
Colonial Governors; Order of First Families of Virginia; Sons of
American Revolution (Past State Registrar,IL); Soc. of War of
1812 (Past State Treasurer,IL). Occup: Certified Real Estate
Broker, Illinois. Address: 725 South Crescent Avenue, Park
Ridge, IL 60068. Descended from:

1 George Yeardley, Governor of Virginia 1618-27

Continue with the lineage of his mother Virginia Marie Healy
Meyer (Mrs. Harold I.) #195-B.

    Inheritor: Brent Rogers Meyer (son)

MEYER, ROBERT BEESON BROOKS

Nat. #265-B. Elected 22 Sep 1975. b. Chicago,IL 3 Dec 1939.
m. Evanston,IL 25 Oct 1969, Barbara Jean Miller, b. Evanston
12 Aug 1940. Issue: Eric Clingman Meyer, b. Houston,TX 12 Dec
1972. Educ: Northwestern University, B.A., M.A.
Member: Hereditary Order of Desc. of Colonial Governors; Order
of First Families of Virginia; Sons of American Revolution;
Soc. of War of 1812. Occup: Computer Sciences Co. of Philadelphia,PA. Address: 529 East Drive, Shady Lane, Barrington,IL
60008. Descended from:

1 George Yeardley, Governor of Virginia 1618-27

Continue with the lineage of his mother Virginia Marie Healy
Meyer (Mrs. Harold I.) #195-B.

    Inheritor: Eric Clingman Meyer (son)

MEYER, VIRGINIA MARIE HEALY (MRS. HAROLD I.)

Nat. #195-B. Elected 18 Sep 1972. b. Chicago,IL 25 Dec 1901.
m. Kankakee,IL 29 May 1937, Harold Irving Meyer, M.D., b. Central
City,IL 21 Mar 1897. Issue: Paul Rogers Meyer, b. Chicago 7 Nov
1938; Robert Beeson Meyer, b. Chicago 3 Dec 1939. Educ:
University of Chicago; University of Illinois; Chicago Business
College. Member: Hereditary Order of Desc. of Colonial
Governors; Dau. of American Revolution (Past State Librarian,IL);
Colonial Dames of America; U.S. Dau. of 1812 (Past Rec. Sec.,IL);
Order of First Families of Virginia; Dau. of Colonial Wars (Past
Vice Pres.,IL); Illinois, Pennsylvania, Chicago, and London
Genealogical Societies. Occup: Genealogist. Address:
434 Arlington Place, Chicago,IL 60614. Descended from:

1 George Yeardley, Governor of Virginia 1618-27

2 Argoll Yeardley   (1)   Frances Knight
   Virginia 1620/1   Middlesex Co.   -----
                             England
   Northampton Co.VA 1655 9 Mar 1635   Northampton Co. c. 1649

3 Argoll Yeardley   Sarah Michael
   Northampton Co. 1644   Northmptn.Co.   c.1656
   Northampton Co. 1683   Jan 1671   c.1695

4 Frances Yeardley   John West
   Northampton Co.   Virginia   -----
     by 9 Aug 1678
   af. 1702   af. 29 Mar   -----
                            1694

5 Argoll Yeardley West   Comfort
   -----   -----   -----
   w.p. Accomac Co.VA   -----   -----
     6 Jul 1736

6 Sarah Yeardley West   Americus Scarburgh
   bf. 4 Apr 1736   -----   Accomac Co. 17 Sep
                                                 1723
   -----   -----   c.1773

7 John Scarburgh   Mary Pitts Jacob
   Virginia   -----   -----
   Northampton Co.   14 Jun 1784   Portsmouth,OH
     c.1793   11 Feb 1853

8 Vienna P. Scarburgh   John Russell Turner
   Northampton Co.   Northmptn.Co.   Northampton Co.
     3 Dec 1790   25 Jun 1787
   btw. 1832-52   17 Oct 1807   Portsmouth 15 Oct 1859

9 Sarah Parker Turner   John Bright Clingman
   Portsmouth 28 Oct 1811 Portsmouth   PA 12 May 1803
   Cedarville,IL 22 Apr   1 May 1828   Cedarville 4 Feb 1886
     1863

10 Lewis Pressell   Mary Elizabeth Morgan
     Clingman
   Cedarville 4 Jun 1844   Chicago,IL   Chelsea,MA 15 Aug 1848
   Chicago 31 Dec 1924   23 Jun 1869   Chicago 9 Jul 1925

11 Edna Morgan Clingman   Edward Brennan Healy
   Chicago 26 Sep 1877   Chicago   Detroit,MI 13 Jan 1863
   Chicago 31 May 1952   14 Jun 1899   Chicago 12 Mar 1933

12 Virginia Marie Healy   Harold Irving Meyer
   Chicago 25 Dec 1901   Kankakee,IL   Central City,IL
                                                 21 Mar 1897

                           29 May 1937

MIKESELL, MARIAN L. LEE (MRS. JOHN W., JR.)

Nat. #80-B. Elected 13 Apr 1963. b. Detroit,MI 21 Nov 1920.
m. Lordsburg,NM 15 Feb 1947, John Wadsworth Mikesell, Jr., b.
Washington,PA 19 Nov 1920. Issue: Helen Joy Mikesell, b.
Tucson,AZ 18 Dec 1947; Linda Ann Mikesell, b. Tucson 9 May 1949;
John Wadsworth Mikesell III, b. Tucson 23 Aug 1950; Henry Bourne
Mikesell, b. Tucson 23 Sep 1952; James Frederick Mikesell, b.
Tucson 2 Aug 1954. Member: Hereditary Order of Desc. of
Colonial Governors; Dau. of American Revolution; Soc. of May-
flower Desc.; U.S. Dau. of 1812; Dau. of Colonial Wars; Dau. of
Founders and Patriots of America. (From Society's Records).
Descended from:

1 William Bradford, Governor of Plymouth Colony 1621-33, 1635-57

2 William Bradford   (1)   Alice Richards
   Plymouth,MA 17 Jun   Plymouth   Weymouth,MA 16 Jun
     1624   1627
   Plymouth 20 Feb 1703/4   28 Jan 1650/1   Plymouth 12 Dec 1671

3 Alice Bradford Adams   (2)   James Fitch
   Plymouth 1661   Norwich,CT   Saybrook,CT 2 Aug 1649
   Canterbury,CT 15 Mar   8 May 1687   Canterbury 10 Nov 1727
     1745

4 Ebenezer Fitch   Bridget Brown
   Norwich 10 Jan 1689/90   Canterbury   -----
   Windham,CT 24 Nov 1724   18 Sep 1712   Windham

5 Alice Fitch   John Fitch
   Windsor 30 Jan 1713   Windsor,CT   Windham 18 Mar 1705
   1796   25 Jan 1730/1   Windsor 12 Feb 1760

6 James Fitch   Ann Hulbert
   Windham 9 Apr 1739   Windsor   Windham 14 Apr 1730
   Windsor 7 Nov 1815   23 May 1763   Windsor 3 Feb 1821

7 Anna Theresa Fitch   George Phelps
   Windham 16 Oct 1765   Windsor   Windsor 7 Dec 1755
   Windsor 29 Oct 1854   23 May 1784   Windsor 16 Feb 1807

8 Rhoda Phelps   Elihu Newberry
   Windsor 16 Aug 1793   Windsor   Windsor 3 Feb 1788
   Romeo,MI 16 Oct 1877   19 Dec 1815   Romeo 13 Mar 1860

9 John Stoughton   Helen Handy
     Newberry
   Waterville,NY 18 Nov   Cleveland,OH   Cleveland 15 Nov 1835
     1826
   Detroit,MI 2 Jan 1887   6 Oct 1859   Detroit 17 Dec 1912

10 Helen Hall Newberry   Henry Bourne Joy
   Detroit 9 Jun 1869   Grss.Pnt.Frm.   Detroit 23 Nov 1864
   Grosse Pointe Farms,   11 Oct 1892   Grosse Pointe Farms
     MI 13 Mar 1958   6 Nov 1936

11 Helen Bourne Joy   Howard Barker Lee
   Detroit 20 Mar 1896   Grss.Pnt.Frm.   Detroit 13 Aug 1891
                            16 Jun 1917   Detroit 28 Feb 1962

MILLER, LOUISE HOLLAND McNEILL (MRS.)

Nat. #249-B. Elected 6 Feb 1975. b. Tacoma,WA 10 Jun 1904.
m. Montesano,WA 9 Aug 1930, George Edward Miller, b. St. Paul,
MN 7 Sep 1907. Educ: University of Puget Sound and University
of Washington. Member: Hereditary Order of Desc. of Colonial
Governors; Colonial Dames XVII Century; Dau. of American Revolu-
tion; Dau. of American Colonists; Virginia Genealogical Soc.;
Virginia Historical Soc.; Seattle Opera Guild; Tacoma Art
Museum; Women's Philharmonic Assn.; Freedom Foundation at Valley
Forge. Address: 7845 South Pine, Tacoma,WA 98409. Descended fr:

1 Edward Digges, Governor of Virginia 1655-56

2 Dudley Digges   Susannah Cole
   York Co.VA 1662/5   -----   Virginia 1674
   18 Jan 1710   -----   9 Dec 1708

3 Cole Digges   Elizabeth Power
   Virginia 1691/2   York Co.VA   -----
   Virginia 1744   -----   -----

4 Dudley Digges   Martha Armistead
   1729   -----   -----
   Yorktown,VA 3 Jun   -----   -----
     1790

5 Martha Digges   Nathaniel Burwell
   York Co. 10 Aug   -----   James City Co.VA 1750
     1750/57
   Virginia 1848   1780   Botetourt Co.VA
                                                      10 Mar 1801/2

6 Frances Thacker Burwell   Lewis Harvey
   King William Co.VA   Botetourt Co.   Botetourt Co. 4 Nov
     28 Feb 1781   1785
   Roanoke Co.VA 24 Nov   25 Sep 1807   Roanoke Co. 14 Feb
     1864   1842

7 Robert H. Harvey   Julia Holland
   Roanoke Co. 15 Jan   -----   20 Sep 1812
     1815
   Roanoke Co. 31 Mar   20 Nov 1839   Virginia
     1883

8 Louisa Burwell Harvey   John Abner Persinger
   Roanoke Co. 20 Feb   Roanoke Co.   Roanoke Co. 6 Jul 1841
     1847
   Roanoke Co. 11 Mar   12 Sep 1866   Roanoke Co. 3 Mar 1913
     1887

9 Emma Petty Persinger   Charles Frederick
                                                      McNeill
   Sedalia,MO 28 Jan 1875 Austin,TX   Austin 10 Jun 1875
   Puyallup,WA 19 May   25 Jan 1897   Steilacoom,WA 14 Dec
     1953   1946

MIRICK, JULIA M. KERBY (MRS. LAURENCE P.)

Nat. #44-B. Elected 31 Jan 1962. b. Oxon Hill,MD 20 Nov 1893.
m. 3 Jun 1943, Laurence Payson Mirick, b. Malden,MA 4 Feb 1895,
d. Bethesda,MD 29 Aug 1957. Educ: Maryland State College.
Member: Hereditary Order of Desc. of Colonial Governors; Dau. of
American Revolution; Dau. of Colonial Wars; Dau. of Founders and
Patriots of America (Past State Pres.,DC); Colonial Daughters of
XVII Century; Assn. for Preservation of Virginia Antiquities;
Magna Charta Dames. Occup: Former teacher and principal.
Address: C/o Robert Henry Kerby, 8407 Indian Head Highway,
Oxon Hill,MD 20022. (From Society's Records). Descended from:

1 Robert Brooke, Governor of Maryland 1652

2 Thomas Brooke   Eleanor Hatton
     Battle, Eng. 23 Jun   Calvert Co.   England 1642
       1632   MD
     Calvert Co. 1676   c.1659   Maryland 1725

3 Clement Brooke   Jane Sewall
     Calvert Co.   Maryland   St. Mary's Co.MD
       bf. 25 Oct 1676
     Prince George's Co.   bf.31 Aug 1704 Prince George's Co.
       MD 1736/7   1761

4 Henry Brooke   Margaret
     Prince George's Co.1704 Maryland   -----
     Prince George's Co.1751 -----   Prince George's Co.
                                              bf.3 Jan 1792

5 Nicholas Brooke   Miss Hill
     Prince George's Co.1752 Maryland   Prince George's Co.
     Prince George's Co.1797 -----   -----

6 Clement Hill Brooke   Ann Carroll
     Prince George's Co.   Surrattsville, Surrattsville 1799
       c.1778   MD
     Prince George's Co.   -----   Silver Hill,MD
       28 Aug 1854   23 Jul 1879

7 Clement Hill Brooke   Margaret Elizabeth
                                              Jenkins
     Surrattsville   Washington,DC   Surrattsville
       25 Feb 1832   15 Jan 1844
     Silver Hill 4 Apr 1917 23 Dec 1869   Silver Hill 5 Dec 1915

8 Eugenia Brooke   John Henry Kerby
     Silver Hill   -----   Oxon Hill,MD 10 Aug
       10 Jul 1870   1864
     Washington,DC   7 Feb 1893   Oxon Hill 29 Jun 1936
       19 Nov 1954

     Inheritor: Robert Henry Kerby, 8407 Indian Head Highway,
     Oxon Hill,MD 20022.

MOORE, CAROLINE L. TIEDEMAN (MRS. HAROLD A.)

Nat. #71-B. Elected 26 Mar 1963. b. Savannah,GA 1 Aug 1907.
m. Charleston,SC 17 Nov 1934, Harold A. Moore, b. McClellanville,
SC 17 Jan 1906. Issue: Sara R. Moore Salley, b. 23 Aug 1939.
Educ: Ashley Hall; College of Charleston. Member: Hereditary
Order of Desc. of Colonial Governors; Huguenot Soc. of SC
(Membership Chrm.); National Huguenot Soc. (KS Chrm.); Huguenot
Soc. of Founders of Manakin,VA; Dau. of American Revolution
(Founder and First Regent, Fort Sullivan Chap.); Children of
American Revolution (Senior Pres., SC); Dau. of Barons of Runne-
mede (Past 3rd Vice Pres.); Dau. of Colonial Wars(Past 3rd Vice
Pres.); Order of First Families of Virginia; Colonial Dames of
XVII Century); Order of Americans of Armorial Ancestry); Order
of Crown of Charlemagne in U.S.A.); United Dau. of Confederacy;
National and SC Genealogical Societies; SC Historical Soc.;
British American Soc. of America. Publisher of Abstracts of Wills
of the State of SC from 1670 to 1784. Address: 307 Stono Drive,
Charleston,SC 29412. Descended from:

*1 Samuel Mathews, Governor of Virginia 1656-60

2 Francis Mathews   -----
   Virginia   -----   -----
   York Co.VA 16 Feb 1674   -----   -----

3 Baldwin Mathews   -----
   York Co. 1670   -----   -----
   York Co. 1737   -----   -----

4 Mary Mathews   Philip Smith
   York Co.   -----   Gloucester Co.VA
                                                     1 Jun 1695
   -----   19 Feb 1711   Northumberland Co.VA
                                                     1743

5 Jane Smith   John Payne
   -----   -----   Goochland Co.VA
                                                     4 Dec 1713
   -----   23 Jun 1757   Goochland Co. 28 Jun
                                                     1784

6 Smith Payne   Margaret Morton Payne
   Goochland Co. 18 Jun   -----   -----
     1764
   -----   -----   -----

7 George Morton Payne   Susan Lewis
   Goochland Co. 4 Feb   -----   Cumberland Co.VA
     1796
   Micanopy,FL 1855   10 Oct 1815   Buckingham Co.VA 14 Apr
                                                     1821

8 George B. Payne   Catherine Gabriella
                                                     Penn
   Goochland Co. 24 Sep   -----   Amherst Co.VA 19 Jun
     1816   1819
   Micanopy 22 Nov 1859   9 Oct 1839   Micanopy 6 Jul 1859

9 Sarah P. Payne   James C. Rembert
   Micanopy 4 Jul 1852   Savannah,GA   Elbert Co.GA 28 Nov
                                                     1849
   Savannah 13 May 1932   28 Oct 1870   Columbus,GA 10 Nov 1881

* See Preface

10 James C. Rembert   John Otto C. Tiedeman
   Columbus, 5 Sep 1881   Savannah   Charleston,SC 11 Jun
                                                   1878
   Columbia,SC 26 Jan   17 Nov 1904   Charleston 31 Jan 1940
      1952

Inheritor: Sara Rembert Moore Salley (Mrs. Michael G.),
1734 John Wesley Drive, Orangeburg,SC 29115.

MORGAN, DIANA MAE SWEENEY (MRS. JAMES P., JR.)

Nat. #56-B. Elected 24 Sep 1962. b. New York,NY 24 Nov 1939.
m. James P. Morgan, Jr. Educ: Columbia University, B.S. 1962.
Member: Hereditary Order of Desc. of Colonial Governors; Dau. of
American Revolution; Ancient and Honorable Artillery Co. of MA;
Soc. of Desc. of Colonial Clergy. Address: 486 North Street,
Greenwich,CT 06830. Descended from:

1 John Alden, Governor of Plymouth Colony 1663-4, 1667

2 John Alden   (2)   Elizabeth Phillips
                                                 Everett
   Duxbury,MA/Plymouth,MA   -----   -----
      1622/26
   Boston,MA 14 Mar 1701   -----   1695

3 William Alden   Mary Drury
   Boston 10 Sep 1669   Boston   Boston 10 Jul 1672
   Dedham,MA 9 Feb 1729   21 May 1691   Boston 11 Feb 1727

4 Elizabeth Alden   Thomas Betterly
   Boston 10 Mar 1695   Boston   England c.1688
   Boston 23 Feb 1753   23 Aug 1720   Boston 12 Feb 1733

5 Thomas Betterly   (2)   Elizabeth Carson
   Boston 17 Nov 1723   Boston   Boston 22 Mar 1732
   Boston 28 Jul 1775   6 Apr 1749   Boston 7 Aug 1775

6 Thomas Betterly   Lydia Warren
   Boston 28 Apr 1751   Boston   Boston 12 Sep 1751
   Newfane,VT 25 Jun 1836   24 Dec 1772   Newfane 26 Nov 1839

7 Thomas Betterly   (2)   Hannah Rogers
   Worcester,MA c.1773   Guilford,VT   Guilford c.1770
   Dummerston,VT Mar 1854   c.1800/2   Newfane 1 Feb 1862

8 William C. Betterly   Lucretia Pedee
                                                 Templeton
   Newfane 1805   -----   c.1817
   Newfane 15 Mar 1875   16 Feb 1834   Newfane bf. 1870

9 Mary Augusta Betterly   Nathaniel Whitcomb
                                                 Stacy
   Newfane 25 Sep 1838   Chicopee,MA   Prescott,MA 6 Aug 1820
   Boston 4 Jun 1937   23 Feb 1859   Springfield,MA 13 Jan
                                                 1896

10 Edna Inez Stacy   Anthony J. Sweeney
   Chicopee 8 Sep 1869   Jersey City,   St. Catherines,Canada
                            NJ   1 Jul 1850
   Philadelphia,PA   18 Jun 1890   Mansfield,OH 26 Oct
    9 May 1944   1928

11 Henry Whitcomb Stacy   Mae Edith Fichter
   Sweeney
   Springfield,MA   New York,NY   NYC 11 May 1901
    12 Sep 1898   12 Jun 1934

MORSE, MARY GENEVIEVE FORBES (MRS. FREDERICK TRACY)

Nat. #16-B. Elected 20 Oct 1959. b. New Rochelle,NY 8 Jun 1905.
m. Charlottesville,VA 1 Jan 1926, Frederick Tracy Morse, b.
Unadilla,NY 11 Sep 1902. Issue: Robert Frederick Morse, b.
Ruston,LA 14 Oct 1927. Educ: Louisiana Polytechnic Institute,
B.A. Member: Hereditary Order of Desc. of Colonial Governors
(Hon. Governor General); Dau. of American Revolution (Past Vice
Pres. General and Curator General); Dau. of Colonial Wars (Past
National Pres.); Dau. of American Colonists; Order of the Crown
in America; Americans of Royal Descent; Dau. of the Barons of
Runnemede; Soc. of Desc. of Colonial Clergy; Magna Charta Dames;
Colonial Dames of America; Soc. of Desc. of William I, the
Conqueror; British American Soc.; Gavel Club; Nat. Trust for
Historic Preservation; American Heritage Soc.; Smithsonian
Associates. Address: Box 6127, University Station,
Charlottesville,VA 22906. Descended from:

1 William Leete, Governor of Connecticut 1676-83

2 John Leete   Mary Chittenden
   Guilford,CT 1639   Guilford   Guilford 1647
   Guilford 25 Nov 1692   4 Oct 1670   Guilford 9 Mar 1712

3 Anne Leete   John Collins
   Guilford 5 Aug 1671   Guilford   Guilford 1665
   Guilford 2 Nov 1724   23 Jul 1691   Guilford 24 Jan 1751

4 Avis Collins   Peter Buell
   Guilford 1 Apr 1714   Litchfield,CT   Lebanon,CT 22 May 1710
   Litchfield 1 Nov 1754   26 Dec 1734   Litchfield 4 May 1784

5 Peter Buell   Abigail Seymour
   Litchfield 12 Oct 1739   Litchfield   Harwinton,CT 30 Apr
                                               1745
   Litchfield 30 Jan 1797   25 Dec 1766   Litchfield 16 May 1806

6 Abigail Buell   Melancthon Woolsey
                                               Welles
   Litchfield 3 May 1770   Litchfield   Stamford,CT 6 Dec 1770
   Elyria,OH 6 Nov 1847   7 Feb 1794   Lowville,NY 7 Feb 1857

7 George W. Welles   Mary Ann Bardin
                                               Richardson
   Shaftsbury,VT 31 Dec   -----   New York,NY 8 Jun 1802
    1796
   af. 1876   18 Jun 1822   af. 1876

8 Mary Elizabeth Welles   James Frederick
                                        Blauvelt
   New York 25 Oct 1825   -----   New York 14 Aug 1823
   Brooklyn,NY 14 Jun   17 Jul 1854 Brooklyn 17 May 1884
     1912

9 Genevieve Blauvelt   William Winterbourne
                                        Sabin
   Newton,NY 19 May 1856   Brooklyn   Chestnut Hill,PA
                                         12 Aug 1850
   New York 16 Mar 1947   12 Aug 1874 Asheville,NC 5 Sep 189?

10 Mabel Sabin   James Forbes
   England 15 Nov 1882   Hollis,NY   England 9 Jan 1874
                           9 Jan 1904 Yonkers,NY 26 Nov 1935

                        SUPPLEMENT NO. 1

1 John Webster, Governor of Connecticut 1656

2 Robert Webster   Susannah Treat
   England c.1627   Middletown,CT England bp. 8 Oct 1629
   Hartford,CT 1676   1652   Hartford 1705

3 Sarah Webster   Joseph Mygatt
   Middletown 30 Jun 1655 Hartford   Hartford
   Hartford Feb 1744   15 Nov 1672 Hartford Mar 1698

4 Dorothy Mygatt   Jonathan Steele
   Hartford 26 Jan 1696   Hartford   Hartford bp. 13 Sep
                                         1693
   Hartford 8 Nov 1775   5 May 1715   Hartford 6 Jan 1753

5 Sarah Steele   Zachariah Seymour
   Hartford 8 Jan 1715/6 Hartford   Hartford 24 Sep 1712
   Hartford 26 Mar 1759   25 Apr 1739 Hartford 24 Aug 1777

6 Abigail Seymour   Peter Buell

   Continue with Generation 5 of her lineage from Governor
   William Leete.

   Inheritor: William Tracy Morse

                              183

MORTON, ANN MAYO TILDEN (MRS. DONALD JOHN, SR.)

Nat. #365-B. Elected 15 Oct 1979. b. Concord,NH 3 Dec 1931.
m. Mesilla Park,NM 16 Aug 1968, Donald John Morton, Sr., b.
Brooklyn,NY 11 Jan 1931. Educ: New Mexico State University,
B.S. in Biology, Glendale (CA) School of Medical Technology.
Member: Hereditary Order of Desc. of Colonial Governors; Dau. of
American Revolution (State Vice Regent); Dau. of Colonial Wars;
Soc. of Desc. of Colonial Clergy; Colonial Dames of XVII Century;
New England Women; Soc. of Mayflower Descendants. Address:
12 Westchester Drive, Auburn,MA 01501. Descended from:

1 Thomas Prence, Governor of Plymouth Colony 1634-35, 1638-73

2 Mercy Prence   John Freeman
   Plymouth c.1631   Eastham,MA   England 1627
   Eastham 28 Sep 1711   13 Feb   Eastham 28 Oct 1719

3 Hannah Freeman   John Mayo 3d
   Eastham 1665   -----   15 Dec 1652
   Hingham,MA 15 Feb 1743 14 Apr 1681   Hingham 1 Feb 1728

4 Joseph Mayo   Abigail Myrick
   Hingham 22 Dec 1696   Harwich,MA   1700
   Harwich 1774   20 Feb 1717/8   -----

5 Thomas Mayo   Elizabeth Wing
   Harwich 1 Apr 1725   Harwich   28 Feb 1729
   Newport,RI 1778   5 Oct 1752   Harwich 11 Feb 1816

6 Elnathan Mayo   (int.)   Susan (Paine) Chapman
   Harwich 4 Jun 1762   -----   Eastham,MA 26 Oct 1789
   Harwich 23 Oct 1839   23 Mar 1821   Boston,MA 18 Aug 1856

7 Joseph Mayo   Maria Louise
                                            Huntington
   Brewster,MA 27 Jan   Brewster   East Weare,NH 6 Dec
     1822   1824
   East Weare 24 Jan 1906 5 May 1846   Worcester,MA 20 Feb
                                              1884

8 Ann Maria Mayo   Charles Houghton
                                            Tilden
   Antrim,NH 1 Oct 1847   Concord,NH   South Boston,MA
                                              29 Apr 1842
   East Weare 8 Nov 1936 4 Jul 1866   Worcester 28 Nov 1890

9 Joseph Mayo Tilden   Gertrude Estelle
                                            Bennett
   Worcester 12 Mar 1873 Worcester   Georgetown,CT 4 Nov
                                              1874
   Concord 23 Feb 1928   28 Jul 1898   Clermont,FL 20 Jun
                                              1957

10 Sidney Edward Tilden   Wanda Louise Tapp
   Brooklyn,NY 4 Oct 1899 Galesburg,IL   Galesburg 27 Sep 1900
   Wichita,KS 31 Jul 1944 2 Aug 1924   El Paso,TX 24 Jan 1978

MOSS, ETHEL MAUDE (MISS)

Nat. #173-B. Elected 13 Feb 1971. b. Agnes City, Lyon Co.,KS 17 Jan 1888. Educ: Kansas State Emporia College, A.B.; University of California at Berkeley, M.A.; graduate work, University of Chicago, University of Colorado, and Southern California. Member: Hereditary Order of Desc. of Colonial Governors; Dau. of American Revolution (Past Regent, Santa Barbara Chap.); Dau. of American Colonists (Regent, S.B. Chap.); Colonial Dames XVII Century (First Vice President); Dames of the Court of Honor; Women Desc. of the Ancient and Honorable Artillery Co. of MA; Dau. of Colonial Wars; National Huguenot Soc.; Magna Charta Dames; U. Nations Assn. of Santa Barbara. Occup: Retired High School and College Teacher. Address: 506 East Sola St., Santa Barbara,CA 93103. Descended from:

1 Thomas Roberts, Governor of New Hampshire 1641

2 Hester Roberts   John Martin
   New Hampshire 1628   New Hampshire Devon,Eng. 1620
   Piscataway,NJ 6 Dec   1646   Piscataway 5 Jun 1687
      1687

3 Joseph Martin   Sarah Trotter
   New Hampshire 1657   New Jersey   NJ 3 May 1663
   New Jersey 1723   25 Nov 1677   NJ af.1700

4 James Martin   Hannah Smith
   NJ 14 Dec 1680   Piscataway   Woodbridge,NJ 1685
   NJ af.1721   4 Sep 1701   NJ 1715

5 Ephraim Martin   Keziah Runion
   NJ 25 Jan 1708   Woodbridge   NJ c.1713
   NJ 1771   c.1730   NJ

6 Ephraim Martin   Catherine Stelle
   Somerset Co.NJ   Stelton,NJ   Stelton 1734
      Dec 1733
   New Brunswick,NJ   c.1754   New Brunswick 5 Oct
      28 Feb 1806   1805

7 Ephraim Martin   Mercy Alward
   Sparta,NJ Sep 1760   New Jersey   NJ c.1760
   Campbell Co.GA 1840   c.1776/7   NJ 1782

8 Martha Martin   Samuel Stites
   Somerset Co. 18 May   Somerset Co.   Somerset Co. 31 Oct
      1779   1776
   Trenton,IL 16 Dec 1838   14 Sep 1794   Trenton,IL 16 Aug 1839

9 Anna Stites   Anthony W. Casad
   Somerset Co.10 Dec 1796 Fairfield,OH   Sussex Co.NJ 2 May 1791
   Lebanon,IL 16 Jul 1838   6 Feb 1811   Lebanon 16 Dec 1857

10 Isaac D. Casad   Mary E. James
   Lebanon 6 Apr 1829   Island Grove,   Georgetown,IL 24 Apr
                               IL   1841
   Spring Hill,KS 7 Mar   22 Nov 1859   Los Angeles,CA 22 May
      1886   1930

11 Cornelia A. Casad   Charles Moss
   Summerfield,IL 29 Sep   Ocheltree,KS   Springfield 19 Aug 1854
      1861
   Santa Barbara,CA   29 Sep 1881   Emporia,KS 5 Aug 1914
      10 Mar 1948

185

MOUSSETTE, VIRGINIA KING (MRS.)

Nat. #302-B. Elected 15 Nov 1979. b. Portland,OR 15 Jul 1909.
m. New York,NY 29 May 1942, Everett Moussette b. Brooklyn,NY
10 Jun 1910, d. c.1965 (div.). Educ: University of Washington.
Member: Hereditary Order of Desc. of Colonial Governors; Dau. of
American Revolution; Colonial Dames of XVII Century; Dau. of the
American Colonists; Soc. of Desc. of Mayflower. Address:
1214 North West 121, Seattle,WA 98177. Descended from:

1 Thomas Prence, Governor of Massachusetts 1673

2 Mercy Prence   John Freeman
   Plymouth c.1631   Plymouth   Billinghurst, Sussex,
                                         Eng. 26-8 Jan 1626
   Eastham,MA 28 Sep 1711 13 Feb 1649/50 Eastham 28 Nov 1719

3 Edmund Freeman   Sarah Mayo
   Eastham 15 Jun 1657   -----   Boston,MA 10 Dec 1660
   Eastham 10 Dec 1719   -----   Boston 1775

4 Ebenezer Freeman   Abigail Young
   Eastham   Eastham   -----
   Eastham   12 Oct 1710   -----

5 Thankful Freeman   Ebenezer Newcomb
   Eastham 15 Feb 1714/5 Eastham   -----
   -----   -----   -----

6 Thankful Newcomb   Jonathan Rich
   -----   Truro,MA   Truro 1 Nov 1737
   -----   17 Oct 1760   Yorktown,VA 1777

7 Jonathan Rich   Ruth Slate
   Truro 26 Aug 1771   -----   1767
   Fort Covington,NY   1790   1841
     7 Apr 1844

8 Samuel Rich   Mary Gray
   Gill,MA 26 Aug 1794   -----   -----
   Palatine,IL 24 Jan   -----   -----
     1871

9 Julius Rich   Harriet Hoyt
   Fort Covington   -----   -----
     10 Mar 1831
   -----   -----   -----

10 Herman Rich   Alice Lyon
   Bangor,NY 23 Jun 1854 Independence, Earlville,IA
                            IA   24 Oct 1857
   Portland,OR 6 Feb   23 Oct 1876   Portland 19 May 1924
     1919

11 Elsie Rich   David King
   Des Moines,IA 8 Sep   Prosser,WA   Elk Falls,KS 21 Apr
     1881   1878
   Seattle,WA 14 Jul   27 Apr 1908   Seattle 13 Feb 1927
     1949

Inheritor: Elaine Moussette King (same address)

MUNGER, ELIZABETH MACK (MRS. ROBERT CUSHWAY)

Nat. #320-B. Elected 7 Dec 1977. b. Nazareth,PA 28 Jul 1906.
m.(1) Michigan City,IN 23 Apr 1932, Bonver Ridgeway Hitchcock,
b. Memphis,TN 28 Nov 1897, d. Berwyn,IL 28 Dec 1940. M.(2)
Almont,MI 7 Aug 1949, Robert Cushway Munger, b. Hart,MI 4 Oct
1896, d. Hart 12 Nov 1960. Issue: Gilbert Ridgway Hitchcock,
b. 25 Jun 1934; John Lathrop Hitchcock, b. 18 Jun 1936; both b.
Chicago,IL. Educ: University of Illinois, B.S.; Northwestern
University, M.A. Member: Hereditary Order of Desc. of Colonial
Governors; Soc. of Mayflower Desc.; Dau. of American Revolution;
Women Desc. of Ancient and Honorable Artillery Co.; Colonial
Dames of XVII Century; Dau. of American Colonists; Dau. of
Colonial Wars; Dau. of Founders and Patriots; Magna Charta Dames;
Soc. of Huguenots; Soc. of Desc. of Colonial Clergy; Dau. of
1812; Dames of Court of Honor; Order of Americans of Armorial
Ancestors; Desc. of Founders of Hartford; New England Women;
Sons and Dau. of Pilgrims. Address: 500 Marquette Trail,
Michigan City,IN 46360. Descended from:

1 John Webster, Governor of Connecticut 1656

2 Robert Webster   Susannah Treat
  England 1627   Middletown,CT   bp.Pitminster,Eng.
                                        8 Oct 1629
  Hartford,CT 31 May 1676 1652   Hartford 19 Nov 1705

3 Mary Webster   Thomas King
  Hartford c.1672   Hartford   Northampton,MA 14 Jul
                                        1662
  Hartford 27 Sep 1706   2 Nov c.1690   Hartford 26 Dec 1711

4 Robert King   Elizabeth Barnard
  c.1695   Hartford   Hartford bp.28 May 1699
  c.1748   17--   Hartford 26 Feb 1783

5 Sarah King   Thomas Burr
  Hartford 9 Feb 1725/6   Hartford   Hartford 4 Oct 1719
  Hartford 5 Oct 1799   17--   Hartford 27 Oct 1777

6 Samuel Burr   Rebecca Stillman
  Hartford 20 Jan 1744/5   Rocky Hill   Wethersfield,CT 4 Aug
                                        1747
  Wethersfield 18 Feb   17 Jun 1773   Hartford 7 Oct 1831
    1792

7 Rebecca Stillman Burr   Ephriam Robins, Jr.
  Hartford bp.24 Oct   Hartford   Mansfield,CT 29 Mar
    1785   1784
  26 May 1818   21 May 1812   Cincinnati,OH Feb 1845

8 Rebecca Amelia Robins   Samuel Ely Mack
  Boston,MA 3 Apr 1815   Amherst,MA   Middlefield,MA 8 Nov
                                        1815
  Sacramento,CA 2 Jan   7 Sep 1841   St.Louis,MO 16 Dec
    1899   1866

9 Henry Ely Mack   Sarah Grace Lathrop
  Covington,KY 19 Oct   St.Louis   Northampton,MA 7 Apr
    1851   1851
  Philadelphia,PA 7 Nov   9 Oct 1876   Chicago,IL 14 May 1935
    1916

10 Joseph Lathrop Mack   Roberta Covington Smith
  San Francisco,CA   Philadelphia   Denton,MD 28 Jul 1877
    28 Sep 1877
  Chicago 22 Jul 1952   20 Oct 1904   Michigan City,IN
                                     30 Apr 1945

MUNSEY, KENNETH BERNARD

Nat. #333-B. Elected 24 Jan 1979. b. Washington,DC 13 May 1936.
m. Washington,DC 14 May 1960, Janette Evans, b. Norfolk,VA 7 Jan
1939. Educ: The American University, Washington,DC, B.S.
Member: Hereditary Order of Desc. of Colonial Governors; Soc. of
Desc. of Colonial Clergy; Soc. of Mayflower Descendants.
Address: 82 Pelham Island Road, Sudbury,MA 01776. Descended from:

1 Thomas Prence, Governor of Plymouth 1634-38, 1657-73

2 Hannah Prence   (1)   Nathaniel Mayo
   bf.1635   Eastham,MA   England c.1627
   bf. 23 Nov 1698   13 Feb 1649   Eastham af.19 Dec 1661

3 Thomas Mayo   Barbara Knowles
   Eastham 7 Dec 1650   Eastham   Eastham 28 Sep 1656
   Eastham 22 Apr 1729   13 Jun 1677   Eastham 23 Feb 1714

4 Mercy Mayo   Jonathan Godfrey
   Eastham 19 Jan 1685   Eastham   Eastham 24 Jun 1682
   -----   30 Oct 1707   Chatham,MA bf.24 Apr
                                             1765

5 Thomas Godfrey   (1)   Bethiah Eldredge
   Chatham c.1708   Chatham   Chatham
   Chatham c.1778   7 Jun 1733   -----

6 Hannah Godfrey   Ebenezer Ryder
   Chatham c.1738   -----   Provincetown,MA 1735
   Provincetown af.1779   12 Aug 1756   16 Mar 1809

7 Samuel Ryder   Lydia Atkins
   13 Dec 1757   Truro,MA   Truro 5 Jul 1761
   Orrington,ME   19 Jun 1781   Orrington af.Jun 1819

8 Deborah Ryder   Moses Blaisdell
   Provincetown 2 Feb 1798 Bucksport,ME   2 May 1790
   Eddington,ME 20 Sep   5 Sep 1818   Bucksport 9 Jan 1868
   1870

9 Ann H. Blaisdell   George Manning Wood
   Hampden,ME 16 Jun   Bucksport   Orrington 5 May 1815
   1819
   Eddington 14 Feb 1896   31 Jan 1837   Eddington 5 Apr 1890

10 George Weston Wood   Sarah E. Ames
   Orrington 15 Mar 1840   Eddington   Prospect,ME 15 Oct 1845
   Eddington 29 Jun 1907   Jun 1864   Eddington 1 Jan 1884

11 George Manning Wood   Ethel Emma Gilbert
   Eddington 7 May 1881   Bangor,ME   Douglas,N.B.,Can. 8 Nov
                                             1881
   Bangor 30 Jul 1966   26 Nov 1901   Bangor 7 Apr 1974

12 Mildred Lovenia Wood   Virdell Everard Munsey
   Eddington 11 Feb 1905   Bangor   New Castle,ME 8 Oct
                                             1899
                           1 Feb 1924

Inheritor: Deborah Constance Munsey

MUNSEY, MILDRED L. WOOD (MRS. VIRDELL)

Nat. #286-B. Elected 4 May 1976. b. Eddington,ME 11 Feb 1905.
m. Bangor,ME 1 Feb 1924, Virdell Everard Munsey, b. New Castle,
ME 8 Oct 1899. Member: Hereditary Order of Desc. of Colonial
Governors; Dau. of American Revolution (Past Board of Governors,
DC, State Officer's Club); Dau. of Colonial Wars (State Regis-
trar); Soc. of Mayflower Descendants (Past Board of Assistants);
Soc. of Desc. of Colonial Clergy. Address: 22 Laurel Road,
Weston,MA 02193. Descended from:

1 Robert Treat, Governor of Connecticut 1683-98

2 Samuel Treat   Jane Tapp
   Pitminister,Eng. 1624   Milford,CT   1628
   Milford 12 Jul 1710   c.1647   Milford Oct 1703

3 Samuel Treat   Elizabeth Mayo
   Milford bp.3 Sep 1648   Eastham,MA   Boston,MA bp.22 May
                                             1653
   Eastham 18 Mar 1716   16 Mar 1674   Eastham 4 Dec 1696

4 Jabez Snow   Elizabeth Treat
   Eastham 6 Sep 1669/70   Eastham   Eastham 24 Jul 1671
   Eastham 14 Oct 1750   24 Jul 1695   Eastham 3 Mar 1755

5 Sylvanus Snow   Hannah Cole
   Eastham 16 Feb 1704   Eastham   Eastham 1712
   Eastham 23 Mar 1772   1 Feb 1733   Eastham 3 Aug 1750

6 Edward Snow   Betty Myrick
   Eastham 25 Jun 1745   Eastham   Eastham
   Orrington,ME Sep 1791   18 Feb 1768   Hampden,ME 25 Jul 1822

7 Sarah H. Snow   Manning Wood
   Orrington 26 Mar 1776   Orrington   Mendon,MA 1 Apr 1778
   Orrington 12 Jan 1851   16 Jun 1806   Orrington 7 Jun 1856

8 George Manning Wood   Ann H. Blaisdell
   Orrington 5 May 1815   Bucksport,ME   Hampden 16 Jun 1819
   Eddington,ME 5 Apr   31 Jan 1837   Eddington 14 Feb 1896
     1890

9 George Weston Wood   Sarah E. Ames
   Orrington 15 Mar 1840   Eddington   Prospect,ME 15 Oct
                                             1845
   Eddington 29 Jun 1907   5 Nov 1864   Eddington 1 Jan 1884

10 George Manning Wood   Ethel Emma Gilbert
   Eddington 7 May 1881   Bangor,ME   Douglas,N.B., Can.
                                             8 Nov 1881
   Bangor 30 Jul 1966   26 Nov 1901   Bangor 7 Apr 1974

MUSSO, LAURIE E. DUSTON (MRS. VINCENT J.)

Nat. #199-B. Elected 12 Feb 1973. b. Springfield,MA 6 Jan 1919.
m. San Francisco,CA 5 Sep 1946, Vincent John Musso, b. Los
Angeles,CA 22 Oct 1914. Issue: Dean Duston Musso, b. 15 Oct
1955; Dwight Vincent Musso, b. 1 Jan 1957; both b. Orange,CA.
Educ: Universities of Washington and California. Member:
Hereditary Order of Desc. of Colonial Governors; Dau. of the
American Revolution (State Chairman,CA); Dau. of Founders and
Patriots of America; Colonial Dames XVII Century; Magna Charta
Dames; Knights of the Garter; The Huguenot Society of CA; Women
Desc. of Ancient and Honorable Artillery Co.; Soc. of Mayflower
Descendants; U.S. Dau. of 1812; Americans of Royal Descent;
Colonial Order of the Crown; Dames of the Court of Honor; Duston-
Dustin Family Assn. Occup: Mathematician and Computer Technician
(ret.) Address: 1820 Skyline Drive, Fullerton,CA 92631.
Descended from:

1 Tristram Coffin, Governor of Nantucket 1671-73

2 John Coffin   Deborah Austin
   Haverhill,MA 30 Oct   Massachusetts   -----
      1647
   Nantucket,MA 5 Nov 1711 -----   -----

3 Samuel Coffin   Miriam Gardner
   Nantucket 12 Feb 1680   Nantucket   14 Jul 1685
   Nantucket 22 Feb 1764   1705   17 Nov 1750

4 Mary Coffin   William Barnard
   Nantucket 1724   Nantucket   23 Nov 1724
   Nantucket 28 Aug 1777   5 Jan 1743   11 Jul 1771

5 Tristram Barnard   Margaret Folger
   Nantucket 5 May 1743   Nantucket   27 Jun 1747
   Stokes Co.NC wp. 1807   2 Jan 1766   -----

6 Mary Barnard   William Macy
   Stokes Co. 14 Mar 1782 Stokes Co.   Nantucket 2 Feb 1772
   Union Co.IN 26 Aug   1799   Union Co. 26 Aug 1850
      1850

7 Obed Macy   Lucinda Polk
   New Garden,NC 14 Dec   Indiana   Knox Co.IN 6 Jan 1808
      1801
   Los Angeles,CA   17 Oct 1824   Los Angeles 4 Aug 1872
      9 Jul 1857

8 Urania Macy   David W. Cheesman
   IN 5 Apr 1828   Daviess Co.IN   IN 20 Dec 1824
   Medford,OR 17 Mar 1916 17 Oct 1849   San Francisco,CA
                                               3 Nov 1884

9 Laura Giddings   Edward Stephens Clark
      Cheesman
   Oakland,CA 19 Oct 1872 San Francisco   Paris,KY 28 Sep 1856
   Seattle,WA 15 Jan 1951 13 Oct 1896   Napa,CA 30 May 1900

10 Laura Estelle Clark   Arthur Given Duston
   Alameda,CA 3 Aug 1897   Medford,OR   Marlborough,MA 10 May
                                               1889
                           9 Sep 1916   27 Sep 1972

NESTOR, ELIZABETH D. GOODRIDGE (MRS. ROY C.)

Nat. #272-B. Elected 11 Nov 1975. b. Florence,KY 3 May 1907.
m. 9 Mar 1941, Roy C. Nestor, b. Cincinnati,OH 30 Jan 1910.
Issue: Virginia Royale Nestor Kohl (Mrs. Harold D.). Educ:
University of Kentucky. Member: Hereditary Order of Desc. of
Colonial Governors; Dau. of American Revolution (Organized Boone
County Chapter); Children of American Revolution (Organized
Boone Trail Soc., Past State Pres.); Huguenot Society of KY
(Past State Pres.); Sons and Dau. of the Pilgrims (State Regis-
trar); Dau. of American Colonists; United Dau. of Confederacy;
Magna Charta Dames; Kentucky Historical Society; Kentucky
Bi-Centennial Commission. Address: 259 Main Street, Florence,
KY 41042. Descended from:

1 Josias Fendall, Governor of Maryland 1656-60

2	Mary Fendall		John Theobald
	1673	-----	1666
	1751	-----	24 Jul 1713

3	William Theobald		-----
	-----	-----	-----
	w.p. 2 Nov 1751	-----	-----

4	Clement Theobald		Sara Phillips
	-----	-----	-----
	w.p. Sep 1837	23 Feb 1789	-----

5	John P. Theobald		Elizabeth M.V. Muncy
	-----	-----	-----
	1 Mar 1842	15 Nov 1830	-----

6	Elizabeth Virginia Theobald		George Washington Grant
	11 Oct 1831	-----	Grant Co.KY 25 Apr 1829
	Florence,KY 1901	11 Dec 1849	-----

7	Margaret Adel Grant		John Milton Finch
	Sherman,KY 23 Dec 1857	-----	Florence 12 Jan 1844
	Florence 8 Jun 1916	7 Dec 1871	Madison,IN 17 Nov 1935

8	Virginia Corey Finch		William Horace Goodridge
	Florence 11 Oct 1879	Florence	Florence 12 May 1861
	Florence 6 Nov 1967	7 Nov 1903	Florence 1 Dec 1925

Inheritor: Virginia Royale Nestor Kohl (Mrs. Harold Douglas),
8 Spruce Drive, Union, KY 41091.

NEWSOME, SAMUEL HENDRIXSON

Nat. #107-B.   Elected 11 Feb 1965.   b. Chester,PA 2 Jun 1902.
Educ: American Institute of Banking; Rutgers University Grad.
School of Banking. Member: Hereditary Order of Desc. of
Colonial Governors (Treasurer General); Order of Three Crusades
(Treasurer General); Americans of Royal Descent (Treasurer
General); Baronial Order of Magna Charta; Sons of American
Revolution; Sons of the Revolution; National Huguenot Society;
Order of the Crown in America; Order of Crown of Charlemagne in
the USA; Americans of Armorial Ancestry; DuBois Family Assn.
(Vice President); Silver Circle Club (First Pres. and Founder);
Colonial Club of Chester; Delaware Co. Historical Soc. (Pres.
the past 12 years); Paperweight Collectors Soc. Occup: Retired
Vice Pres. and Trust Officer of the Delaware County National
Bank of Chester,PA. Received the Order of Merit Award; Silver
Beaver Award and Vigil Honor Award from the Valley Forge Council
Boy Scouts of America and the Delmont Lodge, Order of the Arrow.
Address: 493 S. Middletown Rd., Media,PA 19063. Descended from:

1 Jeremiah Clarke, Governor of Rhode Island 1652

2	Jeremiah Clarke		Anne Dudley
	Newport,RI c.1643	Newport	Boston,MA c.1645
	Newport 16 Jan 1729	-----	·Newport 15 Dec 1732

3	Anne Clarke		William Greenman
	1676	-----	-----
	-----	c.1702/3	-----

4	Jeremiah Greenman		Sarah Blackman
	-----	-----	3 Apr 1705
	-----	6 Sep 1720	-----

5	Amey Greenman		Peter DuBois
	24 Oct 1727	-----	10 Apr 1734
	2 Jun 1807	1758	21 Aug 1795

6	Joel DuBois		Elizabeth Sparks
	22 Oct 1759	-----	6 Jul 1764
	29 Jun 1808	-----	c.1834

7	Rachel DuBois		William Holston
	c.1787	-----	-----
	28 May 1867	-----	-----

8	Maria DuBois Holston		Isaac Hendrixson
	20 Jun 1812	-----	17 Apr 1808
	2 Nov 1889	28 Nov 1833	11 Sep 1880

9	William H. Hendrixson		Miranda Richman Ford
	8 Nov 1836	-----	20 May 1840
	4 Mar 1910	29 Aug 1861	14 Oct 1924

10	Florine Bailey		Frank Newsome
	Hendrixson		
	2 Nov 1877	-----	2 Apr 1872
		19 Jun 1901	22 Oct 1935

Inheritor: Harry Edward Berry, 1234 Waverly St., Philadelphia,
PA

NICKERSON, LT. GEN. HERMAN, JR. (RET.)

Nat. #273-B. Elected 27 Oct 1975. b. Boston,MA 30 Jul 1913.
m. San Francisco,CA 8 Jun 1939, Phyllis Anne Winters b. 27 Jul
1918, Tacoma,WA. Issue: John Herman Nickerson b. San Diego,CA
30 Jul 1941; Dennis Anne Nickerson Higgenbotham b. Oakland,CA
17 Jan 1951. Educ: Boston University, B.S., B.A. Member:
Hereditary Order of Desc. of Colonial Governors; Soc. of Mayflower
Desc.; Soc. of the Cincinnati; Sons of American Revolution; Sons
of the Revolution; Soc. of Colonial Wars; Hereditary Order of
Desc. of Loyalists and Patriots (Past Gov. Gen.); Order of the
Founders and Patriots of America; Ancient and Honorable Artillery
Co. of MA; Desc. of Colonial Clergy; Disabled American Veterans;
Hereditary Register of US (Pres.); National Genealogical Soc.;
Order of Americans of Armorial Ancestry; Legion of Valor of the
USA; Masonic Lodge; Ambassador at Large, Sudan Temple; Retired
Officers Association; American Legion. Honors: Distinguished
Service Medal w/Gold Star; Silver Star; Legion of Merit; Bronze
Star Medal; Air Medal; WW II Victory Medal; United Nations
Service Medal; Outstanding Public Service Award. Occup: Lt.Gen.
U.S. Marine Corps (Ret); Administrator, National Credit Union
Administration. Address: Lake Lane, Rock Creek, Jacksonville,
NC 28540. Descended from:

1 Thomas Prence, Governor of Plymouth Colony 1634-73

2 Mercy Prence   John Freeman
   Plymouth c.1631   Eastham,MA   England 28 Jan 1626
   Eastham 28 Sep 1711   13 Feb 1649   Eastham 28 Oct 1719

3 John Freeman   Sarah Merrick
   Eastham Dec 1651   Eastham   Eastham 1 Aug 1654
   Eastham 27 Jul 1721   18 Dec 1672   Harwich,MA 21 Apr 1696

4 Mary Freeman   Judah Berry
   -----   -----   Yarmouth,MA
   Harwich 18 Aug 1719   -----   Harwich

5 Lemuel Berry   Lydia Clark
   Harwich 21 Feb 1713   Harwich   Harwich 7 Mar 1716
   Harwich 27 Aug 1767   20 May 1741   -----

6 Scotto Berry   Hanna Mayo
   Harwich 20 Oct 1745   -----   12 Dec 1806
   Brewster,MA 12 Jan 1832 -----   Brewster

7 Nancy Berry   Eleazer Nickerson
   Brewster 11 May 1793   Harwich   Yarmouth 25 May 1786
   Dennis 29 Oct 1877   3 Jan 1811   Dennis 29 Dec 1831

8 John Harding Nickerson   Phebe Kelly Baker
   Dennis 8 Dec 1811   Yarmouth   Yarmouth 21 Feb 1815
   -----   6 Nov 1833   Yarmouth 21 May 1849

9 John Freeman Nickerson   Susan Sophia Robinson
   Yarmouth 21 Sep 1837   Boston,MA   Boston 5 Apr 1840
   Boston 7 Nov 1917   13 Jan 1864   Boston 23 Mar 1878

10 Herman Nickerson   Emma Eva Carver
   Boston 20 May 1870   Lincolnville   Lincolnville 5 Sep 1885
   Lincolnville,ME   12 Oct 1912   Living
      10 Jun 1954

NILE, ABBOTT HOWE

Nat. #254-B. Elected 4 Apr 1975. b. Rumford,ME 13 Jun 1901.
m. Boston,MA 12 Sep 1928, Winona Russell Coleman b. Somerville,
MA 6 Aug 1906. Issue: Winona T. Nile Eddy; Russell Abbott Nile;
Lawrence Brackett Nile. Educ: Cornell University, A.B. Member:
Hereditary Order of Desc. of Colonial Governors; Soc. of Mayflower
Desc.; Sons of American Revolution; Old Plymouth Colony Desc.;
Soc. of Desc. of Colonial Clergy; Pilgrim John Howland Soc.;
National Huguenot Soc.; The Augustan Soc.; New England Historical
and Genealogical Soc.; Piscataqua Pioneers; Bunker Hill Monument
Soc.; Waltham Historical Soc.; Sons and Daughters of First Set-
tlers of Newbury,MA. Address: 40 Manning Road, Waltham,MA
02154. Descended from:

1   Thomas Roberts, Governor of New Hampshire 1640-41

2   John Roberts   Abigail Nutter
    Dover,NH c.1629   Dover   -----
    Dover 1695   c.1650   -----

3   Mary Roberts   Timothy Robinson
    Dover   -----   c.1667
    -----   -----   -----

4   Mary Robinson   Joseph Estes
    Dover 1695   -----   Dover 26 Aug 1696
    Dover 26 Dec 1777   -----   -----

5   Mary Estes   Moses Varney
    Dover 8 Jun 1737   Dover   10 Nov 1734
    Dover 4 Mar 1825   25 Mar 1761   -----

6   Anne Varney   Samuel Abbott
    Dover 13 May 1769   -----   22 Jun 1767
    -----   -----   -----

7   Richard Abbott   Hannah Locklyn
    Tuftonboro,NH 1790   -----   -----
    Rangeley,ME 27 May   Apr 1813   -----
      1851

8   John Abbott   Hulda Matilda Peary
    Wolfeboro,NH 18 Oct -----   22 Mar 1816
      1812
    Rangeley 1886   2 Apr 1835   Rangeley 1892

9   Aribelle Peary Abbott   Luther Nile
    Rangeley 4 Apr 1849 -----   Rangeley 4 Dec 1837
    Rangeley 17 Sep 1888 29 Jan 1865   -----

10 Joseph Abbott Nile   Mary Esther Howe
    Rangeley 25 Aug 1873 Rumford,ME   Norway,ME 18 Nov 1875
    Hickory,NC 30 Dec   1 Jun 1900
      1964

NORRIS, ABELL A., JR.

Nat. #45-B. Elected 2 Feb 1962. b. Gaithersburg,MD 30 Jun 1905.
m. Washington,DC 30 Jun 1934, Mary Shafer Hershey, b. Comus,MD
9 Jul 1908. Issue: Janet A. Norris Woodruff, b. 25 Aug 1938;
Abell A. Norris III, b. 16 Apr 1940; James Edward Norris, b.
31 Jul 1941; all b. Wash.,DC. Educ: Georgetown University, B.S.;
University of Maryland, M.Ed. Member: Hereditary Order of Desc.
of Colonial Governors (Past Genealogist Gen.); Soc. of Colonial
Wars (Governor, DC); Soc. of War of 1812 (Asst. Gen.Gen.); Desc.
of Lords of Maryland Manors (First Vice Pres.); Sons of Revolu-
tion (Past Pres.,DC); Soc. of War of 1812 (Asst.Historian,MD);
Baronial Order of Magna Charta; Americans of Royal Descent; Order
of First Families of VA; Military Order of Crusades; Jamestowne
Soc.; Order of Crown of Charlemagne in USA; Soc. of Ark and Dove;
Colonial Soc. of PA; Colonial Order of the Crown; Order of Wash-
ington; Sons of American Revolution; St. Andrews Soc.; St.
George's Soc.; Maryland Historical Soc.; Montgomery Co.MD Hist.
Soc. (First Vice Pres.); St. Mary's Co. Hist. Soc.; National
Genealogical Soc.; Augustan Soc.; Historic Area Comm., City of
Rockville,MD (Charter Chrm.). Occup: College Coordinator,
Montgomery Co.MD Public Schools (Ret.). Honor: Lion's Internatl.
"Master Key" for service to community. Address: 134 South Adams
St., Rockville,MD 20850. Descended from:

1 Robert Brooke, Governor of Maryland 1652

2 Thomas Brooke   Eleanor Hatton
   Battle,Eng. 23 Jun 1632 Maryland   England 1642
   Calvert Co. 25 Oct 1676 c.1658   Calvert Co.MD 1725

3 Thomas Brooke   (2)   Barbara Dent
   Calvert Co. 1659   -----   St.Mary's Co.MD 1676
   Prince George's Co.MD   bf.4 Jan 1699 Prince George's Co.
     7 Jan 1730/1   1754

4 Elizabeth Brooke   George Beall
   MD 1709   Maryland   Upper Marlboro,MD 1695
   Georgetown,DC 2 Oct   1728   Georgetown 15 Mar 1780
     1768

5 George Beall   Ann -----
   Georgetown 26 Feb 1729 Maryland   -----
   Georgetown 15 Oct 1807 c.1757   Georgetown

6 Levin Covington Beall   Esther Belt
   Georgetown 7 Jun 1760   Maryland   Maryland
   Montgomery Co. 1802   1781   Montgomery Co.MD 1830

7 John Beall   Charlotte Jones
   Montgomery Co.   Montgomery Co. MD 18 Feb 1787
     23 Dec 1781
   Montgomery Co.   1808   Montgomery Co.
     26 Aug 1831   22 Jan 1867

8 William Rufus Beall   Martha Elizabeth McAtee
   Montgomery Co.   -----   Montgomery Co. c.1811
     24 Feb 1814
   Dranesville,VA   -----   Montgomery Co. 1895
     3 Jan 1884

9 Charles Edward Beall   Mary Elizabeth Clements
   Barnesville,MD   Georgetown   Barnesville 22 Jun 1853
     8 Oct 1849
   Gaithersburg,MD   20 Jun 1883   Gaithersburg 1 Jan 1935
     6 Nov 1913

10 Mary Emma Beall   Abell Archibald Norris
   Toledo,OH 22 Mar 1884   Rockville,MD   Leonardtown,MD 20 Feb
                                               1875
   Gaithersburg 27 Aug   30 Aug 1904   Gaithersburg 23 Oct
     1940   1955

Inheritor: James Edward Norris (son)

NORTH, SUSAN MERRIMAN (MISS)

Nat. #293-B-S. Elected 12 Jul 1976. b. Meriden,CT 29 Jan 1954.
Member: Hereditary Order of Desc. of Colonial Governors.
Address: 44 William Ave., Meriden,CT 06450. Descended from:

1 Thomas Welles, Governor of Connecticut 1655, 1658

2 Samuel Welles   Elizabeth Hollister
   England 1630   -----   Wethersfield
   Wethersfield,CT   1659   Wethersfield
     15 Jul 1675

3 Sarah Welles   Ephraim Hawley
   Wethersfield   Trumbull,CT   N.Stratford 7 Aug 1659
    29 Sep 1664
   N.Stratford,CT   4 Dec 1683   -----
    29 Jun 1694

4 Gideon Hawley   Anna Bennett
   Bridgeport,CT 30 Jan   Stratford   Bridgeport 1691
    1687
   Bridgeport 16 Feb 1730 4 Feb 1711   Stratford 14 Nov 1727

5 James Hawley   Eunice Jackson
   Bridgeport 29 Jan 1713 Fairfield,CT   Bridgeport
   Bridgeport 7 Oct 1746   18 Jul 1733   Bridgeport 6 Sep 1796

6 Deacon E. Hawley   Mercy Bennett
   Bridgeport 30 Dec 1744 Weston,CT   Weston 31 Dec 1751
   Penfield,OH 11 Aug   27 Feb 1772   Penfield 18 Oct 1847
    1825

7 Huldah Hawley   Stephen Hoyt
   New Fairfield,CT   Danbury,CT   Danbury 27 Aug 1767
    24 Jan 1775
   Danbury 23 Jul 1848   2 Mar 1796   Danbury 11 Oct 1835

8 Harriet Hoyt   John Abbott
   Danbury 28 Jan 1809   Danbury   London,Eng. May 1795
   Bethel,CT 26 Dec 1895 1835   Danbury 5 Apr 1865

9 Susan M. Abbott   Abraham Baldwin
   New Canaan,CT 4 Sep   Danbury   Woodbridge,CT 15 Feb
    1837   1827
   Bethel,CT 6 Jun 1922   4 Apr 1861   Bethel 29 Feb 1924

10 Martha Baldwin   Lawrence Douglass
     Bethel 29 Jul 1870   Bethel   Pepperell,MA 27 Jun
                                                        1865
     New Haven,CT 6 Jan   31 Jul 1895   New Haven 12 Jun 1954
        1955

11 Helen Douglass   David Alden North
     Danbury,CT 15 Oct 1903   -----   New Haven 1 Sep 1903
     -----   -----   -----

12 Lawrence Douglass North   Barbara Merriman
                                                        Backes
     New Haven 27 Jan 1931   Wallingford,CT New Haven 16 May 1931
                                 10 Jun 1952

NORWOOD, PEARL P. NEVES (MRS. ROBERT W.)

Nat. #178-B. Elected 13 Sep 1971. b. Roby,TX 7 Oct 1912.
m. Boise,ID 12 Apr 1943, Robert Worth Norwood, b. Burleson,TX
27 Sep 1904. Member: Hereditary Order of Desc. of Colonial
Governors; Dau. of American Revolution (Regent, John Davis
Chap.); Dau. of 1812 (Vice Pres., John Hudnall Chap.); Dau. of
American Colonists (Treas. William Norwood Chap.); Colonial Dames
of XVII Century (Registrar); Magna Charta Dames (Sec., West Texas
Col.); United Daughters of the Confederacy (Sec.-Treas., Tom
Green Chap.). Occup: Business career, banking. Address:
1410 Orange St., Abilene,TX 79601. Descended from:

1 John West, Governor of Virginia 1635-37

2 John West   Unity Croshaw
     c.1632   -----   -----
     c.1691   1667   -----

3 Anne West   Henry Fox
     -----   York Co.VA   -----
     -----   1695   -----

*4 Henry Fox   (2)   Martha Keen
     c.1702   Charleston,SC   -----
     1770   20 Aug 1738   -----

5 William Fox   Sarah Carroll
     SC 1743   Richland Dist.   -----
                                 SC
     Richland,SC 1816   c.1766   -----

6 Henry Fox   Sarah Harrell
     Richland 12 Jun 1768   -----   30 Jul 1772
     18 Jan 1852   c.1790   1848

7 Jacob Fox   Mary Ann Hughs
                                                         Finnell
     Richland Co. 19 Jan   Tuscaloosa Co. South Carolina 20 Nov
        1808   AL   1811
     8 Dec 1884   26 Mar 1829   MS 25 Oct 1896

* See Preface

8   Dorcas Ann Fox   John P. Bennett
    Tuscaloosa 17 Dec 1833   -----   1829
    Pickens Co.AL 4 Sep   c.1849   Pickens Co. 18 Sep
      1893   1853

9   William T. Bennett   Telula E. Linebarger
    Pickens Co. 22 Sep   Carrollton Co. Pickens Co. 19 Jun
      1852   AL   1860
    Roby,TX 27 Sep 1934   19 Jun 1878   Roby 21 Nov 1926

10 Susie P. Bennett   Hugh T. Neves
    Palmetto,AL 27 Sep   Roby   26 Dec 1885
      1886
    Abilene,TX 26 Nov 1965   6 Oct 1907   Roby 18 Mar 1960

NOTTINGHAM, WILLIAM PROSSER

Nat. #229-B. Elected 4 Apr 1974. b. Onancock,VA 27 Apr 1911.
m.(1) Staunton,VA 5 Jan 1933, Dorothy Louise Oliver, b. Atlanta,
GA 21 Mar 1910. Issue: William Prosser Nottingham, Jr., b. 8 Aug
1938. Div. 20 Jun 1957. m.(2) Indianapolis,IN 20 Dec 1957,
Gwynne Roads Dulin. Educ: Emory University, Pre-law; University
of Virginia, LLB and JD. Member: Hereditary Order of Desc. of
Colonial Governors; Soc. of Colonial Wars; Order of Crown of
Charlemagne in the USA; Baronial Order of Magna Charta;
Americans of Royal Descent; Military Order of the Crusades; Order
of Three Crusades. Address: 7177 Williams Creek Drive,
Indianapolis,IN 46240. Descended from:

1   Thomas Dudley, Governor of Massachusetts 1634-35, 1640-41,
    1645-46, 1650-51

2   Joseph Dudley   Rebecca Tyng
    Roxbury,MA 23 Sep 1647   Massachusetts Boston,MA 13 Jul 1651
    Roxbury 2 Apr 1760   1669   MA 21 Sep 1722

3   Ann Dudley   John Winthrop
    MA bp.31 Aug 1684   Massachusetts Boston 26 Aug 1681
    MA 29 May 1776   16 Dec 1707   Sydenham,Eng. 1 Aug
                                                   1747

4   Mary Winthrop   Joseph Wanton (Gov.RI)
    MA 18 Sep 1708   -----   Newport,RI 15 Aug 1705
    Newport 25 Feb 1767   c.1729   Newport 19 Jul 1780

5   Elizabeth Wanton   Thomas Wickham
    Newport 22 Oct 1742   Newport   Newport 5 Apr 1736
    Newport 25 Aug 1814   28 Dec 1762   Newport 21 Feb 1816

6   Elizabeth Wickham   Walter C. Gardiner
    Newport 2 Nov 1773   -----   RI bp.1790
    Somerset Co.MD   -----   Northampton Co.VA
      15 Aug 1803   Mar 1817

7   Mary S.P. Gardiner   Richard Nottingham
    Newark,NJ 28 Nov 1798   Northmptn.Co. Northampton Co. c.1783
    Northampton Co.   19 Jul 1814   Northampton Co. c.1823
      15 Mar 1823

8 Luther Nottingham   (2)   Catherine E. Dalby
   Northampton Co. 1817   Northmptn.Co.   Northampton Co. 6 Jan
                                                   1828
   Northampton Co.   1 Oct 1849   Northampton Co.
     27 Oct 1867   af. 1867

9 Arthur M. Nottingham   Laura A. Toulson
   Northampton Co.   Baltimore,MD   Ewell,MD 19 Apr 1875
     17 Mar 1856
   Onancock,VA 30 Aug   25 Jul 1900   Westfield,IN 16 Jan
     1920   1968

SUPPLEMENT NO. 1

1 John Winthrop, Governor of Massachusetts 1629-49

2 John Winthrop, Jr., Governor of Connecticut 1657-67

3 Wait Still Winthrop   Mary Browne
   Boston,MA 27 Feb 1642   -----   Salem,MA 16 Jan 1656
   Boston 7 Nov 1717   -----   MA 14 Jun 1690

4 John Winthrop   Ann Dudley

Continue with Generation 3 of his lineage from Governor
Thomas Dudley.

SUPPLEMENT NO. 2

1 Nicholas Easton, Governor of Rhode Island 1650, 1672-74

2 Peter Easton   Ann Coggeshall
   Lymington,Eng. 1622   Newport,RI   England
   Newport 12 Feb 1694   15 Nov 1643   Newport 6 Mar 1687/9

3 Nicholas Easton   Elizabeth Barker
   Newport 12 Nov 1644   Newport   Newport
   Newport 1 Feb 1677   30 Nov 1666   Newport 5 Jul 1676

4 Nicholas Easton   Mary Holmes
   Newport 24 Feb 1668   Newport   Newport c.1664
   Newport 11 May 1711   -----   Newport 12 Dec 1741

5 Jonathan Easton   Patience Rodman
   Newport 1699   Newport   Newport 5 Jun 1706
   Newport 4 Mar 1782   -----   Newport 9 May 1739

6 Amey Easton   Samuel Gardiner
   Rhode Island   -----   RI 16 Jan 1719/20
   Rhode Island 1810   12 Jul 1749   Rhode Island 1802

7 Walter Clarke Gardiner   Elizabeth Wickham

Continue with Generation 6 of his lineage from Governor
Thomas Dudley.

SUPPLEMENT NO. 3

1 Jeremy Clarke, Governor of Rhode Island 1652

2 Walter Clarke, Governor of Rhode Island 1686, 1696-98

3 Hannah Clarke   Thomas Rodman
   Newport 28 Oct 1667   Newport,RI   England 26 Dec 1640
   Newport 22 Oct 1732   26 Nov 1691   Newport 11 Jan 1728

4 Patience Rodman   Jonathan Easton

   Continue with Generation 5 of his lineage from Governor
   Nicholas Easton.

SUPPLEMENT NO. 4

1 William Wanton, Governor of Rhode Island 1732-33

2 Joseph Wanton, Governor of Rhode Island 1769-75

3 Elizabeth Wanton   Thomas Wickham
   Newport 22 Oct 1742   Newport,RI   Newport 5 Apr 1736
   Newport 25 Aug 1814   28 Dec 1762   Newport 21 Feb 1816

4 Elizabeth Wickham   Walter Clarke Gardiner

   Continue with Generation 7 of his lineage from Governor
   Nicholas Easton.

SUPPLEMENT NO. 5

1 Joseph Dudley, Governor of Massachusetts 1702-15

2 Ann Dudley   John Winthrop

   Continue with Generation 3 of his lineage from Governor
   Thomas Dudley.

SUPPLEMENT NO. 6

1 John Coggeshall, Governor of Rhode Island 1647

2 Ann Coggeshall   Peter Easton

   Continue with Generation 2 of his lineage from Governor
   Nicholas Easton.

Inheritor: William Prosser Nottingham, Jr., 2501 Calvert St.,
N.W. #16, Washington, DC 20008

NOWACEK, CHARLES JAMES, M.D.

Nat. #222-B. Elected 5 Nov 1973. b. Lincoln,NE 25 Nov 1938.
m. Cleveland,OH 6 Jun 1964, Donna Virgene Graham, M.D., b.
Marietta,OH 18 Jul 1935. Issue: Charles Graham Nowacek,
b. 28 Mar 1966; David Michael Nowacek, b. 31 May 1968; Paul
Douglas Nowacek, b. 11 Nov 1969; all b. Cleveland. Educ:
University of Chicago, B.S. 1960; Western Reserve University,
M.D. 1964; University of New York, Intern; Orthopedic University
Hospital, Cleveland, Resident. Member: Hereditary Order of Desc.
of Colonial Governors; Soc. of Mayflower Desc., DC; Virginia
County Medical Soc.; U.S. Army Medical Corps 1970-72. Occup:
Orthopedic Surgeon. Honors: Diplomate of American Board of
Orthopedic Surgery, 1973. Address: 2289 Stillman Road, Cleveland
Heights,OH 44118. Descended from:

1 Thomas Mayhew, Governor of Martha's Vineyard 1647-81

2 Martha Mayhew   Thomas Tupper
   Watertown,MA c.1638   Sandwich,MA   Sandwich 16 Jan 1638
   Sandwich 15 Nov 1717   27 Dec 1661   Sandwich 26 Apr 1706

3 Israel Tupper   Elizabeth Gifford
   Sandwich 22 Sep 1666   Sandwich   Falmouth,MA 25 Feb 1664
   Sandwich 1745   c.1690   Sandwich 19 Oct 1701

4 Thankful Tupper   Josiah Clark
   Sandwich 9 Oct 1696   Sandwich   Plymouth,MA 1690
   -----   30 Oct 1718   -----

5 Israel Clark   Deborah Pope
   Plymouth 10 Sep 1720   Plymouth   Sandwich 23 Feb 1725
   Plymouth Oct 1788   13 May 1742   -----

6 Abigail Clark   Josiah Cornish
   Plymouth 13 May 1756   Plymouth   Plymouth 15 Oct 1760
   -----   15 Dec 1786   Lee Center,NY 10 Oct
                                                 1844

7 Allen Cornish   Clarissa Cornish
                                                  (cousin)
   Plymouth 1 Sep 1789   Plymouth   Plymouth 2 Nov 1792
   Lee Center 6 Apr 1853 18 Apr 1808   Lee Center 9 Jun 1864

8 George Cornish   Mary Tucker
   Lee Center 28 May 1825 New York   New York 2 May 1831
   Lee Center 3 Dec 1894 c.1848   Rome,NY 28 Apr 1898

9 Alice Cornish   Patrick Henry O'Donnell
   Lee Center 5 Nov 1853 Rome,NY   Newport,NY 6 Nov 1850
   Albany,NY 24 May 1916 16 Apr 1862   Rome 18 Apr 1916

10 Mary Catherine   Charles Herbert Thurtle
      O'Donnell
   Elgin,IL 16 Mar 1875   Lincoln,NE   Knowlesville,NY
                                                    12 Oct 1877
   Euclid,OH 28 Mar 1948 2 Jun 1906   Lincoln,NE 13 May 1947

11 Mary Lucille Thurtle   Charles George Nowacek
   Lincoln 21 Mar 1912   Lincoln   Plattsmouth,NE
                                                    22 Feb 1912
                          10 Jun 1937

NOWACEK, MARY L. THURTLE (MRS. CHARLES G.)

Nat. #181-B. Elected 15 Nov 1971. b. Lincoln,NE 21 Mar 1912.
m. Lincoln 10 Jun 1937, Charles G. Nowacek, b. Plattsmouth,NE
22 Feb 1912. Issue: Charles James Nowacek, b. Lincoln 26 Nov
1938; John Edward Nowacek, b. Lincoln 26 Mar 1940; Mary Virginia
Palmer, b. Lincoln 7 May 1941; George Arthur Nowacek, b. Lincoln
9 Sep 1942; Robert Joel Nowacek, b. Cleveland,OH 23 Sep 1944;
Thomas Joseph Nowacek, b. Cleveland 27 Sep 1945; Helen Ruth Cusa
b. Cleveland 19 Apr 1947; Paul Victor Nowacek, b. Cleveland
1 Dec 1950. Educ: Nebraska University, A.B. and B.S.; Ohio
State University at Cleveland, B.S. in Education. Member:
Hereditary Order of Desc. of Colonial Governors; Soc. of May-
flower Desc. in DC and OH; Soc. of Desc. of Colonial Clergy;
Dau. of American Revolution; Magna Charta Dames. Occup:
Elementary School Teacher, Manhasset, L.I., NY. Author of
"Heritage of Manhasset." Address: Kent Court, Apt. #13A,
15 Norwood Ave., Summit,NJ 07901. Descended from:

1 Thomas Mayhew, Governor of Martha's Vineyard 1647-81

2	Martha Mayhew		Thomas Tupper	
	Watertown,MA c.1638	Sandwich,MA	Sandwich 16 Jan 1638	
	Sandwich 15 Nov 1717	27 Dec 1661	Sandwich 26 Apr 1706	

3	Israel Tupper		Elizabeth Gifford	
	Sandwich 22 Sep 1666	Sandwich	Falmouth,MA 25 Feb 1664	
	Sandwich 1745	c.1690	Sandwich 19 Oct 1701	

4	Thankful Tupper		Josiah Clark	
	Sandwich 9 Oct 1696	Sandwich	Plymouth,MA 1690	
	-----	30 Oct 1718	-----	

5	Israel Clark		Deborah Pope	
	Plymouth 10 Sep 1720	Plymouth	Sandwich 23 Feb 1725	
	Plymouth Oct 1788	13 May 1742	-----	

6	Abigail Clark		Josiah Cornish	
	Plymouth 13 May 1756	Plymouth	Plymouth 15 Oct 1760	
	-----	15 Dec 1786	Lee Center,NY 10 Oct 1844	

7	Allen Cornish		Clarissa Cornish (cousin)	
	Plymouth 1 Sep 1789	Plymouth	Plymouth 2 Nov 1792	
	Lee Center 6 Apr 1853	18 Apr 1808	Lee Center 9 Jun 1864	

8	George Cornish		Mary Tucker	
	Lee Center 28 May 1825	New York	New York 2 May 1831	
	Lee Center 3 Dec 1894	c.1848	Rome,NY 28 Apr 1898	

9	Alice Cornish		Patrick Henry O'Donnell	
	Lee Center 5 Nov 1853	Rome,NY	Newport,NY 6 Nov 1850	
	Albany,NY 24 May 1916	16 Apr 1862	Rome 18 Apr 1916	

10	Mary Catherine O'Donnell		Charles Herbert Thurtle	
	Elgin,IL 16 Mar 1875	Lincoln,NE	Knowlesville,NY 12 Oct 1877	
	Euclid,OH 28 Mar 1948	2 Jun 1906	Lincoln 13 May 1947	

OBENAUER, RUTH E. HALLOCK (MRS. FREDERICK H.)

Nat. #303-B. Elected 9 Mar 1977. b. Center Village 2 May 1916.
m. Oxford,NY 26 Jun 1943, Frederick Holmes Obenauer, b. Norwich,
NY 24 Aug 1912. Educ: New York State College for Teachers, A.B.
Member: Hereditary Order of Desc. of Colonial Governors; Colonial
Dames of XVII Century; Dau. of American Revolution. Address:
43 Milwaukee St., Box 7, Malone,NY 12953. Descended from:

1 William Leete, Governor of Connecticut 1676-83

2	John Leete Guilford,CT Guilford 25 Nov 1692	Guilford 4 Oct 1670	Mary Chittendon 1647 9 Mar 1712
3	Benjamin Leete Guilford 26 Dec 1686 Durham,CT 1741	----- -----	Rachel Champion Lyme,CT 1 Dec 1697 26 Oct 1713/4
4	Leah Leete Guilford 7 May 1740 -----	Guilford 28 May 1758	Edward Benton Guilford 12 Apr 1740 Albany,NY 3 Oct 1794
5	Clarinda Benton Guilford 31 Jan 1764 Worcester,NY af.1806	----- -----	William Hallock Waywanda,NY 1753 Worcester 9 Nov 1821
6	David Hallock Worcester 1806 Unadilla,NY 3 May 1887	Worcester c.1829	Margaret ----- 1810 4 Feb 1876
7	Thomas Hallock Unadilla 16 Mar 1837 Sand Hill 22 Jul 1900	Sidney Center, NY Feb 1859	Elizabeth Bishop Sidney Center 12 Mar 1839 New Woodstock,NY 13 Feb 1921
8	Clyde Leslie Hallock Unadilla 20 Nov 1879 San Juan,TX 1 Aug 1963	Center Vlg., NY 18 May 1915	Cora Ann Martin Center Village 22 Dec 1888 San Juan 6 May 1967

ORNDORFF, VERNA S. ROSS (MRS. JOHN R.)

Nat. #118-B. Elected 7 Apr 1966. b. Newton,IA 7 Feb 1901.
m. Oak Park,IL 20 Jun 1940, John Roseberry Orndorff, b. Chicago,
IL 12 Apr 1908. Issue: Alice Orndorff Gordon. Member: Hereditary
Order of Desc. of Colonial Governors; Soc. of Mayflower Desc.,IL;
Founders and Patriots of America; Women Desc. of Ancient and
Honorable Artillery Co.; Dau. of Colonial Wars; National Huguenot
Soc.; New England Women; Magna Charta Dames; Soc. of Desc. of
Knights of Most Noble Order of Garter; Pilgrim Soc. of Massachu-
setts; Americans of Royal Descent; Dau. of American Revolution.

Address: 1009 Bonniebrae, 3B, River Forest,IL 60305. Descended from:

1 Thomas Mayhew, Governor of Martha's Vineyard 1647-81

2 Hannah Mayhew   Thomas Doggett
   Watertown,MA 15 Apr   -----   Watertown c.1630
   1635
   Martha's Vineyard,MA   1657   Martha's Vineyard 1691
   1722

3 Jemima Doggett   Thomas Butler
   c.1666   -----   c.1654
   bf. 1727   27 Nov 1682   20 Oct 1732

4 Mary Butler   William Worth
   c.1693   -----   27 Nov 1674
   Aug 1756   24 Oct 1719   16 Oct 1780

5 Damaris Worth   Edward Starbuck
   8 Feb 1722   -----   28 Nov 1719
   10 Jan 1789   11 Jul 1742   12 Nov 1798

6 Matthew Starbuck   Lydia Barney
   Jan 1750   -----   Nantucket,MA 25 Sep
                                                1755
   1815   28 Nov 1776   Nantucket 2 Nov 1781

7 Sally Starbuck   James Coffin
   Nantucket 26 Jun   Deep River,   Guilford,NC 26 Jun
   1788   NC   1783
   Guilford 23 Aug 1822   10 Oct 1805   Lewisville,IN 28 Mar
                                                1838

8 Matthew Starbuck Coffin   Martha Ellen Thompson
   Guilford 25 Mar 1811   Indiana   Washington Co.IN
                                                20 May 1819
   IN 18 Mar 1884   7 Nov 1841   Washington Co. 30 Jul
                                                1857

9 Mary Frances Coffin   Vernon William Skiff
   Salem,IN 25 Oct 1842   Chillecothe,   Hume,NY 23 Jan 1841
                           MO
   Oak Park,IL 29 Dec   23 Jan 1867   Oak Park 29 Apr 1926
   1918

10 Blanche Skiff   Franklin Pierce Ross
   Newton,IA 24 Jan 1873 Newton   Wind Ridge,PA 22 Jul
                                                1869
                          8 Feb 1899   Brookline,MA 27 Feb
                                                1947

Inheritor: Alice Coffin Orndorff Gordon (Mrs. Donald R.),
103 Laurel Crest Road, Madison,CT 02043

PAGEL, WILLIAM RUSH

Nat. #106-B. Elected 16 Jan 1965. b. Egan,SD 4 Nov 1901.
m. Chicago,IL 19 Aug 1939, Dorothy Loretta Johnsen, b. Chicago
6 Dec 1910. Issue: William Kingston Pagel, b. 15 May 1942;
Diane L. Pagel Harsh, b. 12 Aug 1943; both b. Chicago. Educ:
University of South Dakota and University of Wisconsin, B.A. Cum
Laude. Member: Hereditary Order of Desc. of Colonial Governors;
Aztec Club of 1847; Sons of Union Veterans of Civil War; Soc. of
Colonial Wars; Soc. of Mayflower Descendants (KS, Historian);
Sons of American Revolution (IL, Past Vice Pres.); Huguenot Soc.
(IL, Past Pres.); Desc. of Colonial Clergy; South Dakota Histori-
cal Soc.; Illinois Genealogical Soc.; Heart of America Genealogi-
cal Soc. Distinguished Service Award and Patriot's Medal from
the SAR. Occup: Retired Commercial Personnel Supervisor, Ill.
Bell Telephone Co. Address: 5208 West 96th St., Shawnee Mission,
KS 66207. Descended from:

1 Robert Treat, Governor of Connecticut 1683-98

2 Samuel Treat   Elizabeth Mayo
  Milford,MA 3 Sep 1648   Eastham,MA   Eastham 22 May 1653
  Eastham 18 Mar 1716   16 Mar 1674   Eastham 4 Dec 1696

3 Jane Treat   Constant Freeman
  Eastham 6 Dec 1675   Eastham   Eastham 31 Mar 1669
  Eastham 1 Sep 1729   11 Oct 1694   Truro,MA 8 Jun 1745

4 Robert Freeman   Mary Payne
  Truro 12 Aug 1696   Canterbury,CT Eastham 1 Feb 1695
  Pomfret,CT 27 Sep 1755   5 Apr 1722   -----

5 Rebecca Freeman   Abraham Paine
  Truro 23 Sep 1724   Canterbury   Canterbury 2 May 1722
  Hamilton,NY 25 Dec   8 Mar 1743   Hamilton 21 Apr 1801
  1810

6 Anne Paine   Uriah Cross
  Amenia,NY 11 Aug 1754   Coventry,CT   Coventry 3 Apr 1750
  Stafford,NY 1825   -----   Georgetown,NY 4 Apr
                                          1835

7 Anna Cross   Noah Cross
  Rutland,VT 2 Feb 1785   New York   VT 1 Nov 1783
  Parkman,OH 23 Jan   9 Apr 1805   Parkman 22 Aug 1846
  1872

8 Noah A. Cross   Olive A. McKee
  Stafford 28 Feb 1824   Chardon,OH   Adams,NY 4 Oct 1827
  Bradford,IA 20 Feb   25 Jun 1846   Egan,SD 27 Feb 1923
  1895

9 Frances A. Cross   Jacob Rush
  IL 3 Dec 1848   Richland,IA   Danby,VT 8 Mar 1829
  Egan 23 Mar 1922   19 Feb 1873   Egan 6 Oct 1887

10 Carrie E. Rush   William R. Pagel
   Rock Co.MN 18 Jan   Luverne,MN   Fond du Lac,WI 9 Jun
   1886   1874
   Egan 22 Jun 1947   9 Nov 1898   Egan 1 Dec 1951

PALMER, ELMER HALL

Nat. #309-B. Elected 5 Apr 1977. b. Boston,MA 25 Dec 1926.
m. Providence,RI 11 Jun 1948, Anne Dorothy Foster, b. Fall River,
MA 17 Oct 1928. Issue: Richard Leslie Hall Palmer, b. Provi-
dence 11 Sep 1960. Educ: Rhode Island School of Design. Member:
Hereditary Order of Desc. of Colonial Governors; Sons of American
Revolution (RI, Past Pres.); Founders and Patriots of America;
Soc. of Desc. of Colonial Clergy; Soc. of Colonial Wars; Flagon
and Trencher; Roger Williams Family Assn.; Dennison Soc.;
Knights Templar (MA and RI, Past Grand Commander). Address:
1401 South County Trail, East Greenwich,RI 02818. Descended from:

1 Benedict Arnold, Governor of Rhode Island 1657-69

2 Caleb Arnold   Abigail Wilbur
   19 Dec 1644   -----   Portsmouth,RI
   9 Feb 1719   -----   17 Nov 1730

3 Samuel Arnold   Mary George
   Portsmouth 1677   Block Island   -----
   -----   17 May 1706   -----

4 Joseph Arnold   Hannah Gifford
   16 Sep 1712   -----   -----
   c.1766   -----   -----

5 Caleb Arnold   Hannah Taylor
   17 Mar 1754   -----   -----
   Centerville,RI   -----   21 Jul 1827
    8 Nov 1844

6 Experience Arnold   Samuel Wightman
   Exeter,RI 21 Jan 1789   East Greenwich   East Greenwich
                                             1 Oct 1780
   East Greenwich   11 Jul 1811   East Greenwich
    29 Sep 1865   3 Oct 1839

7 Patience Wightman   John Tillinghast
    (Whitman)   Gardner Sweet
   East Greenwich   -----   Exeter 12 Sep 1828
    18 May 1832
   East Greenwich   22 Nov 1852   Exeter 24 Feb 1904
    26 Oct 1904

8 Emma Patience Sweet   Rowland Briggs Palmer
   Exeter 9 Sep 1866   -----   Richmond,RI 16 Feb
                                             1870
   15 Dec 1918   1 Jan 1894   Exeter 7 Apr 1933

9 Earl Sweet Palmer   Jennie Frances Hall
   Providence 24 Apr 1896 Pawtucket   Pawtucket,RI 28 Mar
                                             1897
                          11 Oct 1918

PALMER, MARY V. NOWACEK (MRS. ROBERT C.)

Nat. #214-B. Elected 21 Aug 1973. b. Lincoln,NE 7 May 1941.
m. Smithtown,NY 24 Nov 1964, Robert Carl Palmer, Jr., b. Cleve-
land,OH 17 Oct 1940. Issue: Mary Sue Palmer, b. Bronxville,NY
5 Aug 1969; Emy Lyn Palmer, b. Summit,NJ 12 Feb 1971; Carl
Patrick Palmer, b.Summit 8 Jul 1973. Educ: Kent State Univer-
sity, B.A. in Ed., 1962; Columbia University Teachers College,
M.A., 1964. Member: Hereditary Order of Desc. of Colonial
Governors; Junior League of Summit; A.A.U.W.; N.E.A. Occup:
Former teacher. Address: 108 Bellevue Ave., Summit,NJ 07901.
Descended from:

1 Thomas Mayhew, Governor of Martha's Vineyard 1647-81

2 Martha Mayhew   Thomas Tupper
   Watertown,MA c.1638   Sandwich,MA   Sandwich 16 Jan 1638
   Sandwich 15 Nov 1717   27 Dec 1661   Sandwich 26 Apr 1706

3 Israel Tupper   Elizabeth Gifford
   Sandwich 22 Sep 1666   Sandwich   Falmouth,MA 25 Feb
                                          1664
   Sandwich 1745   c.1690   Sandwich 19 Oct 1701

4 Thankful Tupper   Josiah Clark
   Sandwich 9 Oct 1696   Sandwich   Plymouth,MA 1690
   -----   30 Oct 1718   -----

5 Israel Clark   Deborah Pope
   Plymouth 10 Sep 1720   Plymouth   Sandwich 23 Feb 1725
   Plymouth Oct 1788   13 May 1742   -----

6 Abigail Clark   Josiah Cornish
   Plymouth 13 May 1756   Plymouth   Plymouth 15 Oct 1760
   -----   15 Dec 1786   Lee Center,NY 10 Oct
                                          1844

7 Allen Cornish   Clarissa Cornish
                                            (Cousin)
   Plymouth 1 Sep 1789   Plymouth   Plymouth 2 Nov 1792
   Lee Center 6 Apr 1853 18 Apr 1808   Lee Center 9 Jun 1864

8 George Cornish   Mary Tucker
   Lee Center 28 May 1825 New York   New York 2 May 1831
   Lee Center 3 Dec 1894 c.1848   Rome,NY 28 Apr 1898

9 Alice Cornish   Patrick Henry O'Donnell
   Lee Center 5 Nov 1853 Rome   Newport,NY 6 Nov 1850
   Albany,NY 24 May 1916 16 Apr 1862   Rome 18 Apr 1916

10 Mary Catherine   Charles Herbert Thurtle
     O'Donnell
   Elgin,IL 16 Mar 1875   Lincoln,NE   Knowlesville,NY
                                            12 Oct 1877
   Euclid,OH 28 Mar 1948 2 Jun 1906   Lincoln,NE 13 May 1947

11 Mary Lucille Thurtle   Charles George Nowacek
   Lincoln 21 Mar 1912   Lincoln   Plattsmouth,NE
                                            22 Feb 1912
   Living   10 Jun 1937   Living

PERDUE, DAVID RUSSELL

Nat. #260-B. Elected 22 Sep 1975. b. Pine Bluff,AR 3 May 1934.
m. Joplin,MO 23 Sep 1956, Karen Dare Terry, b. 4 Apr 1936.
Issue: Melissa Dare Perdue, b. Wichita Falls,TX 7 Jul 1957;
David Russell Perdue, Jr., b. Pine Bluff,AR 21 Feb 1960; Paul
Terry Perdue, b. Pine Bluff, AR 25 Jun 1963. Educ: University
of Arkansas, B.A., 1956. Member: Hereditary Order of Desc. of
Colonial Governors; Arkansas History Commission Chairman; Ruling
Elder, Presbyterian Church; U.S.A.F. Reserve (Ret.) Occup:
The Perdue Co., Inc., Printing and Office Products. Address:
28 Mockingbird Lane, Pine Bluff,AR 71611. Descended from:

1 Leonard Calvert, Governor of Maryland 1633-47
   William Stone, Governor of Maryland 1649-54

Continue with the lineage of his father John Armer Perdue, Jr.,
Nat. #13-B.

PERDUE, JOHN ARMER, JR.

Nat. #13-B. Elected 25 Aug 1959. b. Pine Bluff,AR 14 Jul 1903.
m. Selma,AL 30 Jun 1927, Ruby Elise Russell, b. Selma 5 Mar
1904. Issue: John Armer Perdue, III, b. 1930; David Russell
Perdue, b. 1934; Richardson Milam Perdue, b. 1938. Educ:
University of Alabama; Harvard Graduate School of Business
Administration. Member: Hereditary Order of Desc. of Colonial
Governors. (From Society's Records). Address: Box 6696, Pine
Bluff,AR 71611. Descended from:

1 Leonard Calvert, Governor of Maryland 1633-47
   William Stone, Governor of Maryland 1649-54

2	William Calvert England 1603 MD 10 Jan 1682	----- 1621/2	Elizabeth Stone MD 1603 MD af. 1682
3	George Calvert St.Mary's Co.MD 1668 af.1739	----- 1690	Elizabeth Doyne ----- -----
4	John Calvert MD 1690 Prince William Co.VA 1739	(1) ----- 1711	Jane ----- ----- -----
5	George Calvert 1712 Culpeper Co.VA 19 May 1782	----- c.1750	Anne Crupper ----- Prince William Co.
6	Ann Calvert 1751 Fairfax Co. 1822	----- c.1766	William Lindsay Fairfax Co.VA 1743 Fairfax Co. 15 Sep 1798
7	Sarah Lindsay 1785 29 Apr 1837	----- 4 Dec 1805	George Triplett Fairfax Co. 1777 6 Oct 1821

8	Charles Hector Triplett		Esther Dunlap
	Fairfax Co. 13 Aug 1809	Fairfax	Alexandria,VA 7 Jan 1811
	Pine Bluff,AR 22 Sep 1887	7 Feb 1833	Marven,AR 7 Feb 1858
9	George William Triplett		Sue Milam
	Marven 16 Apr 1848	Pine Bluff	Laurens Co.SC 4 Jun 1853
	Pine Bluff 31 Dec 1878	3 Dec 1873	Pine Bluff 16 Nov 1923
10	Miriam Reeder Triplett		John Armer Perdue
	Tucker,AR 15 Nov 1874	Pine Bluff	Champagnole,AR 15 Jan 1873
		19 Feb 1895	Pine Bluff 5 Nov 1943

PERDUE, JOHN ARMER, III

Nat. #262-B. Elected 22 Sep 1975. b. Pine Bluff,AR 1930.
Member: Hereditary Order of Desc. of Colonial Governors.
Address: P.O. Box 6696, Pine Bluff,AR 71611. Descended from:

1 Leonard Calvert, Governor of Maryland 1633-47
   William Stone, Governor of Maryland 1649-54

Continue with the lineage of his father John Armer Perdue, Jr.,
Nat. #13-B.

PERDUE, RICHARDSON MILAM

Nat. #261-B. Elected 22 Sep 1975. b. Pine Bluff,AR, 1938.
Member: Hereditary Order of Desc. of Colonial Governors.
Address: 14 Jefferson Place, Pine Bluff,AR 71611. Descended from:

1 Leonard Calvert, Governor of Maryland 1633-47
   William Stone, Governor of Maryland 1649-54

Continue with the lineage of his father John Armer Perdue, Jr.,
Nat. #13-B.

PETERLE, HELEN JOY LEE (MRS.)

Nat. #74-B. Elected 31 Mar 1963. b. New York, New York 19 Aug 1919. m. Hailey,ID 21 Jun 1947, Agustas Peterle, b. Amesbury, MA 28 Nov 1916. Issue: George Bednar Peterle, b. Lakeland,FL 19 Mar 1951; Helen Agusta Peterle, b. Lakeland 13 Mar 1954; Miles Agustas Newberry Peterle, b. New London,CT 22 Nov 1958. Educ: Columbia University Teachers College, NY. Member: Hereditary Order of Desc. of Colonial Governors; Dau. of American Revolu- tion; United States Dau. of 1812; Soc. of Mayflower Descendants. Address: Route 2, Box 2, Stonington,CT 06378. (From Society's Records.) Descended from:

1 William Bradford, Governor of Plymouth Colony 1621-33

Continue with the lineage of her sister Marian Lawson Lee Mikesell (Mrs. John W., Jr.), Nat. #80-B.

PHILBRICK, GEORGE DARY

Nat. #300-B. Elected 1 Feb 1977. b. Lexington,MA 13 Jun 1896. m. Rising Sun,MD 28 May 1941, Esther Crawford Macardell, b. Middletown,NY 25 Jul 1910, d. Germantown,PA 22 Jan 1969. Member: Hereditary Order of Desc. of Colonial Governors; Soc. of Mayflower Descendants,MA; Jamestowne Society; Order of Founders and Patriots of America,VA. Address: 1717 Bellevue Ave., #A-907, Richmond, VA 23227. Descended from:

1 Robert Treat, Governor of Connecticut 1683-98

2 Samuel Treat		Elizabeth Mayo
bp. 3 Sep 1648	-----	1652
18 Mar 1716/7	16 Mar 1674	Eastham,MA 4 Dec 1696
3 Elizabeth Treat		Jabez Snow
Eastham 24 Jul 1676	-----	Eastham 6 Sep 1670
3 Mar 1755	c.1695	14 Oct 1750
4 Tabitha Snow		John Mayo
21 Mar 1707	-----	14 Oct 1707
-----	7 Oct 1731	1759
5 Susannah Mayo		John Mores
Orleans,MA 11 Jun 1739	-----	-----
-----	29 Dec 1774	-----
6 Treat Mores		Mercy Briggs
Eastham 5 Dec 1775	-----	Provincetown,MA 3 Aug 1780
Eastham 1840	-----	-----
7 Phebe Horton Mores		Daniel Peterson
Eastham 12 Aug 1804	Duxbury,MA	Duxbury 7 Sep 1803
Ashburnham,MA 1884	1823	Boston,MA 18 Dec 1878

8	Jerusha Peterson		Henry Remick Philbrick
	Duxbury 12 Jul 1839	Boston	Kittery,ME 5 Jun 1834
	Dorchester,MA 21 Apr	25 Jul 1857	Norfolk,VA 15 Feb 1902
	1900		

9	Harry Clifford Philbrick		Jeannette Tuttle Dary
	Kittery 10 Aug 1870	Roxbury	Newton,MA 19 May 1870
	Braintree,MA 8 Mar	31 Oct 1894	Dansville,NY 16 Feb
	1954		1912

PITTMAN, CHALMERS VAN ANGLEN

Nat. #68-B. Elected 17 Mar 1963. b. Trenton,NJ 25 Jul 1904.
m. Wilmington,DE 10 Aug 1929, Margaret E. Hallett, b. Lansdowne,
PA 12 Dec 1905. Issue: Janet McLellan Henley, b. Dallas,TX
10 May 1939. Educ: Haverford College, B.S. Member: Hereditary
Order of Desc. of Colonial Governors; Sons of American Revolu-
tion; Soc. of Colonial Wars; Huguenot Society, TX; Soc. of Desc.
of Colonial Clergy; Desc. of Knights of the Garter; American
Assn. of Petroleum Geologists; Soc. of Exploration Geophysicists;
Board of Managers of Haverford College. Occup: Geophysicists.
Address: 3909 Miramar Avenue, Dallas,TX 75205. Descended from:

1 John Winthrop, Governor of Massachusetts 1629-49

2	John Winthrop		Elizabeth Reade
	12 Feb 1606	-----	-----
	5 Apr 1676	1635	1672

3	Margaret Winthrop		John Corwin
	1646	-----	28 Jul 1638
	Nov 1711	May 1665	12 Jul 1683

4	George Corwin	(2)	Lydia Gedney
	26 Feb 1665	-----	-----
	12 Apr 1696	-----	1700

5	Bartholomew Corwin		Esther Burt
	21 Jun 1693	-----	-----
	9 May 1747	-----	-----

6	Samuel Corwin		-----
	10 Mar 1728	-----	-----
	1776	-----	-----

7	Samuel Corwin		Rachel Newman
	28 Dec 1762	-----	26 Dec 1763
	20 May 1837	26 Dec 1786	12 Jun 1839

8	Richard Corwin		Hannah Soothoof
	27 Feb 1803	-----	-----
	Apr 1829	-----	-----

9	Hannah C. Corwin		Stephen S. Voorhees
	12 Feb 1827	-----	16 Sep 1816
	17 Mar 1905	28 May 1845	5 Jul 1885

```
10  Eliza E. Voorhees                              Samuel S. Van Anglen
    15 Apr 1846              -----               2 May 1841
    28 Jul 1935              20 Sep 1864         26 Jul 1912

11  Evanna C. Van Anglen                           Raymond H. Pittman
    13 Oct 1876             -----                6 Mar 1874
    4 Jul 1961             11 Oct 1899           30 Jun 1960

    Inheritor: Janet Pittman Henley (Mrs. Ronald R.)
```

PITTMAN, MARGARET HALLETT (MRS. CHALMERS V.)

Nat. #19-B. Elected 5 Feb 1960. b. Lansdowne,PA 12 Dec 1905.
m. Wilmington,DE 10 Aug 1929, Chalmers Van Anglen Pittman, b.
Trenton,NJ 25 Jul 1904. Issue: Janet McLellan Henley, b. Dallas,
TX 10 May 1939. Educ: Friends School, Philadelphia; School of
Design for Women with a degree in Fine Arts. Member: Hereditary
Order of Desc. of Colonial Governors; Dau. of American Revolu-
tion; Soc. of Mayflower Descendants,TX; New England Women; Sons
and Dau. of the Pilgrims; Old Plymouth Colony; Magna Charta
Dames; Dau. of Colonial Wars; U.S. Dau. of 1812; The Pilgrim
John Howland Soc.; Dau. of American Colonists; Colonial Dames of
XVII Century; Dames of the Court of Honor; Dau. of Founders and
Patriots of America; Soc. of Desc. of Colonial Clergy; Huguenot
Society,TX; Adams Hawkes Family Assn. Address: 3909 Miramar
Avenue, Dallas,TX 75205. Descended from:

```
1  John Coggeshall, Governor of Rhode Island 1647

2  Anne Coggeshall                                 Peter Easton
   Essex,Eng. c.1622      -----                  England 1622
   Newport,RI 6 Mar       1643                   RI 12 Feb 1693/4
     1688/9

3  Waite Easton                                    John Carr
   Newport 5 Nov 1668     Newport                Newport c.1664
   Newport 3 Aug 1725     -----                  Newport c.1714

4  Patience Carr            (2)                   Edward Estes
   Newport c.1700         Portsmouth,NH          Lynn,MA 20 Feb 1703/4
   Durham,ME 13 Dec 1788  27 Aug 1730            Royalsboro,ME 13 Dec
                                                   1788

5  Waite Estes                                     Lemuel Jones
   Hanover,MA 31 May 1733 -----                  North Yarmouth,ME
                                                   30 May 1730
   -----                  1751                   af. 1774

6  Mercy Jones                                     Nathaniel Hawkes
   4 May 1752             -----                  1740
   af. 1800               27 Jul 1771            c.1815/6

7  Lemuel Hawkes                                   Abigail Winslow
   Windham,ME 7 Aug 1774  -----                  Falmouth,ME 1776
   Manchester,ME 16 Nov   30 Oct 1799            15 Nov 1851
     1840
```

8	Winslow Hawkes 1800 1 Aug 1882	----- 6 Oct 1829	Lydia McLellan ----- -----
9	Winslow Hawkes Hallowell,ME 19 Nov 1830 Portland,ME 7 Jan 1910	----- 7 Mar 1867	Lucy Amy Nichols Saugus,ME 1811 Hallowell 1887
10	Gertrude Amy Hawkes Windham,ME 10 Jan 1873 -----	Pittsburgh,PA 21 Feb 1894	George Hervey Hallett Manchester,ME 30 Dec 1870 West Chester,PA 12 Aug 1947

Inheritor: Janet Pittman Henley (Mrs. Ronald R.)

PLATZ, LUCIA CELISTA COLLINS (MRS. HARRY W.)

Nat. #209-B. Elected 21 Jun 1973. b. Spokane,WA 12 Mar 1906.
m. Seattle,WA 18 Feb 1927, Harry William Platz, b. Roslyn,WA
23 May 1900. Issue: Marian Celista Spath, b. Seattle 17 Nov
1928. Educ: Eastern Washington College of Education. Member:
Hereditary Order of Desc. of Colonial Governors; Dau. of American
Revolution; Colonial Dames of XVII Century; Soc. of Colonial
Wars (Treas.); Dau. of Founders and Patriots of America (Corres.
Secretary); New England Women (Pres. Elizabeth Glover Dunston
Col.); Women Desc. of the Ancient and Honorable Artillery Co.;
Soc. of Desc. of Colonial Clergy; Huguenot Society, WA; Magna
Charta Dames; Soc. of Mayflower Descendants; Washington Family
Desc.; Dau. of American Colonists; Dau. of Pioneers of Washington
prior to 1870 (Treas.). Occup: U.S. Civil Service Secretary
(ret.). Address: 6511 - 44th Avenue, S.W., Seattle,WA 98136.
Descended from:

1 Peleg Sanford, Governor of Rhode Island 1680-83

2	Ann Sanford Newport,RI 1675/6 Noyes's Beach,RI	Rhode Island 1703	James Noyes Stonington,CT 2 Aug 1677 Noyes's Beach 1718
3	Dorothy Noyes Noyes Beach 1 Oct 1712 Stonington 16 Oct 1772	Stonington 4 Jul 1728	John Brown Newport 1702 Stonington c.1782
4	John Brown Stonington 25 Jul 1735 Stonington 25 Jul 1777	Stonington 2 Jul 1767	Mary Holmes Stonington 9 Aug 1745 Stonington 12 Sep 1809
5	Clark Brown Stonington 25 Jan 1771 MD 12 Jan 1817	Brimfield,MA 1 Dec 1799	Tabitha Moffatt Brimfield 1 May 1780 Salem,OR 4 May 1858

213

6　Pherne Tabitha Brown　　　　　　　　　　Virgil Kellogg Pringle
　　Montpelier,VT 22 Mar　　St.Charles,MO　Harwinton,CT 29 Jul
　　　1805　　　　　　　　　　　　　　　　　　1804
　　Salem,OR 21 May 1891　　4 May 1827　　Salem 24 Mar 1887

7　Clark Spencer Pringle　　　　　　　　　Catherine Carney Sager
　　Warren Co.MO 17 Apr　　Salem　　　　　Union Co.OH 15 Apr
　　　1830　　　　　　　　　　　　　　　　　　1835
　　Spokane,WA 19 Oct 1914　29 Oct 1851　Spokane 10 Aug 1910

8　Lucia Naomi Pringle　　　　　(1)　　　Dayton Carpenter
　　　　　　　　　　　　　　　　　　　　　　　Collins
　　Linn Co.OR 24 Nov 1871　Colfax,WA　　Middlesex,NY 13 Jan
　　　　　　　　　　　　　　　　　　　　　　　1855
　　Shelton,WA 25 Dec 1944　22 Jun 1890　Seattle 7 Oct 1940

SUPPLEMENT NO. 1

1　William Leete, Governor of Connecticut 1676-83

2　John Leete　　　　　　　　　　　　　　Mary Chittenden
　　Guilford,CT 1639　　　　Guilford　　　Guilford 1647
　　Guilford 25 Nov 1692　　4 Oct 1670　　9 Mar 1712

3　Anne Leete　　　　　　　　　　　　　　John Collins
　　Guilford 4 Aug 1671　　Guilford　　　Branford, CT 1665
　　Guilford 2 Nov 1724　　25 Jul 1691　　Guilford 24 Jan 1751

4　Timothy Collins　　　　　　　　　　　Elizabeth Hyde
　　Guilford 13 Apr 1699　　Connecticut　Lebanon,CT 1703
　　Litchfield,CT 7 Feb　　16 Jan 1723　　Litchfield
　　　1777

5　John Collins　　　　　　　　　　　　　Lydia Buell
　　Litchfield 1 Jun 1739　Litchfield　　Goshen,CT 11 Nov 1742
　　Litchfield 1792　　　　　-----　　　　Litchfield

6　Hiram Collins　　　　　　　　　　　　Annar Cadwell
　　Litchfield 9 Nov 1781　Onondaga Co.,　East Hartford,CT
　　　　　　　　　　　　　　　　NY　　　　　15 Jun 1787
　　Troy,NY 23 Sep 1834　　14 Jul 1807　　Grass Lake,MI 23 Mar
　　　　　　　　　　　　　　　　　　　　　　　1879

7　Norman Collins　　　　　　　　　　　Sarah Delinda Dayton
　　Middlesex,NY 21 May　　Middlesex　　Gorham,NY 23 Oct 1818
　　　1816
　　Grass Lake 17 Nov 1890　6 Jul 1837　Grass Lake 19 Mar 1882

8　Dayton Carpenter Collins　　　　　　Lucia Naomi Pringle

Continue with Generation 8 of her lineage from Governor
Peleg Sanford.

SUPPLEMENT NO. 2

1 William Coddington, Governor of Rhode Island 1638-40, 1675-78

2 Mary Coddington   Peleg Sanford
   Newport,RI 16 May 1654   Rhode Island   10 May 1639
   Newport Mar 1693   Dec 1674   Newport 1701

3 Ann Sanford   James Noyes

Continue with Generation 2 of her lineage from Governor
Peleg Sanford.

SUPPLEMENT NO. 3

1 Jeremiah (Jeremy) Clarke, Governor of Rhode Island 1652

2 James Clarke   Hope Power
   1649   -----   Providence,RI 1650
   1 Dec 1736   -----   Providence 27 Feb 1713

3 Ann Clarke   James Brown II
   Providence   -----   Newport 1680
   Newport   Sciate,RI 1756

4 John Brown   Dorothy Noyes

Continue with Generation 3 of her lineage from Governor
Peleg Sanford.

SUPPLEMENT NO. 4

1 John Webster, Governor of Connecticut 1656

2 Robert Webster   Susannah Treat
   England c.1627   Wethersfield   Wethersfield,CT
                                              bp. 8 Oct 1629
   Wethersfield c.31 May   1652   -----
     1676

3 Elizabeth Webster   John Seymour
   Hartford,CT bp.8 Feb   Hartford   Hartford 12 Jun 1666
     1673
   Hartford 15 May 1754   19 Dec 1693   Hartford 17 May 1748

4 John Seymour   (2)   Hannah Ensign
   Hartford 25 Dec 1694   Hartford   Hartford 19 Jan 1711/2
   New Hartford 25 Jul   7 May 1733   -----
     1758

5 Sarah Seymour   Abraham Kellogg, Jr.
   Hartford Jul 1750   New Hartford   Hartford 27 Jan 1750
   Hartford 4 Mar 1802   6 Feb 1772   Hartford 29 Apr 1812

6 Sarah Kellogg   Norman Pringle (Prindle)
   Nw.Hartford 4 Jun 1783 New Hartford   Harwinton,CT 21 Feb
                                              1702
   Warren Co.MO   3 Nov 1803   Warren Co.

7 Virgil Pringle   Pherne Tabitha Brown

Continue with Generation 6 of her lineage from Governor
Peleg Sanford.

Inheritor: Mrs. Marian C.P. Spath, 6006 46th Ave., S.W.,
Seattle,WA 98136

215

POPE, MARGUERITE JONES (MRS. D. STUART, JR.)

Nat. #270-B. Elected 11 Nov 1975. b. Newton,MA 9 Feb 1902.
m. Newton 16 Jun 1927, Daniel Stuart Pope, Jr., b. Yonkers,NY
22 Jul 1904. Issue: Barbara Barton Pope Peckham (Mrs. Douglas
W.), b. Dover,MA 29 Nov 1928; Daniel Stuart Pope, III, b.
Rochester,NY 8 Aug 1930; Robert Gardner Pope, b. Newton 13 Aug
1936. Educ: Vassar College, A.B. Member: Hereditary Order of
Colonial Governors; Dau. of American Revolution (Past Chap.
Regent); Children of American Revolution (Past Pres.,CT); New
England Women; Women Desc. of Ancient and Honorable Artillery Co.
(Past Treas.,CT); Soc. of Mayflower Descendants,CT); Dames of the
Court of Honor (Past Vice Pres.); Huguenot Society, CT ; Living
Descendants of Blood Royal; CT Soc. of Genealogists. Address:
1199 Whitney Ave., Hamden,CT 06517. Descended from:

1 Thomas Dudley, Governor of Massachusetts 1634-35, 1640-41,
   1645-46, 1650-51

2 Samuel Dudley   (3)   Elizabeth
   Northampton,Eng.c.1606   -----   c.1628
   Exeter,NH 10 Feb   by 1650   aft.1702
      1682/3

3 Dorothy Dudley   Moses Leavitt
   Exeter c.1663   Exeter   Exeter 12 Aug 1650
   -----   25 Sep/Oct   Exeter c.1731
                               1681

4 Moses Leavitt   Alice
   -----   Exeter   -----
   -----   -----   btw. 1740-46

5 Love Leavitt   Thomas Chase
   1717   Stratford,NH Stratford 26 Jun 1720
   Stratford 27 Nov 1802   c.1740   Stratford 15 Jan 1757

6 Jonathan Chase   Abigail Wilson
   Stratford 22 Feb 1748   Stratford   -----
   Wolfeboro,NH   1774   -----
      21 Mar 1835

7 Polly Chase   Isaac Jones
   Madbury,NH 8 Mar   Wolfeboro   Madbury 4 Dec 1773
      1775
   Wolfeboro 21 Feb 1818   4 Apr 1794   Wolfeboro 28 Dec 1816

8 Isaac Jones Jr.   Susan Chase
   Wolfeboro 24 Sep 1803   Boston,MA   Wolfeboro 5 Nov 1808
   Melrose,MA 14 Nov   22 Nov 1825   Melrose 3 Jan 1899
      1874

9 William Thompson   Sarah Amelia Everett
      Jones
   Melrose 16 Jan 1840   Boston   Boston 23 May 1843
   Melrose 2 Oct 1886   10 Jul 1865   Melrose 5 Apr 1874

                                          Elizabeth Damon
10 Gardner Irving Jones   Boston 13 Oct 1864
   Melrose 12 Aug 1869   Newton,MA
   Brookline 13 Feb 1937   20 Dec 1897   Hamden,CT 7 Jan 1958

PRUITT, PEARL CLARA RAMSEY (MRS. HENRY LEE)

Nat. #298-B. Elected 25 Sep 1976. b. Ralston,OK 7 Jan 1902.
m. Ponca City,OK 6 Sep 1931, Henry Lee Pruitt, b. Ft. Scott,KS
30 May 1886, d. Drumright,OK 14 Mar 1948. Educ: Oklahoma State
University, B.S., M.S. Member: Hereditary Order of Desc. of
Colonial Governors; Order of Crown of Charlemagne; Magna Charta
Dames; Americans of Royal Descent; Soc. of Desc. of Colonial
Clergy; Soc. of Mayflower Descendants; Women Desc. of Ancient and
Honorable Artillery Co.; Colonial Dames of XVII Century; Dau. of
American Colonists; Desc. of Knights of Most Noble Order of the
Garter; United Dau. of the Confederacy; Dau. of American Revolu-
tion; Doane Family Assn.; Pioneer Historical Society of Oklahoma.
Address: 35 Pioneer Place, 715 Monument Road, Ponca City, OK
74601. Descended from:

1 Thomas Prence, Governor of Plymouth Colony, 1633-34, 1636-37,
   1644-45

2 Mercy Prence   John Freeman
   Plymouth,MA 1631   Eastham,MA   Billinghurst,Eng.
                                               c.1621-27
   Eastham 28 Sep 1711   13 Feb 1649   Eastham 28 Oct 1719

3 Edmond Freeman   Ruth Merrick
   Eastham Jun 1655   Eastham   Eastham 15 May 1652
   Eastham 10 Dec 1717   Jan 1677   Eastham 1680

4 Ruth Freeman   Israel Doane
   Eastham 1680   Eastham   Eastham 1672
   Eastham 7 Jun 1728   -----   Eastham af.1732

5 Elnathan Doane   Martha Paddock
   Eastham 9 Apr 1709   Eastham   -----
   Doansburg af.1778   25 Feb 1736/7   Doansburg,NY

6 Daniel Doane   Elizabeth Merrick
   Eastham 4 Apr 1741   -----   Harwich,MA 23 Jul 1747
   Doansburg af.1787   1771   Plainfield,NY c.1798/9

7 Joseph Doane   Esther Markham
   Dutchess Co.NY 1773   Dutchess Co.   Enfield,CT 17 Feb 1778
   Lyon,MI 29 Mar 1847   1797   Lyon 18 Dec 1851

8 Erastus Doane   Hester Stringham
   Brookfield,NY 6 Jan   Scipio,NY   Scipio 16 Feb 1802
     1798
   Green Oak,MI 13 Aug   1827   Green Oak 27 Nov 1883
     1861

9 Jemima Zilla Doane   William Lloyd Webb
   Sempronius,NY 17 Aug   South Lyon,MI   England 1823
     1828
   South Lyon 8 Apr 1908   10 Apr 1851   South Lyon 5 Mar 1867

10 Janet Webb   William Thomas Ramsey
   Northville,MI 16 Apr   Butler Co.,KS   Pittsylvania Co.,VA
     1853   16 Oct 1842
   Ripley,OK 4 Feb 1913   20 Sep 1875   Ripley 31 May 1913

11 John Newman Ramsey   Anna Stazia Jones
   Greenwood Co.KS   Stillwater,OK   Marshfield,MO 28 Sep
     8 Apr 1880   1880
   Boise,ID 25 Jun 1964   20 Nov 1900   Ponca City,OK 26 Mar
                                            1951

PRYOR, MARIANNA L. BRAND (MRS. WILLIAM YOUNG)

Nat. #40-B. Elected 30 Aug 1961. b. Wilmington,DE 8 Apr 1909.
m. Montclair,NJ 29 Jul 1944, William Young Pryor, b. Newark,NJ
24 Oct 1908. Issue: Ann Love Pryor, b. Montclair 28 Mar 1946;
William Brand Pryor, b. Montclair 13 Aug 1947. Educ: Kimberly
School, Montclair and Scudder,NYC. Member: Hereditary Order of
Desc. of Colonial Governors; Dau. of Colonial Wars, NJ; Dau. of
American Revolution, NJ; Huguenot Society, NJ; Dau. of Society
of War of 1812, NJ; Soc. of Desc. of Colonial Clergy. Address:
64 Fellswood Dr., Essex Fells,NJ 07021. (From Society's Records)
Descended from:

1 Nicholas Greenbury, Governor of Maryland 1694

2 Anne Greenbury   John Hammond
   England c.1672   -----   1675
   c.1700   1693   -----

3 Comfort Hammond   (2)   John Worthington
   15 Aug 1701   -----   MD 1689
   -----   1728   MD 1763

4 Samuel Worthington   Mary Tolley
   MD 1733/4   Joppa,MD   1740
   MD 7 Apr 1813   17 Jan 1759   1777

5 Martha Worthington   (2)   Thomas Love
   9 Apr 1775   -----   Cecil Co.MD 25 Mar
                                             1753
   21 Jan 1846   2 Sep 1802   Baltimore Co.MD
                                             1 Mar 1821

6 Rufus K. Love   Mary Amelia Brown
   Cockeysville,MD 2 Feb Philadelphia,   22 Dec 1830
     1815   PA
   Cincinnati,OH 28 Jul   1 Jul 1853   14 Mar 1893
     1856

7 Annie F. Love   J. Morton Poole
   Cincinnati 23 Apr   Wilmington,DE   Wilmington 29 Mar 1855
     1854
   Detroit,MI 14 Jun   14 Jun 1880   Wilmington 22 Apr 1913
     1936

8 Ethel Love Poole   Graton S. Brand
   Wilmington 17 Jan 1882 Wilmington   Essex Co.VT 11 Dec
                                             1878
                          4 Jun 1908   Verona,NJ 7 Oct 1946

   Inheritor: Ann Love Pryor

PRYOR, WILLIAM YOUNG

Nat. #29-B.   Elected 3 Dec 1960.   b. Newark,NJ 24 Oct 1908.
m. Montclair,NJ 29 Jul 1944, Marianna Love Brand, b. Wilmington,
DE 8 Apr 1909.   Issue: Ann Love Pryor, b. Montclair 28 Mar 1946;
William Brand Pryor, b. Montclair 13 Aug 1947.   Educ: Columbia
University, B.A.; New York University, J.D.   Member: Hereditary
Order of Desc. of Colonial Governors (Hon. Gov. Gen.); St.
Nicholas Soc., NY; St. Andrews Soc., NY; Ancient and Honorable
Order of the Jersey Blues; Soc. of Colonial Wars, NJ; Sons of
American Revolution; Sons of Revolution; Soc. of War of 1812;
Huguenot Society, NJ; Sons and Dau. of the Pilgrims; New Jersey
Genealogical Soc.; New York Genealogical and Biographical Soc.
Occup: Attorney.   Address: 64 Fellswood Dr., Essex Fells,NJ
07021.   (From Society's Records).   Descended from:

1   Robert Treat, Governor of Connecticut 1683-98

2   Mary Treat   Azariah Crane
    Milford,CT 1 May 1652   Newark,NJ   Branford,CT 1649
    Newark,12 Nov 1704   c.1675   Newark 5 Nov 1730

3   Azariah Crane   Rebecca
    Newark 1682   Newark   1691
    Cranetown,NJ af.1753   c.1706   Cranetown 1739

4   Stephen Crane   Rhoda Holloway
    Cranetown c.1725   Orange,NJ   Southold,NY 1730
    West Bloomfield,NJ   1752   West Bloomfield
      1794   by 1800

5   Rhoda Crane   Linus Baldwin
    W.Bloomfield 12 Mar   Bloomfield,NJ Orange 18 Mar 1760
      1764
    W.Bloomfield 2 Oct 1821 1783   Newark 16 Dec 1836

6   Rhoda L. Baldwin   Richard C. Bush
    W.Bloomfield 10 Jun   Bloomfield   Caldwell,NJ 26 Nov
      1802   1800
    Newark 11 Oct 1875   7 Apr 1822   Newark 16 Nov 1835

7   Mary Jane Bush   Hercules M. Wilson
    Bloomfield 16 Jun 1827   Newark   New York,NY 15 Mar
                                              1825
    Newark 20 Apr 1911   25 Mar 1846   Newark 21 Nov 1905

8   Mary Ella Wilson   David Young
    Newark 4 Oct 1850   Newark   Alloa,Scotland 6 May
                                              1849
    Towaco,NJ 29 Jul 1929   10 May 1871   St.Petersburg,FL
                                              6 Feb 1939

9   Annie May Young   William W. Pryor
    Newark 5 Sep 1872   Newark   Newark 7 Sep 1869
    Verona,NJ 3 Jun 1952   3 Feb 1904   Montclair,NJ 30 Dec
                                              1947

    Inheritor: William Brand Pryor

PUTNAM, JOSEPHINE W. PHELPS (MRS. HENRY W., JR.)

Nat. #171-B. Elected 13 Feb 1971. b. Carthage,MO 23 Jun 1908.
m. Los Angeles,CA 19 Aug 1932, Henry Walter Putnam, Jr., b.
Carthage 27 Aug 1906, d. St. Louis,MO 8 Jun 1947. Educ: University of Cal. at L.A. Member: Hereditary Order of the Desc.
of Colonial Governors; Dau. of American Revolution; Dau. of
American Colonists. Address: 3663 San Remo Drive, #5-M, Santa
Barbara, CA 93105. Descended from:

1 William Leete, Governor of Connecticut 1676

2 John Leete   Mary Chittenden
  Guilford,CT 1639   -----   Guilford 1647
  Guilford 25 Nov 1692   4 Oct 1670   Guilford 9 Mar 1712

3 Sarah Leete   Eliakim Marshall
  Guilford 16 Dec 1677   -----   10 Jul 1669
  -----   23 Aug 1704   Windsor,CT

4 Eliakim Marshall   Sarah Hodge
  Windsor 15 Jul 1720   -----   -----
  -----   10 Nov 1743   -----

5 Dinah Marshall   John Phelps
  Windsor 1 Apr 1749   -----   Colebrook,CT 4 Jul 1750
  -----   -----   Norfolk,CT 1812

6 Harlow Phelps   Lucy Bennett
  Windsor 12 Jul 1786   -----   Bennetsburg,NY 19 Jun
                                                 1790
  Haskell Flats,NY   6 Mar 1808   Cuba,NY 2 Feb 1865
    19 Jun 1851

7 Cyrus Phelps   Charlotte Howe
  Lansing,NY 26 Jul   Haskell Flats   Haskell Flats 4 Feb
    1813   1821
  Haskell Flats 4 Jan   20 Dec 1840   Carthage,MO 16 Jun 1880
    1874

8 William Harlow Phelps   Lois J. Wilson
  Haskell Flats 16 Oct   Northfield,OH   Northfield 6 Nov 1846
    1845
  Rochester,MN 26 Jul   8 Feb 1868   St.Louis,MO 25 Nov
    1916   1894

9 William H. Phelps   Laura A. Bigley
  Carthage,MO 13 Sep   Chicago,IL   Bradford,PA 5 Jan 1885
    1881
  Los Angeles,CA 13 Aug   4 Aug 1904
    1927

QUINN, ALICE CAROLINE HAWKINS (MRS. JOHN L.)

Nat. #238-B. Elected 30 May 1974. b. Wilmington,DE 28 Jun
1899. m. Brooklyn,NY 4 May 1936, John Leo Quinn, b. California
5 Dec 1903. Issue: Caroline Quinn Epperson; James Matthew
Quinn. Educ: New York University. Member: Hereditary Order of
Desc. of Colonial Governors; Huguenot Society of SC; Dau. of
American Revolution (Nat. Vice Chairman of General Records);
Dau. of War of 1812 (Historian and Librarian, AZ); United Dau.
of Confederacy (Past Pres.,CA); New England Women; Dau. of
Founders and Patriots of America (Nat. Membership Chrm.); Soc.
of Desc. of Colonial Clergy; National Historical Soc.; Smith-
sonian Associates. Occup: Legal Secretary, ret. Address:
P.O. Box 2249, Prescott,AZ 86301. Descended from:

1 Robert Gibbes, Governor of South Carolina 1710-11

2 William Gibbes   Alice Culcheth
  Charlestown,SC 2 Feb   Charlestown   Ireland c.1700
    1689
  10 Mar 1733   9 Aug 1716   Johns Island,SC 31 Aug
                                                1739

3 William Gibbes   (2)   Elizabeth Hasell
  Johns Island 8 Jan   -----   14 Jan 1725
    1722/3
  Charlestown 20 Feb   18 Feb 1747/8   2 Jun 1762
    1789

4 William H. Gibbes   (2)   Mary P. Wilson
  Charlestown 16 Mar   -----   Charlestown 4 Jun 1772
    1754
  13 Feb 1834   21 Jan 1808   21 Apr 1844

5 Robert W. Gibbes   Caroline E. Guignard
  Charlestown 8 Jul 1809   Columbia,SC   Columbia 14 Apr 1811
  Columbia,SC 15 Oct 1866 20 Dec 1827   Columbia 1 Feb 1865

6 Harriet H. Gibbes   John F. Dozier
  Columbia 29 Jun 1848   Columbia   Columbia 2 Oct 1847
  Georgetown,SC 14 May   21 Jul 1868   Georgetown 30 Jan 1907
    1946

7 Harriet G. Dozier   Courtland K. Hawkins
  Georgetown 21 May 1879   Charlestown   Georgetown 14 Jul 1877
  Myrtle Beach,SC 18 May   6 Sep 1898   Georgetown 25 Mar 1943
    1964

Inheritor: James Matthew Quinn, 13076 Osage Road, Apple Valley,
CA 92307.

RAMSEY, HOMER LLOYD

Nat. #285-B. Elected 4 May 1976. b. Fairfax, Osage Co., Indian
Territory 11 Jul 1904. m. Wausau,WI 7 Nov 1932, Gertrude Emma
Wiechmann, b. Wausau 1 Apr 1909. Educ: University of Oklahoma.
Member: Hereditary Order of Desc. of Colonial Governors; Sons of
American Revolution; Ancient and Honorable Artillery Co. of MA;
Soc. of Mayflower Descendants (Past Gov. and Past Treas., TX);
Baronial Order of Magna Charta; Order of Crown of Charlemagne;
Soc. of Descendants of Colonial Clergy. Military: World War II.
Address: 3722 Nottingham, Houston,TX 77005. Descended from:

1 Thomas Prence, Governor of Plymouth Colony 1633-34, 1636-37,
   1644-45

Continue with the lineage of his sister Pearl Clara Ramsey Pruitt
#298-B, his daughter Mildred M. Ramsey Kemper #297-B, and his
grandson John William Kemper #299-B.

READ, LILLIAN EVELYN HUNTINGTON HITCHCOCK (MRS. GEORGE D.)

Nat. #350-B. Elected 6 Aug 1979. b. Buffalo,NY 18 Nov 1908.
m. Bath,NY 24 Dec 1928, George David Read, b. Avoca,NY 17 Aug
1901. Member: Hereditary Order of Desc. of Colonial Governors;
Dau. of American Revolution; Dau. of American Colonists; Colonial
Dames XVII Century; Dau. of Founders and Patriots of America;
United States Dau. of 1812 (NY State Pres.); Dau. of Colonial
Wars. Address: 41 Robie St., Bath,NY 14810. Descended from:

1 William Bradford, Governor of Plymouth Colony 1621-57

2	William Bradford		Alice Richards
	Plymouth,MA 17 Jun 1624	Plymouth	Weymouth,MA 16 Jun 1627
	Plymouth 20 Feb 1703/4	28 Jan 1650/1	Plymouth 12 Dec 1671
3	Hannah Bradford		Joshua Ripley
	Windham,CT c.1663	Plymouth	Hingham,MA 19 Nov 1658
	Windham 28 May 1738	28 Nov 1682	Windham 18 May 1739
4	Joshua Ripley		Mary Backus
	Windham 13 May 1688	-----	1692
	Windham 18 Nov 1773	3 Dec 1712	bur.Windham 1770
5	Joshua Ripley		Elisabeth Lathrop
	Windham 30 Oct 1725	-----	Barnstable,MA 9 Mar
			1731
	-----	26 Mar 1749	-----
6	Olive Ripley		Jabez Fitch, Jr.
	Windham 13 Sep 1756	Windham	Windham 2 Mar 1747/8
	-----	7 Nov 1773	23 Jun 1789
7	Fanny Fitch		Elias Parmalee
	11 Jan 1776	Windham	New Haven 26 Sep 1765
	-----	2 Feb 1795	-----

```
8  Jabez Fitch Parmalee                          Sallie Ketchum
   Lansingburgh,NY 12 Jan  -----                 -----
   1797
   Brooklyn 28 Apr 1849    12 Jan 1819           21 Oct 1855

9  Elisabeth Parmalee                            William James Hitch-
                                                   cock
   16 Jan 1837             New York City         Lee,NY 29 Apr 1836
   Buffalo,NY 20 Feb       2 Jul 1859            Buffalo 18 May 1894
   1910

10 Edwin Terry Hitchcock                         Harriet Elaine
                                                   Ostrander
   NYC 17 May 1862         Buffalo               Kanona,NY 4 Mar 1873
   Pittsburgh,PA 26 Sep    30 Dec 1903           Bath,NY 22 Nov 1946
   1912
```

REYNOLDS, MARY OLA (MISS)

Nat. #347-B. Elected 24 Jul 1979. b. Lorain Co.,OH 10 Jun 1913.
Educ: Michigan State University, B.A.; Northwestern University;
University of Michigan, M.S.W. Member: Hereditary Order of Desc.
of Colonial Governors; Dau. of American Revolution; Soc. of
Mayflower Descendants; Old Plymouth Colony Descendants; National
Assn. of Social Workers and Assn. of Certified Social Workers,
Charter Member. Address: 4734 Colonial Drive, Apt. 3, Saginaw,
MI 48603. Descended from:

```
1  William Bradford, Governor of Plymouth Colony 1621-33, 1635-
   36, 1637-38, 1645-57

2  William Bradford            (3)             Mary (Atwood) Holmes
   Plymouth,MA 17 Jun         -----           -----
   1623/4
   Plymouth 20 Feb 1703/4     -----           Plymouth 6 Jan 1714/5

3  Ephraim Bradford                           Elizabeth Brewster
   1680                       Kingston,MA      Kingston c.1690
   1746                       13 Feb 1709/10  Kingston 5 Dec 1741

4  Simeon Bradford                            Phebe Whiton
   Plymouth 28 Aug 1729       Plympton,MA      Plympton 15 Mar 1736/7
   Springfield,VT 7 Oct       25 Jan 1755     -----
   1793

5  Lucy Bradford                              John McRoberts
   Kingston 2 Oct 1761/2      Springfield      Scotland 1759
   Pittsfield,OH 1845         3 - 1782         Whiting,VT 4 Apr 1813

6  Peter McRoberts                            Eliza Waite
   Springfield 10 Feb         Sudbury,VT       Shoreham,VT 23 Aug
   1804                                          1803
   Pittsfield 1847            13 Dec 1828     Pittsfield 26 Jan 1896

7  Volney McRoberts                           Celia Pomeroy
   Wellington,OH 12 May       Pittsfield       Pittsfield 22 Nov 1841
   1841
   Oberlin,OH 12 Dec          18 Aug 1863     Pittsfield 15 Feb 1875
   1915
```

8 Cora Eliza McRoberts   Charles Clayton
                                        Reynolds
    Pittsfield 29 Aug 1865 Pittsfield   Sheffield,OH 25 Jan
                                         1860
    Oberlin 15 Mar 1935   15 Oct 1887   Oberlin 26 Jun 1926

9 Shirley Garfield   Lulu Helen Bockius
    Reynolds
    Lorain,OH 27 Mar 1890   Detroit,MI   Port Huron,MI 9 Dec
                                         1888
    Frankenmuth,MI 23 Oct 11 Sep 1912 (living)
    1976

    Inheritor: Tammy Jo-An Finner, 1625 Arthur St., Saginaw,MI
    48602.

RIGGS, LUCIE O. DONALSON (MRS. EDGAR R.)

Nat. #25-B. Elected 1 Jul 1960. b. 18 Jun 1875. m.(1) Donal-
sonville,GA 30 Jun 1896, John Peel Donalson, b. 7 Mar 1867,
d. 21 Jul 1941. m.(2) Edgar Ryerson Riggs. Educ: Brenau
College, Gainesville,GA; Columbia University, NYC. Member:
Hereditary Order of Desc. of Colonial Governors; Dau. of
American Revolution; Dau. of American Colonists; Colonial
Dames of XVII Century. Address: 808 Elm Street, Graham,TX
76046. (From Society's Records.) Descended from:

1 James Moore, Governor of South Carolina 1700-02, 1719, 1721

2 James Moore   (2)   Carolina Elizabeth
                                         Beresford
    1683   -----   1686
    Mar 1724   1700   -----

3 James Moore   Sarah Waring
    1703   So. Carolina 1706
    Sep 1772   1723   -----

4 James Moore   Ann Davis
    1724   So. Carolina 1728
    1779   1744   -----

5 Ann Moore   John Cowdrey
    1778   So. Carolina 1774
    -----   1794   25 Dec 1804

6 Harriet Cowdrey   James Shackelford
    15 Sep 1800   So. Carolina 1786
    20 Jan 1867   1814   26 Dec 1866

7 Harriet Eugenia   Charles James Munnerlyn
    Shackelford
    13 Oct 1825   So. Carolina 1822
    19 Feb 1887   28 Feb 1845   16 May 1898

8 Eugenia Munnerlyn   Lucie Otey Branch
    27 Nov 1847   Camilla,GA   28 Feb 1850
    27 Nov 1916   28 Dec 1871   23 Sep 1892

ROBBINS, REV. WILLIAM RANDOLPH

Nat. #94-B. Elected 1 Apr 1964. b. West Hartford,CT 22 May
1912. m. Princeton,NJ 6 Jun 1942, Sarah Craig Wright, b. Phila-
delphia,PA 9 Oct 1920. Issue: Henry Craig Robbins, b. 10 Jul
1943; Sarah Franklin Robbins Jenks, b. 7 Sep 1945; Thomas Nelson
Robbins, b. 18 Jul 1948. Educ: Trinity School, NYC; DeVeaux
School, Niagara Falls,NY; Princeton University, B.A.; Oxford
University; Yale University, Master of Divinity. Member:
Hereditary Order of Desc. of Colonial Governors (Chaplain
General); Soc. of Desc. of Colonial Clergy; Military Order of
Loyal Legion (Chaplain); Military Order of Foreign Wars (Chap-
lain General); Comite' Francais du Souvenir de LaFayette
(Chaplain); Oxford Univ. Union Soc.; Oxford Cricket Club;
Princeton Club of NYC; U.S. Coast Guard Auxiliary (District
Chaplain); Founders and Patriots of America; Sons of American
Revolution. Occup: Rector, St. Thomas Episcopal Church, New
Haven,CT; Pres. St. Thomas Day School. Address: St. Thomas
Episcopal Church, New Haven, CT 06511. Descended from:

1 Thomas Prence, Governor of Plymouth Colony 1634-35, 1638-39,
   1657-73

2 Hannah Prence   Nathaniel Mayo
   Plymouth,MA 1627/8   Eastham,MA   England c.1627
   bf. 23 Nov 1698   13 Feb 1649/50   Eastham 1661/2

3 Samuel Mayo   Ruth Hopkins
   Eastham 12 Oct 1655   -----   Jun 1653
   29 Oct 1738   -----   -----

4 Mary Mayo   Ralph Smith
   -----   Eastham   1682
   Middle Haddam,CT   23 Oct 1712   Middle Haddam 8 Apr
      13 Jul 1744   1762

5 Isaac Smith   Mary Sparrow
   Eastham 17 Nov 1720   Eastham   10 Mar 1718
   East Hampton,CT   9 Mar 1738   Middle Haddam 17 Apr
                                                 1785

6 Phoebe Smith   Ezekiel Wright
   Chatham,MA 22 Apr 1753 -----   Plymouth 20 Jun 1747
   East Hartland,CT   2 Feb 1775   Granby,CT 9 Jun 1812
      5 Jun 1828

7 Lucy Wright   Robert Robbins
   1780   Hartland,CT   Sandisfield,MA 13 Jul
                                                 1773
   St.Louis,MO Mar 1858   27 Sep 1796   St.Louis 10 May 1831

8 Ezekiel W. Robbins   Elizabeth Hickox
   Verona,NY 20 Aug 1802 -----   Hartford,CT 21 Sep 1801
   Chester,IL 25 Jul   22 Feb 1824   Fort Collins,CO 4 Dec
      1852   1895

9 Washington I. Robbins   Helen Mar Robinson
   Jefferson Co.NY   -----   4 May 1837
      8 Mar 1826
   Fargo,ND 14 Jun 1919   25 Jul 1855   26 Sep 1919

10 Harry E. Robbins   Matilda S. Franklin
   Chicago,IL 19 Jul 1869 Chicago,IL   Covington,KY 3 Dec 1878
   Brooklyn,NY 21 Dec   15 Aug 1894   21 Nov 1962
      1921

   Inheritor: Henry Craig Robbins (son)

ROWELL, GEORGE BARKER

Nat. #37-B. Elected 2 May 1960. Educ: Dartmouth, A.B.; Harvard
Law School, LLB; Suffolk University, J.D. (Honorary). Member:
Hereditary Order of Desc. of Colonial Governors; Order of Three
Crusades; Soc. of Colonial Wars; Baronial Order of Magna Charta;
Boston, Massachusetts, American and International Bar Assns.;
American Judicature Soc.; Cambridge Club. Address: 358 Beacon
Street, Boston,MA 02116. (From Society's Records). Descended fr:

1 Thomas Dudley, Governor of Massachusetts 1634-35, 1640-41
  Simon Bradstreet, Governor of Massachusetts 1679-86, 1689-92

2 Ann Dudley   Simon Bradstreet
  Northamptonshire,Eng.   Hardingstone,   Lincolnshire,Eng.
    c.1612   Eng.   bp. Mar 1603
  Andover,MA 16 Sep 1672 c.1628   Salem,MA 27 Mar 1697

3 Dorothy Bradstreet   Seaborn Cotton
  -----   -----   At sea 12 Aug 1633
  Hampton,NH 26 Feb 1671 14 Jun 1654   Hampton 19 Apr 1686

4 Anna Cotton   George Carr
  Hampton 22 Aug 1661   Salisbury,MA   Salisbury 15 Apr 1644
  Boston,MA   8 Nov 1677   Portsmouth,NH c.1697

5 Ann Carr   Robert Bettel
  Amesbury,MA   Amesbury   Newbury,MA 5 Jan 1764/5
  -----   11 Nov 1702   c.1740

6 Martha Bettel   Israel Young
  Amesbury 10 Nov 1703   Amesbury   Haverhill,MA c.1700
  -----   21 Jan 1724/5 Salem,NH c.1770

7 Mary Young   Philip Rowell
  Amesbury 20 Aug 1725   Salem   Haverhill bp. 7 Jul
                              1728
  -----   28 Sep 1742   Salem c.1797/8

8 Joseph Rowell   Dorcas Redington
  Salem,NH bp. 1745   Tolland,CT   Haverhill c.1756
  Allentown,NH c.1826   c.1776   Salem 15 Dec 1798

9 Adoniram J. Rowell   Ann Bartlett
  Salem 7 May 1787   Plaistow,NH   Plaistow 20 May 1791
  Montpelier,VT 7 Jan   17 Nov 1812   Waterville,VT 2 Jul
    1870   1833

10 George B. Rowell   Lucy Ann Richardson
  Waterville 4 Nov 1818   Methuen,MA   Methuen 16 Apr 1818
  North Troy,VT 24 Dec   15 Jun 1841   North Troy 16 Apr 1895
    1864

11 George Barker Rowell   (2)   Esther Rowan Grant
  North Troy 20 Mar   Pembroke,   Pembroke 5 Oct 1867
    1846   Can.
  Orleans,VT 16 Jan 1918 1 Sep 1891   Orleans 8 Sep 1952

  Inheritor: Dorothy Frances Rowell

ROYALL, JOHN WELDON, JR.

Nat. #258-B-S. Elected 22 May 1975. Member: Hereditary Order of Desc. of Colonial Governors. Descended from:

1 Alexander Spotswood, Governor of Virginia 1710-1722

2 Dorothea Spotswood   Nathaniel West Dand-
                                                  ridge
   1727   -----   1729
   1773   1747   1786

3 Dorothea Dandridge   (2)   Patrick Henry
   25 Sep 1757   -----   29 May 1736
   1781   1777   6 Jun 1799

4 Elizabeth Henry   Philip Aylett
   23 Apr 1779   -----   12 Mar 1767
   1842   1786   11 Sep 1835

5 Mary Macon Aylett   Philip Fitzhugh
   5 Dec 1793   -----   1796
   6 Oct 1836   13 Jul 1815   31 Dec 1836

6 Lafayette Henry   Ann Eliza Bullitt
      Fitzhugh
   9 May 1829   -----   9 Mar 1831
   Caroline Co. 1 Aug 1905 13 Jul 1851   Dallas,TX 25 Jan 1908

7 Lillian Lee Fitzhugh   Samuel Hamilton
                                                  Milliken
   Nottaway Co.VA 10 Dec   -----   Dallas 9 Feb 1844
      1865
   Dallas 19 Dec 1932   1885   Dallas 1931

8 Anna Mae Milliken   John Weldon Royall
   Dallas 29 Jun 1888   -----   -----
   -----   -----   -----

RUSSELL, ELSIE WELLS (MRS. JOHN PAUL)

Nat. #205-B. Elected 10 Apr 1973. b. Farina,IL 16 Sep 1901.
m. Washington,DC 24 Dec 1925, Dr. John Paul Russell, b. Washing-
ton,DC 24 Feb 1901, d. Berkeley,CA 17 Mar 1941. Issue: John
Randolph Russell, b. Washington,DC. Educ: Battle Creek College,
B.S.; Univ. of California at Berkeley, MPH; Univ. of Michigan.
Member: Hereditary Order of Desc. of Colonial Governors; Dau. of
American Revolution; Huguenot Soc. of California; Dau. of
Founders and Patriots; Dau. of American Colonists; Women Desc. of
Ancient and Honorable Artillery Co.; U.S. Dau. of 1812; Colonial
Dames of America; Magna Charta Dames; Plantagenet Soc.; Colonial
Dames of XVII Century. Occup: Nutritionist. Address: 3315-B
San Amadeo, Laguna Hills,CA 92653. Descended from:

1 William Coddington, Governor of Rhode Island 1640-47

2 Mary Coddington   Peleg Sanford
   Newport,RI 16 May 1654 Newport   Portsmouth,RI 10 May
                                                  1639
   Newport 1701   1 Dec 1674   Newport 1693

3 Elizabeth Sanford   Thomas Noyes
   Newport 1680   Newport   Stonington,CT 15 Aug
                                                1679
   Newport 23 Oct 1760   13 Sep 1705   Stonington 26 Jun 1755

4 Joseph Noyes   Barbara Wells
   Stonington 9 Oct 1727   Stonington   1 Aug 1734
   Stonington 13 Mar 1802   31 Jul 1753   Stonington 7 Sep 1814

5 Sanford Noyes   Martha Babcock
   Stonington 18 Jun 1761   Westerly,RI   30 Aug 1781
   Stonington 8 Aug 1843   2 Feb 1800   30 Sep 1860

6 Anna M. Noyes   Robert Brown
   Stonington 6 Jul 1801   Lockport,NY   Westerly 16 Dec 1796
   23 Jun 1858   4 Apr 1831   28 Nov 1858

7 Emma L. Brown   George C. Wells
   Lockport 15 Apr 1843   Royalton,NY   Hopkinton,RI 20 Jan
                                                1844
   Farina,IL 5 Mar 1909   16 Feb 1868   Farina 5 Oct 1918

8 Oscar C. Welles   Inez V. FitzRandolph
   Farina 27 Sep 1869   Farina   Farina 11 Oct 1870
   Farina 3 Apr 1958   21 Feb 1891   Farina 5 Feb 1947

   Inheritor: Jeffrey Evans Russell, 13674 Sarahills Drive,
   Saratoga, CA 95070

RYMAL, MARY L. BARNARD (MRS. GRANT V.)

Nat. #190-B. Elected 26 Jun 1972. b. Geneseo,IL 1 Nov 1903.
m.(1) Los Angeles,CA 7 May 1925, James Connachan, b. Banff, Canada 12 Nov 1903. Issue: Patricia M. Connachan, b. Los Angeles
4 Mar 1926; Joanne Connachan, b. Los Angeles 2 Oct 1928. m.(2)
Santa Ana,CA 25 Jul 1936, Roland Main, b. New York,NY 4 Feb 1894.
m.(3) Reno,NV 17 Jun 1957, Grant Vernon Rymal, b. Hamilton,
Canada 24 Apr 1895. Educ: University of South California; Univ.
of California at L.A.; Univ. of Oklahoma, Graduate School of
Social Work. Member: Hereditary Order of Desc. of Colonial
Governors; Dau. of American Revolution (Regent, Santa Ana Chap.);
Soc. of Mayflower Descendants; Desc. of Founders and Patriots;
Colonial Dames XVII Century (Pres., Cavalier Chap.); Dau. of
American Colonists (Regent, Hannah Hatch Chap.); Dames of Court
of Honor (CA, Corresponding Sec.); Court of Assistants; Women
Desc. of Ancient and Honorable Artillery Co. (State Vice Pres.);
Huguenot Society (CA, Librarian); Magna Charta Dames; Soc. of
Desc. of Hartford; Roger Williams Family Assn.; Thomas Angell
Family Assn.; New England Historic and Genealogical Soc.; CT Soc.
of Genealogists; IL Genealogical Soc. Occup: Professional Social
Worker; Councilor. Address: 2402 Plaza a la Playa, San Clemente,
CA 92672. Descended from:

1 Roger Williams, Governor of Rhode Island 1654-57

2 Daniel Williams   Rebecca (Rhodes) Power
   Providence 15 Feb 1641   Providence,RI   Providence
   Providence 14 May 1712   7 Dec 1676   Providence 1727

3   Mary Williams   Epenetus Olney
    Providence Jun 1676   Providence   Providence 18 Jan 1675
    Providence 1740   -----   Gloucester,RI 18 Sep
                                                   1740

4   Martha Olney   Stephen Angell
    Gloucester 16 May 1707   Providence   Johnston,RI 1705
    Johnston   16 May 1728   Johnston Jan 1772

5   James Angell   Amey Day
    Johnston 18 Apr 1736   Johnston   Johnston 9 Dec 1743
    Johnston 1817   1 Feb 1760   Johnston

6   Ezekiel Angell   Sarah Sprague
    Johnston 24 Mar 1771   Smithfield,RI   Smithfield 4 Mar 1771
    Greenfield,NY 20 Sep   2 Apr 1795   Greenfield 5 Oct 1847
      1847

7   James Angell   Sally H. Lincoln
    Greenfield 19 Aug 1805   Greenfield   Greenfield 5 Mar 1814
    South Corinth,NY   22 Jan 1835   South Corinth 7 Aug
      18 Feb 1877   1847

8   Henry L. Angell   Lucy J. Talcott
    South Corinth 27 Sep   Rock Island   Rock Island Co.
      1839   Co.,IL   16 Oct 1848
    Henry Co.,IL 2 Jul   2 Jul 1866   Geneseo,IL 27 Apr 1915
      1916

9   Jessie L. Angell   Allison F. Barnard
    Rock Island Co.   Decatur,IL   Lyme,OH 30 Nov 1868
      18 Aug 1872
    Chicago,IL 17 Jul 1911   21 Jun 1893   Seymour,IA 7 Jul 1948

Inheritor: Joan Main Ayotte (Mrs. Normand J.).

                                    S

SALOT, HELEN BALCH (MRS. NEVIN E.)

Nat. #98-B. Elected 27 Jul 1964. b. Topsfield,MA 26 Nov 1910.
m. Fort Myers,FL 20 Jul 1939, Nevin E. Salot, b. Dubuque,IA
6 Jan 1910. Issue: Susan H. Salot Gaumer, b. Washington,DC
30 Apr 1942. Educ: Banking and Art Schools, Washington,DC.
Member: Hereditary Order of Desc. of Colonial Governors; Soc. of
Mayflower Descendants; Dau. of American Revolution; Colonial
Dames of XVII Century; Dau. of Founders and Patriots. Occup:
Artist. Address: 3311 West Riverside Drive, Fort Myers, FL
33901. Descended from:

1   Thomas Dudley, Governor of Massachusetts 1634-35, 1640-41,
    1645-46, 1650-51
    Simon Bradstreet, Governor of Massachusetts 1679-86, 1689-92

2   Ann Dudley   Simon Bradstreet
    Northamptonshire, Eng.   Hardingstone,   Lincolnshire, Eng.
      c.1612   Eng.   bp. Mar 1603
    Andover,MA 16 Sep 1672   c.1628   Salem,MA 27 Mar 1697

3 John Bradstreet   Sarah Perkins
   Andover,MA 22 Jul 1653   -----   2 Mar 1657
   Topsfield,MA 17 Jan   11 Jun 1677   Apr 1745
      1717/8

4 Samuel Bradstreet   Sarah Clarke
   Andover 4 Aug 1699   -----   -----
   -----   3 Apr 1722   19 Jun 1736

5 Anne Bradstreet   Benjamin Bixby
   Topsfield 23 Nov 1724   -----   Salem Village,NH
                                                  13 Nov 1724
   Warren,NH 10 Nov 1808   20 Mar 1745/6   Salem,NH 13 Feb 1790

6 Benjamin Bixby   Peggy Peabody
   Topsfield 2 Jan 1747   -----   Topsfield 13 Apr 1748
   3 Feb 1830   9 Oct 1770   23 Jan 1805

7 Elizabeth Bixby   Daniel Pingree
   Salem 18 Aug 1779   -----   6 Mar 1769
   Rowley,MA 27 Sep 1862   5 Dec 1799   3 Nov 1866

8 Jewett Pingree   Mary Perkins
   Bridgewater,NH 24 Jan   -----   Topsfield 29 Apr 1812
      1809
   Michigan 1904   31 May 1832   14 Apr 1844

9 Caroline P. Pingree   Benjamin Johnson Balch
   Rowley,MA 25 May 1833   Topsfield   Topsfield 9 Sep 1826
   Topsfield 6 Mar 1918   26 Sep 1871   Topsfield 9 Feb 1912

10 Franklin Balch   Helen King Smith
   Topsfield 15 Jan 1876   Chicago,IL   Akron,OH 12 Aug 1885
   Topsfield 24 Jun 1962   26 Jun 1909

   Inheritor: Susan Helen Salot Gaumer (Mrs. H. Richard),
   7324 Beryl, New Orleans,LA 70124.

SANBORN, EARL BOYCE, JR., M.D.

Nat. #289-B. Elected 14 Jun 1976. b. Pekin,IL 2 Apr 1911. m.
Williamsport,PA 4 May 1946, Edna Frisbie Turner, b. Philadelphia,
PA 1 Oct 1919. Educ: Northwestern University, B.S., B.M., M.D.;
University of Illinois, M.S. in Surgery. Member: Hereditary
Order of Desc. of Colonial Governors; Society of Cincinnati;
Sons of Revolution; Soc. of Colonial Wars (IL, Council); Hugue-
not Society (IL, Past Pres.); Sons of American Revolution (IL,
Vice Pres.); Sons of Union Veterans of Civil War; Soc. of Desc.
of Colonial Clergy; Americans of Royal Descent; Ancient and
Honorable Artillery of MA; Order of Crown of Charlemagne;
Military Order of the Crusades; Baronial Order of Magna Charta;
Soc. of Genealogists, London; New England Historical Genealogi-
cal Soc.; Sons and Dau. of Pioneer Rivermen; many Military
Organizations and Professional Societies. Address: Box 304,
Kenilworth,IL 60043. Descended from:

1 Thomas C. Welles, Governor of Connecticut, 1655, 1658

2   Ann Welles
    Essex,Eng. 1619   Hartford,CT
    Farmington,CT   14 Apr 1646
      by Dec 1680
    Thomas Thomson
    England 1617
    Farmington 25 Apr 1655

3   John Thomson
    Farmington 1649   Farmington
    Farmington 21 Nov 1711   24 Oct 1670
    Mary Steele
    Farmington 20 Nov 1646
    Farmington

4   John Thomson, Jr.
    Farmington 29 Dec 1671   Farmington
    Farmington 9 Aug 1741   2 Nov 1699
    Margaret Orton

    -----

5   Solomon Thomson
    Farmington 11 Apr 1716   Farmington
    Farmington bf. 1 Aug   26 Dec 1745
      1790
    Susannah Gridley
    Farmington 25 Jul 1721
    Farmington 19 Jun 1761

6   Thankful Thomson
    Farmington btw.1747-   Farmington
      1751
    -----   6 Feb 1769
    Ebenezer Porter
    Farmington 1746
    Stamford,VT 1800

7   Deidamia Porter
    Farmington c.1778   Pawlet,VT
    Pawlet 7 Jul 1840   25 Feb 1799
    Oliver Hanks
    Pawlet 7 Dec 1778
    Pawlet 20 Jun 1859

8   Ermina Hanks
    Pawlet 24 Sep 1812   -----
    Olive,OH 24 Jul 1891   -----
    William H. Packard
    Lebanon,NH 1809
    Olive 30 Sep 1889

9   Marcia Ermina Hanks
    Chester,OH 11 Jun 1836   Shade River,
        OH
    Reedsville,OH 13 Feb   14 Dec 1854
      1914
    John Oliver Sanborn
    Cincinnati,OH 2 Oct
      1832
    Reedsville 17 Mar 1917

10 William Wallace Sanborn
    Meigs Co.,OH 3 Jun   Middleport,
      1856   OH
    Middleport 7 Jun 1890   25 Jun 1879
    Caroline Susan Boyce
    Indiana 19 Aug 1855
    Middleport 3 Nov 1928

11 Earl Boyce Sanborn
    Middleport 7 Dec 1882   Pekin,IL
    Pekin 24 Jun 1968   14 Feb 1906
    Minnie Annetta Albert-
      sen
    Pekin 16 Aug 1879
    Pekin 27 Mar 1960

SATTERTHWAITE, PENNINGTON

Nat. #66-B. Elected 28 Feb 1963. b. Manhattan,NY 20 Dec 1911.
Educ: The Harvey School, Hawthorne,NY. Member: Hereditary Order
of Desc. of Colonial Governors; Soc. of Colonial Wars;
St. Nicholas Soc. of New York City; Order of Colonial Lords of
Manors in America; Desc. of Signers of Declaration of Independence; Sons of Revolution; Huguenot Society of America; NJ
Historical Society; St. Andrews Soc. of NY. Address: 439 East
51st St., New York,NY 10022. (From Society's Records). Descended
from:

1 Lewis Morris, Governor of New Jersey 1719-20, 1731-32,1738-46

2 Lewis Morris   Tryntje Staats
   23 Sep 1698   -----   4 Apr 1697
   3 Jul 1762   17 Mar 1723   11 Mar 1731

3 Lewis Morris   Mary Walton
   8 Apr 1726   -----   Feb 1727
   22 Jan 1798   24 Sep 1749   11 Mar 1794

4 Helen Morris   John Rutherfurd
   1762   -----   20 Sep 1760
   6 Oct 1840   30 Oct 1782   23 Feb 1840

5 Anna Rutherfurd   John Watts
   1 Mar 1794   -----   New York 1786
   New York,NY 15 Feb 1876 1813   New York 4 Feb 1831

6 Helen R. Watts   Archibald Russell
   New York 22 Jun 1815 -----   Edinburgh,Scot. 24 Dec
                                              1811
   New York 11 Apr 1906 1836/7   New York 17 Apr 1871

7 Eleanor E. Russell   Arthur John Peabody
   New York 22 Apr 1849 New York   Zanesville,OH 8 Oct
                                              1835
   New York 4 Nov 1910 9 May 1871   New York 13 Jan 1901

8 Helen M. Peabody   Pennington Satter-
                                              thwaite
   New York 3 Apr 1879 New York   Newark,NJ 6 Oct 1870
   Short Hills,NJ 28 Oct 28 Jun 1909   Summit,NJ 27 Apr 1946
      1958

   Inheritor: Franklin Bache Satterthwaite, Jr.

SAUNDERS, ALDEN CLINTON

Nat. #228-B. Elected 4 Apr 1974. b. Providence,RI 10 Jul 1912.
m. Providence 4 Oct 1941, Lora Beattie Thurber, b. Cranston,RI
18 Nov 1913. Educ: University of Rhode Island, B.S.; Rhode
Island College, M.E.; Brown and Boston Universities for graduate
work. Member: Hereditary Order of Desc. of Colonial Governors;
Society of Mayflower Descendants, RI; Sons of American Revolu-
tion; Order of Founders and Patriots; Soc. of Desc. of Colonial
Clergy; National Huguenot Society. Occup: Supt. of Schools,
Retired. Address: Box #142, Apple Hill Drive, North Scituate,
RI 02857. Descended from:

1 John Alden, Governor of Plymouth Colony 1663-67

2 Joseph Alden   Mary Simmons
   -----   Plymouth   -----
   Bridgewater,MA 8 Feb -----   -----
      1696

3 John Alden   Hannah White
   c.1674   -----   Weymouth,MA 5 May 1681
   Middleboro,MA 29 Sep -----   Middleboro 5 Oct 1732
      1730
                          232

4 Hannah Alden   Thomas Wood
   Middleboro 24 Mar 1709   -----   Middleboro 20 Jan 1703
   Middleboro 24 Mar   1729   Halifax,MA 27 Jan
     1743/4   1744/5

5 Priscilla Wood   John Pratt
   Middleboro 26 Feb 1729   -----   Middleboro 20 Apr 1729
   Scituate,RI   9 Sep 1749   Scituate 19 Dec 1777
    af. 19 Dec 1777

6 Hannah Pratt   Abraham Phillips
   Middleboro 31 Aug 1753   Scituate   Scituate 28 Feb 1755
   Foster,RI 19 Feb 1828   27 Feb 1780   Foster 17 Oct 1828

7 Elizabeth Phillips   Parley Round
   Foster   Foster   Scituate 6 Jan 1782
   Scituate 1 Jan 1841   -----   Foster 21 Aug 1808

8 Alden P. Round   Hannah M. Angell
   Foster 3 Jul 1810   Coventry,RI   S. Kingston,RI 25 Aug
                                      1819
   Foster 3 Mar 1895   25 Nov 1849   Foster 18 Jan 1901

9 Sarah E. Round   Byron W. Sweet
   Foster 14 Jun 1850   Foster   Foster 1 Sep 1849
   Providence,RI 19 Aug   30 Dec 1875   Providence 21 Nov 1908
    1931

10 Vera G. Sweet   Winthrop H. Saunders
   Foster 20 Jun 1881   Providence   Westerly,RI 7 Dec 1884
   Foster 22 Nov 1963   20 Jun 1911   Warwick,RI 27 Aug 1957

SAUNDERS, LORA B. THURBER (MRS. ALDEN C.)

Nat. #231-B. Elected 4 Apr 1974. b. Cranston,RI 18 Nov 1913.
m. Providence,RI 4 Oct 1941, Alden Clinton Saunders, b. Provi-
dence 10 Jul 1912. Member: Hereditary Order of Desc. of Colonial
Governors; Society of Mayflower Descendants; Dau. of American
Revolution; Dau. of Founders and Patriots; Soc. of Desc. of
Colonial Clergy. Address: Box #142, Apple Hill Drive, North
Scituate, RI 02857. Descended from:

1 Roger Williams, Governor of Rhode Island 1654-57

2 Mercy Williams   (2)   Samuel Winsor
   Providence 15 Jul 1640   Providence,RI Providence 1644
   Providence 1705   2 Jan 1677   Providence 19 Sep 1705

3 Samuel Winsor   Mercy Harding
   Providence 18 Nov 1677   Providence   -----
   Providence 17 Nov 1758   7 Jan 1703   Providence af. 1749

4 Joseph Winsor   Deborah Matheson
   Glocester,RI 4 Oct   -----   Glocester c.1714
    1713
   Glocester 4 Sep 1802   -----   Glocester 23 Aug 1785

5 Mary Winsor   Benjamin Comstock
  Glocester 2 Apr 1755   Providence   Providence 7 Mar 1747
  Providence 7 Nov 1825   -----   Providence 30 Sep 1828

6 Ann B. Comstock   Samuel Thurber, Jr.
  Providence 15 Dec 1784   Providence   Providence 21 Jan 1785
  Providence 23 Aug 1868   20 Nov 1808   Providence 1 Jul 1821

7 George J. Thurber   Sarah J. Taft
  Providence   Providence   -----
  Providence 6 Jan 1856   23 Sep 1839   Providence af.15 Jan
                                                   1856

8 Cyrus T. Thurber   Ida Adele Simmons
  Providence 1852   Providence   Cranston,RI 21 Feb 1855
  Providence 10 May 1898   12 Nov 1873   Cranston 16 Dec 1935

9 Arthur N. Thurber   Fanny Dartt Haven
  Providence 4 Jan 1875   Cranston   Cranston 14 Sep 1876
  Providence 10 Nov 1953   10 Oct 1899   Cranston 23 Oct 1918

SCHMITT, ROGER MICHAEL LAURENCE

Nat. #345-B. Elected 23 Jul 1979. b. New York 21 Oct 1952.
Educ: Westminster College. Member: Hereditary Order of Desc. of
Colonial Governors; Saint Nicholas Society; Sons of the Revolu-
tion. Address: Johnson & Higgins, 95 Wall St., Personal, New
York, NY 10005; also Syosset,NY. Descended from:

1 Thomas Lee, Governor of Virginia, 1740-45

2 Richard Henry Lee   Anne Gaskins Pinckard
  Westmoreland Co.VA 1732.Westmoreland   Westmoreland Co.
                                                  bf. 1769
  Westmoreland Co. 1794   1769   Westmoreland af.1770

3 Anne Lee   Charles Lee
  Westmoreland 1770   Westmoreld.Co.   Westmoreland 1758
  Westmoreland Co. 1804   1789   Westmoreland 1815

4 Anne Lucinda Lee   Walter Jones, Jr.
  Westmoreland Co. 1790   Westmoreld.Co.   Hanover Co.VA 1777
  Westmoreland Co. 1835   1808   Hanover Co. 1861

5 Anne Harriotte Jones   Matthew Harrison
  Loudon Co.VA c.1830   -----   Loudon Co. 18 Dec 1826
  Loudon Co. af.1875   1851   Loudon Co. 26 Jan 1875

6 Thomas Walter Harrison   (2)   Nellie Cover
  Winchester,VA 12 Apr   -----   Cockeysville,MD 4 Jan
    1856   1866
  Winchester 19 May 1935   6 Jul 1903   Winchester 17 Mar 1936

7 B. Powell Harrison   Elizabeth C. Brady
  Winchester 2 Jul 1904   Oyster Bay,NY   Oyster Bay 6 Sep 1903
  Winchester 29 Dec 1975   10 Jun 1925   London,Eng. 10 Aug 1932

8 Alexandra B. Harrison   A. Lyman Schmitt
  Syosset,NY 2 Sep 1927   Oyster Bay   New York 23 Nov 1919
  New York 11 Dec 1974   10 Oct 1948   New York 6 Jun 1971

SCHNEIDER, MARGARET P. O'CONNOR (MRS. SAMUEL G.)

Nat. #57-B. Elected 22 Oct 1962. b. Bogue,KS 20 Mar 1915.
m. Memphis,TN 29 Jun 1933, Samuel George Schneider, b. Memphis
30 Oct 1908. Issue: Samuel Charles Schneider, b. Memphis 10 Sep
1934. Member: Hereditary Order of Desc. of Colonial Governors.
Address: 809 North Brown St., El Paso,TX 79902. (From Society's
Records). Descended from:

1 William Coddington, Governor of Rhode Island 1640-47

2 Mary Coddington   Peleg Sanford
  Newport,RI 16 May 1654 Portsmouth,RI   Portsmouth 10 May 1638
  Newport 1701   1 Dec 1674   Newport 1701

3 Elizabeth Sanford   Thomas Noyes
  Newport 1680   Newport   Stonington,CT 15 Aug
                                              1679
  Newport 23 Oct 1762   3 Sep 1705   Stonington 26 Jun 1755

4 Elizabeth Noyes   Ichabod Palmer
  Stonington 22 Dec 1706 Stonington   25 Oct 1702
  Stonington 24 Dec 1760 29 Apr 1723   1749

5 Elias S. Palmer   Phebe Palmer
  Stonington 12 Mar 1742 -----   5 Sep 1742
  1824   15 Mar 1761   -----

6 Luther Palmer   Sarah Kenyon
  25 Nov 1774   -----   Westerly,RI 1776
  22 Feb 1864   12 Dec 1799   3 Jul 1815

7 Sarah Palmer   Paul Greene
  25 Feb 1805   Hopkinton,RI   Westerly 31 Jan 1803
  1891   31 Jan 1826   1883

8 Sarah Greene   John L. Starkweather
  21 May 1831   Hopkinton   Preston,CT 12 Apr 1830
  7 May 1892   28 Nov 1855   28 Nov 1909

9 John P. Starkweather   Jennie Means Holt
  Riley Co.KS 4 Sep 1861 Ottowa,KS   Garnett,KS 6 Aug 1865
  Clay Center,KS 21 Sep   17 Aug 1888   Pine Bluff,AR
    1917

10 Anne Starkweather   James C. O'Connor
   Clay Center 8 May 1889 -----   Esban,KS 6 Oct 1876
                           -----   Jul 1920

   Inheritor: Samuel Charles Schneider

SCHROEDER, ELIZABETH P. CARLTON (MRS. HENRY JOHN, JR.)

Nat. #236-B. Elected 1 May 1974. b. Portsmouth,VA 24 Nov 1942.
m. Washington,DC 15 Apr 1972, Brig. Gen. Henry John Schroeder,
Jr., b. Long Branch,NJ 3 May 1921. Issue: Mary Byrd Schroeder,
b. Richmond,VA 27 Aug 1973. Educ: Sweet Briar College, B.A.;
Medical Research Specialist, University of Virginia Medical
School; Research Aide, Memorial Sloan-Kettering Institute of
Cancer Research, NYC; College of William and Mary, post graduate
work; Virginia Teacher's Certificate. Member: Hereditary Order
of Desc. of Colonial Governors; Jamestowne Society; Magna Charta
Dames; Order of Crown of Charlemagne in USA. Occup: Teacher;
Exchange Teacher to England. Address: 3115 Savoy Road, Fairfax,
VA 22031. Descended from:

1 Robert Carter, Governor of Virginia 1726-27

2 Anne Carter   Benjamin Harrison
  Virginia c.1702   Charles City   Berkeley,VA c.1705
                          Co.,VA
  -----   1722   1745

3 Benjamin Harrison   Elizabeth Bassett
  Berkeley 22 Aug 1726   -----   New Kent Co.VA
  Berkeley 24 Apr 1791   13 Dec 1730   -----

4 Ann Harrison   David O'Shields
                                           Coupland
  Berkeley 21 May 1753   Berkeley   Nansemond Co.VA 3 Aug
                                           1749
  Berkeley 30 Apr 1821   9 Mar 1775   Surrey Co.VA 29 Jun
                                           1822

5 Elizabeth B. Coupland   Stephen Woodson Trent
  Henrico Co.VA 1 Jan   Cumberland Co.   Cumberland Co. 20 Jan
  1776   1769
  Cumberland Co.VA   12 Nov 1794   Cumberland Co. 12 Mar
  13 March 1844   1853

6 Thomas W. Trent   Catherine Ann Gannaway
  Cumberland Co. 9 Dec   Buckingham Co.   Buckingham Co. 25 Dec
  1821   1830
  Buckingham Co.VA   16 Jan 1867   Buckingham Co. 6 Feb
  7 Feb 1903   1915

7 Stephen W. Trent   Anna Harrison Trible
  Buckingham Co. 4 Nov   Baltimore,MD   Buckingham Co. 20 Mar
  1871   1882
  Cumberland Co. 10 Mar   16 Jun 1915   Essex Co.VA 28 Sep
  1949   1964

8 Nannie Nicholas Page   Emory Linwood Carlton
  Trent
  Buckingham Co. 18 Aug   Buckingham Co.   King & Queen Co.VA
  1916   15 Jul 1906
                          28 Jun 1941

SCHROEDER, ENRIETTE L. LEWIS (MRS. HENRY JOHN)

Nat. #159-B. Elected 11 Apr 1970. b. Fort Riley,KS 18 Oct 1896.
m. New Orleans,LA 15 Dec 1917, Henry John Schroeder, b. Portland,
OR 6 Jun 1893; d. Bethesda,MD 25 Apr 1968. Issue: Henry John,
Jr., b. Long Branch,NJ 3 May 1921; William Rising, b. West Point,
NY 16 Feb 1925; Robert Lewis, b. Fort Sam Houston,TX 13 Aug 1930.
Educ: University of Oregon. Member: Hereditary Order of Desc.
of Colonial Governors; Dau. of American Revolution (Past Regent,
Army and Navy Chap., DC); Women Desc. of Ancient and Honorable
Artillery Co. (Past Treas., DC Court of Assistants); Colonial
Dames of America in VA; Order of First Families of VA; Jamestowne
Society; Desc. of Lords of Maryland Manors; Soc. of Dau. of
Colonial Wars; U.S. Dau. of 1812; Order of the Crown in America;
Dau. of Barons of Runnemede; United Dau. of the Confederacy; Dau.
of U.S. Army; DAR State Officers Club; Club of Colonial Dames;
Army-Navy Town Club. Address: 6204 Redwing Court, Bethesda,MD
20034. Descended from:

1 Thomas Welles, Governor of Connecticut 1655-58

Continue with the lineage of her son Brig. Gen. Henry John
Schroeder, Jr. #227-B.

SCHROEDER, BRIG. GEN. HENRY JOHN, JR.

Nat. #227-B. Elected 4 Apr 1974. b. Long Branch,NJ 3 May 1921.
m. Washington,DC 15 Apr 1972, Elizabeth Page Carlton, b. Ports-
mouth,VA 24 Nov 1942. Issue: Mary Byrd Schroeder, b. Richmond,
VA 27 Aug 1973; Henry John Schroeder III, b. Atlanta,GA 14 Dec
1947; Thomas Andrew Schroeder, b. Washington,DC 3 Feb 1956.
Educ: George Washington University, M.A. in International
Affairs; Georgia Inst. of Technology, MSEE; U.S. Military
Academy, B.S. Member: Hereditary Order of Desc. of Colonial
Governors; Society of the Cincinnati; Baronial Order of Magna
Charta; Jamestowne Society; Sons of American Revolution; Lords
of Maryland Manors. Military: Commissioned 2nd Lt. US Army,
1943, advanced through grades to Brigadier General, 1970; retired
1972. Honors: Distinguished Service Medal; Legion of Merit; DFC;
Bronze star w/V devise awarded 4 times; Air Medal w/V devise
awarded 24 times. Occup: Senior Analyst and Dep. Dir., Tactical
Warfare Center, Gen. Research Corp., McLean,VA. Address:
3115 Savoy Road, Fairfax,VA 22031. Descended from:

1 Thomas Welles, Governor of Connecticut 1655-58

2 John Welles   Elizabeth Bourne
     England c.1621   Stratford,CT   Stratford c.1627
     Fairfield,CT 1659   1647   Fairfield c.1660

3 Robert Welles   Elizabeth Goodrich
     Wethersfield,CT 1648 Wethersfield Wethersfield 1658
     Wethersfield 22 Jun   9 Jun 1675   Wethersfield 17 Feb
       1714   1697

4	Robert Welles		Sarah Wolcott
	Wethersfield 1684	Wethersfield	Wethersfield 14 Aug 1686
	Wethersfield 22 Jun 1738	12 Dec 1706	Wethersfield 1738

5	Sarah W. Welles		Jonathan Robbins
	Wethersfield 1 Feb 1708	Wethersfield	Wethersfield 28 Dec 1694
	Wethersfield 15 May 1776	21 Nov 1728	Wethersfield 15 Aug 1777

6	Solomon Robbins		Mary Harmon
	Wethersfield 30 Mar 1743	Sandisfield	Sandisfield 1750
	Sandisfield,MA 1 Dec 1794	10 May 1770	Sandisfield 26 Mar 1812

7	Eunice Robbins		Edward Stevens
	Sandisfield 4 Feb 1784	New Marlboro	New Marlboro 18 Apr 1778
	New Marlboro,MA 15 Jun 1858	1801	New Marlboro 15 Sep 1854

8	Eunice R. Stevens		James C. Rising
	New Marlboro 16 Jan 1826	New Marlboro	Suffield,CT 14 Aug 1818
	New Marlboro 19 Apr 1892	17 Oct 1848	New York,NY 12 Aug 1904

9	Emma Rising		Thomas J. Lewis
	New Marlboro 26 Sep 1856	New York	New Orleans,LA 6 Apr 1857
	Lake Toxaway,NC 13 Aug 1913	29 Jul 1880	Baltimore,MD 19 Jan 1920

10	Enriette Lawson Lewis		Henry John Schroeder
	Ft. Riley,KS 18 Oct 1896	New Orleans	Portland,OR 6 Jun 1893
		15 Dec 1917	Bethesda,MD 25 Apr 1968

Inheritor: Mary Byrd Schroeder

SCHROEDER, COL. ROBERT LEWIS

Nat. #235-B. Elected 1 May 1974. b. Fort Sam Houston,TX 13 Aug 1930. m. Fort Meyer,VA 22 Jul 1961, Margaret Mary Beurket, b. Washington,DC 9 Dec 1934. Issue: Robert Lewis Schroeder, Jr., b. Columbus,OH 17 Jul 1962; William David Schroeder, b. Washington,DC 12 Jan 1966. Educ: U.S. Army Artillery School; Command and General Staff College; U.S. Army War College; U.S. Military Academy, B.S.; Ohio State University, M.S. Member: Hereditary Order of Desc. of Colonial Governors; Sons of American Revolution; Desc. of Lords of Maryland Manors; Society of the Cincinnati in VA. Honors: Army Commendation Medal for Valor and Achievement w/2 Oak Leaf Clusters; RVN Gallantry Cross w/Bronze and Silver Stars; RVN Armed Forces Honor Medal, 1st Class; RVN Gallantry Cross w/Palm, Unit Award; Army of Occupation Medal (Germany); Vietnam Service Medal. Occup: Colonel, U.S. Army, Organization of the Joint Chiefs of Staff, Washington,DC.

Address: 3715 - 49th Street, N.W., Washington,DC 20016. Descended from:

1   Thomas Welles, Governor of Connecticut 1655-58

Continue with the lineage of his brother Brig. Gen. Henry John Schroeder, Jr. #227-B.

   Inheritor: William David Schroeder, 3715 - 49th Street, N.W., Washington, DC 20016.

SHEPARD, JOHN SANFORD

Nat. #184-B.   Elected 10 Jan 1972.   b. Franklin,NH 15 Sep 1901. m. Douglas,MA 24 Jun 1933, Ruth Gertrude Crockett, b. North Uxbridge,MA 18 Dec 1908.   Issue: John S. Shepard, III,b.Whitins-ville,MA 7 Jul 1934; Ruth A. Shepard Kurtz, b. Franklin 19 Oct 1936; Rosamond Robinson Shepard, b. Franklin 4 Mar 1938. Educ: Harvard College, A.B.; Boston University, M.A.   Member: Heredi-tary Order of Desc. of Colonial Governors; Soc. of Mayflower Descendants (NH, Past Gov.); Soc. of Colonial Wars (NH, Registrar, Genealogist); Sons of American Revolution; Huguenot Society; Piscataqua Pioneers; New Hampshire Historical Soc.; N.E. Historic Genealogical Soc.   Occup: Realtor, Lakes Region Realtors Assn. Received Senior Counsellor's Jewel, Concord Council #559 UCT and Fifty year Veteran Medal, NH Grand Lodge F.& A.M.   Address: 94 View Street, Franklin,NH 03235.   Descended from:

1   William Bradford, Governor of Plymouth Colony 1621-33, 1635-57

2	William Bradford	(1)	Alice Richards
	Plymouth,MA 17 Jun 1624	Plymouth	Weymouth,MA 16 Jun 1627
	Plymouth 20 Feb 1703/4	28 Jan 1650	Plymouth 12 Dec 1671
3	Hannah Bradford		Joshua Ripley
	Plymouth 9 May 1662	Plymouth	Hingham,MA 9 Nov 1658
	Windham,CT 28 May 1738	28 Nov 1682	Windham 8 May 1739
4	Faith Ripley		Samuel Bingham
	Hingham 20 Sep 1686	Windham	Norwich,CT 28 Mar 1685
	Windham 11 Feb 1720	5 Jan 1708	Windham 1 Mar 1760
5	Jerusha Bingham		Benjamin Robinson
	Windham 2 Feb 1708	Windham	Tisbury,MA 23 Feb 1703
	Stafford,CT 29 Apr 1774	4 Mar 1729	Stafford 12 Apr 1772
6	Lydia Robinson		Daniel Blodgett
	Windham 5 Feb 1741	-----	Stafford 13 Oct 1739
	-----	1 Nov 1760	New York,NY 12 Nov 1776
7	Nathan Blodgett		Anna Perrin
	Stafford 27 Sep 1761	Lebanon	1764
	Lebanon,NH 26 Aug 1798	3 Mar 1785	Lebanon 26 Apr 1838

8 Roxanna Blodgett   John Shepard
   Lebanon 31 Mar 1798   Lebanon   New Chester,NH 23 Nov
                                                           1796
   Canaan,NH 3 Jun 1871   21 Jun 1823   Lebanon 8 May 1868

9 John Sanford Shepard   Theoda Hews Clark
   Canaan 25 Apr 1825   Canaan   Canaan 11 Dec 1827
   Canaan 3 Nov 1867   19 Jul 1855   Franklin,NH 4 May 1916

10 John Sanford Shepard   Alice Maude Robinson
   Canaan 28 Dec 1860   Bangor,ME   Bangor 11 Aug 1870
   Concord,NH 20 Nov 1937   18 Sep 1895   Franklin 3 Nov 1959

   Inheritor: John Sanford Shepard,III, Apt. 17, Garden Crescent
   Apts., 30 Middlesex Circle, Waltham,MA 02154.

SHEPARD, WILLIAM DURELL

Nat. #168-B. Elected 4 Jan 1971. b. Waterbury,CT 11 Mar 1896.
m. Chicago,IL 20 Oct 1937, Myrtle Thelma Lind b. Grand Forks,ND
7 Mar 1904. Educ: Mass. College of Pharmacy and Mass. Institute
of Technology. Member: Hereditary Order of Desc. of Colonial
Governors; Sons of American Revolution; M.I.T. Club of Chicago.
Occup: Retired Partner, Shepard Laboratories. Address: American
Embassy, APO New York 09253. Descended from:

1 John Webster, Governor of Connecticut 1656

2 Robert Webster   Susannah Treat
   Cossington,Eng. 1628   Middletown,CT   Pitminster,Eng. 1629
   Hartford,CT 31 May   1652   Hartford Nov 1705
     1676

3 John Webster   Sarah (Whiting)Mygatt
   10 Nov 1653   -----   -----
   8 Dec 1694   -----   -----

4 Ebenezer Webster   Hannah Webster
   bp. 14 Jul 1689   -----   7 Nov 1695
   12 Feb 1776   -----   11 Nov 1775

5 Medad Webster   Elizabeth Holten
   bp. 5 Jan 1723/4   -----   -----
   Hartford 9 Apr 1793   10 Nov 1748   Hartford 28 Aug 1805

6 Samuel Webster   Huldah Skinner
   Hartford Sep 1749   Hartford   -----
   Hartford 25 Mar 1813   c.1770   Hartford 1 Apr 1813

7 Mary Webster   Phineas Shepard
   1 Sep 1772   -----   2 Nov 1766
   1848   24 Nov 1791   1840

8 Almeron Shepard   Ruth Bunce
   20 Oct 1795   -----   1796
   Hartford 15 Nov 1849   9 Jun 1822   Hartford 1 Feb 1858

9 Daniel B. Shepard   Lucy Townshend
   26 Oct 1835   -----   England
   New Britain,CT 24 May   27 Mar 1864   -----
      1912

10 William M. Shepard   Gertrude D. Hinman
   17 Jun 1868   Bristol,CT   Forestville,CT 4 Oct
                                                            1871
   Waterbury,CT 26 Jan   -----   Wethersfield,CT
      1898   Apr 1956

SHEPARD, WILLIAM SETH

Nat. #332-B. Elected 1 Feb 1979. b. Boston,MA 7 Jun 1935.
m. Westbrook,CT 25 Jun 1960, Lois Rosalie Burke, b. Hartford,CT
1 Feb 1938. Issue: Stephanie Lee Shepard, b. Charlottesville,
VA 18 May 1962; Cynthia Robin Shepard, b. Charlottesville 2 May
1963; Warren Burke Shepard, b. Singapore 3 May 1966. Educ:
Wesleyan University, Middletown,CT A.B.; Harvard Law School,
J.D. Member: Hereditary Order of Desc. of Colonial Governors;
Soc. of Mayflower Descendants; Sons of American Revolution;
Flagon and Trencher; Bars of U.S. Supreme Court and Supreme
Court of New Hampshire. Occup: Career Diplomat, U.S. Department
of State. Address: American Embassy, APO New York 09253.
Descended from:

1 Tristram Coffin, Governor of Nantucket 1671-73

2 Tristram Coffin, Jr.   Judith Greenleaf
   England 1632   -----   England 2 Sep 1625
   4 Feb 1704   2 Mar 1652/3   Newbury,MA 15 Dec 1705

3 Judith Coffin   John Sanborn, Jr.
   4 Dec 1653   -----   1649
   17 May 1724   19 Nov 1674   23 Sep 1727

4 John Sanborn   Mehitable Fifield
   1683   -----   9 Apr 1687
   4 Jan 1732   1 Jan 1707   -----

5 Abigail Sanborn   Elisha Swett
   Hampton Falls,NH   -----   30 Sep 1705
      6 May 1713
   10 Mar 1802   10 Feb 1736   -----

6 Stephen Swett   Sarah Garland
   Kingston,NH 21 May 1739 -----   Hampton Falls 1741
   -----   25 Feb 1761   11 Nov 1772

7 Abigail Swett   Moses Shepard
   Gilmanton,NH 28 Aug   East Kingston,   South Hampton,NH
      1772   NH   11 Apr 1768
   Canaan,NH 26 Mar 1838   21 Nov 1793   Canaan 8 Dec 1826

8 John Shepard   Roxanna Blodgett
   New Chester,NH 23 Nov   Lebanon,NH   Lebanon 31 Mar 1798
      1796
   Lebanon 8 May 1868   2 Jun 1823   Canaan 3 Jun 1871

9 John Sanford Shepard   Theoda Hewes Clark
   Canaan 25 Apr 1825   Canaan   Canaan 11 Dec 1827
   Canaan 3 Nov 1867   19 Jul 1855   Franklin,NH 4 May 1916

10 John Sanford Shepard   Alice Maude Robinson
   Canaan 28 Dec 1860   Bangor,ME   Bangor 11 Aug 1870
   Concord,NH 20 Nov   19 Sep 1895   Franklin 3 Nov 1959
   1937

11 Robinson Shepard   Myra Ellen Foster
   Bangor 23 Aug 1896   Orford,NH   17 Oct 1906
                           30 Mar 1931

SHERMAN, F. LYNETTE (MISS)

Nat. #329-B. Elected 10 Aug 1978. b. Waukegan,IL 15 Feb 1915.
Educ: Northwestern University. Member: Hereditary Order of Desc.
of Colonial Governors; Dau. of American Revolution; National
Huguenot Soc.; Dau. of Founders and Patriots of America; Dau. of
Colonial Wars; Soc. of Mayflower Descendants. Address: 6713 N.
Caldwell Ave., Chicago,IL 60646. Descended from:

1 Thomas Welles, Governor of Connecticut 1655, 1658

2 John Welles   Elizabeth Bourne
   England c.1621   Stratford,CT   Stratford c.1627
   Fairfield,CT 1659   1647   Fairfield c.1660

3 Sarah Welles   Ambrose Thompson
   c.1658   -----   Stratford 1 Jan 1651/2
   Stratford 23 Mar 1730   -----   Stratford 7 Sep 1742

4 Ambrose Thompson   Ann Booth
   Stratford 1682   -----   c.1688
   Stratford 3 May 1768   22 May 1707   Stratford 22 Sep 1774

5 Joseph Thompson   Temperance Nichols
   Stratford 30 Jul 1708   -----   -----
   -----   31 Dec 1731   -----

6 Jerusha Thompson   Nathaniel Sherman
   7 May 1735   -----   Stratford bp.30 Mar
                                                 1729
   Stratford c.1797   Dec 1754   Trumbull,CT 1799

7 David Sherman   Mabel Lamkin
   Stratford 20 Dec 1755   -----   Huntington,CT 1764
   Trumbull,CT 30 Oct   -----   Trumbull 4 Mar 1829
   1826

8 David Thompson Sherman   Sarah Cables
   Trumbull 1796   Woodbury,CT   Oxford,CT 1799
   Berkshire,OH 9 Mar   9 Feb 1819   Berkshire 30 Jun 1868
   1867

9 Henry S. Sherman   Esther Hattie Young
   18 Apr 1825   Delaware Co.OH 24 Feb 1826
   Berkshire 13 May 1880   -----   Berkshire 11 Nov 1876

10 Charles Henry Sherman   Ann Shannon
    Berkshire 21 May   Cicero,IL   MN 1 Aug 1863
      1858/9
    Waukegan,IL 3 Nov 1935   27 Sep 1885   Waukegan 29 Dec 1933

11 Charles Everett Sherman   Bertha Arnesen
    Chicago,IL 12 Jan 1887   Kenosha,WI   Chicago 8 Apr 1890
    Chicago 9 Dec 1946   11 May 1913   Chicago 14 Mar 1961

SHIPMAN, RUTH M. WEBB (MRS. WILLIAM L.)

Nat. #352-B. Elected 6 Aug 1979. b. Tuscarora,NY 15 Jun 1916.
m. Richmond,VA 20 Dec 1941, Dr. William LeRoy Shipman, b. Utica,
NY 10 Feb 1918. Educ: University of Buffalo, B.E.; Albright
School of Fine Arts, Buffalo. Member: Hereditary Order of Desc.
of Colonial Governors; Dau. of American Revolution; U. S. Dau.
of 1812; Colonial Dames of XVII Century; Dau. of American
Colonists; Dau. of Colonial Wars; Dau. of Founders and Patriots
of America; Central NY Genealogical Soc.; Twin Tiers Genealogical
Soc.; Steuben Co. Historical Soc. Address: Lake Road, R.D. #1,
Bath,NY 14810. Descended from:

1 John Webster, Governor of Connecticut, 1656

2 Thomas Webster   Abigail Alexander
   -----   -----   -----
   1686   16 Jun 1663   bf. Mar 1690

3 John Webster   Elizabeth
   Northampton,MA 11 Sep   -----   -----
     1672
   Lebanon,CT 3 Nov 1735   -----

4 John Webster   Mary Dewey
   Lebanon 10 Jul 1702   -----   Lebanon 24 Oct 1704
   Lebanon 1750   20 Aug 1724   -----

5 Daniel Webster   Bridget Holdridge
   Lebanon 29 Apr 1740   -----   Hebron,CT 21 Jun 1740
   Ames,NY 4 Apr 1835   30 Oct 1765   5 Apr 1780

6 Abigail Webster   Aaron Baxter, Jr.
   Lebanon 25 Sep 1766   -----   Hebron 1766
   Tuscarora,NY 19 Feb   1786   Tuscarora 6 Dec 1836
     1833

7 Ira Baxter   Betsy Manley
   Canaan,NY 29 Jun 1787   -----   Otsego,NY 22 May 1795
   Nelson 26 Jan 1838   15 May 1814   Nelson,PA 10 May 1871

8 Susan Vedder Baxter   Joseph Stedman Bottum
   Addison,NY 6 Sep 1831   -----   Mansfield,CT 30 Apr
                                     1820
   Addison 24 Aug 1914   18 Dec 1848   Addison 5 Feb 1897

9 Phebe Elizabeth Bottum   Loren Monroe Webb
   Nelson 16 Mar 1850   -----   Tuscarora 10 Oct 1843
   Addison 31 Dec 1921   4 Aug 1869   Addison 1 Oct 1919

10 Loren Heberling Webb   Alice Elizabeth Currey
   Tuscarora 19 Aug 1892   Addison   Passaic,NJ 8 Jul 1893
   New Brunswick,NJ   28 Apr 1915   Urbana,NY 15 Aug 1962
     3 Feb 1920

SIMS, OLIVIA J. KERBY (MRS. HENRY M.)

Nat. #63-B. Elected 9 Mar 1963. b. Oxon Hill,MD 16 Jan 1898.
m. 10 Oct 1925, Henry McCoy Sims, b. Brevard,NC 10 Feb 1891.
Educ: University of Maryland, B.Sc. (cum laude). Member: Hereditary Order of Desc. of Colonial Governors; Dau. of American
Revolution; Gray Ladies Service at NIH, Bethesda,MD. Address:
503 West Montgomery Ave., Rockville,MD 20850. (From Society's
Records). Descended from:

1 Robert Brooke, Governor of Maryland 1652

2 Thomas Brooke   Eleanor Hatton
   Battle, Eng. 23 Jun   Maryland   England 1642
     1632
   Calvert Co.MD c.1676   1658   Portland Manor,MD
                                              c.1725

3 Clement Brooke   Jane Sewall
   Calvert Co. c.1676   Maryland   St. Mary's Co.,MD
   Prince George's Co.,MD   bf.31 Aug 1704 Prince George's Co.
     c.1736/7   1761

4 Henry Brooke   Margaret
   Prince George's Co.   Maryland   -----
     1704
   Prince George's Co.   -----   Prince George's Co.
     1751   1792

5 Nicholas Brooke   Miss Hill
   Prince George's Co.   Maryland   Prince George's Co.
     1752
   Prince George's Co.   -----   -----
     1797

6 Clement Hill Brooke   Ann Carroll
   Prince George's Co.   Surrattsville   Surrattsville,MD
     c.1778   1799
   Prince George's Co.   -----   Silver Hill,MD 23 Jul
     28 Aug 1854   1879

7 Clement H. Brooke   Margaret E. Jenkins
   Surrattsville 25 Feb   Washington,DC   Surrattsville 15 Jan
     1832   1844
   Silver Hill 4 Apr 1917   23 Dec 1869   Silver Hill 5 Dec 1915

8 Eugenia Brooke   John H. Kerby
   Silver Hill 10 Jul   -----   Oxon Hill,MD 10 Aug
     1870   1864
   Washington,DC 19 Nov   7 Feb 1893   Oxon Hill 29 Jun 1936
     1954

   Inheritor: Henry Kerby, 8407 Indian Head Hwy., Oxon Hill,MD
   20022

SLOWINSKI, ANNETTE C. ROBERTS (MRS. WALTER A.)

Nat. #348-B. Elected 28 Jul 1979. b. Washington,DC 21 Jul 1928.
m. Washington,DC 31 Jan 1953, Walter Aloysius Slowinski, b. 28
Oct 1920. Member: Hereditary Order of Desc. of Colonial
Governors; Society of Colonial Dames, MD; Desc. of Maryland
Manors; Jamestowne Society; Dau. of the Cincinnati; Junior
League; Cosmos Club. Address: 4400 Edmunds St., N.W., Washing-
ton,DC 20007. Descended from:

1 Edward Digges, Governor of Virginia 1655-56

2 William Digges   Elizabeth Sewell
  York Co.VA   -----   -----
  Prince George's Co.,   -----   Prince George's Co.
    MD 1697/8   1710

3 Charles Digges   Susanna Maria Lowe
  Prince George's Co.   -----   16--
    168-
  Prince George's Co.   17--   17--
    1744

4 Mary Digges   Clement Hill III
  Compton Basset,MD   -----   Prince George's Co.
    11 Jan 1715   4 Jan 1707
  Prince George's Co.   11 Jan 1737   Prince George's Co.
    16 Jan 1756   12 Feb 1782

5 Clement Hill IV   Eleanor Brent
  Upper Marlboro,MD   Pr.Geo.Co.   Charles Co.MD 17--
    6 Nov 1743
  Upper Marlboro   13 Dec 1774   Upper Marlboro 8 May
    6 Feb 1807   1827

6 Richard Smith Hill   Elizabeth Snowden Hall
  Upper Marlboro 27 Dec   Up. Marlboro   Prince George's Co.
    1816   1831
  Upper Marlboro 1878   1 May 1854   Washington,DC 1898

7 Francis William Hill   Grace Harrison Claggett
  Upper Marlboro 20 Oct   Up. Marlboro   Upper Marlboro 16 Dec
    1866   1864
  Washington,DC 9 Dec   16 Oct 1889   Washington,DC 7 Nov
    1947   1955

8 Mary Hill   Joseph William Roberts
  Upper Marlboro 31 Jul   Washington,DC   Landover,MD 22 Oct
    1897   1892
  Washington,DC 4 Nov   25 Aug 1925   Charles Co.MD 17 Nov
    1973   1962

SUPPLEMENT NO. 1

1 Giles Brent, Governor of Maryland 1643-44

2 Giles Brent   Mary Brent (cousin)
  Stafford Co.VA 5 Apr   -----   -----
    1652
  Middlesex Co.VA   c.1670   -----
    2 Sep 1679

3 William Brent   Sarah Gibbons
   Richland,VA c.1677   Stafford Co.MD -----
   Middlesex,Eng. 26 Nov 12 May 1709   -----
      1709

4 William Brent   Jane
   England 6 Mar 1710   -----   -----
   Aquia,MD 17 Aug 1742   Jun 1730   -----

5 William Brent   Eleanor Carroll
   Richland 26 Jul 1733   -----   -----
   Jan-Apr 1782   1754   May 1827

6 Eleanor Brent   Clement Hill IV

Continue with Generation 5 of her lineage from Governor
Edward Digges.

                    SUPPLEMENT NO. 2

1 Robert Brooke, Governor of Maryland 1652

2 Thomas Brooke   Eleanor Hatton
   Battle,Eng. 23 Jun   -----   London,Eng. 1642
      1632
   w.p. 29 Dec 1676   1658   Feb 1725

3 Thomas Brooke   Barbara Dent
   Prince George's Co.MD Maryland   MD 1676
      c.1659
   Prince George's Co.   -----   MD 1754
      7 Jan 1730/1

4 Jane Brooke   Alexander Contee
   -----   -----   Barnstable, England
                                            Apr 1693
   Jun 1779   1720   24 Dec 1740

5 Catherine Contee   John Harrison
   1732   -----   -----
   -----   31 Jul 1831   -----

6 Sarah Contee Harrison   Henry Waring, Jr.
   Jun 17--   -----   Jun 1779
   -----   1802   -----

7 Grace Harrison Waring   Richard Henry Clagett
   1812   Up.Marlboro,MD 1809
   -----   19 Nov 1866   1851

8 Henry Waring Clagett   Martha Chum Bowling
   1840   -----   -----
   6 Jun 1914   -----   -----

9 Grace Harrison Clagett   Francis William Hill
   Upper Marlboro   Up.Marlboro   Upper Marlboro 20 Oct
      16 Dec 1864   1866
   Washington,DC 7 Nov   16 Oct 1889   Washington,DC 9 Dec
      1955   1947

Continue with Generation 7 of her lineage from Governor
Edward Digges.

1 Richard Bennett, Governor of Maryland 1652

2 Richard Bennett   Henrietta Marie Neal
   -----   -----   Spain 27 Mar 1647
   1667   -----   Talbot Co.MD 21 May
                                                        1697

3 Susannah M. Bennett   (2)   Henry Lowe
   1667   -----   c.1660
   28 Jul 1714   -----   St.Mary's Co.MD 1717

4 Susanna Maria Lowe   Charles Digges

   Continue with Generation 3 of her lineage from Governor
   Edward Digges.

   Inheritor: Mary Carroll Slowinski, 4400 Edmunds St., NW,
   Washington,DC 20007.

SMALLWOOD, GRAHAME THOMAS, JR.

Nat. #21-B. Elected 17 Mar 1960. b. Toledo,OH 26 Feb 1919.
Educ: Collège Moderne, Geneva,Switzerland; Lycée de St. Gilles,
Brussels, Belgium. Member: Hereditary Order of Desc. of Colonial
Governors (Hon. Governor General); Order of Founders and Patriots
of America (Past Governor General); Americans of Royal Descent
(Past President General and Life Member); Order of Americans of
Armorial Ancestry (Past President and Life Member); Order of
Three Crusades (Past 2nd Vice President General, Past Registrar
General, Life Member); Order of the Crown of Charlemagne (2nd
Vice President General, Life Member); Order of the Crown in
America (Registrar General for life, Life Member); Military Order
of the Crusades (Commander General, Life Member); Baronial Order
of Magna Charta (Past Marshal, Life Member); Americans of
Lafayette (Past National President); Ancient and Honorable
Artillery Co. of MA (Life Member); Order of First Families of
Virginia; Jamestowne Society of Virginia; National Huguenot
Society (Past Vice President General and Curator General); Soc.
of Desc. of Colonial Clergy (Life Member); Colonial Society of
PA (Past Treasurer); Sons and Dau. of Pilgrims (Past Councillor
General and District Governor); Sons of American Revolution
(Past Librarian and State President); Children of American
Revolution (Honorary Senior National Vice President); Gen. Soc.
of War of 1812 (Vice President,PA); Gen. Soc. of Colonial Wars
(Past Assistant Registrar, DC, Verifying Genealogist PA Soc.);
Soc. of Sons of St. George of Philadelphia (Historian and
Treasurer); Royal Soc. of St. George, London, Eng.; Soc. of Desc.
of Knights of the Garter, Windsor Castle (Life Member); Dutch
Colonial Society of Delaware (Genealogist); Netherland Society of
Philadelphia (Past Membership Chairman and Executive Board);
Dutch Settlers Society of Albany; Sons of Revolution (PA, Verify-
ing Genealogist); St. Nicholas Society of NYC; Military Order of
Loyal Legion, PA Commandery; Military Order of Foreign Wars in
U.S., PA Commandery; Sons of Union Veterans of Civil War; St.
Andrews Soc. of NY and Philadelphia; Flagon and Trencher Soc.;
Welsh Soc. of Philadelphia; Society of Mayflower Desc. in PA

(Deputy Governor); Hereditary Order of Loyalists and Patriots
of America (Past Treasurer General); Military and Hospitaller
Order of St. Lazarus of Jerusalem; Knight of Grace; International
Constantinian Order, Chevalier; Sovereign Military Order of the
Temple of Jerusalem (Knight Grand Croix); Genealogical and
Historical Societies of PA; National Genealogical Society; PA
Academy of Fine Arts; Soc. of Genealogists, London, England;
National Gavel Club (Treasurer); Utah Genealogical Soc.;
American Legion (Vice Commander, Benjamin Franklin Post, Phila.);
Boy Scouts of America (National Board and Regional Board Member);
English Speaking Union; Honorary Order of Kentucky Colonels.
Awards: Boy Scouts - Silver Beaver Award; SAR Minuteman and
Patriot's Medal Award; Citation for Outstanding Performance,
Crusade for Freedom, in support of Radio Free Europe from Henry
Ford II; Certificate of Appreciation from the American Red Cross
for serving as company recruiter for the Washington Regional
Blood Center for ten years. Occup: Trans World Airlines, Reg.
Mgr. (Ret.). Address: 45 East 200 North, Apt. 6, Salt Lake City,
UT 84103. Descended from:

1 John Leverett, Governor of Massachusetts 1672-79

2 Rebecca Leverett   James Lloyd
   Boston 5 Dec 1664   Boston,MA   England 1646
   1738/9   3 Nov 1691   Boston Jul 1693

3 Rebecca Lloyd   James Oliver
   Boston 4 May 1694   Boston   Boston 27 Oct 1687
   1739   11 Jan 1711   -----

4 Mary Oliver   William Ellsworth
   Boston 21 Nov 1712   -----   Windsor,CT 15 Apr 1702
   -----   16 Jun 1737   Harwinton,CT 19 Jan
                                             1759

5 Jemina Ellsworth   David Hayden
   Harwinton 4 Sep 1742   Harwinton   Haydens,CT 8 Oct 1738
   Angelica,NY 13 Feb   11 Mar 1761   Angelica 3 Feb 1813
   1828

6 Jemina Hayden   Nehemiah Hubbell
   Harwinton 25 Feb 1764 -----   Fairfield,CT 7 Apr
                                             1764
   Bath,NY 20 Dec 1842   5 Oct 1797   Painted Post,NY 21 Jun
                                             1835

7 William Spring Hubbell   Maria McCall
   Painted Post 17 Jan   -----   Ovid,NY 18 Jun 1801
   1801
   Bath 8 Nov 1873   5 Sep 1822   Bath 18 Mar 1858

8 William Butler Hubbell   Mary Eliza Parmelee
   Bath 11 Jul 1833   Buffalo,NY   Lockport,NY 17 Aug 1841
   Bath, 25 Aug 1905   11 Jul 1865   Gulfport,MS 15 Mar 1914

9 Edward Parmelee Hubbell   Ermina Cadwell Pheatt
   Buffalo 7 Feb 1869   Toledo,OH   Toledo 28 Dec 1869
   Washington,DC 8 Aug   12 Feb 1895   Washington,DC 9 Feb
   1951   1956

10 Dorothy Hubbell   Graeme Thomas Smallwood
   Toledo 17 Dec 1895   Washington,DC   Revere,MA 2 Aug 1897
   Living in Washington,DC 12 Mar 1918   Washington,DC 25 Apr
                                          1947

SUPPLEMENT NO. 1

1 Thomas Roberts, Governor of New Hampshire 1640-41

2 Anne Roberts   James Philbrick
  -----   -----   Bures,Eng. bp.2 Dec
                                       1619
  -----   -----   Hampton,NH 16 Nov 1674

3 Thomas Philbrick   Mehitable Dalton Ayres
   Hampton 14 Mar 1659   -----   Hampton 3 Nov 1658
   Kingston,NH 1 Jan   14 Apr 1681   -----
     1712

4 Ann Philbrick   Stephen Berry
   Hampton 12 Mar 1691   -----   New Castle,NH 18 Jan
                                       1690/1
  -----   4 Jan 1716   NH 1762-5

5 Stephen Berry   Mary Allen
   New Castle 21 Apr 1724 -----   -----
   4 Apr 1792   -----   -----

6 Lydia Berry   David Allard
   11 Feb 1741   -----   Rochester,NH 14 Oct
                                       1743
   Eaton,NH 18 Feb 1839   -----   Eaton 28 Nov 1831

7 Betsy Allard   Joseph Clark
  -----   -----   Rochester,NH 1755
   Eaton 9 Jun 1841   1783   Tamworth,NH 17 Aug 1849

8 Samuel Clark   Patience Mooney
   Porter,ME 3 Jan 1787   Eaton   Eaton 2 Jan 1794
   Eaton 2 Feb 1849   11 Nov 1813   Eaton 3 Mar 1859

9 Phoebe Ann Clark   Richard Wesley Robinson
   Eaton 10 Sep 1827   Lowell,MA   Warwick,Eng. 20 Dec
                                       1826
   Washington,DC 9 Jan   15 Oct 1845   Revere,MA 8 Jan 1910
     1906

10 Della Graeme Robinson   George Thomas Smallwood
   Lawrence,MA 27 Apr   Dorchester,MA Newton,MA 21 Jan 1854
     1862
   Washington,DC 7 Feb   27 Jun 1888   Washington,DC 9 Sep
     1930   1929

11 Graeme Thomas Smallwood   Dorothy Hubbell

Continue with Generation 10 of his lineage from Governor John
Leverett.

1 John Coggeshall, President of Newport Colony, Rhode Island 1647-48

2 John Coggeshall II, Acting Governor of Rhode Island 1686-90

			Elizabeth Baulstone
	England 1620	Newport	England Aug 1629
	Newport 1 Oct 1708	17 Jun 1647	Portsmouth 1 Oct 1700

3 John Coggeshall   Elizabeth Timberlake
  Portsmouth 12 Feb   Newport   -----
    1649/50
  Portsmouth 9 Nov 1706   24 Dec 1670   -----

4 Mary Coggeshall   William Anthony
  Portsmouth 18 Sep 1675 Portsmouth   Portsmouth 31 Oct 1675
  af. 1737   14 Mar 1695   Swansea,RI 28 Dec 1744

5 James Anthony   Alice Chace
  Swansea,RI 9 Nov 1712   Swansea,RI   3 Mar 1717
  Swansea,MA 31 May 1748 11 Dec 1734   Swansea,MA 1748

6 Hannah Anthony   Marmaduke Mason
  Swansea 19 Feb 1735/6   Swansea,MA   Swansea 14 Sep 1732
  Warren,RI 25 Feb 1774   25 Feb 1752   Warren 28 Jun 1798

7 Joseph Mason   Lovina Rounds
  Warren 12 Aug 1759   Swansea,MA   Warren 1758
  Herkimer,NY c.1796   9 Sep 1778   Herkimer,NY

8 Lovina Mason   Eli Frink
  Warren 15 Apr 1788   Fairfield,NY   Peru,MA 11 Jun 1783
  Herkimer 26 Jul 1816   10 Sep 1806   Rochester,NY 14 Mar
                                              1829

9 Ermina Frink   Isaac Tichenor Pheatt
  Herkimer 15 Sep 1809   Rochester   Liverpool,NY 15 Apr
                                              1808
  Toledo,OH 11 Oct 1881   3 Dec 1829   Toledo 11 May 1859

10 Zebulon Converse Pheatt   Sarah Amanda Cadwell
   Cape Vincent,NY   Cape Vincent   Turin,NY 17 Feb 1832
     21 Dec 1832
   Toledo 7 Jul 1901   21 May 1867   Toledo 27 Aug 1903

11 Ermina Cadwell Pheatt   Edward Parmelee Hubbell

Continue with Generation 9 of his lineage from Governor John Leverett.

Inheritor: Paul M. Niebell, Jr., 7825 Mary Cassatt Drive, Potomac, MD 20854.

SMITH, ARNOLD

Nat. #246-B. Elected 20 Oct 1974. b. Ogdensburg,NY 9 Apr 1900.
Educ: Hamilton College; Harvard University, M.B.A. Member:
Hereditary Order of Desc. of Colonial Governors; Sons of Ameri-
can Revolution; Soc. of Mayflower Descendants (MA and VA); Soc.
of Colonial Wars; Phi Beta Kappa. Address: 7 Lake Road,
Farmington, Charlottesville,VA 22901. Descended from:

1 Gregory Dexter, Governor of Rhode Island 1653-54

2	James Dexter Providence,RI 6 May 1650	-----	Esther Arnold 22 Sep 1647
	1676	af.1671	af.1688
3	James Dexter ----- 23 Jan 1732	----- -----	Sarah ----- af.1732
4	Peleg Dexter ----- Glocester,RI 26 Sep 1789	Providence 15 Feb 1732/3 -----	Mary Smith ----- -----
5	Gideon Dexter Providence c.1795	----- -----	Freelove ----- -----
6	Mercy Dexter c.1775 -----	Glocester Mar 1800	Arnold Smith ----- Hammond,NY 21 Mar 1853
7	Chauncey Smith Morristown,NY 2 Jan 1815 Hammond 22 Apr 1875	----- 9 Jan 1840	Elizabeth E. Pond Addison,VT 30 May 1817 -----
8	Arnold Smith Hammond 2 Feb 1841 16 Jan 1914	Ogdensburg,NY 14 Apr 1864	Almira L. Brown ----- -----
9	Edwin C. Smith Ogdensburg 8 Aug 1867 21 Nov 1942	Ogdensburg 24 Apr 1899	Edith F. Ives ----- -----

SMITH, BARBARA JEAN CARVER (MRS. WILLIAM A.)

Nat. #216-B. Elected 15 Sep 1973. b. Long Branch,NJ 14 Dec
1932. m. Avon-by-the-Sea,NJ 29 May 1954, William Alfred Smith,
b. Linden,NJ 2 Sep 1928. Issue: Suzanne Patricia Smith, b.
Neptune,NJ 18 Apr 1956; William Douglas Smith, b. Neptune 11 Aug
1958; Michele Diane Smith, b. Neptune 3 Jul 1963. Educ: Mon-
mouth Adult Education School, Medical Secretary. Member:
Hereditary Order of Desc. of Colonial Governors (Recording
Secretary General); Dau. of American Revolution; Dau. of American
Colonists; Soc. of Desc. of Colonial Clergy; Colonial Dames of
XVII Century (Charter member of NJ Chap.); Monmouth County
Historical Soc.; New England Women; Huguenot Soc. of NJ. Occup:
Part-time Medical Secretary. Address: 227 Garfield Ave., Avon-
by-the-Sea,NJ 07717. Descended from:

1 Thomas Roberts, Governor of New Hampshire 1640-41

```
2  Hester Roberts                          John Martin
   Dover,NH 1628           Dover          Devon,Eng. 1620
   Piscattaway,NJ 6 Dec    -----          Piscattaway 7 Jul 1687
      1687

3  Joseph Martin                           Sarah Trotter
   NH 1652                 -----           Elizabethtown,NJ
   Piscattaway 1723        25 Nov 1679     -----

4  Joseph Martin                           Elizabeth Merritt
   Piscattaway 1682        Woodbridge,NJ   -----
   Piscattaway Jun 1757    1725            -----

5  William Martin                          Sarah Moore
   Woodbridge 1727         Woodbridge      1728
   Woodbridge 1804         -----           Woodbridge 1795

6  Sarah Martin                            Edward Crowell
   Woodbridge 16 Mar 1756  Woodbridge      Woodbridge 3 Apr 1761
   Woodbridge 31 Dec 1820  -----           Woodbridge 11 Nov 1800

7  James Crowell                           Betsey Lee
   Woodbridge 20 Dec 1781  Woodbridge      2 Apr 1785
   Woodbridge 30 Jan 1864  -----           Woodbridge 25 May 1824

8  Joseph L. Crowell                       Hannah Langstaff
   Woodbridge 16 Jul 1816  Perth Amboy     Philadelphia,PA 20 Apr
                                              1819
   Perth Amboy,NJ 14 Jun   5 Feb 1840      At Sea 3 Jun 1852
      1886

9  Caroline V. Crowell                     Silas W. Barton
   Richmond,VA 2 Jul 1849  Perth Amboy     Adelphia,NJ 31 May 1847
   Neptune,NJ 3 Aug 1915   1868            Spring Lake Heights,NJ
                                              4 Apr 1931

10 James S. Barton                         Lillian M. Alexander
   Ocean Grove,NJ 13 Jul   West Grove,NJ   Hoboken,NJ 22 Jun 1879
      1878
   Asbury Park,NJ 14 Jul   29 Jan 1905     Long Branch,NJ 4 Nov
      1956                                    1931

11 Charlotte Virginia                      Carroll Noel Carver
      Barton
   Asbury Park 29 Jan      Elkton,MD       Bradley Beach,NJ
      1907                                    8 Dec 1904
                           30 Jan 1927     Neptune 9 Nov 1970
```

SUPPLEMENT NO. 1

```
1  Thomas Mayhew Sr., Governor of Martha's Vineyard 1647-81

2  Thomas Mayhew, Jr.                      Jane Paine
   England c.1620/1        Edgartown,MA    London,Eng. c.1625
   At Sea 1657             c.1647          Martha's Vineyard

3  Jerusha Mayhew             (2)          Thomas Eaton
   Tisbury,MA 1654         -----           England
   Shrewsbury,NJ           12 Dec 1684     Shrewsbury 26 Nov 1688
```

4 John Eaton
   Shrewsbury 26 Mar 1689   Shrewsbury
   Shrewsbury 1 Apr 1750   -----

   Joanna Wardell
   Shrewsbury
   af.1750

5 Joseph Eaton   (2)
   Shrewsbury 1716   -----
   Shrewsbury 5 Apr 1761   -----

   Lucy Mayhew
   Chilmark,MA 4 Jul 1716
   Shrewsbury

6 John Eaton
   Shrewsbury 1747   -----
   -----   -----

   Lydia Brinley
   Shrewsbury 3 Jun 1751
   -----

7 Elizabeth Eaton
   Shrewsbury 21 Sep 1773   Shrewsbury
   Ocean,NJ 20 Aug 1862   2 Oct 1791

   Samuel Slocum
   Shrewsbury 19 Aug 1764
   Shrewsbury 13 May 1842

8 Rebecca Slocum
   Shrewsbury 7 Mar 1812   Shrewsbury
   Eatontown,NJ 16 May   17 Oct 1829
     1898

   Gavin Drummond White
   Hamilton,NJ 3 Aug 1811
   Hamilton 17 May 1872

9 Asbury B. White
   Hamilton 29 Oct 1847   -----

   Neptune,NJ 7 Aug 1920   c.1875

   Deborah Annie Truex
   Burrsville,NJ 8 Jan
     1858
   Neptune 21 Jul 1918

10 Lizzie Truex White
   Burrsville 24 Aug 1878   -----

   Bradley Beach,NJ   24 Aug 1898
     8 May 1950

   Asher Curtis Carver
   Point Pleasant Beach,NJ
     17 May 1878
   Bradley Beach 5 Jul
     1946

11 Carroll Noel Carver,Sr.

   Charlotte Virginia
   Barton

Continue with Generation 11 of her lineage from Governor
Thomas Roberts.

SMITH, HELEN SALOME TUTTLE (MRS. LEN YOUNG)

Nat. #338-B. Elected 10 Apr 1978. b. East St. Louis,IL 28 Jun
1903. m. Buchanan,MI 7 Aug 1930, Len Young Smith, b. Nicholas-
ville,KY 20 Oct 1901. Issue: Margaret Helen Smith (Mrs. Roger
Dean Smith); William Ransom Tuttle Smith. Educ: Northwestern
University, B.S.; University of Wisconsin, M.S. Member: Heredi-
tary Order of Desc. of Colonial Governors; Desc. of John &
Eliz. Curtiss; Dau. of Founders and Patriots (Past Natl. Presi-
dent); Dau. of American Revolution (Past Vice President General);
Order of Americans of Armorial Ancestry (Past Natl. President);
Huguenot Society; Colonial Dames of America; New England Women;
Dau. of American Colonists; Soc. of Mayflower Descendants;
Colonial Dau. of 17th Century; Women Desc. of Ancient and Honor-
able Artillery Co.; Dau. of Colonial Wars; National Gavel Soc.;
U.S. Daughters of 1812; Descendants of Hartford; John Howland
Soc.; Order of Crown of Charlemagne; Colonial Coverlet Guild.
Address: 109 Fuller Lane, Winnetka,IL 60093. Descended from:

1 Thomas Welles, Governor of Connecticut 1655, 1658

2	John Welles		Elizabeth Bourne
	England 1621	Stratford,CT	Stratford c.1627
	Stratford 7 Aug 1659	1647	Fairfield,CT c.1662
3	Robert Welles		Elizabeth Goodrich
	Stratford c.1648	Wethersfield	Wethersfield,CT 1658
	Wethersfield 22 Jun 1714	9 Jun 1675	Wethersfield 17 Feb 1698
4	Prudence Welles		Anthony Stoddard
	Wethersfield c.1682	-----	Northampton,MA 9 Aug 1678
	16 Apr 1715	20 Oct 1700	Woodbury,CT 6 Sep 1760
5	Eliakim Stoddard		Joanna Curtiss
	Woodbury 30 Apr 1705	-----	Woodbury 5 Sep 1708
	Woodbury 30 Sep 1749	4 Dec 1729	-----
6	John Stoddard		Mary Atwood
	Watertown,CT 26 Jan 1730	-----	20 Apr 1733
	Harwinton,CT 22 Jan 1795	15 Apr 1751	Charleston,NY 16 Jan 1802
7	Samson Stoddard		Amy Goodwin
	25 Oct 1752	-----	Litchfield,CT 10 Jul 1753
	11 Nov 1809	22 Nov 1780	15 Sep 1827
8	Anna Stoddard		William Ransom Tolles
	17 Aug 1788	-----	18 Jan 1787
	Burton,OH 14 Sep 1846	9 Apr 1809	Burton 24 Sep 1846
9	Abigail Theresa Tolles		John Tuttle
	Woodbury 23 Jun 1812	Watertown,CT	Woodbury 15 Aug 1810
	Burton 6 Jun 1881	29 Feb 1836	Burton 12 Dec 1863
10	Albert John Tuttle		Sarah Thompson
	Burton 18 Sep 1840	Middlefield,OH	Middlefield 6 Jan 1842
	Burton 23 Feb 1921	6 Jan 1865	Oberlin,OH 21 Apr 1909
11	William Ransom Tuttle		Fannie Lesbia Beardsley
	Burton 10 Oct 1868	Buchanan,MI	17 Oct 1870
	Buchanan 16 Jul 1941	7 Aug 1902	Evanston,IL 11 Apr 1956

Inheritor: Mrs. Roger Dean Smith, 1238 Hayward Ave., Cincinnati, OH 45226.

SMITH, CDR. JOHN HENRY BRONSON

Nat. #211-B. Elected 23 Jul 1973. b. Chicago,IL 1 Jul 1897. m.(1) Seattle,WA 11 Jul 1920, Elsie L. Steele, b. Clarmont,FL 8 Nov 1898. Issue: John Stephen Bronson Smith. m.(2) Seattle, WA 24 Oct 1942, Angie Margaret Messner, b. Calumet,MI 10 Feb 1900. Educ: Univ. of Washington, Seattle, B.S.F. in Logging Engr. Member: Hereditary Order of Desc. of Colonial Governors; Soc. of Mayflower Desc. in DC (Past Treas.); Sons of American Revolution; Military: CDR. U.S.N.(Ret.), Bronze Star. Address: 5601 Seminary Rd., Apt. #510-N., Falls Church,VA 22041. Descended fr:

1 Thomas Mayhew, Governor of Martha's Vineyard 1647-81

2 Hannah Mayhew   Thomas Doggett
   Watertown,MA 15 Apr   -----   Watertown c.1630
   1635
   Edgartown,MA 1722   -----   Edgartown c.1691

3 Thomas Doggett   Elizabeth Hawes
   Edgartown c.1658   -----   Yarmouth,MA 5 Oct 1662
   Edgartown 23 Aug 1726   23 Jan 1683   Edgartown 1732/3

4 Jemima Doggett   Malachi Butler
   c.1694   -----   -----
   c.1789   -----   -----

5 Benjamin Butler   Dorcas Abbott
   Windham,CT 19 May 1729   Andover,NH   Andover 11 May 1729
   Nottingham,NH 26 Dec   5 May 1753   Nottingham 19 Apr 1789
   1804

6 Mary Butler   Abraham Brown
   Nottingham 30 Mar 1760   Epping,NH   Nottingham 8 May 1753
   Northfield,NH 1846   27 May 1777   Northfield 8 Mar 1824

7 Henry Butler Brown   Laura Ticknor
   Northfield 4 Jul 1802   Plainfield,NH Plainfield 11 Jun 1804
   Big Rapids,MI 13 Dec   24 Jan 1829   Chicago,IL 21 Dec 1867
   1872

8 Katherine M. Brown   Stephen Bronson
   Windsor,VT 26 Nov 1829   Wheaton,IL   Broome Co.NY 3 Aug 1817
   Seattle,WA 8 Dec 1915   14 Feb 1867   Big Rapids 19 Jul 1896

9 Katherine L. Bronson   Coy J. Smith
   Big Rapids 10 Jul 1870   Big Rapids   Barry Co.MI 24 Oct 1873
   Arlington,VA 29 Jun   30 Jun 1896   Coronado,CA 18 Feb 1952
   1956

   Inheritor: John Stephen Bronson Smith

SMITH, LOIS ELIZABETH DODSON (MRS. ROBAH LEE)

Nat. #144-B. Elected 20 Jun 1968. b. Walnut Cove,NC 24 Jun
1918. Educ: Draughan Business College, Winston-Salem,NC.
Member: Hereditary Order of Desc. of Colonial Governors; Dau. of
American Revolution; Colonial Daughters of Seventeenth Century.
Occup: Administrative Assistant of Federal Home Loan Bank,
Greensboro,NC and Ft. Lauderdale,FL. Address: P.O. Box 52,
Walnut Cove,NC 27052. Descended from:

1 William Stone, Governor of Maryland 1648-53

2 John Stone   Elizabeth Warren
   Accomac Co.VA 1640   -----   -----
   Maryland 1698   -----   -----

3 Thomas Stone   Martha Hoskins
   1677   -----   Charles Co.VA c.1680
   1727   -----   -----

4	Thomas Stone		Mary Butler
	Charles Co. c.1700	-----	-----
	Prince William Co.VA	c.1720	-----
	24 Nov 1748		

5	John Stone		Miss Corder
	Virginia c.1747	-----	-----
	Surry Co.NC af.1780	-----	-----

6	Enoch Stone, Sr.		Nancy Anthony
	Surry Co.	Surry Co.	-----
	Surry Co. Aug/Sep 1823	c.1784	-----

7	Enoch Stone, Jr.		Elizabeth Gordon
	Surry Co. 8 Nov 1791	Surry Co.	Surry Co. 28 Mar 1797
	Surry Co. 11 Oct 1874	21 Oct 1819	Surry Co. 26 Mar 1877

8	John Clayborn Dodson		Rhoda Elizabeth Stone
	Surry Co. 4 Apr 1831	Surry Co.	Surry Co. 1 Jun 1833
	Surry Co. 8 Aug 1891	2 May 1861	Surry Co. 20 Jul 1891

9	Wesley Greenville Dodson	(2)	Salome (Dolly) Fair
	Surry Co. 27 Nov 1867	-----	Madison,NC 9 Sep 1881
	Walnut Cove,NC 23 Sep 1924	17 May 1917	Walnut Cove 24 Oct 1956

SNIFFEN, ELEANOR A. SAUER (MRS. ALLAN M., III)

Nat. #151-B. Elected 14 Jul 1969. b. Bridgeport,CT 4 Dec 1924. m. Fairfield,CT 20 Nov 1954, Dr. Allan Mead Sniffen III, b. Hackensack,NJ 7 May 1926. Issue: Allan Mead Sniffen IV, b. 4 Nov 1957; Daniel Burr Sniffen, b. 16 Dec 1959; both b. Nyack, NY. Educ: Middlebury College, B.A. Member: Hereditary Order of Desc. of Colonial Governors; National Huguenot Soc.; Dau. of American Revolution (Reg., Chappaqua,NY Chap.); Dau. of American Colonists; Dau. of Founders and Patriots; Dames of Court of Honor; Soc. of Desc. of Colonial Clergy; Soc. of Founders of Hartford. Address: Wood Road, Bedford Hills,NY 10507. Descended from:

1 Thomas Welles, Governor of Connecticut 1655-58

2	John Welles		Elizabeth Bourne
	England 1621	Stratford,CT	Stratford c.1627
	Stratford 7 Aug 1659	1647	Fairfield,CT c.1662

3	John Welles		Mary Hollister
	Stratford c.1648	-----	Wethersfield,CT
	Stratford 1713	c.1669	1732

4	Robert Welles		Eunice Curtis
	Stratford Sep 1688	Stratford	1 Aug 1699
	Stratford 1758	24 Oct 1720	-----

5	Samuel Welles		Hannah
	Stratford 24 Apr 1736	-----	-----
	Stratford 1782	-----	-----

6   Hannah Welles   William Fairchild
    Stratford bp. Jun 1767   Stratford   Stratford 1769
    Stratford 8 Oct 1835   by 1793   Stratford 27 Sep 1841

7   Susan Fairchild   William Plumb
    Stratford 1804   Stratford   Stratford 31 Dec 1797
    Stratford 1848   19 Oct 1823   Stratford 11 Oct 1880

8   Mary E. Plumb   Truman Hotchkiss
    Stratford 22 Nov 1824   Stratford   Derby,CT 10 Apr 1816
    Stratford 3 Mar 1914   31 Dec 1845   Stratford 11 Sep 1880

9   William D. Hotchkiss   Eleanora R. Choate
    Stratford 10 Jul 1848   New York City New York 23 Oct 1853
    Fairfield,CT 15 Dec   13 Sep 1876   Fairfield 29 Sep 1925
      1925

10 Ethel A. Hotchkiss   Frederick Sauer
    NY 21 Jun 1891   New York City NY 17 Dec 1890
                     27 Oct 1923

SUPPLEMENT NO. 1

1   Andrew Ward, Governor of Connecticut 1635-36

2   Ann Ward   Caleb Nichols
    c.1629   -----   -----
    Woodbury,CT 23 Jul   c.1649   Woodbury 14 Aug 1690
      1718

3   Mary Nichols   Joseph Hull
    Stratford c.1665   Derby,CT   Stratford 16 Feb 1668
    Derby 6 Apr 1733   20 Jan 1691   Derby 5 Oct 1744

4   Samuel Hull   Anna Riggs
    Derby 15 Nov 1692   Derby   Derby 10 Jun 1704
    Derby   15 Jan 1724   Derby 22 Mar 1731

5   Eunice Hull   John Wooster
    Derby 19 Nov 1727   Derby   Derby 22 Dec 1719
    Derby 17 Nov 1799   18 Jun 1746   Oxford,CT 2 Aug 1804

6   Elizabeth A. Wooster   Truman Loveland
    Derby 1766   Oxford   Watertown,CT bp.12 Oct
                                      1760
    Seymour,CT 31 Mar 1842   -----   Humphreysville,CT
                                      12 Mar 1839

7   Ruth A. Loveland   David Hotchkiss
    Oxford 18 May 1790   Derby   Derby 13 Feb 1788
    Stratford 29 Apr 1875   24 Oct 1811   Stratford 10 Mar 1845

8   Truman Hotchkiss   Mary E. Plumb

Continue with Generation 8 of her lineage from Governor Thomas Welles.

Inheritor: Allan Mead Sniffen IV and Daniel Burr Sniffen

SOOY, HELEN GIBERSON (MRS. LESLIE M.)

Nat. #223-B. Elected 1 Dec 1973. b. Smithville,NJ 12 May 1899.
m. Oceanville,NJ 20 Sep 1925, Leslie M. Sooy, b. Leeds Point,NJ
28 Jan 1897. Educ: Atlantic City High School. Member: Heredi-
tary Order of Desc. of Colonial Governors; Lafayette Dau. of
American Revolution; Huguenot Society of NJ; Eastern Star (Worthy
Matron and Secretary); Church Executive Board (Past Pres.);
AARP. Address: 1300 New York Road, Oceanville,NJ 08231.
Descended from:

1 John Endicott, Governor of Massachusetts 1629-65

2 Zerubabel Endicott   Mary Smith
   Salem,MA 1635   Salem   Salem c.1636
   Salem Jan 1684   1654   Salem 20 Jun 1667

3 Joseph Endicott   Hannah
   Salem 1672   -----   -----
   Burlington Co.NJ 1747   -----   -----

4 John Endicott   Hannah Fellon
   -----   -----   -----
   -----   -----   -----

5 Benjamin Endicott   Susannah Doughty
   NJ 1741   -----   Gloucester Co.NJ
   Higbeetown,NJ 31 May   c.1749   Higbeetown 15 Jun 1805
      1792

6 Mary Endicott   Jesse S. Higbee
   c.1785   Higbeetown   Galloway,NJ 7 Dec 1782
   2 Mar 1858   -----   c.1824

7 Nicholas E. Higbee   Eliza Smith
   Smithville,NJ 11 Nov   Smithville   Smithville 16 Nov 1813
      1804
   Atlantic City,NJ   -----   Smithville 29 Aug 1888
      23 Apr 1891

8 John Higbee   Abigail Baremore
   Smithville 18 Aug 1840 Absecon,NJ   Brigantine,NJ 12 Aug
                                                 1849
   Smithville 21 Sep 1928 31 Dec 1868   Smithville 31 Dec 1920

9 Eva Higbee   Harvey A. Giberson
   Brigantine,NJ 6 Dec   New Gretna,NJ   Oceanville,NJ 4 Jan
      1869   1870
   Smithville 15 Mar 1947 4 Jul 1893   Smithville 31 Aug 1934

SOUTHERLAND, HENRY DeLEON, JR.

Nat. #95-B. Elected 1 Apr 1964. b. Birmingham,AL 8 Sep 1911.
m. Tuscaloosa,AL 22 Jan 1955, Louise Harris Wilson, b. Jackson,
MS 25 Jul 1912. Issue: Carolyn Wilson Long (Step Dau), b.
Birmingham 31 Jan 1941; Mary Neil Southerland, b. Knoxville,TN
5 Nov 1948. Educ: University of Georgia, B.S.; University of
Tennessee, M.S.; Columbia University, J.D.; Ordnance School;
Command and General Staff College. Member: Hereditary Order of
Desc. of Colonial Governors; Society of the Cincinnati; Sons of
the Revolution (General Vice Pres.); Soc. of War of 1812, AL;
Huguenot Society, SC; Soc. of Desc. of Colonial Clergy; First
Families of Virginia; Military Order of the World Wars; St.
Andrews Soc.; Soc. of Colonial Wars, AL (Deputy Governor);
Fellow, American Soc. of Civil Engineers; American, Alabama, and
Birmingham Bar Assns. Occup: Licensed Engineer, TN (Ret.).
Address: 47 Greenway Road, Birmingham, AL 35213. Descended from:

1 Richard Bennett, Governor of Virginia 1652-55

2 Anne Bennett   Theodoric Bland
   Weyanoke,VA c.1640   Weyanoke   London,Eng. bp.16 Jan
                                                   1629
   Wharton's Creek,MD   1660   Westover,VA 23 Apr 1671
     Nov 1687

3 Richard Bland   (2)   Elizabeth Randolph
   Charles City Co.VA   Henrico Co.VA   Henrico Co. c.1680
     11 Aug 1665
   Charles City Co. 6 Apr   11 Feb 1701   Williamsburg,VA 22 Jan
     1729   1719

4 Anne Bland   Robert Munford
   VA 25 Feb 1711   Virginia   Virginia
   Virginia   -----   VA Dec 1744

5 Robert Munford   Anne Beverley
   Virginia   Virginia   Virginia
   Mecklenburg Co.VA 1784   -----   VA 1784

6 Elizabeth Beverley   Richard Kennon
     Munford
   Mecklenburg Co.   Mecklenburg   VA 1759
     28 Mar 1762   Co.
   Mecklenburg Co.c.1825   16 May 1780   Mecklenburg Co. 1805

7 Erasmus Kennon   Nancy Carter Nelson
   Mecklenburg Co. 19 Sep   Mecklenburg   Mecklenburg Co. 1790
     1786   Co.
   Mecklenburg Co. 1840/2   c.Nov 1808   Mecklenburg Co. 1831

8 Lucy P. Kennon   Edwin A. Williams
   Mecklenburg Co. 3 Oct   Mecklenburg   Charlotte Co.VA 14 Apr
     1817   Co.   1806
   Mecklenburg Co. 17 Oct   4 Mar 1841   Mecklenburg Co. 28 Oct
     1892   1879

9 Edwin A. Williams   Sarah J. Hamilton
   Mecklenburg Co. 6 May   Athens,GA   Columbia Co.GA 2 Feb
     1843   1849
   Rome,GA 10 Oct 1880   5 Mar 1873   Athens 18 Dec 1920

10 Edwina H. Williams   Henry DeLeon
                                                  Southerland

    Rome 13 Jan 1880   Athens   Wilmington,NC 12 Feb 1879

                          2 Oct 1907   Athens 22 Jan 1957

SUPPLEMENT NO. 1

1 William Claiborne, Governor of Maryland 1652

2 Thomas Claiborne   Sarah Fenn
   Romancoke,VA 17 Aug   Virginia   -----
   1647
   Romancoke 7 Oct 1683   c.1670   -----

3 Thomas Claiborne   (3)   Ann West Fox
   Romancoke 16 Dec 1680 King William New Kent Co.VA 20 Jun
                     Co.VA   1684
   VA 16 Aug 1732   -----   VA 4 May 1733

4 Leonard Claiborne   Martha Burnell
   Virginia   Virginia   King William Co. 1 Jan
                               1701
   King William Co.   -----   VA 3 Apr 172-
   af. 1740

5 Martha Claiborne   Patrick Napier
   King William Co.   Albermarle Co. Albermarle Co. 13 Feb
   27 Nov 1717   1713
   Albermarle Co.VA   -----   Goochland Co.VA 23 Aug
   23 Aug 1784   1774

6 Thomas Napier   (2)   Chole Napier
   VA 1736   Goochland Co. Goochland Co. c.1740
   Columbia Co.GA   -----   -----
   c.Mar 1804

7 Ann Fox Napier   James Hamilton
   Albermarle Co.   Fluvanna Co.VA Ulster,Ireland 1746/7
   Columbia Co. 30 Jan 5 Mar 1782   Columbia Co. 31 Jul
   1807   1817

8 Thomas Napier Hamilton   Sarah Sherwood Bugg
   Columbia Co. 3 Feb   Columbia Co. Columbia Co. 28 Oct
   1788   1797
   Athens,GA 7 Nov 1858 14 Jan 1814   Athens 11 Mar 1876

9 James Sherwood   Rebecca Appling
    Hamilton   Crawford
   Columbia Co. 23 Apr Columbia Co. Columbia Co. 25 Oct
   1817   1824
   Athens 28 Oct 1888   26 Sep 1843   Athens 18 Dec 1896

10 Sarah J. Hamilton   Edwin A. Williams

   Continue with Generation 9 of his lineage from Governor
   Richard Bennett.

SUPPLEMENT NO. 2

1 John West, Governor of Virginia 1635-37

```
2  John West                             Unity Croshaw
     Chiskack,VA 1632      Virginia       Poplar Neck,VA
     New Kent Co.VA c.1691  c.1667        VA af.1707

3  Anne West                             Henry Fox
     King William Co.VA    York Co.VA     VA c.1650
     Virginia             1695           King William Co. c.1714

4  Anne West Fox                         Thomas Claiborne, Jr.

   Continue with Generation 3 of his lineage from Governor
   William Claiborne.

   Inheritor: Frank A. White
```

STEARNS, PARLEY MARK, II

Nat. #363-B. Elected 15 Oct 1979. b. Havre-de-Grace,MD 1943.
m.(1) Ft.Hood,TX 9 Oct 1966, Helen Myrle Smallwood, b. Washing-
ton,DC 9 Mar 1945. m.(2) Birmingham,AL 23 Dec 1976, Rebea
Eleaine Roberts, b. Eva,AL 21 Mar 1944. Member: Hereditary
Order of Desc. of Colonial Governors; Soc. of Mayflower Descen-
dants; Founders and Patriots of America; Barons of the Magna
Charta, Sons of American Revolution. Address: Apt. #A, 719 Exec
Ctr Dr., West Palm Beach,FL 33401. Descended from:

```
1  Thomas Prence, Governor of Plymouth Colony 1634-35, 1638-39,
     1657-73

2  Mercy Prence                          John Freeman
     Plymouth,MA 1631      Eastham,MA     England 1621
     Eastham 28 Sep 1711   13 Feb 1649/50 Eastham 28 Oct 1719

3  John Freeman                          Sarah Merrick
     Eastham Dec 1651      Eastham        Eastham 1 Aug 1654
     Hardwick,MA 27 Jul 1721 18 Dec 1672  Eastham 21 Apr 1696

4  John Freeman                          Mercy Watson
     Eastham Jul 1678      -----          -----
     -----                c.1701          -----

5  John Freeman                          Joanna Rickett
     Hardwick 3 Aug 1709   Plympton,MA    Plympton Oct 1709
     Hardwick 24 Jun 1804  29 Jan 1730/1  Hardwick 29 Mar 1797

6  Sarah Freeman                         Stephen Gorham
     Rochester,MA 15 Oct   Hardwick       Yarmouth,MA 29 Jul 1735
       1737
     Hardwick 27 Mar 1820  16 Mar 1758    Hardwick 28 Jan 1806

7  Eli Gorham                            Olive Stearns
     Hardwick 10 May 1775  Dover,VT       Douglas,MA 8 Jun 1779
     Fulton Co.IL 20 Apr   17 Aug 1800    Fulton Co. 4 Mar 1860
       1861

8  Fidelia Octavia Gorham                Edwin Gay Hills
     Homer,NY Feb 1809     Groton,NY      East Hartford,CT
                                            16 Mar 1805
     Belmont,NY Mar 1849   14 Dec 1829    Belmont 3 Jan 1894
```

9 Mary Fidelia Hills   Madison Cleveland
                                                      Stearns
      Belmont 9 Feb 1832   Avon,IL   Naples,NY 10 Mar 1822
      Brady,TX 17 Mar 1924   9 May 1852   Kingfisher,OK 11 Aug
                                                      1899

10 Edwin DeLaney Stearns   Sarah Almena Vredenburgh
      Fulton Co. 26 Apr 1853   Logan,IA   Lamoni,IA 27 Dec 1865
      San Antonio,TX 6 Jan   12 Nov   San Antonio 1 Aug 1951
        1946

11 Roe Vredenburgh Stearns   Ester Belle Knoy
      Preparation,IA   Brady,TX   Pocahontas,AR 5 Aug
        1 Dec 1886   1887
      Mason,TX 19 Nov 1939   22 Feb 1911   Fort Worth,TX 6 Jun
                                                      1944

12 Parley Mark Stearns   Mary Louise Gantt
      Brady 9 Mar 1919   Fort Worth   Fort Worth 27 Oct 1923
                                5 Feb 1942

                          SUPPLEMENT NO. 1

1 John Alden, Governor of Plymouth Colony 1663-4, 1667

2 Elizabeth Alden   William Peabodie
      Plymouth,MA c.1624   Duxbury,MA   England c.1620
      Little Compton,RI   6 Dec 1644   Little Compton 13 Dec
        31 May 1717   1707

3 Mercy Peabodie   John Simmons
      Duxbury 2 Jan 1649/50   Duxbury   Duxbury c.1642
      Duxbury bf.8 Nov 1728   c.1642   Duxbury bf.11 Feb 1715

4 William Simmons   Abigail Church
      Duxbury 24 Feb 1672   Duxbury   Duxbury 1680
      Duxbury 1765   1696   Little Compton 4 Jul
                                                      1720

5 Joseph Simmons   Rebecca Wood
      Little Compton 4 Mar   Little Compton   Little Compton 26 Dec
        1702   1704
      Little Compton 17 Jul   28 Mar 1726   Little Compton
        1778

6 Johanthan Simmons   Abigail Bailey
      Little Compton 20 Aug   Little Compton   Little Compton 27 Oct
        1736   1736
      Little Compton   5 May 1759   Little Compton

7 Sarah Simmons   Timothy Chase
      Little Compton 18 May   Little Compton   Little Compton 14 Feb
        1761   1760
      Little Compton 28 Aug   2 Nov 1784   18 Apr 1832
        1836

8 Abner Chase   Amy Scott
      Little Compton 26 Apr   -----   Rupert,VT 5 Oct 1789
        1784
      21 Mar 1824   2 Nov 1808   -----

9 Ames Scott   Sarah Silsby
  Lincoln,VT 18 Dec 1820   -----   Callaraugus Co.NY
                                               14 Apr 1823
  Little Sioux,IA   4 Jan 1848   Harrison Co.IA 17 Jan
    22 Nov 1879   1906

10 Amy Anjean Scott   Charley Vredenburg
   Harrison Co. 30 Oct   -----   Wayne Co.NY 27 Sep
     1850   1832
   Lamoni,IA 19 Mar 1926   19 Nov 1864   Pisgah,IA 8 Jan 1915

11 Sarah Almena Vredenburg   Edwin DeLaney Stearns

Continue with Generation 10 of his lineage from Governor
Thomas Prence.

SUPPLEMENTS No. 2 AND 3

1 John Coggeshall, Governor of Rhode Island 1647

2 John Coggeshall II, Governor of Rhode Island 1686-90

                                               Elizabeth Baulston
   Halstead,Essex,Eng.   Newport,RI   Portsmouth,RI Aug 1629
     c.1620
   Newport 1 Oct 1708   17 Jun 1647   Newport 1 Oct 1700

3 John Coggeshall III   Elizabeth Timerlake
   Portsmouth 12 Feb 1649 Portsmouth   -----
   Portsmouth 9 Nov 1706   24 Dec 1669   -----

4 Mary Coggeshall   William Anthony
   Portsmouth 18 Sep 1675 Portsmouth   Portsmouth 31 Oct 1675
   af.1737   14 Mar 1694/5   Portsmouth 28 Dec 1744

5 Alice Anthony   James Chase
   Portsmouth 22 May 1705 Portsmouth   Swansea,MA 12 Feb
                                                 1705/6
   Middletown,RI Mar 1762 11 May 1727   Middletown 20 Apr 1782

6 James Chase   Hulda Winslow
   Swansea,MA 27 Oct 1729 -----   Freetown,MA 10 Mar
                                                 1729/30
   af.1780   20 Jul 1749   -----

7 Timothy Chase   Sarah Simmons

Continue with Generation 7 of his lineage from Governor John
Alden.

STEVENS, GRACE M. SOUTHMAYD (MRS. LEONARD W.)

Nat. #359-B. Elected 19 Sep 1979. b. Sandpoint,ID 19 Jul 1909.
m. 25 Jul 1936, Leonard Woodbury Stevens, b. Seattle,WA 10 Dec
1907, d. Seattle 28 Dec 1977. Educ: University of Washington,
B.A. Member: Hereditary Order of Desc. of Colonial Governors;
Dau. of American Revolution; Dau. of American Colonists; Dau. of
Colonial Wars; Dau. of Founders and Patriots of America; Ancient
and Honorable Artillery Co.; Soc. of Mayflower Descendants; Soc.
of Desc. of Colonial Clergy; Colonial Dames XVII Century; New
England Women; Huguenot Society; Washington Family Descendants;
Thomas Rogers Descendants; Richmond Family Assn.; Magna Charta;
Freedoms Foundation at Valley Forge; Archivist for Seattle
Genealogical Society; Soc. of Genealogists, CT; Kentucky Histori-
cal Soc. Address: 146 34th Avenue E., Seattle,WA 98112.
Descended from:

1 Thomas Prence, Governor of Plymouth Colony 1634-73

2 Mercy Prence   John Freeman
   Plymouth,MA 1631   Eastham,MA   Eastham 1621
   Eastham 28 Sep 1711   13 Feb 1649/50   Eastham 28 Oct 1719

3 Thomas Freeman   Rebecca Sparrow
   Eastham Sep 1653   Eastham   Eastham 30 Oct 1655
   Harwich,MA 9 Feb   31 Dec 1673   Harwich Feb 1740
     1715/16

4 Prince Freeman   Mary Doane
   Harwich 3 Jan 1689/90   Eastham   Orleans,MA 15 Nov 1691
   -----   20 Mar 1711/2   Middletown,CT

5 Moses Freeman   Susanna Brooks
   Harwich 11 Nov 1730   Middletown   Haddam,CT 11 Aug 1732
   At sea 1782   28 Aug 1753   Haddam 12 Feb 1783

6 Cynthia Freeman   Joseph Southmayd
   Chatham,CT 29 Sep 1769 -----   Middletown 2 Mar 1769
   Portland,CT 14 Jul   Jul 1793   Durham,CT 2 Sep 1824
     1851

7 John Bulkeley Southmayd   Elizabeth Perkins
   Durham 11 Jun 1794   Middletown   Bath,Eng. 17 May 1795
   Worcester,MA 11 Apr   28 Nov 1815   Middletown 12 Nov
     1870   1851

8 Ogden Augustus   Lucy Richmond
     Southmayd
   Middletown 6 Feb   New York   Livonia,NY 4 Mar 1836
     1837
   Muskogee,OK 9 May   10 Apr 1859   Muskogee 9 Nov 1910
     1910

9 John Bulkeley Southmayd   (2)   Minnie Lee Hawker
   Columbus,WI 18 Jul   Rathdrum,ID   Warren,MO 6 Feb 1880
     1863
   Spokane,WA 30 Nov 1924 12 Sep 1908   Spokane 8 Apr 1967

   Inheritor: Terry Towle Stevens (son)

STONE, POLLY A. MARINER (MRS. STANLEY)

Nat. #S-730. b. Milwaukee,WI 7 Mar 1898. m.(1) Milwaukee 7 Apr 1923, Emmett Donnelly. Issue: Deirdre Donnelly Kieckhefer. m.(2)Milwaukee 5 May 1932, Stanley Stone, b. Chicago,IL 24 Jan 1896. Educ: Masters School, Dobbs Ferry,NY. Member: Hereditary Order of Desc. of Colonial Governors; Colonial Dames of America, WI; Chairman of the Committee that operates the old Indian Agency House at Portage,WI, restored by the Colonial Dames and is now a museum; Junior League of Milwaukee; Woman's Club of WI; Milwaukee Country Club. Address: 7820 North Club Circle, Milwaukee,WI 53217. Descended from:

1 William Bradford, Governor of Plymouth Colony 1621-33

2 William Bradford   (1)   Alice Richards
   Plymouth,MA 17 Jun   Plymouth   Weymouth,MA 16 Jun
      1624   1627
   Plymouth 20 Feb 1703/4 bf.28 Jan 1650 Plymouth 12 Dec 1671

3 Samuel Bradford   Hannah Rogers
   Plymouth c.1668   Plymouth   Duxbury,MA 16 Nov 1668
   Duxbury 11 Apr 1714   31 Jul 1689   Milton,MA af.16 Jul
                                                 1733

4 Perez Bradford   Abigail Belcher
   Plymouth 28 Dec 1694   Dedham,MA   Dedham 22 Aug 1695
   Attleborough,MA   14 Apr 1720   Attleborough 15 Nov
      19 Jun 1746   1746

5 George Bradford   Sarah Carpenter
   Milton bp. 22 Oct   Attleborough   Attleborough 23 Feb
      1732   1736
   Woodstock,CT 11 May   28 Apr 1756   Cooperstown,NY
      1795   8 Feb 1832

6 Eseck Bradford   Huldah Skinner
   Cumberland,RI   -----   Woodstock 29 Sep 1771
      21 Mar 1769
   Cooperstown 2 Feb 1842 c.1790   Cooperstown 6 Jun 1829

7 Harvey Sabin Bradford   Mary Stacy
   Cooperstown 30 Aug   Cherry Valley,   Windham,CT 27 Nov 1806
      1800   NY
   Toledo,OH 5 Jan 1842   12 May 1824   Chicago,IL 6 Aug 1880

8 Sophia M. Bradford   Albert Antisdel
   Toledo 26 Aug 1841   Middlefield,   Roseboom,NY 7 May 1840
                           NY
   Milwaukee,WI 10 Feb   20 Jun 1861   Milwaukee 31 Oct 1906
      1915

9 Mary F. Antisdel   John W. Mariner
   Chicago 6 Aug 1869   Chicago   Milwaukee 8 Feb 1868
   Milwaukee 16 Apr 1952   17 Oct 1894   Milwaukee 25 Jun 1930

STORM, WALTER KERR

Nat. #319-B. Elected Sep 1977. b. Mount Vernon,NY 28 Apr 1925.
Educ: Duke University, A.B.; Columbia University, M.B.A.; New
York University, graduate work. Member: Hereditary Order of
Desc. of Colonial Governors; Sons of American Revolution;
American Marketing Assn. Military: Lieutenant j.g. USNR in WW
II. (5 ribbons, 3 silver stars). Address: 149 Harmon Avenue,
Pelham,NY 10803. Descended from:

1 William Pynchon, Governor of Connecticut 1635-36

2 Mary Pynchon   Elizur (Elizear)
                                          Holyoke
   England c.1662   Springfield,MA England bf.1630
   Springfield 26 Oct 1657 20 Nov 1640   Springfield 6 Feb 1676

3 Hannah Holyoke   Samuel Talcott
   Springfield 9 Jun 1644 Springfield   Hartford,CT c.1635
   Wethersfield,CT 2 Feb   7 Nov 1661   Wethersfield 10 Nov
     1677/8   1691

4 Benjamin Talcott   Sarah Hollister
   Wethersfield 1 Mar 1674 Wethersfield Wethersfield 25 Oct
                                           1676
   Glastonbury,CT   5 Jan 1699   Glastonbury 15 Oct 1715
     12 Nov 1727

5 John Talcott   Lucy Burnham
   Glastonbury 17 Dec   -----   -----
     1704
   Provincetown,MA   1731   -----
     25 Aug 1745

6 John Talcott   Abiah Phelps
   Hebron,CT 23 Sep 1732   Hebron   21 Feb 1736
   Hebron 15 Jul 1760   23 Dec 1752   Hebron 23 Jun 1804

7 Mary Talcott   David Mack
   Hebron 21 Sep 1757   Hebron   10 Dec 1750
   Middlefield,MA   24 Apr 1774   Middlefield 24 Mar
     11 Jul 1827   1845

8 Zilpha Mack   Azariah Smith
   Middlefield 3 Feb   Manlius,NY   Middlefield 7 Dec 1784
     1788
   Manlius 13 Mar 1871   29 Apr 1811   New Haven,CT 12 Nov
                                           1846

9 Zilpha Smith   Walter Storm
   Manlius 1 Apr 1825   New York,NY   New Hamburg,NY 3 Sep
                                           1820
   Syracuse,NY 21 Feb   5 Mar 1845   Jersey City,NJ 9 Aug
     1901   1878

10 Bertrand Evart Storm   Esther Keziah Everson
   Bergen,NJ 22 May 1864   Alexandria   Alexandria Bay 27 May
                           Bay,NY   1867
   Miami,FL 19 Dec 1956   7 Jun 1892   Mount Vernon,NY
                                           18 Dec 1955

11 Walter Everson Storm   Martha Lillian Kerr
   Evanston,IL 28 Sep   Brooklyn,NY   Mamaroneck,NY 27 Jun
   1898   1894
   -----   8 Mar 1924   New Rochelle,NY
                                        24 Dec 1968

STRONG, CORNELIA LIVINGSTON VAN RENSSELAER (MISS)

Nat. #M-202. b. New Brunswick,NJ 16 Nov 1902. Member: Heredi-
tary Order of Desc. of Colonial Governors; Colonial Lords of
Manors; Descendants of Signers of the Declaration of Indepen-
dence; The Colonial Dames of America (Past President General);
Daughters of Holland Dames. (From Society's Records).
Descended from:

1 Thomas Dudley, Governor of Massachusetts 1634-35, 1640-41,
   1645-46, 1650-51
   William Leete, Governor of Connecticut 1676-83

2 Mercy Dudley   John Woodbridge
   Northampton, Eng.   -----   Stanton, Eng. 1613/4
      27 Sep 1621
   Newbury,MA 1 Jul 1691 1641   Newbury 17 Mar 1694/5

3 John Woodbridge   Abigail Leete (Dau. of
                                       Governor Leete)

4 John Woodbridge   Jemima Eliot

5 John Woodbridge   Martha Clarke

6 Sophia Woodbridge   Joseph Strong

7 Theodore Strong   Lucy Dix

8 Woodbridge Strong   Harriet Anne Hartwell

9 Theodore Strong   Cornelia Livingston
                                       Van Rensselaer

* The details of birth etc. were lost by the Society.

STUART, HAROLD LEONARD

Nat. #119-B. Elected 16 May 1966. b. Providence,RI 29 Aug 1881.
Educ: Brown University; Lewis Institute, Chicago. Member:
Hereditary Order of Desc. of Colonial Governors; Society of the
Cincinnati; Soc. of Mayflower Desc.; Soc. of War of 1812; Sons
of American Revolution; Order of Founders and Patriots of
America; Soc. of Desc. of Colonial Clergy; Ancient and Honorable
Artillery Co. of MA; Order of Washington; Plantagenet Society;
Soc. of Desc. of Knights of the Most Noble Order of the Garter;
Sovereign Colonial Society of Americans of Royal Descent; Order
of Crown of Charlemagne; Magna Charta Barons; Colonial Order of
the Crown; Soc. of Colonial Wars. Occup: Halsey, Stuart & Co.
President. Address: 999 Lake Shore Drive, Chicago,IL 60611.
(From Society's Records). Descended from:

1 Roger Williams, Governor of Rhode Island 1654-57

2 Mercy Williams   Resolved Waterman
   Providence 15 Jul 1640   Providence,RI Providence 1638
   Providence 1705   c.1659   Providence 1670

3 Waite Waterman   John Rhodes
   Providence c.1668   Warwick,RI   Warwick 1658
   Warwick af.1711   12 Feb 1685   Warwick 14 Aug 1716

4 Phoebe Rhodes   Samuel Aborn
   Warwick 30 Nov 1698   Warwick   Providence 1697
   Providence af.1761   c.1722   Providence 16 Mar 1761

5 James Aborn   Hannah Westgate
   Providence 28 Sep   Warwick   Warwick 1 Jun 1735
     1734
   Providence 4 Apr   6 Nov 1755   Providence 9 May 1819
     1801

6 James Aborn   Mary L. Greene
   Providence 9 Apr   Providence   Providence 19 Sep 1780
     1763
   Providence 4 Oct   19 Apr 1801   Providence 1 Jun 1809
     1845

7 Eliza G. Aborn   George L. Barnes
   Providence 24 Feb   Providence   Providence 6 Oct 1797
     1806
   Providence   21 Apr 1831   Providence 27 Nov 1869

8 James A. Barnes   Abbie N. Bishop
   Providence 14 Oct   Seekonk,RI   Seekonk 18 Jul 1834
     1833
   Providence 28 Feb 1869   22 Mar 1853   Fox Lake,IL May 1898

9 Eliza A. Barnes   George Stuart
   Norton,MA 12 Apr   Providence   Cranston,RI 29 Sep 1843
     1856
   Kenilworth,IL   12 Apr 1874   Chicago,IL 19 Nov 1944
     6 Jul 1912

   Inheritor: Elizabeth Barnes Stuart

SWANSTROM, KATHRYN C. RAYMOND (MRS. LUTHER D.)

Nat. #351-B. Elected 8 Aug 1979. b. Milwaukee,WI 5 Sep 1907.
m. Valpariaso,IN 27 Aug 1934, Luther David Swanstrom, b. Linds-
borg,KS 9 Nov 1884, d. Chicago,IL 11 Nov 1962. Issue: William
Hyland Raymond Swanstrom, b. Chicago 3 Jun 1935. Educ: Bryand &
Stratton Business College. Member: Hereditary Order of Desc. of
Colonial Governors; Colonial Dames of America (Treasurer, Chap.
XIV); Americans of Armorial Ancestry; Order of Crown of Charle-
magne; Soc. of Mayflower Desc.; National Huguenot Soc. (President
General); Dames of Court of Honor; Dau. of American Colonists;
Dau. of American Revolution; Dau. of Barons of Runnemede; Dau. of
Colonial Wars; Dau. of Founders and Patriots of America; Magna
Charta Dames; New England Women; Soc. Old Plymouth Colony Desc.;
Sons & Dau. of Pilgrims (IL, Organizing Secretary General);
Women Desc. Ancient and Honorable Artillery Co. (National Presi-
dent); U.S. Dau. of 1812; Americans of Royal Descent. Occup:
President, Kay C. Raymond Associates (Convention Management).
Address: 9027 South Damen Ave., Chicago,IL 60620. Descended from:

1 John Alden, Governor of Plymouth Colony 1644-65, 1677

2	Joseph Alden		Mary Simmons
	Duxbury,MA c.1623	Bridgewater	-----
	Bridgewater,MA	-----	-----
	8 Feb 1696/7		

3	Hopestill Alden		Joseph Snow
	Duxbury c.1669	Bridgewater	Bridgewater bf.1670
	Bridgewater	c.1689	Bridgewater 18 Dec 1754

4	James Snow		Ruth Shaw
	Bridgewater 16 Aug	Bridgewater	Bridgewater c.1698
	1693		
	Bridgewater	c.1719	Bridgewater

5	Nathan Snow		Mary Mansfield
	Bridgewater 9 Jul 1725	Abington,MA	12 Nov 1728
	2 Aug 1803	20 Oct 1748	-----

6	Jacob Snow		Susanna Brett Gannett
	Abington 12 Apr 1756	Abington	Bridgewater 30 Sep 1760
	-----	7 Jul 1783	Windsor,MA 26 Jul 1845

7	Susanna (Sukey) Snow		Cyrus Bird
	Cummington,MA 11 Mar	Windsor	Windsor 14 Feb 1783
	1789		
	Medina Co.OH Sep 1814	27 Oct 1808	Windsor 16 May 1813

8	Susanna (Susan) Bird	(int.)	Roswell Packard
	Williamstown,MA	Williamstown	Plainfield,MA 14 Feb
	7 Apr 1809		1808
	Racine,WI 21 Jul 1890	14 Jul 1832	Racine 25 Apr 1883

9	Cornelia Lily Packard		George Seymour Bliss
	Burlington,WI 31 Aug	Racine	Buffalo,NY 14 Sep 1844
	1850		
	Racine 29 Feb 1932	14 Oct 1869	Racine 20 Feb 1896

10	Jessie Viola Bliss		William Hyland Raymond
	Racine 13 Aug 1872	Racine	Racine 19 Dec 1869
	Chicago,IL 26 Feb	30 Aug 1892	Chicago 17 Jan 1957
	1938		

Inheritor: William Hyland Raymond Swanstrom (son)

SWITZER, OPAL RISDON (MRS. E. CLAIR)

Nat. #282-B. Elected 1 Mar 1976. b. Iowa Co.,IA 20 Aug 1894.
m. Iowa Co. 20 Aug 1913, E. Clair Switzer, b. Iowa Co. 20 Jul
1888, d. Long Beach,CA 22 Jul 1962. Educ: University of Southern
California, B.S. and M.S. Member: Hereditary Order of Desc. of
Colonial Governors; Dau. of American Revolution; Colonial Dames
XVII Century; Women Desc. Ancient and Honorable Artillery Co.;
Huguenot Society of CA; Magna Charta Dames; Dames, Guild of St.
Margaret of Scotland; Desc. of Royal Order of Knights of the
Garter. Address: 1500 East 3rd St., Apt. 3, Long Beach,CA
90802. Descended from:

1 Samuel Gorton, Governor of Rhode Island 1651-52

2 Ann Gorton   John Warner
  -----   -----   1 Aug 1645
  -----   7 Aug 1670   22 Apr 1712

3 Ann Warner   Jabez (Jacob) Browne
  -----   -----   Providence,RI 1675
  Providence 25 Feb 1727   -----   Providence 9 Sep 1724

4 William Browne   Patience Arnold
  Providence 1708   -----   -----
  Smithfield,RI 27 Jan   c.1728   -----
    1756

5 Eleazer Browne   Sarah Scott
  Smithfield 31 Dec 1736   Smithfield   Smithfield 18 Oct 1738
  Fayette Co.PA   14 Dec 1758   -----
    w.p. 23 Mar 1822

6 Joseph Browne (Brown)   Sarah Hewitt
  Smithfield 10 Jun 1764   Fayette Co.   Pennsylvania
  Stark Co.OH   8 Apr 1802   Stark Co.

7 Eliza Brown   Jesse Hawley
  1806   -----   Chester Co.PA 10 Feb
                                                   1796
  Stark Co. 1852   c.1827   Cedar Co.IA 31 Jul 1880

8 Elvira Hawley   Thomas Maudlin
  Stark Co. 14 Mar 1838   -----   Wayne Co.IN 28 Aug 1818
  Ladora,IA 14 Oct 1928   16 Feb 1860   Iowa Co.IA 10 Feb 1896

9 Euretha (Retha) Maudlin   William J. Risdon
  Iowa Co. 13 May 1873   Iowa Co.   Iowa Co. 28 Apr 1873
  Iowa Co. 15 Feb 1919   1 Jan 1894   Riverside,CA 15 Sep
                                                   1937

TAYLOR, ALMA V. DENNY (MRS. ROBY E.)

Nat. #138-B. Elected 24 Feb 1968. b. Pilot Mountain,NC 28 Mar 1900. m. Raleigh,NC 21 Oct 1921, Roby Ellis Taylor, b. Ararat, NC 21 Oct 1900. Issue: Robert Edwin Taylor, b. 14 Aug 1922; Peggy Aileen Taylor, b. 7 Jan 1924; Elizabeth Ellen Taylor, b. 14 Dec 1927; John Anderson Taylor, b. 17 Sep 1930; Alma Janet Taylor, b. 19 Oct 1937; all b. Winston-Salem,NC. Member: Hereditary Order of Desc. of Colonial Governors; United Dau. of the Confederacy; Dau. of American Revolution; Order of the Crown of Charlemagne; Colonial Daughters of XVII Century. Address: 2720 Windsor Road, Winston-Salem,NC 27104. Descended from:

1 William Stone, Governor of Maryland 1648-53

2 John Stone   Elizabeth Warren
    Accomac Co.VA 1640   -----   -----
    Maryland 1698   -----   -----

3 Thomas Stone   Martha Hoskins
    Maryland 1677   -----   Charles Co.MD c.1680
    Virginia 1727   -----   -----

*4 Thomas Stone   Mary Butler
    Charles Co. c.1700   -----   -----
    Prince William Co.VA c.1720   -----
      24 Nov 1748

5 John Stone   Miss Corder
    Virginia c.1727   -----   -----
    Surry Co.NC   c.1780   -----

6 Enoch Stone   Nancy Anthony
    Surry Co.   Surry Co.   -----
    Surry Co. Sep 1823 c.1784   -----

7 Enoch Stone   Elizabeth Gordon
    Surry Co. 8 Nov 1791 Surry Co.   Surry Co. 28 Mar 1797
    Surry Co. 11 Oct 1874 21 Oct 1819 Surry Co. 26 Mar 1877

8 Francis R. Stone   Sarah C. Poindexter
    Surry Co. 6 Mar 1828 -----   26 Dec 1833
    Ararat,NC 30 Mar 1918 4 Mar 1851   Ararat 5 Jul 1911

9 Sarah D. Stone   Gabriel Denny
    Pilot Mountain,NC   Pilot Mtn.   Surry Co. 20 Dec 1842
      7 Dec 1852
    Pilot Mountain   14 Jun 1868 Pilot Mountain 14 Jul
      12 Aug 1905   1927

10 Oliver J. Denny   Minerva E. Pell
    Surry Co. 30 Nov 1871 North Carolina Westfield,NC 15 Jul
                                     1875
    Winston-Salem,NC   21 Apr 1895 Winston-Salem
      7 Mar 1951   21 Jul 1923

Inheritor: Mrs. Benjamin Earl Winstead, Jr.

* See Preface

TAYLOR, DOROTHY E. RUSS (MRS. DAROLD W.)

Nat. #370-B. Elected 17 Nov 1979. b. Akron,OH 23 Jun 1917.
m. Summit Co.OH 12 Oct 1940, Darold William Taylor, b. Summit
Co. 24 Apr 1914. Member: Hereditary Order of Desc. of Colonial
Governors; Society of Mayflower Descendants, DC; Dau. of American
Revolution; Daughters of Founders and Patriots of America,DC;
Women Desc. of Ancient and Honorable Artillery Co., VA; Daughters
of Colonial Wars, NM; U.S. Daughters of 1812, VA. Address:
2101 Wakefield Street, Alexandria,VA 22308. Descended from:

1 John Alden, Governor of Plymouth Colony 1663-64; 1667

2 Elizabeth Alden   William Pabodie
     Plymouth,MA 1624   Duxbury,MA   England 1619
     Little Compton,RI   26 Dec 1644   Little Compton 13 Dec
       31 May 1717   1707

3 Lydia Pabodie   Daniel Grinnell
     Duxbury 3 Apr 1667   Duxbury   Little Compton 1665
     Saybrook,CT 13 Jul 1748 1683   Saybrook 17 Jan 1740/1

4 George Grinnell   Mary Post Bull
     Saybrook 12 Apr 1702 Saybrook   Saybrook 22 Apr 1708/9
     Saybrook 11 Nov 1759 31 Jan 1725   Saybrook 20 Sep 1775

5 Mary Grinnell   Jedediah Chapman
     Westbrook,CT 25/26 Dec Westbrook   Westbrook 15 Dec 1726
       1731
     Westbrook 11 Jul 1776 1755   Westbrook 29 Feb 1816

6 Constant Chapman   Jemima Kelsey
     Westbrook 27 Dec 1761 Westbrook   Killingworth,CT 18 Oct
                                              1762
     Brimfield,OH 24 Sep   27 Jan 1785   Portage Co.OH 13 Sep
       1847   1849

7 Joseph Gela Chapman   Elizabeth Boszor
     Westbrook 23 May 1802 Portage Co.   Portage Co. 12 Dec
                                              1805/6
     Brimfield 4 Mar 1878   13 Mar 1824   Portage Co. 3 Oct 1880

8 Leroy Milton Chapman   Permelia Alice
                                              Haughawout
     Brimfield 9 Jan 1834   Portage Co.   Juniata Co.PA 7 Aug
                                              1833
     Brimfield 1 Sep 1912   24 Dec 1868   Portage Co. 30 Jun 1927

9 Rhoda Ellen Chapman   Ernest Lester Russ
     Brimfield 22 Oct 1869 Chatauqua Co.   Brimfield 6 Jan 1863
     Alexandria,VA 20 Nov   25 Nov 1885   Portage Co. 4 Jan 1947
       1952

TAYLOR, MARJORIE ELLEN (MISS)

Nat. #255-B. Elected 12 Apr 1975 as an inheritor of the membership of Miss Agnes Virginia Dodson, No. 83-B. Member: Hereditary Order of Desc. of Colonial Governors. Address: 3246
Paddington Lane, Winston-Salem,NC 27106. Descended from:

1   William Stone, Governor of Maryland 1649-54

2   John Stone   Elizabeth Warren
    Accomac Co. VA 1640   -----   -----
    Maryland 1698   -----   -----

3   Thomas Stone   Martha Hoskins
    1677   -----   Charles Co. MD c.1680
    1727   -----   -----

*4 Thomas Stone   Mary Butler
    Charles Co. c.1700   -----   -----
    Prince William Co.   c.1720   -----
       24 Nov 1748

5   John Stone   Miss Corder
    Virginia c.1727   -----   -----
    Surry Co.NC c.1780   -----   -----

6   Enoch Stone   Nancy Anthony
    Surry Co.   Surry Co.   -----
    Surry Co. Sep 1823   c.1784   -----

7   Enoch Stone   Elizabeth Gordon
    Surry Co. 8 Nov 1791   Surry Co.   Surry Co. 28 Mar 1797
    Surry Co. 11 Oct 1874   21 Oct 1819   Surry Co. 26 Mar 1877

8   Rhoda E. Stone   John C. Dodson
    Surry Co. 1 Jun 1833   Surry Co.   Surry Co. 4 Apr 1831
    Surry Co. 20 Jul 1891   2 May 1861   Surry Co. 8 Aug 1891

9   Wesley G. Dodson   Salome Dair
    Surry Co. 27 Nov 1867   Walnut Cove   Madison,NC 9 Sep 1881
    Walnut Cove,NC 23 Sep   17 May 1916   Walnut Cove 24 Oct
       1924   1956

TAYLOR, ROBY ELLIS

Nat. #172-B. Elected 13 Feb 1971. b. Ararat,NC 21 Oct 1900.
m. Raleigh,NC 21 Oct 1921, Alma Vane Denny, b. Pilot Mountain,
NC 28 Mar 1900. Issue: Robert Taylor, b. 14 Aug 1922; Peggy
Taylor, b. 7 Jan 1924; Elizabeth Taylor, b. 14 Dec 1927; John
Taylor, b. 17 Sep 1930; Janet Taylor, b. 19 Oct 1937; all b.
Winston-Salem,NC. Educ: Elon College and La Salle Extension
University, Certified Public Accountant. Member: Hereditary
Order of Desc. of Colonial Governors; Order of Crown of Charle-
magne. Occup: Oil Dealer. Address: 2720 Windsor Rd., Winston-
Salem,NC 27104. Descended from:

1   William Stone, Governor of Maryland 1649-54

*   See Preface

273

2 John Stone   Elizabeth Warren
   Accomac Co.VA 1640   -----   -----
   Maryland 1698   -----   -----

3 Thomas Stone   Martha Hoskins
   Maryland 1677   -----   Charles Co.MD c.1680
   Maryland 1727   -----   -----

*4 Thomas Stone   Mary Butler
   Charles Co. c.1700   -----   -----
   Prince William Co.VA c.1720   -----
      24 Nov 1748

5 John Stone   Miss Corder
   Virginia c.1727   -----   -----
   Surry Co.NC   -----   -----

6 Enoch Stone   Nancy Anthony
   Surry Co.   Surry Co.   -----
   Surry Co. Sep 1823   c.1784   -----

7 Enoch Stone   Elizabeth Gordon
   Surry Co. 8 Nov 1791 Surry Co.   Surry Co. 28 Mar 1797
   Surry Co. 11 Oct 1874 21 Oct 1819   Surry Co. 26 Mar 1877

8 Francis R. Stone   Sarah C. Poindexter
   Pilot Mountain,NC   -----   Yadkin Co.NC 26 Dec
      6 Mar 1828   1833
   Ararat,NC 30 Mar 1918 4 Mar 1851   Ararat 5 Jul 1911

9 Sarah D. Stone   Gabriel Denny
   Pilot Mountain 7 Dec Pilot Mtn.   Surry Co. 20 Dec 1842
      1852
   Pilot Mountain 12 Aug 14 Jun 1868   Pilot Mountain 14 Jul
      1905   1927

10 Virginia E. Denny   Augustine J. Taylor
   Pilot Mountain 6 Jun Pilot Mtn.   -----
      1858
                        24 Dec 1874   Pilot Mountain 12 Dec
                                            1942

THATCHER, DOROTHY L. DOUGLASS (MRS. LYNDON)

Nat. #123-B. Elected 10 Aug 1966. b. Danbury,CT 16 Jan 1899.
m. New York, 2 Apr 1937, Dr. Lyndon Thatcher. Educ: Smith
College, A.B.; Columbia University, M.A., Ed.D. Member: Heredi-
tary Order of Desc. of Colonial Governors; Dau. of American
Revolution,CT; Dau. of Founders and Patriots,NY; New England
Women, New Haven; Sons and Dau. of Pilgrims,CT; Women Desc. of
Ancient and Honorable Artillery Co. of MA; New Haven Historical
Soc. Address: 194 Knoll Drive, Hamden,CT 06518. (From
Society's Records). Descended from:

1 Thomas Welles, Governor of Connecticut 1655-58

2 Samuel Welles   Elizabeth Hollister
   Glastonbury,Eng. 1630 -----   Wethersfield,CT
   Wethersfield, 15 Jul 1659   Glastonbury,CT 1673
      1675
* See Preface

3 Sarah Welles   Ephraim Hawley
  Wethersfield 29 Sep   Trumbull,CT   New Stratford 7 Aug
    1664   1659
  New Stratford,CT   4 Dec 1683   -----
    29 Jun 1694

4 Gideon Hawley   Anna Bennett
  Bridgeport,CT 30 Jun   Stratford,CT Bridgeport 1691
    1687
  Bridgeport 16 Feb   4 Feb 1711   Stratford 14 Nov 1727
    1730/1

5 James Hawley   Eunice Jackson
  Bridgeport 29 Jan   Fairfield,CT 1714
    1713
  Bridgeport 7 Oct 1746   18 Jul 1733 Bridgeport 6 Sep 1796

6 Deacon E. Hawley   Mercy Bennett
  Bridgeport 30 Dec 1744 Weston,CT   Weston 31 Dec 1751
  Penfield,OH 11 Aug   27 Feb 1772 Penfield 18 Oct 1847
    1825

7 Huldah Hawley   Stephen Hoyt
  New Fairfield 24 Jan   Danbury,CT   Danbury 27 Aug 1767
    1775
  Danbury 23 Jul 1848   2 Mar 1796   Danbury 11 Oct 1835

8 Harriet Hoyt   John Abbott
  Danbury 28 Jan 1809   Danbury   London,Eng. May 1795
  'Bethel,CT 26 Dec 1895 1835   Danbury 5 Apr 1865

9 Susan M. Abbott   Abraham Baldwin
  New Canaan,CT 4 Sep   Danbury   Woodbridge,CT 15 Feb
    1837   1827
  Bethel 6 Jun 1922   4 Apr 1861   Bethel 29 Feb 1924

10 Martha Baldwin   Lawrence A. Douglass
  Bethel 29 Jul 1870   Bethel   Pepperell,MA 27 Jun
                                    1865
  New Haven,CT 6 Jan 1955 31 Jul 1895 New Haven 12 Jun 1954

Inheritor: Richard Baldwin North, Vineyard Point, Sachems
Head, Guilford,CT 06437.

THOMAS, INA MERLE (MISS)

Nat. #183-B. Elected 28 Nov 1971. b. Ozark,AL 27 Sep 1907.
Educ: Louisiana State University, B.A.; Columbia University,M.A.
Member: Hereditary Order of Desc. of Colonial Governors;
Daughters of the Confederacy; Dau. of American Revolution;
Colonial Dames of 17th Century (St. 3rd Vice President); Magna
Charta Dames (St. Parliamentarian); Soc. of Desc. of Knights of
Most Noble Order of the Garter; Americans of Royal Descent.
Occup: Retired teacher. Address: 3912 Polk St., Monroe,LA
71201. Descended from:

1 Samuel Mathews, Governor of Virginia 1656-60

2 John Mathews   Elizabeth Tavernor
   Warwick Co.VA 1661   York Co.VA   -----
   King & Queen Co.VA   1683   -----
      1702

3 Samuel Mathews   (1)   Miss Paullin
   King & Queen Co. 1682   -----   -----
   Richmond Co.VA 1718   -----   -----

*4 Mary Mathews   Isaac Mathews
   Virginia   King & Queen   King & Queen Co.VA
                               Co.
   South Carolina af.1718   1723   SC 19 Sep 1769

5 Thomas Mathews   -----
   VA 1727   -----   -----
   Moore Co.NC   -----   -----

6 James Mathews   Nancy Dickenson
   VA 1756   -----   Moore Co. 1774
   SC 1812   1792   Jackson Co.GA 1830

7 Willis Dickenson   Rebecca Allgood
      Mathews
   Moore Co. 20 Mar 1804   -----   Walton Co.GA 21 Feb
                                                      1807
   Alexander City,AL   14 Sep 1824   Alexander City 9 Dec
      27 Jun 1864   1874

8 Willis Dickenson   Georgia Ann Gilbert
      Mathews
   Meriwether Co.GA   -----   Talbot Co.GA 23 Jul
      6 Apr 1841   1845
   Hanover,AL 28 Nov   10 Dec 1865   Hanover 31 May 1891
      1890

9 Linnie Mathews   Frank Lee Thomas
   Alexander City 27 Sep   Ozark,AL   Ozark 16 Sep 1875
      1878
   Monroe,LA 13 May 1958   20 May 1903   Monroe 5 Nov 1927

THOMAS, ROBERT LANCEFIELD, M.D.

Nat. #157-B. Elected 7 Mar 1970. b. Forest Grove,OR 23 Feb
1909. m. Fall River,MA 29 Nov 1958, Lois Jane Hodgson, b. Fall
River 6 Oct 1935. Issue: Randolph Woodson Thomas, b. Oakland,
CA 11 Apr 1960; Suzanne Chilton Thomas, b. Berkeley,CA 24 Aug
1962. Educ: Stanford University, A.B.; Harvard University
School of Medicine, M.D. Member: Hereditary Order of Desc. of
Colonial Governors; Soc. of Mayflower Desc. (Surgeon General,
Governor,CA); Sons of American Revolution; National Huguenot
Soc.; Jamestowne Soc.; Soc. of the Cincinnati, RI; Order of
First Families of Virginia; Soc. of California Pioneers; Sons and
Dau. of Oregon Pioneers. Military: U.S. Navy (Ret). Occup:
Surgeon, Psychiatrist. Honors: SAR Good Citizenship Medal.
Address: P.O. Box 7213, Imola,CA 94558. Descended from:

1 Nicholas Easton, Governor of Rhode Island 1650-74

* See Preface

2 Peter Easton
England 1622   England   Ann Coggeshall
RI 12 Feb 1693/4   15 Nov 1643   England c.1622
     Newport,RI 6 Mar 1688/9

3 Waite Easton   John Carr
Newport 5 Nov 1668   Newport   Newport c.1664
Newport 3 Aug 1725   -----   Newport 1714

4 Patience Carr   Edward Estes
Newport c.1700   Portsmouth,NH   Lynn,MA 20 Feb 1703/4
Durham,ME 13 Dec 1788   27 Aug 1730   Durham 13 Feb 1788

5 Caleb Estes   Lydia Bishop
Hanover,MA 26 Nov 1747   -----   Harpswell,ME 20 Aug
     1749
Durham Nov 1822   24 Jun 1769   4 May 1815

6 Thomas Estes   Betsy H. Alden
Durham 20 Aug 1784   Greene,ME   Greene 19 Oct 1786
South Durham 16 Oct   Dec 1811   Durham 23 Jan 1857
   1870

7 Horace Estes   Elizabeth Derbyshire
South Durham 14 Jun   Bucks Co.PA   Bucks Co. 8 Nov 1819
   1819
Ashawa,IA 23 Feb 1884   1845   Dubuque,IA 12 Jul 1856

8 Mary E. Estes   Arthur B. Thomas
Galena,IL 20 Jun 1847   Dubuque   Cascade,IA 11 Mar 1848
Forest Grove,OR   23 Jun 1881   Forest Grove 5 Mar
   25 Jan 1935   1936

9 Horace E. Thomas   Georgia C. Lancefield
Ames,IA 16 Nov 1882   Amity,OR   Yamhill Co.OR 20 Sep
     1886
Portland,OR 2 Aug 1969   28 Apr 1908   Portland 13 Jun 1963

SUPPLEMENT NO. 1

1 Caleb Carr, Governor of Rhode Island 1695

2 John Carr   Waite Easton

Continue with Generation 3 of his lineage from Governor
Nicholas Easton.

SUPPLEMENT NO. 2

1 John Coggeshall, Governor of Rhode Island 1647

2 Ann Coggeshall   Peter Easton

Continue with Generation 2 of his lineage from Governor
Nicholas Easton.

SUPPLEMENT NO. 3

1 John Alden, Governor of Plymouth Colony 1663-64, 1667

2 Joseph Alden   Mary Simmons
1624   -----   -----
Bridgewater,MA 8 Feb   c.1657   -----
   1697

3 Joseph Alden   Hannah Dunham
Duxbury,MA 1667   -----   1670
Bridgewater 22 Dec   1690   Bridgewater 13 Jan
   1747   1748

4 Daniel Alden   Abigail Shaw
   Bridgewater 29 Jan 1691 -----   1694
   Stafford,CT 3 May 1767 1717   Stafford 12 Jul 1755

5 Joseph Alden   Susanna Packard
   Bridgewater 20 Nov 1718 Bridgewater   Bridgewater 11 Mar
                                                       1724
   Worcester,MA 2 Jan 1768 16 Dec 1742   Bridgewater bf.1760

6 Benjamin Alden   Betty Hayford
   Stafford 1758   Turner,ME   Pembroke,MA 12 Mar 1765
   Greene,ME 1842   24 Nov 1785   12 Mar 1862

7 Betsy H. Alden   Thomas Estes

   Continue with Generation 6 of his lineage from Governor
   Nicholas Easton.

THOMAS, SUZANNE CHILTON (MISS)

Nat. #253-B. Elected 4 Mar 1975. b. Berkeley,CA 24 Aug 1962.
Member: Hereditary Order of Desc. of Colonial Governors.
Address: 136 Overhill Rd., Orinda,CA 94563. Descended from:

1 Caleb Carr, Governor of Rhode Island 1695

2 John Carr   Waite Easton
   Newport,RI c.1664   -----   Newport 5 Nov 1668
   Newport 1714   -----   Newport 3 Aug 1725

3 Patience Carr   Edward Estes
   Newport c.1700   Portsmouth,NH   Lynn,MA 20 Feb 1720
   Durham,ME 13 Dec 1788   27 Aug 1730   Durham 13 Feb 1788

4 Caleb Estes   Lydia Bishop
   Hanover,MA 26 Nov 1747 -----   Harpswell,ME 20 Aug
                                                       1749
   Durham Nov 1822   24 Jun 1769   4 May 1815

5 Thomas Estes   Betsy H. Alden
   Durham 20 Aug 1784   Greene,ME   Greene 19 Oct 1786
   South Durham 16 Oct   Dec 1811   Durham 23 Jan 1857
    1870

6 Horace Estes   Elizabeth Derbyshire
   South Durham 14 Jun   Bucks Co.PA   Bucks Co. 8 Nov 1819
    1819
   Ashawa,IA 23 Feb 1884   1845   Dubuque,IA 12 Jul 1856

7 Mary E. Estes   Arthur B. Thomas
   Galena,IL 20 Jun 1847   Dubuque   Cascade,IA 11 Mar 1848
   Forest Grove,OR 25 Jan 23 Jun 1881   Forest Grove 5 Mar
    1935   1936

8 Horace E. Thomas   Georgia C. Lancefield
   Ames,IA 16 Nov 1882   Amity,OR   Yamhill Co.OR 20 Sep
                                                       1886
   Portland,OR 2 Aug 1969 28 Apr 1908   Portland 13 Jun 1963

9 Robert L. Thomas   Lois Jane Hodgson
   Forest Grove 23 Feb   Fall River,MA   Fall River 6 Oct 1935
    1909
                           29 Nov 1958

THURTLE, ROBERT GLENN

Nat. #176-B. Elected 8 Jun 1971. b. Lincoln,NE 2 Aug 1908.
m. Omaha,NE 5 Jun 1934, Mary Virginia Doyle, b. Greeley,NE 8 May
1908. Issue: Robert J.P. Thurtle, M.D., b. St. Louis,MO 18 Mar
1935; Maureen Katherine Allen, b. Plainfield,NJ 17 Feb 1939.
Educ: Creighton University, Omaha, AB 1931; LLB 1934; JD 1967.
Member: Hereditary Order of Desc. of Colonial Governors (Asst.
Genealogist General); Soc. of War of 1812 (District Deputy
President General; DC, Past Vice President); Sons of the Revolu-
tion (DC, Past Secretary); Sons of American Revolution (National
Auditing Comm.; George Mason Chap., Past Vice President); Soc.
of Mayflower Descendants (Assistant Deputy Governor General;
DC, Past Governor, Historian); Order of Founders and Patriots in
America (DC, Past Genealogist); Soc. of Colonial Wars (Publica-
tion Comm.); Hereditary Order of Loyalists and Patriots
(Governor General); Order of Americans of Armorial Ancestry;
Sons and Dau. of Pilgrims; Colonial Lords of Manors in America;
Soc. of Desc. of Colonial Clergy (Past Member of Council);
Colonial Order of the Crown; Soc. of Knights of the Most Noble
Order of the Garter; Somerset Chapter, Magna Charta Barons;
Soc. of Pilgrims of St. Mary's; Sovereign Military Order of the
Temple of Jerusalem; Richard Warren Soc. (Secretary); Desc. of
Robert Bartlett, Plymouth,MA; Columbia Historical Soc.; National
Genealogical Soc.; Alpha Chi Kappa; Alpha Sigma Nu; Nebraska
State Bar Assn. Occup: Attorney, Office of the Chief Counsel,
IRS (ret.). Address: 2000 South Eads Street, Apt. 719,
Arlington,VA 22202. Descended from:

1 Thomas Mayhew, Governor of Martha's Vineyard 1647-81

2 Martha Mayhew   Thomas Tupper
   Watertown,MA c.1638   Sandwich,MA   Sandwich 16 Jan 1638
   Sandwich 15 Nov 1717 27 Dec 1661   Sandwich 26 Apr 1706

3 Israel Tupper   Elizabeth Gifford
   Sandwich 22 Sep 1666 Sandwich   Falmouth,MA 25 Feb
                                          1664
   Sandwich 1745   c.1690   Sandwich 19 Oct 1701

4 Thankful Tupper   Josiah Clark
   Sandwich 9 Oct 1696   Sandwich   Plymouth,MA 1690
   -----   30 Oct 1718   -----

5 Israel Clark   Deborah Pope
   Plymouth 10 Sep 1720 Plymouth   Sandwich 23 Feb 1725
   Plymouth Oct 1788   13 May 1742   -----

6 Abigail Clark   Josiah Cornish
   Plymouth 13 May 1756 Plymouth   Plymouth 15 Oct 1760
   -----   15 Dec 1786   Lee Center,NY 10 Oct
                                          1844

7 Allen Cornish   Clarissa Cornish
                                          (Cousin)
   Plymouth 1 Sep 1789   Plymouth   Plymouth 2 Nov 1792
   Lee Center 6 Apr 1853 18 Apr 1808   Lee Center 9 Jun 1864

8 George Cornish   Mary Tucker
   Lee Center 28 May 1825 New York,NY   NY 2 May 1831
   Lee Center 3 Dec 1894 c.1848   Rome,NY 28 Apr 1898

9 Alice Cornish   Patrick Henry O'Donnell
   Lee Center 5 Nov 1853   Rome,NY   Newport,NY 6 Nov 1850
   Albany,NY 24 May 1916   16 Apr 1862   Rome 18 Apr 1916

10 Mary Catherine O'Donnell   Charles Herbert Thurtle
   Elgin,IL 16 Mar 1875   Lincoln,NE   Knowlesville,NY
                                              12 Oct 1877
   Euclid,OH 28 Mar 1948   2 Jun 1906   Lincoln 13 May 1947

   Inheritor: Robert J.P. Thurtle, M.D., 418 North "M" St.,
   Livermore,CA 94550.

TOWNE, ANITA MOREY (MRS. LEIGH C.)

Nat. #152-B. Elected 11 Aug 1969. b. Schuyler Lake,NY 25 Feb
1901. m. Frankfort,NY 1 Jan 1960, Leigh Towne, b. Frankfort
26 Jul 1897. Member: Hereditary Order of Descendants of Colonial
Governors; Dau. of American Revolution in Frankfort,NY; New
England Women in Syracuse,NY; Dau. of American Colonists; Dau. of
Colonial Wars in NY State; Women Desc. of Ancient and Honorable
Artillery Co.; Flagon and Trencher; Soc. of Desc. of Colonial
Clergy; Soc. of Mayflower Descendants. Address: Schuyler Lake,
NY 13457. Descended from:

1 Thomas Dudley, Governor of Massachusetts 1634-35; 1640-41;
   1645-46; 1650-51

2 Mercy Dudley   John Woodbridge
   Northampton,Eng.   -----   Stanton,Eng. 1613/4
      27 Sep 1621
   Newbury,MA 1 Jul 1691   1641   Newbury 17 Mar 1694/5

3 Martha Woodbridge   Samuel Ruggles
   -----   Roxbury,MA   1 Jun 1658
   1738   6 Jul 1680   25 Feb 1715/6

4 Timothy Ruggles   Mary M. White
   Roxbury 3 Nov 1685   -----   27 Aug 1688
   Rochester,MA 24 Oct   27 Dec 1710   Rochester 23 Jan 1749
      1768

5 Samuel Ruggles   Alice Sherman
   Rochester 5 Jul 1715   Roxbury   29 Jul 1719
   -----   25 Jun 1738   -----

6 Sarah Ruggles   John Rider
   Rochester 27 Apr 1739   -----   Rochester 11 Nov 1739
   -----   26 Jun 1764   Exeter,NY 1820

7 Stephen Rider   Levica
   Rochester 1769   -----   -----
   af. 1855   -----   -----

8 Sallie Rider   Alanson Morey
   Exeter 23 Dec 1803   -----   CT 16 Apr 1804
   Schuyler Lake,NY   20 Oct 1825   Exeter 15 Feb 1883
      29 Jan 1861

9 Nathan Smith Morey   Arzelia M. Veber
   Exeter 3 Mar 1839   Herkimer,NY   Exeter 8 May 1841
   New Berlin,NY   20 Jun 1860   New Berlin 23 Jul 1913
      13 Mar 1912

10 Adelmar G. Morey		Grace A. Engell
Schuyler Lake	-----	Lawrence,MI 1 Mar 1868
10 Jul 1868		
Cooperstown,NY	18 Jun 1891	Utica,NY 9 Aug 1944
31 Jul 1940		

TROXEL, NAVENA HEMBREE (MRS. VESTER O.)

Nat. #358-B. Elected 6 Sep 1979. b. Blackwell,OK 5 Feb 1929. m.(2) Tucumcari,NM 23 May 1953, Vester Orville Troxel, b. Noble, OK 12 Jan 1923. Member: Hereditary Order of Desc. of Colonial Governors; Dau. of American Revolution,NJ; Dau. of American Colonists, NJ; Colonial Dames XVII Century, NJ; Soc. of Desc. of Colonial Clergy, NJ; Soc. of Mayflower Descendants, NJ; Flagon and Trenchers, NJ; North Central Texas Genealogical and Histori- cal Soc., TX. Address: 1309 Melrose Drive, Richardson,TX 75080. Descended from:

1 Thomas Dudley, Governor of Massachusetts 1634-35; 1640-41; 1645-46; 1650-51

2 Mercy Dudley		John Woodbridge
England 27 Sep 1621	Newbury,MA	England 1613
1 Jul 1691	1639	17 Mar 1695

3 John Woodbridge		Abigail Leete
Andover,MA 1644	-----	-----
1690	26 Oct 1671	-----

4 John Woodbridge		Jemina Eliot
1678	-----	14 Nov 1679
West Springfield,MA	14 Nov 1699	-----
10 Jun 1718		

5 John Woodbridge		Typhena Ruggles
West Springfield	South Hadley	22 Jun 1707
25 Dec 1702		
South Hadley,MA	-----	South Hadley 10 Jan
10 Sep 1783		1749

6 Typhena Woodbridge		Samuel Preston
South Hadley 31 Jul	South Hadley	South Hadley 29 Oct
1731		1715
South Hadley 18 Aug	-----	South Hadley 18 Jan
1777		1799

7 Samuel Preston		Jemima Ingram
South Hadley 22 Apr	-----	3 Apr 1758
1759		
South Hadley 12 Dec	-----	South Hadley 1 May 1823
1806		

8 Emerence Preston		Abner Downing
South Hadley 2 Jul	South Hadley	Windham,CT 1 Mar 1778
1782		
Mt. Carroll,IL	23 Oct 1802	Mt. Carroll 18--
20 May 1859		

```
9   Heman Downing                            Rachel Holbrook
    South Hadley 28 Jul    Princeton,IL      Richmond,NH 17 ? 1812
      1810
    Princeton 29 Apr 1882  7 Jan 1836        Council Bluff,IA
                                               1 Nov 1896

10  Enos Holbrook Downing                    Ella Anderson
    Mt. Carroll 3 Nov 1849 Princeton         Sweden 10 Nov 1858
    Sharon,KS 15 Oct 1927  23 Dec 1878       Longmont,CO 23 Nov 1937

11  Flora Belle Downing                      James Dee Hembree
    Attica,KS 15 Feb 1880  Attica            Wright Co.MO 28 Aug
                                               1877
    Oklahoma City,OK       25 Dec 1901       Blackwell,OK 9 Jan 1961
      16 Mar 1937

12  Jess Enos Hembree                        Cleo Almeda Merrill
    Sharon 16 Aug 1904     Perry,OK          Joplin,MO 8 Jun 1909
    Oklahoma City 6 Sep    19 Jul 1927       Oklahoma City 17 Mar
      1943                                     1957
```

TUTTLE, ELEANOR BROOKE PERRY STIEFEL (MRS. FREDERICK BURTON)

Nat. #188-B. Elected 24 Apr 1972. b. Maryland 9 Apr 1906.
m.(1) Queen Anne's Co.MD 4 Jun 1923, Dr. Charles Valentine
Stiefel, b. Washington,DC 11 Oct 1894. Issue: Eleanor B. Stiefel
McDonald, b. Washington,DC 8 Apr 1929. m.(2) Frederick Burton
Tuttle, b. New Haven,CT 12 Jul 1908. Educ: Mt. St. Agnes
College, Baltimore Co.MD, A.A. Member: Hereditary Order of Desc.
of Colonial Governors; Dau. of Founders and Patriots of America
(Past President, DC); Ark and Dove (Board Member); Colonial
Dames of America (VA, Recording Secretary); Desc. of Lords of
the Maryland Manors (National President); Jamestowne Society;
Dau. of the Cincinnati; Magna Charta Dames; Soc. of Americans of
Royal Descent; Washington Club (Genealogy and Heraldry Comm.).
Honor: Certificate of Merit from Institute of Genealogy.
Address: 3133 Connecticut Ave., N.W., Washington,DC 20008.
Descended from:

```
1   Leonard Calvert, Governor of Maryland 1633-47

2   Ann Calvert                              Baker Brooke
    England c.1640         Calvert Co.MD     Battle,Eng. 16 Nov
                                               1628
    Maryland 1713          1664              Calvert Co. 1679

3   Baker Brooke                             Katherine Marsham
    Calvert Co.            -----             -----
    St.Mary's Co.MD 1698   -----             -----

4   Leonard Brooke                           Ann
    -----                  -----             -----
    Prince George's Co.    -----             Prince George's Co.
      MD 1736                                  1770
```

5 Leonard Brooke   Elizabeth Maxwell
   Prince George's Co.   England   -----
     1728
   Prince George's Co.   c.1755   -----
     1785

6 Esther Brooke   Henry Hill
   Prince George's Co.   Pr.Geo.Co.   Prince George's Co.
     1755   1750
   Prince George's Co.   23 Apr 1780   Prince George's Co.
     1842   1832

7 Mary Ann Hill   James Brooke
   Prince George's Co.   Pr.Geo.Co.   Charles Co.MD 1758
     25 Aug 1795
   Kent Co.MD 14 Jun   25 Oct 1814   Annapolis,MD 2 Feb
     1849   1822

8 Henrietta E. Brooke   George H. Willson
   Prince George's Co.   Kent Co.   Kent Co. 25 May 1810
     25 Jun 1820
   Kent Co. 17 Apr 1877   13 Jun 1837   Kent Co. 2 Apr 1873

9 Mary G. Willson   Francis A. Wallis
   Kent Co. 13 Feb 1842   Chestertown,MD   Kent Co. 28 Mar 1828
   Queen Anne's Co.MD   26 Apr 1864   Queenstown,MD 21 Jun
     10 May 1906   1904

10 Henrietta E. Wallis   Elton H. Perry
   Kent Co. 9 Nov 1869   Chestertown   Talbot Co.MD 11 Nov
                                               1861
   Hyattsville,MD   25 Jun 1895   Queenstown 11 Feb
     17 Jun 1959   1923

SUPPLEMENT NO. 1

1 Robert Brooke, Governor of Maryland 1652

2 Baker Brooke   Ann Calvert

Continue with Generation 2 of her lineage from Governor
Leonard Calvert.

SUPPLEMENT NO. 2

1 Richard Bennett, Governor of Virginia 1652

2 Richard Bennett   Henrietta M. Neale
   -----   -----   Spain 27 Mar 1647
   1667   -----   Talbot Co.MD

3 Susannah M. Bennett   (2)   Henry Lowe
   1667   -----   -----
   28 Jul 1714   -----   St. Mary's Co.MD 1717

4 Dorothy Lowe   Francis Hall
   1704   -----   c.1696
   Feb 1803   -----   Prince George's Co.MD
                                               1785

283

```
5   Francis Hall                              Martha Neale
    1732                      -----           1739
    Queen Anne's Co.MD        -----           31 May 1789
       13 Feb 1798

6   Mary T. Hall                              Thomas B. Willson
    1760                      -----           1729
    10 Aug 1814               26 Aug 1776     1819

7   Thomas B. Willson                         Anna M. Smyth
    1778                      -----           1784
    Kent Co. MD 1859          3 Jun 1806      1823

8   George H. Willson                         Henrietta E. Brooke
```

Continue with Generation 8 of her lineage from Governor
Leonard Calvert.

SUPPLEMENT NO. 3

```
1   Edward Digges, Governor of Virginia 1655-56

2   William Digges                            Elizabeth Sewell
    -----                     -----           -----
    Charles Co.MD 1697        -----           Charles Co. 1710

3   Elizabeth Digges                          Anthony Neale
    -----                     -----           -----
    -----                     -----           Charles Co. 1723

4   Edward Neale                              Mary Lowe
    Charles Co. 1700          -----           -----
    Queen Anne's Co.MD        -----           -----
       28 Dec 1760

5   Martha Neale                              Francis Hall
```

Continue with Generation 5 of her lineage from Governor
Richard Bennett.

Inheritor: Eleanor Brooke Stiefel McDonald (Mrs. Thomas Ely),
20365 Seaboard Road, Malibu,CA 90265.

TUTTLE, FREDERICK BURTON, M.D.

Nat. #239-B. Elected 30 May 1974. b. New Haven,CT 12 Jul 1908.
m.(1) Jonesboro,AR 3 Sep 1936, Mary Emily Armstrong, b. 10 Jul
1914, d. Jul 1972. Issue: Frederick Burton Tuttle, Jr.; James
Armstrong Tuttle; Allen Carter Tuttle; Margaret Emily Tuttle.
m.(2) Eleanor Brooke Perry Stiefel, b. Maryland 9 Apr 1906.
Educ: Yale, BA 1930; Yale, PhD 1942. Member: Hereditary Order
of Desc. of Colonial Governors; Founders and Patriots; Sons of
American Revolution; Sons of the Revolution; Soc. of Colonial
Wars; Soc. of Desc. of Colonial Clergy; Royal Soc. of St. George;
Loyalists and Patriots; Knights of Temple of Jerusalem; Baronial
Order of Magna Charta; Order of Crown of Charlemagne; Yale Club,
DC; Mount Vernon Yacht Club; Cosmos Club. Occup: Dir. of Educa-
tional Programs, Nat. Aeronautics and Space Administration.
Citation for Service to Aviation by the Commission for Celebra-
ting the Fiftieth Anniversary of Powered Flight. Address:
3133 Connecticut Ave.,N.W.,Washington,DC 20008. Descended from:

1 James Bishop, Governor of Connecticut 1683-84

2 Hannah Bishop   John Morris
   New Haven 29 May 1651   New Haven,CT   New Haven bp. 8 Mar
                                                1664
   New Haven 12 Jun 1701   12 Aug 1669   New Haven 10 Dec 1711

3 Mary Morris   John Hemingway
   East Haven,CT 9 Sep   -----   East Haven 29 May 1675
     1673
   East Haven 8 Dec 1743   -----   East Haven 3 Feb 1736

4 Desire Hemingway   Moses Thompson
   New Haven 2 Mar 1707   New Haven   New Haven 1 Nov 1699
   East Haven 30 Dec 1765   10 Dec 1724   Cheshire,CT 17 Feb
                                                1768

5 Desire Thompson   Nicholas Street
   East Haven 5 Jul 1745   East Haven   New Haven 21 Feb 1730
   East Haven 27 Jan 1765   6 Dec 1758   New Haven 8 Oct 1806

6 Lucinda Street   (2)   Titus Allen
   East Haven 17 Jul 1763   East Haven   East Haven bp.12 Sep
                                                1756
   East Haven 7 Oct 1843   27 Jan 1789   -----

7 Sylvia Allen   Aner Brown
   East Haven bp.21 Feb   East Haven   East Haven 13 Oct 1786
     1790
   East Haven af.1850   -----   3 Oct 1838

8 Sarah Brown   Ruel Pardee Tuttle
   East Haven 7 Jan 1825   East Haven   East Haven 11 Oct 1825
   New Haven 5 Jun 1918   14 Dec 1846   New Haven 15 Jan 1913

9 Frederick Ruel Tuttle   Henrietta Frisbie
   East Haven 14 Jan 1848   East Haven   Branford,CT 31 Jul
                                                1848
   New Haven 15 Jul 1903   21 Dec 1870   East Haven 16 Sep 1902

10 Burton Linsey Tuttle   Alta Carter
   East Haven 22 Apr 1876   New Haven   New Haven 13 Apr 1874
   New Haven 18 Jan 1948   11 Oct 1906   New Haven 13 Jul 1962

TYNG, FRANKLIN SOMES

Nat. #177-B. Elected 8 Jun 1971. b. Jamaica Plain,MA 25 Jan
1924. m. Charlottesville,VA 18 Dec 1948, Jean Louise Firth.
Educ: Harvard College, AB; University of Virginia Law School LLB.
Member: Hereditary Order of Desc. of Colonial Governors; Virginia
State Bar Assn.; American Bar Assn.; American Judicature Soc.;
Former Judge, People's Court of Harford Co.MD; Maryland Golf and
Country Club; Harvard Club of MD. Address: R.D. #3, Wheel Road,
Bel Air, MD 21014. (From Society's Records). Descended from:

1 Thomas Dudley, Governor of Massachusetts 1634-35, 1640-41,
   1645-46, 1650-51

2 Joseph Dudley   Rebecca Tyng
   Roxbury,MA 23 Sep 1647   -----   13 Jul 1651
   Roxbury 2 Apr 1720   1668/9   21 Sep 1722

3 Mary Dudley   (2)   Joseph Atkins
   2 Nov 1692   -----   Sandwich,Eng.
                                            bp. 4 Nov 1680
   19 Nov 1774   1730   Newbury,MA 25 Jan 1773

4 Dudley Atkins   Sarah Kent
   Newbury Jan 1731   -----   -----
   Newburyport,MA   4 May 1752   1810
     24 Sep 1767

5 Dudley Atkins Tyng   Sarah Higginson
   Newburyport 3 Sep 1760 -----   Salem,MA 11 Jun 1766
   Newburyport 1 Aug 1829 18 Oct 1792   Boston,MA 2 Nov 1808

6 Stephen Higginson Tyng   Anne Griswold
   Newburyport 1 Mar 1800 -----   5 Oct 1805
   Irvington,NY 3 Sep   5 Aug 1821   16 May 1832
     1885

7 Dudley Atkins Tyng   Catherine M. Stevens
   Prince George's Co.MD   Castle Point   Castle Point,NJ
     12 Jan 1825
   Philadelphia,PA   1847   21 Apr 1888
     20 Apr 1858

8 Stephen Higginson Tyng   Elizabeth Walworth
   Castle Point 2 Aug   Newton,MA   Boston 5 Aug 1852
     1851
   Cataumet,MA Sep 1911   8 Sep 1880   New York,NY 1937

9 Walworth Tyng   Ethel Atkinson Arens
   Dorchester,MA 3 Jan   Newburyport   Boston 25 Oct 1887
     1885
   Cambridge,MD 27 May   19 Jun 1912
     1960

TYNG, JOHN STEVENS

Nat. #165-B. Elected 4 Jan 1971. b. Kuling, Kiangsi, China,
31 May 1915. m. Richmond,VA 28 Nov 1942, Camilla Brown Haden,
b. Palmyra,VA 13 Jul 1916. Issue: Catherine Walworth Tyng;
Eleanor Sloan Tyng; Edward Atkins Tyng. Educ: Trinity College,
Hartford,CT. Member: Hereditary Order of Desc. of Colonial
Governors; Sons of the American Revolution; Fluvanna County
Historical Soc.; American Institute of Certified Public
Accountants; Virginia Soc. C.P.A. (Fellow); American Accounting
Assn. Occup: Certified Public Accountant. Honors: Seven battle
stars and Purple Heart. Address: 501 Grove Avenue, Charlottes-
ville,VA 22902. (From Society's Records). Descended from:

1 Thomas Dudley, Governor of Massachusetts, 1634-35, 1640-41,
   1645-46, 1650-51

   Continue with the lineage of his brother, Franklin S. Tyng,
   #177-B.

   Inheritor: Edward Atkins Tyng (son)

TYNG, WILLIAM WARK

Nat. #169-B. Elected 13 Feb 1971. b. Changsha, Hunan, China,
2 Dec 1918. m. Naples, Italy 31 Dec 1945, Anna Teresa Schiavo,
b. Naples 17 Mar 1925. Issue: Robert Campbell Tyng, b. Trieste,
Italy 6 Jul 1947; Mary E. Tyng, b. Charlottesville,VA 9 Sep 1948;
Cynthia Walworth Tyng, b. Rome, Italy 30 May 1952; William
Schiavo Tyng, b. Charlottesville 9 Apr 1954. Educ: Kent School,
Kent,CT; Harvard College, AB cum laude; Senior Seminar in
Foreign Policy, U.S. State Dept. Member: Hereditary Order of
Desc. of Colonial Governors; Harvard Club, Washington,DC; Church
Council St. Christopher's Church, Saigon, Vietnam. Military:
First Lieutenant, U.S. Army. Occup: U.S. State Dept. Address:
3916 Livingston St., N.W., Washington,DC 20015. Descended from:

1 Thomas Dudley, Governor of Massachusetts, 1634-35, 1640-41,
  1645-46, 1650-51

  Continue with the lineage of his brother, Franklin S. Tyng,
  #177-B.

  Inheritor: Robert Campbell Tyng (son)

                              U - V

VAN ANTWERP, LEE DOUGLAS, M.D.

Nat. #148-B. Elected 29 Nov 1968. b. Pittsburgh,PA 3 Aug 1900.
m. Chickasha,OK 8 Mar 1946, Helen B. Anstey, b. Massena,IA
5 Sep 1911. Educ: University of Michigan, AB 1923; MD 1931.
Member: Hereditary Order of Desc. of Colonial Governors; Soc. of
Mayflower Desc. (Past Gov. Gen. and recipient of Gov. Gen.
Award; Past Surgeon Gen.;Chairman, Five Generations Project);
Sons of American Revolution (National Membership Award and
Registrar of IL Soc.); Holland Soc. of New York (Pres., Mid West
Branch); Illinois Huguenot Soc. (Member, Board of Directors);
Order of Founders and Patriots (Registrar); Soc. of Colonial
Wars; Soc. of War of 1812; Flagon and Trencher; Knight of Grace,
Military and Hospitaller Order of St. Lazarus of Jerusalem;
Knight, Supreme Order of the Hospital of St. John of Jerusalem
in Denmark; Knight, Supreme Military Order of the Temple in
Jerusalem; American College of Physicians (Life Fellow);
American Medical Soc.; Illinois and Cook Co. Medical Societies;
American Medical Writers' Assn.; Board Member for Certification
of Genealogists. Occup: Physician (Ret.) Address: 2050 Plymouth
Lane, Northbrook,IL 60062. Descended from:

1 William Bradford, Governor of Plymouth Colony 1621-33,
  1635-57

2 William Bradford   (1)   Alice Richards
  Plymouth,MA 17 Jun   Plymouth   c.1627
    1624
  Plymouth 20 Feb 1703/4 bf.28 Jan 1650 Plymouth 12 Dec 1671

3 Hannah Bradford   Joshua Ripley
  Plymouth 9 May 1662   Plymouth   Hingham,MA 9 Nov 1658
  Windham,CT 28 May 1738 28 Nov 1682   Windham 8 May 1739

4	Faith Ripley		Samuel Bingham
	Hingham 20 Sep 1686	Windham	Norwich,CT 28 Mar 1685
	Windham 11 Feb 1720	5 Jan 1708	Windham 1 Mar 1760
5	Abisha Bingham		Mary Tubbs
	Windham 29 Jan 1710	-----	Lyme,CT 2 Apr 1710
	-----	28 Dec 1731	-----
6	Abisha Bingham		Ann Sawyer
	Windham 28 Feb 1735	Windham	Windham 28 Feb 1734/5
	-----	Feb 1755	Windham 29 Oct 1813
7	Sarah Bingham		Adroyal Simmons
	Windham 24 Jul 1758	Windham	Windham 2 Feb 1757
	Luzerne Co.PA Jul 1802	8 Mar 1781	Bradford Co.PA 11 Oct 1828
8	Levi Simmons		Rhoda Ward
	21 Dec 1785	-----	-----
	Belmont,NY 5 Nov 1870	-----	Belmont c.1831
9	John A. Simons		Lany Ann Utter
	Belmont 2 Nov 1822	Friendship,NY	Friendship 25 Apr 1826
	Sparta,MI 25 Feb 1899	Sep 1846	Sparta 17 Apr 1917
10	Mary Frances Simons		William Lewis Van Antwerp
	Sparta 16 Jun 1850	Sparta	Schenectady,NY 21 Feb 1843
	Clare,MI 16 Apr 1934	17 Sep 1868	Grand Rapids,MI 27 Feb 1912
11	Herbert Adelbert Van Antwerp		Marie Freda Deffinger
	Sparta 27 Mar 1872	Filer City,MI	Sherman,PA 25 May 1876
	East Grand Rapids,MI 19 Jan 1952	31 Dec 1895	Grand Rapids,MI 2 Apr 1966

SUPPLEMENT NO. 1

1	Benedict Arnold, Governor of Rhode Island 1688-89		
2	Caleb Arnold		Abigail Wilbor
	Providence,RI 19 Dec 1644	-----	-----
	Newport,RI 9 Feb 1719	10 Jun 1666	Newport 17 Nov 1730
3	Samuel Arnold		Mary George
	Portsmouth c.1677	Block Island	-----
	-----	17 May 1706	-----
4	Elizabeth Arnold		Josiah Utter
	North Kingston,RI	New Shoreham	Westerly,RI c.1717
	6 Nov ----	27 May 1736	Connecticut
5	Josiah Utter		Mary Ketcham
	CT 1755	Greenwich,CT	1759
	Friendship,NY 1812	4 Feb 1779	NY 1848
6	Joshua Utter		Helena Rhynders
	Greenwich 5 Sep 1791	-----	Poughkeepsie,NY 27 Oct 1792
	Friendship 17 Nov 1861	-----	Friendship 1828
7	Lany Utter		John A. Simons

Continue with Generation 9 of his lineage from Governor
William Bradford.

VAN ARSDALE, RUTH TORR (MRS. HOWARD C.)

Nat. #101-B. b. Lynn,MA 20 Jan 1901. m. Hillside,MD 3 Apr
1947,Howard Campbell Van Arsdale, b. Newport News,VA 13 Sep
1901. Educ: Macalester College, St. Paul,MN; University of
Minnesota, B.Sc. in Physics. Member: Hereditary Order of Desc.
of Colonial Governors; Dames of the Court of Honor; Dau. of
American Revolution (Past Treasurer); Dau. of 1812; National
Huguenot Soc. (Past Treasurer); Huguenot Soc. Memorial of
Oxford; Soc. of Desc. of Colonial Clergy; Soc. of Dau. of
Colonial Wars; Sons and Dau. of the Pilgrims; New England Women;
Piscataqua Pioneers (Past President); Magna Charta Dames; Most
Noble Order of the Garter; Americans of Royal Descent (Listed in
Blood Royal); Listed in the Royal Blue Book, National Register
and Green Book of Washington,DC. Occup: High school teacher and
former court reporter. Address: 8704 Eaglebrook Court,
Alexandria,VA 22308. Descended from:

1 Thomas Dudley, Governor of Massachusetts 1634-35, 1640-41,
   1645-46, 1650-51

2 Samuel Dudley   (3)   Elizabeth
   Northampton,Eng.   -----   c.1628
      c.1606
   Exeter,NH 10 Feb   by 1650   af.1702
      1682/3

3 Stephen Dudley   Sarah Gilman
   c.1650   -----   -----
   c.1735   12 Mar 1684   -----

4 Nicholas Dudley   Elizabeth Gordon
   Exeter 27 Aug 1694   -----   -----
   1766   -----   -----

5 Joseph Dudley   Hannah Leavitt
   Brentwood,NH 1728   -----   -----
   -----   -----   -----

6 Trueworthy Dudley   Sarah Stevens
   Brentwood 5 Jan 1757   -----   Lebanon,ME 10 Jan 1760
   York Co.ME   -----   -----

7 William Dudley   Harriet Hardy
   Portland,ME 1804   -----   Portland
   Gorham,ME 25 Mar 1852   -----   Portland 21 Aug 1828

8 Caroline F. Dudley   John Stevens Torr
   Portland 21 Aug 1828   Peabody,MA   -----
   Peabody 27 Jan 1899   1850   5 Aug 1894

9 Charles Stevens Torr   Rose Belle Hurlburt
   Peabody 2 Jun 1869   Danvers,MA   Digby,Nova Scotia
                                              26 Feb 1873
   Minneapolis,MN   17 Jul 1895   Bethesda,MD 10 May
      9 Jul 1933   1950

VAN RENSSELAER, EDNA TRETHEWAY (MRS.)

Nat. #269-B. Elected 11 Nov 1975. b. Oakland,CA 13 Sep 1909.
m. Los Angeles,CA 13 Sep 1931, Robert Schuyler Van Rensselaer,
b. Chicago,IL 19 Sep 1903, d. Oxnard,CA 22 Dec 1972. Educ:
Univ. of Southern California. Member: Hereditary Order of Desc.
of Colonial Governors; Dau. of American Revolution; Local Mitz
Khan a Khan; Magna Charta Dames; Sovereign Colonial Soc. of
Americans of Royal Descent; Knights of Most Noble Order of the
Garter; Order of Crown of Charlemagne; Plantagenet Society;
Francis Bacon Literary Society of England. Address: 191 West
Fiesta Green, Port Hueneme,CA 93041. Descended from:

1 John Alden, Governor of Plymouth Colony 1663-64, 1667

2 Jonathan Alden   Abigail Hallet
   Plymouth,MA c.1632   Duxbury,MA   c.1644
   Duxbury 14 Feb 1697   10 Dec 1672   Duxbury 17 Aug 1725

3 Jonathan Alden   Elizabeth Arnold
   Barnstable af.1686   Marshfield,MA   -----
   Gorham,ME 10 Jul 1770 17 Jan 1717   af. 3 Apr 1727

4 Austin Alden   Salome Lombard
   Marshfield 25 Mar   -----   Gorham 10 Jun 1736
     1729
   Gorham 23 Mar 1804   25 Nov 1756   Gorham bf. 1781

5 Josiah Alden   Sarah Robinson
   Gorham 31 Mar 1761   -----   Cape Elizabeth,ME 1757
   Gorham Nov 1834   25 Nov 1782   Gorham 21 Aug 1820

6 Hannah Alden   Jotham Sedgley
   Gorham 20 Jan 1791   -----   York,ME 8 Mar 1780
   Limerick,ME Nov 1876 18 Jan 1812   Limerick 31 Jan 1857

7 John Sedgley   Elizabeth A. Smith
   Limerick 10 Jan 1822 -----   England 1827
   Alameda,CA 20 Mar 1903 -----   Alameda 23 Dec 1918

8 Emmie L. Sedgley   Thomas Tretheway
   San Francisco,CA   -----   Cornwall,Eng. 1850
     12 Aug 1855
   Alameda 1935   12 Aug 1875   San Francisco 1880

9 Charles Frederick   Edna Elsie Bishop
     Tretheway
   Alameda 12 Nov 1879   San Francisco   Chico,CA 14 Feb 1882
   Alameda 19 Aug 1931   14 Feb 1900   Bakersfield,CA
                                            17 Mar 1919

Inheritor: Mrs. Ethel Tretheway Spangler (sister)

VOSBURG, VIRGENE CAREY (MRS. DELBERT JAMES)

Nat. #284-B. Elected 1 Mar 1976. b. Ladora,IA 2 Mar 1920.
m.(1) Cedar Rapids,IA 20 Jun 1936, Rex Wilmot Atherton, div.
8 Jan 1940. m.(2) Encinitas,CA 24 Jun 1940, Delbert James
Vosburg, b. Denver,CO 22 Aug 1917. Educ: Long Beach State, Long
Beach,CA; UCSD, LaJolla,CA. Member: Hereditary Order of Desc.
of Colonial Governors; Dau. of American Revolution; Colonial
Dames XVII Century; Women Desc. of Ancient and Honorable
Artillery Co. (CA, Court of Assistants); Huguenot Society of
California; Magna Charta Dames; Dames, Guild of St. Margaret of
Scotland; Sovereign Colonial Society of Americans of Royal Des-
cent. Address: 179 Allington St., Long Beach,CA 90805. Descended
from:

1 Samuel Gorton, Governor of Rhode Island, 1651-52

2 Ann Gorton   John Warner
   -----   -----   1 Aug 1645
   -----   7 Aug 1670   22 Apr 1712

3 Ann Warner   (Jacob) Jabez Browne
   -----   -----   Providence,RI 1675
   Providence 25 Feb 1727   -----   Providence 9 Sep 1724

4 William Browne   Patience Arnold
   Providence 1708   -----   -----
   Smithfield,RI 27 Jan   c.1728   -----
     1756

5 Eleazer Browne   Sarah Scott
   Smithfield 31 Dec 1736   Smithfield   Smithfield 18 Oct 1738
   Fayette Co.PA w.p.   14 Dec 1758   -----
     23 Mar 1822

6 Joseph Browne (Brown)   Sarah Hewitt
   Smithfield 10 Jun 1764   Fayette Co.   Pennsylvania
   Stark Co.OH   8 Apr 1802   Stark Co.

7 Eliza Brown   Jesse Hawley
   1806   -----   Chester Co.PA 10 Feb
                                                    1796
   Stark Co. 1852   c.1827   Cedar Co.IA 31 Jul 1880

8 Elvira Hawley   Thomas Maudlin
   Stark Co. 14 Mar 1838   -----   Wayne Co.IN 28 Aug 1818
   Ladera,IA 14 Oct 1928   16 Feb 1860   Iowa Co.IA 10 Feb 1896

9 Euretha (Retha) Maudlin   William J. Risdon
   Iowa Co. 13 May 1873   Iowa Co.   Iowa Co. 28 Apr 1873
   Iowa Co. 15 Feb 1919   1 Jan 1894   Riverside,CA 15 Sep
                                                    1937

10 Alma Retha Risdon   Ora Forest Carey
   Iowa Co. 27 Mar 1897   Adel,IA   Iowa Co. 27 Jun 1898
   -----   5 Jul 1919   Encinitas,CA 29 Jan
                                                    1956

WAGNER, MARY WENDELL WOODWARD (MRS. JOHN WRIGHT)

Nat. #323-B. Elected 17 Feb 1978. b. Philadelphia,PA 7 Jul 1913. m. Philadelphia 19 Oct 1940, John Wright Wagner, b.Philadelphia 7 Jul 1908. Educ: Agnes Irwin School, Rosemont,PA. Member: Hereditary Order of Desc. of Colonial Governors; Dau. of American Revolution (NJ, Past Vice Regent, Bicentennial Comm.) Occup: Former Executive Secretary. Address: 6743 Rogers Avenue, Merchantville,NJ 08109. Descended from:

1 Thomas Hinckley, Governor of Plymouth Colony 1680-85, 1689-92

2 Ebenezer Hinckley
  Barnstable,MA 23 Sep   Barnstable
  1673
  Braintree,MA 17 Oct   17 Nov 1706
  1721

Mary Stone
Sudbury,MA 19 Feb 1682

1743

3 Ebenezer Hinckley, Jr.
  Braintree 14 Mar 1713   Braintree
  West Indies   11 Jul 1732

Hannah Nightingale
Milton,MA 25 Oct 1712
-----

4 Ebenezer Hinckley,3rd
  -----   Boston,MA
  Westford,MA 15 Aug   22 Oct 1765
  1812

Anna Morton
Dorchester,MA
Dorchester 24 Jun 1820

5 John Hinckley
  MA 19 Feb 1768   Littleton,MA
  Albany,NY   22 Aug 1800

Eunice Warren
Littleton 11 Aug 1779
Albany

6 Mary Hinckley
  Albany 3 Dec 1820   Albany
  Poughkeepsie,NY   3 Sep 1844
  3 Oct 1909

Cornelius Wendell
Albany 20 Feb 1813
Northampton,MA 9 Oct
  1870

7 Blanche Wendell

  Albany 2 Dec 1846   Washington,DC

  Washington,DC 31 Mar   3 Feb 1870
  1896

Joseph Janvier
  Woodward
Philadelphia,PA
  30 Oct 1833
Media,PA 17 Aug 1884

8 Graham Cox Woodward
  Washington,DC 6 Sep   Philadelphia
  1880
  Philadelphia 13 Feb   -----
  1946

Alice Weber
3 Jan 1875

Philadelphia 14 Oct
  1943

WALEN, HARRY LEONARD

Nat. #312-B. Elected 27 Jun 1977. b. Winchester,MA 26 Jun 1915.
m. Somerville,MA 26 Jun 1939, Elizabeth Rowe Benson, b. Somerville
25 Jan 1915. Educ: Harvard AB, AM. Member: Hereditary Order of
Desc. of Colonial Governors; Sons of American Revolution (MA,
Vice President; Minuteman Chap., President); Soc. of Mayflower
Descendants; Pilgrim John Howland Soc.; Order of Founders and
Patriots; Soc. of Desc. of Colonial Clergy. Listed in Who's
Who in the East and Directory of American Scholars. Address:
Penzance Road, Rockport,ME 01966. Descended from:

1 Thomas Dudley, Governor of Massachusetts 1634-35, 1640-41,
   1645-46, 1650-51

2 Patience Dudley   Daniel Denison
   England   Cambridge,MA   England 1612
   8 Feb 1690   18 Oct 1633   Ipswich,MA 20 Sep 1682

3 Elizabeth Denison   John Rogers
   Ipswich c.1641   Ipswich   Assington,Eng. c.1630
   Ipswich·13 Jun 1723   14 Nov 1660   Cambridge,MA 20 Jul
                                             1684

4 John Rogers   Martha Whitingham
   Ipswich 7 Jul 1666   Ipswich   c.1670
   Ipswich 28 Dec 1745   4 Mar 1690   Ipswich 9 Mar 1759

5 John Rogers   Susannah Whipple
   Ipswich 27 Jan 1692   Ipswich   -----
   Kittery,ME 16 Oct 1773 6 Sep 1718   Kittery 22 Oct 1779

6 Daniel Rogers   Elizabeth Gorham
   Kittery 25 Oct 1734   Gloucester   Barnstable 10 Dec 1739
   Gloucester,MA 4 Jan   6 Nov 1759   Gloucester 4 Mar 1769
     1800

7 John Gorham Rogers   Mercy Rogers (cousin)
   Gloucester 16 Apr   Gloucester   Gloucester 27 Oct 1770
     1763
   Gloucester 27 Nov   27 Oct 1790   Gloucester 30 Dec 1845
     1802

8 Daniel W. Rogers   Eliza (Betsey) Kimball
   Gloucester 31 Aug   Gloucester   Gloucester 1 Oct 1798
     1791
   Gloucester 9 Mar 1834 2 Dec 1819   Gloucester 27 Aug 1877

9 John Kimball Rogers   Sarah McLennen Niles
   Gloucester 31 Jan 1821 Gloucester   Boston,MA Nov 1829
   Brookline,MA 27 Jan   31 Jan 1854   Brookline 12 Apr 1862
     1888

10 Sarah McLennen Rogers   Joseph Everett Garland
   Brookline 28 Oct 1861 Brookline   Gloucester 17 Nov 1851
   Newton,MA 16 Jul 1931 23 Feb 1887   Gloucester 16 Dec 1907

11 Alice Garland   Harry Leonard Walen
   Gloucester 20 Mar 1888 Gloucester   Gloucester 18 May 1888
   living in 1977   4 May 1914   Gloucester 23 Feb 1923

WALLER, JAMES WITHERS

Nat. #219-B. Elected 23 Oct 1973. b. Roanoke,VA 7 May 1935.
Educ: Virginia Polytechnic Inst. and State University, Blacks-
burg,VA, BS; University of North Carolina, MS. Member:
Hereditary Order of Desc. of Colonial Governors; Sons of American
Revolution; Washington Family Desc.; Desc. of Signers of the
Declaration of Independence; Jamestowne Society; Soc. of Colonial
Wars; Virginia Historical Soc. Address: 808 Preston Avenue,
Blacksburg,VA 24060. Descended from:

1 John West, Governor of Virginia 1635-37

2 John West   Unity Croshaw
  New Kent Co.VA 1632   York Co.VA   York Co.
  1689   c.1667   -----

3 Nathaniel West   Martha W. Macon
  New Kent Co. c.1672   -----   -----
  1723   -----   -----

4 Unity West   William Dandridge
  West Point,VA c.1700   -----   England
  1753   18 Mar 1719   King William Co.VA
                                                   c.1743

5 Nathaniel W. Dandridge   Dorothy Spotswood
  King & Queen Co.VA   -----   1733
    7 Sep 1729
  Hanover Co.VA 16 Jan   -----   -----
    1786

6 Elizabeth Dandridge   Philip Payne
  12 Sep 1764   -----   Goochland Co.VA 29 Mar
                                                   1760
  26 Apr 1833   13 Nov 1783   Campbell Co.VA 7 Sep
                                                   1840

7 Evalina W. Payne   Edward B. Withers
  Campbell Co. 24 Feb   Campbell Co.   Fauquier Co.VA 10 Jan
    1801   1797
  -----   1819   Campbell Co. 20 May
                                                   1849

8 Walter S. Withers   Mary M. Clark
  Campbell Co. 10 Feb   Lynchburg,VA   Campbell Co. 15 Mar
    1829   1836
  Campbell Co. 7 Nov   5 Oct 1859   Fayetteville,NC
    1896   29 Mar 1918

9 Zuleika I. Withers   Thomas C. Nelson
  Bedford Co.VA 20 Apr   Pelham,NC   Jefferson Co.WV 7 Jan
    1869   1868
  Lynchburg,VA 25 Aug   1 Mar 1889   Lynchburg 30 Jan 1938
    1948

10 Nina Withers Nelson   James A. Waller, Jr.
   Rustburg 3 Sep 1898   Rustburg,VA   Hebron,MD 29 Aug 1889
                           11 Nov 1924

WALLER, NINA WITHERS NELSON (MRS. JAMES A., JR.)

Nat. #162-B. Elected 14 Aug 1970. b. Rustburg,VA 3 Sep 1898.
m. Rustburg 11 Nov 1924, James A. Waller, Jr., b. Hebron,MD
29 Aug 1889. Issue: Thomas Nelson Waller, b. 10 Oct 1930;
James Withers Waller, b. 7 May 1935; both b. Blacksburg,VA.
Educ: Randolph Macon Woman's College. Member: Hereditary Order
of Desc. of Colonial Governors; Dau. of American Revolution
(Past Regent); Washington Family Descendants; Huguenot Society
of Founders of Manakin in Colony of Virginia; Dau. of Colonial
Wars; Clan MacDougall Soc. of U.S. and Canada; Signers of the
Declaration of Independence; Soc. of Desc. of Colonial Clergy;
Dau. of American Colonists; Americans of Royal Descent; Order of
Three Crusades; Order of First Families of Virginia; Americans
of Armorial Ancestry; Dau. of Founders and Patriots of America;
Dau. of Cincinnati; Colonial Dames of XVII Century; Jamestowne
Society; Magna Charta Dames. Address: 808 Preston Avenue,
Blacksburg, VA 24060. Descended from:

1 John West, Governor of Virginia 1635-37

Continue with the lineage of her son, James Withers Waller,
Nat. #219-B.

WALSH, MYLES ALEXANDER, II

Nat. #217-B. Elected 21 Sep 1973. b. Oradell,NJ 21 Jun 1912.
m. Chicago,IL 29 Nov 1941, Ruth Elizabeth Berg, b. Chicago 19
Jul 1920. Issue: Josephine Louise Walsh, b. Santiago de Cuba,
Cuba 8 Jan 1943; Myles Alexander Walsh, III, b. Santiago de Cuba
13 Mar 1944; Fraser MacFarland Walsh, b. Red Sea 19 Feb 1947.
Educ: Harvard University, BS, Mining Engineering 1933. Member:
Hereditary Order of Desc. of Colonial Governors; Soc. of
Mayflower Desc., NJ; Soc. of Desc. of Colonial Clergy; Order of
Colonial Lords of the Manors in America; Soc. of Economic
Geologists; American Inst. of Mining, Metallurgical and Petro-
leum Engineers; Soc. of Harvard Engineers and Scientists; Harvard
Club of NYC; NY Academy of Sciences; Mining Club of NY; Mining
and Metallurgical Soc. of America. Occup: Consultant Mining
Engineer. Address: 143 No. Main St., Cranbury, NJ 08512.
Descended from:

1 Thomas Mayhew, Governor of Martha's Vineyard 1641-81

2	Martha Mayhew		Thomas Tupper
	Martha's Vineyard 1642	Martha's Vnyd.	Sandwich 16 Jun 1638
	Sandwich,MA 15 Nov 1717	27 Dec 1661	Sandwich 28 Apr 1706
3	Anne Tupper		Benjamin Gibbs
	Sandwich 14 Dec 1679	-----	Sandwich Dec 1673
	-----	1698/9	Sandwich 1757
4	Silvanus Gibbs		Bathsheba Pope
	Sandwich 20 Apr 1702	-----	Sandwich 2 Dec 1713
	Dec 1749	-----	-----

5	Bathsheba Gibbs Sandwich 29 Aug 1740		John Perry Sandwich 26 Jul 1739
		Monument Beach,MA	
	-----	26 Jul 1763	Sandwich 11 May 1809
6	John Perry Sandwich 23 Aug 1768	-----	Mary Swift Falmouth,MA 1768
	Nantucket,MA 26 Oct 1804	20 Jan 1793	Sandwich 16 Sep 1864
7	Lydia Perry Sandwich 26 Nov 1793	-----	Ellis H. Blackwell Sandwich 22 May 1789
	Sandwich 29 Dec 1851	30 Dec 1819	Sandwich 30 Jan 1848
8	Russell Blackwell Sandwich 21 Apr 1824	-----	Lydia B. Phinney Sandwich 20 Dec 1827
	Bourne,MA 17 Nov 1898	6 Sep 1848	Bourne 20 Apr 1907
9	Ada B. K. Blackwell Monument Beach 15 Jul 1851	Bourne	Robert T. Newman Koenigsburg, Prussia 1831
	Oradell,NJ 24 Feb 1920	2 Oct 1877	Monument Beach 28 Aug 1903
10	Louise P. Newman New York City 21 Dec 1878	Bourne	Myles A. Walsh London,Eng. 15 Nov 1874
	Hackensack,NJ 17 Jun 1960	30 Jun 1903	Westwood,NJ 5 Feb 1968

WALSH, RUTH ELIZABETH BERG (MRS. MYLES A.)

Nat. #208-B. Elected 14 Jun 1973. b. Chicago,IL 19 Jul 1920.
m. Chicago 29 Nov 1941, Myles Alexander Walsh, b. Oradell,NJ
21 Jun 1912. Issue: Josephine Louise Walsh, b. Santiago de Cuba,
Cuba 8 Jan 1943; Myles Alexander Walsh III, b. Santiago de Cuba
13 Mar 1944; Fraser MacFarland Walsh, b. Red Sea 19 Feb 1947.
Educ: Stephens College, Columbia,MO; Northwestern University,BS;
Columbia University, MAT. Member: Hereditary Order of Desc. of
Colonial Governors; Soc. of Mayflower Descendants, NJ; Soc. of
Desc. of King William the Conqueror, London; Magna Charta Dames;
Sovereign Colonial Soc. Americans of Royal Descent; Desc. of
Knights of the Garter; Plantagenet Soc.; Huguenot Soc. of America
NYC; British American Soc. of America, London; Order of Crown of
Charlemagne; Washington Family Desc.; Soc. of Desc. of Colonial
Clergy; Dau. of American Revolution (Francis Hopkinson Chap.,
Vice Regent); Life and State Promoter CAR; Bicentennial Ch. 1974-
1977; SAR Medal of Appreciation; Cranbury,NJ Historical and
Preservation Soc. (Historian); N.E. Historical and Genealogical
Soc.; Stetson Kindred; Dickinson Family Assn. Address: 143 North
Main St., Cranbury,NJ 08512. Descended from:

1 Thomas Prence, Governor of Plymouth Colony 1634-73

2	Elizabeth Prence Duxbury,MA c.1642	-----	Arthur Howland Marshfield,MA
	-----	9 Dec 1667	-----

3	Thomas Howland		Mary
	Marshfield 26 Sep 1672	-----	-----
	-----	-----	-----
4	Rebeckah Howland		Samuel Thomas
	Marshfield 13 Nov 1704	Duxbury	Marshfield 7 Dec 1685
	13 Mar 1798	15 Feb 1727	22 Sep 1768
5	Bethiah Thomas		Israel Rogers
	Marshfield 23 Jan 1728	Marshfield	Marshfield 22 Nov 1722
	15 Jun 1819	31 Dec 1747	29 Nov 1811
6	Bethiah Rogers		Anthony E. Hatch
	Marshfield 24 Feb 1761	-----	Marshfield 18 Apr 1753
	23 Jul 1844	28 Feb 1782	10 Sep 1842
7	Calvin Hatch		Ruth Webber
	Marshfield 14 Apr 1794	-----	Canada 31 Dec 1800
	Burton, Canada 31 May 1877	14 Apr 1817	Burton 21 Jun 1880
8	Anthony R. Hatch		Charlotte Kinney
	Burton 8 Mar 1826	Oromocto	Oromocto 10 Nov 1829
	Oromocto,N.B., Canada 27 Jun 1894	c.1848	Oromocto 13 May 1913
9	Josephine L. Hatch		Thomas Millidge Gratz
	Lincoln,N.B., Canada 26 Oct 1859	Lincoln	Lincoln 8 Jul 1855
	Lake Villa,IL 14 Dec 1918	14 Jun 1870	Libertyville,IL 13 Feb 1930
10	Grace Gratz		Frederick A. Berg
	Waasis,N.B., Canada 22 Aug 1887	Wheaton,IL	Chicago,IL 4 Aug 1889
	Chicago 17 Aug 1969	6 Dec 1916	

Inheritor: Mr. Myles Alexander Walsh, IV, 60 Barnabas Road, Falmouth,MA 02540.

WALTERS, FRANCES HERNDON (MRS. AUGUSTUS)

Nat. #196-B. Elected 8 Nov 1972. b. Franklin,GA 30 Aug 1890. m. Toccoa,GA 3 Jul 1949, Augustus Walters, b. 11 Nov 1879, d. Jacksonville,FL 3 Nov 1951. Educ: Georgia State College for Women. Member: Hereditary Order of Desc. of Colonial Governors; Dau. of American Revolution; Colonial Dames of XVII Century; National Soc. of Magna Charta Dames. Occup: Former teacher. Address: none. (From Society's Records). Descended from:

1   Edward Digges, Governor of Virginia 1655-56

*2 Catherine Digges   William Herndon
    Virginia 1654   Virginia   England 1649
    Virginia 1727   1677   New Kent Co.VA 1722

3   Edward Herndon   Mary Waller
    Virginia 1678   Virginia   c.1680
    Virginia 1745   1698   Virginia 1727

*4 William Herndon   Ann Drysdale
    Virginia 1706   Virginia   Virginia 1711
    Virginia 1783   1730   Virginia 1777

5   Edward Herndon   Mary Gaines
    Spotsylvania Co.VA   Virginia   Culpeper Co.VA 1742
      16 Jul 1738
    Madison Co.VA 1831   1762   Virginia 1829

6   Benjamin Herndon   Susan Ahart
    Virginia 1765   Virginia   Virginia 1769
    Elbert Co. GA 1805   20 Nov 1786   1835

7   Michael Herndon   Sarah J. Seals
    VA 26 Apr 1788   Elbert Co.   Elbert Co. 26 Aug 1788
    Elbert Co. 6 Apr   12 Apr 1812   Elbert Co. 22 Nov 1837
      1857

8   Michael A. Herndon   Frances Roberts
    Elbert Co. 26 Apr   -----   Franklin Co.GA 21 Jul
      1837   1836
    Lavonia,GA 3 Jun   18 Dec 1859   Hopeville,GA 23 Jan
      1917   1915

9   George H. Herndon   Lucy P. Moseley
    Franklin Co.   Franklin Co. Franklin Co. 20 May
      18 Jun 1862   1863
    Fort Worth,TX c.1932 14 Jan 1885 Orlando,FL 17 Dec
                                      1955

SUPPLEMENT NO. 1

1   Hugh Drysdale, Governor of Virginia 1722-26

*2 Ann Drysdale   William Herndon

    Continue with Generation 4 of her lineage from Governor
    Edward Digges.

    Inheritor: Mary Lucy Herndon (Mrs. Frank Mikell)

WARD, NICHOLAS DONNELL

Nat. #198-B. Elected 11 Dec 1972. b. New York,NY 30 Jul 1941.
m. Washington,DC 6 Sep 1968, Elizabeth Reed Lowman, b. Takoma
Park,MD 12 Nov 1944. Educ: Columbia College, New York,NY, BA;
Georgetown University Law Center, Washington,DC, LLB.
Member: Hereditary Order of Desc. of Colonial Governors (2nd
Deputy Governor General); Soc. of War of 1812 (DC, Historian);
Military Order of the Loyal Legion, DC; Sons of Revolution, DC,
NY; Sons of Union Veterans of Civil War, Lincoln Cushing Camp
#2; Sons of American Revolution (DC, Assistant Secretary);
Military Order of Foreign Wars of U.S.; Soc. of Colonial Wars;
Soc. of Mayflower Descendants (DC, Assistant Captain); Order of
Founders and Patriots of America; Baronial Order of Magna
Charta; Order of Americans of Armorial Ancestry; Soc. of Desc.
of Colonial Clergy; Order of Crown of Charlemagne in U.S.A.;
National Huguenot Soc. (DC, Treasurer); Order of La Fayette;
Flagon and Trencher; Friends of St. George; Desc. of Knights of
the Garter; Jaycees (DC, Director); Selden Society; University
Club, Washington,DC; Alpha Delta Phi. Honors: Downtown Jaycees,
"Man of the Year," 1971-72; Listed: Outstanding Young Men of
America, 1972 Ed., Hereditary Register. Occup: Partner in
Hamilton & Hamilton Law Firm. Address: 6654 Barnaby Street, NW,
Washington, DC 20015. Descended from:

1 Benedict Arnold, Governor of Rhode Island 1657-60, 1662-66,
  1669-72, 1677-78

2 Caleb Arnold   Abigail Wilbur
  Providence,RI 19 Dec   -----   -----
    1644
  Newport,RI 9 Feb 1719   10 Jun 1666   Newport 17 Nov 1730

3 Penelope Arnold   George Hazard
  Newport 3 Aug 1669   Rhode Island   Kingston,RI
  South Kingston,RI   -----   South Kingston 1743
    af. 1742

4 George Hazard   Sarah Carder
  North Kingston 9 Oct   Rhode Island   RI 14 May 1705
    1700
  South Kingston 24 Jun   -----   RI 1738
    1738

5 Carder Hazard   Alice Hazard
  South Kingston 11 Aug   Rhode Island   South Kingston 30 Aug
    1734   1737
  South Kingston 24 Nov   5 Mar 1761   South Kingston 13 Jan
    1792   1793

6 George C. Hazard   Jane Hull
  South Kingston 13 Apr   So.Kingston   South Kingston 24 Sep
    1763   1781
  South Kingston 29 Sep   16 May 1807   South Kingston 13 Apr
    1829   1862

7 Laura Hazard   Attmore Robinson
  South Kingston 4 Nov   Wakefield,RI   South Kingston 23 Apr
    1819   1804
  Wakefield 12 Mar 1915   17 Mar 1841   Wakefield 2 Aug 1890

8 George Hazard Robinson		Sarah Delamater
Wakefield 20 Apr 1847	New York City	NYC 12 Dec 1846
NYC 5 Sep 1919	14 Jun 1869	NYC 20 Dec 1929
9 Ruth Robinson		Harry Ellingwood Donnell
NYC 28 Mar 1870	New York City	Portland,ME 2 May 1867
NYC 22 May 1949	10 Oct 1894	NYC 25 Feb 1959
10 Sarah Delamater Donnell		Francis Xavier Ward
NYC 16 Oct 1906	Northport,NY	NYC 14 Jul 1904
NYC 25 Jun 1962	28 Aug 1933	living in 1973

WARFIELD, JOHN OGLE, JR., M.D.

Nat. #218-B. Elected 23 Oct 1973. b. Baltimore,MD 3 Apr 1900. m. Baltimore Co.MD 16 Dec 1924, Rachel Elisabeth Baldwin, b. Harford Co.MD 5 Jun 1896. Issue: Elisabeth Baldwin Warfield, b. Baltimore 11 Oct 1926; John Ogle Warfield III, b. Washington, DC 8 Apr 1930. Educ: St. John's College, Annapolis, BA, MA; University of Maryland Medical School, Baltimore,MD. Member: Hereditary Order of Desc. of Colonial Governors; Soc. of Colonial Wars, (MD, DC, Past Governor and Past Deputy Governor General); Sons of Revolution, DC; Baronial Order of Magna Charta (Surety); Military Order of Crusades; Order of Crown of Charlemagne in USA; Soc. of Americans of Royal Descent (Councillor); Huguenot Society, MD; Order of Three Crusades; Desc. of Knights of the Garter; Order of First Families of Virginia; Desc. of Lords of Maryland Manors; numerous medical societies; Cosmos Club; Kappa Alpha; Nu Sigma Nu. Occup: Physician. Honors: Awarded Grant of Armorial Bearings, American College of Arms; Living Desc. of Blood Royal. Address: 3544 Williamsburg Lane, N.W., Washington,DC 20008. Descended from:

1 Nicholas Greenberry, Governor of Maryland 1692-94

2 Katherine Greenberry		Henry Ridgely
England c.1668	Maryland	Anne Arundel Co.MD 3 Oct 1669
Anne Ar.Co. 1703	c.1690	Anne Ar.Co. 19 Mar 1699
3 Anne Ridgely		Joshua Dorsey
Anne Ar.Co. c.1691	Anne Ar.Co.	Anne Ar.Co. c.1686
Anne Ar.Co. 1771	16 May 1711	Anne Ar.Co. 28 Nov 1747
4 Henry Dorsey		Elizabeth Worthington
Anne Ar.Co. 8 Nov 1712	Anne Ar.Co.	Anne Ar.Co. 6 Oct 1717
Anne Ar.Co. Feb 1770	1 Jul 1735	Anne Ar.Co. 1776
5 Ann Dorsey		Davidge Warfield
Anne Ar.Co. 7 Feb 1741	Maryland	Anne Ar.Co. 15 Feb 1729
Anne Ar.Co. bf.1810	bf.1770	Anne Ar.Co. 25 Jun 1810
6 Mary Ann Warfield		Edward Warfield
Anne Ar.Co. 28 Mar 1773	Anne Ar.Co.	Anne Ar.Co. 5 Jun 1769
Anne Ar.Co. 6 Sep 1824	7 Oct 1794	Howard Co.MD 25 Jan 1853

7　John D. Warfield
　　Anne Ar.Co. 4 Mar 1799　Anne Ar.Co.　Corrilla E. Hobbs
　　Howard Co. 31 Jul 1865　7 Dec 1826　Anne Ar.Co. 3 Mar 1806
　　　　　　　　　　　　　　　　Howard Co. 23 Jul 1880

8　Cecilius E. Warfield
　　Anne Ar.Co. 15 Aug　Frederick Co.　Laura W. Thomas
　　　1841　MD　Frederick Co. 1 Dec
　　Baltimore Co.MD　18 Jan 1870　　1844
　　　8 Sep 1915　　Baltimore Co. 19 Jan
　　　　　　　　　　　　　　　　1912

9　John Ogle Warfield
　　Frederick Co. 21 May　Baltimore Co.　Louyse D. Spragins
　　　1871　　Baltimore Co. 19 Nov
　　Montgomery Co.PA　26 Oct 1898　　1869
　　　16 Mar 1950　　Montgomery Co. 6 Jul
　　　　　　　　　　　　　　　　1948

WARNER, LOUISE, PhD

Nat. #335-B. Elected 13 Mar 1979. b. Dixon,IL 14 Aug 1916.
Member: Hereditary Order of Desc. of Colonial Governors.
Address: 4644 Reservoir Road,N.W., Washington,DC 20007.
Descended from:

1　Thomas Welles, Governor of Connecticut 1655-58

2　Sara(h) Welles
　　England 1631　Wethersfield　John Chester
　　　　　　　　　　　　Watertown,CT 5 Aug
　　　　　　　　　　　　　1653
　　Wethersfield,CT 12 Dec　Feb 1653/4　Wethersfield 23 Feb
　　　1698　　1698

3　Stephen Chester
　　Wethersfield 26 May　Wethersfield　Jemima Treat
　　　1659/60　　15 May 1668
　　Wethersfield 9 Feb　17 Dec 1691　25 May 1755
　　　1697/8

4　Dorothy Chester
　　·CT 5 Sep 1692　-----　Martin Kellogg
　　　　　　　　　　　　Deerfield,MA 26 Oct
　　　　　　　　　　　　　1686
　　Wethersfield 20 Sep　13 Jan 1716　Wethersfield 13 Nov
　　　1754　　1753

5　Dorothy Kellogg
　　Newington Parish,CT　-----　Eliphalet Whittlesey
　　　24 Dec 1716　　Newington,CT 10 May
　　　　　　　　　　　　　1714
　　Washington,CT 14 Apr　16 Dec 1736　Washington 12 Jul 1786
　　　1772

6　Dorothy Whittlesey
　　Newington 5 Sep 1755　-----　Perry Averill
　　　　　　　　　　　　Rehoboth,MA 18 Sep
　　　　　　　　　　　　　1754
　　12 Jul 1824　21 Sep 1774　10 Jul 1842

7　Patience Matilda
　　　Averill　　David Whittlesey
　　New Preston,CT　New Preston　New Preston 18 Aug
　　　5 Jan 1790　　1787
　　New Preston 31 Dec　30 Sep 1816　New Preston 20 Apr
　　　1845　　1869

8 Sarah Deming Whittlesey   Leman Ackley Warner
   Washington 25 May 1822   Washington   Olcott,NY 6 May 1817
   Freeport,IL 6 Jun 1893   7 Mar 1847   Freeport 17 Oct 1894

9 Andrew Clinton Warner   Myra Ophelia Brookner
   New Preston 3 Apr 1850   Dixon,IL   Dixon 5 Apr 1858
   Dixon 2 Jul 1927   16 Dec 1875   Alaska 20 Jul 1928

10 Henry Chester Warner   Lucile Mertz
   Dixon 19 Dec 1876   Chicago,IL   Burnettsville,IN
                                                    19 Jul 1888
   Chicago 12 Apr 1960   19 Sep 1912   living in 1978

   Inheritor: Nancy A. Nichols. 421 E. Everett St., Dixon,IL
   61021. (niece)

WATKINS, SUSAN CAROLINE FINLAY (MRS. WILLIAM H.)

Nat. #158-B. Elected 24 Mar 1970. b. Melrose,MA 12 Mar 1942.
m. William H. Watkins. Educ: University of Massachusetts, BA;
Salem State College, Salem,MA MA; New York State University.
Member: Hereditary Order of Desc. of Colonial Governors; Dau. of
American Revolution; U.S. Dau. of 1812 (MA, State Vice Presi-
dent); Soc. of Mayflower Descendants; Women Desc. of Ancient and
Honorable Artillery Co.; Dau. of Colonial Wars; Soc. of Desc. of
Colonial Clergy; Magna Charta Dames; New England Women; Flagon
and Trencher; Dau. of American Colonists; NY State Historical
Assn.; Arizona Pioneers Historical Soc.; Balch House Associates.
Address: R.D. #1, Military Road, Dolgeville,NY 13329. Descended
from:

1 John Endicott, Governor of Massachusetts 1629-65

2 Zerubbabel Endicott   Mary Smith
   Salem c.1635   Salem,MA   Salem 1636
   Salem Jan 1683/4   1654   Salem 20 Jun 1677

3 Samuel Endicott   Hannah Felton
   1659   -----   bp. 20 Jun 1663
   1694   1684   -----

4 Ruth Endicott   Martyn Herrick
   1689   -----   Salem 26 Jan 1679
   -----   17 Jul 1710   Salem 1739

5 Samuel Herrick   Elizabeth Jones
   1713   -----   Woburn,MA 31 Aug 1720
   Reading,MA 1792   1742   1759

6 Susanna Herrick   Stephen Putman
   Reading 30 Jun 1750   Reading   Salem Village,MA
                                                    22 Feb 1742
   Danvers,MA 25 Feb 1825 15 Dec 1774   Danvers 8 Jun 1809

7 Eben Putman   Betsey Webb
   Danvers 5 Feb 1785   Danvers   Danvers 11 Dec 1790
   Danvers 19 Oct 1876   8 Oct 1809   Danvers 19 Apr 1842

8 Margaret D. Putman   Joseph W. Ropes
   Danvers 24 Dec 1817   Danvers   Salem 14 Mar 1816
   Danvers 11 Jan 1895   8 Apr 1840   Danvers 24 Mar 1880

9 Caroline E. Ropes		John E. Dow
Danvers 9 Dec 1847	Danvers	Quincy,MA 16 Sep 1846
Danvers 19 Jan 1928	20 Mar 1873	Beverly,MA 28 Feb 1938
10 Waldo H. Dow		Nettie C. Morgan
Danvers 28 Jul 1882	Beverly	Beverly 19 Jul 1885
	21 Aug 1907	Beverly 1 Oct 1964
11 Lydia R. Dow		Christopher A. Finlay
Beverly 18 Apr 1912	Pelham,NH	24 Feb 1905
	27 Feb 1937	

WATROUS, DOROTHY A. POOLE STEVENS (MRS. PHILIP M.)

Nat. #48-B. Elected 10 Apr 1962. b. Philadelphia,PA 26 Oct 1917. m.(1) Philadelphia 29 Apr 1944, Lawrence Lewis Stevens, Jr., b. Ocean City,NJ 29 Jul 1915. Issue: Edward Malpass Stevens, b. Philadelphia 29 Jun 1945; Mark Lewis Stevens, b. Philadelphia 24 May 1948. m.(2) Philip M. Watrous. Member: Hereditary Order of Desc. of Colonial Governors (Councillor General); Society of Colonial Dames,PA; Society of Little Gardens of Philadelphia (President); Bryn Mawr Hospitality House Committee (Former Chairman); Acorn Club. Address: 462 Montgomery Ave., Haverford,PA 19041. Descended from:

1 Nicholas Greenbury, Governor of Maryland 1694

2 Anne Greenbury		John Hammond
England 1672	-----	1675
-----	1693	-----
3 Comfort Hammond	(2)	John Worthington
15 Aug 1701	-----	MD 1689
-----	1728	MD 1763
4 Samuel Worthington		Mary Tolley
MD 1733/4	Joppa,MD	1740
MD 7 Apr 1813	17 Jan 1759	1777
5 Martha Worthington	(2)	Thomas Love
9 Apr 1775	-----	Cecil Co.MD 25 Mar 1753
21 Jan 1846	2 Sep 1802	Baltimore Co.MD 1 Mar 1821
6 Rufus K. Love		Mary A. Brown
Cockeysville,MD	Philadelphia,	22 Dec 1830
2 Feb 1815	PA	
Cincinnati,OH	1 Jul 1853	14 Mar 1893
28 Jul 1856		
7 Annie Florence Love		J. Morton Poole
Cincinnati 23 Apr 1854	Wilmington,DE	Wilmington 29 Mar 1855
Detroit,MI 14 Jun 1936	14 Jun 1880	Wilmington 22 Apr 1913
8 John M. Poole		Caroline M. Stamback
Wilmington 12 Jan 1884	Haverford,PA	Philadelphia 20 May 1887
Villanova,PA 10 Aug 1942	12 Oct 1912	

Inheritor: Edward Malpass Stevens (son)

WEAVER, ELIZABETH J. CASE (MRS. JOHN FRANKLIN, SR.)

Nat. #316-B. Elected 1977. b. Chicago,IL 17 Sep 1917. m.
Evanston,IL 12 May 1956, John Franklin Weaver, b. South Rockwood,
MI 13 Aug 1916. Educ: Beloit College, Wisconsin, BS. Member:
Hereditary Order of Desc. of Colonial Governors; Dau. of American
Revolution (National Vice Chairman, Honor Roll); Dau. of American
Colonists (MI State Historian); Dau. of Colonial Wars (National
Recording Secretary); Colonial Dames of XVII Century (Elizabeth
Patch Chap., Past President); Colonial Daughters of Seventeenth
Century (MI, Corresponding Secretary); New England Women (Sarah
Sibley Colony, Organizing President); Women Desc. of Ancient and
Honorable Artillery Company (MI, Court of Assistants, President);
Dames of Court of Honor; Huguenot Society,MI; Soc. of Desc. of
Colonial Clergy; Flagon and Trencher; Magna Charta Dames; Old
Plymouth Colony Desc.; Piscataqua Pioneers; Sons and Dau. of
First Settlers of Newbury,MA; Sons and Dau. of Pilgrims; U.S.
Dau. of 1812; Soc. of Mayflower Desc.; Order of Crown of Charle-
magne. Address: 305 West Elm Ave., Monroe,MI 48161. Descended
from:

1 John Alden, Governor of Plymouth Colony 1633-34, 1667

2	Joseph Alden Plymouth,MA 1624 Bridgewater,MA 8 Feb 1697	----- 1657	Mary Simmons Duxbury,MA Bridgewater af.1697
3	Mary Alden Plymouth 1671 -----	----- 1700	Samuel Allen III Bridgewater 4 Dec 1660 Braintree,MA 25 Aug 1724/5
4	Abigail Allen E. Bridgewater,MA 1712 Shaftsbury,VT 6 Sep 1799	Bridgewater 14 Oct 1730	Shubael Waldo Windham,CT 7 Apr 1707 Alstead,NH 12 May 1776
5	Daniel Waldo Mansfield,CT 30 Jan 1744 Chesterfield,NH 18 Dec 1825	Haverhill,NH 1768	Hannah Carlton Haverhill 16 Aug 1745 Chesterfield 2 Dec 1825
6	Shubael Waldo Alstead 2 May 1777 Chesterfield 5 Oct 1857	Alstead 9 Mar 1800	Rebeckah Crosby Alstead 7 Feb 1779 Chesterfield 10 May 1823
7	Daniel Waldo Alstead 6 Jan 1802 Meredosia 5 Oct 1881	Meredosia,IL 31 Mar 1836	Emily Fox Batavia,NY 8 Apr 1813 Meredosia 23 Jan 1855
8	Frances Elmina Waldo Meredosia 26 Mar 1841 Meredosia 7 Oct 1880	Meredosia 3 Oct 1860	Burrette Allen New York 21 Apr 1838 Waco,TX 16 Nov 1879
9	Frances Elsie Allen Toledo,OH 15 Dec 1862 Chicago,IL 14 Oct 1941	Meredosia 14 Jul 1881	Douglas Emanuel Case Minneapolis,MN 2 Oct 1857 Sioux Falls,SD 8 Sep 1900

10 Burrette Allen Case

    Lyons,KS 12 May 1888   Chicago

    Evanston,IL 26 Jun 1957 14 Jun 1914

Ivey Elizabeth
   Kortlander
Grand Rapids,MI 28 Mar
   1885
living in 1977

Inheritor: John Franklin Weaver, Jr. (son)

WELCH, INEZ GRAHAM (MISS)

Nat. #170-B. Elected 13 Feb 1971. b. Colusa,CA 6 Jan 1894.
Educ: Mills College, Oakland,CA. Member: Hereditary Order of
Desc. of Colonial Governors; Dau. of American Revolution; Dau.
of 1812; Magna Charta Dames; New England Women; Dau. of Founders
and Patriots of America; Huguenot Society; Colonial Order of the
Crown; Soc. of Mayflower Descendants; John Alden Kindred;
Americans of Royal Descent; Calif. Hist. and Genealogical
Societies. Address: 3875 Clay St., San Francisco,CA 94118.
Descended from:

1 John Alden, Governor of Plymouth Colony 1663-64, 1667

2 David Alden
  Duxbury,MA 1646   Duxbury
  Duxbury 20 Mar 1719   by 1670

  Mary Southworth
  Duxbury
  Duxbury

3 Priscilla Alden
  Duxbury 1679   Duxbury
  Stonington,CT   4 Jan 1699

  Samuel Chesebrough
  Stonington 14 Feb 1674
  Stonington 19 Jan
    1735/6

4 Amos Chesebrough
  Stonington 2 Feb 1709 Stonington
  Stonington 13 Sep 1770 2 Dec 1729

  Desire Williams
  New London,CT
  Groton,CT

5 Hannah Chesebrough
  Stonington 27 Sep 1745 Stonington
  Groton 1835   22 Apr 1767

  Joseph Stanton
  Stonington 31 May 1739
  Groton 1832

6 John Stanton
  Groton 25 Jul 1768   Groton
  Syracuse,NY   c.1790

  Mary Palmer
  Groton c.1770
  Syracuse

7 Joseph Stanton
  Syracuse c.1794   Canton,PA
  Hancock Co.IL Mar 1865 1832

  Clarissa Griffin
  Middleton,CT Sep 1798
  Colusa,CA 30 Nov 1881

8 Asenath L. Stanton
  Hancock,IL 5 Apr 1834 Carthage,IL

  College City,CA 20 Mar 22 Mar 1855
    1904

  Edwin R. Graham
  Hamilton Co.OH 19 Jun
    1827
  Arbuckle,CA 4 Nov
    1896

9 Elva Graham
  Grimes,CA 24 Apr 1870 Colusa

  San Francisco,CA   12 Nov 1887
    14 Apr 1962

  Robert L. Welch
  Woodland,CA 22 Jul
    1861
  San Francisco 9 Aug
    1937

Inheritor: Mrs. James Theodore Wood, Jr., 829 So. Madre St.,
Pasadena,CA 91107.

WELDER, KATIE SMITH (MRS. PATRICK HUGHES)

Nat. #304-B. Elected 9 Mar 1977. b. Lufkin,TX 27 Dec 1920.
m. Matamoras, Tamps Mexico 2 Jan 1955, Patrick Hughes Welder,
b. 15 Oct 1930. Issue: Patrick Hughes Welder III b. 3 Oct 1957;
Robert Hughes Welder b. 3 Oct 1957; Patti Kay Welder b. 4 Sep
1959. Member: Hereditary Order of Desc. of Colonial Governors;
Colonial Dames XVII Century; Dau. of American Colonists; Dau. of
American Revolution; United States Dau. of 1812; United Dau. of
Confederacy. Address: 604 North Craig, Victoria,TX. Descended
from:

1 James Moore I, Governor of South Carolina 1700-02, 1719, 1721

2	Nathaniel Moore	(2)	Elizabeth Webb
	c.1699	-----	-----
	bf. 1748	bf. 1735	-----

3	Margaret Moore		William Hill
	Brunswick,NC Dec 1735	Orton,NC	Boston,MA 15 Apr 1737
	Brunswick 3 Nov 1788	29 Sep 1757	Wilmington,NC 26 Aug 1783

4	Thomas Hill		Susannah Mabson
	Hanover Co.NC 28 Nov 1770	-----	Wilmington 1770
	Pittsboro,NC 27 Jul 1818	18 Oct 1792	Pittsboro

5	Arthur J. Hill		Anne Waddell
	New Hanover Co.NC 25 Feb 1799	-----	c.1801
	Wilmington 23 Nov 1874	22 Jan 1822	-----

6	William Henry Hill		Mary Gregg
	Chatham Co.NC 1823	-----	Marion Co.SC 1833
	Livingston,TX Dec 1909	1851	Livingston 1867

7	Arthur J. Hill		Mary Molly Jones
	Soda,TX 1853	-----	Groveton,TX 9 Apr 1865
	Angelina Co.TX 1900	9 Feb 1882	Humble,TX 30 Jan 1957

8	Eva Hill		William Robert Smith
	Lufkin,TX 1 Apr 1894	-----	Trinity Co.TX 20 Jul 1880
	living	29 Dec 1909	Camaron Co.TX 20 Jul 1952

WESTBROOKE, GILBERTA WOOD (MRS. EDWARD LYNN)

Nat. #131-B. Elected 21 Jan 1968. b. St. Paul,MN 7 Oct 1904.
m. Memphis,TN 1 Nov 1928, Edward Lynn Westbrooke b. Jonesboro,AR
26 Jul 1900, d. Jonesboro 10 Feb 1974. Educ: Smith College,
Northampton,MA. Member: Hereditary Order of Desc. of Colonial
Governors; Dau. of American Revolution (Registrar General);
Dau. of Founders and Patriots of America (AR, Past President);
Colonial Dames of America; Soc. of Mayflower Descendants (AR,
Deputy Governor); Alden Kindred; Dames of Court of Honor; Life
Judge of Flower Shows. Address: 1221 West Washington Ave.,
P.O. Box #248, Jonesboro,AR 72401. Descended from:

1   John Alden, Governor of Plymouth Colony 1663-64, 1667

2   Elizabeth Alden   William Pabodie
    Plymouth,MA c.1624   Duxbury,MA   c.1619
    Little Compton,RI   6 Dec 1644   Little Compton 13 Dec
      31 May 1717   1707

3   Elizabeth Pabodie   John Rogers
    Duxbury 24 Apr 1647   Duxbury   c.1640
    af. 3 May 1677   16 Nov 1666   Barrington,MA 28 Jun
                                                 1732

4   Elizabeth Rogers   Silvester Richmond
    Barrington 1673   Barrington   Little Compton 1672
    Little Compton 23 Oct   1693   Dartmouth,MA 20 Nov
      1724   1754

5   William Richmond   Anna Gray
    Little Compton 10 Oct   Little Compton   Little Compton 29 Jan
      1694   1702
    Little Compton 22 Feb   8 Jul 1720   Bristol,RI 9 Oct 1762
      1770

6   Abigail Richmond   Peter Pitts
    Little Compton 28 Feb   Little Compton   Dighton,MA 15 Sep 1737
      1744
    Honeoye,NY 26 Jul   29 Dec 1764   Richmond,NY 15 Dec
      1807   1812

7   Abigail Pitts   Abel Short
    Dighton 1776   Honeoye   Bristol Co.MA 18 Mar
                                                 1776
    Honeoye af.1809   c.1799   af. 1809

8   Abigail R. Short   Samuel Crooks
    Honeoye 20 Jul 1807   Honeoye   Richmond 7 Nov 1802
    Kalamazoo,MI 17 Jan   c.1828   Kalamazoo 1 Nov 1881
      1900

9   Phoebe C. Crooks   Gilbert A. Watkins
    Kalamazoo 3 Jan 1841   Portage,MI   Athens,MI 28 Dec 1837
    Detroit,MI 26 Aug 1915 7 Mar 1866   Detroit 17 Mar 1907

10 Alice M. Watkins   William C. Wood
    Detroit 31 May 1878   Detroit   Haddonfield,NJ 25 Mar
                                                 1868
    Memphis,TN 4 Oct 1965   9 Jan 1902   Rochester,MN 16 May
                                                 1927

WHEELER, GERALDINE HARTSHORN (MRS. LLOYD FRANKLYN)

Nat. #99-B. Elected 26 Aug 1964. b. Pomona,CA 5 Feb 1919.
m. Pomona 2 Dec 1938, Lloyd F. Wheeler, b. Pomona 23 Jun 1916.
Issue: Russell Lloyd Wheeler, b. Pomona 6 Dec 1939; Robert
Gerald Wheeler, b. Upland,CA 28 Jul 1944. Educ: Santa Barbara
City College, A.A. Member: Hereditary Order of Desc. of Colonial
Governors (Past 2nd Deputy Governor General); Colonial Dames of
America (2nd Vice President of Chap. V); Magna Charta Dames (So.
California, Past Regent); Colonial Order of the Crown; Plantage-
net Society; Sovereign Colonial Society, Americans of Royal
Descent; Desc. of Most Nobel Order of the Garter; Dau. of
Founders and Patriots of America (CA, Registrar and Vice Presi-
dent); Dames of Guild of St. Margaret of Scotland (Serene Grand
Dame; Editor of Journal published quarterly); Dau. of Colonial
Wars (CA, Past Registrar and Historian); Huguenot Society (CA,
Past Chaplain); Women Desc. of Ancient and Honorable Artillery
Co. (CA, Past Assistant Corresponding Secretary); Soc. of
Mayflower Desc. (CA, Past State Board of Assistants); Dau. of
American Colonists; Dames of Court of Honor (CA, Past 2nd Vice
President); Dau. of American Revolution (CA, Past State Chair-
man,DAR Schools); Military and Hospitaller Order of St. Lazarus
of Jerusalem (Dame of Grace, Publishing Editor of newsletter six
times a year); Hereditary and Noble Order of St. Beggs
(Sovereign); Family Assn. of True and Bradbury Descendants
(Chairman); Prentice-Prentiss-Bubier-Angier and Oakes Family
Group (Chairman); Desc. of John Perkins (Chairman); Native Dau.
of Golden West; Pioneer Soc. of Pomona Valley (Founding Pres.);
New England Historic Genealogical Soc.; National Genealogical
Soc.; Pilgrim Soc.; Marblehead Historical Soc.. Listed in
Who's Who of CA; Southwest Blue Book; Los Angeles Blue Book;
Hereditary Register. Occup: Co-owner of"Atheling's" limited
edition publishers. Address: 1047 Baseline Road, Claremont,CA
91711. Descended from:

1 Samuel Jennings, Governor of New Jersey 1681-84

2	Mercy Jennings		John Stevenson
	Burlington,NJ 27 Jun 1687	Burlington	Newtown,NY c.1678
	Burlington c.1720/4	6 Mar 1706	Hunterdon Co.NJ 1744
3	Thomas Stevenson		Sarah Whitehead
	Burlington Co. 1707/8	Jamaica,LI,NY	Jamaica 18 Apr 1713
	-----	30 Apr 1730	-----
4	John Stevenson		Mercy King
	Hunterdon Co. 22 Nov 1732	New Jersey	Amwell,NJ 26 Oct 1739
	Sussex Co.NJ 12 Apr 1812	12 Jul 1760	-----
5	Joseph Stevenson		Susannah Kester
	NJ 19 Mar 1767	New Jersey	NJ 16 Nov 1770
	NJ 4 Aug 1841	26 Sep 1796	NJ 11 May 1870
6	Samuel K. Stevenson		Alice Dawes
	Hunterdon Co. 24 Nov 1803	Lebanon,NJ	Lebanon 18 Jul 1809
	Ottawa,IL 7 Feb 1876	4 Oct 1831	Allen,KS 16 Feb 1898

7	Eliza M. Stevenson Scotch Plains,NJ 16 May 1836 Pomona 23 Oct 1902	Ottawa,IL 31 May 1857	George A. True Boston,MA 30 Jun 1831 Los Angeles,CA 22 Jul 1898
8	Angeline True La Salle Co.IL 4 Mar 1858 La Verne,CA 13 Aug 1947	Waltham,IL 24 Nov 1886	Eugene Hartshorn Waltham 10 Oct 1865 La Salle,IL 17 Nov 1953
9	Albion T. Hartshorn La Verne 23 Jan 1892	Pomona 29 Jun 1916	Beatrice O. Barnes Colon,NE 4 Jan 1892

Inheritor: Russell Lloyd Wheeler

WHITECOTTEN, DR. GLENN LEE

Nat. #331-B. Elected 15 Aug 1978. b. Terre Haute,IN 28 Aug
1937. m. 22 May 1967, Grace Oralee Young, b. 21 Apr 1941.
Educ: Purdue University BS, MS; University of Wisconsin Medical
School, MD; Urology Residency, Cleveland,OH; Anesthesiology
Residency, Naval Medical Center, Bethesda,MD. Member: Hereditary
Order of Desc. of Colonial Governors; Soc. of Mayflower Descen-
dants, DC; Sons of American Revolution, MD; Somerset Chapter of
Magna Charta Barons; F. & A. Masons, Savannah,GA. Address:
Naval Regional Medical Center, Guam, F.P.O. San Francisco,CA
96630. Descended from:

1   John Alden, Governor of Plymouth Colony 1663-64, 1677

2	Elizabeth Alden Plymouth,MA c.1624 Little Compton,RI 31 May 1717	Duxbury,MA 6 Dec 1644	William Pabodie c.1619 Little Compton 13 Dec 1707
3	Mary Pabodie Duxbury 7 Aug 1648 -----	----- 16 Nov 1669	Edward Southworth Duxbury Duxbury c.1727
4	Mercy Southworth Duxbury c.1670 c.1728	----- c. 1701	Moses Soule Duxbury Duxbury c.1748
5	Isaac Soule Duxbury 1702 Pembroke 22 Oct 1775	Pembroke,MA 1725	Agatha Perry Pembroke 5 Jan 1703 Pembroke 22 Jul 1775
6	Moses Soule Pembroke 2 Apr 1738 New York 4 Apr 1796	Marshfield,MA 7 May 1761	Eleanor Williams Massachusetts Pittsfield,MA 26 Oct 1782

7 William Soule   Jemima Butler
   Marshfield 17 Sep 1766   New York   MA Sep 1773
   Vigo Co.IN 9 Sep 1820   -----   Vigo Co. 3 Oct 1832

8 William Soule   Almira Baker
   New York 28 Feb 1796   Vigo Co.   Warren,MA Sep 1800
   Vigo Co. 10 Oct 1857   20 Jun 1820   Vigo Co. 9 Nov 1882

9 Origen Brigham Soule   Frances Ann Watkins-
                                            Draper
   Vigo Co. 22 Jul 1826   Vigo Co.   Rockridge Co.VA 22 May
                                            1826
   Vigo Co. 12 Feb 1908   Apr 1854   Vigo Co. 22 Jul 1912

10 Julia Esther Soule   George Franklin Sankey
   Vigo Co. 2 Jan 1855   Vigo Co.   Vigo Co. 26 Jun 1853
   Vigo Co. 3 Sep 1948   22 Sep 1875   Vigo Co. 4 Mar 1934

11 Charles Origen Sankey   Nettie Van Owsley
   Vigo Co. 20 Jul 1876   Vigo Co.   Winchester,KY 2 Nov
                                            1875
   Darke Co.OH 28 Oct   5 Feb 1899   Vigo Co. 8 Jun 1959
     1962

12 Elizabeth Evelyn Sankey   John Paul Whitecotten
   Vigo Co. 8 Nov 1912   -----   Vigo Co. 3 May 1907
   living in 1978   16 Sep 1934   Fort Meyers,FL 8 Dec
                                            1977

WHITEHEAD, LOUIS HENRY

Nat. #129-B. Elected 8 Apr 1967. b. Burlington,PA 25 May 1903.
m. 19 Aug 1927, Dorothy May Hawthorne, b. 16 Aug 1905. Educ:
University of Pennsylvania, BS; Syracuse and Harvard Universities.
Member: Hereditary Order of Desc. of Colonial Governors; Sons of
American Revolution; Order of Founders and Patriots of America;
Soc. of Desc. of Colonial Clergy; Baronial Order of Magna Charta;
Soc. of Colonial Wars; NY Soc. of Security Analysts; Masonic
orders. Listed in Who's Who in East and in Commerce and Industry.
Address: Hornblower, Weeks,Hemphill Noyes, Inc., 8 Hanover St.,
New York,NY 10004. Descended from:

1 Andrew Ward, Governor of Connecticut 1635-36

2 Samuel Ward   (2)   Hannah Nichols
   -----   -----   -----
   Fairfield,CT bf.1693   -----   -----

3 Hannah Ward   Peter Bulkeley
   -----   Stratfield,CT   Fairfield 21 May 1684
   Fairfield 1772   25 Oct 1709   Fairfield 15 Oct 1752

4 Peter Bulkeley   (2)   Hannah Sherwood
   Fairfield bp.9 Oct   -----   -----
     1715
   Fairfield 1801   -----   -----

5 Olive Bulkeley   Hezekiah Whitehead
   Fairfield c.1771   -----   27 Jul 1764
   New Milford,CT   -----   Kent,CT 1813
      26 Dec 1867

6 John Bulkeley Whitehead   Emmaline West
   Kent 1 Apr 1793   -----   19 Aug 1798
   Bradford Co.PA   18 Mar 1816   bur.16 Dec 1854
      16 Apr 1874

7 Henry West Whitehead   Annie Barbara Smith
   Kent 23 Sep 1843   Dushore,PA   15 Dec 1840
   Mar 1923   22 Feb 1869   21 Mar 1917

8 Dorsey John Whitehead   Anna Wharton Thompson
   Dushore 28 Aug 1875   -----   New Albany,PA 31 Jul
                                                 1878
      26 May 1945   21 Jan 1899   14 Apr 1965

WIENER, ELLANORE STONE BROWN (MRS. ALEXANDER LODER)

Nat. #278-B. Elected 10 Feb 1976. b. Grosse Pointe,MI 9 Feb
1913. m. Grosse Pointe 19 May 1934, Alexander Loder Wiener,
b. Philadelphia,PA 18 Feb 1908. Educ: Miss Porter's School,
Farmington,CT. Member: Hereditary Order of Desc. of Colonial
Governors; Colonial Dames in America, NJ, MI; Soc. of Mayflower
Descendants, MI; National Huguenot Society, MI. Address:
6 Woodland Place, Grosse Pointe,MI 48230. Descended from:

1 Thomas Roberts, Governor of New Hampshire 1640-41

2 Esther Roberts   John Martin
   New Hampshire c.1626   -----   Durham,Eng. c.1620
   Piscataway,NJ 12 Dec   c.1646   Piscataway 5 Jul 1687
      1687

3 John Martin, Jr.   Dorothy Smith
   Dover,NH 1647   -----   -----
   Piscataway 1703   26 Jun 1677   28 Mar 1698

4 Patience Martin   Daniel Sutton
   -----   -----   Piscataway 25 Feb 1682
   -----   31 Oct 1704   Piscataway 1761

5 Patience Sutton   Jonathan Doty
   Piscataway 23 May 1719 Basking Ridge   Piscataway c.1724
   -----   c.1752   Basking Ridge,NJ

6 William Doty   Elizabeth Parker
   Basking Rdg. 8 Oct 1767 Somerset Co.   Somerset Co.NJ 1774
   Groveland,NY 13 Apr   c.1793   Groveland 13 Mar 1845
      1853

7 Jonathan Doty   Margaret Salmon
   Basking Ridge c.1796   Groveland   Bloom,PA 20 Nov 1796
   Dansville,NY 29 Mar   6 Sep 1818   Dansville 13 Mar 1881
      1875

8   Harriet Newell Doty   Alexander Brown
    Groveland 20 Aug   Rochester,NY   North Hampton,NY 2 Aug
      1819   1812
    Darien,NY 5 Apr 1901   10 Oct 1839   Darien 2 Apr 1892

9   James Doty Brown   Sarah Melissa Andrus
    Dansville,NY 2 Apr 1844 Buffalo,NY   Evans,NY 13 Jul 1852
    Cleveland,OH 13 Jan   9 Nov 1870   Cleveland 28 Aug 1949
      1937

10 Edwin Hewitt Brown   Olive Marie McIntosh
    Chicago 14 Feb 1879   Cleveland   Cleveland 22 Aug 1883
    Grosse Pointe,MI   6 Nov 1907   Grosse Pointe 3 Aug
      16 Aug 1939   1932

    Inheritor: Edward McIntosh Wiener

WIGGIN, ELMER S.

Nat. #204-B. Elected 9 Apr 1973. b. Boscawen,NH 29 Oct 1903.
m. Boscawen 6 Jun 1929, Marjorie M. Ellsworth, b. Boscawen
12 Jul 1901. Issue: Cabot Ellsworth Wiggin, b. Worcester,MA
2 Nov 1931. Educ: University of New Hampshire; Clark University.
Member: Hereditary Order of Desc. of Colonial Governors; Sons of
American Revolution; Soc. of Founders and Patriots of America;
Boscawen Historical Soc. Address: 10 Sweatt St., Penacook,NH
03301. (From Society's Records.) Descended from:

1   Thomas Wiggin, Governor of New Hampshire 1631-36

2   Andrew Wiggin   Hannah Bradstreet
    Stratham,NH 1635   Andover,MA   Ipswich,MA 1642
    Stratham 9 Feb 1710   3 Jun 1659   Stratham 1707

3   Bradstreet Wiggin   Ann Chase
    Stratham 25 Mar 1676   -----   9 Jan 1676/7
    Stratham 18 Jan 1708/9 21 Aug 1697   -----

4   Joseph Wiggin   Patience Piper
    Stratham 30 Mar 1707   -----   -----
    Stratham 5 May 1788   c.1753   -----

5   Noah Wiggin   Sarah Goss
    Stratham 23 Sep 1755   Stratham   Greenland,NH 2 Apr 1758
    Loudon,NH 14 Nov 1835   10 Oct 1779   Loudon Oct 1841

6   Thomas Wiggin   Sarah Whitney
    Loudon 21 Oct 1796   Loudon   1795
    28 Mar 1825   26 Mar 1816   Concord,NH 1842

7   Stephen Wiggin   Rosella G. Boyce
    Loudon 19 Aug 1822   -----   5 Jul 1828
    Boscawen,NH 10 Jun   26 Nov 1846   13 Aug 1886
      1898

8   Charles S. Wiggin   Mary A. Canham
    Boscawen 30 Apr 1854   Boscawen   England 14 Jan 1851
    Boscawen 25 Jun 1929   24 Nov 1875   Boscawen 22 Jul 1928

9　Leon E. Wiggin　　　　　　　　　　　　Blanche I. Dockham
　　Boscawen 22 Jun 1880　　Gilford,NH　　Lowell,MA 9 Aug 1882
　　Boscawen 22 Jul 1957　　25 Dec 1902

　　Inheritor: Cabot Ellsworth Wiggin, 7 Winchester St.,
　　Northfield, MA 01360

WILCOX, JANICE ESTELLE LaMACK (MRS. LLOYD HAWKINS)

Nat. #346-B.　Elected 23 Jul 1979.　b. Racine,WI 18 May 1929.
m. Racine 7 Jun 1955, Lloyd Hawkins Wilcox.　Educ: Lawrence
College, Appleton,WI, B.S.; University of Wisconsin, Milwaukee,
Elem. Teaching Certif.　Member: Hereditary Order of Desc. of
Colonial Governors; Dau. of American Revolution.　Address:
2924 West Bonnie Brook Lane, Waukegan,IL 60085. Descended from:

1　Nicholas Easton, Governor of Rhode Island 1672-74

2　Peter Easton　　　　　　　　　　　　　Ann Coggeshall
　　Wales 1622　　　　　　　Newport,RI　　England c.1626/8
　　Newport 12 Dec 1693　　15 Nov 1643　　Newport 6 Mar 1687

3　Patience Easton　　　　　　　(2)　　　Thomas Rodman
　　Newport 20 Nov 1655　　-----　　　　　Barbedoes 26 Dec 1640
　　Newport 21 Nov 1690　　7 Jun 1682　　So.Kingston 11 Jan 1727

4　Thomas Rodman　　　　　　　　　　　　Katherine Frye
　　Newport 11 Nov 1683　　Newport　　　　1683
　　South Kingston,RI 1775　20 Sep 1706　　So.Kingston 4 Mar 1740

5　Joseph Rodman　　　　　　　　　　　　Tabitha Mumford
　　South Kingston 1 Oct　　Rhode Island　-----
　　　1713
　　Columbia Co.NY 1762/7　c.1730　　　　-----

6　Joseph Rodman　　　　　　　　　　　　Mary West
　　South Kingston 23 Mar　New York　　　bp. Newtown,NY
　　　1733　　　　　　　　　　　　　　　　20 Jul 1740
　　Hillsdale,NY 24 Mar　　c.1757/8　　　Columbia Co. af.1804
　　　1811

7　John Rodman　　　　　　　　　　　　　Hannah Goss
　　Hillsdale 22 Sep 1764　Hillsdale　　　Hillsdale 5 May 1770
　　Syracuse,NY 1834　　　1787　　　　　Syracuse 1830

8　Asa Rodman　　　　　　　　　　　　　Asenath Dixon
　　Schoharie Co.NY　　　　Ontario Co.NY　Mayfield,NY 17 Jun 1811
　　　8 May 1797
　　Gorham,NY 18 Jul 1868　22 Dec 1829　　Gorham,NY 10 Nov 1885

9　Jacob Rodman　　　　　　　　　　　　Lanah Altanah Lewis
　　Schoharie Co. 9 Apr　　Gorham　　　　Forham,NY 24 Apr 1847
　　　1839
　　Gorham 15 Feb 1903　　1 Feb 1872　　Gorham 21 Apr 1923

10　Hattie Lee Rodman　　　　　　　　　Byron Charles Reed
　　Gorham 19 Dec 1874　　Gorham　　　　Mt.Pleasant 19 Aug 1873
　　Mt.Pleasant,WI　　　　1 Oct 1896　　Racine,WI 9 Aug 1936
　　　27 Mar 1907

11 Hattie Edna Reed   Lester Joseph LaMack
   Mt.Pleasant 7 Mar 1907 Fort Wayne,IN -----
                           8 Jun 1926

   Inheritor: Jane Elva Wilcox, 2924 West Bonnie Brook Lane,
   Waukegan,IL 60085

WILLIAMS, BERNICE FLETCHER (MRS. MARION H.)

Nat. #75-B. Elected 1 Apr 1963. b. Mendon,IL 18 Feb 1893.
m. Mendon 8 Jun 1921, Rev. Marion H. Williams, b. Zalma,MO
23 Mar 1900. Issue: Winston Fletcher Williams, b. Mendon 31 Oct
1924. Member: Hereditary Order of Desc. of Colonial Governors;
Dau. of American Revolution (Past State Chaplain); Dau. of
American Colonists (Past State Regent); Huguenot Society, IA;
Dau. of the Nile (Chaplain). Occup: Former teacher. Address:
3325 Mansfield Ave., S.E., Cedar Rapids,IA 52403. Descended fr:

1 James Moore, Governor of South Carolina 1700-21

2 James Moore   Margaret Berringer
   England 1644   -----   -----
   South Carolina 1706   1676   South Carolina

3 James Moore   Elizabeth Nimmer
   1677   -----   -----
   1740   -----   -----

4 Margaret Moore   William Sanders
   1707   -----   -----
   1775   1738   -----

5 James Sanders   Sarah Slann
   -----   -----   -----
   Yellow Springs   -----   1799
      17 Sep 1778

6 Mary Sanders   William Gallemore
   1760   South Carolina Randolph Co.NC 14 Feb
                                        1750
   1800   1780   10 Apr 1794

7 William A. Gallemore   Esther C. Bullen
   Salisbury,NC 11 Nov   Salisbury   Gold Hill,NC 22 Feb
      1784   1788
   Adams Co.IL 11 Jan 1848 1806   Lima,IL 15 Jan 1862

8 John A. Gallemore   Catherine Ann Proctor
   NC 8 Dec 1811   Adams Co.IL   Canada 6 Feb 1825
   Lima 22 Jan 1869   4 May 1843   Adams Co. 26 Oct 1868

9 Millicent Gallemore   George Fletcher
   Lima 30 Apr 1846   Lima   MO 19 Aug 1839
   Camp Point,IL 22 Nov 25 Dec 1865   Camp Point 22 Jul 1920
      1900

```
10 Cora A. Fletcher                            Charles A. Fletcher
   Grayson Co.TX 30 Nov    Camp Point          Adams Co. 27 Sep 1866
     1868
   Cedar Rapids,IA         14 Oct 1891         Mendon,IL 2 Dec 1928
     10 Mar 1953

   Inheritor: Winston Fletcher Williams
```

WILLSON, RICHARD EUGENE

Nat. #317-B. Elected 1977. b. Kenton,OH 1 Jan 1933. m. Marion, OH 3 May 1958, Ruth Ann Simpson, b. Kenton 24 Oct 1932. Issue: Richard Alexander Willson, b. Akron,OH 30 Nov 1959. Educ: Bowling Green State University, BA; Case Western Reserve University, MS. Member: Hereditary Order of Desc. of Colonial Governors; Sons of American Revolution (Founder and Past President, Firelands Chap., Lorain,OH); Soc. of Colonial Wars; First Families of Ohio; Somerset Chapter Magna Charta Barons. Occup: Librarian, Executive Director, Starved Rock Library System, Ottawa,IL. Address: P.O. Box 354, Ottawa,IL 61350. Descended fr:

```
1  Samuel Jennings, Governor of New Jersey 1681-84

2  Mercy Jennings                            John Stevenson
   Burlington,NJ 27 Jun    Chesterfield,     Newtown,LI,NY c.1678
     1687                    Friends,NJ
   c.1720-24               c. 6 Mar 1706     Hunterdon Co.NJ 1744

3  Abigail Stevenson                         Peter Schmuck
   -----                   Chester.Fr.       -----
   -----                   5 Jun 1742        -----

4  Abigail Schmuck                           Jonathan Willson, Sr.
   27 Mar 1748             Hardwick          Philadelphia Co.PA
                            Friends,NJ         8 Aug 1741
   Lycoming Co.PA 4 Aug    15 Apr 1767       Lycoming Co. 23 Sep
     1824                                      1824

5  Robert Willson                            Rhoda Dell
   Sussex Co.NJ 17 Sep     Morris Co.NJ      Morris Co. 28 Dec 1773
     1777
   bf. 8 May 1833          8 May 1800        af. 8 May 1833

6  Elisha Willson                            Huldah Dennis Shotwell
   Warren Co.NJ 14 Mar     Warren Co.        Warren Co. 10 Apr 1814
     1810
   Sycamore,OH 18 May      8 May 1833        Sycamore 1 Dec 1907
     1866

7  Jehu Roy Willson, Sr.                     Samantha Lavina
                                               Longabaugh
   Sycamore 19 Jul 1838    Wyandot Co.OH     Wyandot Co. 10 Nov
                                               1842
   Blanchard,OH 12 Jul     7 Dec 1865        Blanchard 7 Nov 1919
     1911
```

```
8   Jehu Roy Willson, Jr.                          Pearl Gertrude Jones
    Sycamore 4 Jan 1874      Dunkirk,OH            Washington,OH 15 Oct
                                                     1882
    Tymochtee,OH 22 Mar      6 Mar 1906            Upper Sandusky,OH
      1940                                           20 Apr 1964

9   Richard Earl Willson                           Mary Arilla Hogue
    Blanchard 23 Oct 1906    Newport,KY            Kenton,OH 11 Sep 1913
                             12 May 1931

    Inheritor: Richard Alexander Willson
```

WOODBRIDGE, FREDERIC LEONIDAS, JR.

Nat. #324-B. Elected 2 Mar 1978. b. Newark,OH 20 Nov 1900.
m. Wooster,OH 2 Sep 1927, Maybelle Josephine Fischer, b. Wooster
2 Oct 1896, d. Cincinnati,OH 11 Sep 1975. Educ: College of
Wooster,OH, BS. Member: Hereditary Order of Desc. of Colonial
Governors; Sons of American Revolution; Society of Colonial
Wars (OH, Past Councillor); Baronial Order of Magna Charta;
Founders and Patriots; First Families of OH; Military Order of
the Crusades. Address: 2645 Erie Avenue #42, Cincinnati,OH
45208. Descended from:

```
1   Thomas Dudley, Governor of Massachusetts 1634-35, 1640-41,
    1645-46, 1650-51

2   Mercy Dudley                                   John Woodbridge
    Northant,Eng. 27 Sep     -----                 Stanton, Wiltshire,
      1621                                            Eng. 1613/4
    Newbury,MA 1 Jul 1691    1639                  Newbury 17 Mar 1695

3   Timothy Woodbridge          (2)                Mrs. John Howell
    Barford, St.Martin,      Hartford,CT           Hartford
      Eng. 13 Jan 1656
    Hartford 30 Apr 1737     c.1703                Hartford

4   Ashbel Woodbridge                              Mrs. Jerusha Pitkin
                                                     Edwards
    Hartford 10 Jun 1704     Hartford              Hartford
    Hartford 6 Aug 1758      17 Nov 1737           Hartford 31 Jul 1799

5   Howell Woodbridge                              Mary Plummer
    Hartford 17 Mar 1746     Glastonbury           Glastonbury,CT 1760
    Glastonbury 13 Jun       26 Nov 1778           Glastonbury 1 Oct 1794
      1796

6   Howell Woodbridge                              Mary Hollister
    Glastonbury bp. 1 Oct    Glastonbury           Glastonbury 17 Mar
      1786                                           1788
    Glastonbury 6 Jan 1823   3 Nov 1808            Newark,OH 3 Jan 1861

7   William Woodbridge                             Martha Jane Houston
    Glastonbury 13 Nov       Newark                Newark 20 Mar 1825
      1812
    Newark 1 Jun 1883        8 Oct 1846            -----
```

8 Frederic Leonidas   Irene Alice Prichard
   Woodbridge, Sr.
   Newark 18 Jul 1861   Newark   Newark 10 Dec 1879
   Newark 30 Nov 1935   11 Oct 1899   Newark 7 Jun 1962

WOODFIELD, DR. DENIS B.

Nat. #180-B. Elected 1 Nov 1971. b. New York,NY 23 Oct 1933.
m. London,Eng. 16 Feb 1963, Rosemary Humphries, b. Leeds, Eng.
24 Jul 1938. Issue: Katherine Rapalye Woodfield, b. Port
Chester,NY 15 Nov 1966; Nicholas Wyckoff Woodfield, b. Port
Chester 12 Mar 1968; Elizabeth Dudley Woodfield, b. Port Chester
25 Jun 1971. Educ: Harvard College, BA; Oxford University,
England, PhD. Member: Hereditary Order of Desc. of Colonial
Governors; Soc. of Mayflower Descendants; Order of Founders and
Patriots; St. Nicholas Soc.; Soc. of Colonial Wars; Huguenot Soc.;
Crown of Charlemagne; Barons of Magna Charta; American Yacht
Club, Rye,NY; Grolier Club of NYC; Harvard Club of NYC. Occup:
Director, Captain and Banking, Pan American World Airways.
Author of: "An Ordinary of English Armorial Bookbindings, London
1958" and "Surreptitious Printing in England." Address: The Box
Stall, 883 Lawrenceville Rd., Princeton,NJ 08540. Descended from:

1 Thomas Dudley, Governor of Massachusetts 1634-35, 1640-41,
   1645-46, 1650-51

   Simon Bradstreet, Governor of Massachusetts 1679-86, 1689-92

2 Anne Dudley   Simon Bradstreet
   Northamptonshire,   Hardingston,   Lincolnshire, Eng.
   Eng. c.1612   Eng.   bp. Mar 1603
   Andover,MA 16 Sep 1672 c.1628   Salem,MA 27 Mar 1697

3 John Bradstreet   Sarah Perkins
   Andover 22 Jul 1653   -----   2 Mar 1657
   Topsfield,MA 17 Jan   11 Jun 1677   Apr 1745
   1717/8

4 Mercy Bradstreet   John Hazen
   Topsfield 2 Jun 1689   -----   Boxford,MA 23 Mar
                                                1687/8
   Norwich,CT 22 Nov 1725 1710   24 Feb 1772

5 Caleb Hazen   Sarah Hamlin
   Norwich 4 Apr 1720   -----   Barnstable,MA 16 Mar
                                                1720/1
   Carmel,NY 5 Mar 1777   Mar 1740   Carmel Dec 1814

6 Eleazar Hazen   Hannah Fuller
   Carmel 1755   -----   1755
   Carmel 20 Sep 1793   -----   Red Mills,NY 13 Dec
                                                1839

7 Mercy Hazen   Francis Gailor
   Carmel 1 Jan 1780   -----   17 Sep 1770
   Lockport,NY 14 Oct   -----   Hudson,NY 25 Dec 1803
   1857

8	Hazen Amzi Gailor		Lucinda Mallory
	6 Feb 1803	Warren,CT	Warren 6 Aug 1809
	Albion,NY 3 Sep 1877	12 Sep 1826	Albion 28 Nov 1880
9	Mary Martha Gailor		Minot Hoyt
	Warren 20 Feb 1830	Lockport	Wayland,MI 1823
	Lockport 16 Dec 1851	19 Oct 1848	Wayland 9 Dec 1878
10	Hazen Leuertes Hoyt		Margaret Isabella Brunton
	Lockport 30 Aug 1849	New York,NY	Perth, Scotland
	Mineola,LI,NY 10 Aug 1924	10 Nov 1881	Great Neck,LI,NY 27 Dec 1925
11	John Robertson Hoyt		Katherine Van Nostrand
	New York 17 Sep 1882	New York,NY	Brooklyn,NY 9 Aug 1886
	Dallas,TX 9 Jun 1946	30 Sep 1908	-----
12	Margery Brunton Hoyt		William Frederick Woodfield
	Great Neck 13 Oct 1911	New York,NY	Morristown,NJ 29 Aug 1901
	-----	27 Mar 1931	Matinecock,LI,NY 29 Apr 1968

WOODRUFF, JANET ANN NORRIS (MRS. FREDERICK EDWARD)

Nat. #88-B. Elected 24 Aug 1963. b. Georgetown,DC 25 Aug 1938.
m. Rockville,MD 10 Oct 1959, Frederick Edward Woodruff, b.
Michigan City,IN 25 Apr 1935. Issue: Carolyn Marie Woodruff, b.
18 Jan 1961; Mary Elizabeth Woodruff, b. 25 Feb 1965; both b.
Michigan City. Educ: University of Maryland. Member: Hereditary
Order of Desc. of Colonial Governors. Address: 315 Golfview Rd.,
Michigan City,IN 46360. Descended from:

1 Robert Brooke, Governor of Maryland 1652

2	Thomas Brooke		Eleanor Hatton
	Battle,Eng. 23 Jun 1632	Maryland	England c.1642
	Calvert Co.MD 25 Oct 1676	c.1658	Calvert Co. 1724/5
3	Thomas Brooke	(2)	Barbara Dent
	Calvert Co. c.1659	Maryland	St.Mary's Co.MD 1676
	Brookfield,MD 7 Jan 1730/1	bf.4 Jan 1699	Prince George's Co.MD 1754
4	Elizabeth Brooke		George Beall
	Maryland 1709	Maryland	Upper Marlboro,MD 1695
	Georgetown,DC 2 Oct 1768	1728	Georgetown 15 Mar 1780
5	George Beall		Ann
	Georgetown 26 Feb 1729	Maryland	-----
	Georgetown 15 Oct 1807	c.1759	-----

6 Levin C. Beall   Ester Belt
   Georgetown 7 Jun 1760   Maryland   -----
   Montgomery Co.MD   1781   MD c.1830
      c.1802

7 John Beall   Charlotte Jones
   Montgomery Co. 23 Dec   Montgomery Co. MD 18 Feb 1787
      1781
   Montgomery Co. 26 Aug   1808   Montgomery Co. 22 Jan
      1831   1867

8 William R. Beall   Martha E. McAtee
   Montgomery Co. 24 Feb   Montgomery Co. Montgomery Co. c.1811
      1814
   Dranesville,VA 3 Jan   -----   Darnestown,MD 1895
      1884

9 Charles E. Beall   Mary E. Clements
   MD 8 Oct 1849   Georgetown   MD 22 Jun 1853
   Gaithersburg,MD   20 Jun 1883   Gaithersburg 1 Jan
      6 Nov 1913   1935

10 Mary E. Beall   Abell A. Norris
   Toledo,OH 22 Mar 1884   Rockville,MD   Leonardtown,MD
                                              20 Feb 1875
   Gaithersburg 27 Aug   20 Aug 1904   Gaithersburg 23 Oct
      1940   1955

11 Abell Archibald Norris   Mary Shafer Hershey
   Gaithersburg   Georgetown   Comus,MD 9 Jul 1908
      30 Jun 1905
                            30 Jun 1934

WORTHING, CLIFFORD ARTHUR

Nat. #127-B. Elected 16 Dec 1966. b. Greenville,ME 12 Jul
1924. m. Cincinnati,OH 16 Sep 1947, Louise Pugh, b. Cincinnati
2 Jul 1919. Issue: Sharon L. Worthing, b. Tucson,AZ 19 Jul
1952. Educ: University of Maine, BA. Member: Hereditary Order
of Desc. of Colonial Governors; Soc. of Colonial Wars; Soc. of
Founders and Patriots of America, ME; Soc. of Desc. of Colonial
Clergy; Baronial Order of Magna Charta; National Trust for
Historic Preservation; Soc. for Preservation of New England
Antiquities; Piscataqua Pioneers; Camden Rockport Historical
Soc.; Knox Co.,Maine Agricultural Soc. Occup: Investments.
Address: 802 Wakefield Drive, Cincinnati,OH 45226. Descended fr:

1 Thomas Dudley, Governor of Massachusetts 1634-35, 1640-41,
   1645-46, 1650-51

2 Samuel Dudley   (3)   Elizabeth
   Northampton,Eng.   -----   c.1628
      c.1606
   Exeter,NH 10 Feb   by 1651   af. 1702
      1682/3

3 Samuel Dudley   Elizabeth Thing
   Exeter c.1668   -----   5 Jun 1664
   -----   -----   -----

4	Mary Dudley		David Watson
	-----	-----	c.1684
	-----	-----	c.1747

5	Sarah Watson		Nathaniel Doe
	Dover,NH	-----	Durham,NH 5 Jan 1718
	-----	c.1750	-----

6	Dudley Doe		Anna Dyer
	Durham 25 May 1750	-----	Portland,ME 20 Mar 1748
	-----	11 Dec 1773	16 Feb 1833

7	Jonathan Doe		Mary McLaughlin
	Sidney,ME 14 Feb 1792	-----	China,ME
	3 Aug 1873	2 Sep 1816	-----

8	William Dudley Doe		Leonora Willey
	Winslow,ME 11 Oct 1824	-----	Stillwater,ME
	Belfast,ME 12 Jul 1894	-----	-----

9	Lizzie B. Doe		Albert Tewksbury Worthing
	Albion,ME 8 Aug 1860	Belfast	Boston,MA 17 Dec 1858
	Bangor,ME 1952	5 Jan 1879	-----

10	Chester Clifford Worthing		Antonia Wilhelmina Holman
	Chelsea,MA 4 Apr 1886	-----	11 Dec 1894
		23 Dec 1919	

WRIGHT, HELEN GREY HENNING (MRS. DOUGLAS CHANDLER)

Nat. #232-B. Elected 1 May 1974. b. Brooklyn,NY 28 May 1914.
m. Elkton,MD 20 Jun 1933, Douglas Chandler Wright, b. Acton,Eng.
13 Mar 1914. Issue: Douglas Chandler Wright, Jr., b. Montclair,
NJ 13 Dec 1934; Roxlyn Grey Wright, b. Glen Ridge,NJ 6 Jun 1938.
Educ: Maryland College for Women, Lutherville,MD. Member:
Hereditary Order of Desc. of Colonial Governors (Councillor
General); Dau. of American Revolution (Shrewsbury Towne Chap.,
Past Registrar); New England Women; Huguenot Society,NJ; Dau. of
American Colonists (Corresponding Secretary); Dau. of Colonial
Wars (NJ, State President); Dau. of Founders and Patriots.
Address: 462 Point Road, Little Silver,NJ 07739. Descended from:

1 Robert Treat, Governor of Connecticut 1683-98

2	Mary Treat		Azariah Crane
	Milford,CT 1 May 1652	Newark,NJ	Branford,CT 1649
	Newark 12 Nov 1704	c.1675	Newark 5 Nov 1730

3	Jane Crane		John Richards
	Newark 1686	Newark	c.1687
	Newark 12 Sep 1741	-----	Newark 16 Mar 1748

4 David Richards   Edus Crane
   Newark c.1720   Newark   -----
   Hanover,NJ 1781   -----   Hanover 1781

5 Hannah Richards   Daniel Corey
   Hanover   Hanover   -----
   -----   1 Jan 1781   -----

6 Electa Cory   Barzillai Campfield
   7 Sep 1788   Afton,NJ   Afton 29 Jun 1781
   Florham Park,NJ   13 Jul 1809   Afton 28 Mar 1863
     20 Jun 1872

7 Alfred W. Campfield   Elvina Miller
   Florham Park 26 Aug Rockaway   Rockaway Valley,NJ
     1811   Valley   24 Dec 1817
   Vailsburg,NJ 29 Oct 6 Mar 1837   South Orange,NJ
     1878   May 1905

8 Alfred L. Campfield   Helen Ada Grubb
   Rockaway Valley 25 Aug Chicago,IL   Chicago 3 Aug 1852
     1842
   Glen Ridge,NJ 23 Jan 3 May 1871   Chicago 11 Aug 1904
     1923

9 Rosabell Grey Campfield   Norman H. Henning
   Chicago 29 Dec 1883   Chicago   Wingham, Ontario,Can.
                                                       10 Aug 1884
   Long Branch,NJ   16 Jul 1908   Montclair,NJ
     21 Sep 1969   13 Jun 1951

Inheritor: Roxlyn Grey Wright Cole (Mrs. Allan A.),
6431 West Arbor Ave., Littleton,CO 80123.

ADDENDUM

Lineages of new members received too late to be included in the Member Section.

ABBOTT, JOHN TUCKER

Nat. #360-B. Elected 19 Sep 1979. b. Boston,MA 26 Sep 1914. m. Rochester,NH 26 Sep 1943, Anne Elisabeth Skelly, b. Dover,NH 24 Jan 1918. Educ: Springfield College, Springfield,MA,BSc. Member: Hereditary Order of Desc. of Colonial Governors; Sons of American Revolution (MA, Continental Color Guard); Order of the Founders and Patriots of America; Sons and Dau. of Pilgrims; Soc. of Desc. of Colonial Clergy; Piscataqua Pioneers; Sons and Dau. of First Settlers of Newbury,MA; Bedford Historical Soc. (Past Pres.); Bedford Historical Comm.; New England Historical Genealogical Soc.; Hereditary Register of USA. Occup: Configura- tion Engineering, Product Records and Documentation with the Raytheon Co. (ret.). Address: 118 Wilson Road, Bedford,MA 01730. Descended from:

1   Thomas Mayhew, Governor of Martha's Vineyard 1647-81

2   Thomas Mayhew   Jane Paine
    Southampton,Eng. 1620/1 -----   England 1625
    At sea 1657   1647   -----

3   Matthew Mayhew   Mary Skiffe
    Tisbury,MA 1648   Chilmark,MA   Sandwich,MA 24 Mar 1650
    Edgartown,MA 19 May   1 Mar 1674   Edgartown 1 May 1690
       1710

4   Paine Mayhew   Mary Rankin
    Chilmark 31 Oct 1677   Chilmark   Boston,MA 1676
    Chilmark 8 May 1761   8 Dec 1699   Chilmark 17 Feb 1753

5   Mary Mayhew   Jethro Athearn
    Chilmark 26 Sep 1700   Chilmark   Tisbury 30 Jun 1693
    Tisbury 7 Apr 1778   8 Sep 1720   Tisbury 3 Feb 1784

6   Martha Athearn   James Allen
    Tisbury 9 Aug 1733   Chilmark   Chilmark 28 Mar 1732
    Chilmark 26 Oct 1826   1755   Chilmark 3 Nov 1815

7   William Allen   Love Coffin
    Chilmark 5 Jan 1756   Edgartown   Edgartown 3 May 1756
    Industry,ME 5 Nov 1842   10 Mar 1779   Industry 5 Jun 1831

8   William Allen   Hannah Titcomb
    Chilmark 16 Apr 1780   Farmington,ME   Topsham,ME 15 Nov 1780
    Norridgewock,ME   3 Sep 1807   Norridgewock 26 Mar
       1 Jul 1873   1859

9   Elizabeth Titcomb Allen   John Stevens Abbott
    Norridgewock 24 Sep   Norridgewock   Temple,ME 6 Jan 1807
       1813
    Norridgewock 27 Jul   6 Oct 1835   Watertown,MA 12 Jun
       1858   1881

10 John Edward Abbott   Alice Greeley Cochrane
    Norridgewock 30 Nov   Compton   Compton,Quebec,Canada
    1845   22 Mar 1855
    Watertown 1 Dec 1915   12 Jun 1878   Watertown 26 Dec 1930

11 Charles Matthew Abbott   Frances Tucker
    Brooklyn,NY 4 Apr 1879   Paget   Paget,Bermuda 19 Apr
                                                           1878
    Boston 2 Oct 1956   26 Jun 1913   Paget 25 Dec 1945

ATKINS, DOREEN A. CORNWALL (MRS. ERNEST G.)

Nat. #377-B. Elected 14 Jan 1980. b. Niles,MI 23 Jan 1910.
m.(2) Elkton,MD 29 Mar 1943, Lt.Col. Ernest G. Atkins, b. Wash-
ington,DC 10 Apr 1906. Member: Hereditary Order of Desc. of
Colonial Governors; Magna Charta Dames; Desc. of Knights of Most
Noble Order of Garter; Soc. of Desc. of Colonial Clergy; Women
Desc. of Ancient and Honorable Artillery Co. (FL, Court of
Assistants); Dau. of American Revolution; Colonial Dames XVII
Century; Soc. of Desc. of Henry Wolcott (FL, Past State Pres.);
Hereditary Register of USA. Address: Orlando Lutheran Towers,
300 E. Church St., Apt.1401, Orlando,FL 32801. Descended from:

1 Thomas Welles, Governor of Connecticut 1655-58

2 John Welles   Elizabeth Bourne
   England c.1621   Stratford,CT   Stratford c.1627
   Stratford 7 Aug 1659   Jul 1647   -----

3 Robert Welles   Elizabeth Goodrich
   Wethersfield,CT 1651   Wethersfield   Wethersfield 1658
   Wethersfield 22 Jun   9 Jun 1675   Wethersfield 17 Feb
   1714   1697/8

4 Robert Welles   Sarah Wolcott
   Wethersfield c.1684   Wethersfield   Wethersfield 14 Aug
                                                           1686
   Wethersfield c.1738   12 Dec 1706   Wethersfield 1738

5 Judith Welles   Josiah Robbins
   Wethersfield 4 Mar   Wethersfield   Wethersfield 17 Dec
   1730   1724
   Wethersfield 1 May   21 Dec 1749   -----
   1771

6 Rhoda Robbins   Gershom Wolcott
   Wethersfield 6 Apr   Wethersfield   Wethersfield 11 Apr
   1755   1748
   Wethersfield 20 Oct   10 Oct 1774   Wethersfield 29 Nov
   1795   1782

7 Gershom Nott Wolcott   Eunice Willard
   Wethersfield 13 Feb   Wethersfield   Wethersfield 23 Jul
   1776   1779
   Jordan,NY 15 Jul 1845   17 May 1798   Rome,NY 3 Mar 1854

8 Emily Louisa Wolcott
   Trenton,NY 7 May 1809   Jordan,NY   Henry Duncan
   Sherwood,MI 13 Sep   1839   Bennington,VT 1812
   1861   Burr Oak,MI 24 Sep
                                            1864

9 Helen Amelia Duncan   Ransom Edward Stephens
   Jordan 2 Jul 1841   Burr Oak   Palmyra,NY 13 Nov 1824
   Burr Oak 2 Feb 1918   18 Oct 1876   Kalamazoo,MI 1 Apr
                                            1919

10 Lulu Bell Stephens   Fred H. Cornwall
   Coldwater,MI 28 Oct   Colon,MI   Colon 22 Feb 1879
   1877
   LaGrange,IN 12 Jan   29 Apr 1900   LaGrange 15 May 1958
   1933

   Inheritor: Denise Anne Turner (granddaughter)

BROEMMER, H. RICHARD

Nat. #374-B. Elected 4 Dec 1979. b. Cape Girardeau,MO 17 Aug
1943. m.(1) Albuquerque,NM 21 Aug 1965, Christal Loring Jane
(Chastain) Sullivan, b. Topeka,KS 11 Sep 1943. m.(2) Albuquer-
que 3 Jun 1972, Billie Sue Meyer, b. Santa Fe,NM 12 Nov 1948.
Issue: Andrew Patrick Broemmer, b. 17 Sep 1968; Lara Lindsey
Broemmer, b. 22 Mar 1977; Brandon Ahric Broemmer, b. 14 Aug 1979;
all b. Albuquerque. Educ: New Mexico State University, BS;
University of New Mexico, MS. Member: Hereditary Order of Desc.
of Colonial Governors. Address: 11137 Newcomb, N.E.,
Albuquerque,NM 87111. Descended from:

1 John West, Governor of Virginia 1635-37

2 John West   Ursula Unity Croshaw
   New Kent Co.VA c.1632   -----   1634-36
   New Kent Co. 1689   1652   York Co.VA 1709

3 Anne West   Henry Fox
   King William Co.VA   Virginia   Gloucester Co.VA
   1662   1660
   -----   -----   Virginia 1714

4 N. Fox   -----
   Virginia   -----   -----
   -----   -----   -----

5 Amy Fox   John Kendrick
   Virginia 1740   Virginia   1735
   1760   -----   1802

6 Thomas Kendrick   Dolly Lawson
   -----   -----   -----
   -----   -----   -----

7 Joseph Kendrick   Lavinia Suggs
   1784   North Carolina NC 11 Oct 1793
   -----   1812   Ripley,MS 1883

8 John Warren Kendrick   Martha Craig Glenn
   Lincoln Co.NC 14 Mar   -----   9 Jun 1813
   1813
   Booneville,MS 19 Apr   -----   Booneville 26 Feb 1895
   1884

9	Margaret Josephine Kendrick		Mose McCarley	
	Tippah Co.MS 23 May 1843	Mississippi	Tennessee 1830	
	Booneville,MS 11 Mar 1923	19 Feb 1861	Booneville 13 Sep 1882	

10 Moses Glenn McCarley
   Ripley,MS 24 Mar 1862 Booneville
   Booneville 24 Feb 1926 16 Oct 1888

   Inez Smith
   Baldwyn,MS 3 Dec 1867
   Booneville 17 Jun 1943

11 Marguerite McCarley
   Booneville 22 Jun 1891 Booneville

   Albuquerque,NM 19 Feb 1976   19 Sep 1914

   Roy Lee Cox
   Middleton,TN 13 Jun 1880
   Albuquerque 19 Apr 1962

12 Margaret Josephine Cox
   Phoenix,AZ 9 Jul 1915 Albuquerque

   -----   2 Jan 1938

   Howard Richard Broemmer
   St. Louis,MO 14 Jul 1914

BROOKS, JANE ARNOLD BOYER (MRS. WILBUR STARR)

Nat. #369-B. Elected 17 Nov 1979. b. North Adams,MA 13 Feb 1921. m. New York,NY, Dr. Wilbur Starr Brooks, b. East Hampton, CT 20 Nov 1904. Educ: New York University, BS. Member: Hereditary Order of Desc. of Colonial Governors; Dau. of American Revolution; Dau. of Founders and Patriots of America; Soc. of Mayflower Descendants; Dau. of American Colonists. Address: 312 Rugby Road, Syracuse,NY 13203. Descended from:

1 John Winthrop, Governor of Massachusetts 1629-34, 1637-40, 1642-44, 1646-49

2 Mary Winthrop
   England 1612   -----

   Salisbury,MA 16 Apr 1643   1632

   Samuel Dudley
   Northamptonshire,Eng. 1610
   Exeter,NH 10 Feb 1682/3

3 Ann Dudley
   Salisbury 16 Oct 1641   -----
   -----   c.1658

   Edward Hilton
   Exeter btw.1626-29
   Exeter 28 Apr 1699

4 Jane Hilton   (2)
   c.1668   -----
   c.1738   c.1699

   Richard Mattoon

   Exeter 23 Jul 1706

5 Mary Mattoon
   -----   Exeter
   21 Jan 1772   c.1720

   Richard Smith
   Exeter
   bur.Newmarket,NH 22 Apr 1765

6 Richard Smith
   c.1720   -----
   -----   bf.1745

   Mary Hardy

   -----

7 Abigail Smith 7 Oct 1762 Berwick,ME 1846/7	----- 19 Mar 1785	John Burleigh 22 May 1754 Gilmanton,NH 1 Jun 1827
8 William Burleigh Gilmanton 24 Oct 1785 South Berwick 2 Jul 1827	South Berwick 1 Jan 1817	Deborah Currier Dover,NH 7 Dec 1784 Somersworth,NH 18 Dec 1864
9 Micajah Currier Burleigh South Berwick 15 Jan 1818 Great Falls 5 Mar 1881	Great Falls,NH (Somersworth) 9 Dec 1846	Mary Frances Russell Great Falls 4 Aug 1881 Great Falls 29 Nov 1889
10 Charlotte Russell Burleigh Somersworth 6 Sep 1862 Exeter 23 Jun 1930	----- 2 Oct 1884	Edmund Swalm Boyer Pottsville,PA 21 Oct 1857 Exeter 10 Mar 1930
11 Francis Burleigh Boyer Reading,PA 12 Dec 1885 Boston,MA 6 Apr 1937	North Adams,MA 15 Jun 1915	Jane Arnold Bond North Adams 31 Oct 1885 living

SUPPLEMENT NO. 1

1 Thomas Dudley, Governor of Massachusetts 1634, 1640, 1645,
  1650-51

2 Samuel Dudley   Mary Winthrop

Continue with Generation 2 of her lineage from Governor John
Winthrop.

BUNNELL, IRENE TUTTLE (MRS. RICHARD W.)

Nat. #372-B. Elected 23 Nov 1979. b. Salt Lake City,UT 12 Sep
1914. m. Salt Lake City 1 Jun 1935, Richard W. Bunnell, b. Salt
Lake City 2 Apr 1906. Member: Hereditary Order of Desc. of
Colonial Governors; Soc. of Mayflower Desc.; Dau. of American
Revolution; Dau. of American Colonists; Dau. of Founders and
Patriots; Soc. of Desc. of Colonial Clergy; Huguenot Society;
Colonial Dames XVII Century; Washingtons Army at Valley Forge;
Dames of Court of Honor; Americans of Royal Descent; Magna Charta
Dames; Dau. of Colonial Wars; Sons and Dau. of Pilgrims, Soc. of
War of 1812; New England Women; New England, Kentucky, and
Suffolk Co. Historical Societies; Marchand and Conover Family
Assns.; Hereditary Register of USA. Address: 401 North Adams,
Fullerton,CA 92632. Descended from:

*1 Francis Lovelace, Governor of New York 1668-73

2 Edward Lovelace c.1662 1714	----- c.1680	----- ----- -----

* See Preface

```
3  John Lovelace
   England c.1690          Dutchess Co.NY  -----
   Syracuse,NY             c.1725          -----

4  George Lovelace                         -----
   c.1735                  Kentucky        -----
   Bourbon Co.KY af.1803   c.1755          -----

5  John Lovelace                           Rachael Van Hook
   New York c.1760         Bourbon Co.     c.1760
   Syracuse,NY 1835        c.1777          -----

6  Joseph Loveless                         Dorothy Rogers
   Marysville,KY 3 Mar     Kentucky        TN 25 Feb 1781
     1778
   Illinois                c.1806          OH 18 Oct 1834 or 1838

7  John Loveless               (1)         Mahala Anderson
   Caldrean,OH 24 Jun 1807 Perry,OH        Hampshire Co.VA 25 Aug
                                             1805
   Payson,UT 6 Dec 1880    25 Jan 1826     UT 25 Oct 1891

8  James W. Loveless           (1)         Matilda Elizabeth
                                             McClellan
   Fairfield Co.,OH        Council         Nashville,TN 15 Dec
     23 Dec 1828             Bluffs,IA       1829
   Provo,UT 7 May 1889     9 Mar 1847      Provo 1 Mar 1909

9  Juliet Elizabeth                        Abram Conover
     Loveless
   Provo 7 Mar 1861        Provo           Provo 24 Jul 1858
   Ferron,UT 29 Jul 1937   4 Dec 1879      Ferron 29 Jul 1937

10 Alta Jeanette Conover                   Mark Tuttle
   Ferron 15 Apr 1882      Ferron          Manti,UT 14 Jan 1880
   Orange,CA 13 Feb 1956   17 Dec 1902     Salt Lake City,UT
                                             9 Jun 1949
```

COFFIN, KENNETH DIX

Nat. #340-B. Elected 25 Jul 1979. b. Carthage,IN 11 Oct 1894.
m. 12 Dec 1920, Ellen Shirk, b. Indianapolis,IN 22 May 1893.
Educ: Purdue University, BSCE; Indiana University, MA. Member:
Hereditary Order of Desc. of Colonial Governors; Sons of American
Revolution; Somerset Chapter Magna Charta Barons; Huguenot Soc.
of Indiana and Florida; Indiana Pioneers; Nantucket, Dukes Co.,
and various local Historical Societies; Officers Assns.; Various
Masonic Bodies. Address: 512 North Riverside Drive, New Smyrna
Beach,FL 32069. Descended from:

```
1  Tristram Coffyn, Governor of Nantucket 1671

2  John Coffyn                             Deborah Austin
   30 Oct 1647             -----           -----
   5 Sep 1711              1668            4 Feb 1724

3  Samuel Coffyn                           Miriam Gardner
   Nantucket 12 Dec 1680   -----           Nantucket 24 Jul 1685
   Nantucket 22 Feb 1764   1705            17 Apr 1750
```

4	William Coffin	(2)	Priscilla Paddock
	Nantucket 4 Nov 1720	-----	Nantucket 18 Jul 1722
	New Garden,NC 10 Nov	8 Nov 1740	New Garden 15 Jul 1803
	1803		

5	Bethuel Coffin		Hannah Dicks
	New Garden 6 Feb 1756	-----	New Garden 16 Jun 1757
	New Garden 1837	5 May 1776	New Garden 10 Oct 1820

6	Zachariah Coffin		Phebe Starbuck
	New Garden 6 Apr 1782	Guilford Co.	Guilford Co. 8 Mar
		NC	1782
	Westland,IN 21 Aug 1845	25 Jul 1803	Westland 18 Dec 1852

7	Nathan Dix Coffin		Mary H. Wheeler
	Westland 6 Nov 1818	-----	Guilford Co. 25 Oct
			1818
	Westland 13 Sep 1908	30 Aug 1838	Westland 22 Dec 1891

8	Orlando Shubael Coffin		Mary Blacklidge
	Westland 7 Nov 1886	-----	Rust Co.IN 24 Oct 1862
	Indianapolis,IN	14 Apr 1886	Indianapolis 11 Oct
	4 Mar 1929		1894

Inheritor: John Shirk Coffin, 5617 Crestview Ave.,
Indianapolis,IN 46220

CRUSE, MAURINE R. MORLEY (MRS. CHARLES D.)

Nat. #361-B. Elected 19 Sep 1979. b. Rooks Co.KS 16 Feb 1907.
m. Salina,KS 12 Nov 1932, Charles David Cruse, b. Kenesaw,NE
29 Dec 1889, d. Abilene,KS 6 Aug 1965. Educ: University of
Kansas, BA. Member: Hereditary Order of Desc. of Colonial
Governors; Dau. of American Revolution; Dau. of American
Colonists; National Huguenot Society, KS; U.S. Dau. of 1812;
Dau. of Colonial Wars; DuBois Family Assn.; Huguenot and
Dickinson Co.KS Historical Societies. Address: 204 North Vine,
Abilene,KS 67410. Descended from:

1 Charles Calvert, Governor of Maryland 1675-1715

2	Mary Calvert		John Chinoweth, Sr.
	1680-85	England	Meneage,Cornwall Co.,
			Wales 1682/3
	-----	c.1705	w.p. Frederick Co.VA
			6 May 1746

3	John Chinoweth, Jr.		Mary Smith
	Baltimore Co.MD 1706	Baltimore Co.	-----
	w.p. Frederick Co.	26 Nov 1730	-----
	5 Mar 1771		

4	William Chennerworth,Sr.		Ruth Calvert
	Baltimore Co. 8 Jan	-----	-----
	1732		
	w.p. Frederick Co. 1772	-----	-----

5 William Chenoweth, Jr.   Mary Van Meter Henton
   Frederick Co.   Elizabethtown, VA 11 Feb 1757
      10 Jun 1760   KY
   Nelson Co.KY 16 Apr   Oct 1781   Nelson Co. 29 Jun 1832
      1828

6 Jacob Van Meter   Mary Haycraft
      Chenoweth
   Nelson Co. 2 Mar 1784 Elizabethtown   Elizabethtown 15 Apr
                                              c.1787
   Pike Co.IL 29 Jul 1851 7 Jan 1808   Bushnell,IL 27 Jul
                                              1868

7 Mary Chenoweth   William Hudson Jaques
   KY 13 May 1820   Pike Co.   NY 10 Mar 1816
   Sullivan Co.MO   15 May 1838   Sullivan Co. 22 Sep
      28 Apr 1899   1892

8 Hester Chenoweth Jaques   John George Smith
                                              (Schmidt)
   Pike Co. 7 Nov 1845   Milan,MO   Bucheurenth,Bavaria,
                                              Ger. 20 Nov 1843
   Lawrence,KS 1 Mar 1925 26 Oct 1876   Rooks Co.KS 17 Oct
                                              1905

9 Clara Viola Smith   Marcus Stanley Morley
   Rooks Co. 20 Aug 1879 Rooks Co.   Marshall,MI 13 May
                                              1874
   Halstead,KS 13 Dec   19 Jun 1900   Abilene,KS 4 May 1966
      1941

DAZEY, MARGARET H. TOLLES (MRS. DONALD A.)

Nat. #362-B. Elected 19 Sep 1979. b. Sioux City,IA 16 Feb 1928.
m. Caldwell,ID 22 Dec 1945, Donald Arthur Dazey, b. Homedale,ID.
Member: Hereditary Order of Desc. of Colonial Governors; Soc. of
Mayflower Desc. (Board of Assistants); Huguenot Soc. of Washing-
ton State (Registrar); Dau. of American Revolution (Chap.
Registrar); Colonial Dames XVII Century; Dau. of American
Colonists; Dau. of Colonial Wars; Soc. of Desc. of Colonial
Clergy; Magna Charta Dames; Colonial Order of the Crown; Plan-
tagenet Society; Seattle Genealogical Soc.; Connecticut Soc. of
Genealogists. Address: 1309-164th Place,N.E., Bellevue,WA
98008. Descended from:

1 Thomas Welles, Governor of Connecticut 1655-58

2 Ann Welles   Thomas Thompson
   Essex,Eng. c.1619   -----   -----
   Farmington,CT   14 Apr 1646   Farmington 20 Apr 1655
      bf. Dec 1680

3 Ester Thompson   Samuel Gridley
   Farmington 17 Jun 1655 Farmington   Farmington 25 Nov 1647
   -----   bf.2 Dec 1680   Farmington 1712

4 Thomas Gridley   Hannah Wilcoxson
   Farmington 1685   Farmington   Farmington 18 Sep 1685
   Farmington 1785   31 Oct 1704   c.1724

```
5  Timothy Gridley                               Esther Porter
   Farmington 1711         Farmington           -----
   Farmington 1758         1737                 Farmington 1762

6  Timothy Gridley                               Rhoda Woodruff
   Farmington c.1739       Farmington           Farmington 7 Jul 1746
   Farmington              8 May 1766           Farmington

7  Bede Gridley                                  Carlos Cowles
   Farmington 1772         West Hartford,       Farmington 2 Nov 1770
                           CT
   Farmington              22 Jan 1796          Weathersfield,VT 1846

8  Nancy Cowles                                  Clark Tolles, Jr.
   Wolcott,CT 30 Oct 1796  -----                Weathersfield 22 Sep
                                                   1787
   Weathersfield 1 Jan     17 Nov 1814          Weathersfield 4 Oct
      1840                                         1869

9  Franklin Tolles                               Martha Theodotia
   Weathersfield 9 Jan     Springfield          Springfield,VT 29 Jun
      1818                                         1823
   Weathersfield 1 Jul     28 Nov 1843          Weathersfield 13 Feb
      1895                                         1897

10 Louis Clark Tolles                            Sarah Augusta Ankeny
   Weathersfield 17 Nov    Cedar Co.NE          JoDaviess Co.IL 10 Dec
      1847                                         1854
   Laurel,NE 17 Nov 1917   24 Feb 1874          Long Beach,CA 17 Feb
                                                   1925

11 Perry Kenneth Tolles                          Bernice Viola Petersen
   Laurel 21 Oct 1893      Lyons,NE             Lyons 20 Jan 1890
   Boise,ID 28 Nov 1971    18 Jan 1916          living
```

Inheritor: Donald Joseph Dazey, 1309-164th Place, N.E.,
Bellevue,WA 98008. (son)

DOYLE, MABEL GRAYBILL HUNT (MRS.)

Nat. #376-B. Elected 17 Jan 1980. Educ: Wellesley College,
Massachusetts, AB. Member: Hereditary Order of Desc. of Colonial
Governors; Desc. of Loyalists and Patriots of American Revolu-
tion; Women Desc. of Ancient and Honorable Artillery Company.
Occup: U.S. Civil Service (ret.) and CDR U.S. Naval Reserve
(ret.). Address: 2700 Virginia Ave., N.W., Washington,DC 20037.
Descended from:

1 Tristram Coffin, Governor of Nantucket 1671-73

```
2  James Coffin                                  Mary Severance
   Devonshire,England      Salisbury,MA         Salisbury 5 Aug 1645
      12 Aug 1640
   Nantucket 28 Jul 1720   3 Dec 1663           Nantucket 1724

3  Dinah Coffin                                  Nathaniel Starbuck,Jr.
   Nantucket 29 Aug 1674   Nantucket            Nantucket 9 Aug 1668
   Nantucket 1 Aug 1750    20 Nov 1690          Nantucket 9 Feb 1753
```

4 Paul Starbuck   Ann Tibbets
   Nantucket 29 Aug 1694   Nantucket   Nantucket 8 Jul 1698
   Nantucket 20 May 1759   26 Sep 1718   Nantucket 29 Jul 1736

5 William Starbuck   Jane Taylor
   Nantucket 28 Nov 1719   Guilford Co.NC   North Carolina
   Nantucket 11 Dec 1798   1 May 1776   Nantucket 23 Nov 1803

6 Thomas Starbuck   Eleanor Leonard
   New Garden,NC 10 Sep   North Carolina   Guilford Co. 10 Mar
     1778   1780
   NC 18 Mar 1834   28 Apr 1804   Guilford Co.

7 Abigail Starbuck   Thomas Henley
   Guilford Co. 2 Aug   Guilford Co.   Randolph Co.NC 18 Aug
     1804   1803
   Henry Co.IN 1 Dec 1878   5 Mar 1829   Carthage,IN 6 Jun 1893

8 Anne Henley   Aaron Betts Hunt
   Randolph Co. 24 May   Little Blue   Leesburg,OH 26 Feb
     1835   River,IN   1830
   Carthage 19 May 1912   8 May 1868   Martinsville,OH
                                                29 Mar 1883

9 Gurney L. Hunt   Millie Elizabeth
                                                Graybill
   Martinsville 4 May   York,PA   York 16 Jun 1897
     1873
   Washington,DC 8 Nov   -----   -----
     1935

EDWARDS, JAMES MacDONALD

Nat. #364-B. Elected 22 Oct 1979. b. Jackson,GA 15 Apr 1914.
Educ: University of Georgia, BCS, BBS. Member: Hereditary Order
of Desc. of Colonial Governors; Sons of American Revolution;
Sons and Dau. of Pilgrims; Sons of Confederate Veterans; Order
of Stars and Bars; Magna Charta Barons; National Gavel Society;
Washington Family Descendants; Order of El Cid; Huguenot Soc. of
Tennessee. Address: 1941 Twin Falls Road, Decatur,GA 30032.
Descended from:

1 Edward Digges, Governor of Virginia 1655-56

2 Catherine Digges   William Herndon
   Bellfield,VA 1654   -----   England 1649
   King & Queen Co.VA   1677   St. Stephen's Par.
     1727   King & Queen Co.VA
                                                1722

3 Edward Herndon   Mary Waller
   1678   -----   Newport Pagnell,Co.
                                               Bucks,Eng. 23 May
                                               1674
   1758/9   1698   England 1727

4	William Herndon King & Queen Co. 1706 1783	----- 1730	Ann Drysdale 1711 1757
5	Edward Herndon, Sr. Spotsylvania Co.VA 16 Jul 1738 Madison Co.VA 11 May 1831	Orange Co. 30 Nov 1762	Mary Gaines Orange Co.VA 10 May 1742 Orange Co. 15 Jun 1829
6	Edward Herndon, Jr. Madison Co. 6 May 1768 Elbert Co.GA 22 Sep 1827	Culpeper Co. VA 18 Aug 1791	Nancy Rucker Madison Co. 8 May 1768 Elbert Co. 11 Apr 1845
7	Frances Herndon Orange Co. 21 Nov 1800 Jasper Co. 21 Nov 1840	Elbert Co. Jun 1820	James Adams Franklin Co.VA 5 Mar 1795 Jasper Co. 2 Aug 1857
8	Edward Herndon Adams Jasper Co. 7 Feb 1824 Jasper Co. 14 Jun 1893	Jasper Co. 12 Dec 1841	Julia Ann Hancock Jasper Co. 18 Dec 1828 Twiggs Co.GA 28 Dec 1905
9	Georgia Ann Adams Jasper Co. 8 Aug 1843 Jasper Co. 5 Jun 1920	(1) ----- 24 Oct 1860	Robert Mayne Lane Putnam Co.GA 19 Apr 1839 Richmond,VA Jun 1862
10	Roberta Mayne Lane Gladesville,GA 25 May 1862 Atlanta,GA 17 Jun 1947	Jasper Co. 25 Jan 1880	James Byrd Edwards Monroe Co.GA 27 Sep 1858 Jackson,GA 22 May 1932
11	James Lane Edwards Flovilla,GA 12 Aug 1891 Atlanta 13 Oct 1971	Jackson 13 Mar 1913	Florrie Alamo Harp 12 Feb 1894 -----

Inheritor: Vera Jones Edwards Martin (Mrs. William L., Jr.),
2969 King Alfred Drive, Macon,GA 31204.

HAGEDORN, BEATRICE DOROTHY MEAD (MRS. ALFRED ARTHUR)

Nat. #375-B. Elected 8 Dec 1979. b. 27 Sep 1919. m. 10 Jul 1943, Alfred Arthur Hagedorn, b. 11 Apr 1919. Issue: Dr. Alfred Arthur Hagedorn III; Dr. George Allan Hagedorn. Educ: Cornell University, Engineering College. Member: Hereditary Order of Desc. of Colonial Governors; Dau. of American Revolution; Sons and Dau. of Pilgrims; Huguenot Society of Colorado; Dau. of Founders and Patriots of America; Dau. of American Colonists; Bidwell, Parsons, and Welles Family Assns.; Connecticut Soc. of Genealogists. Occup: Vice President and Secretary, Mid Colorado Investment Co.; Director, Austrado Pty Ltd, Australia. Address: 13 Loma Linda Drive, Colorado Springs,CO 80906. Descended from:

1 John Webster, Governor of Connecticut 1656

2 Robert Webster
England 1627
Hartford,CT 1676
\-\-\-\-\-
1652
Susanna Treat
Pitminster, Eng. 1629
Hartford 1705

3 Jonathan Webster
Hartford 1657
Hartford 1735
Hartford
1681
Dorcas Hopkins
\-\-\-\-\-
Hartford 1694

4 Mehitable Webster
Hartford 1691
\-\-\-\-\-
\-\-\-\-\-
\-\-\-\-\-
David Bidwell
Hartford 1687
Hartford 1758

5 David Bidwell
Canaan,CT 1720
Stillwater,NY c.1793
\-\-\-\-\-
\-\-\-\-\-
Esther Lawrence
Canaan 1729
Stillwater 1809

6 Esther Bidwell
Canaan 1750
Stillwater 1809
\-\-\-\-\-
1770
Charles Moore
1741
Stillwater 1827

7 Gideon Moore
Stillwater 1781
Stillwater 1858
\-\-\-\-\-
\-\-\-\-\-
Minerva Soulard
Bemis Heights,NY 1785
Stillwater 1844

8 Maria Louisa Moore
Stillwater 1781
Stillwater 1858
\-\-\-\-\-
\-\-\-\-\-
Cornelius Sanford Mead
West Charlton,NY 1816
Chatham,NY 1879

9 Sanford Montgomery
Mead
Rotterdam,NY 1846
St.Louis,MO 1931
\-\-\-\-\-
1873
Katherine Collard
New York,NY 1849
Brooklyn,NY 1931

10 Albert Raynor Mead
Philadelphia,PA
20 Jan 1884
Amityville,NY
29 Jun 1955
Brooklyn
22 Feb 1916
Eloise Jennie Baxter
27 Nov 1894
8 Jun 1977

Inheritor: Dr. Alfred A. Hagedorn, III, 158-A Cedar Lane, Highland Park,NJ 08904.

HAUPT, GRACE ELEANOR MAINES (MRS. GEORGE W.)

Nat. #301-B. Elected 17 Nov 1979. b. Clearfield Co.PA 23 May
1896. m. Philadelphia,PA 31 Jan 1925, Dr. George Webster Haupt,
b. Sunbury,PA 15 Jun 1900, d. Philadelphia 9 Jun 1955. Educ:
Bucknell University, AB. Member: Hereditary Order of Desc. of
Colonial Governors; Ancient and Honorable Artillery Co.; New
England Women; Olde Plymouth Colony Descendants; U.S. Dau. of
1812; Dau. of Founders and Patriots of America. Address:
Northwood Apts., Apt. A-1, Woodbury,NJ 08096. Descended from:

1 Brian Pendleton, Governor of Maine 1680-81

2 James Pendleton   (2)   Hannah Goodenow
   Watertown,MA c.1628   Sudbury,MA   Sudbury 28 Nov 1639
   Stonington,CT 29 Nov 29 Apr 1656   Stonington af.1725
     1709

3 Ann Pendleton   Eleazer Brown
   Sudbury 12 Nov 1667   Stonington   Lynn,MA 5 Aug 1670
   Stonington 1723   18 Oct 1693   Stonington 30 Nov 1734

4 Ann Brown   Thomas Main
   Stonington   Stonington   Stonington 19 Jul 1700
     Feb 1699/1700
   North Stonington   20 Apr 1720   North Stonington
     11 Mar 1766   w.p. 6 Sep 1771

5 Ezekiel Main   (1)   Deborah Meacham
   North Stonington   Stonington   Norwich,CT 20 Apr 1746
     8 Jul 1742
   Bridgewater,PA   25 Nov 1763   -----
     btw.1790-1800

6 Nehemiah Maine   Phebe Bunnell
   Bristol,CT bf.1774   Connecticut   af.1774
   Clearfield Co.PA   bf.1800   Clearfield Co.
     adm.6 May 1841   af. May 1841

7 Seth Maine(s)   Nancy Forcee(ey)
   Centre Co.PA 1808   Clearfield Co. Delaware 26 Oct 1799
   Clearfield Co.   bf.1829   Clearfield Co.
     w.p. 17 May 1859   15 Sep 1882

8 David B. Maines   Louisa C. Vought
   Clearfield Co. 1838 Clearfield Co. Clearfield Co. 1844
   Amelia Co.VA   bf.1865   Amelia Co. Nov 1887
     22 Mar 1892

9 Edgar W. Maines   Tacey Elizabeth Glace
   Clearfield Co.   Clearfield Co. Lock Haven,PA 3 Feb
     btw.15 Jun-6 Aug   1872
     1869
   Clearfield Co.   25 Oct 1892   Northumberland Co.PA
     Jan 1896   5 Aug 1936

Inheritor: (Miss) Erika Christine Haupt, 3345 Kensington
Circle, Napa,CA 94558. (grand-daughter)

HELM, HERSCHEL H.

Nat. #368-B. Elected 17 Nov 1979. b. Owensboro,KY 13 Aug 1916.
m. Washington,DC 19 Sep 1952, Rosalie Nease, b. Buffalo,WV
1 Dec 1925. Issue: Nan McDowall Helm, b. Saigon,Vietnam, 3)ct
1956. Educ: George Washington University, AB, MA; University
of Mexico. Member: Hereditary Order of Desc. of Colonial
Governors; Jamestowne Society (Past Governor, Member at Large
of Council). Military: U.S. Army Air Force, Lt. Counter-
Intelligence Corps. Occup: Government Service; Foreign Service,
Dept. of State; Retired, Member of DACOR. Address: 4106-27th
Road North, Arlington,VA 22207. Descended from:

1 William Stone, Governor of Maryland 1649-54

2	Mary Stone Accomac,VA 1642 Charles Co.MD 1685	Charles Co. 1674	Robert Doyne Ireland 1640 Charles Co. 1689

3	Mary Doyne
	Charles Co. 1682/3
	Prince George's Co.MD
	  1734
		Charles Co.
		c.1704/6
			Nicholas Dawson
			St.Mary's Co.MD 1682/3
			Prince George's Co.
			  1727

4	Nicholas Dawson Pr.Geo.Co. c.1706 -----	----- c.1736	Sarah Ellen ----- -----
5	George Dawson Pr.Geo.Co. 10 Mar 1750 Adair Co.KY 1790	Maryland 1780	Hannah Asbury Pr.Geo.Co. 1764 Kentucky 1837
6	Enoch W. Dawson Pr.Geo.Co. 1783 Simpson Co.KY 1846	Adair Co. 20 Dec 1808	Nancy Chapman Orange Co.VA c.1783 Simpson Co.
7	Elizabeth A. Dawson Allen Co.KY 1 Jan 1810 KY 21 Jul 1885	Allen Co. 18 May 1829	Hugh Nelson Morehead VA 27 May 1807 McLean Co.KY 30 Feb 1895
8	Jesse W. Morehead Simpson Co. 19 Feb 1833 Indian Territory 15 May 1862	Butler Co.KY 6 May 1858	Mary J. Kuykendall Butler Co. 16 Mar 1837 Butler Co. 23 Jan 1879

9	Mary J. Belle Morehead
	Honey Grove,TX
	  15 Jan 1861
	Morgantown,KY 19 Nov
	  1901
		Butler Co.
		27 Nov 1878
			William Avilette Helm
			Butler Co. 25 Jan 1857
			Morgantown 16 Feb 1921

10	Herschel Horace Helm
	Morgantown 27 Sep 1879
	Arlington,VA 2 Jan
	  1971
		Hawesville,KY
		16 Jul 1915
			Lucy Jane Hancock
			Hancock Co.KY 24 Jan
			  1893
			Owensboro,KY 15 Dec
			  1931

Inheritor: Nan McDowall Helm, 4106 27th Road North,
Arlington,VA 22207. (daughter)

LEONARD, DANIEL, JR.

Nat. #371-B. Elected 4 Dec 1979. b. Evanston,IL 27 Jul 1935.
m. Chicago,IL 7 Nov 1959, Elizabeth Anne Dix Chamberlain, b.
Binghamton,NY 17 Feb 1937. Educ: Amherst College, AB; University of Chicago, MMA. Member: Hereditary Order of Desc. of
Colonial Governors; Soc. of Mayflower Descendants; Mensa
Society. Address: Cricket Hill Drive, Amherst,NH 03031.
Descended from:

1 William Bradford, Governor of Plymouth Colony 1621-57

2 William Bradford, Jr.   Alice Richards
   Plymouth 17 Jun 1624   Plymouth   Weymouth,MA 16 Jun 1627
   Plymouth 20 Feb 1703/4   28 Jan 1650   Plymouth 12 Dec 1671

3 Hannah Bradford   Joshua Ripley
   Plymouth 9 Sep 1662   Plymouth   Hingham,MA 9 Nov 1658
   Windham,CT 28 May 1738   28 Nov 1682   Windham 18 May 1739

4 Joshua Ripley, Jr.   Mary Backus
   Hingham 13 May 1688   Windham   Windham 8 Nov 1692
   Windham 18 Nov 1773   3 Dec 1712   Windham 19 Oct 1770

5 Ebenezer Ripley   Mehitable Burbank
   Windham 22 Jun 1729   -----   Suffield,CT 28 Jul
                                                  1729
   Windham 11 Jun 1811   11 Jun 1752   West Springfield,MA
                                                  20 May 1813

6 Eleanor Ripley   Daniel Leonard
   Windham 16 Aug 1754   -----   West Springfield
                                                  16 Jun 1747
   West Springfield   1776   West Springfield
      15 Oct 1815   18 Apr 1824

7 Daniel Leonard   Nancy Fenn
   West Springfield   -----   Plymouth,CT 5 Sep
      7 Jul 1781   1785
   West Springfield   26 Aug 1805   West Springfield
      19 May 1813   7 Mar 1810

8 James Leonard   Mary Rood
   W.Springfield 25 May   W.Springfld.   W.Springfield 18 Apr
      1806   1802
   W.Springfield 13 Dec   24 Mar 1830   W.Springfield 17 Jul
      1882   1880

9 Daniel Leonard   Mary Elizabeth Cotrell
   W.Springfield 3 Oct   Albany,NY   Albany 1 May 1840
      1839
   Albany 26 Oct 1917   11 Jun 1861   Albany 9 May 1897

10 Harriet Olcott Leonard   John Robert Leonard
   Albany 17 Nov 1873   Albany   New York,NY 19 Sep
                                                  1864
   Winnetka,IL 28 Feb 1923 16 Feb 1897   Winnetka 5 Nov 1945

11 Daniel Leonard II   Sarah May Morey
   Albany 26 Jan 1901   Winnetka   Evanston,IL 18 Dec
                                                  1905
   -----   3 Feb 1934   -----

337

McGEE, MARIAN E. JUMP (MRS. RALPH E.)

Nat. #373-B. Elected 4 Dec 1979. b. Selma,IN 18 May 1910.
m. Wasseon,OH 25 Mar 1933, Ralph Edward McGee, b. Muncie,IN
15 Apr 1901, d. Los Angeles,CA 5 Nov 1955. Educ: Indiana
University, BA, MA. Member: Hereditary Order of Desc. of
Colonial Governors; Colonial Dames of XVII Century (State Pres.);
Dames of Court of Honor (Organizing President, Past President,
Corresponding Secretary General); Dau. of American Colonists
(IN State Chaplain, Chap. Regent); Dau. of Colonial Wars (State
Registrar); New England Women; Dau. of American Revolution;
Magna Charta Dames; Order of Washington; National and Delaware
Co.IN Historical Societies. Address: 125 E. Beverly Dr.,
Indianapolis,IN 46205. Descended from:

1 William Leete, Governor of Connecticut 1676-83

2 John Leete   Mary Chittendon
 Guilford,CT 1637 ----- Guilford 1647
 25 Nov 1692 4 Oct 1670 9 Mar 1712

3 Ann Leete   John Collins
 5 Aug 1671 ----- 1665
 1724 23 Jul 1691 1751

4 Avis Collins   Peter Buell
 ----- Connecticut 22 May 1710
 1 Nov 1754 26 Dec 1734 -----

5 Lucretia Buell   Benjamin Webster
 26 Apr 1742 ----- Litchfield,CT 8 Dec
           1736
 23 Mar 1809 10 Feb 1759 Litchfield 29 Oct 1782

6 Elijah Webster   Lois Coe
 Litchfield 19 Mar 1761 ----- 24 Mar 1762
 1791 Jan 1783 1841

7 Uri Webster   Mercy Ashley
 Litchfield 30 Nov 1783 Whitesboro,NY Winchester,NH 24 Nov
           1789
 West Bloomfield,NY 6 Jan 1812 Petersburgh,KY 14 Feb
 28 Sep 1851   1858

8 Seraph Webster   Othaniel Gilbert
 Whitesboro 27 Apr 1814 W.Bloomfld. Bristol,NY 23 Sep 1808
 Yorktown,IN 2 Oct 1890 26 Apr 1832 Yorktown 21 Aug 1892

9 Mary Sophia Gilbert   Samuel Vaughn Jump
 East Bloomfield,NY Delaware Co. Dover,DE 27 Jun 1822
 6 Apr 1839 IN
 Muncie,IN 1908 28 Mar 1872 New Burlington,IN
           13 Aug 1887

10 Samuel Gilbert Jump   Fay Tima Lithco
           Jackson
 New Burlington New Burlingtn. Perry,IN 21 Dec 1875
 3 Mar 1873
 West Lafayette,IN 6 Jun 1900 -----
 11 May 1938

Inheritor: Mrs. E. Kenneth Parson, 800 W. Adams St.,
Muncie,IN

OXX, WILLIAM GARDNER, III (aka William Garderner Oxx, III)

Nat. #378-B. Elected 20 January 1980. b. Newport,RI 19 Jan
1923. m. Portuguese Bend,CA 11 Feb 1956, May Isobel Anderson,
b. LaFléche, Saskatchewan, Canada 24 Jul 1930. Issue: William
Anderson Oxx, IV, b. 16 Mar 1960; Sheri Lynn Oxx, b. 18 May 1963;
Jonathan James Oxx, b. 8 Oct 1965. Educ: University of Redlands,
Cal., AB, MA; grad. studies, Inst. of Russian Affairs, Columbia
University,NY. Military: U.S. Naval Intelligence, Chief of Naval
Operations, WWII; USNR. Occup: Educator, Author, Illustrator.
Published 26 articles and 2 books on foreign affairs, military-
naval history, government and religion; educator in Los Angeles
schools; instructor of Russian history, military-naval history,
government, U.S. history; coach of speech and debate teams with
72 first and second place championship awards. Member:
Hereditary Order of Desc. of Colonial Governors; Sons of American
Revolution; Sons of Revolution; Soc. of Mayflower Descendants;
Soc. of Colonial Wars (CA, State Governor); Soc. of War of 1812,
MA; St. George's Soc. of NY; St. Andrew's Soc. of San Francisco;
Sons and Dau. of Pilgrims; John Howland Soc.; Military Order of
World Wars. Address: 3806 Mainsail Circle, Westlake Village,CA
91361. Descended from:

1 Benedict Arnold, Governor of Rhode Island 1657-60, 1662-63,
   1663-66, 1669-72, 1677-78

2 Damaris Arnold   John Bliss
   Newport,RI 23 Feb   -----   Sandwich,MA c.1645
     1648/9
   c.1717   24 Jun 1666   Newport 4 May 1717

3 Josiah Bliss   Miss Belcher
   Middletown,RI c.1685/6   -----   -----
   Rhode Island 1747/8   -----   -----

4 Henry Bliss   Susan
   Middletown 1722   -----   c.1732
   Newport 10 May 1805   1743   3 Jul 1813

5 Amy Bliss   -----
   Newport c.1778/80   -----   -----
   Rhode Island   -----   -----

6 Leonard S. Bliss,Sr.   Hannah Pratt Clarke
   Newport 1801   -----   Newport c.1800
   Newport 18 Jun 1872   16 May 1821   Newport 18 Dec 1833

7 Hannah May Bliss   Gordon Dixon Oxx
   Newport 20 Dec 1823   Newport   Newport 16 Dec 1818
   Newport c.1857   17 Jun 1841   Newport 12 Jul 1899

8 William Bliss Oxx   Priscilla W. Gardner
   Newport 10 Jun 1848   -----   Nantucket Island,MA
                                             23 Nov 1840
   Newport 23 Feb 1911   4 May 1873   Newport 26 Jun 1901

9 William Gardner Oxx   (2)   Mary Elizabeth Björkman
   Newport 2 Mar 1877   -----   Gloucester,MA 29 Aug
                                             1896
   Newport 31 Dec 1943   17 May 1922   San Diego,CA 20 Sep
                                             1964

Inheritor: William Anderson Oxx, IV, Class of 1983, United
States Naval Academy, Annapolis,MD.

QUALIFYING ANCESTORS WITH THE LIFE MEMBERS

WHO REPRESENT THEM

JOHN ALDEN, PLYMOUTH
    Cornett, Robert Fielding, Jr.
    Cross, J. Alan
    Gallagher, Genevieve J. Sherman (Mrs. Edward E.)
    Goodell, Col. Ralph Harmer, Jr.
    Grinnell, Henry Stephen
    Howe, Helen D. Bailey (Mrs. Elden L.)
    Hultander, Ethel Russell (Mrs. Martin E.)
    Knowles, Grace Fuller (Mrs. W. Herbert)
    Morgan, Diana M. Sweeney (Mrs. James P., Jr.)
    Saunders, Alden Clinton
    Stearns, Parley Mark, II
    Swanstrom, Kathryn C. Raymond (Mrs. Luther D.)
    Taylor, Dorothy E. Russ (Mrs. Darold W.)
    Thomas, Robert Lancefield, M.D.
    Van Rensselaer, Mrs. Edna Tretheway
    Weaver, Elizabeth J. Case (Mrs. John F., Sr.)
    Welch, Miss Inez Graham
    Westbrooke, Gilberta Wood (Mrs. Edward L.)
    Whitecotten, Dr. Glenn Lee

BENEDICT ARNOLD, RHODE ISLAND
    Almond, Roxanne M. Elmquist (Mrs. Richard W.)
    Benson, Newell Barton, Jr.
    Hills, Col. J. Huntington
    Oxx, William Gardner, III
    Palmer, Elmer Hall
    Van Antwerp, Lee Douglas, M.D.
    Ward, Nicholas Donnell

GERARDUS BEEKMAN, NEW YORK
    Chatfield, Florence M. Van Tine (Mrs. Charles H.)
    Foster, Giraud Van Nest

RICHARD BENNETT, VIRGINIA
    Bailey, Miss Mary Ethel
    Baird, Miss Stella
    Klein, Catherine C. Taylor (Mrs. George)
    Slowinski, Annette C. Roberts (Mrs. Walter A.)
    Southerland, Henry DeLeon, Jr.
    Tuttle, Eleanor B. P. Stiefel (Mrs. Frederick B.)

JAMES BISHOP, CONNECTICUT
    Darlington, Thomas
    Tuttle, Frederick Burton, M.D.

WILLIAM BRADFORD, PLYMOUTH
    Alper, Alice Gaskins (Mrs. Theodore)
    Barrington, Laurence W. L.
    Batchelder, Clarke Gilman
    Bauermann, Helen G. Benedict (Mrs. Werner F.)
    Fenn, Ruth A. Jones (Mrs. Clyde B.)

Foss, Philip Emery
Frische, Harriet Ross (Mrs. Carl A.)
Fuller, Eunice B. Lee (Mrs. William H.)
Fuller, Robert Stevens
Goodsell, Percy Hamilton
Hallowell, Thomas Jewett, Jr.
Harris, Florence E. Clarke (Mrs. Frank L.)
Jones, Cereno St. Clair
Leonard, Daniel, Jr.
Mikesell, Marian L. Lee (Mrs. John W., Jr.)
Peterle, Mrs. Helen J. Lee
Read, Lillian E. H. Hitchcock (Mrs. George D.)
Reynolds, Miss Mary Ola
Shepard, John Sanford
Stone, Polly A. Mariner (Mrs. Stanley)
Van Antwerp, Lee Douglas, M.D.

SIMON BRADSTREET, MASSACHUSETTS
Anderson, Dr. John Sherburne
Aurelius, Brynn Frederic
Bradstreet, William Carner
Dyer, Eleanor E. Folsom (Mrs. William W., Jr.)
Loucks, Barbara W. Haupt (Mrs. Charles E.)
Rowell, George Barker
Salot, Helen Balch (Mrs. Nevin E.)
Woodfield, Dr. Denis B.

WILLIAM BRATHWAYTHE (BRATHWAITHE), MARYLAND
Belding, Sicily A. Sparkman (Mrs. Paul B.)

GILES BRENT, MARYLAND
Anderson, Dr. John Sherburne
Slowinski, Annette C. Roberts (Mrs. Walter A.)

WILLIAM BRENTON, RHODE ISLAND
Barrington, Lois B. Hall (Mrs. Laurence W. L.)

ROBERT BROOKE, MARYLAND
Bartlett, Leah C. Ford (Mrs. Bradford)
Carruth, Mrs. Margaret Scruggs
Cram, Henry Sergeant
Dorman, John Frederick
Fisher, Clara C. Kerby (Mrs. Adrian P.)
Martell, Miss Helen M. Contee
Mirick, Julia M. Kerby (Mrs. Laurence P.)
Norris, Abell A., Jr.
Sims, Olivia J. Kerby (Mrs. Henry M.)
Slowinski, Annette C. Roberts (Mrs. Walter A.)
Tuttle, Eleanor B. P. Stiefel (Mrs. Frederick B.)
Woodruff, Janet A. Norris (Mrs. Frederick E.)

CHARLES CALVERT, MARYLAND
Cooke, Robert George
Cruse, Maurine R. Morley (Mrs. Charles D.)

LEONARD CALVERT, MARYLAND
  Fullerton, Tommie F. Triplett (Mrs. Samuel B., Jr.)
  Kuhn, Miss Virginia Florence
  McKnight, Elise McDaniel (Mrs. Stephen D.)
  Perdue, David Russell
  Perdue, John Armer, Jr.
  Perdue, John Armer, III
  Perdue, Richardson Milam
  Tuttle, Eleanor B. P. Stiefel (Mrs. Frederick B.)

CALEB CARR, RHODE ISLAND
  Johnson, Ross Byron
  Thomas, Robert Lancefield, M.D.
  Thomas, Miss Susanne Chilton

ROBERT CARTER, VIRGINIA
  Buonassisi, Louisa C. Frost (Mrs. Charles B.)
  Lindsey, Julia E. Hobson (Mrs. Charles F. P.)
  Schroeder, Elizabeth P. Carlton (Mrs. Henry J., Jr.)

WILLIAM CLAIBORNE, MARYLAND
  Southerland, Henry DeLeon, Jr.

JEREMIAH (JEREMY) CLARKE, RHODE ISLAND
  Johnson, Ross Byron
  Kupillas, Mary Anna C. Martin (Mrs. Lawrence O.)
  Martin, William Raymond
  Newsome, Samuel Hendrixson
  Nottingham, William Prosser
  Platz, Lucia C. Collins (Mrs. Harry W.)

WALTER CLARKE, RHODE ISLAND
  Chadwick, Mrs. Margaretta L. Woodbridge
  Nottingham, William Prosser

WILLIAM CODDINGTON, RHODE ISLAND
  Platz, Lucia C. Collins (Mrs. Harry W.)
  Russell, Elsie Wells (Mrs. John P.)
  Schneider, Margaret P. O'Connor (Mrs. Samuel G.)

TRISTRAM COFFIN (COFFYN), NANTUCKET
  Barbara, Elizabeth O. Munsey (Mrs. Anthony A.)
  Clark, Janet Collier (Mrs. Richard G.)
  Coffin, Kenneth Dix
  Doyle, Mrs. Mabel G. Hunt
  Haden, Miss Eunice Barnard
  Musso, Laurie E. Duston (Mrs. Vincent J.)
  Shepard, William Seth

JOHN COGGESHALL, RHODE ISLAND
  Fleming, Elaine Briggs (Mrs. Kenneth S.)
  Johnson, Charles Owen
  Johnson, Ross Byron
  Mason, Judson Philip
  Nottingham, William Prosser
  Pittman, Margaret Hallett (Mrs. Chalmers V.)
  Smallwood, Grahame Thomas, Jr.
  Stearns, Parley Mark, II
  Thomas, Robert Lancefield, M.D.

JOHN COGGESHALL, II, RHODE ISLAND
  Smallwood, Grahame Thomas, Jr.
  Stearns, Parley Mark, II

ROGER CONANT, CAPE ANN AND MASSACHUSETTS
  Fisher, Elva Jean B. Paul (Mrs. Craig B.)
  McPeck, Dorothy E. Mooney (Mrs. Edwin K.)

JOHN CRANSTON, RHODE ISLAND
  Gibbs, Marion B. Jones (Mrs. Frederick R.)
  McDonnell, Gladys B. Holcombe (Mrs. Joseph F., Jr.)

SAMUEL CRANSTON, RHODE ISLAND
  Gibbs, Marion B. Jones (Mrs. Frederick R.)
  Lovejoy, Col. Charles Douglas

THOMAS DANFORTH, MAINE
  Bogardus, Ethel K. Samson (Mrs. Emory A.)

GREGORY DEXTER, RHODE ISLAND
  Smith, Arnold

EDWARD DIGGES, VIRGINIA
  Conkey, CDR Clement Snowden
  Edwards, James MacDonald
  Miller, Mrs. Louise Holland McNeill
  Slowinski, Annette C. Roberts (Mrs. Walter A.)
  Tuttle, Eleanor B. P. Stiefel (Mrs. Frederick B.)
  Walters, Frances Herndon (Mrs. Augustus)

HUGH DRYSDALE, VIRGINIA
  Walters, Frances Herndon (Mrs. Augustus)

JOSEPH DUDLEY, MASSACHUSETTS
  Nottingham, William Prosser

THOMAS DUDLEY, MASSACHUSETTS
Abaire, Madeline Phelps (Mrs. Orlando)
Anderson, Dr. John Sherburne
Brooks, Jane A. Boyer (Mrs. Wilbur S.)
Coudekerque-Lambrecht, Mme. Beatrice Cowles
Fenton, Margaret S. Haines (Mrs. John G.)
Gibson, Aimee B. Frost (Mrs. Zachary L.)
Goodsell, Percy Hamilton
Halberstadt, James Franklin, Jr.
Heaney, Marjorie A. Stubbs (Mrs. Richard C.)
Hedrick, Gale Holbrook, II
Higgins, Mary A. Tyng (Mrs. Charles A.)
Loucks, Barbara W. Haupt (Mrs. Charles E.)
McRae, Miss Nancy Jane
Nottingham, William Prosser
Pope, Marguerite Jones (Mrs. D. Stuart, Jr.)
Rowell, George Barker
Salot, Helen Balch (Mrs. Nevin E.)
Strong, Miss Cornelia Livingston
Towne, Anita Morey (Mrs. Leigh C.)
Troxel, Navena Hembree (Mrs. Vester O.)
Tyng, Franklin Somes
Tyng, John Stevens
Tyng, William Wark
Van Arsdale, Ruth Torr (Mrs. Howard C.)
Walen, Harry Leonard
Woodbridge, Frederic Leonidas, Jr.
Woodfield, Dr. Denis B.
Worthing, Clifford Arthur

NICHOLAS EASTON, RHODE ISLAND
Nottingham, William Prosser
Thomas, Robert Lancefield, M.D.
Wilcox, Janice E. LaMack (Mrs. Lloyd H.)

THEOPHILUS EATON, NEW HAVEN COLONY
Beard, Timothy Field
Faricy, Norma A. Hauser (Mrs. William T.)
McCrea, Mrs. Bernie Chesley

JOHN ENDICOTT, MASSACHUSETTS
Emerson, Col. Maxwell
Finlay, Lydia R. Dow (Mrs. Christopher A.)
Gibbs, James Wenrich
Sooy, Helen Giberson (Mrs. Leslie M.)
Watkins, Susan C. Finlay (Mrs. William H.)

JOSIAS FENDALL, MARYLAND
Nestor, Elizabeth D. Goodridge (Mrs. Roy C.)

ROBERT GIBBES, SOUTH CAROLINA
Quinn, Alice C. Hawkins (Mrs. John L.)

STEPHEN GOODYEAR, CONNECTICUT
Jones, Malcolm Murray
Jones, Norma Hopson (Mrs. S. Murray)

SAMUEL GORTON, RHODE ISLAND
  Carey, Alma R. Risdon (Mrs. Ora F.)
  Loucks, Maj. Gen. Charles Ernest
  Switzer, Opal Risdon (Mrs. E. Clair)
  Vosburg, Virgene Carey (Mrs. Delbert J.)

NICHOLAS GREENBERRY (GREENBURY), MARYLAND
  Hardy, Miss Ann Ridgely
  Pryor, Marianna L. Brand (Mrs. William Y.)
  Warfield, John Ogle, Jr., M.D.
  Watrous, Dorothy P. Stevens (Mrs. Philip M.)

JOHN GREENE, RHODE ISLAND
  Johnson, Charles Owen

THOMAS GREENE, MARYLAND
  Kranz, Ysabelita H. J. H. (Mrs. Martin E.)
  Martin,Ysabelita L. K. (Mrs. Jack L.)

THOMAS HARVEY, NORTH CAROLINA
  Addis, Virginia B. Downes (Mrs. Roland T.)

JOHN HAYNES, CONNECTICUT-MASSACHUSETTS
  Goodsell, Percy Hamilton

THOMAS HINCKLEY, MASSACHUSETTS
  Edwards, Elsie M. Dunn (Mrs. Chester E.)
  Hope, Craig Leonard
  Wagner, Mary W. Woodward (Mrs. John W.)

WILLIAM HOOKE, MAINE
  Garrett, Margaret L. Zeller (Mrs. Clarence J.)
  Gross, Miriam I. Zeller (Mrs. Russell C.)

WILLIAM HUTCHINSON, RHODE ISLAND
  Hills, Col. J. Huntington

SAMUEL JENNINGS, NEW JERSEY
  Elkins, Willard Eugene
  Wheeler, Geraldine Hartshorn (Mrs. Lloyd F.)
  Willson, Richard Eugene

THOMAS LEE, VIRGINIA
  Schmitt, Roger Michael L.

WILLIAM LEETE, CONNECTICUT
  Goodsell, Percy Hamilton
  Jones, Malcolm Murray
  Jones, Norma Hopson (Mrs. S. Murray)
  Leet, Ernest Delos
  Leet, John Daskam
  Lewis, Ruth Ahlert (Mrs. George S.)
  McGee, Marian E. Jump (Mrs. Ralph E.)
  Morse, Mary G. Forbes (Mrs. Frederick T.)
  Obenauer, Ruth E. Hallock (Mrs. Frederick H.)
  Platz, Lucia C. Collins (Mrs. Harry W.)
  Putnam, Josephine W. Phelps (Mrs. Henry W., Jr.)
  Strong, Miss Cornelia Livingston

JOHN LEVERETT, MASSACHUSETTS
  Smallwood, Grahame Thomas, Jr.

THOMAS LLOYD, PENNSYLVANIA
  Leet, Irene Haines (Mrs. John D.)

FRANCIS LOVELACE, NEW YORK
  Bunnell, Irene T. (Mrs. Richard W.)

ROGER LUDLOW, CONNECTICUT
  Andersen, Elizabeth F. O'Hanlon (Mrs. Thor B.)

JOHN MASON, CONNECTICUT
  Kessler, Elizabeth M. Hill (Mrs. Lewis H.)

SAMUEL MATHEWS, VIRGINIA
  Brooks, Virginia Walton (Mrs. Berry B.)
  Curtius, Catherine R. Pelot (Mrs. Benjamin L., Jr.)
  Moore, Caroline L. Tiedeman (Mrs. Harold A.)
  Thomas, Miss Ina Merle

THOMAS MAYHEW, MARTHA'S VINEYARD
  Abbott, John Tucker
  Allen, Maureen Thurtle (Mrs. Robson H.)
  Cleland, Mrs. R. Hilton
  Emerson, Col. Maxwell
  Fulweiler, Spencer Biddle
  Gregg, Col. Clifford Cilley
  Hall, Miss Catherine Eichhorn
  Hall, Miss Margaret S.
  Hall, Miss Sarah L.
  Hall, Warren Smith, Jr.
  McKay, Miss Margaret Ione
  Nowacek, Charles James, M.D.
  Nowacek, Mary L. Thurtle (Mrs. Charles G.)
  Orndorff, Verna S. Ross (Mrs. John R.)
  Palmer, Mary V. Nowacek (Mrs. Robert C.)
  Smith, Barbara J. Carver (Mrs. William A.)
  Smith, CDR J. H. Bronson
  Thurtle, Robert Glenn
  Walsh, Myles Alexander, II

JAMES MOORE, SOUTH CAROLINA
  Fraser, Alexander Herbemont
  Riggs, Lucie O. Donalson (Mrs. Edgar R.)
  Welder, Katie Smith (Mrs. Patrick H.)
  Williams, Bernice Fletcher (Mrs. Marion H.)

LEWIS MORRIS, NEW JERSEY
  Satterthwaite, Pennington

JOSEPH MORTON, SOUTH CAROLINA
  Getzinger, Virginia A. Tardy (Mrs. Philip L.)

BRIAN PENDLETON, MAINE
  Haupt, Grace E. Maines (Mrs. George W.)
  Loucks, Barbara W. Haupt (Mrs. Charles E.)

THOMAS PRENCE, PLYMOUTH
  Atwood, Roswell Levi
  Custer, Caroline Hallett (Mrs. Jacques R.)
  Freeman, Myron Frederick
  Hathaway, Ruth H. Jordan (Mrs. Chester E.)
  Johns, Miss Dorothy Mae
  Kemper, John William
  Kemper, Mildred M. Ramsey (Mrs. William)
  Morton, Ann M. Tilden (Mrs. Donald J., Sr.)
  Moussette, Mrs. Virginia King
  Munsey, Kenneth Bernard
  Nickerson, Lt. Gen. Herman, Jr.
  Pruitt, Pearl C. Ramsey (Mrs. Henry L.)
  Ramsey, Homer Lloyd
  Robbins, Rev. William Randolph
  Stearns, Parley Mark, II
  Stevens, Grace M. Southmayd (Mrs. Leonard W.)
  Walsh, Ruth E. Berg (Mrs. Myles A.)

WILLIAM PYNCHON, CONNECTICUT
  Storm, Walter Kerr

JOHN READING, NEW JERSEY
  DuBois, Frederic Marshall

THOMAS ROBERTS, NEW HAMPSHIRE
  Mann, Vandelia D. Smith (Mrs. William M., Jr.)
  Moss, Miss Ethel Maude
  Nile, Abbott Howe
  Smallwood, Grahame Thomas, Jr.
  Smith, Barbara J. Carver (Mrs. William A.)
  Wiener, Ellanore S. Brown (Mrs. Alexander L.)

PELEG SANFORD, RHODE ISLAND
  Armin, Sadie Collins (Mrs. Lot W.)
  Platz, Lucia C. Collins (Mrs. Harry W.)

THOMAS SOUTHWORTH, MAINE
  Howland, McClure Meredith

ALEXANDER SPOTSWOOD, VIRGINIA
  Lane, Elizabeth C. Chapman (Mrs. E. Sam)
  Royall, John Weldon, Jr.

JOHN STEELE, CONNECTICUT
  Bacon, Ralph Hoyt

WILLIAM STONE, MARYLAND
  Crowell, Della Dodson (Mrs. Clyde O., Sr.)
  Denny, Miss Josephine
  Dodson, Miss Lois Elizabeth
  Fullerton, Tommie F. Triplett (Mrs. Samuel B., Jr.)
  Helm, Herschel H.
  Howard, Mrs. Helen Denny
  Marsh, Mrs. Elizabeth L. Dodson
  Martin, Carolyn Ashburn (Mrs. Warren D.)
  Perdue, David Russell
  Perdue, John Armer, Jr.
  Perdue, John Armer, III
  Perdue, Richardson Milam
  Smith, Lois E. Dodson (Mrs. Robah L.)
  Taylor, Alma V. Denny (Mrs. Roby E.)
  Taylor, Miss Marjorie Ellen
  Taylor, Roby Ellis

ROBERT TREAT, CONNECTICUT
  Buck, J. Orton
  Chatfield, Benjamin Vantine
  Crayne, Lynn Myers
  Jakobsson, Mrs. Donna R. Johnson
  Munsey, Mildred L. Wood (Mrs. Virdell)
  Pagel, William Rush
  Philbrick, George Dary
  Pryor, William Young
  Wright, Helen G. Henning (Mrs. Douglas C.)

RIP VAN DAM, NEW YORK
  Burden, Ordway Partridge
  Fryer, Appleton
  Fryer, Livingston, Jr.

HENRY VANE, MASSACHUSETTS
  Cox, Paul Vernon

JOSEPH WANTON, RHODE ISLAND
  Nottingham, William Prosser

WILLIAM WANTON, RHODE ISLAND
  Nottingham, William Prosser

ANDREW WARD, CONNECTICUT
  Hofmeister, Virginia L. Hageman (Mrs. George C., Sr.)
  Sniffen, Eleanor A. Sauer (Mrs. Allan M., III)
  Whitehead, Louis Henry

JOHN WEBSTER, CONNECTICUT
  Abell, Elizabeth A. Porter (Mrs. Walter W., II)
  Amos, Eugene Paul
  Barker, C. Austin
  Beyers, Bernice West (Mrs. Robert A.)
  Bryan, Leslie Aulls
  Cherry, Charlotte E. Spencer (Mrs. Lee W.)
  Goodell, Col. Ralph Harmer, Jr.
  Goodsell, Percy Hamilton
  Hagedorn, Beatrice D. Mead (Mrs. Alfred A.)
  Hamm, Ruth T. Bitting (Mrs. James J.)
  Harris, Edward Park
  Lockwood, Randolph Scott Dewey
  Marmaduke, Virginia F. Clayton (Mrs. Donald S.)
  Morse, Mary G. Forbes (Mrs. Frederick T.)
  Munger, Elizabeth Mack (Mrs. Robert C.)
  Platz, Lucia C. Collins (Mrs. Harry W.)
  Shepard, William Durell
  Shipman, Ruth M. Webb (Mrs. William L.)

THOMAS WELLES, CONNECTICUT
  Atkins, Doreen A. Cornwall (Mrs. Ernest G.)
  Bacon, Ralph Hoyt
  Buck, J. Orton
  Davis, Ellsworth Marcus
  Davis, The Reverend Ralph Milton
  Dazey, Margaret H. Tolles (Mrs. Donald A.)
  Goodsell, Percy Hamilton
  Gross, Mrs. Martha MaWhinney
  Guffey, Mrs. Verité L. Greene
  Lewis, A. Sidney
  Lewis, Mary K. Curtius (Mrs. Leroy R.)
  McCall, Miss Beth Ada
  North, Miss Susan Merriman
  Sanborn, Earl Boyce, Jr.
  Schroeder, Enriette L. Lewis (Mrs. Henry J.)
  Schroeder, Brig. Gen. Henry John, Jr.
  Schroeder, Col. Robert Lewis
  Sherman, Miss F. Lynette
  Smith, Helen S. Tuttle (Mrs. Len Y.)
  Sniffen, Eleanor A. Sauer (Mrs. Allen M., III)
  Thatcher, Dorothy L. Douglass (Mrs. Lyndon)
  Warner, Louise, Ph.D.

JOHN WEST, VIRGINIA
  Broemmer, H. Richard
  Coulter, Phebe D. Frost (Mrs. John L.)
  Estill, Alice Garth (Mrs. George C.)
  Hill, Ms. Mary M. Ayres
  King, George H. S.
  Norwood, Pearl P. Neves (Mrs. Robert W.)
  Southerland, Henry DeLeon, Jr.
  Waller, James Withers
  Waller, Nina W. Nelson (Mrs. James A., Jr.)

THOMAS WIGGIN, NEW HAMPSHIRE
  Anderson, Dr. John Sherburne
  Dyer, Eleanor E. Folsom (Mrs. William W., Jr.)
  Wiggin, Elmer S.

ROGER WILLIAMS, RHODE ISLAND
  Rymal, Mary L. Barnard (Mrs. Grant V.)
  Saunders, Lora B. Thurber (Mrs. Alden C.)
  Stuart, Harold Leonard

Edward Winslow, Plymouth
  Bird, Jackson

JOHN WINTHROP, MASSACHUSETTS
  Brooks, Jane A. Boyer (Mrs. Wilbur S.)
  Nottingham, William Prosser
  Pittman, Chalmers Van Anglen

JOHN WINTHROP, JR., CONNECTICUT
  Nottingham, William Prosser

ROGER WOLCOTT, CONNECTICUT
  Goodsell, Percy Hamilton

GEORGE WYLLYS (WILLYS), CONNECTICUT
  Cummins, Dr. James William
  Goodsell, Percy Hamilton

GEORGE YEARDLEY, VIRGINIA
  Meyer, Paul Rogers
  Meyer, Robert Beeson Brooks
  Meyer, Virginia M. Healy (Mrs. Harold I.)

INDEX OF LIFE MEMBERS' RESIDENCES

ALABAMA
    Birmingham
        Southerland, Henry DeLeon, Jr.
ARIZONA
    Prescott
        Quinn, Alice C. Hawkins (Mrs. John L.)
    Scottsdale
        Frische, Harriet Ross (Mrs. Carl A.)
        Gallagher, Genevieve J.M. Sherman (Mrs. Edward E.)
    Sun City
        Hultander, Ethel Russell (Mrs. Martin E.)
    Tucson
        Guffey, Mrs. Verité L. Greene
ARKANSAS
    Jonesboro
        Westbrooke, Gilberta Wood (Mrs. Edward L.)
    Pine Bluff
        Perdue, David Russell
        Perdue, John Armer, Jr.
        Perdue, John Armer, III
        Perdue, Richardson Milam
    Warren
        Fullerton, Tommie F. Triplett (Mrs. Samuel B., Jr.)
CALIFORNIA
    F.P.O. San Francisco
        Whitecotten, Dr. Glenn Lee
    Alhambra
        Lewis, Ruth Ahlert (Mrs. George S.)
    Anaheim
        Cummins, Dr. James William
    Burlingame
        McRae, Miss Nancy Jane
    Capitola
        Johns, Miss Dorothy Mae
    Claremont
        Wheeler, Geraldine Hartshorn (Mrs. Lloyd F.)
    Encinitas
        Carey, Alma R. Risdon (Mrs. Ora F.)
    Fullerton
        Bunnell, Irene Tuttle (Mrs. Richard W.)
        Musso, Laurie E. Duston (Mrs. Vincent J.)
    Imola
        Thomas, Robert Lancefield, M.D.
    Laguna Hills
        Russell, Elsie Wells (Mrs. John P.)
    La Jolla
        Gregg, Col. Clifford Cilley
    Long Beach
        Switzer, Opal Risdon (Mrs. E. Clair)
        Vosburg, Virgene Carey (Mrs. Delbert J.)
    Oakland
        Baird, Miss Stella
    Orinda
        Thomas, Miss Susanne Chilton

CALIFORNIA (Continued)
    Palo Alto
        Leet, Irene Haines (Mrs. John D.)
        Leet, John Daskam
    Port Hueneme
        Van Rensselaer, Mrs. Edna Tretheway
    San Clemente
        Rymal, Mary L. Barnard (Mrs. Grant V.)
    San Francisco
        Welch, Miss Inez Graham
    Santa Barbara
        Moss, Miss Ethel Maude
        Putnam, Josephine W. Phelps (Mrs. Henry W., Jr.)
    Westlake Village
        Oxx, William Gardner, III

COLORADO
    Aurora
        Jones, Malcolm Murray
    Colorado Springs
        Hagedorn, Beatrice D. Mead (Mrs. Alfred A.)
    Denver
        Marmaduke, Virginia F. Clayton (Mrs. Donald S.)
    Lakewood
        Johnson, Ross Byron

CONNECTICUT
    Bridgeport
        Bauermann, Helen G. Benedict (Mrs. Werner F.)
        Chatfield, Florence M. Van Tine (Mrs. Chester H.)
    Cheshire
        Goodsell, Percy Hamilton
    Essex
        Bird, Jackson
    Greenwich
        Morgan, Diana M. Sweeney (Mrs. James P., Jr.)
    Guilford
        Davis, Ellsworth Marcus
    Hamden
        Pope, Marguerite Jones (Mrs. D. Stuart, Jr.)
        Thatcher, Dorothy L. Douglass (Mrs. Lyndon)
    Meriden
        North, Miss Susan Merriman
    New Haven
        Robbins, Rev. William Randolph
    Sharon
        Hardy, Miss Ann Ridgely
    Stonington
        Peterle, Mrs. Helen J. Lee
    West Hartford
        Freeman, Myron Frederick
        Hathaway, Ruth H. Jordan (Mrs. Chester E.)
    Windsor
        Foss, Philip Emery

DELAWARE
    Wilmington
        Buonassisi, Louisa C. Frost (Mrs. Charles B.)
        Chadwick, Mrs. Margaretta L. Woodbridge

DISTRICT OF COLUMBIA
          Alper, Alice Gaskins (Mrs. Theodore)
          Atwood, Roswell Levi
          Coulter, Phebe D. Frost (Mrs. John L.)
          Dorman, John Frederick
          Doyle, Mrs. Mabel Graybill Hunt
          Faricy, Norma A. Hauser (Mrs. William T.)
          Gibbs, Marion B. Jones (Mrs. Frederick R.)
          Haden, Miss Eunice Barnard
          Martell, Miss Helen M. Contee
          Schroeder, Col. Robert Lewis
          Slowinski, Annette C. Roberts (Mrs. Walter A.)
          Tuttle, Eleanor B.P. Stiefel (Mrs. Frederick B.)
          Tuttle, Frederick Burton, M.D.
          Tyng, William Wark
          Ward, Nicholas Donnell
          Warner, Louise, Ph.D.

FLORIDA
     Coral Gables
          Howe, Helen D. Bailey (Mrs. Elden L.)
     DeLand
          Heaney, Marjorie A. Stubbs (Mrs. Richard C.)
     Fort Myers
          Salot, Helen Balch (Mrs. Nevin E.)
     Miami
          Cross, J. Alan
          Estill, Alice D. Garth (Mrs. George C.)
     New Smyrna Beach
          Coffin, Kenneth Dix
     Orlando
          Atkins, Doreen A. Cornwall (Mrs. Ernest G.)
          Elkins, Willard Eugene
     West Palm Beach
          Stearns, Parley Mark, II
     Winter Haven
          Fuller, Eunice B. Lee (Mrs. William H.)
     Winter Park
          McPeck, Dorothy E. Mooney (Mrs. Edwin K.)

GEORGIA
     Atlanta
          Lewis, A. Sidney
     Decatur
          Edwards, James MacDonald
     Douglas
          Gross, Mrs. Martha MaWhinney

ILLINOIS
     Barrington
          Meyer, Robert Beeson Brooks
     Champaign
          Bryan, Leslie Aulls
     Chicago
          Meyer, Virginia M. Healy (Mrs. Harold I.)
          Sherman, Miss F. Lynette
          Stuart, Harold Leonard
          Swanstrom, Kathryn C. Raymond (Mrs. Luther D.)
     Hudson
          Hamm, Ruth T. Bitting (Mrs. James J.)

ILLINOIS (Continued)
    Kenilworth
        Sanborn, Earl Boyce, Jr., M.D.
    LaGrange
        Hedrick, Gale Holbrook, II
    Northbrook
        Van Antwerp, Lee Douglas, M.D.
    Ottawa
        Willson, Richard Eugene
    Park Ridge
        Meyer, Paul Rogers
    River Forest
        Orndorff, Verna S. Ross (Mrs. John R.)
    Waukegan
        Wilcox, Janice E. LaMack (Mrs. Lloyd H.)
    Winnetka
        Smith, Helen S. Tuttle (Mrs. Len Y.)

INDIANA
    Decatur
        Halberstadt, James Franklin, Jr.
    Indianapolis
        McGee, Marian E. Jump (Mrs. Ralph E.)
        Nottingham, William Prosser
    Michigan City
        Munger, Elizabeth Mack (Mrs. Robert C.)
        Woodruff, Janet A. Norris (Mrs. Frederick E.)

IOWA
    Cedar Rapids
        Williams, Bernice Fletcher (Mrs. Marion H.)
    Des Moines
        DuBois, Frederic Marshall

KANSAS
    Abilene
        Cruse, Maurine R. Morley (Mrs. Charles D.)
    Burlington
        Garrett, Margaret L. Zeller (Mrs. Clarence J.)
    Mission Hills
        Kessler, Elizabeth M. Hill (Mrs. Lewis H.)
    Overland Park
        Goodell, Col. Ralph Harmer, Jr.
    Shawnee
        Amos, Eugene Paul
    Shawnee Mission
        Pagel, William Rush

KENTUCKY
    Florence
        Nestor, Elizabeth D. Goodridge (Mrs. Roy C.)

LOUISIANA
    Baton Rouge
        Anderson, Dr. John Sherburne
        Hofmeister, Virginia L. Hageman (Mrs. George C., Sr.)
    Covington
        Kranz, Ysabelita H.J.Hamiton (Mrs. Martin E.)
        Martin, Ysabelita L. Kranz (Mrs. Jack L.)
    Monroe
        Thomas, Miss Ina Merle

MAINE
    ROCKPORT
        Walen, Harry Leonard

MARYLAND
    Baltimore
        Abell, Elizabeth A. Porter (Mrs. Walter W., II)
        Klein, Catherine C. Taylor (Mrs. George)
    Bel Air
        Tyng, Franklin Somes
    Bethesda
        Jones, Cereno St. Clair
        Schroeder, Enriette L. Lewis (Mrs. Henry J.)
    Oxon Hill
        Cox, Paul Vernon
        Fisher, Clara C. Kerby (Mrs. Adrian P.)
        Mirick, Julia M. Kerby (Mrs. Laurence P.)
    Potomac
        Martin, William Raymond
    Rockville
        Conkey, CDR Clement Snowden
        Norris, Abell A., Jr.
        Sims, Olivia J. Kerby (Mrs. Henry M.)
    Towson
        Benson, Newell Barton, Jr.

MASSACHUSETTS
    Auburn
        Morton, Ann M. Tilden (Mrs. Donald J., Sr.)
    Bedford
        Abbott, John Tucker
    Boston
        Rowell, George Barker
    Cambridge
        Jones, Norma Hopson (Mrs. S. Murray)
    Peabody
        Finlay, Lydia R. Dow (Mrs. Christopher A.)
    Sudbury
        Munsey, Kenneth Bernard
    Waltham
        Nile, Abbott Howe
    Wayland
        Barbara, Elizabeth O. Munsey (Mrs. Anthony A.)
    Weston
        Munsey, Mildred L. Wood (Mrs. Virdell)
    Worcester
        Barrington, Laurence W. L.
        Barrington, Lois B. Hall (Mrs. Laurence W.)

MICHIGAN
    Grosse Pointe
        Wiener, Ellanore S. Brown (Mrs. Alexander L.)
    Monroe
        Weaver, Elizabeth J. Case (Mrs. John F., Sr.)
    Saginaw
        Reynolds, Miss Mary Ola

MINNESOTA
    St. Paul
        Cooke, Robert George

MISSOURI
    Higginsville
        Lewis, Mary K. Curtius (Mrs. Leroy R.)

NEVADA
    Reno
        Allen, Maureen Thurtle (Mrs. Robson H.)

NEW HAMPSHIRE
    Amherst
        Leonard, Daniel, Jr.
    Franklin
        Shepard, John Sanford
    Penacook
        Wiggin, Elmer S.

NEW JERSEY
    Avon-by-the-Sea
        Smith, Barbara J. Carver (Mrs. William A.)
    Cranbury
        Walsh, Myles Alexander, II
        Walsh, Ruth E. Berg (Mrs. Myles A.)
    Essex Fells
        Pryor, Marianna L. Brand (Mrs. William Y.)
        Pryor, William Young
    Little Silver
        Wright, Helen G. Henning (Mrs. Douglas C.)
    Maplewood
        Andersen, Elizabeth F. O'Hanlon (Mrs. Thor B.)
    Merchantville
        Wagner, Mary W. Woodward (Mrs. John W.)
    Moorestown
        Davis, The Reverend Ralph Milton
    Morris Plains
        Gross, Miriam I. Zeller (Mrs. Russell C.)
    Morristown
        Hall, Miss Catherine Eichhorn
        Hall, Miss Margaret S.
        Hall, Miss Sarah L.
        Hall, Warren Smith, Jr.
    Oceanville
        Sooy, Helen Giberson (Mrs. Leslie M.)
    Princeton
        Howland, McClure Meredith
        Woodfield, Dr. Denis B.
    Rahway
        Cleland, Mrs. R. Hilton
    Short Hills
        Darlington, Thomas
    Summit
        Nowacek, Mary L. Thurtle (Mrs. Charles G.)
        Palmer, Mary V. Nowacek (Mrs. Robert C.)
    Woodbury
        Haupt, Grace E. Maines (Mrs. George W.)

NEW MEXICO
    Albuquerque
        Broemmer, H. Richard

NEW YORK
      APO New York
            Shepard, William Durell
            Shepard, William Seth
      Auburn
            Fenn, Ruth A. Jones (Mrs. Clyde B.)
      Bath
            Read, Lillian E.H. Hitchcock (Mrs. George D.)
            Shipman, Ruth M. Webb (Mrs. William L.)
      Bedford Hills
            Sniffen, Eleanor A. Sauer (Mrs. Allan M., III)
      Brewster
            Bacon, Ralph Hoyt
      Buffalo
            Fryer, Appleton
      Dolgeville
            Watkins, Susan C. Finlay (Mrs. William H.)
      Frankfort
            McKay, Miss Margaret Ione
      Jamestown
            Leet, Ernest Delos
      Malone
            Obenauer, Ruth E. Hallock (Mrs. Frederick H.)
      New City
            Bogardus, Ethel K. Samson (Mrs. Emory A.)
      New York City
            Almond, Roxanne M. Elmquist (Mrs. Richard W.)
            Beard, Timothy Field
            Burden, Ordway Partridge
            Fryer, Livingston, Jr.
            Fulweiler, Spencer Biddle
            Kupillas, Mary A.C. Martin (Mrs. Lawrence O.)
            Satterthwaite, Pennington
            Schmitt, Roger Michael Laurence
            Whitehead, Louis Henry
      Northport
            Hallowell, Thomas Jewett, Jr.
      Pelham
            Storm, Walter Kerr
      Rye
            Barker, C. Austin
      Schuyler Lake
            Towne, Anita Morey (Mrs. Leigh C.)
      Syracuse
            Brooks, Jane A. Boyer (Mrs. Wilbur S.)
      White Plains
            Fisher, Elva J.B. Paul (Mrs. Craig B.)

NORTH CAROLINA
      Asheville
            Bailey, Miss Mary Ethel
      Burlington
            Martin, Carolyn A. Ashburn (Mrs. Warren D.)
      High Point
            Marsh, Mrs. Elizabeth Louise Dodson
      Jacksonville
            Nickerson, Lt.Gen. Herman, Jr.
      Walnut Cove
            Smith, Lois E. Dodson (Mrs. Robah L.)
      Winston-Salem
            Crowell, Della Dodson (Mrs. Clyde O., Sr.)
            Dodson, Miss Lois Elizabeth
            Taylor, Alma V. Denny (Mrs. Roby E.)
            Taylor, Miss Marjorie Ellen
            Taylor, Roby Ellis

OHIO
    Akron
        Grinnell, Henry Stephen
    Canfield
        Fleming, Elaine Briggs (Mrs. Kenneth S.)
    Cincinnati
        Woodbridge, Frederic Leonidas, Jr.
        Worthing, Clifford Arthur
    Cleveland Heights
        Nowacek, Charles James, M.D.
    Dayton
        Harris, Edward Park
    Lakeside
        Cherry, Charlotte E. Spencer (Mrs. Lee W.)

OKLAHOMA
    Ponca City
        Pruitt, Pearl C. Ramsey (Mrs. Henry L.)
    Tulsa
        Curtius, Catherine R. Pelot (Mrs. Benjamin L., Jr.)

PENNSYLVANIA
    Easton
        Bradstreet, William Carner
    Harrisburg
        Fuller, Robert Stevens
    Haverford
        Addis, Virginia B. Downes (Mrs. Roland T.)
        Watrous, Dorothy A.P. Stevens (Mrs. Philip M.)
    Jefferson
        Crayne, Lynn Myers
    Media
        Newsome, Samuel Hendrixson
    Philadelphia
        Gibbs, James Wenrich
    Warren
        Mann, Vandelia D. Smith (Mrs. William M., Jr.)
    Waynesburg
        Denny, Miss Josephine
        Howard, Mrs. Helen Denny

RHODE ISLAND
    East Greenwich
        Palmer, Elmer Hall
    North Scituate
        Saunders, Alden Clinton
        Saunders, Lora B. Thurber (Mrs. Alden C.)

SOUTH CAROLINA
    Bluffton
        Cram, Henry Sergeant
    Charleston
        Moore, Caroline L. Tiedeman (Mrs. Harold A.)
    Mullins
        Lipscomb, Mrs. Margaret Smith

SOUTH DAKOTA
    Sioux Falls
        Armin, Sadie Collins (Mrs. Lot W.)

TENNESSEE
    Memphis
        Brooks, Virginia Walton (Mrs. Berry B.)
        Emerson, Col. Maxwell
        Hill, Ms. Mary M. Ayres
    Murfreesboro
        Lane, Elizabeth C. Chapman (Mrs. E. Sam)
        McKnight, Elise McDaniel (Mrs. Stephen D.)
    Nashville
        Buck, J. Orton
    Sewanee
        Higgins, Mary A. Tyng (Mrs. Charles A.)

TEXAS
    Abilene
        McCrea, Mrs. Bernie Chesley
        Norwood, Pearl P. Neves (Mrs. Robert W.)
    Dallas
        Beyers, Bernice West (Mrs. Robert A.)
        Carruth, Mrs. Margaret Scruggs
        Fenton, Margaret S. Haines (Mrs. John G.)
        Pittman, Chalmers Van Anglen
        Pittman, Margaret Hallett (Mrs. Chalmers V.)
    Eagle Lake
        Kemper, Mildred M. Ramsey (Mrs. William)
    El Paso
        Schneider, Margaret P. O'Connor (Mrs. Samuel G.)
    Graham
        Riggs, Lucie O. Donalson (Mrs. Edgar R.)
    Houston
        Aurelius, Brynn Frederic
        Ramsey, Homer Lloyd
    Katy
        Kemper, John William
    Longview
        Belding, Sicily A. Sparkman (Mrs. Paul B.)
    Richardson
        Troxel, Navena Hembree (Mrs. Vester O.)
    San Antonio
        Fraser, Alexander Herbemont
        Hills, Col. J. Huntington
        Lockwood, Randolph S. Dewey
    Victoria
        Welder, Katie Smith (Mrs. Patrick H.)
UTAH
    Salt Lake City
        Smallwood, Grahame Thomas, Jr.

VERMONT
    Rutland
        Clark, Janet Collier (Mrs. Richard Gilman

VIRGINIA
  Alexandria
      Taylor, Dorothy E. Russ (Mrs. Darold W.)
      Van Arsdale, Ruth Torr (Mrs. Howard C.)
  Arlington
      Chatfield, Benjamin Vantine
      Helm, Herschel H.
      Johnson, Charles Owen
      Loucks, Barbara W. Haupt (Mrs. Charles E.)
      Loucks, Maj. Gen. Charles Ernest
      McDonnell, Gladys B. Holcombe (Mrs. Joseph F., Jr.)
      Thurtle, Robert Glenn
  Blacksburg
      Waller, James Withers
      Waller, Nina W. Nelson (Mrs. James A., Jr.)
  Bluefield
      Lindsey, Julia E. Hobson (Mrs. Charles F.)
  Charlottesville
      Morse, Mary G. Forbes (Mrs. Frederick T.)
      Smith, Arnold
      Tyng, John Stevens
  Fairfax
      Schroeder, Elizabeth P. Carlton (Mrs. Henry J., Jr.)
      Schroeder, Brig. Gen. Henry John, Jr.
  Falls Church
      Smith, CDR J. H. Bronson
  Fredericksburg
      King, George Harrison Sanford
  Hampton
      Getzinger, Virginia A. Tardy (Mrs. Philip L.)
  Lancaster
      Mason, Judson Philip
  Richmond
      Knowles, Grace Fuller (Mrs. W. Herbert)
      Philbrick, George Dary
  Vienna
      Jakobsson, Mrs. Donna Rae Johnson

WASHINGTON
  Bellevue
      Dazey, Margaret H. Tolles (Mrs. Donald A.)
  Seattle
      Lovejoy, Col. Charles Douglas
      Moussette, Mrs. Virginia King
      Platz, Lucia C. Collins (Mrs. Harry W.)
      Stevens, Grace M. Southmayd (Mrs. Leonard W.)
  Tacoma
      Miller, Mrs. Louise H. McNeill

WEST VIRGINIA
  Bluefield
      Cornett, Robert Fielding, Jr.
  Charleston
      Kuhn, Miss Virginia Florence

WISCONSIN
  Frankville
      Harris, Florence E. Clarke (Mrs. Frank L.)
  Milwaukee
      Stone, Polly A. Mariner (Mrs. Stanley)

FRANCE, PARIS
      Coudekerque-Lambrecht, Mme. Beatrice Cowles de
PERU, LIMA
      Custer, Caroline Hallett (Mrs. Jacques R.)

Albertine, Frederick P.	M-260		Lambdin, Mrs. Samuel H.	62-B
Ashburn, Mrs. Arthur Lee	143-B		Lee, Mrs. Helen	22-B
Ayres, Mrs. Willis E.	35-B		Leete, Harry O.	87-B
			Lenning, John L.	338-S
			Lucas, Mrs. Anthony F.	186-B
Bailey, Mrs. Ernest H.	17-B			
Baird, Stella	200-B			
Barker, Russell F.	70-B		MaWhinney, Mrs. William T.	79-B
Barker, Mrs. Russell F.	49-B		Mayo, Rev. Harold E.	32-B
Barrow, Mrs. Edward R.	6-B		McCorkle, Mrs. Donald	26-B
Bartlett, Adm. Bradford	206-B			
Bartlett, Mrs. Bradford	207-B			
Bassett, Col. William H.	259-B		North, Mrs. David A.	124-B
Bauer, Mrs. Frederick	4-B			
Beall, Dr. Otho T.	241-B			
Boden, Mrs. Harry C.	102-S		Oberly, Mrs. Eugene L.	104-B
Booth, Francis A.	116-B		Ordway, Col. Frederick	
Bradley, John M.	61-B		Ira., Jr.	150-B
Brady, Judge Thomas P.	147-B			
Brown, Mrs. Robert Allen	91-B			
Bryan, Mrs. William J.	M-259		Paul, Mrs. Joseph B.	2-B
Bull, Dr. Charles B.	146-B		Pearson, Mrs. Raymond W.	77-B
			Powers, Mrs. Earle Ray	85-B
Carpenter, Mrs. Clovis L.	117-B			
Chapman, Miss Elizabeth C.	20-B		Read, Mrs. Frank W.	12-B
Clymer, William B.	155-B		Rowell, Hugh G., M.D.	14-B
Cowan, Mrs. George J.	39-B		Royall, Mrs. John W.	76-B
Dies, Edward J.	43-B		Starch, Mrs. Daniel	109-B
Dodson, Agnes V.	83-B		Stein, Charles F.	54-B
Dodson, Miss Nannie E.	92-B		Stevens, John Grier	52-B
Donohoe, Mrs. S. Dolan	46-B		Stuart, Mrs. Harriet F.	120-B
Duryee, Miss Ruth M.	15-B		Sweeney, Miss Diana	56-B
			Sweeney, Henry W.	55-B
Fisher, Miss Mary E.	65-B			
Fuller, Stanley	145-B		Thorndike, Mrs. Augustus	M-420
			Treadwell, Miss Shirley	139-B
Gatterdam, Eugene A.	41-B			
			Walsh, Mrs. William T.	140-B
			Warfield, Dr. John Ogle,Jr.	218-B
Hance, Percy L.	1008		Whitman, Charles S.	772-S
Hull, Miss Guy W.	175-B		Whittekin, Mrs. William H.	69-B
Hunter, Mrs. Paul P.	8-B		Willcox, Robert Irving	97-B
			Wilson, Mrs. Hansel D.	M-258
			Winslow, Lorenzo S.	M-270
Johns, Miss Elsie	122-B			
Johnson, Mrs. Ivan T.	60-B			
Keech, Miss Mabel L.	M-603			
Kerby, Miss Mary E.	64-B			
Kinney, Mrs. James E.	7-B			
Kirshman, Mrs. Ortan A.	27-B			
Knorr, Mrs. Herman A.	883			
Koenig, Mrs. Frederick G.	11-B			

This is a comprehensive index of the names in this Register. One entry can include several persons because of the use of only the middle initial, but the full name will usually be found in the text. A name designated by an asterisk (*) indicates that the person was a Colonial Governor.

ATHEARN, Jethro, 47,
  323
  Margaret, 48
  Martha, 323
  Zerviah, 47
ATHERTON, Rex W., 291
ATKINS, Doreen A.,324
  Dudley, 119, 286
  Ernest G., 324
  Joseph, 119, 286
  Lydia, 188
ATKINSON, Sarah, 19
ATWOOD, Alden, 13
  Henry R., 13
  Levi, 13
  Mary, 152, 254
  Roswell, 13
  Roswell L., 13
  Solomon, 13
AUDLEY, Ann, 134
AUGIER, Harriet L., 6
AULLS, Anna, 35
  Ephraim, 35
  Frank M., 35
AURELIUS, Brynn F.,14
  Campbell K., 14
  Dunham M., 14
  William M., 14
AUSTIN, Deborah, 190,
  328
AVERILL, Patience M.,
  301
  Perry, 301
AVERY, Annis, 140
  Jonathan, 140
AYLETT, Mary M., 227
  Philip, 227
AYLEWORTH, Mary, 133
AYOTTE, Joan M., 229
AYRES, Mehitable D.,
  249
  Willis E., 120

BABCOCK, Abigail, 35
  Corinne G., 105,106
  Martha, 228
BACKES, Barbara M.,197
BACKUS, Mary, 222, 337
BACON, Alexander E.,17
  Andrew, 16
  Levi A., 15
  Mary A., 17
  Ralph F., 15
  Ralph H., 15
  Rebecca M., 112
  Samuel, 15, 16
BAILEY, Abigail, 262
  Arthur H., 126
  Ashley, 17
  Caleb, 134
  Cicero F., 17
  Isaac, II, 156
  Louis M., Jr., 126
  Louise, 104
  Mabel, 13

Mary, 148
Mary E., 17
Temperance, 156
Waite, 133, 134
BAIRD, Carroll, 18
  Lydia S., 90
  Samuel, 90
  Stella, 18
  Thomas, 90
BAKER, Almira, 310
  Claire M., 129
  John, 80
  John S., 70
  Kenelm, 80
  Marguerite M., 70
  Phebe K., 193
  Ruth, 80
BALCH, Benjamin J.,230
  Franklin, 230
BALDWIN, Abraham, 196,
  275
  Hannah, 61
  Linus, 219
  Martha, 197, 275
  Mary E., 22
  Rachel E., 300
  Rhoda L., 219
  Timothy, 61
BALL, Elizabeth L., 38
  James, 33
  Jesse, 33
  John S., 33
  Nancy O., 33
BALLARD, Lurana B.,171
BANE, Mary J., 55
BANNING, Sarah, 113
BARBARA, Anthony A., 19
  Elizabeth O., 19
BARCALOW, Ann, 18
BAREFOOT, Sarah, 11
BAREMORE, Abigail, 258
BARKER, Beverly J., 19
  C. Austin, 19
  Clarence G., 20
  Elisha, 20
  Elizabeth, 34, 199
  Fidelia, 20
  Marcus G., 20
  Moses B., 20
  Orlando, 20
  Ruth, 80
  Steven W., 19, 20
BARNARD, Allison F.,
  229
  Elizabeth, 187
  Eunice S., 107
  Mary, 190
  Tristram, 190
  William, 190
BARNES, Beatrice O.,
  309
  Eliza A., 268
  George L., 268
  James A., 268
BARNEY, Lydia, 204
BARR, Isabel, 94
BARRINGTON, Catherine,
  162

Laurence W., 21
Lois B., 21
Robert W., 21
BARTHOLOMEW, Charlotte
  C., 61
  Mary E., 52
BARTLETT, Ann, 226
  Benjamin, 50
  Bradford, 22
  Leah C., 22
  Ruth, 50
BARTON, Benjamin, 159
  Caleb, Jr., 28
  Charlotte V., 252,
  253
  Damaris, 28
  Eveline, 74
  Henry, 28
  James S., 252
  Martin, 74
  Phebe, 159
  Silas W., 252
BASSETT, Eliza, 61
  Elizabeth, 236
BATCHELDER, Clarke G.,
  23, 24
  Jacob, 24
  Sarah, 116
  Timothy, 116
  Warren A., 24
  William F., 24
BATES, Emily C., 33
  Frederick, 33
BAUERISE, Caroline, 93
BAUERMANN, Helen G.,24
  Richard W., 24, 25
  Werner F., 24
BAULSTON(E), Elizabeth
  167, 250, 263
BAXTER, Aaron, Jr.,243
  Eloise J., 334
  Ira, 243
  Susan V., 243
BAYLISS, William H.,3
BEACH, Jennet, 43
BEALL, Arietta M., 23
  Charles E., 195,319
  Frances, 27
  George, 195, 318
  John, 195, 319
  Levin C., 195, 319
  Mary E., 196, 319
  Nathaniel, 27
  Otho B., 23
  Otho R., 23
  Richard, 23
  Samuel, 23, 66
  Samuel B., 23
  Sarah, 27
  Susannah, 66
  Walter, 66
  Washington J., 23
  William, 27
  William R., 195, 319
BEALS, Ann F., 26

BEARD, Maximillian C.,
26
Stuart M., 26
Timothy F., 25
Walter J., 26
BEARDSLEY, Abraham,151
Curtis, 151
Fannie L., 254
Mary A., 151
BEAVANS, Nathaniel,142
Tabitha C., 142
BEDINGER, Ann E., 102
David, 102
BEEBE, Ellen R., 152
BEEKMAN, Christopher,
44
Elizabeth, 81
*Gerardus, 44, 81
Gerardus C., 44
Mary, 44
BEEMAN, Abigail, 7
BEESON, Ann, 53
Benjamin, 53
Charity, 70
Edward, 70
Richard, 53, 70
BELCHER, Abigail, 265
BELDING, Paul B., 27
Sicily A., 27
BELL, Mary, 55, 108
BELT, Catherine, 10
Esther (Ester), 54,
195, 319
John, 10
BENEDICT, Harold G.,25
BENNETT, Anna(e), 17,
18, 196, 259, 275
Elizabeth, 142
Gertrude E., 184
John P., 198
Judith, 91, 104
Louisa J., 95
Lucy, 220
Mercy, 196, 275
Miranda, 41
Oliver, 41
*Richard, 17, 18,142,
247, 259, 283
Richard, 283
Stephen, 91, 104
Susannah M., 247,283
Susie P., 198
William T., 198
BENSON, Anne D.,28, 29
Elizabeth R., 293
Joshua L., 29
N. Barton, Sr., 29
Newell B., Jr., 28
Sallie W., 29
Thomas J., 28
BENTON, Clarinda, 203
Edward, 203
Susan E., 107
BERESFORD, Carolina E.
224
BERG, Frederick A.,297
Ruth E., 295

BERKELEY, Edmund, 154
Lewis, 154
Mary L., 154
BERRINGER, Margaret,
314
BERRY, Abigail A., 169
Eleanor, 23
Harry E., 192
Judah, 193
Lemuel, 193
Lydia, 249
Nancy, 193
Scotto, 193
Stephen, 249
BERSFORD, Carolina E.,
82
BETTEL, Martha, 226
Robert, 226
BETTERLY, Mary A., 181
Thomas, 181
William C., 181
BEURKET, Margaret M.,
238
BEVERLEY, Anne, 259
BEYERS, Arthur L., 29
Bernice W., 29
Robert A., 29
Robert W., 29
BIDDLE, Lydia M., 90
William M., 90
BIDWELL, David, 334
Esther, 334
BIGELOW, Aimee S., 95
Andrew, 95
Timothy, 95
BIGGS, Charity, 8
BIGLEY, Laura A., 220
BILL, Lydia, 127
Mary, 90
BINGHAM, Abisha, 288
Faith, 25
Jerusha, 84, 239
Samuel, 25, 84, 239,
288
Sarah, 288
BIRCH, Sarah C., 38
BIRD, Benjamin N., 31
Cyrus, 269
Jackson, 30
Susanna, 269
BISHOP, Abbie N., 268
Anna, 60
Edna E., 290
Elizabeth, 203
Hannah, 285
*James, 60, 285
John, 60, 137
Lydia, 277, 278
Rebecca, 137
Wealthy, 26
BITTING, Frank L., 112
Samuel, 112
BIXBY, Benjamin, 230
Elizabeth, 230
BJÖRKMAN, Mary E., 339
BLACKLIDGE, Mary, 329
BLACKMAN, Sarah, 146,
166, 192

BLACKMORE, Rebecca,
63, 125
William, 63, 125
BLACKWELL, Ada B., 296
Ellis H., 296
Katherine, 171
Russell, 296
BLAISDELL, Ann H.,188,
189
Moses, 188
BLAKE, Mehitable, 24
BLAND, Ann(e), 17, 259
Richard, 17, 259
Theodoric(k), 17,259
BLAUVELT, Genevieve,
183
James F., 183
BLISS, Amy, 339
George S., 269
Hannah M., 339
Henry, 339
Jessie V., 269
John, 339
Josiah, 339
Leonard S., 339
Mary, 112
BLODGETT, Daniel, 239
Irene, 84
John, 84
Nathan, 239
Roxanna, 240, 241
BOCKIUS, Lulu H., 224
BOGARDUS, Emory A., 31
Ethel K., 31
BOGGS, Sarah E., 25
BOND, Jane A., 327
BOOTH, Ann, 242
BOSZOR, Elizabeth, 272
BOTSFORD, Elnathan, 61
Hannah, 61
BOTTCHER, Dana C., 24
BOTTUM, Joseph S., 243
Phebe E., 243
BOURNE, Elizabeth,105,
151, 152, 237, 242,
254, 256, 324
BOUTWELL, Clark C., 78
Henry T., 79
Jean M., 79
John T., 79
Nehemiah, 78
BOWEN, Fannie B., 36
BOWERS, Robert, 3
Thomas M., 3
BOWLBY, Thelma, 13
BOWLING, Elizabeth C.,
164
Martha C., 246
BOYCE, Caroline S.,231
Rosella G., 312
BOYER, Edmund S., 327
Francis B., 327
BOYLES, Nonnie M., 165
William J., 165
BOYNTON, Lydia, 46

BRADFORD, Alice, 6, 98
Anna, 24
Aseneth H., 78
Elizabeth, 115
Ephraim, 223
Eseck, 265
George, 265
Hannah, 25, 84, 87, 110, 135, 222, 239, 287, 312, 337
Harvey S., 265
Irene, 74
James, 24
John, 6
Joseph, 74
Lucy, 223
Mercy, 21
Perez, 265
Samuel, 114, 135,265
Sarah, 80
Simeon, 223
Sophia M., 265
Thomas, 24
*William, 6, 21, 74, 80, 84, 86, 87, 98, 110, 114, 135, 177, 210, 222, 223, 239, 265, 287, 337
William, 24, 25,222, 223, 239, 265, 287
William, Jr., 337
BRADSTREET, Anne, 67, 68, 230
Austin, 32
Dorothy, 226
Hannah, 117
Jacob G., 32
John, 32, 107, 157, 158, 230, 317
Mercy, 9, 14, 107, 157, 317
Samuel, 9, 10, 32, 230
*Simon, 9, 10, 14, 32, 67, 158, 226, 229, 317
Simon, 107, 117, 157
William C., 32
William H., 32
BRADY, Elizabeth C., 234
BRAITHWAYTHE, Margaret 27
BRAMLETTE, Olive S.,96
BRANCH, Lucie O., 224
BRAND, Graton S., 218
Marianna L., 219
BRASHEAR, Benjamin, 10
Martha, 11
Tobias, 10
BRASHEARS, Mary B., 23
BRATHWAYTHE (BRATH-WAITE), *William, 27
BRAY, Cynthia, 91, 105
Ebenezer, 91, 104
Thomas, 91, 105
BRAYTON, Evangeline,41
Francis M., 41

BRAZER, Anne W., 31
John, 31
BRENT, Eleanor, 49, 245, 246
*Giles, 10, 245
Katherine, 10
Mary, 245
William, 246
BRENTON, Sarah, 22
BRENTON, *William, 22
BREWSTER, Daniel, 8
Edward, 8
Elizabeth, 223
Hannah, 126
John, 8
Nathaniel, 8
Sarah, 8
BRICE, Margaret C., 54
BRIGGS, Henry, 80, 132
Henry D., 80, 132
Mary B., 76
Mercy, 210
Michael, 79, 132
Michael P., 80, 132
Ollie, 80
Sue S., 132
BRINLEY, Lydia, 253
BRINSMADE, John, 103
Mary, 103
Paul, 103
BRISCOE, Ann M., 42
James M., 42
Ralph, 42
BRISTOW, Sarah, 42
BRITT, Mary A., 155
Reddin, 155
BROCKETT, Grace C., 1
BROCUS, Martha, 10
BROEMMER, Andrew P., 325
Brandon A., 325
Howard R., 326
H. Richard, 325
Lara L., 325
BRONSON, Katherine L., 255
Stephen, 255
BROOKE, Anne, 41
Baker, 282, 283
Clement, 77, 179,244
Clement H., 78, 179, 244
Eleanor, 23, 66
Elizabeth, 195, 318
Esther, 283
Eugenia, 78, 179,244
Henrietta E., 283, 284
Henry, 77, 179, 244
James, 283
Jane, 164, 246
Leonard, 282, 283
Mary, 53
Nicholas, 77, 179, 244
*Robert, 22, 41, 53, 65, 77, 164, 179, 195, 244, 246, 283, 318

Roger, 41
Sarah, 23
Thomas, 22, 23, 53, 66, 77, 164, 179, 195, 244, 246, 318
BROOKNER, Myra O., 302
BROOKS, Berry B., Jr., 33
Jane A., 326
Martha E., 28
Susanna, 264
Virginia F., 33
Wilbur S., 326
William T., 27
BROWN, Abraham, 255
Alexander, 312
Almira L., 251
Aner, 285
Ann, 158, 335
Bridget, 86, 177
Catherine A., 14
Clark, 12, 213
Edwin H., 312
Eleazer, 158, 335
Eliza, 40, 270, 291
Emma L., 228
Henry B., 255
James, II, 215
James D., 312
John, 12, 213, 215
Katherine M., 255
Mary A., 218, 303
Mary E., 19
Pherne T., 12, 214, 215
Robert, 228
Roswell H., 14
Ruth, 64
Sarah, 285
BROWNE, Eleazer, 40, 270, 291
Jabez, 270, 291
Jacob, 40
Joseph, 40, 270, 291
Mary, 199
William, 40, 270,291
BROWNING, Mary W., 170
BRUMBAUGH, Daniel D., 34
Hugh H., 35
Peter P., 34
Stiles D., 34
William B., 34
BRUNER, Mary, 42
BRUNTON, Margaret I., 318
BRUSH, Florence A.,60
BRYAN, Daniel B., 35
George G., 35
Leslie A., 35
Leslie A., Jr., 35
Sarah J., 150
BRYANT, Emma A., 92, 105
John E., 92, 105
Lucy J., 47
BRYCE, Edith C., 54
Joseph S., 54
Lloyd S., 54

COGGESHALL (Continued)
Joshua, 79, 131, 133
Mary, 167, 250, 263
COGSWELL, Sarah, 36,37
Stephen, 37
William, 37
COLE, Ann, 122
Bessie M., 144
Hannah, 189
John, 122
Mareeta, 63
Martha, 127
Mary A., 130
Roxlyn G., 321
Susannah, 178
William, 122
William H., 143
COLEMAN, Winona R.,194
COLLARD, Katherine,334
COLLIER, Abram T., 47
Charles, 46
Chloe H., 94, 170
Forrest F., 47
Jane G., 151
COLLINS, Avis, 182,338
Daniel, 101
Dayton C., 12, 214
Elizabeth L., 153
Hiram, 214
John, 100, 153, 182,
214, 338
John, III, 136
Laura, 100, 101
Mercy, 136
Norman, 153, 214
Polly, 87
Sybilla, 93
Timothy, 153, 214
COLLISON, Harry W.,Jr.
95
Lee G., 95
COLTON, Benjamin, 57
Eli, 57
Eliza A., 57
Pliney, 57
COLWELL, Mary R., 136
COMEGYS, Elizabeth,113
COMSTOCK, Ann B., 234
Benjamin, 234
CONANT, Betsy, 173
John, 78, 173
Lot, 78, 173
Peter, 173
Rebecca, 78
Robert, 173
*Roger, 78, 173
CONEY, Mehitable, 31
CONKEY, Clement S., 48
Clement S., Jr., 48
George L., 49
CONLAN, Clyde M., 172
CONNACHAN, James, 228
Joanne, 228
Patricia M., 228
CONOVER, Abram, 328
Alta J., 328
CONTEE, Alexander,
164, 246

Catherine, 246
Charles S., 164
Helen F., 164
John, 164
Richard A., 164
CONWAY, Agatha, 33
Louisa, 34
COOK, Hezekiah, 161
John, 161
Phoebe, 28
Rebecca, 111
Samuel, 111
Sarah, 161
COOKE, Joseph R., 50
Robert G., 49
COOLEY, Abiah, 57
COOPER, Edith, 54
COPENHAVER, Eunice M.,
51
Thomas, 51
COREY, Daniel, 321
CORNETT, Fielding R.,
51
Robert F., Jr., 50
Walter M., 51
CORNISH, Alice, 4,201,
202, 207, 280
Allen, 4, 201, 202,
207, 279
Clarissa 4, 201,202,
207, 279
George, 4, 201, 202,
207, 279
Josiah, 4, 201, 202,
207, 279
CORNWALL, Fred H., 325
Lois, 101
CORWIN, Bartholomew,
211
George, 211
Hannah C., 211
John, 211
Richard, 211
Samuel, 211
CORY, Electa, 321
COTRELL, Mary E., 337
COTTON, Anna, 226
Seaborn, 226
COUCH, Asenath, 55
Ebenezer, 55
COUDEKERQUE-LAMBRECHT,
André de, 51
Beatrice C., 51
COULTER, David D., 51
John L., 51
John L., Jr., 51
Kirkley S., 51
Phebe D., 51
COUPLAND, David O.,236
Elizabeth B., 236
COVER, Nellie, 234
COWDREY, Harriet, 224
John, 224
COWING, Ruth, 136
COWLES, Carlos, 331
Nancy, 331
COX, Francis E., 53
Henry B., 53

Margaret J., 326
Paul V., 52
Roy L., 326
CRAM, Henry S., 53
John S., 54
Ruth, 118
CRANE, Azariah, 54,
129, 219, 320
Edus, 321
Hazel M., 7
Jane, 320
Joseph, 7
Mary, 57
Rhoda, 219
Silas, 54, 129
Stephen, 219
CRANSTON, Caleb, 160
James, 94, 170
*John, 94, 170
John, 160
Lucretia K., 160
Lucy J., 170
Mary, 94
Richard, 170
Richmond, 94, 170
*Samuel, 94, 160
Samuel, 170
Samuel N., 160
Thomas, 160
CRAWFORD, Rebecca A.,
260
CRAYNE, David B., 55
Hallie, 55
Jane, 129
Lynn M., 54, 55
Samuel, 54
Stephen, 55
CRESWELL, Phoebe T.,
52
CRIPPS, Theophila, 93
CRITTENDEN, Lydia, 148
CROCKER, Anna, 124
Hannah, 69
Joseph, 124
Josiah, 68, 124
Seth, 69
Thomas, 69, 124
CROCKETT, Ruth G., 239
CROFTS, Alexander, 85
Margaret L., 85
CROOKS, Phoebe C., 307
Samuel, 307
CROSBY, Danford M.,106
Rebeckah, 304
CROSHAW, Unity, 52,72,
120, 141, 197, 261,
294
Ursula U., 325
CROSS, Anna, 205
Frances A., 205
J. Alan, 55
James F., 56
Noah, 205
Noah A., 205
Uriah, 205
CROSSWELL, Abigail, 29
CROSWELL, Andrew, 71
Emily C., 71

DOTY, Hannah, 143
  Harriet N., 312
  Jonathan, 311
  Patience, 80
  William, 311
DOUGHTY, Susannah,258
DOUGLAS, David, 52
  Mary C., 160
  Samuel C., 52
  Zemula W., 52
DOUGLASS, Helen, 197
  Lawrence, 197
  Lawrence A., 275
  Nancy, 58
DOW, Emma K., 117
  John E., 77, 303
  Jonathan, 117
  Lydia R., 303
  Waldo H., 77, 303
  William H., 117
DOWNES, John L., 3
DOWNING, Abner, 281
  Enos H., 282
  Flora B., 282
  Heman, 282
DOYLE, Mabel G., 331
  Mary V., 4, 279
DOYNE, Elizabeth, 88,
  145, 172, 208
  Mary, 63, 125, 336
  Robert, 63, 125, 336
DOZIER, Harriet G.,221
  John F., 221
DRAPER, Frances A.,
  310
DREW, Franklin, 161
  George F., 161
  John, 161
  Vandelia E., 161
DRING, Delaney, 97
  Philip, 97
  Thomas, 97
DRURY, Mary, 181
DRYSDALE, Ann, 298,333
  *Hugh, 298
DuBOIS, Cornelius, 67
  Floyd R., 67
  Frederic M., 66
  Joel, 192
  Peter, 146, 166, 192
  Peter C., 67
  Phebe, 146, 166
  Rachel, 192
  Thomas, 146, 166
DuBOIS de CORBEIN,
  Rose U., 11
DUDLEY, Abigail, 148
  Ann(e) (a), 9, 26,
  64, 107, 117, 146,
  157, 166, 192, 198,
  199, 200, 226, 229,
  317, 326
  Caroline F., 289
  David, 26
  Dorothy, 118, 174,
  216
  James, 75
  *Joseph, 198, 200

  Joseph, 119, 285,289
  Mary, 76, 119, 286,
  320
  Mercy, 1, 99, 267,
  280, 281, 316
  Nicholas, 289
  Patience, 95, 293
  Samuel, 64, 75, 118,
  174, 216, 289, 319,
  326, 327
  Stephen, 75, 289
  *Thomas, 1, 9, 51,
  64, 75, 95, 99, 107,
  117, 118, 119, 157,
  174, 198, 216, 226,
  229, 267, 280, 281,
  285, 286, 287, 289,
  293, 316, 317, 319,
  327
  Trueworthy, 289
  William, 289
DUKE, Martha, 42
DULANY, Mary G., 127
DULIN, Gwynne R., 198
DUNCAN, Helen A., 325
  Henry, 325
DUNHAM, Elizabeth, 14
  Frederick, 14
  Hannah, 277
DUNLAP, Esther, 209
  Virginia E., 89
DUNN, Charles W., 69
  Harvey, 69
  John A., 69
DUSTON, Arthur G., 190
DUVALL, Jeannette E.,
  97
DYE, Catharine, 133
  Richard, 133
DYER, Anna, 320
  Eleanor E., 67
  Penhallow F., 67
  William W., Jr., 67

EASTON, Amey, 199
  Jonathan, 199, 200
  *Nicholas, 199, 276,
  313
  Nicholas, 199
  Patience, 313
  Peter, 199, 200,212,
  277, 313
  Waite, 212, 277,278
EATON, Elizabeth, 253
  Hannah, 26, 73
  Joanna, 90
  John, 89, 253
  Joseph, 253
  Mary, 169
  *Theophilus, 26, 73,
  169
  Thomas, 89, 252
EBERT, Shirley E., 118
EDDY, Winona T., 194
EDELEN, Joseph, 144
  Theresa C., 144

EDMUNDS, Phebe, 130
EDWARDS, Chester C.,
  68, 69
  Chester E., 68
  Elsie M., 68
  Elsie P., 68
  James B., 333
  James L., 333
  James M., 332
EICHHORN, Rita W.,109
ELDREDGE, Bethiah,188
ELEY, Algernon S., 27
  Amelia, 27
ELIOT, Anne, 22
  Jemima, 267, 281
  Joseph, 22
ELKINS, Willard E.,69
  Willard L., 70
ELLEN, Sarah, 336
ELLENBERGER, Willodean
  107
ELLET, Charles, 149
  John I., 149
  Mary S., 149
  Thomas C., 149
ELLIOTT, John D., 66
  Lucinda P., 66
  William, 66
ELLIS, Caroline S., 2
  Henry P., 31
  Katherine, 31
ELLSWORTH, Jemina, 248
  Marjorie M., 312
  William, 248
ELMQUIST, Roy E., 5
EMERSON, David M., 71
  George D., 71, 72
  Howard, 71
  John P., 71
  June A., 71
  Maxwell, 71
ENDICOTT, Benjamin,258
  Hannah, 93
  *John, 72, 76, 93,
  258, 302
  John, 258
  Joseph, 258
  Mary, 72, 258
  Ruth, 76, 302
  Samuel, 76, 302
  Zerubbabel, 72, 76,
  93, 258, 302
ENGELL, Grace A., 281
ENSIGN, Hannah, 215
EPPERSON, Caroline Q.,
  221
ESTES, Caleb, 277, 278
  Edward, 212, 277,278
  Horace, 277, 278
  Joseph, 194
  Mary, 194
  Mary E., 277, 278
  Thomas, 277, 278
  Waite, 212
ESTILL, Alice D., 72
  George C., 72
ETHERIDGE, Caroline S.
  10
  John A., 9, 10

373

374

FRYER, Appleton, 85
  Appleton, Jr., 85
  Catherine A., 85,86
  Daniel K., 85
  Livingston, Jr.,85,
  86
  Robert L., 85, 86
  William J., 85
FULLER, Bradford N.,
  86
  Byron J., 88
  Eunice B., 86
  Hannah, 317
  Henry, 45
  James B., 88
  Merritt G., 144
  Michael B., 86
  Robert S., 87
  Stanley C., 88
  Susan, 46
  William H., 86
  William H., Jr., 86
FULLERTON, Samuel B.,
  Jr., 88
  Samuel B., III, 88,
  89
  Tommie F., 88
FULWEILER, Hull P.,89
  Marie L., 89
  Pamela S., 89
  Spencer B., 89
  Spencer B., Jr., 89
  Walter H., 90
FURBER, Mary, 169
  Mary E., 48

GAEDKE, Joan F., 82
GAILOR, Francis, 317
  Hazen A., 318
  Mary M., 318
GAINES, Mary, 298, 333
GALLAGHER, Edward E.,
  90
  Edward S., 90
  Genevieve S., 90
  Shannon G., 91
GALLEMORE, John A.,314
  Millicent, 314
  William, 314
  William A., 314
GANNAWAY, Catherine A.
  236
GANNETT, Susanna B.,
  269
GANTT, Mary L., 262
GARDINER, John I., 144
  Josephine M., 145
  Mary S., 198
  Samuel, 199
  Walter C., 198, 199,
  200
GARDNER, Miriam, 190,
  328
  Priscilla W., 339

GARLAND, Alice, 293
  Joseph E., 293
  Sarah, 241
GARRETT, Clarence J.,
  91
  Margaret L., 91
GARTH, Jesse W., 73
  Lena, 73
  William W., 73
  Winston F., 73
GASKILL, Edward, 93
  Mary, 93
  Samuel, 93
GASKINS, Charles T.,6
GAULDEN, Ethel E.,
  10, 11
  Thomas C., 11
GAUMER, Susan H., 229,
  230
GEDNEY, Lydia, 211
GELDER, Gertrude C.,35
GEORGE, Mary, 206, 288
GERBER, Susie, 168
GETZINGER, Margaret A.
  92
  Philip L., 92
  Virginia A., 92
GIBBES, Harriet H.,221
  *Robert, 221
  Robert W., 221
  William, 221
  William H., 221
GIBBONS, Sarah, 246
GIBBS, Alvin J., 93
  Bathsheba, 296
  Benjamin, 295
  Frederick R., 94
  James W., 93
  Joshua, 93
  Lewis L., 93
  Marion B., 94
  Silvanus, 295
  Stephen V., 93
GIBERSON, Harvey A.,
  258
GIBSON, Aimee B., 95
  Sarah, 173
  Zachary L., 95
GIFFORD, Elizabeth, 4,
  201, 202, 207, 279
  Hannah, 206
GILBERT, Ethel E.,
  188, 189
  Georgia A., 276
  Mary L., 36
  Mary S., 338
  Nathaniel, 135
  Othaniel, 338
  Welthea, 135
GILLETTE, Annie, 115
  Anson, 61
  Eli, 61
  Jeremiah, 61
  Mary, 61
GILMAN, Alice, 117
  Antipas, 117
  Joanna, 117
  John, 117

  Samuel, 117
  Sarah, 75, 289
GLACE, Tacey E., 158,
  335
GLENN, Martha C.,325
GODFREY, Hannah, 188
  John, 134
  Jonathan, 188
  Mary, 134
  Penelope, 94, 160,
  170
  Thomas, 188
GOOCH, Eleanor B., 155
GOODALE, Allie M., 7
  Jude, 7
GOODELL, Elmer E., 96
  James A., 96, 97
  Layton B., 97
  Mary, 97
  Ralph H., 97
  Ralph H., Jr., 96
  Ralph H., III, 96,
  97
  Samuel, 97
GOODENOW, Hannah, 158,
  335
GOODLIFFE, Hannah A.,
  60
GOODMAN, Florence, 2
  Henry H., 2
  Moses, 2
  Timothy S., 2
GOODRICH, Elizabeth,
  152, 237, 254, 324
GOODRIDGE, William H.,
  191
GOODSELL, Percy H.,
  98, 99
GOODWIN, Abigail C.,30
  Amy, 254
  Ebenezer, 29
  Harley, 30
  William, 29
GOODYEAR, Rebecca, 137
  *Stephen, 137, 138
GORDON, Alice O., 203,
  204
  Elizabeth, 56, 65,
  163, 165, 256, 271,
  289
GORHAM, Eli, 261
  Elizabeth, 293
  Fidelia O., 261
  Stephen, 261
GORTON, Ann, 40, 270,
  291
  *Samuel, 39, 159,
  270, 291
  Susanna, 159
GOSS, Hannah, 313
  Sarah, 312
GOULD, Mary, 160
  Mehitable, 32
GRAHAM, Donna V., 201
  Edwin R., 305
  Elva, 305
GRANT, Esther R., 226
  George W., 191
  Margaret A., 191

HILTON, Ann, 64
  Benjamin, 48, 64
  Benjamin F., 48, 64
  Edward, 64, 326
  Elizabeth, 75
  Ernest, 48
  Jane, 326
  Jeremiah, 64
  Martha, 64
  Richard, 64
HIMES, Adelaide F.,143
  Hanford S., 143
  Sylvester, 143
HINCKLEY, Ebenezer,292
  Ebenezer, Jr., 292
  Ebenezer, 3rd, 292
  John, 292
  Mary, 116, 292
  Melathiah, 68
  Meletiah, 124
  Ralph W., 130
  Samuel, 116
  *Thomas, 68, 124, 292
HINMAN, Gertrude D.,
  240
HITCHCOCK, Ada T., 169
  Bonver R., 187
  Edwin T., 223
  Gilbert R., 187
  John L., 187
  William J., 223
HOBBS, Corrilla E., 301
HOCKADAY, James W., 58
  Nina M., 58
HODGE, Sarah, 220
HODGSON, Lois J., 276,
  278
HOFMEISTER, Eric L.,122
  George C., 122
  George C., Jr., 122
  Lisa L., 122
  Virginia L., 122
HOGGATT, Rachel, 70
HOGUE, Mary A., 316
HOLBROOK, Betsy A., 118
  Rachel, 282
HOLCOMBE, Charles M.,
  170
  Richmond C., 170
HOLDRIDGE, Bridget, 243
HOLLAND, Estelle, 89
  Julia, 178
HOLLISTER, Elizabeth,
  15, 196, 274
  Mary, 105, 151, 256,
  316
  Sarah, 266
HOLLOWAY, Rhoda, 219
  Suzanne, 81
HOLLOWELL, Mary W., 92
HOLLY, Abigail, 137
HOLMAN, Antonia W., 320
HOLMES, Mary, 12, 199,
  213
  Mary A., 223
HOLSTON, Maria D., 192
  William, 192
HOLT, Jennie M., 235

HOLTEN, Elizabeth, 240
HOLYOKE, Elizur, 266
  Hannah, 266
HONE, Emily, 81
  John, 81
HOOK, John T., 63, 125
  Sarah, 63, 125
HOOKE, Mary, 91, 104
  *William, 91, 104
HOOKEY, Sarah, 94, 170
HOOPER, Lula R., 161
HOPE, Craig L., 123
  Leonard G., 124
HOPKINS, Dorcas
  (Dorcus), 71, 29,
  45, 96, 113, 334
  Henry S., 59
  Lulu L., 59
  Mary, 21
  Ruth, 225
HOPSON, Edgar D., 136
  Norma J., 136
  Samuel, Jr., 136
  Simeon, 136
  Simeon, Jr., 136
  William A., 136, 137
HOSKINS, Martha, 56,
  65, 163, 165, 255,
  271, 273, 274
  Sallie, 38
HOSMER, Chester, 34
  Clemence, 20, 156
  Joseph, 34
  Mary A., 35
  Stiles A., 35
  William, 34
HOTCHKISS, David, 257
  Ethel A., 257
  Truman, 257
  William D., 257
HOUSTON, Martha J., 316
HOWARD, Helen D., 124
  Willis G., 124
HOWE, Charlotte, 220
  Elden L., 126
  Helen D., 126
  Mary E., 194
HOWELL, Pauline A., 48
HOWES, Ebenezer, 103
  Sarah, 104
HOWISON, Anne W., 172
HOWLAND, Arthur, 296
  Dulany, 127
  Gardiner G., 127
  Grafton D., 126, 127
  Joseph, 127
  Katherine M., 126
  Mary, 83
  McClure M., 126
  Nathaniel, 127
  Rebeckah, 297
  Thomas, 297
HOXSIE, Buleah B., 160
  James B., 160
  Reynolds, Jr., 160
HOYT, Harriet, 186,196,
  275
  Hazen L., 318

John R., 318
  Mabel R., 15
  Margery B., 318
  Minot, 318
  Stephen, 196, 275
HUBBARD, Margaret, 57
HUBBELL, Dorothy, 249
  Edward P., 248, 250
  Eunice, 50
  Nehemiah, 248
  William B., 248
  William S., 248
HUDDLESTON, Annette K.
  25
HULBERT, Ann, 86, 177
  Elizabeth, 153
HULL, Damaris, 28
  Eunice, 257
  Jane, 121, 299
  John, 28
  Joseph, 257
  Samuel, 257
  Teddeman, 28
HULTANDER, Ethel R.,
  127
  Martin E., 127
HUMPHREYS, Elizabeth
  H., 3
  Parry W., 3
HUMPHRIES, Rosemary,
  317
HUNKIN, Abigail, 64
HUNKINS, Darius, 174
  David, 174
  Miriam, 174
  Sydney C., 174
HUNT, Aaron B., 332
  Abigail, 156
  Charles J., 118
  Ebenezer, 156
  Elizabeth, 9
  Gurney L., 332
  John, 9, 20, 118,156
  John W., 118
  Jonathan, 20, 156
  Mary, 20
  Mary A., 118
HUNTER, Elizabeth, 53
HUNTINGTON, Elizabeth,
  100, 101
  Hannah, 100
  Jabez, 100
  Jedediah, 121
  Joshua, 100
  Lillian, 122
  Maria L., 184
HURLBURT, Rose B., 289
HUSSEY, Deborah, 107
  George, Sr., 107
HUTCHINSON, Hannah, 35
  Susanna, 122
  *William, 122
HYDE, Elizabeth, 153,
  214
  John, 49
  Mary C., 49
  Rachel A., 156

LOVEJOY, Charles D.,
  160
  Emma L., 24
  Hoxsie W., 160
  Isaac W., 160
LOVELACE, Edward, 327
  *Francis, 327
  George, 328
  John, 328
LOVELAND, Ruth A.,257
  Truman, 257
LOVELESS, James W.,328
  John, 328
  Joseph, 328
  Juliet E., 328
LOVELL, Jennie S., 62
LOWE, Dorothy, 283
  Elizabeth, 63, 125
  Henry, 247, 283
  Mary, 284
  Susanna M., 48, 245,
  247
LOWMAN, Elizabeth R.,
  299
LOWRY, Eleanor E., 68
LUDLOW, *Roger, 8
  Sarah, 8
LUMPKIN, Martha E.,64
LUSTER, Mary J., 23
LUTHER, Lydia, 167
LYON, Alice, 186
  Elfleda, 75
LYTLE, Mary C., 43
  Samuel, II, 43
  Samuel, III, 43

MABSON, Susannah, 306
MACARDELL, Esther C.,
  210
MACEY, Edna V., 29
MACGREUTHER, Alexander
  27
MacINTOSH, Barbara E.,
  126
MACK, David, 266
  Henry E., 187
  Joseph L., 187
  Samuel E., 187
  Zilpha, 266
MACKAL, Ann, 42
  James, 41
  John, 42
MACOMBER, Fannie H.,
  71, 72
  Ichabod, 72
  William, 72
MACON, Martha W., 294
MACY, Obed, 190
  Urania, 190
  William, 190
MADDOX, Sara F., 152
MAGEE, Margaret, 141
MAGRUDER, Elizabeth,27
  Mary A., 23
  Samuel, 27

MAIN, Ezekiel, 158,335
  Nehemiah, 158
  Roland, 228
  Thomas, 158, 335
MAINE, Nehemiah, 335
MAINE(S), Seth, 335
MAINES, David B., 158,
  335
  Edgar W., 158, 335
  Grace E., 158
  Seth, 158
MALLORY, Lucinda, 318
MANLEY, Betsy, 243
MANN, Benjamin D., 161
  Teressa V., 161
  Vandelia D., 161
  William M., Jr., 161
  William M., III, 161
  William O., 161
MANSFIELD, Bethia
  (Bethula), 78, 173
  Betsey, 61
  Mary, 269
MANTER, Benjamin, 47
  Elizabeth, 48
  James, 47
MARINER, John W., 265
MARKHAM, Esther, 138,
  217
MARMADUKE, Donald S.,
  162
  Virginia F., 162
MARSH, Alexander W.,
  163
  Chaun A., 163
  Elizabeth L., 163
  Lucy A., 20
  Robert D., 163
MARSHALL, Dinah, 220
  Eleakim, 220
  Rosilla, 67
MARSHAM, Katherine,
  10, 282
  Richard, 10
MARTELL, Charles J.,
  164
  Helen M., 163
MARTIN, Amy W., 112
  Carolyn A., 164
  Clyde D., 146
  Cora A., 203
  Ephraim, 185
  Hamilton L., 166
  Jack L., 166
  James, 185
  Jamie D., 165
  John, 185, 252, 311
  John, Jr., 311
  Joseph, 185, 252
  Martha, 185
  Mary F., 165
  Mary P., 113
  Patience, 311
  Rebekah, 59
  Sarah, 252
  Solon D., 58
  Vera J., 333
  Virginia W., 33

  William, 252
  William H., 58
  William R., 146,147,
  165
  Ysabelita L., 144,
  145, 166
MARTZ, Sarah, 157
MASON, David, 167
  Edward, 167
  *John, 140
  John T., 167
  Joseph, 250
  Judith E., 167
  Judson P., 167
  Judson P., Jr., 167
  Lovina, 250
  Marmaduke, 250
  Nellie A., 74
  Priscilla, 140
  Raymond, 168
MASSEY, Mary, 72
  Thomas, 72
MATHESON, Deborah, 233
MATHEWS, Ann, 82
  Baldwin, 33, 58, 180
  Francis, 33, 58, 180
  Isaac, 276
  James, 276
  John, 276
  Linnie, 276
  Mary, 33, 58, 276,
  180
  *Samuel, 33, 58, 180,
  275
  Samuel, 276
  Thomas, 276
  William, 82
  Willis D., 276
MATTESON, Sophronia,
  80, 132
MATTOON, Amanda L., 130
  Mary, 326
  Richard, 326
  Schuyler, 130
MAUDLIN, Euretha, 40,
  270, 291
  Thomas, 40, 270, 291
MaWHINNEY, William D.,
  104
  William T., 104
MAXWELL, Ada, 71
  Elizabeth, 283
MAYHEW, Hannah, 102,
  109, 204, 255
  Jedediah, 171
  Jerusha, 89, 252
  Lucy, 253
  Martha, 4, 201, 202,
  207, 279, 295
  Mary, 47, 323
  Matthew, 47, 323
  Paine, 47, 323
  Sarah, 71
  *Thomas, 4, 47, 71,
  89, 102, 108, 109,
  171, 201, 202, 204,
  207, 252, 255, 279,
  295, 323

MAYHEW (Continued)
  Thomas, 323
  Thomas, Jr., 47,252
  Zaccheus, 71
MAYO, Ann M., 184
  Barbara, 13
  Elizabeth, 189,205, 210
  Elnathan, 184
  Hanna, 193
  John, 210
  John, 3d, 184
  Joseph, 184
  Judah, 13
  Mary, 225
  Mercy, 188
  Nathaniel, 13, 188, 225
  Samuel, 225
  Sarah, 116, 186
  Susannah, 210
  Thomas, 13, 184,188
McATEE, Martha E., 195, 319
McCALL, Beth A., 168
  Maria, 248
  Roselle S., 169
McCARLEY, Marguerite, 326
  Mose, 326
  Moses G., 326
McCARTHY, Ann, 174
McCLAUGHERTY, Edna,51
McCLELLAN, Matilda E., 328
McCLURE, Marguerite, 127
McCONOUGHEY, Muriel L. 45
McCREA, Bernie C., 169
  Llewellyn W., 169
  Yancey J., 169
  Yancey J., Jr., 169
McDANIEL, Ambrose D., 172
  Arthur J., 172
  John, 172
  Mary M., 80, 81
McDONALD, Eleanor B., 282, 284
  Elizabeth C., 124
McDONEL, Prudence, 110
McDONNELL, Gladys B., 170
  Joseph F., Jr., 170
  Joseph F., III, 170
McDUFFIE, Margaret F., 92
McELROY, Susan M., 20
McGEE, Marian E., 338
  Ralph E., 338
McINTOSH, Olive M.,312
McKAY, Isaac N., 171
  John E., 171
  Margaret I., 171
  Peter, 171
McKee, Olive A., 205
McKnight, Elise M.,172

Katherine E., 172
Stephen D., 172
Stephen D., Jr.,172
McLAUGHLIN, Mary, 320
McLELLAN, Lydia, 213
  Mary, 123
McMICHAEL, Marcia W., 60
McNEILL, Charles F., 178
  Margaret M., 120
  William A., 120
McPECK, Dorothy E., 173
  Edwin K., 173
McPHERSON, Augusta, 144
  Samuel, 144
McRAE, Nancy J., 174
  William M., 174
McROBERTS, Cora E., 224
  John, 223
  Peter, 223
  Volney, 223
MEACHAM, Deborah,158, 335
MEAD, Albert R., 334
  Cornelius S., 334
  Sanford M., 334
MEIGS, Tryal, 123
MELTON, Knowles R.,27
MENDENHALL, Clementina 70
  Isaac, 70
  Mordecai, 70
MEREDITH, Louise, 127
MERIAM, Jonas, 31
  Mehitable, 31
MERRICK, Elizabeth, 138, 217
  Ruth, 138, 217
  Sarah, 193, 261
MERRILL, Cleo A., 282
MERRITT, Elizabeth,252
MERTZ, Lucile, 302
MERWIN, Harriet B., 112
MESSNER, Angie M.,254
METCALF, Charles W., 120
  Rebecca P., 120
MEYER, Billie S., 325
  Brent R., 175
  Eric C., 175
  Harold I., 175, 176
  Paul R., 175
  Robert B., 175
  Virginia M., 175,176
MICHAEL, Sarah, 176
MIKESELL, Helen J.,177
  Henry B., 177
  James F., 177
  John W., Jr., 177
  John W., III, 177
  Linda A., 177
  Marian L., 177
MILAM, Sue, 209

MILLAWAY, Sallie, 45
MILLER, Barbara J., 175
  Elvina, 321
  George E., 178
  Leonard S., 66
  Louisa M., 126
  Louise H., 178
  Mary J., 103
  Sarah, 116
  Sue C., 66
MILLET, Mary B., 71
MILLIKEN, Anna M.,227
  Samuel H., 227
MILLS, Abigail E., 36
  Isaphene, 174
  Jedediah, 36
  Philo, 36
MINCH, Rizpha, 57
MINER, Esther, 79
  Hannah, 128
MIRICK, Julia M., 179
  Laurence P., 179
MITCHELL, Cora M., 50
  Cushing, 6
  Edward, 6
  George, 49
  George B., 50
  George C., 49
  George M., 50
  Henry H., 6
  Jones H., 6
  Maud A., 6
  Nahum, 6
MOFFATT, Tabitha, 12, 213
MOONEY, Harry M., 173
  Patience, 249
MOORE, Ann, 113, 224
  Anna M., 14
  Caroline L., 180
  Charles, 334
  Elizabeth, 82
  George A., 14
  Gideon, 334
  Harold A., 180
  *James, 82, 224, 306, 314
  James, 224, 314
  John, 82
  Margaret, 306, 314
  Maria L., 334
  Nathaniel, 306
  Sarah, 110, 252
MOREHEAD, Hugh N., 336
  Jesse W., 336
  Mary J., 336
MORES, John, 210
  Phebe H., 210
  Treat, 210
MOREY, Adelmar G., 281
  Alanson, 280
  Nathan S., 280
  Sarah M., 337
MORGAN, Amy, 150
  Diana M., 181
  James P., Jr., 181
  Mary E., 176
  Nettie C., 77, 303
  Rachel, 150

SANKEY, Charles O.,
310
  Elizabeth E., 310
  George F., 310
SARGENT, Josephine A.
  60
SATTERTHWAITE,
  Franklin B., Jr.,232
  Pennington, 231, 232
SAUER, Frederick, 257
SAUNDERS, Alden C.,
  232, 233
  Lora B., 233
  Winthrop, 233
SAWYER, Ann, 288
SAYRE, Ann, 8
  John, 8
SCANLON, Jessie M.,110
SCARBURGH, Americus,
  176
  Charles, 142
  Henry, 142
  John, 176
  Tabitha C., 142
  Vienna P., 176
SCHEFFLER, James G., 9
SCHIAVO, Anna T., 287
SCHINDEL, Marie L.,
  157
SCHLEY, George H., 52
  Mary W., 52
SCHMIDT, Jean A., 175
SCHMITT, A. Lyman,234
  Roger M., 234
SCHMUCK, Abigail, 315
  Peter, 315
SCHNEIDER, Margaret P.
  235
  Samuel C., 235
  Samuel G., 235
SCHOTT, James, Jr.,39
  Lilian K., 46
  Margaret R., 39
  Rebecca C., 39
  William E., 39
SCHROEDER, Elizabeth
  P., 236
  Enriette L., 237
  Henry J., 237, 238
  Henry J., Jr., 236,
  237
  Henry J., III, 237
  Mary B., 236, 237
  Robert L., 237, 238
  Robert L., Jr., 238
  Thomas A., 237
  William B., 237
  William D., 238, 239
SCHULTHEIS, Rosalin C.
  135
SCHUYLER, Cornelia,39
SCOFIELD, Hannah J.,
  136, 137
  Ira, 137
  Israel, Jr., 137
SCOTT, Ames, 263
  Amy, 262
  Amy A., 263

  Emma, 156
  Ruth J., 69
  Sarah, 40, 270, 291
  Susan E., 147
SCOUTEN, Margaret, 165
SCRUGGS, Gross F., 42
  Gross R., 42
  James B., 42
SEALS, Sarah J., 298
SEAMANS, Ida M., 171
SEARLE, Constant, 128
  Hannah, 128
  Nathaniel, 97
  Sarah, 97
SEARLES, Nathaniel, 128
SEARS, Edmund, 59
  Paul, 59
  Sally, 59
SEDGLEY, Emmie L., 290
  John, 290
  Jotham, 290
SELLECK, Mary, 137
  Peter, 137
SEVER, Anne W., 31
  William, 30
SEVERANCE, Mary, 331
SEVERANS, Mary, 106
SEWALL, Elizabeth W.,
  48
  Jane, 77, 179, 244
SEWELL, Elizabeth, 245,
  284
SEYMOUR, Abigail, 182,
  183
  Amny, 2
  Catherine, 98
  Charles, 98, 101
  John, 2, 101, 215
  Sarah, 21, 215
  Timothy, 2, 101
  Zachariah, 183
SHACKELFORD, Harriet E.
  224
  James, 224
SHAEFER, Barbara, 93
SHANNON, Ann, 243
  Emma A., 148
SHARP, Aletha J., 20
SHAULL, Elizabeth, 115
SHAW, Abigail, 278
  Lydia, 130
  Ruth, 269
SHEFFIELD, James, 42
  Mary, 42
SHELDON, Ebenezer, 20
  Stephen, 20
  Thankful, 20
SHEPARD, Almeron, 240
  Cynthia R., 241
  Daniel B., 240
  John, 240, 241
  John S., 239, 240,242
  John S., III, 239,240
  Moses, 241
  Phineas, 240
  Robinson, 242
  Rosamond R., 239
  Stephanie L., 241

  Warren B., 241
  William D., 240
  William M., 241
  William S., 241
SHEPHERD, James, 169
SHERBURNE, Catherine,
  11
  Eugene A., 12
  Eugene J., 12
  Henry, 11
  Martha N., 11
  Phebe, 67
  Samuel, 11
  William L., 11
SHERMAN, Alice, 280
  Charles E., 243
  Charles F., 159
  Charles H., 243
  David, 242
  David T., 91, 242
  Edward, 90
  F. Lynette, 242
  Henry S., 242
  Ira, 130
  John, 91
  Maria L., 159
  Nathan, 90
  Nathaniel, 242
  Peleg, 159
  Prence, 130
  Samuel, 130
  Sarah, 91
  Sylvia A., 130
  Thomas, 159
  William B., 91
SHERWOOD, Hannah, 310
  Mary, 140
  Sarah, 140
SHIELDS, Anna, 124
SHIPMAN, Ruth M., 243
  William L., 243
SHIRK, Ellen, 328
SHORT, Abel, 307
  Abigail R., 307
SHOTWELL, Huldah D.,
  315
SILSBY, Sarah, 263
SILVER, Anne W., 141
SIM, Barbara, 54
  Patrick, 53
SIMMONS, Adroyal, 288
  Ida A., 234
  Johanthan, 262
  John, 262
  Joseph, 262
  Levi, 288
  Mary, 232, 269, 277,
  304
  Sarah, 262, 263
  William, 262
SIMONS, John A., 288
  Mary F., 288
SIMPSON, Ruth A., 315
SIMS, Henry M., 244
  Olivia J., 244
SISSON, Elizabeth, 134
SKELLY, Anne E., 323
SKIFF, Blanche, 204
  Vernon W., 204

WILKINSON, Ann, 92
    Christopher, 92
    Francis, 92
WILLARD, Eunice, 324
WILLET, Abigail, 60
WILLEY, Leonora, 320
WILLIAMS, Bernice F.,
    314
    Daniel, 228
    Desire, 305
    Ebenezer, 100
    Edwin A., 259, 260
    Edwina H., 260
    Eleanor, 309
    George C., 124
    Hannah, 100
    Howard, 124
    Isaac, 72
    Margaret, 124
    Marion H., 314
    Mary, 72, 229
    Mary L., 154
    Mercy, 233, 268
    Rebecca, 90
    *Roger, 228, 233, 268
    Simeon, 124
    Thomas, 124
    Wesley, 124
    Winston F., 314, 315
WILLIS, Helen, 79
    Levina, 84
WILLSON, Elisha, 315
    George H., 283, 284
    Jehu R., Sr., 315
    Jehu R., Jr., 316
    Jonathan, Sr., 315
    Mary G., 283
    Richard A., 315,316
    Richard E., 315,316
    Robert, 315
    Thomas B., 284
WILLYS (WYLLYS),Amy,57
    *George, 57, 99
    Mabel, 99
    Samuel, 99
WILSON, Abigail, 216
    Hercules M., 219
    Lois J., 220
    Louise H., 259
    Mary E., 219
    Mary P., 221
WINEGAR, Angeline, 69
    John, 69
WING, Elizabeth, 184
WINGATE, Betsy, 76
WINSLOW, Abigail, 212
    *Edward, 30
    Hulda, 263
    Isaac, 30
    Josiah, 30
    Penelope, 30
WINSOR, Joseph, 233
    Mary, 234
    Samuel, 233
WINTERS, Phyllis A.,
    193

WINTHROP, *John, 63,
    199, 211, 326
    John, 198, 199, 200
    *John, Jr., 199
    Margaret, 211
    Mary, 64, 118, 198,
    326, 327
    Wait S., 199
WISECARVER, Timothy J.
    125
WISWALL, Mary F., 74
WITHERS, Edward B.,
    294
    Walter S., 294
    Zuleika I., 294
WITT, Elizabeth, 145
WOLCOTT, Elizabeth,
    100
    Emily L., 325
    Frederick, 100, 101
    Gershom, 324
    Gershom N., 324
    Oliver, 100, 101
    *Roger, 100
    Sarah, 238, 324
WOLFE, Katherine E.,
    134
WOOD, George M., 188,
    189
    George W., 188, 189
    James T., Jr., 305
    Manning, 189
    Mildred L., 188, 189
    Patience, 83
    Priscilla, 233
    Rebecca, 262
    Thomas, 233
    William C., 307
WOODBRIDGE, Ashbel,316
    Frederic L., Sr.,317
    Frederic L., Jr.,316
    Howell, 316
    John, 1, 99, 267,
    280, 281, 316
    Martha, 280
    Mary, 1, 99
    Richard G., Jr., 43
    Sophia, 267
    Timothy, 1, 99, 316
    Typhena, 281
    William, 316
WOODFIELD, Denis B.,
    317
    Elizabeth D., 317
    Katherine R., 317
    Nicholas W., 317
    William F., 318
WOODMAN, Miriam, 19
WOODRUFF, Carolyn M.,
    318
    Frederick E., 318
    Janet A., 195, 318
    Mary E., 318
    Olive, 43
    Rhoda, 331
    Sarah, 16

WOODWARD, Abigail, 95
    Graham C., 292
    Joseph J., 292
    Martha, 73
    Priscilla F., 133
    Wilson, 133
WOODWORTH, Delaney,97
    Robert W., 97
WOOLSEY, Mary, 41
WOOSTER, Albert M.,36
    Elizabeth A., 257
    Ephraim, 36
    John, 257
    Myra E., 36
    Philo M., 36, 37
    William C., 36
WORMELEY, Elizabeth,38
WORTH, Damaris, 204
    William, 204
WORTHING, Albert T.,
    320
    Chester C., 320
    Clifford A., 319
    Sharon L., 319
WORTHINGTON,
    Elizabeth, 300
    John, 218, 303
    Martha, 218, 303
    Samuel, 218, 303
WRIGHT, Douglas C.,320
    Douglas C., Jr., 320
    Ezekiel, 225
    Helen G., 320
    Lucy, 225
    Roxlyn G., 320
    Sarah C., 225
    Sarah E., 80, 132

YEARDLEY, Argoll, 176
    Frances, 176
    *George, 175
YEATON, Huldah P., 24
YOUNG, Abigail, 186
    Annie M., 219
    David, 219
    Esther H., 242
    Grace O., 309
    Israel, 226
    Lydia, 161
    Mary, 72, 226
    Thomas, 161
YUTZLER, Annie, 60

ZELLER, Julius C.,
    92, 105
ZOLL, Margaret M., 7
ZURAT, Barbara A., 34